The Making of Buckley and District

T. W. Pritchard

The Making of Buckley and District
First published in Wales 2006
by
BRIDGE BOOKS
61 Park Avenue
Wrexham
LL12 7AW

© 2006 T. W. Pritchard
© Typesetting and design Bridge Books

A CIP entry for this book is available from the British Library

ISBN 1-84494-031-4

Printed by
Cromwell Press Ltd
Trowbridge

Contents

Foreword

Buckleyites are indeed fortunate to have had Archdeacon Bill Pritchard undertake the task of recording the history of their town and its surrounding area. He is renowned for possessing the prerequisites of a good historian: dedication to detailed research; consummate analysis; erudition and a bounding enthusiasm for his chosen subject.

In *The Making of Buckley and District* he presents us with the changes the area has undergone during the past two thousand years; from when it was densely forested to it becoming a moorland with isolated settlements; leading to an industrial landscape dotted with tall-chimneyed brickworks and dark colliery headgears — and ultimately — a residential conurbation serving north-east Wales. As one would expect, this gradual development had a profound effect on some sectors of society and not so much on others. In this work both individual successes and failures are dealt with in a balanced and honest manner; there is no dressing-up of facts in this concise and unbiased investigation.

To some readers it might seen odd having to occasionally read about Ewloe, Hawarden and Mold when the book is specifically concerned with Buckley. This is one of the author's strengths. He realises that the ordinary reader is not conversant with the medieval period and therefore places events that took place in Buckley at that time in their historical context. For example, during the Middle Ages (c.1000–c.1500) the place-name Buckley referred to what we call 'The Common'. It was an open expanse of land where the inhabitants of the manor of Ewloe (centred upon the castle) pastured their animals. On the other hand, for religious purposes, Buckley lay within the parish of Hawarden and people had to walk to St Deiniol's to attend public worship. If that doesn't confuse matters, the part of the district to the south of Wylfa Hill, Pren Hill and Lane End roadway was in Bistre township in the parish of Mold. Therefore, to understand fully the author's grasp of the past one is advised to read the full text and study the accompanying maps. Indeed, the serious student of history is also encouraged to consult the informative footnotes found at the end of each chapter. However, having said that, this is a book that the general reader can quite easily dip in and out of at his or her leisure as it is profusely illustrated with over three hundred photographs, maps and sketches; each accompanied by an explanatory caption.

This publication is one in a long line of treatises written about Buckley by authors worthy of note here: James Bentley; Charles Duckworth; Dennis Griffiths; Arthur Jones; John Clifford Jones; Paul Mason and Richard Willett. Up until now everyone's oracle was unquestionably Thomas Cropper, FSA, whose *Buckley and District* (Buckley, 1923) has been out of print since its reprint (Mold, 1987). Once you have read this book you will be left in no doubt that Bill Pritchard's *The Making of Buckley and District* has now replaced that study as the authoritative volume on the town. As local histories go, it is of top-drawer quality and includes many topics hitherto unmentioned in the writings of others. Hopefully, some of the themes the author has only been able to touch upon here will be later expounded by him or others in forthcoming issues of *Buckley*.

The late Alderman Dennis Griffiths realised the uniqueness of Buckley when, in the introduction to his *Out of this Clay* (1960), he said: 'I am glad I stayed in Buckley where, sometimes agreeing, at others unable to agree with my own folk, there has been wide opportunity to use every passing hour with the people and in the place I love the best.' Having read this book I cannot but believe that Bill Pritchard also feels that magic although he never attended the 'Trap College'!

For recording and interpreting Buckley's past so admirably, a huge *Diolch yn Fawr*.

Ken Lloyd Gruffydd, Editor of *Buckley*

Acknowledgments

When I wrote *A History of the Old Parish of Hawarden* I realised that it was impossible to do justice to Buckley and district and, what is more, I was diffident about attempting the task until I received an encouraging letter from Ken Lloyd Gruffydd. When I began my research I discovered that my mother was born in Mill Lane in 1900 and lived there for two years before my grandfather moved to Hawarden. It was on discovering this connection that I gained the confidence to write the history and this book is the result. My anxiety soon melted away with the warmth of the friendship and support I received from so many Buckley people.

Ken Lloyd Gruffydd and J. Brian Lewis both read the entire manuscript and made many constructive suggestions. Ken Lloyd Gruffydd has drawn the maps and diagrams to illuminate the text and indeed they are an ornament to the book, and in addition he has provided the Foreword. Carol Shone, with infinite patience and a great deal of time, opened up the Buckley Society Archive on my behalf and generously organised the photographs with such consummate skill and, together with her husband, David, read the proofs. One of the great delights in writing the book was my introduction to Wednesday afternoon sessions of the Society's Archive, held fortnightly in Buckley Library where I made many friends.

The list of Acknowledgments for the use of material from the Buckley Society Archive is long. James Bentley (with permission from Mrs Margaret Bentley); John Bright; Joe Chesters; K. M. Davies, MBE; Paul Davies; Stephen Duckworth; Neville Dunn (for special assistance with scanning and taking photographs); Glyn Edwards; Bill Fisher; Mervyn Ffoulkes; Neville Fox; A. E. Griffiths; Eric Hayes; Lelia Hewitt; Phil Hodges; Cyril Hodgson; Bill Holmes; Graham Hopwood; D. R. Hughes; Harry Hughes (for the late Mr Robert Edwards); Alwyn Dempster Jones; Mrs Joy Jones; Mary K. Lewis; Arthur Messham; Alan Minnery; Wilf Owens; Marjorie and Elfet Parry; Alyn Roberts; William Arthur Roberts; Arthur Rowlands; the Royal Buckley Town Band; Carol Shone; Ken Weigh (Creative Image Photography). Many other people who assisted with photographs are acknowledged in the captions.

Much of the research was done in the Flintshire Record Office, Hawarden and, as always, the staff were a tremendous help. I am grateful to the Warden of St Deiniol's Library, Hawarden, the Reverend Peter Francis and his staff for their kindness, and to the staff of Buckley Library and the headquarters of the Flintshire County Library for their help. Karen McNiven helped me considerably with my computer. Sir William Gladstone, Bart, KG, has given me every encouragement and support together with Anthony Furse. Alister Williams of Bridge Books has supported me with the benefit of his professionalism and his kindness as a friend.

T. W. Pritchard

Introduction

One way of understanding the way in which Buckley was made is to take a number of steps backwards through the centuries and review the changes which have taken place. To see more clearly these changes we must think of the story as revealed through the exercise of turning over the pages of an illustrated calendar. Each period of time has its own distinctive landscape, with different objects in the picture which illustrate the most significant features of the age.

The first page of the calendar we turn over, as we move backward in time, is the last hundred years. There are significant changes in the picture we see. Many of the things we take for granted to-day have disappeared. Gone are bungalow developments, the shopping precinct, and wide public roads flowing with motor vehicles, driving towards the new by-pass. Gone too are the council housing estates, modern schools, health clinics, car parks, industrial estates and sports centres.

The scene on the second page is of Buckley around the year 1900. It has a smart new Free Library and Council Chambers to mark its coming of age as a new Urban District Council, both of them built on a long main street known as the Roadside which bisects a concentrated industrial community. Innumerable chimneys and kilns of potteries and brickworks dominate the landscape. A ramshackle railway threads its way through these works, calling as it does at various pitheads, each with distinctive winding gear, before falling away downhill with its cargo of clay goods and coal. Nearby are a number of Nonconformist chapels whose members inhabit streets of terraced houses. The sky is mottled with drifting clouds of dense smoke from domestic fire-grates and industrial manufacturing. Within the bounds of the new Urban District Council are other small settlements which have their own collieries, brickworks, and potteries, established on rich seams of coal and clay which characterise the neighbourhood. Many of these settlements have existed for two or three hundred years but are now swollen by an increase of population — Alltami, Burntwood, Pentre, Drury, Lane End, Spon Green, Nant Mawr, Ewloe Green, and on what is the Commons of Buckley Mountain. Below the Mountain and in the distance to the north is the River Dee, canalised in 1737, and crossed by the Hawarden Bridge in 1889 at Shotton Ironworks. It is the scene on this page depicting the making of the landscape from 1737 to 1897, which is the most familiar to Buckley people.

A detail from this landscape is the subject of a separate page of the calendar. For page three we 'zoom in', as it were, on an element in the landscape which helps to provide continuity, and gives an insight into what has been here for at least a thousand years. In 1897 the Urban District Council boundaries were drawn coincident with the two ecclesiastical parishes which had been created in the previous fifty years. The significance of the joining together of these two distinct parts helps us to understand at a greater depth the making of Buckley. In many ways it was a necessary development, in other ways it seemed to some people at the time an artificial union, a forced marriage, an alliance beset from the outset by inherent rivalry, the partnership of extremes. Different ethnic origins had made it so.

The landscape is divided into two. The Bistre half, on the left of the picture, looks west towards its origins in the parish of Mold or more particularly in the Welsh commote of Ystrad Alun. The ecclesiastical parish of Emmanuel Bistre was created in 1844 from the townships of Bistre and Argoed, part of the ancient parish of Mold. The language and customs of the people of this area were Welsh, belonging, as they did for many centuries to the Welsh kingdoms of Powys and Gwynedd. The Buckley half, on the right of the picture looks east towards its origins in the parish of Hawarden. St Matthew's Church, Buckley, was built in 1822 and became a separate parish in 1874. It was created out of the townships of Ewloe Wood, Ewloe Town, Pentrobin and Bannel. Generally speaking this area was more Saxon than Welsh and had been settled from

Cheshire well before the Norman Conquest in the eleventh century. Its language and customs were Saxon and its later influences English.

The next page on the calendar goes back to the fourteenth century. It shows a settled landscape, a result of peace brought to the area by the conquest of Wales by Edward I in 1282. In the centre of the picture is the plateau of Buckley Mountain. It is an idyllic pastoral scene — grazing cattle and the dwellings of the herdsman on the summer pastures. There is very little else. For any activity we must look to the periphery. In the north, at Ewloe, there is the castle built by the Welsh Prince Owain Gwynedd in the twelfth century on his manor there. Bordering this, at Hawarden, is a castle held by the Montalt family until 1329 and a Parish church with a Celtic foundation ascribed to St Deiniol in 545 AD. There are small groups of men involved in digging surface coal, a few using the clay to make pots, others involved in open field farming or the grazing of cattle. There is evidence that a great deal of the area was once covered by a great forest, the Swerdewod, which stretched from the outskirts of Chester as far as Conwy. To the south west there is Mold with its hill crowned by a motte and bailey castle and in its shadow a parish church lately built and dedicated to St Mary.

War and conflict are the subject of the next page of the calendar. It begins with Harold the Saxon's defeat of the Prince of Gwynedd on the eve of the Norman Conquest in 1063 and ends with the conquest of the Welsh in 1282. There is great activity. We see the visit of the clerks of William the Conqueror, sent nation-wide to make a tax valuation of his kingdom. We see pious English monks establishing a priory after the murder of Thomas a Becket in 1170. Nearby, in 1157, King Henry II is ambushed in the Swerdewod. This results in the decision by the English invaders to make safe their progress by a deliberate policy of felling most of the forest. The Welsh fighting men are much in evidence as they push the English further east.

As we turn over the next page of the calendar we come to the beginning of our story of the making of Buckley. We have already seen the main lines of the narrative. The story will not begin until the departure of the Romans at the beginning of the fifth century AD. For the first thousand years we will be concerned with the struggle between the native Welsh inhabitants and the invaders and colonisers who came from the east who we generally identify as Saxons and Normans. The conquest and colonisation was not only concerned with the possession of land but also with the conquest of souls. Political and religious themes are dominant. On the first page we see the establishment of an ancient frontier, Wat's Dyke, defensive strongholds, and early religious sites, all grouped around the edge of Buckley Mountain and the Swerdewod from which Buckley was eventually made.

This study of the making of Buckley has been deliberately divided into sections to give the reader a choice where to begin. Each section is a unit in itself and is written to explain to the reader a particular aspect of the history of Buckley. The aim of all the parts is to discover how Buckley was made over the centuries and for me to share this story with you.

Chapter 1
Diverse origins. Settlers and Conquerors

This first section in our story of the making of Buckley covers a long period in history stretching from the end of the Roman occupation of Britain until the middle of the nineteenth century. It deals with the origins of the area and the change in land ownership over this period. A discussion of industry, religion, education, and social life in Buckley follows in later sections of the book. In order to see the various influences, which went towards the making of Buckley these fifteen or so centuries are divided into time zones and subject matter.

The first main period lasts from the fifth century AD until the account of the area in Domesday Book compiled in 1086. Its major themes are the marking of the western boundary of the area by the creation of defensive earthworks: Wat's Dyke and Offa's Dyke. This artificial frontier was rather like the marker in a tug-of-war contest. The contestants were native Welsh and insurgents from the east. The extent of ground gained depended upon the relative strength of arms of successive leaders and their dynasties; Welsh, Mercian, Saxon, and Norman. The area taken in successive contests was indelibly marked, not only by bloodshed, but deeper and more lastingly, by cultural elements. The most outstanding of these are found in place-names, field patterns and religious sites. The progress of this tug-of-war contest over the area we now know as Buckley is summed up to some extent in the Domesday Book entries of 1086.

The creation of the frontier

We begin with the establishment of the artificial frontier, the two great earthworks, known to posterity as Wat's and Offa's dykes, both of which lie near to Buckley. They were built to provide a demarcation of land colonised by settlers from the Midlands of England and Cheshire who came in search of rich agricultural land to be found in the river valleys of the Alun and the Clwyd. To consolidate their gains they constructed dykes of great length to act as barriers to raiders and make it difficult for them to carry away stolen booty and cattle. The dykes were boundaries rather than political frontiers or defensive obstacles. They were not fortified or garrisoned, but could be used as places to control trade. The dykes were made with a ditch on their west, or Welsh side.

Offa's Dyke is the longest and runs from near Prestatyn in the north to the Wye near Monmouth in the south. Its nearest point to Mold is at Treuddyn. The length of Wat's Dyke is forty miles and is seen at the western extent of modern Buckley at Mynydd Isa. It runs parallel to Offa's Dyke following a more easterly alignment across mostly low-lying agricultural land. The dyke starts from Basingwerk, and follows, the north and east side of the Alun Valley and runs parallel to the Dee estuary, turning towards Wrexham before crossing the Dee at Ruabon and terminating to the south of Oswestry.

Excavations of Wat's Dyke at Sychdyn show it to be a well-engineered earthwork, better built and sited than Offa's. Here the bank probably stood originally some 2m. high with a ditch 2m. deep and 6m. wide and probably topped with a palisade. In all, a formidable obstacle of 6m. high.[1]

There is, however, no consensus of opinion about the date of construction of the two dykes. Although it is generally accepted that the dyke named after Offa, King of Mercia (759–98), was constructed during his reign. The dating of Wat's Dyke varies between the fifth century and the tenth. Most historians favour the

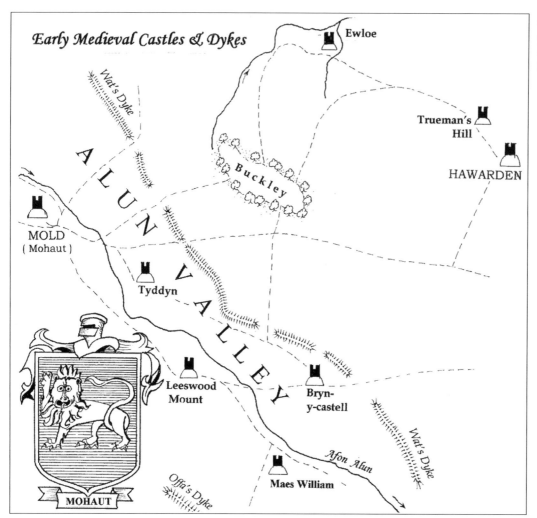

Map showing: Early Medieval Castles & Dykes.
[K. Lloyd Gruffydd]

reign of the Mercian king Aethelbald (716–57).[2] The earliest dating of the dyke was postulated by Hannaford as being a fifth century earthwork. This was based on results from radiocarbon dating of sample excavations carried out on a section of the dyke near Oswestry. He saw the dyke as a political frontier between the post-Roman British Kingdom of the Cornovii and other Welsh tribes further west, the Deceangli and Silures.[3] The latest date is the speculation made by Moore of the dyke being built in the middle of the tenth century 'marking off the reorganised land around Chester from territories controlled by the Welsh'.[4]

Whatever dating we give to the construction of these two great earthworks, we cannot fail to realise the political importance of this area in the relations between the British Tribes, the Welsh Kingdoms of Powys and Gwynedd, and the Mercian, Viking and Norman invaders. Modern Buckley, the area of our study, came from diverse origins. These are the borderland of the Cornovii and Deceangli British Tribes, Ystrad Alun an outlying commote of the Welsh Kingdom of Powys Fadog; and Ewloe, a township in Coleshill for centuries, the furthest commote eastwards of the Cantref Tegeingl, and the area of early Saxon colonisation around Hawarden. Being in such a strategic position the Buckley area became a battlefield, a corridor of invasion; a land colonised by Welsh and English. Warfare was its characteristic for nearly a thousand years.

Warfare

This period in Welsh history is usually known as the Dark Ages, because we know so little about it. What is clear is the warfare here in North Wales between the kingdoms of Powys and Gwynedd and the English invaders from the east. The nearest and most populous city to Buckley, then and now, was Chester. Called

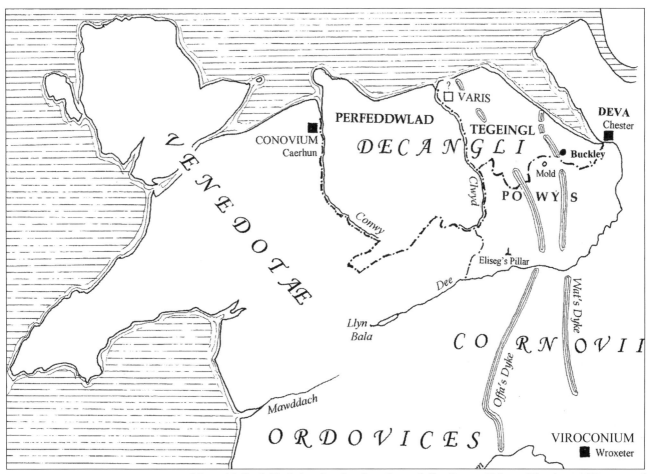

Map with Perfeddwlad – showing four Cantrefedi – Roman Tribes – Kingdoms of Powys and Gwynedd – Chester. [K. Lloyd Gruffydd]

Deva in Roman times, the city of the XX Legion, and although run down in early Saxon times, it remained as the base for invading armies from the first century AD until the revolt of Owain Glyn Dŵr in the fifteenth century. The battleground was usually somewhere between Chester and the river Conwy which marked the eastern frontier of the kingdom of Gwynedd. This disputed territory was known as the *Perfeddwlad*, the Middle Country, made up of the four *cantrefs*: Rhufonig, Rhos, Dyffryn Clwyd and Tegeingl. To reach this area the only passage way by land was along the banks of the Dee or through the gateway of Ystrad Alun. At the height of its power the kingdom of Powys held territory as far north as Hawarden. There were often changes in alliance; sometimes Gwynedd and Powys were united against the English kingdoms, on other occasions, they fought against each other, allied with Northumbria, Mercia and the Vikings, as advantage dictated. Whatever the result of battle the consequence for this area was always the same — destruction and devastation.

Rather than give a catalogue of warfare over this long period, certain events may be mentioned to illustrate the influence upon

Pillar of Eliseg by Moses Griffiths from Thomas Pennant's Tours in Wales.

Hallelujah Monument from Edward Pugh, Cambria Depicta:
a Tour through North Wales *(1816).*

the people of this area made by the supremacy of successive
dynasties and notable events.

Eliseg's Pillar, situated near Valle Crucis Abbey near
Llangollen, shows the strength of the kingdom of Powys in
this area from the end of the Roman occupation *c.* 410 to 855
when, on the death of Cyngen, their power was taken over by
Rhodri Mawr, king of Gwynedd. The inscription on the pillar
traces Cyngen's ancestry back to Brydw, the son of
Gwyrtheyrn (Vortigern) and grandson of the Roman emperor
Magnus Maximus, who seized power in 383. Vortigern is
vilified for inviting the assistance of the German tribes to
Britain in the fifth century. Also mentioned is Cadell the
friend of St Germanus who is reputed to have defeated the
Picts and Scots in the Hallelujah Victory at Maes Garmon near
Mold in 429. Of more substance are the names of Brochwel
and his grandson Selyf, who is said to have been slain in the
battle of Chester.

The battle of Chester *c.*613, marked the end of the hope of
the British tribes taking over the post Roman inheritance and the eventual establishment of Mercia as the
dominant power and expansion of Saxon settlement in North Wales. At the battle, the Northumbrians
successfully defeated the forces of Powys and Gwynedd when the monks of Bangor-is-y-Coed were put to
the sword. An event described by the Saxon chronicler:

> In this year Aethelfrith led his levies to Chester and there slew countless numbers of Welsh: and so was
> Augustine's prophecy fulfilled which he spoke, 'If the Welsh refuse peace with us, they shall perish at the hands
> of the Saxons.' Two hundred priests were also slain there who had come thither to pray for the Welsh host. Their
> leader was called Brochwel, who was one of the fifty who escaped thence.[5]

In the eighth century Mercia became the dominant English kingdom and showed its strength and hunger
for new land by settling beyond the dykes as far as the Conwy until repulsed at the end of the century. This
long period of settlement threatened to make permanent an English kingdom in the region of Hawarden
and beyond into Tegeingl and Ystrad Alun with the construction of the dykes as a symbol of their
confidence. The Mercians were bringing new lands into cultivation by forest clearance — Penley (Penda's
lea), Buckley, Horsley, Bagillt and others. This was the decisive century for the settlement of the area in the
Hawarden portion of Buckley as we will see later.

Mercian power diminished at the beginning of the ninth century. Only the kingdom of Wessex, in
England, was powerful enough to resist the Danes. On the borders of Wales the Danes wasted Chester in
893, but the English re-took the city in 907 with whom the Welsh of Gwynedd and Powys allied themselves
for protection against the Vikings. The construction of Offa's Dyke may have encouraged the Welsh
kingdoms to unite under Rhodri Mawr (d. 877) and later under Hywel Dda (d. 950).

The Welsh dependence on the English in the tenth century is seen in an event, which took place in
Chester in 973. It demonstrated what would become an issue which was to dominate the uneasy
relationship between Welsh rulers and English kings, that is, the nature of overlordship and the paying of
homage in return for recognition. This became more of a necessity after the Norman conquest. In 973 the
newly crowned Edgar, King of the Saxons, arrived in Chester and, as the Anglo-Saxon Chronicler recorded,
'there six kings came to him to make their submission, and pledged themselves to be his fellow workers by
sea and land'.[6] They did this by rowing him up the Dee to his palace, amongst them Iago and Hwyel ab
Idwal of Gwynedd. The meeting was probably to arrange an alliance of the Scots and Welsh against the

Viking marauders. A hundred years later we have the first mention of this area in the government records of the Norman conquerors. The manor of Bistre is mentioned in Domesday Book in 1086, which shows the king's determination to know the fiscal value of his kingdom and its potential for taxation.

Domesday Book, 1086

The entries for Bistre and other manors in North Wales are included in Domesday Cheshire. The book lists those who held land in the reign of Edward the Confessor (d. 1066). We are told that before 1066 Bistre was a manor of Earl Edwin, an ally of Earl Harold. Edwin held other manors at Hawarden and Rhuddlan. These were taken by conquest from Gruffudd ap Llywelyn, king of Gwynedd, in 1063. Gruffudd, soon after becoming king in 1039, allied himself to Mercia and successfully recovered territory which had been lost to the English for centuries, crossing Offa's Dyke and advancing as far as Bistre on Wat's Dyke. He held the land gained in his advance until defeated by Earl Harold and murdered by members of his household in 1063.

The name Bistre is Anglo-Saxon, originating in the late seventh or early eighth centuries. It derives from **biscop** (bishop) + **treow** (tree or wooden cross). It may refer to a boundary marker, or have some religious connection, maybe to commemorate a religious site or person as in Oswestry — Oswald's tree. When Gruffudd ap Llywelyn held the manor of Bistre in the eleventh century, he made good use of it to provision his household.

William the Conqueror's clerks noted in Domesday Book in 1086 that for this part of Flintshire:

> In this hundred of Atis Cross King Gruffydd had 1 manor at BISTRE. He had 1 plough in Lordship; his men, 6 ploughs. When the King came there himself every plough paid him 200 loaves. A barrel of beer and a vessel of butter.[7]

These dues would be used in the Lord's Hall near Wylfa Hill opposite which was a large field called Lord's Meadow. The reference to ploughs or plough teams refers to eight oxen. The English ploughland was the area capable of being tilled by one plough team in a year and able to support a family. It varied between 60 and 180 acres depending on the size of an acre.

Another Domesday entry refers to the great forest, 'ten leagues long and three leagues wide', part of the 'Swerdewod', belonging to the earl of Chester, extending from Dodleston to Coleshill. There is also a list of the outliers of the manor of Bistre which include parts of Nercwys, Gwysaney, Broncoed, Leeswood and Padeswood. The King's clerks note that the land was waste and not hidated, that is, not divided into ploughlands.

> All his land belongs to Bistre. It was waste. It never paid tax nor was it hidated. In this manor the woodland is one league in length and half a league in width; there is a hawk's eerie. The Earl has this woodland, which he has put into a forest.[8]

We cannot over-emphasise the importance of these brief and formal entries in Domesday Book in 1086 for they provide the earliest evidence of settlement in our area. From it we may deduce that in all probability there were two small farms situated where Hill Farm and Garreg Llwyd are to-day. As well as ploughlands there were meadows, woodland, a mill, and two horsepools. The total population is estimated at 18 males with additional family members. Here we begin to see the influence of the feudal system introduced by the Normans in the terminology employed to describe the inhabitants of the manor. There were nine *bordars* — cottagers who were given land for subsistence in return for agricultural and menial services for the lord, free or for a fixed sum; six *villeins* — unfree tenants holding land subject to a range of agricultural services, but above the status of slave. Neither the villein nor his daughter could marry without the lord's permission, and there were other restrictions. Upon his death his heirs paid a 'heriot' (fine). In return he had a land holding and the right to graze a fixed number of cattle on the common pastures and take hay from the common meadow. Lower in status than the villein was the *serf*, who was virtually the slave of his master and could be sold to another person.

The modern Buckley area in 1086 was therefore very thinly populated and based on an agricultural economy exploited and dependent on the laws of a Norman conqueror. A great part was clothed in thick forest, use of which was strictly controlled by the feudal lord. However, the Welsh laws, customs and language still persisted, together with those of the Saxons, who had colonised the area for nearly three hundred years. The only religious presence noticed by Domesday Book was a priest at Gwysaney.

Conflict between Welsh princes and Norman kings (1066–1282)

The next main period was much shorter, from 1066 to 1282, from the conquest of England to the conquest of Wales. The main theme was a struggle between the Welsh princes and the Norman kings. In this struggle the Norman invaders displayed a distinctive superiority in military and fiscal resources to pursue and defeat their enemies. By contrast the Welsh economy was weaker, its military organisation less advanced, and the will and ability to unite against a common foe fickle and unreliable. The result was the inevitable defeat of the Welsh. Out of this conflict the Buckley area was organised into the Norman lordships of Hawarden, Ewloe, and Mold, and received its first recognised religious organisation with the introduction of parishes with churches at Mold, Hawarden and Hope. Of some note in the history of our area in the twelfth century was the short-lived attempt to establish an Augustinian priory at Spon c.1185.

Our review is mainly concerned with the establishment of these military and religious institutions in the region between Mold and Hawarden. In order to understand why it took the English so long to impose their political authority on the Welsh the following points must be made.

The Welsh ability to repel the Norman invasion in North Wales was dependent upon a strong king of Gwynedd, who could command the loyalty of his kingdom and support from other Welsh kingdoms and create an alliance along the March. A combination of diplomatic and military success was necessary.

To pursue a successful policy of political aggrandisement a feudal state needed stability and the loyalty of its barons to fulfil their obligations to the king. During this period the Norman English state was weakened by the anarchy of Stephen's reign, the absence of Richard I, the distrust of John (culminating in Magna Carta in 1215) and the weakness of the long reign of Henry III.

Princes of Gwynedd	*English Kings*
Gruffud ap Cynan (d. 1137)	William I (1066–87) — the Conqueror
Owain Gwynedd (d. 1170)	Stephen (1135–54)
	Henry II (1154–89)
Llywelyn ab Iorwerth (d. 1240) — the Great	Henry III (1216–72)
Llywelyn ap Gruffudd (d. 1282) — the Last	Edward I (1272–1307)

The Conquest of Wales 1284

Attempts at peaceful accommodation between the Welsh princes in the end failed because, in the long run, the English Crown would only allow them to hold certain lands as a tenant-in-chief for which they had to do homage as a recognition of overlordship. This did happen although the princes of Gwynedd regarded it as an alien and repugnant act.

The lands in North Wales which the English Crown claimed to hold by conquest was the Perfeddwlad (see map) resulting in the Buckley area once again becoming an armed camp, the frontline in any military expedition.

The difficulties experienced by the princes of Powys are seen in the rule of Gruffudd ap Cynan (c.1055–1137). He struggled to gain supremacy

Arms of Gruffudd ap Cynan (died 1137), King of North Wales, to be seen on the chapter stalls in Bangor Cathedral

Arms of Owain Gwynedd (died 1170), Prince of North Wales,
to be seen on the chapter stalls in Bangor Cathedral

in Gwynedd, was captured by the Normans near Corwen and imprisoned for some years in Chester. On his release in 1094, he survived invasions in 1098 and 1114 led by Henry I. In return for an oath of homage and the payment of a heavy fine, Gruffudd was left in peace until his death in 1137. He was a survivor and did not rule east of the Conwy. Up to his death the Normans made great headway in North Wales under the leadership of Hugh d'Avranches, Earl of Chester and his soldier cousin, Robert of Rhuddlan. Earl Hugh held Hawarden manor and castle, other motte and bailey castles built at Mold, a defensive position established as at Tyddyn and other sites (see map).

Gruffudd's son and successor Owain Gwynedd (c.1100–70) disturbed the relative peace and security of this region. He was a strong prince, whose rule witnessed the ebb and flow of conflict across the region. The political anarchy in England during the reign of Stephen provided the opportunity for the rulers of Deheubarth and Gwynedd to unite. They overcame the opposition of the ruler of Powys, and Earl Ranulf of Chester. Mold and Ystrad Alun submitted to Owain in 1146, and in 1149 Tegeingl and Iâl were annexed to Gwynedd. However, with the anarchy in England ended, it was the turn of Henry II to reassert the control of the Crown. Henry brought a great force into Wales which set forth from Chester supported by Welsh mercenaries and strengthened by sea with a fleet of ships. His well planned campaign and strong force met with the usual difficulties experienced in Wales: unfavourable weather, difficult terrain, and the guerrilla tactics of lightly armed troops against heavy cavalry. Soon after setting out, Henry II was ambushed in the forest at Ewloe, the Swerdewod, and the skirmish continued into the commote of Coleshill. The Welsh chronicler recounted this dramatic event with some relish:

> Henry, King of England, led a mighty host to Chester, in order to subdue Gwynedd. And there he pitched camp: he was grandson to Henry the Great, the son of William the Bastard. And Owain, prince of Gwynedd, after summoning to him his sons and his leading men, and gathering together a mighty host, encamped at Basingwerk. And he raised a ditch there to give battle to the king. And when the king heard that, he sent his host and many earls and barons beyond number, and with them a strong force fully equipped, along the shore and towards the place, which Owain was holding. And the king and an innumerable host, fearless and ready for battle, came through the wood, which was between them, which was called the wood of Hawarden. And there Cynan and Dafydd, sons of Owain encountered him, and there they gave him a hard battle. And after many of his men had been slain, he escaped to the open country.[9]

The invasion failed. Henry's men met with disaster in Anglesey. Owain was reluctant to throw away what he had and made peace. He did homage to Henry, and agreed to change his official style from 'king' to 'prince', thus accepting the principle of English overlordship, and withdrew his frontier back to the Clwyd. Owain hit back in 1165 and Henry pursued him this time from Shrewsbury. Henry made the mistake of attempting to cross the Berwyns in bad weather and was forced to retreat. In retaliation, Owain pushed his frontier to the estuary of the Dee, in the process repossessing the castle of Mold, and reoccupying the commote of Ystrad Alun. Owain was recognised as one of the great kings of Gwynedd who enlarged his kingdom by diplomatic prudence and military ability. He died in 1170 and was succeeded by his son Dafydd ab Owain Gwynedd (d. 1203).

Dafydd experienced the influences which could impair the power of a prince of Gwynedd. He was weakened by sibling challenges for his kingdom and was forced to seek aid from his father's adversary Henry II. He made the best of this by marrying the king's half-sister, Emma, and sought to find security by paying homage to Henry at Oxford in 1177, in return for which, he held the Perfeddwlad and resided in some style at Rhuddlan. But he lost credence with his subjects and kinsmen, being the first ruler of Gwynedd known to have sworn fealty outside Wales, and appearing to them as an English baron rather than a Welsh prince. Judgement from his peers was inevitable and in 1197 he was removed from power in Gwynedd by his young nephew Llywelyn ab Iorwerth, 'the Great', (1173–1240).

But the years of peace were invaluable to the Welsh economy, the revival of the church on a Norman rather than a Celtic model, and for the invader, providing more time to establish himself in his castles, manors or lordships.

The de Mohaut family, Lords of Mold and Hawarden, *c.*1135–1329

An example of this in the locality is the power exercised by the de Mohaut family as lords of Mold and Hawarden from the middle of the twelfth century onwards. They received their lordships from Earl Hugh of Chester, who bestowed the seneschalcy, or stewardship, of Chester, an hereditary office, upon one of his greatest followers, Hugh fitz Norman. A castle at Mold had been built at the beginning of the twelfth century. The first named baron is Robert de Mohaut I (1135–62) , also known as 'the Black Steward', who established himself at Hawarden in 1147. The barony de Montealto or de Mohaut, 'high mount', is said to have been assumed in reference to the locality. Mold is a corruption of Mohaut. The family was associated with Mold until the death of Robert de Mohaut IV in 1329.[10]

The de Mohaut family

Robert I (1135–62)
Ralph (c. 1162–99)
Robert II (c. 1210–32)
Roger II (1232–60)
Robert III (1260–75)
Roger III (1282–96)
Robert IV (1296–1329)
End of the line of the de Mohauts

The barons had great power in the neighbourhood and beyond as descendants of one of the Conqueror's invasion host. They exercised political and religious patronage and served both the Earl of Chester and

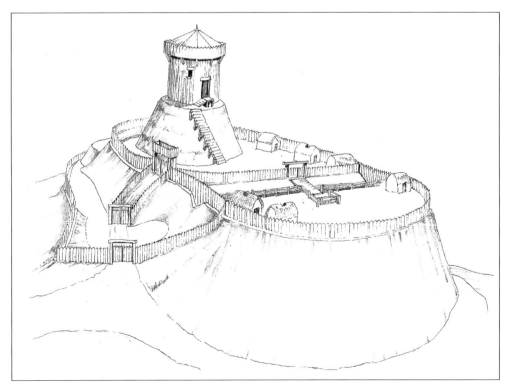

Mold [Mohaut] – motte and bailey castle, c.1100. [K. Lloyd Gruffydd]

attended the English Crown. However, in Mold their power fluctuated with that of the rulers of Gwynedd to whom on more than one occasion, they were forced to yield the castle, sometimes for short periods in the twelfth century, or longer in the thirteenth, when they were compelled to reside at their castle in Hawarden for a number of years during the rule of Llywelyn the Great.

Perhaps the power and influence of the de Mohaut family has been underestimated and forgotten, although they were the major power in the lordships of Hawarden and Mold for almost two hundred years (1147-1329). The reason for this is probably the absence of any remains of their castle at Mold. There are few clues from which to reconstruct their power. We must assume that their castle on Bailey Hill was equal to that at Hawarden and the one built by Llywelyn at Ewloe.

Religious buildings

The de Mohauts were also the patrons of churches. One of these remains at Hawarden and was built by the family after the conquest. Being resident in Hawarden, they were patrons of the parish church that was founded by St Deiniol in the sixth century. The church was mentioned in Domesday Book, and in 1092, Hugh, Earl of Chester, gave the tithes of the manor of Hawarden to the Benedictine abbey of St Werburgh. In 1258 Roger de Mohaut II exchanged with the monks of St Werburgh tithes of parishes in Cheshire in return receiving the chapel and tenement of Spon, and the living and great tithes of Hawarden. The first three recorded rectors of the parish were members of the same family, William de Montalt (1180), Ralph de Montalt (1209) and Hugh de Montalt (1216). Between the years 1315–17 Robert de Mohaut, the last baron, as patron, succesively presented priests to the living of Hawarden. He was also patron at Mold.[11] It is more than likely that Ralph de Mohaut II (1162–99) was responsible for building a stone church at Mold in the twelfth century and for its extensive repair after the conquest of 1282.[12] On November 3 1284, the vicar of Mold received the substantial sum of £26 for compensation for damage. This sum may have included the repair of outlying chapelries at Nercwys and Treuddyn. There is a Norman arch in the west tower of Nercwys church and another tangible memorial of such work at Treuddyn may be the small stained-glass arms of de Mohaut dated c.1330.[13]

A decision was made in the twelfth century to resurrect or make a new diocese between the see of Bangor in the kingdom of Gwynedd and diocese of Chester. The description of the area in 1125, 'without a bishop because of its desolation and barbarousness',[14] led in 1141 to the creation of the diocese of St Asaph as part of the Province of Canterbury. Its episcopal jurisdiction stretched from the Perfeddwlad, 'middle country', and further south to embrace the kingdom of Powys. This provided a permanent episcopal presence under the *de facto* control of the English Crown and Canterbury and as a buffer along the march. The parishes of Mold and Hawarden were included in the deanery of Ystrad Alun. It is probable that Robert de Mohaut I had a hand in its formation. As a marcher lord he knew the volatility of the area which continued to erupt from time to time until 1282. In the middle of the thirteenth century the bishop of St Asaph was forced 'owing to the ruin of the diocese by fire and slaughter, to beg and live on borrowed money'.[15] In the relative calm at the end of the twelfth century Ralph de Mohaut II (1162–99) for the salvation of his soul decided to establish a religious house within his domain.

St Asaph Cathedral. The crossing of 1310–20
[R. J. L. Smith & Associates]

Augustinian Canon. From the cover of Buckley Society Magazine 17.

Capel Spon

It was Ralph de Mohaut II, (1162–99), who invited the abbot of the Augustinian abbey at Haughmond, Shrewsbury, to establish a daughter house in his lordship of Mold. The Augustinian, Austin, or Black Canons arrived at Spon and built their priory about the year 1185. It was dedicated to St Thomas Becket, (*c.*1120–170), Archbishop of Canterbury, who was murdered in his cathedral. Baron Ralph was probably acquainted with him and may have witnessed the act of penitence of his master Henry II.

The new priory consisted of a modest chapel and domestic quarters with a burial place in the enclosure. The Augustinian's occupied the site until 1260 when they were recalled to the mother house in Shropshire during the time of the hostile Roger de Mohaut II (d. 1260) who sought to dispossess the monks of St Werburgh of some of their property. The Annals of Chester recorded that as a result of his misdeeds Roger died in poverty, 'the common people being ignorant of his place of burial'.

The Augustinians were recruited almost exclusively from among a non-Welsh population and were noted for their association with hospitals, which probably accounts for the place-name 'spital fields' nearby at Cold Harbour. It has been suggested that about 1300 Robert de Montalt (Mohaut) (1296–1329) had granted William of Hawarden lepers land, which might be spital fields.[16]

What we do know is that the charters granted to Spon by Ralph de Mohaut gave the Augustinians lands, rights and privileges in Bistre and adjacent townships.[17] These charters are extremely important, for they provide information about the settlement in the Bistre area a hundred years later than Domesday Book. They show that the area was being cleared of forest to provide arable land and pasture for existing inhabitants and new settlers.

The map shows the location of priory lands attached to Spon and their variety, rights, privileges and usage. It was situated in a compact area, whose description from the place names cited in the charter is quite clear.[18] The canons received the whole of Spon and Padeswood for assarting (bringing waste and forest land under cultivation). They were given permission in the forests of Bistre and Swerdewod, immediately adjacent to the priory, to clear, enclose and convert the wood into arable land. They also had the right to feed (pannage) a hundred pigs in those forests. This land was situated in Bistre between Wat's Dyke and the river Alun and more beyond Padeswood towards Rhyd y Defaid. In the northerly direction, the canons received rights of common pasture on Buckley Mountain. An indication that this area had been cleared of forest by earlier settlers. The charter gave them freedom from all secular dues and other taxes. The new priory did not receive endowment from tithes and the monks were expected to subsist on the land given to them with its opportunities of growing crops and pasturing animals. There is no mention of the exact acreage given in the charter although we must assume that it was adequate to provide resources capable of maintaining a small number of monks with permission to convert forest into farmland and possibility of future endowment.

This did not happen because of the temperament and behaviour of the founder's grandson and the canons returned to Haughmond *c.*1260. The history of Capel Spon is uncertain. The owner and occupiers of the building did not appear in the list of those compensated in 1284. By 1392–7 Capel Spon was annexed to 'the free chapel in the castle of Ewloe' and under the jurisdiction of the rector of Hawarden. Edward Lhwyd later lists it (in 1697–9) as one of the three chapelries of Mold together with Nercwys and Treuddyn. He reported great decay, 'whereof a small part of ye wall onely is now to be seen'. Archdeacon C. B. Clough recorded in 1854 that the foundations were being ploughed up. It was in 1989 that a thorough investigation was undertaken and the findings recorded above were made.[19]

Nana Probert's brother's farm was called The Rhyd – in that area

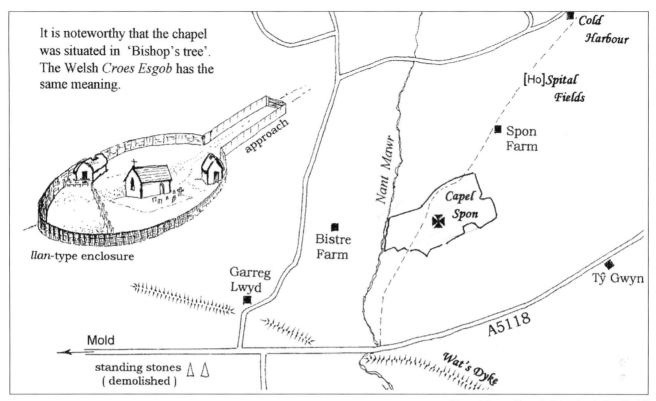

It is noteworthy that the chapel was situated in 'Bishop's tree'. The Welsh *Croes Esgob* has the same meaning.

llan-type enclosure

Garreg Lwyd

Bistre Farm

Nant Mawr

Capel Spon

approach

Cold Harbour

[Ho]*Spital Fields*

Spon Farm

Tŷ Gwyn

A5118

Wat's Dyke

Mold

standing stones (demolished)

Site of Spon Chapel. [K. Lloyd Gruffydd]

The thirteenth century

The canons of Capel Spon prayed for the soul of their founder Ralph de Mohaut slain at Mold in the insurrection of 1199. Once again Mold experienced the ferocity of a Welsh military force intent on reoccupying lost territory. The other members of the de Mohaut family were forced to flee to the safety of their castle at Hawarden. Much destruction was wrought by fire to fortifications described by the poet *'Tyreu poeth, peitiawc pob un'* (burnt towers, destroyed every one).[20] The new prince of Gwynedd, Llywelyn the Great (1173–1240) revived the hopes and fortunes of his people by holding the Perfeddwlad, (apart from its brief loss between 1211–12). Moreover, during his long reign, he maintained peace in Wales and in the March. Llywelyn was prepared to do homage to the English crown to retain his expanded territories. As result of his military skill and diplomatic astuteness the lands which are now Flintshire came under his rule, except for the small strip between Hawarden and Chester. Llywelyn's frontier extended to the manor of Ewloe, which was safeguarded by a former castle built by Owain Gwynedd in the twelfth century and strengthened in 1210. The de Mohauts were kept out of Mold until Llywelyn's death in 1240. Llywelyn married in 1205 Joan, the natural daughter of King John, and it was their son Dafydd who succeeded to Gwynedd.

On his father's death, Dafydd paid homage to his uncle Henry III for his lands in Gwynedd but was not acknowledged as holding outlying territories, which included

Garreg Llwyd Farm 1989, (possibly one of the settlements in Domesday Bistre). [Buckley Library]

Arms of Llywelyn ap Iorwerth (Llywelyn the Great), Prince of North Wales 1196-1240, to be seen on the Chapter Stalls in Bangor Cathedral

Tegeingl, of which the manor Ewloe was part. His half-brother Gruffudd was imprisoned in the Tower of London where he met his death in a fall whilst attempting to escape. Once again the English advanced into Wales and forced a treaty on Dafydd which resulted in the loss of Tegeingl and the return of the lordship of Mold to Roger de Mohaut II, but only for a short time, for he was, once again, deprived of his castle at Mold when the town was retaken by the Welsh in 1245. The issue was settled unexpectedly when Dafydd died childless in 1246.

The end of Welsh independence

Llywelyn ap Gruffudd, (d. 1282), eventually emerged from amongst the contenders to rule Gwynedd, but not until after much misery. When a peace was signed with the English at Woodstock in 1247 the chronicler Matthew Paris recorded that 'Wales had been pulled down to nothing', which summed up the position of Llywelyn, forced to retreat beyond the Conwy. This gave him time to consolidate his power and reunite North Wales from the Dyfi to the Dee given the advantage of the weakness of Henry III and his struggle with Simon de Montfort. One act of Llywelyn's, in about the year 1257, was to strengthen the fortifications of Ewloe Castle by building the round west tower and a stone curtain wall around the upper and lower wards. Llywelyn appointed Ithel ap Bleddyn to the charge of the castle and manor of Ewloe. In 1264 de Montfort, leader of the English barons, conferred with Llywelyn at Hawarden Castle. Unfortunately this alliance was short-lived because of the death of de Montfort in August 1265, but this did not deter Llywelyn from striking a blow against Robert de Mohaut (1260–75) by capturing Hawarden Castle and razing it to the ground in 1265.

By 1267 Llywelyn was at the height of his power. The principality of Wales was formally constituted with Llywelyn and his heirs recognised as princes of Wales, and the Perfeddwlad restored. The prince was to do homage and raise £25,000 to pay for his new dignity. His new position, as tenant-in-chief and quasi-independent prince, was to hinder his freedom of action in the future. One of the clauses in the treaty was the restoration of the lordship of Hawarden to Robert de Mohaut on condition that he did not build a castle there for sixty years.

Relations between the English crown and Llywelyn began to deteriorate on the accession of Edward I in 1272. There was a breakdown in trust between the two and neither would give way, nor did Llywelyn attend the new king's coronation and pay homage. While Llywelyn was bent on independence from the English crown, Edward determined on receiving his submission. Llywelyn was afraid of being seized and imprisoned if he came into the king's presence. The proud and haughty Edward demanded fealty and, impatient of Llywelyn's reluctance to do homage, moved against him, determined to destroy the new principality and humiliate its prince. A wide road was cut through the forest of Ewloe and Coleshill to secure the King's advance towards the Conwy, which brought about a cease-fire and peace was made at Aberconwy.

Llywelyn the Great on his deathbed in 1240, with his grandsons, Gruffudd and Dafydd in attendance. Matthew Paris manuscript. [The Parker Library Corpus Christi College Cambridge. By their kind permission]

Gruffudd falls when trying to escape from the Tower of London where he was imprisoned by Henry III in 1244. Matthew Paris.

The Treaty of 1277 reduced Llywelyn's power by depriving him of the Perfeddwlad and fining him £50,000. Llywelyn vainly sought to exercise patience, particularly with Edward's disregard for Welsh law, customary practice and national identity. Matters came to a head on Palm Sunday 1282, when his brother Dafydd attacked Hawarden Castle. Edward I reported:

Certain Welsh malefactors went by night to the castle of Hawardyn with horses and arms, and assaulted Roger de Clifford (guardian of Roger de Mohaut III) and his familiaries dwelling with him in the same castle, and slew certain of them and burned the houses of the castle, and took Roger and carried him off and held him captive, and, in addition, their raiders went feloniously to the King's castle of Flynt and burned certain houses there as far as possible, and slew certain of the king's men there and committed robberies, homicides, and other enormities there...[21]

Llywelyn and his fellow countrymen smarting under the high-handed attitude of the English king to Welsh institutions, the burden of taxation and the oppression of English officials had little choice than to follow his brother in rebellion. The Welsh were excommunicated, the English demands for peace were impossible, involving Llywelyn's exile to England. They were refused and Llywelyn the 'Last' met his death in a skirmish in mid-Wales on 11 December 1282.

The settlement of 1284 — the Statute of Rhuddlan

'Divine providence has entirely transferred under our proper dominion the land of Wales with its inhabitants, heretofore subject to us in feudal right; and has annexed and united the same into the Crown of the realm (of England)'. This statement certainly applied to the king's lands of North Wales and the county of Flint.

Thus the 'diverse parts' which make up modern Buckley were virtually 'set in stone' in 1284. It is fortunate for the historian that more records survive from this period onwards. The lordships of Moldesdale and Hawarden continued

Ewloe Castle. The Welsh Tower from the east.
[FRO PH 18/39]

Hawarden Castle. [FRO PH 28/d/24]

to be held and appointed by the Crown. The other constituent part, the manor and lordship of Ewloe, was in the hands of the Crown by right of conquest from Llywelyn. Conveniently situated in the cantref of Tegeingl and therefore in the newly established shire of Flint, although enjoying a separate jurisdiction, it was accountable to the king's ministers in Chester. The manor was given to Edward the Black Prince when he was created Earl of Chester in 1333.

The conquest of 1284, and the Edwardian settlement, provides a convenient point to examine the administrative units and place-names, which make up the local community.

Administrative units and place-names[22]

Administrative units in this area varied in size and origin as reflected in their names. This variety is seen particularly in the border area where Welsh, Saxon and Norman influences prevailed. A brief clarification will explain differences and similarities of function.

The townships, which eventually formed part of Buckley Urban District Council on its foundation in 1897, were Ewloe Town, Ewloe Wood, Pentrobin, Bannel, Argoed and Bistre. The Welsh *tref* and Saxon *tun* – townships in Wales, and hundreds in England — was the basic unit of administration and economic organisation of these early societies. They were in essence rural, agriculturally independent, tenurial, social and kinship groups. The people of the township needed a variety of types of land: ploughland, meadowland, rough pasture, woodland, and uncultivated areas known as waste.

The townships, which made up Hawarden ecclesiastical parish, were sixteen in number. Many of these had names of Saxon origin, some with nucleated settlements and open fields, such as Shotton, Aston, Bretton. On the other hand, Pentrobin was an upland Welsh community and Bannel a late pastoral grouping on the common pasture of the plateau. Bistre and Argoed were townships in the Welsh commote and rural deanery of Ystrad Alun, which from the thirteenth century onwards formed the ecclesiastical parish of Mold. The population of the Welsh townships, the *tref*, were made of free tribesmen, *bonedd*, or bondmen and villeins, who were usually a small minority of the population.

The Welsh kingdoms were divided into regions called *cantrefi* (hundreds), each of which was divided into two, three, or more *cymydau* (commotes). Hawarden, as we have seen, was subject to English occupation from the seventh to eighth centuries onwards. It had earlier, been part of the commote of Rhiw, in the Welsh kingdom of Powys Fadog, as was the commote of Ystrad Alun. On the other hand, Ewloe Town and Ewloe Wood were in the commote of Coleshill in the cantref of Tegeingl, which, as we have seen, was part of the Perfeddwlad.

It was through the units of the cantref and commote that the king administered his government and enforced the law.[23] At his *llys*, his court and royal household, the king dwelt with his high-ranking officials, the distain or steward, the judge, the *hebogydd*, or falconer, the court priest, the court bard, and his personal bodyguard. In each cantref and commote the king had a lesser courthouse. This was the centre of local government, the district council or local post office of the day, where the appointed officers exercised their duties. The *rhaglaw*, held the court of the commote, the *maer* collected the dues of the bondmen, and the *rhingyll* or bailiff those of the freemen, the chief rents. Justice was seen to be done and at two seasons of the year the king and his court went on a *tourn* or a progress, to make a formal visitation of his local officials and give decisions in cases of appeal. This custom is recorded in Bistre in the Domesday Book entry when it is noted that the Welsh freemen made a contribution at the *gwestfa*. 'Every plough paid him 200 loaves, a barrel of beer and a vessel of butter.' Later the food and other dues were replaced by a money payment. The bondsmen dwelt in villages whilst the freemen lived in scattered homesteads. They were organized in family groups, or clans, having special right and obligations to them, which were clearly set out in the Welsh laws.

The other administrative units in our area were introduced by means of conquest, settlement, and imposition from the time of the Mercians in the eighth century but more particularly by the Normans from the eleventh century onwards. They were firmly established at the Edwardian conquest by the Statute of Rhuddlan, 1284.

The former cantref of Tegeingl became one of the three cantrefi, which made up the new 'shire' of Flint,

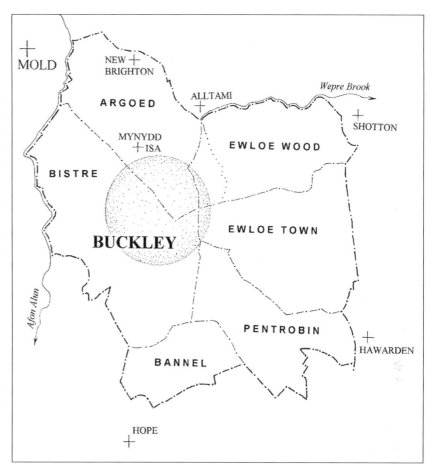

Map showing the position of Buckley in relation to the local townships.
[K. Lloyd Gruffydd]

which was administered by the king's justice of Chester. Our interest in this area arises from the fact that Ewloe Town and Ewloe Wood belonged to the cantref of Tegeingl. Before the conquest they were subject to Welsh law. This Welsh law together with Welsh officials was retained where the Welsh were in the majority. These areas were known as the 'Welshry' and those of the newly introduced settlements as the 'Englishry'.

To complicate matters further, Ewloe had become a royal manor sometime after 1277. It is still known as the manor of Ewloe, and has its lord of the manor. It may have been the Crown's intention to create a borough at Ewloe. Buckley 'pasture' was part of this manor.

The remaining administrative units introduced into this area were the manor of Hawarden and the manor of Mold. These were originally part of Powys Fadog with the commote of Ystrad Alun in particular coming under the influence of the Welsh kingdom of Gwynedd after the twelfth century. Both manors were grouped together to form the lordships of Hawarden and Mold, created as subsidiary buffer lordships under the influence of the earl of Chester, when in 1147, his hereditary *seneschal* or steward, de Mohaut, became the lord.

Marcher lordship was the most common unit of government in Wales after the conquest. By the fourteenth century there were over forty of these independent, self-contained and self-governing lordships which were totally responsible for the conduct of their own affairs. Once appointed by the king the lords enjoyed sovereign rights in their lordships and only forfeited them if they happened to be on the wrong side, as the Montacutes were in upon the abdication of Richard II in 1399.

Most lordships were divided into two parts — as Hawarden and Moldsdale (as the manor of Mold was known), the Englishry and Welshry, each with its own separate officials and courts. This gave some flexibility to the exercise of law and customs and:

> always liable to be modified at the dictates of the lord, who reserved to themselves the right to 'declare, to add to or to reduce the laws, customs, and services of their lordship', though they could do so usually only as a result of a working compromise with the wishes of their tenants.[24]

It is against this background of township, cantref, commote, manor, and lordship under Welsh and English and officials that we can understand the history of this area between the thirteenth and seventeen centuries.

Place-names

We must now examine the meaning of some of these township place-names and others, which deserve explanation.

Ewloe[25]

Ewloe is not Welsh in origin but derives from the English occupation. It means 'the mound by the source of a stream', which may refer to a fortified Mercian settlement or a watchtower strategically situated along the upland ridge. In 1284 it was described:

> Ewelawe and common of pasture in the said wood for all manner of beasts and cattle, saving to the said Welshmen their oak-trees, pannage, honey and sparrow-hawks in the said woods and their small enclosures about their houses within the woods aforesaid.[26]

Swerdewod [27]

The name is lost but reference must be made for its influence on the name of the township, Ewloe Wood, and its historical significance. Swerdewod means 'dark wood' and was the name of part of the great forest of Tegeingl. This is referred to by other names, one of which was 'koet pennardloc', 'wood of Penarlag' (Hawarden).

The forest was of great extent stretching as far as Argoed and Bistre on the Mold side and the Bretton Forest (referred to as Black Wood), on the other side of Hawarden, and into Tegeingl in the west. It is recorded from the twelfth century, when Owain Gwynedd successfully ambushed Henry II in dense forest at Ewloe in 1157. Mention occurs frequently from this date. A great part of the manor of Ewloe was formed out of the forest. The manor changed hands in the thirteenth century. It belonged to the princes of Gwynedd in the first part until King Henry III in 1246 seized it from them and gave it to Roger de Mohaut, who turned the woodlands into a private park. Llywelyn ap Gruffudd recovered the manor and built Ewloe Castle in the corner of the wood in the angle formed by the Alltami and New brooks. By 1277 the Welsh prince was finally expelled and shortly afterwards English settlers were brought into the townships.

Following the attempted ambush of Henry II in 1157, English soldiery took drastic steps to secure their passage through this forest. In his campaign of 1277, Edward I provided guards for his men as they cut a roadway through woodland for over thirty miles from Chester to the river Conwy between April and August. The pathway was one bow shot in breadth — 200–250 yards — resulting in the total clearance of between two and three hundred acres of woodland.[28] In December 1284, another eight hundred woodcutters were assembled at Chester, 'the most powerful, agile and most accustomed to the execution of these offices', each equipped with a strong axe or hatchet paid at the rate of 3d. a day.[29] Others sought to take advantage of the royal policy of clearance for safety. They uprooted and carried off timber in the wood between Mold and Swerdewod, in Argoed township, and 'took fuel throughout and everywhere at their will.'[30]

Other place names in the townships of Ewloe Town and Ewloe Wood refer to the gradual destruction of the great forest over the centuries — Burntwood, Ewloe Green, Hawarden Hayes.

Buckley

The meaning of the place name Buckley has been confused by a variety of spellings from the thirteenth century onwards. George Hawkes[31] favours an explanation derived from a comparison with the use of similar place names in Cheshire. 'Ekwall has written that Bulkeley, pronounced bookli is derived from the Old English *bullucca-leah*, meaning a 'bullock pasture'. The historian, John McNeil Dodgson gives the name as 'bullocks clearing'. He supplies many variations in spelling.[32] Hawkes regards 'bullocks clearing' as reasonable, noticing the grazing of bullocks on Buckley Mountain at the time of the Edwardian conquest and subsequently:

> The pastoral economy of the area was still important as late as 1625 when 57 Welsh farmers from Hawarden parish not only grazed their bullocks on the ancient common of 'Bookley' Mountain (500 acres), but on the cleared pastures of Ewloe Park (300 acres), Ewloe Wood (400 acres), and on the pasturage and lands then lately enclosed. They claimed common on all these grazing grounds.[33]

K. Lloyd Gruffydd has a different explanation of the meaning of Buckley.[34] He argues that the original meaning of the place name derived from 'boc' (beech tree), and was later substituted by 'bucca' (buck, deer), and that the 'The second element in the name is undoubtedly OE *ley*, sometimes *lea* or *legh* 'wood' or 'clearing'. In this instance, possibly the latter, as the equally ancient place-name Aberllanerch appears on Buckley Mountain; Llannerch being the Welsh for 'glade, clearing'. The original meaning of Buckley was therefore 'clearing in a beech wood', and perhaps 'the clearing' as opposed to 'a clearing".[35]

Other place-names in Ystrad Alun reflect forest clearance such as Leeswood, a settlement at the clearing adjacent to a river, and Padeswood.

Pentrobin[36]

A township formerly in the parish of Hawarden. Part of the township became part of the new ecclesiastical parish of St Matthew's Buckley in 1874. *Pentre* is the Welsh for village or hamlet, and Hobyn or Robin is a personal name. The earliest recorded use is in 1532 as 'Pentrabyn'. Edward Lhuyd in 1699 noted the township 'Pentrobyn, Pentre Hobyn y Saeson.' This emphasises the English influence on the settlement. For example, in 1751 Pentrobin Green consisted of three and a half acres of wasteland 'with liberty to erect mills and plant thereon for smelting lead ore'. In the eighteenth and nineteenth centuries it was the scene of coal mining activity. The lands in the township were enclosed by an award dated 20 November 1802.

Bannel[37]

A township formerly in the parish of Hawarden. It became part of the newly created ecclesiastical parish of St Matthew's, Buckley in 1874. Welsh *banadl, banal*, 'broom'. It is a small agricultural township, which, until quite recently, was thinly populated. In 1699 Edward Lhuyd recorded it as part of Pentrobin township with which it was the subject of an enclosure award in 1802.

Argoed[38]

A township formerly totally in the parish of Mold until 1842. Now partly in the ecclesiastical parish of Emmanuel Bistre. The Welsh meaning of the name is 'edge or border of a forest,' or sometimes, a 'circle or enclosure of trees'. Owen concludes that 'The settlement at Argoed was therefore neither opposite a forest, looking towards it, nor within the forest itself'.

Bistre[39]

A township formerly in the parish of Mold until 1842, when it became part of the ecclesiastical parish of Emmanuel Bistre. The name first occurs in the Domesday Book entry for 1086 and may derive from an old English personal name Biscop. Alternatively the element biscop may have an ecclesiastical association. With biscop combined with 'tree' it may suggest a place for preaching — where the bishop set up his Christian cross. On the other hand, the element tree, may refer to a boundary marker with the named person (Biscop) living close to it. The closeness to Wat's dyke may favour this explanation. However it is not impossible that it may have an ecclesiastical association as the furthest extent in this area of Mercian diocesan organisation.

Notes

1. David Hill, *The Archaeology of Clwyd*, Offa's and Wat's Dyke, p.142 passim (Clwyd County Council, 1991).
2. Sir Cyril Fox, *Offa's Dyke* (British Academy, 1965).
3. Hugh Hannaford, *West Midlands Archaeology*, vol. 40, (1997) p.57.
4. David Moore, *The Welsh Wars of Independence, c.410–c.1415*, (Tempus, 2005).
5. G. N. Garmonsway (translator and editor), *The Anglo-Saxon Chronicle*, (J. M. Dent & Sons, Ltd, London, 1972), p.22, see also Leo Sherley-Price, *Bede A history of the English Church and People*, revised by R. E. Latham (Penguin Classics, 1968), p.103.
6. Garmonsway, ibid, p.119.
7. *Domesday Book*, General editor, John Morris, vol.26, Cheshire, editor, Philip Morgan, (Phillimore, Chichester, 1978), p.269b.

8. Ibid ,269b.

9. Thomas Jones, *Brut y Tywysogion or the Chronicle of the Princes* (Board of Celtic Studies, 1952), p.59.

10. Mostyn Lewis, *Stained Glass in North Wales up to 1850*, (Sherratt & Son Ltd, Altrincham, 1970), p.90.

11. D. R. Thomas, *A History of the Diocese of St Asaph*, (Oswestry, 1908–16), 3 vols., vol.2, p.392 and p.406.

12. George Lloyd, 'Carved Stones at Mold,' *Flintshire Historical Society Publications*, vol.18, p.166.

13. See fn 10.

14. Thomas, op.cit vol.1, p.33.

15. ibid, vol.1, p.49.

16. ibid, vol.2, p.360.

17. J. R. Cole and Derrick Pratt, 'Capel Spon', Buckley, Clwyd, Archaeoleg yng Nghymru, *Archaeology in Wales*, vol.33, 1933, pp.25–30.

18. See Ken Lloyd Gruffydd, 'Early Christianity in Ystrad Alun', Ystrad Alun, *Journal of the Mold Civic Society*, Christmas, 2004, p.17, 'land in Bissopestre as far as Bradefort together with the angle of land situated nearby — the whole land of Patdeswde which is for clearing together with common pasture in Bocleghe etc.

19. See fn 17, p.30.

20. Ken Lloyd Gruffydd, 'The Manor and Marcher Lordship of Mold during the Early Middle Ages, 1039–1247', Ystrad Alun, 2002, quoting E. M. Thomas and N. A. Jones, Gwaith Llywarch ap Llywelyn, (Caerdydd, 1991).

21. Frederick C. Suppe, 'Military Institutions on the Welsh Marches, Shropshire, AD 1066-1300', *Studies in Celtic History*, vol.14, (The Boydell Press, 1994), p.12.

22. See in particular Hywel Wyn Owen, *The Place-Names of East Flintshire*, (Cardiff, University of Wales Press, 1994). Hence PNEF.

23. For a map of these and explanation see William Rees, *An Historical Atlas of Wales from Early to Modern Times*, (Faber and Faber, 1959), p.25.

24. Glanmor Williams, *Recovery, Reorientation, and Reformation, Wales, c.1415-1642*, (Oxford, Clarendon Press, 1987), p.37.

25. Hywel Wyn Owen, *Clwyd Historian*, no12, pp.20–2.

26. PNEF, pp.168–70.

27. PNEF, p.154.

28. William Linnard, *Welsh Woods and Forests history and utization*, (National Museum of Wales, 1982) p.23.

29. ibid, p.26.

30. PNEF, p.154.

31. George Hawkes, 'The Place Name of Buckley', *Buckley*, 24.

32. See Hawkes.

33. ibid, fn 10.

34. Ken Lloyd Gruffydd, 'The Manor of Ewloe and the Place-Name Buckley', *Buckley*, 5, pp.25–30.

35. ibid, pp.28–9.

36. PNEF, p.103.

37. PNEF, p.12.

38. Hywel Wyn Owen, 'The names of the Townships of Ystrad Alun', Ystrad Alun, Christmas, 2001.

39. ibid, p.5.

Chapter 2
Shaping the Community. Manor, Lordship, and Gentry, 1284–1640

Introduction

In this chapter we begin to see in more detail the everyday life of the people of this area. We have more details of the way they lived closely together in small communities and the tension this caused. Their existence was tied to the lord of the manor. To them was allotted a multitude of tasks, which earned them little recompense apart from the consolation of their religion and celebration of countless holy days. In the words of the philosopher, life for them was nasty, brutish and short. Although there was the occasional revolt against English rule, this was the beginning of the integration of the native Welsh and immigrant English. They borrowed from one another whatever was convenient and necessary, they inter-married, and the unruly Welsh fought for the English Crown in the Hundred Years War winning a reputation as archers and spearmen. Apart from the year of the pestilence around the Black Death in 1349 and Owain Glyn Dŵr's Rebellion (1400–06) there was prosperity and unprecedented advances in society.

The spectacular emblems of power and authority of this period, which still remain, belong to religion. The parish churches of Mold and Hawarden exhibit the wealth of lordly patron and skill of medieval mason and architect. Although Hawarden parish church has suffered from fire and is mostly a nineteenth century restoration it was rebuilt in the same Early English style of architecture on the same foundations. St Deiniol's Church contains within its walls a list of medieval rectors, and memorials to the emerging gentry families of Whitley and Ravenscroft. Amongst its records are reports of a medieval ecclesiastical court established in the thirteenth century, which controlled the morals of the inhabitants of the parish for seven hundred years. The building of the church was probably undertaken under the patronage of the de Mohaut family who in the years after the Edwardian Conquest rebuilt the Castle at Hawarden. In this enterprise they may have possibly employed Edward I's architect, Master James of St George, to design the new castle and church.[1]

When we speak of Mold parish church we are more certain of our facts. No one may deny the patronage of Thomas Stanley, earl of Derby and his wife Margaret Beaufort, countess of Richmond and Derby. They left their signatures in the superb design of this Perpendicular Church dedicated to St Mary, which replaced an earlier one built by the de Mohaut's. In the stone carving of this magnificent Church are insignia of the Stanley family. The crest of the eagle and child, the eagle's claw badge, the three legs of their kingdom of Man, and the Tudor insignia to show their alliance with the family. The church is big enough to include memorials to the gentry who emerged from the ranks of many of those who had served as officials in the lordship. The Wynnes of Tower, Eytons of Leeswood, Davieses of Gwysaney, and Lloyds of Pentrehobyn. Significantly the importance of the motte-and-bailey castle opposite was reduced and it fell out of use and into disrepair.

Much the same happened at Ewloe castle. Its strategic necessity had disappeared by its replacement by Edward I's stronger castle in the newly created borough of Flint. Ewloe castle was however used as a residence until the sixteenth century, at first in the thirteenth centuries by Bleddyn ab Ithel Annwyl, Forester of Ewloe, and his descendants in the fourteenth century, and in the fifteenth century by the Stanley family

Edward of Caernarfon, created Prince of Wales by his
father in 1301. Matthew Paris.
[The Parker Library, Corpus Christi College, Cambridge. By kind permission]

until the death of Peter Stanley there in 1572.

Our knowledge of the first part of this period is limited. It is derived from records relating to the manor of Ewloe from 1284 onwards which belonged to the Crown and later the Prince of Wales as Earl of Chester and is contained in the accounts of officials who operated from Chester and relate mainly to the fourteenth century. Other records of the manor are few and spasmodic until the seventeenth century. As we shall see later other important records of the manor of Ewloe date from its acquisition by the Davies family of Gwysaney at the beginning of the seventeenth century and continue until the twentieth century. Other records of the area, even in comparison with those of the manor of Ewloe, are meagre. These are two short extracts of the accounts of Baron Thomas Stanley (earl of Derby in 1485), from the accounts of the lordship of Hawarden and Moldsdale in 1474 and 1477. However brief they are we may obtain from them some understanding of the pattern of life in our community, which we cannot find elsewhere.

The manor of Ewloe

The creation of the manor

The ownership and status of the manor was determined by an inquiry in 1311. It is a complicated story, which began between the Crown and Roger de Mohaut in 1282. After the death of Llywelyn ap Gruffudd in 1282, Reginald de Grey, Justice of Chester, took the manor formerly held by the princes of Gwynedd, as forfeited to Edward I by right of conquest. This action brought a protest from the King who alleged that Reginald de Grey was withholding the manor from him, despoiling his woods, and making enclosures in the part of the woodland which had been cleared and converted into arable land by the dwellers in Aston, Shotton and Killins. In 1284, Roger's mother, Joan, when summoned to answer in the court at Flint why she should have dower in Ewloe failed to appear and her right was lost by default. The king took action against her to return to him the *vill* of Killins at Aston with its 97 acres of land and 58 acres at Shotton. In 1290, Roger petitioned parliament alleging that an inquisition taken in 1267–8 confirmed that the lands at Ewloe belonged to his grandfather and they were delivered to Maurice de Croan as his guardian. This inquisition could not be found and a further one held in 1294 rejected Roger's claims. The matter was finally settled at an inquisition at Ewloe in 1311 when it was adjudged that the manor had belonged to Owain Gwynedd and descended through him to Llywelyn ap Gruffydd (killed 1282), which he gave to Bleddyn ab Iorwerth to hold for him. Henry III had wrongly given it to Roger who attached the manor to his own neighbouring lands of Mold and Hawarden, to which it never belonged. Llywelyn had ousted Roger, and King Edward I took the manor in right of his conquest and defeat of the Welsh prince.[2]

Edward I established in the manor a so-called *villa* or *villa anglicana*, an English township, one in four in fourteenth century Englefield, as the *cantref* of Tegeingl was now called.[3] These townships in common with other places, such as the new borough at Flint, were populated by communities of English settlers deliberately introduced amongst the native Welsh to exploit the resources of the area for the benefit of the royal economy and to make less likely the mischief of Welsh insurrection. As an inducement to settle, they were rewarded with grants of land from the royal demesne and given grants and the same privileges as the boroughs.

The extent of the manor

The extent of the manor in 1284 was approximately 2,300 acres containing, as it did then, part of the townships of Shotton, Aston, Hawarden and Pentrobin. The total acreage of the manor in 1785 was about

The Medieval Manor of Ewloe.
[K. Lloyd Gruffydd]

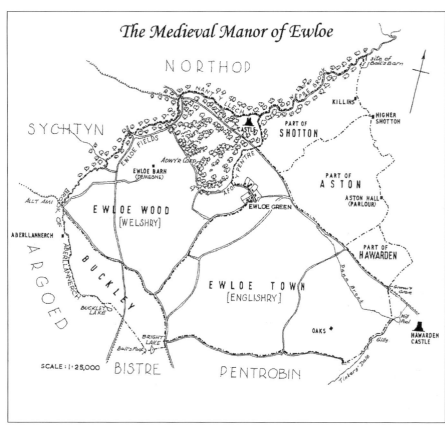

1,844 acres. The map shows the important areas of the manor from the sixteenth to eighteenth centuries. The two townships which made up the manor are Ewloe wood, and the Welshry, where the native community continued to dwell. This contained the lord's demesne lands — what remained of Swerdewod, the castle, and a small nucleated settlement at Ewloe Green on the edge of both townships. The township of Ewloe Town , the Englishry, the land given to the English settlers. To the south of both townships, in the waste, was the pasture land of Buckley.[4]

The value of the manor was revealed at an inquiry made in October 1295:
There are 480 acres of arable land in the demesne worth £14 a year. The two water mills are worth 60s.; the agistment of the pasture (letting of grazing land) of Buckley, 10s; deadwood, 8s.; an iron mine 6s. 8d.; bailiwick of the forestry, 30s.; pannage of the swine, 20s.; (payment for the right to feed pigs in the wood); pleas and perquisites of the court, 21s. Total £21 14s. [sic] Amongst the jurors were Simon de Eweloe, John the Miller, Alcok de Scotton (Shotton), and Madoc ap Rhys.[5]

The people of the manor
The mixture of Welsh and English inhabitants in the manor is shown by a list of those taxed in the subsidy of 1292 whose names appear on the roll for Flintshire.[6] Ewloe was comparatively speaking well-populated with twenty-four English households and twenty of Welsh origin. Their prosperity was disturbed by a native rebellion in 1294–5 aggravated by the punitive subsidy. One of the results of the rising was that Edward I took into temporary custody the lordship of Mold. The population of the manor was to remain stable for the next three hundred years. A rental of *c.*1620 gives a list of tenants, for agricultural purposes in two groups: on the English side twelve and the Welsh side fifty-five.[7]

Manorial courts
We have seen the extent of the manor of Ewloe and the number of people who lived there. The territorial unit of the manor was primarily an economic arrangement with the inhabitants occupying their land by

different kinds of tenure. Villeins, or unfree tenants, bondmen as they were known in Wales, held their land by agricultural services, by working on the lord's demesne and performing 'boon work'. This was seasonal, such as ploughing and harvesting. Villein tenure was known as copyhold and later as leasehold tenure, by which a tenant held a copy of the entry in the rolls of the manorial court baron (see below). On the other hand freemen paid a fixed and often nominal money rent. The payment of a small annual quit rent released a tenant from manorial service.

Life on the manor was controlled by its courts through which the lord was given certain powers to run his estate and to control his tenants. The court baron, normally held every three weeks, dealt with the transfer of copyhold land, upon inheritance or sale, determined the customs of the manor, and enforced obligatory non-payment of services due to the lord. The other jurisdiction exercised by the lord was the court leet and view of frankpledge. The court leet dealt with minor offences law and the order and administration of communal agriculture. The view of frankpledge in reality meant that the male members of the manor carried out a co-operative responsibility for bringing criminals to justice, for the good behaviour of one another, and for their appearance at the court leet to face charges. During the thirteenth century in Wales, and elsewhere, the manorial courts gradually began to use the system of trial by jury. Juries of presentment were charged with the business of enquiring into offences, which lay within their jurisdiction. The other juries were those of inquisition which enquired into all matters of fact, and declared what was the custom of the manor.[8]

It really was a case of everybody minding everybody else's business. The male members of the manor formed a court with a wide range of powers. It could regulate and enforce labour services, and the cropping of the open fields. Punish all types of trespass, offences of violence, and the driving off neighbour's cattle. Prevent overstocking of the common and the too-frequent taking of wood or turves. Impose a fine when a maiden lost her virginity, and reach a decision in civil dispute. It was a rough and ready justice where those presented could hear the 'doom' of the court, the verdict reached by his fellows, before the judgement of the lord was pronounced. It was inconvenient to send people to prison where they would be a charge on the community and their labour would be lost. It was more practicable and profitable to the lord to issue a fine or amercment as it was called. Rather like paying a fixed fine for speeding and just as profitable.

Some of these payments were taken over from the Welsh at the Conquest. *Amobr* was a payment made by a woman or on her behalf, when she married. Ebediw was a succession duty; a fine paid by a man's heirs for the privilege of entering upon the father's possessions. The Welsh *ebediw* has been identified with the Anglo-Saxon *heriot*, which was often his best beast. *Twnc* was a commutation in money for the Welsh *gwestfa*, the rendering of various foodstuffs for the lord. We came across this custom in the Domesday entry for Bistre in 1086. Ancient dues, to Welsh princes, made by bondsmen, included the maintenance for one day and night, of a stallion and groom belonging to the lord. This was commuted to one penny. The same sum was paid to the lord on the first of May for the repair of fences.[9] Another payment was *Porthynant cais*, the maintenance fee for the *cais* or Sergeant of the Peace.[10]

Court procedure

The procedure of the court at Ewloe at the end of the nineteenth century was virtually the same as it was six hundred years earlier.[11] The proclamation at the opening of the Court announced the scope of its traditional jurisdiction. 'All manner of Persons that doe owe Suit and Service to this Court Leet, Court Baron and View of Frankpledge of (the Lord of the manor named) holden in and for this manor of Ewloe'. After the proclamation the steward called the jury and gave his charge after which the foreman and the jury were sworn. The charge to the jury bid them present the deaths of tenants and who are their heirs to succeed them in their estates and what profit accrued to the lord by such death, such as relief, heriot etc. To present suitors who make default in attending the Court and doing their stint and service. To present the forfeiture of any tenant by alienation by waste of any kind, such as cutting timber and the like; by leasing without licence, committing treason or felony. All encroachments or trespasses in the lord's demesne or on the wastelands of the manor. Overstocking the common and any sort of nuisance or offence committed within the bounds of the manor.

Constables were appointed for the townships of Ewloe Town and Ewloe Wood and sworn to make presentment of offences committed within the bounds of the manor. Burleymen (also called beadles or bylawmen) were appointed to enforce the by-laws of the manor.

The commonest presentment made over the centuries was for incroachment on the waste by taking in land and erecting houses. This was the way in which houses in Buckley sprang up around the common and it is to this practice that it owes much of its development. The list of incroachments on Buckley common found in the court leet records provide a means of charting the growth of the clay industry in Buckley. Fines for incroachment and resulting rents were a regular source of income for the lord of the manor. It was the court leet which managed the pinfold in Buckley for impounding stray animals.

An unforgettable day in the lives of both old men and young boys of the manor was the ceremony of beating the bounds. This was a perambulation of the total boundary of the manor along which was a sequence of boundary markers made of stone or iron.[12]

The rights of Commons.[13]

For centuries the tenants of the lord of the manor enjoyed certain rights which were extremely valuable to them. They were entitled to share some of the resources of the manor, which made an important contribution to their lives. In a very practical way these rights of common, as they were called, gave them certain advantages and reduced to some extent the harshness of daily living. They included:

Estovers — the right to take wood and other growing things for building, fencing or fuel, gorse, heather, ferns and bracken for litter for animals.

Turbary — the right to dig turf or peat for fuel.

Rights in the soil — including digging for sand, stone and coal. The rights to timber in copyhold land. The tenants could take trees fit for building and repairing houses usually oak, ash, and elm of a certain dimension and at least twenty years old. There were various forms of the right to take wood from the commons known as 'botes'. House-bote was the taking of timber to repair houses. Fire-bote, the right to take the lops, underboughs and windfalls for fuel. Plough-bote, the use of wood to repair agricultural equipment. Hedge-bote, wood for the repair of fences and gates. Woods differed from forests in regard to restrictions. In them the tenant could exercise his customary rights, as outlined above, but forests had their own 'forest law' designed to protect the sporting-rights of the lord. On copyhold land the lord had no power to enter in and plant trees. Saplings tended to disappear before they were large enough and this speeded up the clearance of woods. In the Survey of Mold in 1653 we will notice that the number of saplings on copyhold land are carefully recorded to prevent destruction and restock the woods.

The lord had the property in the minerals that lay under the land and in the large trees that grew on it.

The copyholder had possession of the land and could refuse access to anyone including the lord. The lord could not touch the minerals without consent of the copyholder.

Ewloe Castle Deer Park.
[Buckley Society Magazine, 8]

The manorial court was responsible for the erection of the pinfold where straying and lost cattle could be impounded. In the bailiff's account for 1435–6 is recorded 'And in the erection of a new fence around the Punfeld, of that lordship in place of another which was blown down by a strong wind and completely destroyed in grosso, 8d.'[14] Pinfold Lane in Buckley was the area where the stray cattle from the pasture were claimed and a fine paid.

Officials of the manor

With the frequent absence of the lord of the manor, and indeed permanent absence from the royal manor of Ewloe, the administration fell upon recognised personnel who were in effect estate managers. At the head of the lord's officials stood the seneschal or steward. He was his master's voice, responsible for ensuring that his lord's property was used to the best advantage. He presided over the manorial courts in place of his lord. An early manual on the running of the manor advised the lord to:

> procure a Seneschal; a man circumspect and faithful, discreet and gracious, humble and chaste and peaceful and modest, learned in the customs of his province and of the duties of a Seneschal; one who will devote himself to guard his Lord's rights in all matters, and who knoweth how to teach and instruct his master's under-bailiffs in their doubts and their errors; merciful to the poor, turning aside from the path of justice neither for prayers nor for bribes.[15]

The official who lived amongst the people of the manor was the bailiff. He was the go-between and his authority was emphasised by the fact that he lived in the manor house at the expense of the lord. In Ewloe the bailiff lived in the castle. He was the official from whom the manorial servants took their orders. He implemented the general agricultural policy which had been decided in consultation with the steward. He met the labourers in the fields and pasture to give orders, make decisions, inspect the work in progress, and if need be exercise discipline. The bailiff had to present an annual written account to the lord's auditors and it is from accounts such as these that we know what happened in the manor of Ewloe in the fourteenth and fifteenth centuries.

Occasionally an official's conduct would be judged intolerable and if there was sufficient cause of complaint by reputable men to support the action he could be indicted for his offences. This happened to Llewelyn ap Bleddyn Goch, bailiff of Ewloe. On the 18 December 1391 he was presented by jurors at Flint on a number of charges of infringing the customs of the manor.

The main complaint was that the English settlers resented what appeared to be the outrageous behaviour of the Welsh bailiff and his wife. It was recited:

> And that whereas according to the custom of the manor of Eulowe, no Welshman ought to be bailiff there, Llewelyn, who is Welsh, has been made bailiff by the steward of the manor and has inflicted from day to day many injuries, extortions and oppressions upon the English tenants there. Wherefore the community of the English tenants of the township ask for a remedy and that Llewelyn be removed from his office.

He was accused that without a licence or grant from the king's officers, of cutting down oak trees from within the park of Ewloe and making a wagon from one, for his own use, and selling another, to Ieuan Decka, smith of Cilcain, and illegally cutting down eight saplings.

> And (they say) that the said Llewelyn illegally and in breach of the peace took several horses and mares belonging to different men at Euwloe in a certain place called Buckley and marked them with various marks, that is to say, of some he cut the ears — of others he cut the hairs of their tails, and of others, the hairs of their manes, and sold them to various strangers.

It maybe that the greatest grievance was that 'no bailiff whilst he is in the office of bailiff keep an ale house' and that the wife of Llewelyn broke this rule and offended the locals by selling very weak ale, overcharging them and serving false measures.[16]

The peasants elected their own representative, the reeve, before final selection by the lord. His job was rather like the foreman on the shop floor, who listened to complaints, settled disputes, and saw that there was fair play.

The hayward was another key worker in the manorial organisation. Up at the crack of dawn he went round the manor setting the men to their seasonal tasks ploughing, harrowing, sowing, and mowing. It was his duty in August:

to assemble the reapers and the boon tenants and the labourers, and see that the corn be properly and cleanly gathered; and early and late watch so that nothing be stolen or eaten by beasts or spoilt. And he ought to tally with the reeve all the seed, and boon-work, and customs and labour which ought to be done on the manor throughout the year.[17]

Another important official was the coroner whose duty was to enquire into sudden or unexplained death, as in Ewloe, when in 1412, on the Tuesday after All Saints day, Richard Saladyn convened a jury to investigate a coal-mining fatality. The finding was that Gronwy Roth while working on his own, and labouring in search of coals, suffered a fatal accident, when the land from the surface fell into the mine on top of him. The Inquest showed that the deceased 'had in goods on the day he died corn in sheaves to the value of 2s. 3d. and a horse priced at 2s. 0d.'[18]

Military service
Fighting for king and country has been an obligation down the ages. After the settlement of 1284 the English king imposed taxes or subsidies on his Welsh subjects to pay for the Hundred Years War (1337–1453) with France. By means of the assize of arms (the weapons and equipment required of each knight) and his commissioners of array (the list of men eligible and available for military service) the king assembled his army. This was the muster roll, and able-bodied men were recruited by various means either as local volunteers or those forced to make up the local quota before being marched off to fight in the wars. Their pay was at least double the one-penny a day for hired fieldwork.

The wild, unruly Welshmen gained a reputation for bravery and fighting spirit. They were skilled with spear and lance, the long knife, with which they delivered the mortal blow in combat, such as the havoc they wrought at Crecy among the unhorsed Frenchmen at arms. In January 1343, writs were issued to the earl of Chester to provide 332 Welshmen, bowmen and spearmen, and 206 archers from the county of Chester and lordships of north-east Wales to reinforce the troops of Edward III in Brittany. Three years later, the chamberlain of Chester was told to buy suitable green and white cloth from Flint for the Welsh soldiers uniforms of a short coat and hat.[19]

The resources and revenues of the manor
It was usual for the manor of Ewloe to be farmed out. The lord leased the resources of the manor to a person who paid him a sum of money for the right to make the best profit he could from these. The potential of the manor is outlined in a Survey of 1295 made at Ewloe before Reginald de Grey, Justice of Chester, and a mixed group of Welsh and English local jurors, Meilir Fychan, Madog ap Cynwrig, William son of William, William son of Biche, John Perrin, Nicholas Bacon, Simon of Ewloe, Richard Champneys, John the Miller, Adam of Allendale, Alcock of Shotton, William of Crowther. They gave the annual revenue of the manor as nearly twenty pounds. It was made up of 480 acres of land in demesne at 6d. per acre £14, the rent of two water mills, £3; the agistment of the pasture at Buckley 10s.; deadwood 8s.; iron mine, 6s. 8d.; bailiwick of the Forest 30s.; pannage of pigs 30s.; pleas and perquisites of the court 20s.

The chamberlain's accounts are invaluable for a statement of the profits obtained from the farm (leasing) of the various resources of the manor the chief of which were noted in 1295. The chamberlain's accounts are extant from 1301 to 1353. This is where we find the accounts as presented for audit by the bailiff and sub-bailiffs of Ewloe manor.[20]

Demesne land
The lord's demesne included the manor house, manor farm, and houses and cottages in the settlement. Originally, the demesne lands were for the sustenance of the lord and his household. The tenants of the manor, both free and bond, performed services on the demesne and cultivated their own plots for subsistence. Later, many lords found it more profitable to enter into a contract with a cultivator and let the demesne for a money rent for a period of time. This arrangement was called a 'farm', either from the Anglo-Saxon *feorm*, meaning food or from the Latin *ferma*, meaning it was for a firm and fixed period[21] and a 'farmer', in this sense, was a collector of taxes who paid the Crown or the lord an agreed sum and made a profit on the collection.

Waste land

The word waste was not used as we might use it in terms of carelessness or profligacy. The wastes of the manor were the open, uncultivated, and unoccupied parcels of the land in the manor as distinguished from the demesne land. As such they were of great variety and of various use for pasture, feeding, warrens, commons, mines, furzes, trees, woods, underwoods, and coppices.[22]

Forest, woods, and timber

We have said a great deal already about the great forest, Swerdewod, and the rights which the tenants of the manor enjoyed. But the lord gained most advantage from the use of the woods and timber. In 1301–02 Kenrick Duy, forester of Ewloe, was paid 60s. for the farm of his bailiwick[23] and timber was taken to the Constable of Flint Castle for repairs to the castle:

> To Jordan de Bradeford for the carriage of timber expended 'to make one great wood work upon the great tower of Flint Castle, together with one noble and beautiful box'. Windows and wooden steps were repaired and in the next year 200 planks and boards were supplied 'for a parapet upon the wall towards the sea.'[24]

Grants in the forest were made to the burghers of Flint in the early period of English settlement. The lord employed foresters and parkers in the woods and the deer park of Ewloe. Their job was to manage the woodland and protect it from the depredations of stray beasts, poachers, and those tempted to reduce its edges.

From time to time attempts were made by the lord to empark part of the wood and make it a private reserve for deer and other sport. Roger de Mohaut made a deer park in the wood in 1241, an enterprise which came to naught when taken down by Llewelyn ap Gruffudd in 1257. The Black Prince enclosed the wood in 1347 surrounding the park with a seven-foot wide and five-foot deep dyke.

By 1320 the Forest of Ewloe was farmed out by the king to one Madoc Stulf for the 'whole life of the same'.[25]

The chamberlain's account for 1349–50 recorded:

> Sale of wood. The same answers for 40s. received for branches and twigs of oaks lately felled for the paling of the new park there, and from the old wood overthrown by the wind, for this amount sold in bulk by view of the chamberlain, and no more, because a certain part of the said branches was delivered for smelting the mine of lead on the condition that the lord shall have every sixth foot of lead smelted with the lord's underwood, whence there fall to the lord this year thirteen and a half feet of lead by measurement for which the chamberlain is charged in his account for this year.[26]

In 1351–02 it was noted, 'for 7s. received from branches of 8 trees felled for timber for divers necessary works to be done about the making of the bridge of Dee and other the lord's works'.[27] It was clearly a valuable resource from the manor of Ewloe, but over the centuries it was gradually dissipated and exhausted by neglect and assarting (taking in the wood for pasture or cultivation). By the beginning of the seventeenth century it was sadly noted that 'in the memory of some that be living, was woods all over, and now not a stick left'.[28]

Pasture

Mixed farming was predominant in the area and, until the eighteenth century, there were open field arable strips probably in Ewloe and certainly in the neighbouring townships of Aston, Shotton and Hawarden.[29] The grazing of cattle on the cleared higher pasture land of Buckley and the keeping of herds of pigs in the wood of Ewloe were an essential part of the manorial economy in the fourteenth century. The bailiff's account for 1301–02 gives returns for pigs sold for ready money which had been fed by pannage, that is the right to graze pigs on acorns and beech mast, and the profit (agistment) for each beast of 1d. 'in the pasture of Eweloe, called 'Bukkelee''. The use of the woods for pasturing continued and the bailiff reported in 1435–6 the receipt 'of 13s. 4d. from the fees for the pasturing of the beasts within the Queen's woods[30] there, so leased to the community of the township for this year, and for 2s. 6d. from the fees for the feeding of pigs there this year as appears in the rolls of the court'.

Perquisites of courts

The profits made from the courts were a regular source of income to the lord. A glimpse into the activities of the manorial courts is provided in the bailiff's account for 1435–6. John Ledsham, bailiff, returned '23s. 2d. from the perquisites of fourteen courts held there this year'. The chief official for this year was Richard Whitely to whom the bailiff recorded 'a certain reward for holding the court there and for the rule and governance of the tenants and superintending the levying of the rents of the same, for a consideration 20s.' There were occasional losses. The rent of 19d. payable by Henry Middilton was written off — 'on account of felonies committed leaving nothing behind him by which the rent could be raised'.

Mills

In 1295 two water mills existed in the manor of Ewloe known as Castle Mill and Lady's Mill. They would be harnessed to one of the brooks, probably Afon y Pentre, which ran close to the castle. The miller was an important figure in the manorial economy, for the use of the lord's mill was compulsory. His method of exacting money for the upkeep of the mill often appeared exorbitant and was a cause of complaint. The fee for grinding, known as multure, was originally a proportion of the flour, one cup in 20 or 24 for free men and one in 13 or 15 for villeins. Later this was commuted for a cash payment. The only detailed medieval record for Ewloe water mills is from 1325–6, 'The Account of the issues of the mills of Ewloe which are in the hand of the lord earl for lack of men willing to take them at farm'. The revenue accounted for by the bailiff was 71s. 10¹/₂d. from the sale of corn, wheat, barley, oats, flour and malt. Most of it was sent to Flint Castle for the provisioning of the garrison, and brewing. The only other customers were local men — Richard de Meysham, and Madoc Stulf to whom the manor was let at farm. The sole expenditure on the mills was 3s. 8d. spent on the purchase of two stones. Richard de Birchoure, carter, was paid 2s. 4d. for the carriage of 6 bushels of corn, malt and flour form the mills to the castle of Flint.[31]

It was essential that the mills were kept in good repair and no one would be more anxious to do this than the bailiff of the manor, to satisfy both his lord, and the tenants dependant upon them. It was probably for these reasons that in 1435–6 John Ledsham the bailiff undertook to be responsible for the farm of Castle Mill. He also undertook to stand surety for Lady's Mill promising to rebuild them both at his own expense and return them 'in a competent state'. The total farm for the two mills was 30s. an indication of the cost of repairs.[32]

Clay

The only mention of the working of clay by potters is in the 1435–6 bailiff's account: 'And for 2s. from the farm of the getting of clay for the making of clay pots so leased to William Potter (12d.), Thomas Potter (nil) and Ralph Gwyn (12d.) as in this year's court roll.'[33]

Coal[34]

Although there was no mention of revenue from coal in the 1295 Survey it was soon being got by some of the newly settled English. Named in the Subsidy list of 1292 were Anes and Sylvester le Colere. In the first years of the fourteenth century and for nearly three hundred years the Crown was to enjoy some revenue from the farm of coal in the manor of Ewloe. It was found near the surface by open cast digging, quarrying or bell-pit work. The coal was got from outcrop seams about six feet thick of Main and Hollin coal covering an area in a belt roughly a mile and a half long. Ewloe coal was valuable for domestic and building use at the castles of Flint and Ewloe and soon found a market in Chester. The farm of coal at first was in the hands of the descendants of Ithel Annwyl, steward at Ewloe in the time of Llywelyn ap Gruffudd (d.1282). Ithel managed to continue in an official capacity under Edward I as bailiff of the manor followed by his descendants until 1389. They were trusted by Welsh and English and frequently, but not successively, occupied the offices of forester or bailiff of the manor. One of them, Bleddyn ab Ithel, died at the time of the Black Death in 1349. To remedy the great disruption to the economy wrought by the pestilence Edward III brought William Trussel, sheriff of Anglesey, and Nicolas de Eccleston to farm the resources of the manor. Eventually Ithel ab Bleddyn succeeded to the office his father previously held until he too died in 1389.

David de Ewloe introduced a competitive note in the getting of coal in the manor by managing mining in 1365 on the lands of the free tenants. He had a successful career as a merchant adventurer in the city of Chester where he served as mayor, collector of customs, and no doubt promoted the marketing of Ewloe coal there. His son John de Ewloe eventually became sole lessee of the manor in 1398 and worked the mines until 1403. The destructive activity of the Glyn Dŵr rebels in the area, who put Wepre and Hawarden to the flame, was a threat to Chester and barred any trade for the next five years. In 1408 John de Ewloe resumed his activities for another decade being succeeded by John de Helegh II.

The trend in the fifteenth century was for the manor to be leased in its entirety. The last to lease coals, separately, was Richard de Whitley, of Aston, in 1436. Robert Moore and Thomas de Poole leased the manor in 1446. In 1461, Peter Stanley I, (d. 1511), (second son of Sir William Stanley of Hooton, a cadet line of the Stanleys of Hawarden Castle) leased the manor which remained in the hands of the family until 1573. Stanley paid an additional sum, by a moiety of coals raised.

Another important development in the extraction of coal in Ewloe was that freeholders were beginning to mine coals upon seisin (possession of property as distinct from ownership). This first appeared in 1433–4 when Roger Boothe paid 2s. for such a right. Later in the fifteenth century Richard de Whitley adopted the same practice of mining coal from freehold land.

By 1606, there was a strong feeling that the three hundred-year venture for digging coal was over when it was reported that 'the Cole mynes are and have bene longe wholli decayed and yields no profits at all to his majesty.'

We began by looking at the state of the resources of the manor listed by the Survey of 1295. At the end of the period, in 1594, a report 'valuing the Farm of the manor, with memorandum on rents and the state of mills and coal mines' revealed depressing neglect and continuing decline.

> The tenants claim for their freehold one pasture called Bookley, which now lyeth open, wherein the inhabitants claim common of pasture, paying a certain rent, and one certain wood called Hedley or Ewloe wood. The wood whereof being at this present altogether destroyed. Township of Ewloe — here were two watermills, a coalmine and perquisites of coal. The mills have been in decay for many years past, and no coals dug here of late because of the great store in other places more convenient and nearer to the sea and where they are dug with less charge.[35]

The lordships of Hawarden and Mold

Two fragmentary records from the 1470s provide the only information we have of life in the manors and lordships of Hawarden and Mold from the fourteenth to seventeenth centuries. They were more extensive than Ewloe and this may be seen in the number of medieval townships: two in Ewloe, twelve in Mold, and thirteen in Hawarden.

After the failure of the male de Mohaut heir in 1329 the lordships of Mold and Hawarden were eventually given to William de Montague created first earl of Salisbury in 1337. The family enjoyed the favour of Edward III and Richard II. When Richard abdicated in 1399 their fortunes suffered an eclipse and the next year Henry IV awarded the lordships in north east Wales to his supporter Sir John Stanley (c.1350–1414). The Stanley we meet in these records of the 1470s is Thomas, second baron Stanley, earl of Derby, in 1486. An astute politician, champion trimmer, known as 'Wily Fox', Stanley, survived the conflicts between the Yorkists and Lancastrians, known as the Wars of the Roses, intact and greatly enriched.

The two fragments of records are part of a Compotus (an estate account), Roll for Hawarden and Mold, dated 1474,[36] and an Account Roll of Thomas Stanley, 1477.[37] I have conflated the information in the documents and discussed them as one, because of their fragmentary nature, the short period of three years between them, and the same personalities and subjects accounted for.

These late fifteenth century accounts for Hawarden and Mold lordships are complementary to those of the manor of Ewloe. Some of the things lacking in the Ewloe records appear here and give further insight into the background of life in this area in the late Middle Ages. The local people would have been familiar with and brought their goods and cattle to the town markets and fairs of Hawarden and Mold. Stories would have been told to frighten little children about the dungeons of Hawarden Castle and persuade them to behave. Some of their elders may have been more acquainted with them and the Court House at Mold. The names and personalities of local officials would have been daily topics of family discourse.

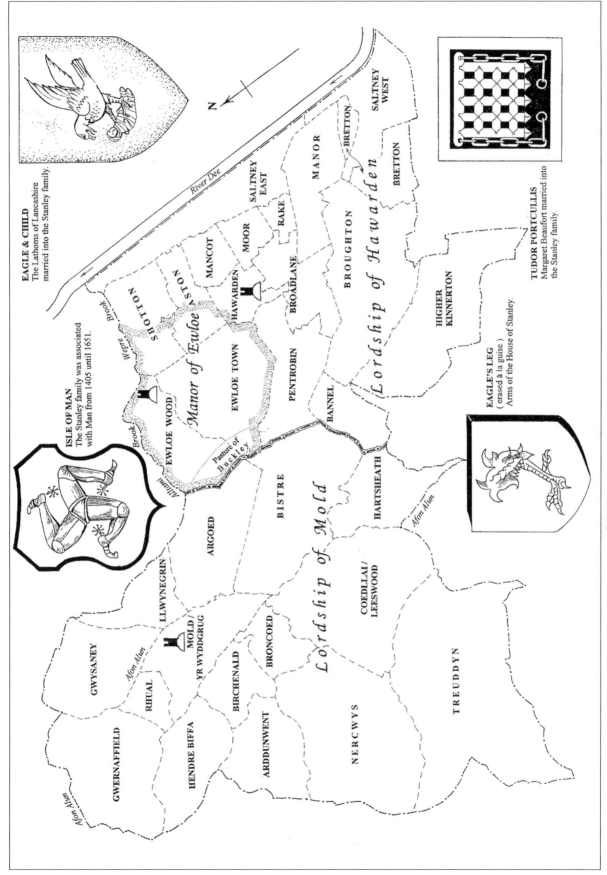

Lordships of Hawarden and Mold and the Manor of Ewloe. K. Lloyd Gruffydd.

Of more lasting memory would be the visits of Thomas, Lord Stanley, and his second wife the Lady Margaret Beaufort, countess of Richmond. Their arrival would involve great preparation, coming as they often did with a large retinue of servants and family, on progress from Knowsley, or from the King's Court, where Thomas Stanley was Lord Steward of the household. This royal connection was increased after 1485 when Lady Margaret's son became King Henry VII, and her husband earl of Derby. The Stanleys were generous and enlightened, particularly in their patronage of local churches, providing church fonts, stained-glass windows, and undertaking major building works of outstanding architectural splendour at Mold, Hawarden, Holywell, Hope, Northop, Gresford and Holt. Many of the local gentry, (the Whitelys, Ledshams, Ravenscrofts, Wynnes, Lloyds, Evanses and Messhams), benefited from their patronage at the universities and Inns of Court.

Richard II at Flint Castle 1399, The King dressed in a monk's habit. The Earl of Salisbury (Lord of Mold and Hawarden) is kneeling, to the left of the picture. From an illuminated MS in the British Museum.

We find the names of the usual officials in charge of business and administration in the lordships. Peter Dutton seneschal or steward of both lordships. Thomas Coverham, the lord's clerk. Nicholas ap Dicus, an official well acquainted with the lands and tenants in both lordships. He was a representative of the rising gentry and grandfather of John Eyton of Leeswood.[38] His work as escheator gave him the responsibility for making sure that the property of a tenant convicted of a felony, or one who died without adult heirs reverted to the lord. Nicholas was buying up tenancies for Stanley. In 1474 he bought 'from 'Blethyn ap Gign' ap Milere three waste tenements and buildings and 10 acres of land with their appurtenances in the town and fields of Mold'.

One of the most influential officers was Robert Lloyd Mayor of Mold in 1477. He virtually ran the business of the town. The reeves were responsible to him, and through them, gave him oversight of the agriculture of the manor of Mold with its town fields, or *maesydd y dre*. The ringilds or bailiffs of the town, Llywelyn ap David ab Ednyfed, and Jankyn ap Hywel, were also under his supervision. In his charge too, were the lord's mills. A corn mill at 'Coliford', now Rhyd y golau, and also, the 'farm of the lord's mill there, called Scaltmylne'. Robert Lloyd and Nicholas ap Dicus were partners together for the farm of a new mill leased to them for 21 years.

More importantly, Robert Lloyd was receiver, the lord's treasurer, whose office was the exchequer of Hawarden. He received money from the burgesses of Mold for the lord of the manor and sums for the farm of the Welshry. As well as his responsibilities in the town of Mold, Lloyd collected money for the farm of the townships of Mold. His assistant as receiver in the lordship of Hawarden was Richard Huxley. At the Castle they met the auditor who scrutinised their accounts. The extent and complexity of the business of the lordship may be seen in the entries:

> for the expenses of auditor, receiver, clerk of the court and of others being at Hawardyne in the month of April for taking and determining accounts there for six days, and to the same 10s. are paid for paper and parchment both for rolls of the court 7s. 8d. and of accounts 2s. 4d. of Hawardyne and Molysdale and for the checker (a counting table).[39]

Estate management was extensive and varied. Hawarden castle was the headquarters for the two lordships and was kept in good repair during this period as the accounts record. In 1474, Lord Stanley repaired the barbican:

> Repairs done about the castle of Hawardyne, making a lime kiln together with breaking stones, the cartage of 50 loads of stone called limestone, breaking stones called asshelers (ashlars), work of stone masons and other

workmen hired by the day both for laying down the steps at the gate of the said hall, a new tower at the gate of the said hall, new axe and iron tools, 188 lbs of iron for making the windows and the doors and seven padlocks bought for divers gates of the castle.

Other building repairs were undertaken. The roof of the grange of the manor was thatched, and tenements repaired in Aston.

One of the most interesting aspects of the 1474 account is the light it throws on the lord's demesne at Hawarden. In spite of the brevity of the accounts we gain the impression of efficiency and purpose. The whole enterprise of farming the demesne centres round the *famuli*, each member of which plays his part. William Griffiths and John Byngley, bailiffs; Thomas Cotyngham, swineherd; Robert Legh, hayward, 'for the custody of the meadows'. There is mention of *selions* (cultivated strips in the open fields) and payments for ploughing fallow and arable land, harrowing, manuring, and sowing barley and oats. Hay is mown and made, the oats and barley reaped. The meadows provide for the stable at the manor, and other land, grain for the lord's household. Attention is paid to the appearance of the manor by 'ditching around' the close, cutting thorns on the path from the park, and making hedges.

Stanley was allowing holdings to fall out of tenancy and intent on getting the best out of his lands. The wasteland at Saltney was used for sheep and a tenement at Broughton was retained by 'the lord himself for an abode by night and guarding of his sheep there', for the use of his shepherd, John Browne who appears in both accounts.

For 1474, 'Paid to John Browne shepherd for buying ointment for the sheep there 2½d., and for leading rushes from Saltney for strewing the sheepfold 2d. and for mending divers defects and the walls of the same house 20d. And paid for washing and shearing 176 lambs this year in all 2s. 6d.'

His accounts for 1477 are more detailed:

Sheep killed for the boon-workers of the manor — 7. (compulsory work on the manor, such as ploughing and harvesting).[7] Sheep killed at the lord's guest chamber at Hawardyn in November 1477, and those killed by foxes this year at the time of lambing 20, and those dead 34, and for 20 stones of wool from 273 shorn fleeces remaining from the last account, and for 26 stones of wool, each stone containing 16 *lbs*. From 280 shorn fleeces obtained from all the sheep, total 46 stones, and there remain in the keeping at Hawarden 20 stones and at Chester with Huxley 26 stones. (Huxley was probably the receiver for Hawarden).

There was a pinfold in Moldsdale farmed in 1474 to Llywelyn ap Grono ap Madog who paid 10s. 'for the farm of the lesser pound'.

The economy of the demesne was directed to providing enough food for the visits of Thomas, Lord Stanley, Lady Margaret Beaufort and their retinues. Expenses in September 1474 over four days, cost the moderate sum of £18 11s. 10d. and included, 'bread, wine, ale, wax, beef, flesh mutton, fresh fish, poultry and other victuals and necessary expenses, together with provender for their horses, with 401 white loaves delivered at Lathom and a carcass of beef and three carcasses of mutton'. Wine was bought in London and Chester.

Security at the castle and the pursuit of criminals throughout the lordship was vigorously prosecuted. There must have been great excitement in 1474 when there was a hue and cry by 'eighty persons of the demesne for their labour in capturing five thieves in Moldesdale'. Their reward was bread and ale. It fell to the lot of Thomas Coney, constable and gaoler at Hawarden, to arrange for their safe custody. He took no chances as the accounts testify. 'Paid to Henry Mason, Nicholas Bellyn and William Leche for watching the said robbers living in the castle.' They stood guard for 12 nights and one Gwyn ap Griffith ap Madog ap Owen may have died in prison.

The 1477 accounts report that the sum of 2s. 3d. was spent on repairing shutters on the windows of a building in Mold called the 'courthouse'. The courthouse was used for centuries for the meeting of the Court leet of the manor and later for the Quarter Sessions when they met in Mold. It was later called the Common Hall of Pleas of the county. At the beginning of the nineteenth century it was owned, as lord of the manor, by Sir Thomas Mostyn. The building was described by Edward Pugh in *Cambria Depicta* in 1816 as a 'barn-like crazy old building appearing better calculated to receive, on an emergency, a set of strolling players, than for the solemnity of a court of justice'. In 1831 the *Chester Chronicle* reported:

We are happy in being able to announce to readers, that, the 'Town Barn' at Mold, which we have so often stigmatised as disgraceful to the County of Flint, will be abandoned to the mice and bats immediately after the ensuing assizes and a handsome County Hall erected in its stead.

The end of lordships as political entities

Lordships were abolished by the Act of Union in 1536 which swept away Marcher lordships and ordained that all Welsh subjects should henceforth enjoy the same freedoms and laws as the king's subjects in England. The Marcher lords were no longer to try pleas of the Crown, though they could continue to hold court baron and court leet jursdiction. The lordship of Mold was included in the county of Flint in 1536. The lordship and manor of Ewloe was part of the shire from 1284. The lordship of Hawarden was transferred from the new county of Denbigh to Flintshire in 1541.

The seventeenth century

This is the century when all the areas of diverse origin begin to coalesce and the community assumes its 'shape' in so many ways. First of all, there is new leadership in the community brought about by the rise of the gentry. Secondly, this new class of gentry, 'middling' squires, new lords of Mold, and the arrival of the more substantial Glynne family at Hawarden (who didn't reside at Hawarden until the beginning of the eighteenth century), take part in an unprecedented change in land ownership. Thirdly, after this share out they begin to exploit the rich deposits of coal and clay by leasing them to entrepreneurs. Fourthly in this way new capital is brought in from outside the area by speculators who are willing to risk taking out these leases sinking collieries, exploiting clay deposits, improving river navigation and other forms of transport. In the seventeenth century too there is a further revolution in religious thought. This is one of the great debates of the Civil War, which slowly brings about after false starts religious toleration and paves the way for religious revival in the eighteenth century and the growth of Nonconformity in the nineteenth century.

The majority of these points are taken up in later chapters. To conclude this chapter we will discuss the rise of the gentry in the area, and the change in land ownership until the beginning of the Civil War in 1640.

The rise of the gentry

There is a marked difference between the fourteenth century effigy of Ithel ab Bleddyn and the figure of Robert Davies V (d. 1728), over three hundred years later. Ithel is clad in a suit of armour and Robert in the dress of a Roman gentleman. But there are similarities. They were both Welsh gentlemen — *uchelwyr, priodorion, boneddig* — high-born, privileged, with a pedigree and lineage which took their roots back to the ancient Welsh families and gave them a place in the exalted ranks of either the five royal tribes of Cambria or the fifteen tribes of north Wales.[41]

Ithel ab Bleddyn, bailiff of the manor of Ewloe, whose family 'farmed' it for the English Crown, emerged from a family who had served the Princes of Gwynedd. His sepulchral effigy representing him as a knight encapsulates the idea of service, chivalry, gentility, and authority. Likewise the dress chosen for Robert Davies's monument demonstrates a more classical expression of these attributes.

The rise of the gentry from the end of the fifteenth century onwards is one of the dominant themes in the history of the Mold, Hawarden, Ewloe, and Buckley district. Exceptional country houses and familiar family names are the legacy of this age of the gentry, whose rule in county affairs lasted until the beginning of the twentieth century. Their fine country houses are clustered like stars in a constellation around the county town of Mold rising as they did within the boundaries of the ancient lordship and expressing the centres of power of a close-knit regional community.

The first opportunities and responsibilities given to the gentry class were, as we have seen, as stewards, bailiffs, ringilds, in the lordships of the Stanley family and the Crown manor of Ewloe. This new administrative class of native Welsh had their origins as uchelwyr, highborn clansmen, in the free townships. Added to the ambition of office was the desire to build up a holding, an estate that they could pass on to their first-born freed from the Welsh custom of partible inheritance. By the Welsh laws of inheritance estates were divided equally between all offspring and made it nigh impossible to build up a lasting and worthwhile patrimony. To overcome this difficulty Welsh jurists developed a legal device which

Effigy of Ithel ab Bleddyn, (c.1395). Colin A. Gresham,
Medieval Stone Carving in North Wales *(p.199).*

allowed land to be alienated by means of a mortgage, *prid*, which if unredeemed after sixteen years, absolute title was gained by the mortgagor. In 1541 Welsh tenurial custom was abolished and land was to be held according to the common law of England.

Ambitious families followed the example of their neighbours gradually adding to their estates by carving out holdings from the waste in the Crown Manor of Ewloe or in the private lordships of Mold and Hawarden. By the middle of the sixteenth century such encroachments were widespread. Welsh freeholders insisted that as tenants of adjoining freeholds they were entitled to enclose and improve them without licence from the lord of the manor. We will see later what effect this action had on the manor of Ewloe. In this way a number of families had risen into the gentry class and were recognisable as a new ruling order in Welsh society from the late fifteenth century onwards.

Gentry families and their houses

These newly emerged families had certain things in common. With the help of the bards, they devised elaborate coats of arms based on their pedigrees which in some cases stretched back to Adam, or at least to the ancient British kings. Some of the English families traced their lineage back to the members of the invading force of 1066. Their newly emblazoned heraldic arms announced their solidarity with others of their class and displayed the arms of families, parent or cadet branches, into which they inter-married. Mostyn, Salusbury, Puleston, Lloyd, Wynn, Evans, Whitley, Ravenscroft these and others of Welsh or English origin formed a new élite. Their increasing power and prosperity was strengthened in this way. The Tudor state relied on them to govern in their localities as local magistrates and arrange between themselves the turns in which they would serve as members of parliament, either for the county or borough. In order to fit them for these responsibilities their sons were educated at the Inns of Court and universities and afterwards elder sons managed the estate, and younger sons followed a career in the law, army, church, or were apprenticed to trade either in Chester or London.

Ewloe families

Ledsham of Farmstile — the family settled in Ewloe in the fourteenth century from which time their name occurred with some frequency. In 1606 George Ledsham endowed Hawarden Grammar School. The brothers George and Richard Ledsham were members of the Inner Temple London. George Ledsham's sister, Ann, married Robert Jones, whose son and heir went to Ireland *c.*1655 as a secretary in Cromwell's army. Farmstile descended to the Leach family who farmed and later exploited the coal and clay in the area.

Messham of Ewloe Hall — Cropper states that 'the long direct line of this name was associated with the place down the centuries and has

Statue of Robert Davies V (1684–1728) Mold Parish Church by
Sir Henry Cheere, Bart. [By permission of Vicar and Churchwardens]

1
GRUFFUDD AP CYNAN
(c.1055-1137)

2
RHYS AP TEWDWR
(d.1093)
The Wynnes of Leeswood Hall
and The Tower, Broncoed.,
decend from this *teulu* 'tribe'

3
BLEDDYN AP CYNFYN
(d. 1075)

**THE FIVE
ROYAL TRIBES
OF WALES**

From Robert Vaughan of Hengwrt's
British Antiquities revived

*

(after Thomas Pennant, *W & H*)

4
ELYSTAN AP GLODRYDD
(*fl.* 1060?)

5
IESTYN AP GWRGANT
(*fl.* c.1081-93)

lately reached its termination with the death of Colonel Messham, DL, JP, of Pontruffydd near Bodfari. The last of the Messhams to reside at Ewloe Hall was Thomas Messham, who was buried in the family grave at Hawarden Church in 1772.[42]

Whitley of Aston Hall — the family arrived in Ewloe in the thirteenth century and played a leading part in its affairs serving as bailiffs, stewards, and 'farming' the manor. They inter-married with the Stanley family of Ewloe Castle in the sixteenth century. In the seventeenth century Thomas Whitley married (i) a Ravenscroft, and (ii) a Brereton, by whom he had issue; five of their sons fought as royalists in the Civil War with Colonel Roger Whitley (1618–97) having an outstanding career. The family continued at Aston Hall and in 1808 James Whitley Deans Dundas married the heiress.[43]

Stanley of Ewloe Castle — a cadet branch of the Stanleys of Hawarden and Latham. King Henry VI gave Peter Stanley, the second son of Sir William Stanley of Hooton, certain rights by letters patent at Ewloe. Peter Stanley married Margery daughter of Sir John Heleigh, who held the manor 1413–4. Their son Pyers Stanley, (d. 1521) 'of Ewloe Castle' married Constance daughter of Thomas Salisbury of Lleweni, and their son, Pyers Stanley, was a gentleman of Henry VIII's household. He was granted the lease of Ewloe manor 'with

Facing: From Thomas Pennant, The Fifteen Tribes of North Wales, in History of the Parishes of Holywell and Whiteford, *plate xxii p 290.*

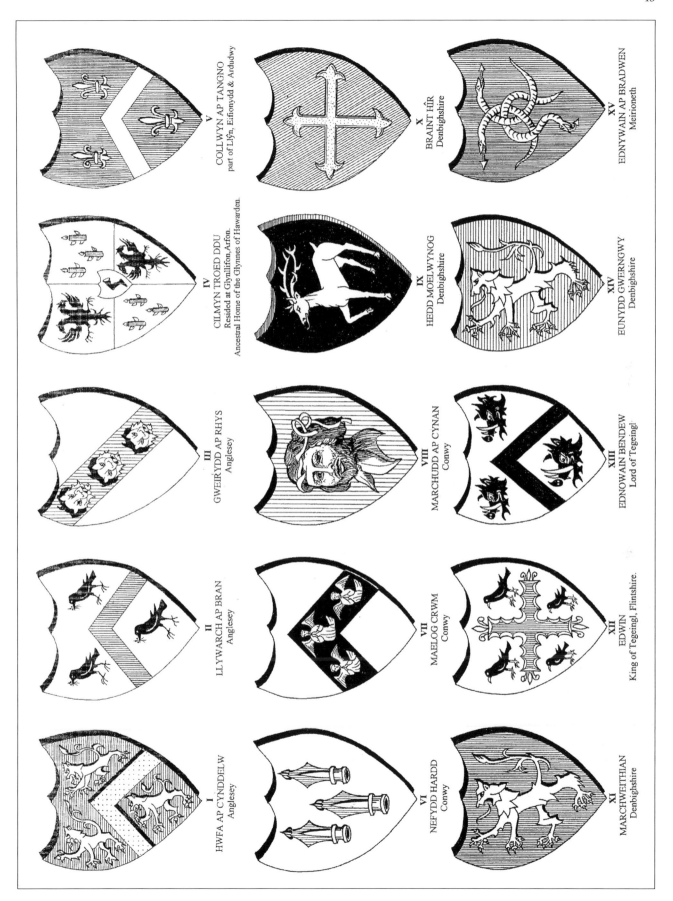

V
COLLWYN AP TANGNO
part of Llŷn, Eifionydd & Ardudwy

X
BRAINT HÎR
Denbighshire

XV
EDNYWAIN AP BRADWEN
Meirioneth

IV
CILMYN TROED DDU
Resided at Glynllifon, Arfon.
Ancestral Home of the Glynnes of Hawarden.

IX
HEDD MOELWYNOG
Denbighshire

XIV
EUNYDD GWERNGWY
Denbighshire

III
GWEIRYDD AP RHYS
Anglesey

VIII
MARCHUDD AP CYNAN
Conwy

XIII
EDNOWAIN BENDEW
Lord of Tegeingl

II
LLYWARCH AP BRAN
Anglesey

VII
MAELOG CRWM
Conwy

XII
EDWIN
King of Tegeingl, Flintshire.

I
HWFA AP CYNDDELW
Anglesey

VI
NEFYDD HARDD
Conwy

XI
MARCHWEITHIAN
Denbighshire

43

Right: Arms and Crest of Davies-Cooke of Gwysaney and Owston from G. A. Usher Gwysaney and Owston nd.

Below: Monumental effigy – John ap Elis Eyton and Elizabeth Calveley (c.1526) St Mary's Church Ruabon.

all mines of sea coal in the Co. of Flint, Flint Mill, fines and profits of the Court, with the tolls of markets and fairs; reserving all woods, quarries of stone, lead, coal except, sea coal, goods of felons &c. paying annually £22 10s. and for the mill four marks &c.' Pyers' heir, Edward, held the manor from the Crown in the reign of Elizabeth. His son Robert married Alice daughter of Thomas Salisbury of Leadbrook. Their only child Anne married John Mostyn of Coed Onn, Flint. Their heiress, Katherine, married John Aldersey of Deiniol's Ash, and in 1636 Anne granted them her extensive estates in Ewloe and several townships in Hawarden parish.

The Ravenscrofts — a family with branches in Ewloe, Shotton, and Bretton. They were of Norman descent and settled in Cheshire with a cadet branch appearing in north Wales in the fourteenth century when Hugh de Ravenscroft was steward of Hope, Hawarden, and Mold. In the seventeenth century they were a large and talented family of strong Protestant sympathies. They inter-married with the Davies family of Gwysaney, and Salusbury of Rug. George Ravenscroft (d.1592) married Dorothy, heiress of John Davies, Constable of Hawarden castle, and owner of Broadlane, which she brought into the family, which in turn by the marriage of the heiress Honora passed into the neighbouring Glynne family in the eighteenth century. We notice the Ravenscroft family later in the Civil War.[44]

The gentry of the parish of Mold

Davies of Gwysaney — they are descended in direct line from Cynric Efell (*fl.*1200) son of Madog ap Maredudd, prince of Powys. The patrynomic name of Davies was first assumed by John ap David in the sixteenth century. Robert Davies I (d.1603) obtained confirmation of family arms, and the crest borne by his descendants from the College of Heralds. The present house of Gwysaney dates from 1603. His eldest son Robert Davies II (1581–1633) succeeded him. His second son, Thomas Davies, (d.1655), became a soldier serving on the continent, and in the court of the young Prince Henry, and later assisting the earl of Bridgewater, Lord President of the Council of Wales. Thomas obtained the purchase of the manor of Ewloe and was a great support to his nephew Robert Davies III in the Civil War. As lords of the Manor of Ewloe from 1633 until the present day the family have played a leading and continuous part in the history of Buckley and district.[45]

Abbreviated pedigree – Davies-Cooke family of Gwysaney and Owston

Robert Davies I (1555–1602)
Robert Davies II (1581–1633)
Robert Davies III (1616–66)
Mutton Davies (1634–1728)
Robert Davies VI (1715–63)
Frances Puleston (1765–1818)
m. Bryan Cooke (1756–1821)
Philip Davies-Cooke (1793–1853)
Philip Bryan Davies-Cooke (1832–1903)
Phillip Tatton Davies-Cooke (1863–1946)
Philip Ralph Davies-Cooke (1896–1970)
Philip Peter Davies-Cooke (1925–2003)

Wynn of 'Coet y llai', old Leeswood Hall — descended from Rhys ap Tewdwr (d.1093), last of the ancient kings of Deheubarth, of the second royal tribe.

Eyton of Leeswood Hall — after 1783 Wynne-Eyton, of Leeswood and The Tower. Same descent as above. Amongst their descendants Nicholas ap Deicus (*fl.*1474) whose grandson married Margaret daughter of John ab Elis Eyton of Rhiwabon. The family inter-married with the neighbouring families of Davies, Gwysaney; Lloyd, Pentrehobyn; and Puleston, Emral. The Reverend Hope Wynne-Eyton was a distinguished vicar of Mold 1792–1825. Amongst other places they owned land and property in Bistre and Argoed. Leeswood Hall was built by Sir George Wynne, Bart, *c.*1724–6.

Wynne, of The Tower, Broncoed — the house was built as a fortified dwelling by Rheinallt ap Gruffydd in 1445. Piers Wynne of The Tower fought with Sir William Stanley when he went to the aid of Sir Philip Sydney in the Low Countries in 1586. David Wynne (d.1626) had a coat of arms with 24 quarterings. In the Leeswood papers are ancient pedigree rolls which trace the family back in the customary manner through the Welsh princes, the ancient British kings, Brutus of Troy, to Adam and Eve. The family were royalists during the Civil War.

Wynne of Nerquis — the house was built by John Wynne, between 1637 and 1640. They were descended from the twelfth tribe of north Wales, Edwin of Tegeingl, in the female line.

Lloyd of Pentrehobyn — the same descent as the family from Nerquis Hall. The present house was built in the early years of the seventeenth century by Edward and Margaret Lloyd although the family were there much earlier.

Lloyd of Plas yn Herseth — descended from the twelfth tribe of North Wales, Edwin of Tegeingl, in the female line. They inter-married with the families of Leeswood, Nerquis, Gwysaney, and the Stanley family of Ewloe. Edward Lloyd was at the surrender of Denbigh in 1646.

Edwards of Rhual — descended from Edwin of Tegeingl. Evan Edwards built the present house of brick in 1634. Evan employed as a clerk in the Exchequer of Chester attracted the attention of Sir Eubule Thelwall. He was admitted to Gray's Inn and became secretary to the third earl of Dorset. In 1625 he became a baron of the Court of the Exchequer and in 1639 Comptroller of Customs for Chester, Beaumaris, and Liverpool. At the beginning of the Civil War he was one of Charles I's Commissioners of Array but by April 1645 was assisting the Parliamentarians in their siege of Hawarden. His brother William was MP for

Nerquis Hall showing the portico which is now at Portmeirion.

The Tower, Broncoed, Mold.

Chester in 1645. The Parliamentarians who suspected Evan's loyalty plundered Rhual in 1645 and fined him £157.

The acquisition of the manor of Ewloe by the Davies family of Gwysaney, 1633

Robert Davies I (d.1603), and his son Robert Davies II (1581–1633), spent their lives busily involved in building up their estate and occupying various administrative offices in North Wales for the Crown. Like their kinsmen the Mostyns, they had an interest in coal pits in Bagillt and were familiar with those at Ewloe.[46] The family maintained a presence at London. In the reign of Elizabeth Robert Davies (d. 1585) was a member of the Yeomen of the Guard and in the next generation another younger son Thomas Davies (d.1655) was familiar with the Court and served as the captain of a regiment on the continent. Their eyes and ears were alert for any advantage, which might come from this quarter. Moreover, they could scrape the cash together if a bargain appeared.

Their interest in the manor of Ewloe extended over a period of forty years before they were able to purchase it. Gwysaney papers show that they were able to monitor the situation there very closely. The earliest document in this series is dated 1594 and is a memorandum on rents and the state of the mills and the coalmines. The Tudors in an age of inflation and seeking to raise money for the defence of the realm and in pursuit of Protestant alliances against Catholic Spain were searching out any possible source of revenue. This is the first of a number of enquiries which were continued in the reign of James I, (1603–25).

Robert Davies I may well have been involved in meeting the Crown officers at Ewloe and providing them with assistance and information.

The Commission of 1594 provided information on the revenue paid by the freehold tenants. They declared that they paid a chief rent (a rent charge) of 18 pence an acre per year for their 480 acres. They also noted:

> one pasture called Bookley, which now lyeth open, wherein the Inhabitants claim Common of Pasture paying a certain yearly rent for the same; and of one certain Wood called Hedley or Ewloe Wood — the wood whereof being at this present altogether destroyed. The Tenants likewise claim Common of Pasture for a certain yearly rent, for which Township here were two watermills, a 'Cole Myne' and perquisites of courts.

This review of the manor's resources and their future must have appeared very gloomy:

> The Mills have been in decay for many years past, and no coals dug here of late because of the great store in other places more convenient and nearer to the sea, and where they are dug with less charge by means whereof her Majesty's Farmers here of late hath received small benefits thereby.[47]

These were from rents and tithes.

In 1599 Robert Davies I and his neighbour, Thomas Ravenscroft, purchased lands from the earl of Derby. Ravenscroft's acquisition was in the three Stanley lordships of Mold, Hope, and Hawarden and Davies's in the lordship of Mold. They paid at the rate of forty times the annual rent. Ravenscroft's annual rent was £8. 15s. 11d. and Davies's £1 15s. 2d. The land cost £422 3s. 4d. and the expenses and gratuities to the earl's agents, and lawyers were £168 10s. 6d.[48] This sale illustrates the importance in carefully building up an estate not only by connections brought about by marriage but local knowledge, and the advantage of being a sitting tenant. Robert Davies was married to Katherine, the sister of Ravenscroft.

In 1606 Robert Davies II (1581–1633), together with John Eyton of Leeswood, acted in an official capacity for the Crown with Thomas Trafford his Majesty's Receiver General of North Wales, who was conducting an enquiry on behalf of a Commission from the Exchequer. Once again they were searching out the rents of the manor of Ewloe.

The jury of fifteen had their charge given to them at the house of Robert Ward in Ewloe on the 5 September 1606. William Griffith, the foreman of the jury, and others, delivered up their findings to Trafford, Davies, and Eyton on the 17 September at 'Kinnerton Green'. They returned information that substantiated the facts of the 1594 memorandum. 'Two water milles and the Cole mynes mencioned in the said commission, wch are and have been longe and whollie decayed and yeld no profite at all to his Majestie'. The chief rents, right of Commons, and perquisites of Court returned £20 10s. or thereabouts. The jury found that the pasture of Buckley and Hedley or Ewloe Wood was of 'no certain profit to his Majesty' and that both 'have been of long time accounted as waste ground belonging to the said manor.'

A note on the back of the document recorded: 'and as touchinge the foure hundred and fourscore acres of land in severalty mencioned in the said commission there is not any suche within the said mannor to the Juries knowledge'. Robert Davies and John Eyton were probably aware that the jury was concealing information.

The manor of Ewloe came into the hands of Charles, who succeeded his late brother Henry, as Prince of Wales, and in 1621 it was leased to Sir John North for 31 years at a rent of £20 15s. There was no attempt to increase revenue and the rent remained the same. The Crown acting under the suspicion that local freeholders were concealing lands of the 'Castle, town and lordship of Ewloe', in 1622/3, instituted proceedings in the Court of the Exchequer when the Attorney General of Charles Prince of Wales, Sir John Walter, prosecuted prominent defendants from Ewloe: Robert Stanley, Ann Moten (Mostyn) widow, Thomas Whitley, Ann Griffiths, Thomas Ravenscroft, Thomas Ledsham, and Thomas Sparke. Members of the families of five out of the seven named had sat on the Jury of enquiry in 1606. The prosecution alleged that, 'Leases were procured of late, by covetous persons, of the whole castle, town and lordship for £20 15s.' They were accused of dividing the demesne lands among themselves, claiming to be freeholders paying a quit rent (to release from manorial obligations of performing specific services). Other allegations included the removing of meres and banks and erecting enclosures. Felling and taking away timber, taking away the stone and lead of the castle. Concealing land and digging coal pits.

In answer the defendants pleaded that 'the meres and bounds are not certain'. They claimed to hold certain messuages and lands in their demesne as of fee together with common pasture in Ewloe wood, Ewloe Park and 'Bookeley'.[49]

They were determined not to be deprived of their privileges and the matter did not rest there, for in the Gwysaney papers are requests to Davies' kinsman, Sir Roger Mostyn, that a Survey be made of the manor of Ewloe. There were reports of the encroachment of freeholders, and a petition, in 1627, for yet another survey of Ewloe Wood.[50]

Another document is more explicit about those 'who digge colles in Ewloe', giving the names of eight prominent freeholders. It also lists the tenants of land for agricultural purposes. Twelve on 'the score (pasture) of Ewloe on the English side', and 'fifty-five on the score of Ewloe on the Welsh side.'[51]

In view of the enterprising and restless attitude of the tenants it is not surprising that the agents of Charles, now King (1625–49), were prepared to sell off the manor and Sir John North relinquish his lease. The king was attempting to rule without parliament and using every expedient to raise revenue such as the notorious ship money. No one was in a better position than Robert Davies to press his suit for the manor. It was a family endeavour and his brother at Court, Captain Thomas Davies, was the instrument by which it was achieved. The soldier brother bought it in his own name, with family money, and received the title of lord of the manor of Ewloe. The Gwysaney papers have two items which reflect this coup — 'An account of expenses incurred on two journeys to London about Ewloe Wood 1631.' And 'Memorandum on the weighing of £300 sent by Robert Davies 1631.'[52] Usher remarks 'This ambition involved him (Thomas Davies) in complicated negotiations' and 'some very shadowy letters passed between him and the earls of Derby and Bridgewater.'[53]

The manor came to the Gwysaney family on 4 November 1633, at a time of mourning, for Robert Davies II had recently died at the age of 52 years. His heir, Robert Davies III (1616–66) was aged 17 years, and two years earlier had married Ann, daughter and sole heiress of the judge Sir Peter Mutton of Llannerch.

Fortunately Captain Thomas Davies, his uncle, was able to give him support and guidance in the critical years leading up to the Civil War.

Any trouble which might have arisen 'on their doorstep' in the manor of Ewloe was wisely settled when Thomas Davies came to an accommodation and agreement with the freeholders. Davies agreed to honour the arrangements previously made by Sir John North designed 'for the pacifying and settling of certain differences and suits between the parties concerning the taking and leasing of stone and marl on the ground called Ewloe Wood, and right to common pasture upon the grounds called Buckley &c.'[54]

This was a significant step in the shaping of the community and established a good relationship between the lord of the manor, the freeholders, and most importantly with those who in later times brought prosperity to Buckley as potters, fire-clay workers, and colliers.

Within twenty years another event occurred which was of equal importance: the change of ownership of the lordships of Mold, Hawarden, and Hope. In the meantime the local population were faced with the agony and devastation of Civil War.

Notes

1. Edward Hubbard, *Clwyd, The Buildings of Wales*, (Penguin Books, University of Wales Press, 1986), p. 364.
2. J. E. Messham, 'Ewloe in the Middle Ages, Part 2: The origins of the Manor and Township of Ewloe', *Buckley*, 13.
3. The others were Mostyn, Prestatyn, and Bachygraig.
4. Map in, K. Lloyd Gruffydd, 'The Manor of Ewloe and the Place-Name of Buckley,' *Buckley* 5.
5. *Cheshire Sheaf*, June 1912.
6. J. E. Messham, 'Ewloe in the Middle Ages, Part 1: Selected documents,' *Buckley* 12, p. 5. Quoting PRO E179/2'52.
7. Hawkes, op cit, *Buckley*, 24.
8. H. S. Bennett, *Life on the English Manor, 1150–1400*, (Cambridge, 1937) p. 196f.
9. Gwilym Usher, 'A Survey of the Honour of Denbigh in 1334,' Denbighshire Historical Society *Transactions*, vol. 3, pp. 14–15.
10. Arthur Jones, 'Flintshire Minister' Account, 1301–1328', *Publications Flintshire Historical Society*, vol. 3, p.xxvi.
11. D/GW/909–11.
12. James Bentley, 'Notes on the manor of Ewloe,' *Buckley*, 13.
13. Christopher Jessel, *The Law of the Manor*, (Barry Rose Law Publishers Ltd., Chichester, 1998), p.167f.
14. J. E. Messham, A Ewloe Bailiff's Account and the origins of the Buckley Pottery Industry, *Flintshire Historical Society Journal*, vol. 32, p.175.
15. Quoted from Bennett op cit, p.158 from *Fleta*, edited by J. Selden, 1647.
16. Messham, op cit., *Buckley*, 12, citing PRO Indictments, Chester, 25/24/, m.25.
17. Quoted by Bennett, op cit, p.179, 'Walter of Henley's Husbandry', together with an 'Annonymous Husbandry, Seneschauncie etc'., E. Lamond, *Royal Historical Society*, 1890, p. 103.
18. Messham, op cit, fn 6.
19. D. L. Evans, 'Flintshire Ministers' Accounts, 1328–1353,' *Flintshire Historical Society Record Series*, no. 2, pp. 1-11.
20. See fns 10, 14, 19.
21. Jessel, op cit, p. 95.
22. ibid, p. 98.
23. See fn 10, p. 7.
24. ibid, 1301–02, p. 15 and p. 33.
25. ibid, p. 76
26. ibid, Ministers Acct, 1349–50, p. 35.
27. ibid, p. 76.
28. FRO D/GW/555/12B.
29. Pritchard, *Hawarden*, p. 43.
30. Katherine widow of King Henry V received the manor as part of her dower.
31. Messham, op cit, *Buckley*, 12, document 4.
32. ibid.
33. For pottery industry in the Middle Ages see chapter on potteries.
34. For a detailed account of the getting of coal in the manor of Ewloe in the Middle Ages see. K. Lloyd Gruffydd, 'Coal Mining in Flintshire during the later Middle Ages,' *Flintshire Historical Society Journal*, vol.30, and 'Medieval Coal Mining in Flintshire,' *Buckley*, 1, and in this book, chapter on collieries.

35. FRO D/GW/555 ff. 4–5.

36. W. B. Jones, Hawarden Deeds, *Flintshire Historical Society Publications*, vol. 7, pp. 32–45.

37. An Account Roll of Thomas Stanley, 1477, FRO D/DM/426 and a report on the manuscript by R. K. Matthias, *Clwyd Record Office Annual Report*, 1974.

38. *Powys Fadog*, vol. v., pp. 206–7.

39. Fn 36, op cit, p. 41.

40. *Chester Chronicle* 8/7/1831. A new hall was built to the designs of Thomas Jones in 1833 and the old building abandoned. After a resolution by the parish vestry in 1845 that 'it was prejudicial to the health of the town' the Mostyns pulled it down in 1849.

41. Thomas Pennant, *The History of the Parishes of Whiteford and Holywell*, (London, 1796), appendix, p. 283.

42. Thomas Cropper, *Buckley and District*, (Buckley, 1923), pp. 244-7. And W. B. Jones, *History of Hawarden* — in manuscript FRO, vol. 4, p. 133.

43. For Roger Whitley and J. W. D. Dundas see *Dictionary of National Biography*.

44. *Dictionary of Welsh Biography*, pp. 821–2.

45. G. A. Usher, *Gwysaney and Owston, a History of the Family of Davies-Cooke*, n.d.

46. ibid p. 32.

47. FRO D/GW/555/ ff. 4–5.

48. FRO D/GW/349. I am grateful to Mr K. Lloyd Gruffydd for transcribing the document for me.

49. T. I. Jeffreys Jones, *Exchequer Proceedings Concerning Wales, James I*, (Cardiff, Univ. of Wales Press, 1955) p. 204.

50. FRO D/GW/ ff. 57–77.

51. See W. B. Jones, fn 42, p. 108, and *Calendar Wynn of Gwydir Papers 1515-1690*, no. 1308, (1614–1625, March 27), NLW, Aberystwyth, 1926.

52. FRO D/DG/555 ff. 78-80.

53. Usher, op cit, p. 41.

54. FRO D/GW/B173.

Chapter 3
Preparing the ground, 1640–1840.
The redistribution of land

The Civil War

To add another dimension to the story of the shaping of Buckley it was in the uncertain and murky conditions of the Civil War and Commonwealth period (1642–1660) that the earliest potters and clay workers began to settle on Buckley Mountain. Adventurers, too, obtained leases of coalmines in the lordship of Mold.

Bentley speculates 'that the presence of contingents of royalist soldiers in this area under the Stanleys and Mostyn may have encouraged the local potters to turn their hands to pipe making.'[1] In 1651 Robert Cotymor from Caernarvon, a Parliamentarian lawyer, obtained possession of the lease for coalmining in the sequestered Stanley lordships. Unfortunately the royalists had disabled the collieries and it took Cotymore until 1657 to restart them.[2] He lived at Plas Onn, Nercwys.

These years, until the Restoration of King Charles II in 1660, brought great upheaval, dislocation, disaster, and death to many. During the Civil Wars it has been estimated that nearly a hundred thousand people were killed and more than that figure taken prisoner. The property of both rich and poor was

ROYALIST OFFICERS

Col. John Robinson of Gwersyllt Uchaf
(1616-81)

Col. Thomas Davies of Gwysaney
(c.1585-1654)

Capt. Robert Davies III of Gwysaney
(1615-66)

Col. Sir Roger Mostyn II of Mostyn
(1624-90)

Lt. Gen. Lord Arthur Capel
(1604-49)

Royalist officers of the Civil War. [Buckley Society Magazine, 28]

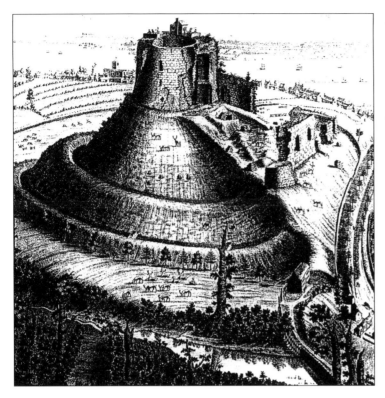

Ruins of the old castle at Hawarden, from Badeslade.

plundered by the soldiers who tended to live off the land. Nearby at Chester, between 22 June 1647 and 20 April 1648, 2,099 people died of the plague.[3] It has been said that 'most of the Welsh lived through the Commonwealth as an enemy occupation'.[4] Wales was vital to the Royalist cause. The Parliamentarian Sir William Brereton regarded the Principality as the magazine whence 'all his Majesty's provisions of victuals and men doe proceed'.[5] Once again in its history this area was the corridor by which opposing armies advanced by land from Chester and Wrexham or by sea from the coast to besiege royalist castles.

The local gentry were almost unanimous in their support for the ill-fated Charles, and Wales was called the 'nursery of the King's infantry' and a 'royal fortress'. The gentry were determined not to be dislodged from the privileged position of leadership given to them by the Tudor monarchy and readily committed themselves to make sacrifices. In one way or another the gentry families of the area became involved in the complex and fragmentary military campaigns between 1642–6. After the execution of the King in January 1649 they suffered for ten years under a military dictatorship and the Commissioners appointed for 'The Act for the Better Promotion of the Gospel in Wales.'

At the beginning of the War Charles appointed Colonels Thomas Davies and Roger Mostyn to lead his forces in Flintshire. Two major campaigns were fought in the area by the Parliamentarian forces during which Hawarden Castle was under siege three times. In November 1643 the Parliamentarians led by Sir Thomas Myddleton and Sir William Brereton crossed over Holt Bridge into Wales and arrived at the gates of Hawarden Castle by the 9 November. To their surprise the gates of the Castle were opened to them by the erstwhile Royalist Governor Colonel Thomas Ravenscroft and his Hawarden neighbour John Aldersey and they promptly marched into the Castle. In the first week of December the Parliamentarians were forced by Colonels Davies and Mostyn to surrender. In the time spent in the town of Hawarden the extreme Puritans in the army took the opportunity to visit the parish church where they smashed the stained-glass windows, broke up the rails around the altar, and tore some pages from a Bible. They defaced the churchyard cross and destroyed others. The Lower Cross by the old House of Correction and the Upper or Aston Cross, where now stands the Memorial Fountain, were destroyed. Advancing through Ewloe to Buckley Mountain, at the west boundary of Hawarden township and the lordships of Mold and Hawarden, they demolished Coningrene Cross.[6]

The second major campaign in the area occurred in 1645. It opened in February when Brereton and Myddleton crossed the Dee with 2,000 men and besieged the castle at Hawarden, but fled because of the presence in the area of royalist troops. The Parliamentarians returned in April when Brereton attempted to intercept an ammunition convoy on its way from Anglesey to Chester. The convoy slipped into Hawarden castle to take refuge. Here the Parliamentarians besieged them until relieved by the Royalists on 19 May.

The destructive nature of war was brought home to the local gentry in April when Brereton's men battered the front door at Gwysaney and took 27 prisoners. Whilst in the neighbourhood a troop of soldiers came to Rhual after which Baron Edwards complained that his house had been stripped and plundered by

Captain Coltham and Captain Viner's men, 'his wife stript out of her cloathes by ye Yorkshire men, a box of jewels taken'.[7]

By the summer of 1645 time was running out for Charles. Cromwell created the new Model Army, which showed its mettle at Naseby in June when the Ironsides annihilated the King's main army. On 24 September the King was in Chester when his forces were cut down at Rowton Heath . He left the city the next morning: '1645 Thursday Sept 25. About 9 and 10 in the morning the King left Chester and went to Harding Castle, governed by Sir Wm. Neale, stayed 3 hours, and that night to Denbigh Castle.'

At the beginning of 1646 Hawarden castle was again under siege. Its fate was sealed by the surrender of Chester in February and on 16 March the Governor, after receiving the written permission of the King, marched out with his colours flying. Like the chorus in a Greek tragedy, the local gentry were involved in the cathartic siege of Denbigh castle which lasted from April until the middle of October, when the vanquished garrison was permitted to leave with honour. Amongst the defenders fined for delinquency in arms were Colonel Thomas Davies, John Eyton, senior, of Leeswood, and his son, John Eyton, junior, and Edward Lloyd, Heartsheath. Robert Davies III was eventually fined £1,300 and imprisoned in Chester castle in 1658. The family with the most outstanding record for service in the Royalist cause in the Civil War were the Whitleys of Aston Hall. Colonel Roger Whitley went into exile with Charles II whilst two of his brothers were killed in action, John at Conway, and Richard at Hawarden.

The war affected all classes. A Ewloe woman was evicted from her home on the pretence that she was behind with her chief rent. She received a visit from Colonel Ravenscroft in company with his Uncle Mr Thomas Whitley, who punished her because she had two sons in the Parliament service. She was advised to write to beg for redress from Robert Davies.[8]

The departure of the Stanleys. New lords of Mold, Hawarden and Hope

The two hundred or so years of dominance by the Stanley family was virtually ended when, in October 1651, James, the seventh earl of Derby, was executed at Bolton for supporting Charles II at the Battle of Worcester. The Stanley estates were confiscated by the Council of State and placed in the hands of Commonwealth trustees. The eighth earl was given the opportunity to redeem them. In his desperation he unwisely entered into a complicated series of transactions by which he received money, signed documents and confirmed others in the ownership of the three confiscated lordships of Mold, Hawarden, and Hope. Time was given for him to redeem these estates but he failed to honour the agreements. Having observed the legal niceties for their conveyance and regarding their purchase as being both honourable and according to law the new owners felt that they had every right to feel secure in their possessions having received double assurance from the earl and Parliamentary trustees.[9]

John Glynne (1603–66)who purchased the castle and manor of Hawarden, was the second son of Sir William Glynne of Glynllifon in Caernarvonshire. The family traced their ancestry back to Cilmin *droed ddu* (Cilmin with the black foot), founder of the fourth of the fifteenth tribes of north Wales. Glynne was a career lawyer and a Parliamentarian who came to notice when he scored a major triumph in the trial of the King's favourite the earl of Strafford. Falling foul of the army, he spent nine months in the Tower, until his release in May 1648. Glynne eventually became Lord Chief Justice of the Upper Bench under Oliver Cromwell and after his death joined the party who welcomed the restoration of the monarchy. As a second son, he was ambitious to build up an estate. In this he succeeded, purchasing estates in Kent, Oxfordshire, and Hawarden. It wasn't until the beginning of the eighteenth century that the Glynnes took up permanent residence in Hawarden. Sir John Glynne (1712–77) the sixth baronet, played a major role in developing coal mining in the area, and

James Stanley, seventh Earl of Derby, executed 1651.
After an original by Van Dyke. [FRO PR/C/5]

Sir John Glynne, 1603-66, Lord Chief Justice. [FRO 28/E/8]

in this way made a significant contribution to the development of Buckley district.[10]

The lordships of Mold and Hope were conveyed by the earl of Derby, to Captain Andrew Ellis, Sir John Trevor, and Colonel George Twistleton.[11] The three purchasers decided by lot their share of the lordships. Sir John Trevor's share was the manor of Hope, the lands there which had belonged to the Stanley family, and a portion of lands in Mold. Captain Andrew Ellis had for his share the manor of Mold, (technically, therefore, he was the lord of the manor), and a portion of lands there. Colonel George Twistleton had the remainder of the lands in Mold. What was significant for the future and for the industrial development of the area was that the mineral rights of the lordships, rich in lead, clay, and coal were divided equally between these three portioners and their successors who became know as the Lords of Mold.

At the Restoration, the earl of Derby and his successors attempted to recover the three lordships. After years of litigation their only success was the recovery of the lordship of Hope when a majority of Judges of the Exchequer decided on a technicality that the manor, having been given by Richard III for services rendered to the Crown by Sir Thomas Stanley, was not alienated from his descendants by the conveyances executed by the eighth earl, Charles, and the grandson of Sir John Trevor II was forced to return it.

The new lords of Mold were influential Parliamentarians, who took the opportunity to buy land, which had become available through confiscation from Royalist grandees. Captain Andrew Ellis was from Althrey Hall, Bangor-is-y-coed and occupied important offices in the Cromwellian administration. And for a time he was Governor of Hawarden castle. This authority was heightened by his marriage to Frances daughter of the Puritan peer Lord Saye and Seele. Their daughter Cecill married Sir Richard Langley and she took with her the manor of Mold into that family. It eventually passed through descendants of the Langleys to Thomas Swymmer Champneys, who by settlement on his marriage in 1792 with Charlotte Margaret, daughter of Sir Roger Mostyn, Bart, vested it in trustees, from whom it was sold to Sir Thomas Mostyn, Bart, and is now part of Mostyn Estates.

Colonel George Twistleton (1617–67) was a Yorkshireman, of Barlow Hall, near Selby. He was a successful Parliamentarian officer serving at Chester, the siege of Denbigh, and defeating the Royalist Sir John Owen of Clenennau in 1648. After the Civil War he served as Governor of Denbigh. He was a Commissioner of Sequestration, and a Commissioner appointed for the trial of Charles I but did not sign the death warrant. He shared the same moderation as John Glynne who disliked both unlimited monarchy and extreme republicanism. He too was a second son and determined to build up an estate and in the endeavour married Mary, daughter and heiress of William Glynne of Lleuar in Caernarfonshire. They had four sons and five daughters. By the beginning of the eighteenth century the Twistleton share of lands in Mold had passed into the hands of Edward Lloyd of Tyddyn, and eventually to their kinsmen the Lloyds of Wigfair and Hafodunos, united by the marriage of Howel Lloyd (d.1729) and Phoebe Lloyd (d.1760). John Lloyd 'The Philosopher' of Wigfair died unmarried in 1815. His title as a Lord of Mold passed to his four sisters, and eventually, through the issue of two of them, into the family of Clough of Denbigh and Howard of Sychdyn and to their descendants.

Sir John Trevor II (d.1673), descended from Tudor Trevor, (*fl*. 940), son-in-law of Hywel Dda, was of Plas Teg to which was added Trefalun, inherited from his uncle Sir Richard. He had a successful career as a Parliamentarian and was accepted as spokesman for north Wales on the chief organs of government.[12] It was unfortunate that his grandson lost the manor of Hope through the appeal of the earl of Derby in 1680

although his family had lands in the lordship of Mold and retained their third portion of minerals as a lord of Mold.

The hey day for the Lords of Mold was in the nineteenth century when a number of collieries and lead mines were producing attractive royalties.

The Argoed estate. Peter Wynne and the earl of Derby

The Argoed estate provides another interesting example of change in land ownership in the lordship of Mold in the seventeenth and eighteenth centuries and its eventual value in the industrial development of Buckley district. The first part of the story shows how tenacious the Stanleys were in hanging on to their land. The estate in question was four hundred or so acres belonging to Argoed Hall. The other protagonist in the conflict was another second son, who had ambitions to create an estate, Peter Wynne (c.1591–1653), the son of John Wyn of Tower. There is an air of at least audacity if not incredulity about the whole matter. The facts are these.[13] It appears that in 1628, Peter Wynne and George Ravenscroft, the earl's agents, had been instructed by their master, to negotiate with three of his sitting tenants for their purchase of three messuages of what later became the Argoed Hall estate. A Mr Foster had agreed to sell his interest in the lease. Peter Wynne then used the earl's money to gain possession of the lease. He told Ravenscroft that the earl had changed his mind had instructed him to buy back the lease in his own name from Foster. He then with the help of his companion William Lloyd evicted the three sitting tenants. On discovering Wynne's actions the earl eventually instigated proceedings against him in the Court of Chancery.

Wynne tried to bluff his way out. He claimed that the earl had sold the lease to him and he bought it with his own money. Unfortunately the documents to prove his claim Wynne alleged were destroyed in a fire. The Court ordered an investigation into the money Wynne had spent on building, improving and repairing the premises at Argoed. With the outbreak of the Civil War and the reversal of the earl's fortunes and execution, Wynne may have felt secure in his possession of Argoed, which passed at his death in 1653 to his son John. Wynne's luck and judgement deserted him towards the end of his life. He had overspent on rebuilding Argoed by at least £800, most of it borrowed from his kinsmen, Evan Edwards, of Rhual, and Edward Lloyd of Pentrehobyn. Eventually he was sent to Flint gaol as a debtor with ample time to meditate on his change of fortune. He never came out alive. It was recorded that 'Peter Wynne of Argoed, beinge in prison fell sicke of a feaver and dyed'.[14]

After the Restoration the new earl re-opened Chancery proceedings and succeeded in evicting Wynne's grandsons from the attractive Argoed estate in 1668. It had land of about 412 acres and included at least three farms. The next year Bishop Isaac Barrow was translated to St Asaph from the diocese of Sodor and Man, where he had been Governor since 1663 and his patron, the earl of Derby, provided Argoed Hall for his grace and favour. This he enjoyed until his death. His body rested at Argoed in 1680 on its journey from Shrewsbury for burial outside the west door of his Cathedral church.

In 1715 the earl of Derby sold the Argoed estate to Charles Roberts, gentleman of Denbigh (d.1740). In 1811 Sarah Roberts bequeathed the property to a niece, Mrs Elizabeth Williamson of Roby Hall, Liverpool, for her life and after her decease to her three daughters.[15] One of these, Mary, married Isaac Gascoyne, a General in the British Army, whose sister in 1831, was Anne Jane Dent, widow, who lived with her sister Elizabeth Williamson, a spinster, in Mayfair. Their lands were leased for collieries and brick works in the nineteenth century.

The ancient house at Tyddyn with lands in Bistre and Argoed passed from the Twistletons to the Lloyds and was mortgaged and later sold at the beginning of the nineteenth century to Jonathan Hobson of Liverpool. In 1847 the estate was leased to John Catherall. A plan shows a tilery lately erected, coal pits, railroads, and a limekiln.[16] The estate was sold to John Wynne Eyton of Leeswood. These are a few examples of the changes in landownership in the seventeenth and eighteenth centuries revealing the increased value of lands in the townships of Bistre and Argoed by industrial development a century later.

The Survey of the manor of Mold, 1653

The defeat of Charles I in the Civil War, and his execution in January 1649, marked, perhaps, the end of the medieval era. With him went the attempt of personal absolutist rule by the monarchy. There was no doubt that Parliament ruled. Throughout society the vestiges of feudalism crumbled. This was seen in our area by the dispersal of the power of the house of Stanley with the break-up of their lordships of Hawarden, Hope, and Mold in the 1650s.

Charles, the eighth earl of Derby, valiantly tried to ward off the dismemberment of his inheritance, brought about by the execution of his father as an enemy of the Commonwealth in September 1651. In the following Spring the new earl appealed to the local royalist gentry, as his tenants, and addressed them confidently as 'my trusted and noble loved friends'. They came from Gwysaney, Leeswood, Tower, Rhual, Heartsheath, and other houses, and included his father's late chaplain Dr Christopher Pashley, recently removed as rector of Hawarden. The beleaguered earl 'empowered and authorised' four or more of the eleven named to act and proceed according to instructions.[17]

But Parliament governed. The earl was unable to meet his promises and the lordship and manor of Mold was lost. The extent of this is seen in a 'Survey of the manor of Mold, parcel of the possessions of James, late Earl of Derby, taken by virtue of a commission under an Act of Parliament, 15 July 1653'.[18] The survey was thorough and may be summarised under a number of headings.

First were listed the traditional courts of the manor, Baron, Frankpledge and Leet, which met in the court house situate at the corner of Mold High Street and New Street, with the manor pound for stray animals behind. The court exercised the same jurisdiction

Charles Stanley, eighth Earl of Derby.
[FRO PR/C/18]

and heard similar pleas to those in Ewloe, which we noted earlier. Two fairs were kept in the manor on the 22 July and 11 November.[19] The tolls of the fairs belonged to the lord of the manor.

The most valuable source of income was the traditional rents paid annually by the tenants. These varied from six or more shillings a year, and never more than twenty shillings, payable at midsummer or Martinmas, with either a fat capon at Easter or a fat hen at Martinmas. Some of the tenants possessed their lands by charter, (a grant confirmed by deed). Seventeen of the gentry living in different townships paid burgage rents presumably as burgess of the borough of Mold.[20] A regular source of income was the payment of heriot. This was a traditional death duty paid to the lord of the manor, originating in feudal times, when on the death of a retainer his family surrendered his horse and armour. It had long been commuted into a money payment varying from 10s to £4. These continued to be paid until the twentieth century.

In the survey of land and tenements five are listed for the township of Argoed and twelve for Bistre. These were usually described as a thatched cottage, with the number of rooms varying between two and five, with a cow house, barn, and oven house attached. The accommodation land varied between thirty-five to sixty acres of statute acre, 40 poles long 4 broad = 4,840 square yards, or 4 roods; although some are given as large measure, the Cheshire acre of 10,240 square yards. The land use was mixed, arable and pasture, with some woodland. The largest dwelling noted in the survey was Gwerney Castle, probably Tyddyn,[21] a messuage and tenement of ten bays of building, with fourteen acres of large measure.

Of frequent notice in the Survey is 'new inclosure and improvement of waste'. This was done by agreement with the lord of the manor in the years immediately before the outbreak of the Civil War. In 1638–9, James Stanley (later seventh earl, d.1651) conducted a policy of improving the value of the lordship by making new contracts with his tenants which included an additional annual rent charge for new inclosures and improvement of waste. By this means the rental value of the lordship was increased tenfold.[22] John Eyton, Esq. of Leeswood made the largest incroachment of 24 acres in Bistre; he claimed to hold his land rent free, 'in lieu of his profession & right of common to his freehold lands within the said Township and Manor'.

The survey carefully recorded the timber in the lordship. The number of trees in Argoed and Bistre were counted as 587 timber trees at 5s. a piece; 1057 pollards and saplings at 3s. a piece. There is no record of the tenants being required to plant trees. In the neighbouring lordship of Hawarden 'Pennant states that in 1666 the timber on the Glynne estate was valued at £5,000 and sold. Sir John Glynne in his diary records that there was only one tree standing about the place in 1730'.[23]

The manor of Mold, as we have seen, was bought in the 1650s by Captain Andrew Ellis and descended through his daughter to the Langleys and by the 1790s had passed by inheritance to Sir Thomas Champneys, Bart, Somerset. The manor had proved a useful asset for raising mortgages and supporting marriage settlements. This was the situation when Champney's son, Thomas Swymmer Champneys. Esq., was betrothed to Charlotte daughter of Sir Roger Mostyn, fifth baronet.

This marriage led to the sale and distribution of land in the parish of Mold when Champneys auctioned the manor in 1801 and included land awarded by the Enclosure Act. In preparation for the marriage settlement the manor of Mold was freed from previous encumbrances. It was described

> with appurtenances and 80 messuages, 50 cottages, 2 dove-houses, 5 tofts, 1 water corn mill, 80 gardens, 50 orchards, 500 acres of land, 500 acres of meadow, 500 acres of pasture, 200 acres of wood, 10,000 acres of furze and heath, 20 acres of land covered with water and all usual rents, rights and courts.[24]

D. Walker of London, made a survey and valuation of the manor in September 1791. This is a most interesting and valuable document. It reviews the value of minerals and gives an interesting account of Spon Colliery, which we quote in another chapter. Walker gave advice on the proposed inclosure and other insights into the condition of the estate.[25] Three notebooks compiled in 1795 for the townships of Bistre, Argoed, and Treuddyn provide information on landowners, tenants, and holdings with field names and acreages.[26]

The major landowners in Argoed township were Mrs Elizabeth Roberts, Argoed Hall, 591 acres; T. S. Champneys, Esq., 172 acres; John Lloyd, Esq., 164 acres; John Jones, 39 acres. In Bistre township, Mrs Allen 373, acres; T. S. Champneys, Esq., 235 acres; Thos. Parker, Gent, 205 acres; Mr Geo. Berks, 73 acres; Ruthin School Trustees, 68 acres; A. B. Messham, 49 acres.

T. S. Champneys' total holding in the parish of Mold (before the Enclosure Award) was 1,395 acres, annual value £1,342 18s. 2d. In addition there were mine royalties — valued in 1789 as £175 for coal and £165 for lead. Champneys increased his land holding in 1800 as a result of the enclosure award, by which he received, 47 acres for some ancient enclosures he gave to the Commissioners, 200 acres, as a proprietor, and 222 acres, as lord of the manor.

The Trustees of Ruthin School held Carreg Llwyd, purchased from Ann Williams for £1,194 13s. 4d. from money left them by the Reverend Edward Lloyd of Ripple in Kent.

Other major beneficiaries in our area of the parish of Mold were the Reverend Hope Wynn Eyton, 186 acres; Trevor Lloyd, 194 acres; Elizabeth Roberts, 62 acres; John Lloyd of Wigfair, 254 acres; Mrs Elizabeth Allen of Chester, for lands in Bistre 42 acres.

Why did John Lloyd of Wigfair receive 254 acres? The answer lies in the fact that he was in 1800 one of the Lords of Mold and was possessed of the share which George Twistleton had bought in the 1650s. This share was extensive, although not as big as Champneys in the manor of Mold. George Twistleton's share was divided by his widow into six parts and left to her children. By the time of his death in 1711 Edward Lloyd of Tyddyn had bought up the six shares. He married in 1690 Elizabeth daughter of Henry Standish of London[27] and had issue three sons and two daughters all of whom died without issue. Edward the last surviving son died in 1776. It was said of him 'that he lived to upwards of eighty years as a bachelor and was possessed of an estate which was let at £1,000 per annum and not only lived within his Income but left behind him some personal property'. His surviving sister Susannah Lloyd lived at Tyddyn and when she died in 1779 the estate passed to her third cousin Howel Lloyd (d.1783), and then to his eldest son John Lloyd (d.1815), of Wigfair and Hafodunos.

The Mold estate was described as:

> 50 messuages, 10 cottages, 20 tofts, 6 water corn grist mills, 10 dove houses, 50 curtilages, 50 gardens, 50 orchards, 600 acres of land, 200 acres of meadow, 700 acres of pasture, 50 acres of wood, 100 acres of furze and heath, 50 acres of marsh, 100 acres of land covered with water, common of pasture for all manner of cattle, common of turbary and piscary… with the appurtenancies in the several parishes of Mold, Northop, and Flint. And also one undivided 3rd part or share, the whole into 3 equal parts or shares to be divided of and in all mines, quarries, ores, minerals, metal, and coals of and in 500 mine pits, 200 lead mine pits, 50 copper mine pits, 100 mine pits of calamine, 50 mine pits of ores of zinc and 100 coal pits and of and in all other mines, quarries and mine pits of what nature or kind soever with the appurtenances in the manor of Mold in the parish of Mold or in either of them in the said County of Flint.[28]

Both Howel Lloyd and John Lloyd used this inheritance as a means of raising money and the mortgage, from the Reverend Edward Hughes of Kinmel had by 1814 reached, £71,450.[29]

The Mold Enclosure Act of 1792, and Award, 1800

The purpose of the Act was for 'Dividing and allotting and inclosing the Commons and Waste lands'. This policy of fencing and consolidating the open-field arable strips, and the waste and common land, had been taking place for centuries. In the eighteenth century the agricultural revolution in crop growing, cattle breeding, and an increase in population, led to a movement by landowners to enclose land by means of Parliamentary legislation. This was done on a parochial basis. Anyone having rights of common could make a claim for an allotment of the newly enclosed land. Commissioners were named in the individual acts and were responsible for surveying, allotting, and enclosing the commons and waste lands. Allotments were sold to pay these costs and create new roads of a statutory size. The landed proprietors received the greatest shares and many of the poorer sort lately incroached upon the commons lost their dwellings.

Mold was a large parish of 18,062 acres of which 4,044 acres (more than six square miles) were commons and wastes. The Act of 1792 was to have an important effect on the shaping of our community in the townships of Argoed and Bistre for it released, reallocated, and led to the improvement of land. Moreover it gave the small landowners in the area the opportunity to purchase land when the commissioners auctioned land to pay for the cost of enclosure and new roads. Twenty-eight local people took this opportunity at three major sales held at the

Front page of Sale Catalogue of Thomas Symmer Champney's Estate Manor of Mold 1801.
[FRO D/KK/269]

THE
PARTICULARS
OF CAPITAL AND VERY VALUABLE
FREEHOLD ESTATES,
situate in the
PARISH OF MOLD,
A BEAUTIFUL AND MOST FERTILE PART OF THE COUNTY OF FLINT:
COMPRIZING THE EXTENSIVE
MANOR OF MOLD,
AND MANY
CAPITAL FARMS.
LYING EXCEEDINGLY CONVENIENT, AND CONSISTING OF EXCELLENT
Grazing, Meadow, and Arable Land,
With suitable Farm Houses and Outbuildings, and let to unexceptionably good Tenants.
WHICH WILL BE
SOLD BY AUCTION,
In Lots,
AT THE GRIFFIN INN, IN MOLD,
On THURSDAY the 30th Day of APRIL, 1801, and the following Days precisely at Two o'Clock.
A Map of the Premises may be seen, and further Information had, at Mr. Wynne's Office, in Mold.

PRINTED BY JOHN MONK, CHESTER.——1801.

Mold Enclosure Commissioners minutes, 1795, showing sale of allotments to local residents. [FRO D/KK/273]

Griffin Inn, Mold, between November 1794 and December 1796.[30] In this way a number of local families established themselves in the townships of Bistre and Argoed. The land they bought was enclosed from Buckley Mountain, Argoed Common, and Bryn-y-baal Common. One group of twelve parcels sold on 27 November 1795 was described as:

> situate upon the south side of Buckley Mountain ranging from the New Turnpike House on the south side of the Turnpike road from Chester to Mold, adjoining the ancient Inclosures belonging to Mrs Allen, in the midst of the Collieries, Brickworks, and Potteries, and are very convenient to build cottages upon, and make gardens for workmen employed in the said works.[31]

Two of the purchasers were Mr Rigby who paid £92 for land on Buckley Mountain and Jonathan Catherall of Ewloe, gentleman, who paid £91 for 9 acres.

Further opportunities arose for the purchase of land in Argoed in Bistre when T. S. Champneys auctioned the manor of Mold in lots in 1801. Seventeen lots were offered in Argoed and Bistre, totalling 595 acres, two thirds of which (c.410 acres) was land he had received as a result of the enclosure award. The sizes of the lots varied. Seven were under six acres, four between ten and thirty acres, one of forty-two acres, and five between seventy-eight and one hundred and five acres. Some were not sold. Amongst the purchasers were William Hancock, 13 acres and the Reverend Mr Eyton, 84 acres.

New roads

George Kay in his General View of the Agriculture of Flintshire, 1792, gave an account:

> The turnpike roads are kept in good repair in general, but the cross or parochial roads are in a very wretched state. They are so very bad, that in many places it is difficult and dangerous to travel on horseback in winter; and to get a carriage to pass along them, appears to be impracticable. They are uncommonly narrow and low, often answering the double purposes of a road and drain'. He concluded that 'new roads are beginning to be formed.'

These new roads came about in our area by two means, as the creation of turnpike trustees and enclosure commissioners. They were made in three stages. The first stage came in the 1750s when turnpike roads were made to link Mold with Chester and Wrexham. The first turnpike road in our area was made c.1757 and crossed from Mold through Argoed and Bistre, continuing through Broughton to Chester. Turnpike roads were made by enterprising landowners determined to improve roads, travel, and trade. An Act of Parliament was needed to set up a Turnpike Trust whose responsibility was to make the roads and pay for their maintenance by charging the users a toll. Toll houses and toll bars became familiar to travellers, carters, and drovers. There was one at the junction of the Mold–Chester road and a new road to Queensferry.

The next stage occurred around 1800 through the efforts of the Enclosure Commissioners appointed to regulate the Acts for the parish of Mold and the townships of Broughton, Pentrobin, and Bannel in the parish of Hawarden. In Mold parish they made a network of well constructed and drained link roads of statutory width across the Commons and Wastes providing access to new allotments. In Hawarden parish the Act stipulated that public carriage roads were to have a breadth of forty feet, between, and exclusive of, ditches. In this way new roads were made to serve our area such as the Pentrobin road leading from the Mold road to Buckley Mountain, and the Smelting House, and White Well road leading out of the Penyffordd road towards Buckley Mountain.

The manor of Ewloe was not subject to an Enclosure Act, as we shall see later. In those townships it was left to tramroads to provide the first transport network linking the many coalmines and brickworks to the river Dee.

The third stage came in October 1826 when the trustees of the King's Ferry Turnpike Roads announced their intention of building new lengths of road by contract. Two of these stretches were designed to link up the river Dee and Mold. The first, lot No. 3, 3,234 lineal yards, was to 'commence on the Mold–Chester road near Pentre Bridge and terminate at Buckley Windmill. The second stretch, lot No. 4, 3,204 lineal yards, was to commence at the termination of lot No. 3, to proceed along present road, past the windmill over Buckley Mountain, and ending at Ewloe Green. Plans and specifications were to be had from Mr Edward Williams, Garreglwydd'.[32] Further along this stretch was the Black Horse Inn, a popular tavern for refreshment. Obviously enjoying an excellent position by reason of the new road, it was advertised as,

The Turnpike House at the Toll Bar Buckley Cross c.1860. [Buckley Society Archive]

> an object worthy of attention, being well adapted as a baiting house for carters, etc., great quantities of lead ore, lime, and coal being carted past daily, and as the new line of road from Mold, etc., to Liverpool is intended to be carried past it, that and other local advantages, it is presumed will make the public house of infinite value.[33]

The final major road link in our area was provided in 1835 by a turnpike which ran 'from Ewloe Green through or near a certain farm called Ewloe Barn, thence through or near another farm called Allt Amy, thence between Mynydd-bychan and Bryn-y-baal farms, thence to the turnpike road leading from Mold to Northop'.[34]

In this way the building of new roads established important and reliable route-ways to the river Dee and other markets at the beginning of industrial development in Buckley and were an important factor in the shaping of our community.

The Broughton, Pentrobin, and Bannel Enclosure Act 1798, and Award 1802

Its most important contribution to the story of the shaping of our district was in the making of the new roads we have described above. It had much less significance compared with the Mold Enclosure Award. There was not as much land involved. A mere six hundred acres compared with the eighteen thousand in Mold. The chief beneficiary in the allotment of land in the townships of Pentrobin and Bannel was Sir Stephen Richard Glynne who received almost five hundred acres.

Buckley Commons

Buckley Commons were not enclosed by Parliamentary legislation. The lord of the manor of Ewloe in which they are situated was reluctant to do so and advised by his agent to be cautious. This is the reason why

Buckley people to-day take such a pride in and receive so much enjoyment from the amenities of the Higher, Middle, and Lower Commons. We have previously stated the rights of common enjoyed from medieval times in the manor of Ewloe. The following quotation and a review of events relating to Buckley Commons over the last two hundred years will show the complex issues surrounding the meaning of the term common land. An expert[35] has described common land in these terms.'

> All common land has an owner; the ambiguous term 'common' refers the right held in common by certain people to use the product of the soil of the commons, by grazing, cutting turf and so on.[36] Yet commons may be said to belong to the people, for although the commoners have an economic interest in the land no doubt they have always used commons, like village greens, for their festivals and holiday activities, a use which has gradually extended to the wider public and is today of considerable importance.[37]

Clayden explains the origins of common land, which will help us understand the way it developed in Buckley:

> Commons are a remnant of the manorial system, which from mediaeval times had been the basis of the country's economy. The manor was the basic unit and was supposed to be self-sufficient. Crops were grown on the better soil and the poor land was the 'waste' used for grazing and gathering of fuel. The lord of the manor owned the whole of the land but the cottagers had rights recognised by the courts. In turn this meant that the lord of the manor could not enclose land without parliamentary authority, hence the unfenced open spaces which we still recognise as the hallmark of a common.[38]

Another important factor in the history of the use of common land in Buckley was the fact that the lord of the manor owned the mineral rights and had the power to lease such rights which led to the growth of the coal and clay industry in Buckley.

The story begins in the eighteenth century and concerns the way in which the lord of the manor dealt with encroachments on common land in Buckley made by potters,[39] brickmakers, and colliers in their exploitation of coal and clay or by individual freeholders or immigrant squatters. The usual practice was for the lord of the manor to accept such practice of encroachment. The procedure was, that each encroachment was presented at the regular meetings of the Court Leet, who imposed a small amercement, which was thereafter paid annually to the Gwysaney estate. These transactions were recorded by the bailiff of the manor, and the Gwysaney agent, as Ewloe manor encroachment rents. The earliest rental of 1759 records 25 names which increased in the next hundred years to 120 persons paying rent for the occupation of about 200 parcels of common land.[40]

There is an interesting episode recorded in Gwysaney correspondence for the year 1817 between the lord of the manor, Bryan Cooke, the agent of Gwysaney, William Williams, of Garreg-lwyd, and Charles Dundas, of Aston Hall. The background is that both Cooke and Dundas were relatively newcomers to the area. Both had married heiresses. Bryan Cooke took as his bride Frances Puleston (1765–1818) and Charles Dundas married the Whitley heiress, to Aston Hall. Cooke was an absentee lord of the manor choosing to live at Owston Hall, Doncaster and letting the Gwysaney estate to a long-term tenant. He was thus dependent upon his agent to keep him abreast of events in the manor. Dundas on the other hand spent more time at Aston and became closely involved in the economic development of the Aston estate. He was one of the promoters of the Aston Tramroad, a shipping Wharf at King's Ferry, and local collieries. Such was his enthusiasm that Cooke's agent regarded his approaches to his master with some alarm and advised caution. Clearly he thought the polite overtures of Dundas and his meeting with the freeholders of Ewloe as dangerous meddling in the affairs of the manor.

Dundas wrote to Cooke saying that on the request of the freeholders he had met them on Buckley Mountain and listened to their complaints, 'that enclosures are made there (which they term encroachments) being without the consent of the Freeholders & the Rents arising from these applied to the sole use of the Lord of the Manor'. He had requested the bailiff on the Mountain to attend, but 'the poor fellow considered, declined & retired'. Later, at Chester, he had called on Cooke's agent, Mr Potts and had advised him, 'that as I was not always resident in Flintshire, Mr Humberstone would act for the Freeholders of Ewloe.' He concluded by suggesting that they should meet and discuss 'a much more beneficial termination, a division of the Mountain, without the expense of an Act of Parliament'.[41]

On the advice of his agent Cooke declined to consider any proposals to divide the Commons in Ewloe amongst the freeholders. William Williams, the agent of Gwysaney informed his master, that 'the uninclosed waste in Buckley when I measured it in 1811 was 149 acres and the Encroachments about 20 years ago was 28 acres, but since then there has been few small Encroachments, and of course, I should presume that the oldest encroachments would become freehold.'[42]

Whilst these matters were being discussed Williams told Dundas 'about the sycamore tree which he had enclosed, in the corner of encroachment n 2, called, the Cross Tree, and by some, Ewloe Cross, and that the tree was considered as belonging to the Lord of the Manor'. Dundas replied 'that it was an ornament and that he enclosed if for fear of it being felled'.[43] The end of the matter was that Dundas made his encroachment, the lord of the manor safeguarded the Cross Tree, and there was no enclosure award to the freeholders.

Disputes which occurred over common land in Buckley during the nineteenth century were brought into the headlines by the dramatic events of 1894.[44] The leading actor in these events was the Reverend Joseph Davies, a local Congregational Minister. His father had farmed in Hawarden, and Davies, a Primitive Methodist, prospered as a grocer in Alltami, before ordination in the 1870s. Davies bore a grudge against the Gwysaney estate and by the 1890s he was in an influential position as one of the first County Councillors elected for Flintshire. As a man of independent means with close connections with local nonconformity, he was able to summon local sympathy. He did this by a number of benefactions, which benefited the newly emerging community. He built a market hall and a large central hall for meetings and concerts, and chapels at Drury, Rivertown, and Mynydd Isa. He was musical, writing hymns and presiding in a flamboyant way at local temperance festivals. But there was also a streak of cunning and mischief, which he used to rouse the rabble in the causes he espoused. No where is this more displayed than in his championship of the rights of local commoners.

A meeting of the Welsh Land Commission at Mold at the end of August 1894 gave him the opportunity and publicity he desired and provided the prelude to events in the following months. Having volunteered to give evidence to the Commission, Davies took the opportunity to attack the policy of the Gwysaney estate in its dealings with encroachments on Buckley's common land. He accused them of unjust evictions of tenants, and rack-renting. There was no foundation in the four cases he brought before the Commission, although the evidence presented by Gwysaney agents did outline the way in which they dealt with encroachments.[45]

After 1850 encroachments were no longer brought before the Court Leet. From September 1872 almost all estate rents were increased by about 50% to enable the lord of the manor to meet rises in rates. At the same time tenants were required to sign a document which in essence acknowledged the estate as owner of the land contained in the encroachment and the building which had been erected by the squatters.[46] It was acknowledged that the Gwysaney estate did not drastically increase their rents and they took into consideration the fact that tenants had built their own dwellings on the encroachments. The legality of the action of the estate in 1872 was upheld by a trial at Mold Assize in 1875.[47]

The evidence to the Land Commission in August 1894 was given in the middle of a conflict over land on the Higher Common. Davies was again posing as the champion of

View of Buckley Common, 1988. [Buckley Library]

The Reverend Joseph Davies. [The Reverend N. J. Lemon]

the underdog, and he took every opportunity to attack his opponent publicly and in the press.

The issue was joined in the summer of 1893 with Major John Merriman Gibson, the commander of the local Buckley Engineers, a Volunteer unit made up mostly of colliers. Gibson, a member of the Commons Preservation Society, had obtained a lease of three acres of ground from the lord of the manor, for a term of fifty years at a rent of 30s. per annum, which he was permitted to take by the Volunteer Act of 1863. However, Davies saw this as an opportunity to defeat the Major and discredit the Gwysaney estate. The piece of land the Major enclosed for the benefit of his Volunteers was crossed by a rarely used public footpath, which could have easily been diverted. Davies informed Gibson of his intention to breach his fences to maintain the right of way. He recruited Samuel Smith, the local Liberal Member of Parliament, to ask a question in the House of Commons, and joined forces with Edward Peters, the local Colliers' agent. They announced their intentions, in the headquarters of Davies, at the Central Hall, before a large public meeting. A week later on Whit-Monday, Davies, Peters, and friends, armed with large hammers destroyed the fences impeding the footpath.

The Major re-erected the fences and built a grandstand on his three acres. Davies issued through his solicitor an ultimatum that if Gibson's fences were not removed by the 15 October he would 'assert his rights over the footpaths'. At 7 a.m. on the morning of the 16 the only attendant at the Volunteers' enclosure was a solitary watchman who was soon joined by a crowd to witness the crusaders Davies and Peters in action. Davies made the most of it and addressed the crowd saying that they were there 'to claim the rights of way, and that in about half an hour, Mr Wright of Queensferry, acting on behalf of the ratepayers and freeholders of the parish of Hawarden, would be there to take everything down'.[48] At 8 a.m. Alfred Wright arrived from Queensferry with his thirty plus heavy mob. He supervised them as they smashed the fences and grandstand. By 9 a.m Major Gibson, alerted by 'Calico' Jack arrived. Gibson and Wright came face to face, with three police officers looking on, but the Major kept his cool and did not resist with his Volunteers and thus prevented a riot. After destroying everything in sight and clearing the enclosure Wright marched his forces to the Cosy Café for refreshments where they were joined by the Reverend Joseph Wright who paid each one of them 5s. for their efforts.

The lord of the manor did not take any action against Davies, Peters, Wright and their companions. The issues at stake were too varied and uncertain. They thought they would not succeed over the rights of way. They were reluctant to ask Wright to prove his rights of common as a freeholder of the parish of Hawarden, and the Major had not received the assent of the freeholders of the manor to proceed with the enclosure. If he wished to continue there would have to be a Board of Agriculture enquiry and approval from the newly instituted Parish Council for enclosure and the removal of the rights of way.

There were other encroachments, but none which attracted the same attention. In 1902 the Clerk of the Buckley Urban District Council wrote to the Board of Agriculture to ask if an enquiry could be held as 20 to 30 acres of Common appeared to have been enclosed by the lord of the manor. They replied pointing out the impossibility of doing anything without his consent. In the late 1920s the Council wished to use part of the common as a playing field and to deal at the same time with a number of complaints. With the assistance of the Commons Preservation Society, the National Playing Field Association, and the involvement of the lord of the manor 18 acres of land were conveyed to the Urban District Council for recreational purposes and a scheme for management drawn up in 1933. Further government legislation was introduced in the Commons Registration Act 1965, and in March 1993, a Buckley Commons Management Plan was published to set out plans to protect and conserve the three main areas, the Higher, Middle and Lower, each regarded as 'quite distinctive in character'.

Land and people in the middle of the nineteenth century

Further distribution of land had taken place by marriage, inheritance, and the sale of land. The pattern at the beginning of the reign of Queen Victoria in 1837, in this area, was a number of proprietors letting their land to tenants, who farmed holdings of between 50 to 100 acres. The ownership of land varied and is best seen by a review of individual townships.[49] Alongside this we may see what other occupational activities were taking place by reference to the Census Returns.

Argoed township.[50] The chief landowners: General Isaac Gascoyne (d.1841) who inherited the Argoed Hall estate formerly held by the descendants of Charles Roberts, Denbigh from 1715–1811. Edward Lloyd Mostyn, second baron, who came into the possession of the residue of the manor of Mold sold by T. S. Champneys in 1801. Mrs Mary Hobson, widow, whose estate was in the townships of Bistre and Argoed. She owned land once possessed by George Twistleton and then by the Lloyds of Tyddyn and Wigfair. Chief occupational activities: coal mining, nail manufacturing, and farming.

Bistre township: the land was shared between over a dozen landowners the chief of whom was Mary Hobson; others were John Wynne Eyton and Samuel Hancock at Padeswood. Chief occupational activities: coal mining, brick manufacturing, and farming.

Ewloe Wood township: Philip Davies Cooke owned the majority of the land. Chief occupational activities: coal mining, brick manufacturing, potteries, farming.

Ewloe Town: Sir Stephen Glynne, Bart. and Sir George Prescott, Bart., are the chief landowners. Chief occupational activities: coal mining, brick manufacturing, potteries, and farming.

Pentrobin township: Pentrobin township: Sir Stephen Glynne owns nearly all the land. Chief occupational activities: coal mining, brick manufacturing, potteries, and farming.

Bannel township: Sir Stephen Glynne owns nearly all the land. Farming is the major occupational activity in this small township.

In our study of this area we have seen that a number of land surveys took place in the various townships in 1653 and 1795 for Argoed and Bistre and in 1839 for all six townships named above. One of the major features of the surveys is the evidence they provide of the field-names. The field-names and place-names of the four townships formerly in Hawarden parish are recorded by Hywel Wyn Owen.[51] The majority of these are of English origin, as we would expect from their settlement in the area from the seventh and eighth centuries onwards. As these may be studied in Owen's book they are not dealt with here. A brief look at some of the field-names in the surveys listed above for Argoed and Bistre provide a suitable note on which to conclude our introduction.

The field-names of the first period of settlement relate to arable cultivation. The medieval Welsh laws demonstrate that farming was a communal enterprise, which demanded co-operation particularly where ploughing was undertaken. The

Major John Merriman Gibson, seated, and his son Richard, in camp with Buckley Volunteers. [Buckley Society Magazine, 10]

Brook Farm Bannel. [FRO PH 11/122]

ideal medieval homestead or *tyddyn* each theoretically contained four acres, *erw* (pl. *erwau*). *Erw* originally indicated the amount of land ploughed in a day by a yoke of oxen. It later became generally used to describe a field or enclosed field. Common pasture, *cytir*, and *gweirglodd*, the common hayfield or meadow occurs often to show the earliest farming in the area.

The second period of settlement and colonisation occurs in the fifteenth and sixteenth centuries. This expansion is seen in the field-names: *cae*, a field or enclosure with a hedge; *coitia*, made up of *coed*, wood, and *cae*, means the field within the hedge; and *cyfer*, from *cyfair* an acre, day's ploughing.

The third phase of the settlement of the land was the process of enclosure around 1800. This newly allocated land was called allotments.

Other field-names occurring in the surveys of Argoed and Bistre may be classified under a number of categories. Here are some examples.

Personal names
Cae Robert Roberts
Coitia Gibbon
Pulford meadow
Frank field
English field
Cae Madoc

Size and age
mawr (big, large, great)
bychan (small)
hir (long, lengthy)
hen (old)
newydd (new)

Location
pella (furthest)
nessa (next to, nearest)
tan (beneath, under)
ysgubor (barn)
canol (middle)
croesffordd (cross roads)
tan y clawdd (below the
    dyke)

Topography
Cae mynydd isaf
Cae pwll marl
Pwll gwair
Erw aber llanerch
Bryn y castell

Conclusion

We have reached the end of the historical introduction to Buckley district and soon we will relate the main themes of its modern development. Our story began with the two dykes which marked the beginning of the age of settlement and conquest; two hundreds years before the Domesday record of Bistre and the building of castles and churches which followed. The main geographical feature of the district was the forest. It was only gradually that the land came under the plough, and pastures were cleared. For a thousand years agriculture provided the livelihood of the population. Welsh tribal society, Norman feudalism, and medieval lordship, provided different kinds of leadership, land ownership, and organisation in society. For centuries the manor was the most important unit of local organisation to regulate agriculture and exploit other resources with control exercised through the lord of the manor by the courts. We have seen that there was a great change in land ownership, more so than in other regions, in the middle of the seventeenth century. The rich corridor of clay and coal was worked according to the technology available from the end of the thirteenth century. In the modern era it was there waiting to be exploited by landowners, independent manufacturers, and joint stock companies.

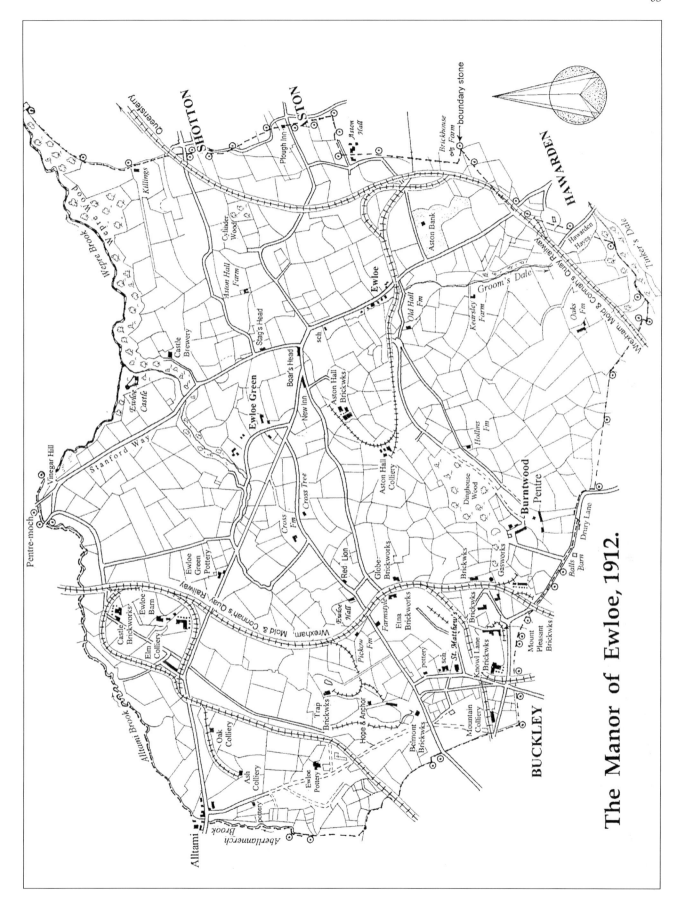

The Manor of Ewloe, 1912.

By the middle of the nineteenth century agricultural and industrial society had assumed its shape. The agricultural revolution was almost complete, and the industrial revolution underway, aided in this area by new roads, tramways, and railways. The opening up and full exploitation of the rich corridor of clay and coal and the influx of an immigrant population finally determined the shape of the community. Buckley became a frontier town. The 'Promised Land' had been entered.

Notes

1 .J. Bentley, 'An aromatic whiff of tobacco,' *Buckley*, 23, p. 6, and J. Bentley, P. J. Davey, and H. M. Harrison, 'Buckley Clay Tobacco Pipes,' *Buckley*, 5.

2, K. Lloyd Gruffydd, 'The Flintshire Coalfield during the sixteenth century,' *Buckley*, 3.

3. John Morrill (ed.), *The Impact of the English Civil War*, (Collins and Brown, London, 1991) p. 20.

4. Gwyn A. Williams, *When was Wales*, (Penguin Books, 1985), p. 132.

5. R. Morris, 'The siege of Chester,' *Chester and North Wales Archaeological and History Society Journal*, xxv, 1923 p. 42.

6. Hywel Wyn Owen, ibid ,PNEF p. 145.

7. N. Tucker, *North Wales in the Civil War*, (Bridge Books, Wrexham, 1992) p. 66.

8. FRO D/GW/555/96, and for the Civil War in the area see Tucker, ibid, and K. Lloyd Gruffydd, 'Hawarden Castle during the First Civil War,' *Buckley*, 28.

9. Henry Taylor, 'The Lords of Mold,' *Publications of the Flintshire Historical Society*, vol. 6.

10. Ibid, and Pritchard, *Hawarden*, and *DNB* and *DWB*.

11. Taylor, op cit.

12. See DNB and DWB for a fuller account of his career.

13. For this information see I. M. Read, 'Argoed Hall, Mold,' *Clwyd Historian*, No. 26, and information kindly supplied by K. Lloyd Gruffydd.

14. Crown Book (Flintshire), 1637–66, p. 126. National Library of Wales.

15. FRO D/KK/638, Isaac Gascoyne (c.1763–1841), MP for Liverpool 1795–1831, see DNB.

16. FRO D/KK/639.

17. FRO D/GW/2104.

18. FRO D/KK/263.

19. By the nineteenth century there were five fairs (3 February, 21 March , 12 May, 2 August, 22 November) listed in *Pigot's Directory*, 1822.

20. I have failed to discover any mention of a Borough Charter. It appears that the locals regarded it so, and burgage rents were paid.

21. I am indebted to K. Lloyd Gruffydd for allowing me to use his transcript of the survey of 1653 from FRO D/KK/263. He suggests that 'Gwerney Castle' is Tyddyn.

22. From £122 16s. 8d. to £1,320 16s. 2d. John Baker, Surveyor General, estimated 'ye whole improved value of the lordship as £1,528 4s. 2d.'

23. Quoted in W. B. Jones *Hawarden* vol. 3., p. 118.

24. FRO D/M/681, 14 April 1691.

25. FRO D/KK/268. Survey and valuation of Thomas Swymmer Champneys' estate in the parish of Mold, made September 1791 by D. Walker, London. It includes a full report on the condition of the estate, proposed inclosure, tithes, lead mines, and Spon Colliery.

26. FRO D/GW/433–5.

27. The entry in Joseph Foster, *Alumni Oxoniensis, 1500–1714*, reads 'Lloyd, Edward, s. David of Tuythin, Flints. Gent. Jesus Coll. Matric 24 April 1668, aged 18; bar-at-law, Gray's Inn, 1678; licensed 21 Sept 1676 to marry Elizabeth Atwood of St Andrews Holborn. Spinster.'

28. Ruthin Record Office, DD/HB/1226.

29. FRO D/KK/629 and 631.

30. FRO D/KK/273.

31. FRO D/KK/273, minutes 27 November 1795.

32. *Chester Chronicle*, 26/10/1826.

33. Cropper, op cit., p. 129, dated 16/3/1826.

34. An Act for improving and keeping in repair certain roads in the counties of Flint and Chester, and for better maintaining the Ferry over the River Dee, called the Lower King's Ferry, 5 & 6 Will. IV, 1835.

35. Paul Clayden, *Our Common Land*. The law and history of commons and village greens, (The Open Space Society, 1985).

36. There are very few people in Buckley who now have rights of common.

37. ibid, p. 1.

38. ibid, p. 1.

39. See in particular the chapter on potteries.

40. FRO D/GW/333–48; Court Leet Books D/GW/909–10; and J. E. Messham, 'Conflict on Buckley Common,' *Flintshire Historical Society Journal*, vol. 32p, 37f.

41. FRO D/GW/555/ ff.275, 28/7/1817.

42. ibid, ff.279 15/8/1817.

43. ibid, ff.278 6/8/1817.

44. Messham, fn. 40.

45. The Royal Commission on Land in Wales and Monmouthshire, Minutes of evidence, The Rev. J. Davies, 58, 485–58, 533.

46. Messham, fn. 40, pp. 36–44.

47. ibid, p. 40.

48. *Chester Chronicle*, 20/10/1894.

49. This information is derived from the Tithe Apportionment Surveys and Awards, for the Parish of Hawarden 1839, FRO MF/24, and the Parish of Mold, P/40/1/36.

50. In 1844 a portion of this township became part of the ecclesiastical district of Bistre.

51. Hywel Wyn Owen, PNEF.

Chapter 4
Potteries

Introduction

Buckley is a frontier community. From the thirteenth century onwards potters began to exploit clay on the mountain and build cottages on the common. Supplies of firewood from the ancient forest lasted for centuries until replaced by coal dug from outcrops. Chester and nearby creeks along the river provided an outlet for clay pipes, pots, pans and sea coals sent to the city, the Welsh coastal ports and Ireland. For inland trade to the neighbouring villages they relied on donkeys and the services of itinerants, gypsies, pedlars and jaggars.

All this changed in the middle of the eighteenth century. Buckley, in common with other parts of the United Kingdom, was transformed in less than two generations by the Industrial Revolution. No longer were the clay and coal used to support a cottage industry but exploited for large-scale production. The first colliers and potters knew of the rich mineral deposits which nature had provided so conveniently in a narrow corridor running from north to south across the mountain. The cottage was replaced by a manufactory; labour was transferred from the home to the works. Fire-clay goods to meet the needs of new towns and a network of railways were produced in conjunction with household earthenware for the rural and urban poor. Coal was mined on a large scale to fuel kilns and later for steamships. From the mountain could be seen the newly canalised channel of the river Dee conveniently placed on the south bank to which tram and railroads tumbled helter-skelter in steep descent to catch the tides to meet the urgent demands of ever-growing markets.

The mountain, so long grazed by goats, sheep and cattle, became a landscape scarred by clay hole, pit head, and rail ravine, hedged in by workshop, drying shed, firing kiln, wagon- infested siding and swathed in smoke from a battalion of chimneys which hovered threateningly over a chaotic environment, which was Buckley. From this great workshop emerged primitive housing and eventually some civic pride. Like the goods they produced the natives became tough, resistant and enduring in their new environment, when the greatest complement that could be bestowed was that of Buckley brick!

The aim of this section on the making of Buckley is to record two centuries of industrial growth and decline by describing in turn the chief enterprises of pottery making, the manufacture of clay goods, and coal mining. All of these relied on efficient transport from coal-pit and clay works to their product's destination.

Pottery making

The Buckley potters established their trade on the mountain because the geology of the area provided easily obtainable clays along the major fault line, which exposed clays and coal. The potters depended upon the boulder clay deposited during the glacial period, which was found at a depth of two to fifteen feet. This is ideal for the manufacture of household goods. Red boulder clay and lighter buff coloured clay was used for the manufacture of household pottery. White-firing clay found in pockets of the carboniferous limestone was used in the making of tobacco pipes. In the upper layers of the coal measures is the Buckley fire-clay group from which cooking pots and saggars were made. In the early pottery industry here, during the

A sixteenth century pottery.
[Buckley Library]

Middle Ages, coal was added to charcoal to fire the kilns. It was not until the middle of the seventeenth century that coal, of which there was abundance, was used exclusively as a firing agent for earthenware goods. The other raw material necessary was lead to glaze the pottery. This too was found locally along the joints and faults and the bedding planes in the limestone, as were iron and manganese oxides, which when added to the glaze produced black and mottled purple-brown finishes.

The settlement area on Buckley Mountain was partly on the eastern side in the lordship of Hawarden, owned by the Glynne family from the 1650s, but primarily on the western side in the lordship of Ewloe, which was, from 1630, possessed by the Davies (later Davies-Cooke) family of Gwysaney. Buckley Mountain was common land and the potters, in order to obtain clay and coal, made gradual inroads onto the land belonging to the lord of manor for which they were initially fined and then charged rent. Such settlements were called encroachments and it is from a record of these that we can trace the potters of the eighteenth century; here they built their cottages, made gardens, and set up workshops and kilns.

Their workplaces next to their small cottages, were so arranged as to enable them to conduct the necessary processes for pottery making. This was little changed over the centuries although, in the early nineteenth century, the larger manufacturers began to introduce machinery. The Reverend Richard Warner of Bath visited Buckley in 1798 and reported:

> Three miles from Hawarden, we ascended Buckley Hill, in order to visit the large potteries scattered over the face of it; fortunately we met with the master of the works on the spot, (*probably Jonathan Catherall*), who was so good as to conduct us round the manufactory, and explain to us the process pursued in forming the various articles which it produces; such as jugs, pans, jars, stone bottles. &c.&c.[1]

It is probably easier to understand the sequence of the stages involved by looking at a sketch made by the late James Bentley.[2]

Each pottery was a separate working unit, usually a family affair, with the labour provided by four or five members. Making pottery was a seasonal occupation conducted after the crops were sown in the spring until the late summer harvest. The first task was to *choose the clay*. In Buckley there was plenty of choice for pot clay with noted fields below St Matthew's Church, others near the Trap and Willow, on the Lower Common, and marl pits in the Liverpool Road area. Jonathan Catherall brought his clay from Hayes field. Pot clay, 'strong clay', coated the surface and was malleable like plasticine. Fire-clay was found under the coal seams and, because the hand cannot press it into shape, is called 'weak clay'. The clays were chosen for their colours and every potter had his secret recipes for mixing strong and weak clays. The clay was brought to the pottery by horse and cart and left sorted in different heaps. The next stage was *blunging*. The clays were purified in a shallow trough or round pit. Water was added to the clay and a horse-powered spindle turned a large toothed beam or paddle which stirred the mixture into a creamy liquid which flowed through fine sieves or screens to remove limestone pebbles and other impurities into large ponds or pans of around forty feet square. The blunged mixture was then allowed to stand over the winter to weather, settle and mature. At the beginning of the next season the clay was wheeled from the pan into the treading or pugging shed and tipped into an area of about six feet. Here water was added and then, as Warner described, 'It is then *tempered* by boys, who tread it under their naked feet for some hours'. This made the clay more plastic

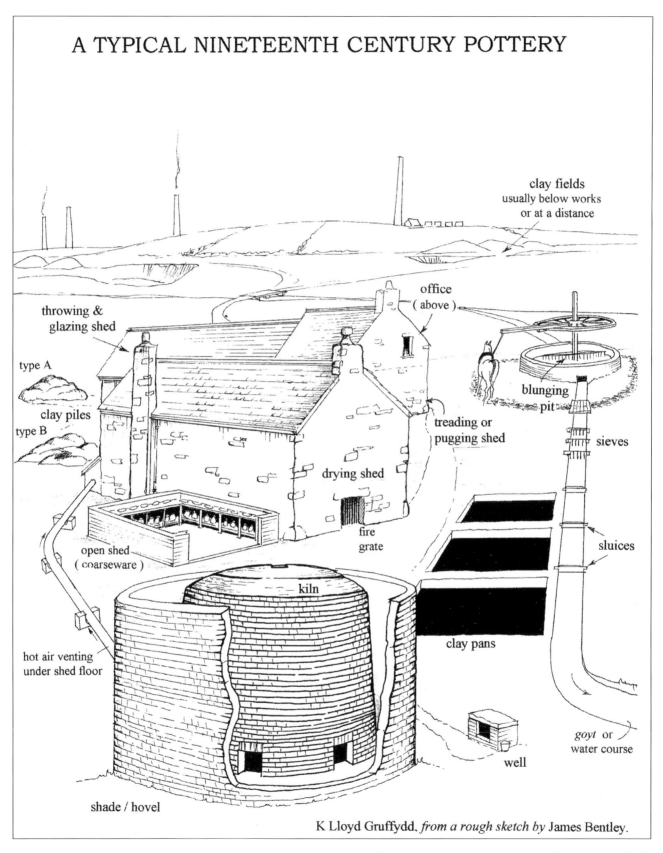

A TYPICAL NINETEENTH CENTURY POTTERY

clay fields
usually below works
or at a distance

office
(above)

throwing &
glazing shed

type A

clay piles

type B

treading or
pugging shed

blunging
pit

sieves

drying shed

open shed
(coarseware)

fire
grate

sluices

kiln

clay pans

hot air venting
under shed floor

well

goyt or
water course

shade / hovel

K Lloyd Gruffydd, *from a rough sketch by* James Bentley.

A Typical nineteenth century pottery. [K. Lloyd Gruffydd]

for the potter. This manual process of treading was later replaced by the pug mill. It was then the turn of the *passer* who weighed, divided and handed the clay in appropriate sized balls to the *thrower* for the clay to be shaped and from thence to be taken by the passer to the *drying shed*. The wheel on which the pots were thrown was attached by a spindle to a large flat disc of stone set rotating by the feet of the potter. The potter moved quickly to throw the pot and to provide decoration. Most of Buckley's domestic ware was wheel-thrown but during the seventeenth century press-moulding was introduced and became the standard method for dishes and plates. The first Buckley moulds were of fire-clay the later ones wooden.

In the drying shed the pots dried out, stiffened and gave opportunity to the *fettler* to carry out repairs, put on handles and, when the ware was hard, to *glaze* it. This was done by dipping the pot or whisking it round with the necessary quantity of slip lead, a thick milky liquid made from a fine powder of hard rock and lead ground in a lead jack and mixed with water. Stoneware, hard-fired bottles and jars used in the liquor trade were glazed by throwing common salt into the hot kiln.

From the drying shed the pots were taken to be *fired in the kiln*. The kilns used in Buckley were shaped like beehives, about fifteen feet in diameter and eight feet in height, and operated on the updraught principle, with the fire lit at the bottom and the hot air circulating upwards. Each pottery had at least one kiln with a capacity for holding up to eight or nine tons of ware. The kiln operators had to carry out three important tasks: loading the ware, firing the kiln, and deciding when the pottery was ready to be withdrawn.

The skill of kiln loading developed in Buckley during the seventeenth century. Examples of kiln furniture, supports for stacking the articles to be burnt and ways of arranging them efficiently were evolved, to allow a variety of ware to be fired at the same time. Large articles like chimney pots and pan mugs were stacked on top of each other in the centre. Small delicate ware was put in saggars; these were ventilated open top cylinders made of a mixture of fire clay and pot clay, which were stacked. Stilts, small cones of clay, allowed larger pots to accommodate smaller ones. Separators, rolls of clay or even half bricks, provided stability and prevented the pots sticking together. Before firing the opening was sealed with loosely cemented bricks and covered with clay plaster.

The walls of the kiln had eight fire grates, or 'bridles', which might take five or six tons of coal to raise the temperature to round a thousand degrees centigrade to enable the lead glazed earthenware to become mature and the pottery properly fired. The potter needed the skill of a good cake maker to be able to judge when the goods were ready. The firing took about forty-eight hours and the completion of a kiln of ware, with the various processes took three weeks.

The history of the Buckley pottery industry

The last pottery closed in the 1940s, but such has been the growth of Buckley over the last sixty years, that many of the pottery sites have disappeared on account of new development. However, thanks to the pioneering work and enthusiasm of a number of scholars, a good account of the industry has emerged. The historian J. E. Messham, a native of Buckley, led the way, when, in 1956, he published a pioneering account of the Buckley Potteries.[3] This aroused the interest of amateur and professional archaeologists led by James Bentley, Martin Harrison, assisted by the Buckley Clay Industries Research Committee, and university lecturer Peter Davey who with colleagues and members of the Buckley Society, (re-established in 1969), identified nineteen sites.[4] Historical research, excavations, field surveys and reports over the last thirty years have preserved much evidence and gathered a representative collection of Buckley Ware. Buckley Library is the home of an excellent display of Buckley pottery which is interpreted by the story boards of an exhibition held at the Mostyn Art Gallery Llandudno in 1983, 'The craft and history of the Buckley potters from the 1340s to the 1940s'.[5] Another collection of Buckley pottery is housed in the Liverpool Museum.[6]

The historical account here relies much on the work of Peter Davey and his colleagues and follows the list of nineteen sites he established as a basis of the study of the Buckley pottery industry and the framework of four periods of pottery activity: medieval, beginning in 1292; pre-industrial *c*.1625–1780, industrial *c*.1780–1860, post-industrial *c*.1860–1940.[7]

The Medieval period

The lordships of Ewloe and Hawarden with their respective castles and the neighbouring one built at Flint in 1277 by Edward I were important strategically for keeping the peace along the border between the English and Welsh. Colonies of English settlers, many of them skilled craftsmen, lived side by side with the native Welsh. It is not surprising therefore that we should find mention of potters. Names of people called *le Potere* (or Potter) can be found as early as 1292 in the lordship of Ewloe. Potters are mentioned in a bailiff's account for the year 1435–6, when John Helegh, the tenant of Potterfield, paid rent for land which was large enough to keep a number of master potters at work. Amongst these were William Potter, Thomas Potter and Ralph Gwyn, occupied 'in getting clay for making clay pots'.[8] Another was John Skot who was accused of theft in 1428.[9] Medieval pottery making in Ewloe was corroborated by the discovery in 1975 by Martin Harrison of medieval pottery sherds and wasters, ranging in date from the thirteenth to nineteenth centuries, in a field on Buckley Mountain. **Site 18**[10] The major finds were jugs, large storage vessels and roofing tiles including a hound's head, which was possibly part of the finial of a roofing tile or some other decorative feature. The products were highly fired white and grey ware with green and brown glazes. The kilns here furnished pots for Chester and the ports of North Wales during the later Middle Ages.

Pre-industrial *c.*1625–1780

This is the most interesting period in the Buckley pottery industry because of the variety and sophistication of the wares produced. The best work was done up to about 1720. Two sites, Brookhill and Pinfold Lane, were discovered and excavated by James Bentley and Martin Harrison.

Brookhill (1640–1720), site 1, was excavated over a long period from 1973 onwards. It is dated by a considerable number of clay tobacco pipes found throughout the excavation. The earliest pipes were made in Chester about *c.*1640 although the majority were made in Buckley between 1680 and 1730, some of which are related in design to pipes made in Broseley, Shropshire, and Chester. Probably the pipes began to be

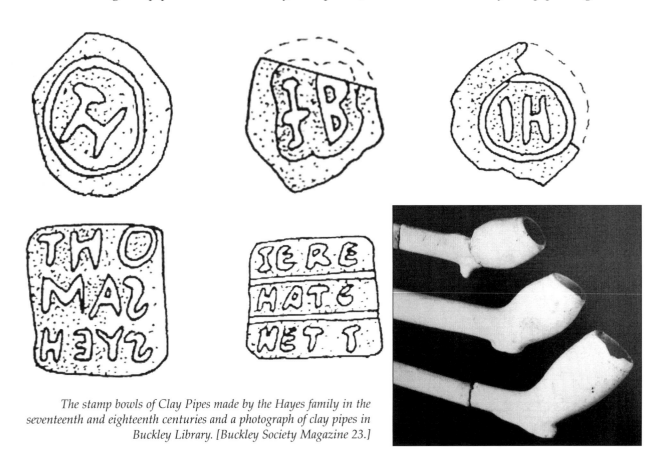

The stamp bowls of Clay Pipes made by the Hayes family in the seventeenth and eighteenth centuries and a photograph of clay pipes in Buckley Library. [Buckley Society Magazine 23.]

made of Buckley white clay during the Civil War when Chester was under siege and both the Royalist and Parliamentarian armies were present from time to time in the neighbourhood of Buckley. Production of pipes at Brookhill was established by the 1660s. Members of the Heyes or Hayes family of Buckley were noted pipe makers of this period. John Hayes *c*.1653–1708, Thomas Hayes 1676–1720 and Thomas Hayes b.1702 left their marks on their clay pipes.[11]

Sgraffito ware is the most interesting of the pottery finds and includes what Davey regards as being 'Perhaps the most distinctive Buckley product … the thrown red-bodied, all over yellow-slipped, lead glazed, sgraffito ware, especially those examples containing 'bestiary' designs with the unusual animal and geometric designs'.[12] Sgraffito (Italian scratched) is a Chinese technique of decorating lead-glazed pottery. In Buckley the earthenware dishes were dipped in a yellow slip, liquid clay, and then scratched in a design form to reveal the colour of the body beneath and then covered in a clear lead glaze. Some of the sgraffito dishes from the Brookhill site are intriguingly decorated with designs from medieval bestiaries, religious books, written to teach moral lessons through the world of nature. Another form of decoration was by slip trailing, that is, when the earthenware pot was covered in a coat of slip, allowed to dry, and then skilfully trailed with a design made in a different liquid clay. The pot was then finished with a clear lead glaze. The colour of the slip could be changed by using white clay or red clay or by adding iron to deepen the colour. The mixing of white and red clay produced agate ware. This method was later replaced by the quicker technique of throwing a pot with red clay and grafting in a sausage of white clay.

Other distinctive finds at Brookhill are a very large tripod-cooking vessel made in a buff fire-clay and a figurine, a female figure, dressed in early seventeenth century costume. The major finds include black glaze ware, slipware, and mottled ware. By about 1700 new ware was emerging which was press-moulded rather than thrown. Dishes were made by pressing out the clay into convex moulds with a variety of fabric used from buff to pink to red and purple. Slip ware bowls were decorated with leaf and tulip designs. Mottled ware jugs, tankards, brown glazed with a mottled appearance was produced by adding manganese to the glaze.

Two vessels found at Brookhill have puzzled historians and archaeologists. They are decorated with motifs obtained from medieval bestiaries, such as, an elephant, a dragon. In addition there is a broken text on the rim of one of the vessels, which may read 'death's sting'.[13] The figures are meant to convey the message of the triumph of goodness over evil for the elephant was regarded as a Christ-like figure, the ambassador of

Above: Brookhill pottery, thrown slip-decorated lead-glazed dish. [National Museum Liverpool]

Right: Brookhill pottery, Sgraffito ware showing elephant's feet and trunk. [National Museum Liverpool]

Buckley sgraffito ware;
bestiary design, c.1625-50.

Brookhill pottery, Bestiary ware,
The cover of Buckley Society Magazine 6.

goodness, and the dragon as possessing all the guile and evil of the biblical serpent. This form of decoration was made to remind pious gentry families who used the pottery on their tables of religious themes. James Bentley's theory that they were commissioned to celebrate the marriage of John Salusbury to Ursula Thelwell in 1586 is a generation too soon.[14] A local display of medieval bestiary motifs is to be seen in Rûg Chapel, Corwen, built in 1634 by Colonel William Salusbury (1580–1660). The interior decoration of the chapel is embellished with a set of bench carvings and a panelled frieze decorated with bestiary figures, which include the elephant and dragon.[15] Both William Salusbury of Rûg and Thomas Davies of Gwysaney were prominent Royalist colonels who served together at the seige of Denbigh in 1646. But, whatever the origin of the design, it shows the vitality and exuberance of the Buckley potters and places them in the mainstream of British craftsmen. This is seen also in the employment of tulip and leaf design. The Brookhill pottery is more than likely to have been patronised by the local gentry during the disturbed political climate of the seventeenth century.

Another important aspect of the Brookhill site is the light it throws on the development of the kiln. Bentley observed that they were in the process of evolution and differed from the typical round pottery kiln used in Buckley during modern times. They were fragile, of a temporary use, being replaced nearby by similar constructions of primitive design. Pits of about five feet diameter were dug and sagger-like stout clay vessels placed in the hole. Slabs of clay about 2-inches thick were laid on top of them to form a floor. A gap left on one side of the perimeter served as an entrance and in all probability a wall of fire-clay sandstone fragments was built round the circumference to a height of about four feet. A series of platform tiers, made up of hollow-pierced clay vessels, were supported on flat slabs of clay laid within. As the packing gradually arose above the walls of the kiln, a wicker beehive shaped dome may have been placed over the kiln and plastered with a mixture of clay and straw with a central vent. When set the kiln was fired. Twelve such kilns were excavated in the area.[16]

Pinfold Lane, site 2, (c.1690–1720) was excavated in 1971 by James Bentley and Martin Harrison. Kiln furniture and clay tobacco pipes similar to those at Brookhill were found together with black glazed ware, simple slip-trailed decorated goods, and mottled ware. The Pinfold Lane site revealed none of the crudely decorated slip-trailed hollow wares discovered at Brookhill but was superior in the size, quality and freedom of expression of its press-moulded dishes. The potters at Pinfold Lane were a generation later than those of Brookhill and probably worked for a different clientele; less for the patron and more for the market place. Their production range was not unlike that of centres at Staffordshire and Prescot, south Lancashire.[17]

The articles made by the Buckley master potters of the seventeenth and eighteenth centuries were of high quality. Earthenware goods, both thrown and press-moulded, glazed, mottled and agate-bodied, slip decorated, when required, were made for the multifarious needs of rural households and the agricultural economy of Welsh and Irish society. Many of the names, forms and uses of the vessels date from medieval times and were to survive unchanged as long as the pottery industry in Buckley remained. Some of these were produced for the kitchen and table: chaffing dish, cooking pot with skillet handle, dripping dish, platter, pipkin, porringer, trencher, jug, bowl, dish, beaker, cup, goblet, flagon, tankard, tyg, and posset cup. The pancheon was the pride of the dairy with a spigot-hole pot. Bleeding bowl, chamber pot, urine and stool pot met the basic needs of the household. No teapots were made until the nineteenth century.

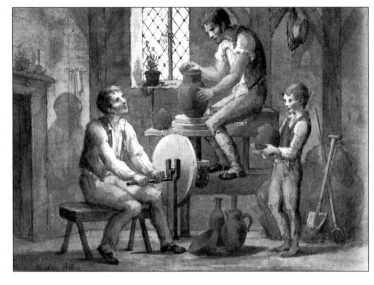

Buckley potters at work, watercolour by
Lady Delamere, 1823.
[By courtesy of Sir William Gladstone]

Stoneware was produced for beer and spirits.

The first potters after the fifteenth century, we can identify by name, are the clay-pipe making family, the Hayes, who appear in the seventeenth century. Their names and those of other potters occur in the Hawarden Parish registers and the probate records of the Peculiar. By the middle the eighteenth century, the sites of the potteries and their associate occupiers appear on maps of the Gwysaney estate, and the neighbouring Glynne estate, both owners of the clay and mineral rights.

The sites were established on encroachments on Buckley Mountain of which there were many. The Gwysaney agent recorded thirty-two in 1759, rising to over a hundred by 1799 and continuing until well into the nineteenth century. 'The uninclosed waste in Buckley when I measured it in 1811', wrote the Gwysaney agent, 'was 149 acres, as the encroachments about twenty years ago was 28 acres, but since then there has been few small encroachments made'.[18]

It is the combination of these records together with archaeological evidence which illuminate the history of the Buckley pottery industry and form the criteria for putting names, dates, and sites to the potters who flourished in Buckley from the seventeenth to the twentieth century. In 1976 Peter Davey published the acknowledged list of nineteen pottery sites, identified by national grid references,[19] and supported by evidence from the Gwysaney estate map of 1757.[20] Other evidence of pottery sites includes maps of the estate, showing the Lordship and Manor of Ewloe with 'the cottages and encroachments thereon', c.1781,[21] and information from the survey of Hawarden Parish, 1815.[22] Invaluable research by Messham provided a list of the eighteenth and nineteenth century potters named in the Clay accounts, in the rentals of the Gwysaney Estate between the years 1783–1810.[23] The list of the nineteen sites is given at the end of this section.

In 1784, Thomas Pennant visited Buckley Mountain and made his famous observation on the newly emerging clay industry.

Within this Lordship are very considerable potteries of coarse earthenware; such as pans, jugs, great pots for butter, plates, dishes, ovens, flower-pots &c. There are fourteen works, which make annually between three and four thousand pounds worth. The ware is mostly exported to Ireland, and the towns on the Welsh coast; particularly to Swansea. There are besides six other works for the making of fire bricks; few clays being better fitted for the purpose of resisting the intense heat of the smelting furnaces. These are made of different sizes; and some which are called bearers weigh two hundred pounds. Great quantities of tiles for barn floors, and for rooms, are also made here; and the annual sale of these two articles amounts to about twelve hundred pounds.

This clay, of a deep ash-colour, is found in beds of great thickness; and is dug up in hard lumps, resembling a shaly rock; after which it is left for a considerable time exposed to the air, in order to effect its dissolution. The bricks made with it are set in the lead-furnaces with the unburnt clay instead of mortar.[24]

Pennant's visit was made at a time when the industry was beginning to separate into two parts, which were to become more apparent in the nineteenth century. The oldest part, the pottery industry, was to remain a domestic concern conducted on the existing pottery sites. The newly emerging industry was the development of larger factory-like establishments for the manufacture of a variety of clay-goods and bricks. Hence, Pennant's observation in Buckley, of fourteen works or potteries and 'six other works for the making of fire bricks', the first of the brick manufactories. Nevertheless Pennant's description of fourteen potteries

Ollive Hayes at work in the thrower's shed, c.1930.
[FRO PH 11/173]

in 1784 and Messham's list of eleven Buckley potteries in 1815 is an interesting starting point for making a list of names and an indication of the continuity of the industry.

The name of Hayes, recorded as pipe-makers in the seventeenth century, spanned the industry until a pottery worked by Ollive Hayes closed in 1942. This was **Ewloe Old Pottery, site ten**. There is frequent mention of the name of Hayes, as in 1757 and 1781, when Jonathan Hayes (d.1809), is the tenant of a public house and mug kiln. His son Jonathan married Elizabeth Jones of Hawarden, and a number of their offspring are mentioned in the nineteenth century. We do not know to which family Elizabeth Hayes belonged. She is described in 1835 as a 'pipemaker' of Hawarden. In 1841 she appears in the Bistre census, living at 'The Square' on Mold Road.

Site two, Pinfold Lane, is recorded as having, over the years, different pottery families working there. The Codrell or Cotrell family, a Benjamin Cottrell was there in the middle of the eighteenth century, and was followed eventually by John Leach occupier in 1815.

John Taylor who in 1815 occupied **site three, near Alltami**, was descended from John Taylor who in 1741 married Mary Codrell, and is recorded in the encroachments of 1781 as having a mug kiln.

The Prices who worked **site eleven**, on the Middle Common were another long surviving family, first mentioned in the 1730s and still there in 1871.

The Whitley or Whitloe family, **site twelve**, came from Prescot to work for Edward Cunnah. Edward Whitley had a mug kiln in 1781. He was succeeded by his son Robert on whose death in 1826 the pottery closed.

John Leach was at **site nine, Ewloe Place**, in 1781, but by 1815 was succeeded by Aaron Sharratt. His father, also Aaron, is reputed to have come from Burslem and to be of Dutch extraction. The son was born in 1751 and became Jonathan Catherall's foreman before setting up as a master potter in 1800. He had four sons Aaron, Moses, Joshua and Jonathan. It eventually became Lamb's Art Pottery and was the last to close in 1945.

The **Willow Pottery, site seven**, was worked by Bartholomew Prescot from 1783 until 1815. The Prescots were another immigrant family who came to Buckley, in the 1770s, to work for Jonathan Catherall or Edward Cunnah. The pottery closed in the 1820s.

Quite naturally, the names of potters disappear, during the history of the Buckley industry, from the seventeenth century onwards; Robert Read, Ewloe, 1679; Thomas Davies, Ewloe, 1681; Thomas Graston, Pentrobin and Joseph Manifold, Ewloe, in the early eighteenth century.

Site 16, at the junction of Church Road and Higher Common Road, worked by Peter Ledsham, (d.1802), came to an end.

At **site 6**, Pinfold, there is no further mention, after 1781, when it was worked by Benjamin Davies.

The Dean family of potters who married into the Hayes family in 1720 is not mentioned after 1791. In the 1815 survey of Hawarden parish there are two potteries worked by potters named John Lewis. **Site 5, Middle Common**, the older Lewis Pottery was worked by Thomas Lewis up to 1799 (d.1801) and in 1815 was in the tenancy of John Leach Senr. **Site 4, Lower Common**, was built by John Lewis Jnr who worked it until his death in 1831 and continued by his widow Jane and was in 1860 tenanted by Thomas Jones who married into the family.

The industrial phase 1780–1860

The Catherall family were natives of Ewloe. They followed the calling of potters in the seventeenth century and from their ranks emerged Jonathan Catherall I (1689–1761), as the leader of this mountain colony and pioneer of the firebrick industry. A long and industrious life blessed with integrity and business sense enabled him to make adequate provision for the continuation of the Catherall progress, as his will directed. The sensible dispersion of his worldly goods between his eldest son John and five daughters gave the prospect of the foundation of a modest dynasty. Although ill-founded, optimism was placed in the future career of his prodigal heirs, who almost dissipated his inheritance before his premature death in 1777. He provided, for his daughter 'Ann, wife of Edward Cunnah, potter, with kiln, work-house, and place to build a house, which my son-in-law useth and occupieth'. To his daughter Martha, the wife of William Hancock, he bequeathed a sum of money, with the gift to his son-in-law of a 'croft or parcel of land called by the name of Hopty Pegg', which adjoined 'the freehold lands of my nephew Benjamin Catherall, potter'.

Looking at the situation thirty years later we see how the fortunes of the various branches of the extended Catherall family faired as master potters after the advantages given them by Jonathan Catherall I in 1761.

Edward Cunnah died in 1782 and his wife Anne carried on the pottery business. She prospered and became the largest user of loads of clay dug in the lordship of Ewloe from 1783/4–90. Ann, (d.1809), retired in 1794 when the pottery fell into obscurity. Benjamin Catherall is not found amongst the Gwysaney clay accounts for this period, neither is his son and heir. This branch mortgaged its inheritance and the younger Benjamin lost the Ewloe brickworks and pottery before he died in 1801. The fate of John, the heir of Jonathan Catherall I, was equally unpromising, but fate was to intervene before his estate was completely dissipated. His profligacy was to love bad women, horses and cocks and he met with a fatal accident, being thrown from his horse in Saltney on his way home from Chester in 1777. He left a widow Martha, three sons, John, Jonathan, and Joseph, and a daughter Ann. The future of his business interests in the pottery and firebrick industry for the next fifteen years fell under the control of his widow Martha until it passed, on her death in 1792, to the eldest son John who proved to be as feckless as his father. Enjoying fully his inheritance, nurtured and augmented by his mother, he too became a victim of irresponsibility and was forced to mortgage and lease some of his estate to his brother Jonathan.

It was this second son, aged 16 years, who was called upon by his mother to share in running the business, paying off creditors, managing the pottery and firebrick works, travelling great distances to secure orders and collect debts. In their partnership over the next fifteen years they enjoyed the satisfaction of seeing the business expand and experiencing a new found religious faith.[25] The zealous Jonathan II built chapels, and developed a strong business sense and intellectual curiosity with regard to pottery making. Together in 1786 they rented two potteries known as the large and small earthenware works, living as tenants at the Hope and Anchor public house, the site of the pottery with its kiln and sheds, **site 8**.

After his mother's death in 1792, Jonathan Catherall II, leased clay, and the tenancy of the brickworks from his eldest brother. In 1796 he built a stoneware works to export jars and bottles to Ireland for the spirit trade. Further expansion occurred in 1810 with the building of Ewloe Place Brickworks. This catalogue of success marked him out as an important and successful Welsh potter.

Jonathan I's daughter Martha, the wife of William Hancock, produced a son William Hancock II (1762–1832) who inherited the business acumen of his maternal grandfather and became the founder of, amongst other enterprises, a successful pottery and firebrick business. In 1792 William Hancock established his pottery in the Brunswick Road area, **site 14**. It was built on land bought by Rigby and Hancock from the Mold enclosure commissioners. A hundred years later it became the site of the first Roman Catholic church in Daisy Hill. The future prosperity of Buckley and the shaping of its destiny was in the hands of the cousins Jonathan Catherall and William Hancock.[26]

The purpose of this section is to review the pottery industry and the discussion here will be limited to the role that the two cousins played in its development. Their involvement in the industrial growth of Buckley was extensive. They built potteries, brickworks, developed coal mines, invested in lead works, pioneered tramways, railroads, and shipping. They shared an ability to market their wares, Jonathan Catherall in Ireland and Wales and William Hancock in England and across the Atlantic in the West Indies

The Hope and Anchor. 1988.
[Buckley Library]

and North America. The goods they produced met two contemporary needs, the growth of urban development, and, secondly, the building of railways. Their vision was that of industrialists, setting them apart from other traditional Buckley potters. They continued the small domestic nature of the cottage industry they had known in the eighteenth century, with a small family labour force and using itinerant carters to distribute their pots. On the other hand, the new generation of Catherall and Hancock harnessed their pottery output to the firebrick and clay goods markets, freighting their products, with other orders in the same cargoes, shipping them mostly, from Connah's Quay, or Aston Wharf, Queensferry. Hancock used the railroad to get to the river whereas Catherall loaded his goods into carts, of which they had over a score, or depended upon the services of carters or jaggers.

Jonathan Catherall had a fifteen-year start on his cousin since he had been forced into responsible adulthood on the death of his father. He learnt early the business of making pots and selling them. Like Cobbett he made his own rural rides around Ireland and North and South Wales. London too was exploited for trade and he made life-long friends in Staffordshire and Chester through religious and business connections. Through his travels to Pwllheli he courted Catherine Jones the daughter the vicar of Llannor and Deneio, and he married her shortly before his mother died in 1792. The previous year Jonathan had a serious illness brought about through years of exhausting travel on horseback in all weathers, from which happily he recovered.

Their marriage began by their building Hawkesbury House which was soon filled with eight children, five of whom died in infancy, to be followed to their graves in 1807 by his wife Catherine. A double tragedy occurred in 1818 when he lost his remaining daughters Martha and Frances of fever within two days of each other. Thereafter he was left with an only son, William, with whom he entered into what proved to be a difficult partnership.

Cropper relates Catherall's correspondence with craftsmen from the pottery towns of Hanley and Burslem. He was interested in their secret recipes for blending clay and preparing glaze and the development of a piece of machinery, the Yorkshire Horse.[27]

Both Catherall and Hancock were supplying day to day utilitarian pots for kitchen, table, dairy, and other household purposes, much as the Buckley potters had done in the eighteenth century. J. E. Messham made a comprehensive list of these domestic wares from the Catherall papers (1838–52)[28] of which this is an abridged list.

Buckley mugs, in shining black, red or yellow, with their simple slip decorations.

Jonathan Catherall's Business Card.
[T. Cropper Buckley and District]

There were cups and tots 18, 24, 30 and 36 to the piece, the most popular size being the 24 to the piece half-pint cups, useful for holding bread and milk. A small number of quart cups were made. Porringers, plates and platters, round and oval were made in large quantities in sizes from 12 to 36 to the piece. Basins were made in three sizes, bowls in five, dishes in five, and there was a wide range of jugs holding from half a pint to two gallons. For the kitchen there were stew-pots and stew-mugs, venison pots, saucepans, beef pots, tureens and collinders, pudding dishes and bread pans. For the dairy there were butter dishes, cream mugs and milk pans, and for the storehouse pickle pots and large oval dishes for salting hams. Large pans were bought as washing pans. Chamberware in six sizes as well as stool-pans, chairpans and pettypans. Flowerpots for the garden, and chimney pots for the house. Numbers of small articles were made, such as candlesticks, button baskets, inkstands, inkhorns, and spitting boxes.[29]

Catherall's trade with Ireland was valuable, although clouded, by the financial crisis of 1820–1. It did not appear that Buckley's 'father of nonconformity' had any moral qualms in supplying the Irish whisky trade with stoneware spirit bottles or pious Roman Catholics with holy water vessels.

There is little documentary evidence about Hancock's enormous pottery trade, which lasted until the Daisy Hill Works closed in 1886. Dennis Griffiths estimated that Hancock's several potteries concentrated on the production of milk and butter pans, baking dishes, and wine and tobacco jars, in coarser than Staffordshire ware, unrivalled for its suitability for heat resistance. Some of it was probably sent to the West Indies and the United States with their other clay goods. Griffiths estimated. that by 1847, the railroad from Hancock's carried 100,000 tons a year in the proportion of 60% firebrick, 40% coal and pottery.[30] Messham states that Hancocks sent down the tramway an average of over 150 tons of earthenware a year from 1839 to 1869.[31]

Bentley's excavation of a small area of the Daisy Hill site revealed commercial goods, conical burnt clay pots, lead pots for Chester lead works as well as household pottery, including pan mugs and spirit jars.[32] Bentley reports that most of the site of the **Daisy Hill Pottery, site 14**, has been built over.

The Buckley pottery industry in the nineteenth century never really met the challenge of the high quality and cheapness of Staffordshire ware. Catherall's never fully recaptured their Irish market after the crisis of the 1820s and the family enthusiasm for pottery declined with the death of Jonathan II's son William in 1875 and their output dwindled. The large number of producers of coarse domestic earthenware led to overproduction and internal competition amongst the Buckley tradesmen which the Brick manufacturers sought to regularise by fixing prices in the 1870s. Hancock's closed their pottery division in 1886 by which time death and competition had reduced their numbers. A new era began in the 1860s.

The last phase, 1860–1940

The potters of the 1820s included three Prices, five Lewises, two Taylors, three Sharratts, five Hayeses, and one Whitley. By the end of the century many of these had gone and were replaced by new firms who struggled to survive and reinvigorate the industry with the production of rustic, art noveau, and novelty ware. To augment their ware, and supply customers with utilitarian Buckley mugs, the small potteries felt it advantageous to buy some of their products from large earthenware manufactures. For these supplies they relied on such large manufacturers as the Ewloe Barn Brick and Tile Co. In the 1890s, Davison's,

Taylor's Pottery 1920s, Alltami, (c.1750–c.1929). [FRO D/JB/109]

supplied flower pots to the Art Pottery, Jones and Gerrard Pottery, Hancock and Co., and Taylor Bros. Pottery.[33] The surviving potters still produced the traditional coarse earthenware for household use, but, reverting to the cottage scale of industry, they were driven by decline to seek new markets with a variety of goods. In a conscious revival of seventeenth methods and styles, sgraffito ware, slip-trailed with patterns and legends as mundane as 'Meat', 'Beef', 'Mutton' was made. Davey described Buckley rustic ware:

as a type of lead glazed earthenware on which the outer surfaces were scratched to produce an effect like the surface of a tree trunk. Small stumps of clay, with blobs of yellow slip on the ends were often added to look like sawn-off branches. The body of this ware is normally brick red throughout. A rectangular panel of yellow slip is usually applied to the body and a legend added in *sgraffito*. The ware was produced from 1896 until at least 1927; a number of pieces having been made in Hayes pottery in 1924 and 1925.[34]

As Tyler pointed out:

The smaller potteries' determination to hang on to their dwindling outlets was valiant and full of cheerful enthusiasm; they leapt on fashion's passing bandwagon and from the last quarter of the 19th century a succession of rustic, 'art' and novelty wares spilled from their kilns. The miscellany of good, indifferent and grotesque, but rarely humourless pots, covered the new and revamped: chick and hen money boxes, cuckoo whistles, puzzle jugs, chests of drawers, tobacco jars; self-watering plant pots, drawer stands, poultry feeders, funeral urns, church collection boxes, door stops and a lot more. The awe-inspiring potters persuaded their clay into forms hitherto unknown in the material.[35]

Few potteries were working during this last phase. Of these, Jones and Gerrard worked Ewloe Green Pottery, **site 17**, from *c.*1870 to 1913. Charles Gerrard from Rainford in Lancashire, an employee of Pilkington's Glass Works, formed a partnership with William Jones of Buckley who had a pottery in Ewloe Green. Firing was carried out in a single kiln. Clay was obtained from a field behind Oak's Farm in Pinfold Lane.[35]

In the 1890s they advertised as manufacturers of all kinds of Buckley ware — garden, rhubarb, and sea-kale pots, chimney pots made to order, Rockingham, jet and fancy teapots, black, brown and yellow glazed earthenware – bread pots, milk pans, flower pots; selling their goods in Chester and North Wales. They closed in 1913.

George Lewis remembered the old firm of Taylor's of Alltami, **site 3**, working into the early twentieth century.

Other potteries did not survive long. A short-lived firm which printed its letter-head 'The Welsh Art Pottery Co., Chester Road, Buckley,' lasted from, between, February 1914 until November 1916, when it surrendered its 'kilns, mortar mill and engine in satisfaction of the debt owed to the Hawarden estate'. The erstwhile potter was Frederick James Holloday of Penyffordd. Works at the Trap and Dirty Mile opened after 1918 soon closed. The pottery reported by George Lewis as beginning in May 1915 by Mr Ernest Wilson, in the meadow at Ewloe Place where Rice Jones was the potter, was short lived. George Lewis (1878–1963) from early manhood kept a diary in which he meticulously recorded the events which affected the lives of Buckley people. He noted the industrial changes which took place, closure of collieries, potteries and brickworks. He always recorded the winner of the Chester Cup. He was the father of George Lewis (1903–72), Secretary of Castle Fire Brick Co. Ltd (1939–54) and a company director.

The most successful and accomplished of the potteries in this last phase was Powell's 'North Walian Art Pottery', situated in the middle of Buckley Common, **site 15**.[37] Its founder in 1853 was George Powell. He was the first local master potter to install a machine to replace hand turning at the wheel. This pressed out a pot in one stroke. Powell's was the only firm in the county which possessed one.[38] This was installed by the ingenious carpenter and jack of all trades Edwin Rogers who recorded on 25 August 1883, 'Finished two new pot wheels to work with the engine. Three wheels work by steam, room for two more wheels.' George Powell was in partnership with his brother Isaac, who had a son also called Isaac. The son was born in 1848 at Ruabon of which place his mother was a native. It was probably the venture of the newly opened enterprise at Buckley which attracted them to move from one clay district to another. The young Isaac became an accomplished violinist, and for a time, taught at Bistre National School. He then began travelling throughout the United Kingdom and the Channel Islands, probably as a salesman for the family business. He was regarded as an authority on earthenware and highly respected as a potter

The Buckley diarist, George Lewis (c.1880–1960), and his wife, Martha Jane (née Wright), 1922.

distinguished for 'making ornamental flower pots and horticultural ware of chaste design in various coloured glazes'. Powell was acknowledged as 'a great student of this ancient industry, and had a library of the world's best books bearing upon the subject. He was a great theorist and had several secret coloured glazes of his own invention'. In 1902 he gained a diploma of honour at the Liverpool Exhibition of Welsh Industries.

The Powell family connection with Ruabon was continued on account of their other branch of clay works there. It could be that be they were related to Jonathan Powell, one of J. C. Edwards' valued workmen. Such an association was particularly valuable to the North Walian Art Pottery for the ideas which emanated from the Trefynant works of J. C. Edwards, situated nearby on the river Dee below Ruabon. Trefynant became internationally famous for its tessellated and encaustic tiles, in competition with firms like Maws, and Craven Dunnill of Shropshire which specialised in ruby, brown and green lustre tiles, producing encaustic tiles in the style of William de Morgan. The famous artist Lewis F. Day the principal exponent in England of slip-outlined decoration designed for J. C. Edwards.[39] Wherever the inspiration for his designs came from, Isaac Powell was certainly a worthy practitioner of the *art nouveau* with its Japanese influence both in the use of slipware decoration and design of jugs, vases and jars. Powell's designs for ceramic

Powell's Pottery 1923, a display of goods made at the pottery, Lower Common (1853–1929). [FRO PH 11/400]

Lamb's Pottery, 1920s, Church Road, (c.1740–1945).
[FRO D/DM/809/48]

tiles are inspirational and a fine example of Buckley ware at its best.

His obituary notice in 1924 expresses the fears of the decline of the industry in the twenties and the difficulties in marketing art nouveau ware, remarking that, 'of late they have returned to the manufacturing of the famous Buckley ware for domestic purposes mainly, such as washing and baking pans, milk, cream and butter pots etc. Their stamp was 'I & W POWELL – BUCKLEY – EWLOE POTTERIES'. Other goods produced were novelties: hat pin holders, pepper and salt cellars and jam and butter dishes. A photograph of 1923 shows around forty high-class art and souvenir pots. Isaac Powell, now aged over seventy years, was in partnership with his brother William and nephew Isaac Willis Powell. They had optimistic plans to continue in business and were considering the prospects of expansion. Writing to a solicitor they informed him that 'we are about to form a company at our Ruabon works for the development of certain branches of the Clay Industries — which are badly needed in the district and would eventually find employment for a considerable number of men who are now on the employment lists'.[40] Nothing came of this project and when Isaac Powell, a bachelor, died the following year, the pottery passed to his brother and nephew who appeared to have disagreed over its future. George Lewis records 'a distress sale there in May 1929'. Mr Price Jones, the thrower, started on his own there, at the Willow Pottery and eventually it closed down in the 1940s.

The same decade saw the end of the Buckley pottery industry when it was forced, by wartime restrictions, to close. No one believed the closure was permanent at the time, although concern was expressed as Hayes family pottery, **site 10**, closed in September 1942, faithfully recorded by George Lewis '1942, Sept 5, Old Ewloe Pottery closed down. G. Dyment potter.'

John Lamb & Son, **site 9**, adjoining the old St Matthew's Infant School, Church Road, the place previously worked by John Leach in the eighteenth century and the Sharrat family in the nineteenth, was the last to close. Lamb's worked there for fifty years. A small, undated, folded card, described their wares,

Established 1740 – Art Pottery – Church Road, Buckley, near Chester. John Lamb & Sons, Manufacturers of all kinds of black, brown and yellow glazes ware, Garden Pots and Chimney Pots (Best Hand-Made Flower Pot List) — (Trade List Pan Mugs, Bread Mugs, Dishes, Milk Coolers).

The end came farcically rather than dramatically. The young potter George Henry Lamb was called up, the kiln was filled, sealed and fired by his father, and left to his son to open on his return from the war in 1945. The young serviceman returned safely, opened the kiln, and found government restrictions over pricing the ware, and obtaining coal and lead, too daunting for him to continue in business.

Attempts at revival — failure and inquest

In 1943 Flintshire County Council began to plan for the revival of industry when the county returned to peace after the war. To this end the Director of Education, Dr Hadyn Williams, made enquiries about the future of the pottery industry. He appointed the County Art Organiser, Mr W. McAllister Turner, to investigate the matter and produce a report. Turner, together with colleagues, made a visit to the Staffordshire potteries, on a fact-finding mission. 'Schools, factories and exhibitions were visited including the very modern plant built by Messrs Wedgwood at Barlaston' in order 'to obtain first hand information on the industry and the value of pottery as a school subject.' Here they met the art director of the Potteries and representatives from local firms. Turner took with him samples of Buckley clay and pottery for inspection by his hosts. Turner's report of his visit was forwarded by the County Council to R. W. Baker, Clay Industries Adviser of the Rural Studies Bureau who replied in some detail.

Baker's report was realistic both in his assessment of the possibility of the long-term benefit of teaching pottery in schools and the success of the future design and marketing of Buckley pottery. Baker was dismissive of Turner's limited recommendations for the teaching of pottery. He was convinced that 'what ought to be established in the beginning of the scheme is the reason for the introduction of pottery in schools. Boys leaving elementary and secondary schools could not be expected to do any decent job in the potteries. Their training would be too scanty. They will be put to 'donkey jobs', which boys these days do not relish.' Turner had reported rather optimistically about the response he had from the experts in the Potteries that 'All were of the opinion that the designs were both obsolete and crude, but with proper direction, a bright and prosperous future was assured'. Turner suggested that local potters should evolve new and distinctive designs in both utility and decorative ware. Baker thought that local potters cannot evolve new and distinctive designs unless they have good taste and are practical in their aims. Turner was of the opinion that the industry should use modern methods of publicity, suggesting as an example, 'You have never tasted milk pudding until made in a Bokkelegh dish.' To which Baker retorted, 'reversion to the old name Bokkelegh is surely incompatible with the desire to produce new and distinctive designs'. Turner and Baker failed to agree on most points and the latter concluded rather blandly. 'If the training in the schools is efficient and produces a live and enthusiastic type of pottery student, the firms of Buckley will, without doubt, take great interest in the teaching of pottery in and around Buckley'. Baker promised the Clerk to Flintshire County Council that he would be 'pleased to test the various Buckley clays with the aim of discovering its possibilities' and suggesting possible uses of the clay, providing recipes of glazes and temperatures and methods of production of various types of wares. He appeared ignorant of the long history of the Buckley pottery industry![41]

In fact pottery had been taught in St Matthew's School. Miss Emily Jones, the excellent head teacher of the Girl' School, reported in the Log Book:

> 1931 January 5. In November two girls, Doris M. Jones and Mary Dyment painted two designs suitable for a cup in two shades of blue. These were sent to the Josiah Wedgwood pottery as ideas of a clean, cheery & free design. The Head Teacher also sent one based on a harebell. The company unexpectedly translated the designs in blue enamel on to china cups & they sent a cup and saucer for each designer.
>
> 1932 April 9. Three of the Girls made 'worm' pottery a few weeks ago. It is now out of the kiln & is interesting from a handwork point of view.
>
> May 23. Some of the articles made by the girls have been baked in local kilns.
>
> July 11. Miss Bevan Evans took some of the younger children to the local pottery for a short time this afternoon. (She was the daughter of the Director of Education, and attended the School for 3 weeks beginning July 4 on school practice).

The final act was a public conference to discuss the revival of Buckley's clay work industry held in the Council Chamber in May 1945. It was a representative gathering attended by Trade Unionists, Ministry of Labour Officials, H.M. Inspector of Schools, the Director of Education and the County Art Organiser and was chaired by Mr Dennis Griffiths.

In the course of the meeting references were made to the pottery industry. Mr Ollive Hayes, a potter, said he could not see why the local pottery trade could not be revived. He believed the local education authority could help in the matter of educational training although he admitted that he had not had an apprentice for thirty years. Mr James Peters, Chairman of the Urban District Council, was sceptical as to the future of what he called 'art pottery'. Not so Mr P. A. Lewis, HMI, who emphasised that there would be a demand for their pottery if they could provide what he public wanted. Why should they all be made in England? There was no reason why their old industry should not be revived and reach new heights of prosperity. The Art Organiser, Mr W. McAllister Turner, shared his optimism and thought there was a demand for artistic

IT'S TIME THE
BUCKLEY POTTERIES GOT GOING AGAIN.

Cartoon: Its time the Buckley Potteries got going again. Buckley Magazine 1 1944.(BYPCA)

pottery if the matter of design were to be handled with foresight. He believed there was a great future for Buckley pottery.[42]

In December 1945 the Urban District Council replied to the Clerk to Flintshire County Council, who had requested details with a view to establishing new industries. They told him 'that three potteries and one brickworks had closed down during the war, but that the brick yard intended to reopen' and stressed 'the importance of the revival of the pottery industry'.

During the following year the Flintshire Education Committee were still exploring the possibilities of the revival of the pottery industry. They had received details of a scheme of apprenticeship for those employed in the Staffordshire industry and were considering the possibility of establishing some form of pottery training centre at Buckley. But it was pointed out that, although the difficulty of providing additional accommodation for this purpose at the present moment made this almost impossible, primary consideration would be given to this need, when the new Technical College, which the Authority proposed to establish, was erected.[43]

In September 1946, the Urban District Council nominated a sub-committee 'to confer with the proprietors of the brick works in Buckley and the pottery industry with a view to exploring the possibilities of developing the industry in the area'. Mr Ollive Hayes (Ewloe Pottery), Mr George Lamb (Art Pottery), W. McAllister Turner, and the proprietors of the brickworks were invited. Nothing came of it. The inquest on the Buckley pottery industry was over. No official verdict was pronounced. Was it neglect, misadventure or natural causes after a very long life?

A list of pottery sites

This information corresponds to the site numbers given in the text above. The list is based on the one produced by P. J. Davey in *Buckley 4*, p.16f, 1976. Some details may have been omitted and others added. 1750 and 1781 refers to details from the Gwysaney Estate Map, 1815 from information provided by J. E. Messham from the Survey of Hawarden and 1871 is the 25" Ordnance Survey of 1871.

Site one: Brookhill. ? 1750.
Site two: Pinfold. ? 1750; 1781 (Benjamin Cottrell); 1815 (John Leach).
Site three: Alltami, Lower Common ? 1750; 1781 (Joseph Codrell's sister); 1815 (John Taylor); 1860 (Taylor and Son); 1871; 1886 (Charles Taylor).
Site four: Lower Common. 1815 (John Lewis jnr); 1871.
Site five: Middle Common. ? 1750, 1781 (Thomas Lewis); 1815 (John Leach sen.); 1871.
Site six: Pinfold ? 1750; 1781 (Benjamin Davies).
Site seven: Willow 1815 (Bartholomew Prescot — closed).
Site eight: Hope & Anchor ? 1750; 1781 (? John Leach); 1815 (Jonathan Catherall); 1869; 1871.
Site nine: Ewloe Place 1781 (John Leach); 1815 (Aaron Sharratt); 1860; 1871; 1886.
Site ten: Old Ewloe ? 1750; 1781 (Jonathan Hayes); 1815 (Phoebe and Joseph Hayes); 1860; 1871; 1886; 1942 (closed).
Site eleven: Middle Common ? 1750; 1815 (Charles Price); 1860; 1871.
Site twelve: Middle Common 1781 (Edward Whitely); 1815 (Robert Whitely).
Site thirteen: Buckley Common ? 1750; 1871.
Site fourteen: Daisy Hill 1815 (William Hancock); 1860; 1871; 1886.

Site fifteen: Lower Common, Powell's Pottery opened 1853 closed 1929. Reopened by Price Jones as Willow Pottery, closed *c*.1940.

Site sixteen: Junction of Church Road and Common Road   ? 1750; 1781 (Peter Ledsham).

Site seventeen: Ewloe Green Pottery 1871 Jones & Gerrard closed 1913.

Site eighteen: Finds of sherds of medieval pottery.

Site nineteen: *c*.1650–80.

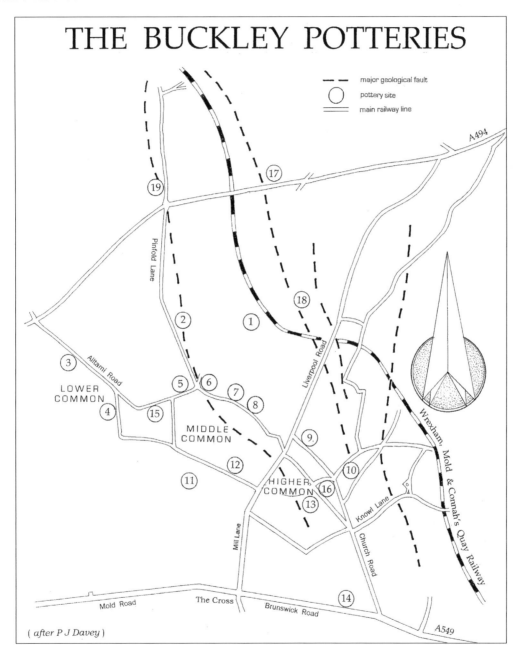

THE BUCKLEY POTTERIES

major geological fault

pottery site

main railway line

(after P J Davey)

Notes

1. Rev. Richard Warner, *Second Walk through Wales* 1798 (1800 edition).
2. Drawn by J.Bentley for Katherine M.Hartley 1984. In 'A History of Buckley Pottery'. Univ. thesis deposited in FRO.
3. J. E. Messham, 'The Buckley Pottery Industry', in *Flintshire Historical Society Publications*, Flintshire Miscellany, vol. 16, 1956.
4. P. J. Davey, 'Recent Fieldwork in the Buckley Potteries', *Buckley*, No. 4.
5. Sheila Tyler, Catalogue, Major exhibition — Mostyn Art Gallery 1983. Sponsored by the Welsh Arts Council and Crafts Council.
6. See lecture 'The Buckley Potteries', 1 March 2001, by Christine Longworth of the National Museums & Galleries on Merseyside. Buckley Library.

7. P. J. Davey, *Buckley Pottery*, (Print Flow: Shotton 1975); P. J. Davey and C. M. Longworth, "The identification of Buckley Pottery" in *Archaeology in Wales*, vol. 41, 2000; James Bentley, *A Short Account of the Buckley Potteries*, 1982.

8. J. E. Messham, 'A Ewloe Bailiff's Account and the origins of the Buckley Pottery Industry' p.169, in *Flintshire Historical Society Journal*, vol. 32, 1989.

9. ibid.

10. *Buckley*, No. 4, p.28, op cit.

11. J. Bentley, P. J. Davey, H. M. Harrison, 'Buckley Clay Tobacco Pipes', *Buckley*, No 5.

12. Davey and Longworth, op cit, p. 66.

13. K. Lloyd Gruffydd, 'Seventeenth-century bestiary ware from Buckley, Clwyd', in *Archaeologia Cambrensis*, vol. 129, pp. 160–3.

14. James Bentley, 'Interesting sgraffito Decorated Pottery', in *Buckley*, No. 19, pp.13–6.

15. CADW: Welsh Historic Monuments, Rûg Chapel, Llangar Church, etc. pp.20–1.

16. James Bentley, 'An early pottery site in Buckley', *Buckley*, No. 7, pp. 8–14.

17. P. J. Davey, 'Further observations on a post-medieval kiln group from Pinfold Lane, Buckley', in B. Vyner and S. Wrathnell (eds), *Studies in Medieval and Later Pottery in Wales*. Presented to J. M. Lewis (Cardiff, University College Dept. of Extra Mural Studies), p. 98.

18. FRO D/GW/55.

19. *Buckley*, No. 4, op cit.

20. FRO D/GW/651, see also Messham, op cit (1956), p.58.

21. FRO D/GW/ 671, 673 and Messham, ibid, p. 58.

22. FRO Survey of Hawarden 1815 and Messham, ibid, p. 61.

23. Messham, ibid, pp.56–7.

24. Thomas Pennant, *Tours in Wales*, (London: 1778) vol. I, p. 115.

25. For Jonathan Catherall see articles by J. E. Messham in *Buckley*, Nos 24, 25, 26, and Thomas Cropper, *Buckley & District*, (Buckley 1923).

26. For William Hancock & Co. see FRO D/DG/48, and H. Morris-Jones, 'The Hancock Family: Industrial Entrepreneurs', *Buckley*, No. 21.

27. Cropper, op cit, p. 62f.

28. FRO D/DM/440/1.

29. Messham, 1956, op cit, p. 50–1.

30. FRO D/DG/48.

31. Messham, 1956, op cit, p. 40, fn 71.

32. FRO NT/195.

33. FRO D/DM/809/33 ND, *c*.1900.

34. Davey, 1975, op cit.

35. See fn 5.

36. James Bentley, 'Jones and Gerard of Alltami, Potters *c*.1870–1930', *Buckley*, 16.

37. *Mold, Deeside and Buckley Leader*, May 9 1824. Obituary of Isaac Powell.

38. ibid.

39. Ifor Edwards, 'Clay Masters and Clay Workers in Ruabon', *Denbighshire Historical Society Transactions*, vol. 35, pp. 92–3.

40. *Buckley*, No. 4, op cit, p. 26.

41. FRO UD/A/1/51–2.

42. *Chester Chronicle*, 2 June 1945.

43. FRO UD/A/1/51.

Chapter 5
Collieries

In the nineteenth century Coal was King. Mined extensively throughout the United Kingdom, it fuelled the steam ships carrying British trade to all corners of the earth; it kept the Empire together, transporting immigrants, administrators and troops. The smoke from the chimney pots of every household and workplace, the soot, which was its hallmark, was an inescapable reminder of its omnipresence. Written in grime were the words, necessity, energy, power, and wealth. The saying, 'where there's muck, there's money', was as relevant to Buckley as it was to any part of the industrial Midlands or North.

One simple fact will make clear the necessity for coal in Buckley in the nineteenth century. The amount of coal consumed in the firing of an up-draught kiln was between 10–16 cwts and down-draught kilns, 8–14 cwts. Even the more sophisticated kilns introduced towards the end of the nineteenth century were capable of burning a great deal of coal.[1] A cheap and plentiful supply of coal was the only means of survival in a cut-throat economy.

An important factor was the geological sequence of coal and fire-clay seams. They were found close together in Buckley. Geological faulting in the area meant that the Middle Coal measures outcropped in several places, or were easily mined, particularly during most of the nineteenth century. In our discussion of the history and location of mining in the area geological considerations are important. Fire-clay, if not on the surface, was found as 'warrant' or underlay to coal seams. The corridor of coal and fire-clay was Buckley's industrial heartland. The coal industry in Buckley lasted as long as the Potteries, although their demise was different. The last industrial coal mine closed in the 1930s.

This review of the coal mining industry in Buckley is chronological. There is a general discussion on coalmining and a list of the main colliery sites dating from the end of the eighteenth century and continuing to the closure of the last colliery in the 1930s. Most of those listed are discussed in the text. There are probably more sites which have gone unrecorded. Some are located by a brief reference in the Tithe maps and schedules for the parishes of Hawarden and Mold in 1839 and on the first detailed Ordnance Survey map published thirty years later. Mr K. Lloyd Gruffydd made a survey of abandoned coalmining shafts in the Urban District of Buckley, which demonstrates their abundance.[2] In the 1920s the Hawarden estate was responsible for the safety of thirty-three disused shafts in their lordship along the eastern side of Buckley.

As with the pottery industry we begin in the Middle Ages. The evidence is derived from the same source, that of the English administrators under the jurisdiction of the Crown and the Earl of Chester, from the end of the thirteenth century until the beginning of the seventeenth century. Mr K. Lloyd Gruffydd has admirably recounted much of the evidence here presented.[3] Buckley was in the manor of Ewloe, and in the records for 1292, colliers are mentioned with English names, Anes and Sylvester le Colere. These early mining ventures would be on a modest scale for domestic and building use at Flint and Ewloe castles, with probably the sale of the surplus at nearby Chester. The coal was got from outcrop seams, about six feet thick, of Main and Hollin coal covering an area in a belt roughly a mile long and half a mile wide. Mining became more active in the fourteenth century but still under control of the Earl of Chester from whom were purchased licences to dig for coal. Because digging this outcrop coal was relatively easy and profitable it is not surprising that the Earl's local official, the Forester, took advantage of his position and obtained the farm

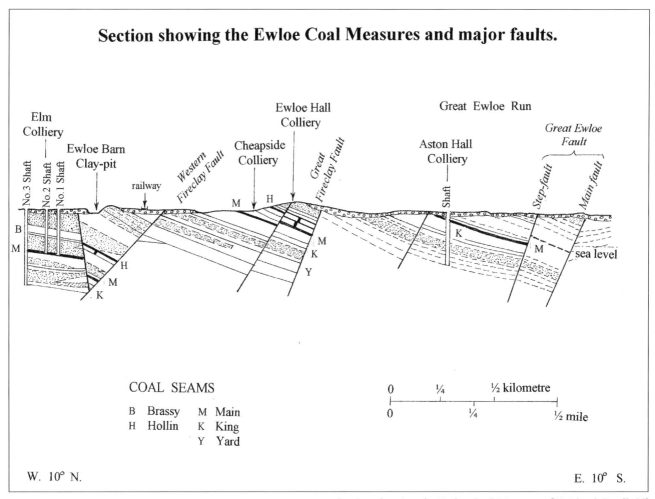

Section showing the Ewloe Coal Measures. [K. Lloyd Gruffydd]

of sea-coals in the earl's demesne lands. Bleddyn ab Ithel Annwyl, the Forester of Ewloe, was granted such a licence and made full use of it by exploiting new mine workings within the wood. From 1322 various pits in the manor were leased to Bleddyn. In 1331 a group of Cheshire men took over the 'farm' of coal for three years at an annual rent of £8, but by 1341 Bleddyn was again the sole lessee, a position he retained until he perished in the Black Death. His son Ithel took his place and paid £5 6s. 8d. for the leases. In 1394 Bleddyn's grandsons were still operating in the manor. Other pits were held from 1365–87 by David de Ewloe, Collector of the Customs at the Port of Chester, and Mayor of Chester in 1381. William de Meysham and Robert Launcelyn, a former sheriff of Chester, followed him. In 1395 the lease of the sea-coals passed to John de Ewloe, Mayor of Chester 1404–10; he acquired a further licence which he held until 1418 to sell coal from his own holdings and from certain other lands rented direct from the Lord at 8d. an acre. The revolt of Owain Glyn Dŵr in 1400 interrupted trade until 1408. There is evidence of a lease of some open workings in Ewloe in 1408. In 1461 the lease of the coalmines of the manor of Ewloe came into possession of the Stanleys of Hawarden who held it until the death of Edward Stanley in 1572.

The economic changes at the end of the Middle Ages led to the emergence of individual tenancy and the demand by freeholders to exercise their right to dig coal. Outside interference was resented. This was seen in 1528 when the coalmine in Ewloe, inherited by John Both, Archdeacon of Hereford, was rendered unworkable by a riotous attack by his Ewloe neighbours. As a result of the affray five men were detained and charged that on 20 June they were guilty of unlawful assembly when twenty persons carrying weapons, staves, swords and bucklers, wrongfully entered the mine and caused damage to the value of three pounds. Not content with this they returned twenty two days later to incapacitate the mine, prevent it operating,

Early Methods of Coal-mining. [K. Lloyd Gruffydd]

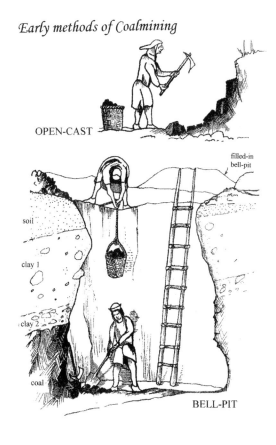

Early methods of Coalmining

and frighten off John Both with the intent of forcing him to relinquish his tenancy. Their method was to flood the mine by digging trenches and making holes. So successful were they that it took four men, forty days to drain the mine by bringing the water to the surface by means of buckets strapped to their backs. They were paid 10d. a day for their labour.[4] In the reign of the Catholic Queen Mary, 1553–58, the Holcroft family successfully defied the Stanleys by appeal to unwritten mining codes of their right to dig coal in their freeholder's land. The lease for coal was taken over by Henry Kingswell in 1575 who relinquished it before it expired in 1594. Litigation in the sixteenth century was symptomatic of the growing shortage. At the end of the sixteenth century the surface coal in the manor of Ewloe appeared to have been worked out, and in 1606, it was said 'the Cole mynes are and have been longe wholli decayed and yeld no profits at all to his Majestie'. Nevertheless coal was worked nearby either in the neighbouring lordship of Hawarden or further south. John Leland observed in 1536 that there were "cole pittes a 3 quarters of a mile from Molesdale towne" probably at Nant Mawr. A sign of much mining activity in this area was the complaint in 1632 of the neglect to re-fill abandoned pits when they were worked out citing ' a Waine leading from Knoule Hill to Eastyn (Caergwrle) and from there to Wrexham full of ould Colepitts. there are within the Townshipps of Bannel and Pentrehobin and bene Dangerous for travoylers and passingers when passeth that waye.'[5]

In many ways the Civil War of the seventeenth century was a turning point in the industrial history of Britain. The restoration of Charles II in 1660 shows Buckley beginning to emerge from the mists of the past. It is perhaps from this date that we may date its formation rather than the more definite and symbolic year of 1737 when the newly canalised channel of the River Dee was opened. We have seen that the 1640s marked the beginning of exciting developments in the pottery industry. Likewise it may be argued that it was in 1661 that significant changes began to develop in coal mining in Buckley.

This began with mining activity in the Lloyd's Hills area, named after George Lloyd and his son John, who in 1661 began leasing what was to become known as Sandycroft Colliery. Here we see new mining methods being used. The old method of working was no longer viable because surface coal was exhausted in the area. This was mining coal by digging shallow pits to reach the seam. The coal was dug until the sides of the pit were in danger of collapsing and then abandoned and another dug nearby. These pits were shaped like bells. When a depth of more than twenty feet was reached to the seam it was then followed and two or more shafts could be joined. This allowed the air to circulate and a network of tunnels could be made from which the coal had been got, separated by pillars of coal left to support the roof. These bell-pits were round and about twelve feet in diameter. By the fourteenth century coal was being reached by shafts and adit levels. This was the method used on hillsides when horizontal tunnels, or levels, were driven in at a slope, to allow the water to drain from the workings. In the sixteenth century the men of Ewloe worked in teams. In 1537 Richard Ledsham and John Fox were part of a team under the direction of John Duckworth who went as 'expert men' to Mancot to dig for coal.[6]

By the end of the seventeenth century and throughout the eighteenth new methods were introduced into this area by coal entrepreneurs from Staffordshire who leased coal workings from the enterprising Sir John Glynne (1712–77), sixth baronet of Hawarden. He made a succession of leases of the coal in the Lordship of Hawarden and astutely became a partner in some of these enterprises. The lands of the lordship were the

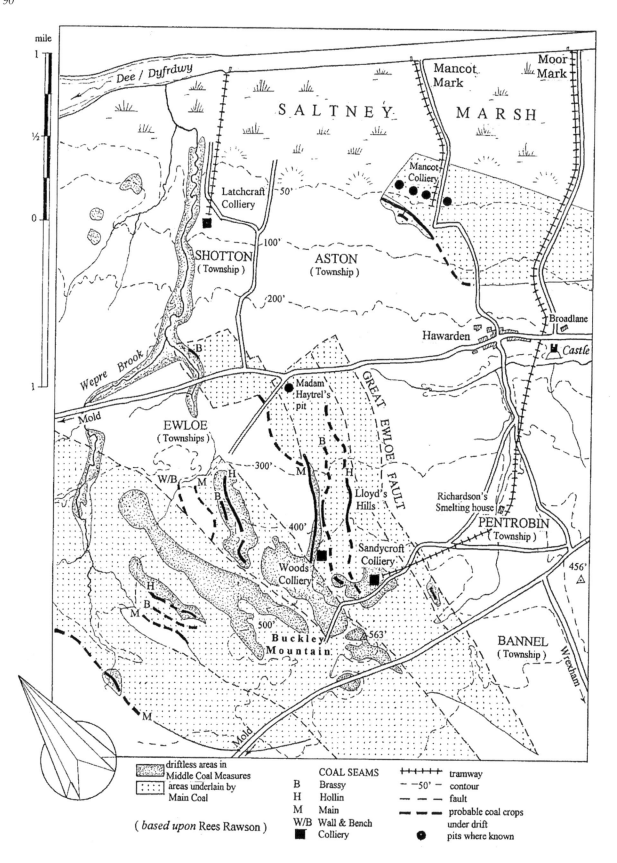

Eighteenth century Collieries in the Lordship of Hawarden on the Glynne estate. [K. Lloyd Gruffydd]

major area of mining activity in Buckley in the eighteenth century. They coincided with the Middle Coal measures stretching from Buckley Mountain to the Dee Estuary. These rocks consisting of shales, clays, thin sandstones, and coals, included up to eighteen coal seams varying in thickness from 6 ins. to 12 ft.[7] The most important of the coal seams are Main, Brassy, Hollin, Premier, Yard and Rough. The seams of clays, shales, sandstones and coal follow in sequence throughout the coalfield. For mining purposes the situation is complicated by major faults and fractures, which mean that coal seams emerge at the surface and then dip for several hundred feet. Many problems faced the pioneers of the industry. At first without any geological understanding they had to find the coal. Mining the coal was fraught with danger, it had to be brought to the surface from a depth which was subject to flooding and the presence of dangerous gases. We may see how they began to overcome these difficulties in the Buckley area by looking at some of the local coal mining operations up to about the year 1800.

From a boy in the 1720s Sir John Glynne would have been familiar with these problems. Perhaps he was taken by the agent Josiah Boydell to inspect the mining operations at Mancot, Ewloe, and the Lloyd's Hill area, where he heard the debate of the best means of getting rid of the water, taking the coals to market, and the exciting propositions of the canalising the Dee and draining the salt marshes. What would he see in the local mines?

Coming to the Buckley area he would visit Lloyd's Hills leased to George Sparrow, later to be called Sandycroft Colliery. There was plenty of activity on the surface. A horse-powered cog-and-rung gin would be used for raising coal and another for bringing water to the surface in large oxhide vessels or dippers. The gin consisted of a horizontally mounted drum with spokes or rungs attached to one end, these engaging with a horizontal wheel having vertical cogs upon it. The axle of the latter carried a long horizontal bar to which a horse was harnessed; the horse was driven in either direction round a circular track whose circumference completely surrounded shaft and gin. The rope, carrying a corfe at either end, was wrapped several times round the drum, as in a windlass. Reversal of winding was made when the horse was driven in the opposite direction. An advance was made by the introduction of the whim gin, which meant faster winding. Everywhere the young man would hear the dialect of the Staffordshire men who played the leading role in the management of the work. Woods Mine, leased to a group of Staffordshire gentlemen, (there were 28 equal shares) possessed a 'Fire-Engine' introduced sometime in 1714–5 by Richard Beech and partners. It was novel, a steam-powered pumping engine, invented by Thomas Newcomen, and introduced at Goal Pit in Staffordshire in 1712. This latest technology cost Beech and his partners a thousand pounds for 'erection and setting up', an expenditure they must have thought worth while.[8]

It was not until 1769 that James Watt patented his improved steam engine. In the early years, the cylinders of the new Watt engine were made at Bersham by John Wilkinson. In 1790 he opened a lead smelt in Buckley. There is evidence that the Hawarden estate was trading with Wilkinson from the 1750s. An excellent description of a steam engine at Spon Colliery was given in 1791 by a Mr Walker, which shows how far the technology had improved.

> There is a Steam Engine on the Old Construction Erected on this Colliery to drain it of Water the Cylinder is 26 Inches Diameter, pipes about 6 Inches Diameter, with two lifts the Engine pit 85 Yards, the thickness of the principal Seam of Coals near 3 Yards thick and excellent Coal. The Engine draws in 8 hours the Water, which runs into the Engine pit in 24 hours. There is also lately Erected at this Colliery a Small Steam Engine on the new Construction for raising the Coals from one of the Working pits. The Cylinder of this Engine is only 14 Inches Diameter length of Stroke about 3 feet and regulated by a Fly.[9]

As well as the horse gin, and fire engine, on the colliery site, there would be piles of timber for lining the shafts, and putting up surface buildings. These would include the 'counting house', occupied by the stewards, foremen or managers; the smithy, for blacksmiths to sharpen tools and repair machinery; and stables for horses. At the pit head labourers would be employed to empty baskets by which coal was brought to the surface, others to work the horses. The darkness underground would be lit by tallow candles, with cutters, fillers, labourers and ponies, each fulfilling their backbreaking tasks. Edwin Rogers' nineteenth century diary records the many different jobs of a carpenter in the opening and maintenance of a Buckley

Fire-Engine. A water-powered pumping engine for drainage of coal pits. Sir Roger Mostyn's engine from Thomas Dineley's Account of the Official Progress of the Duke of Beaufort thro' Wales in 1684.

Colliery, from the lining of the pit shafts when sinking, putting up the whimsies, fitting up the engine, making wagons, to 'makeing Manger and Rack for the Poney'.[10] Local pits became deeper in the eighteenth century. One at Sandycroft Colliery in the 1750s was 264 feet deep. An excellent indication of the nature of coal mining and its progress in the time of Sir John Glynne is seen in a document dated 1 October 1770.[11] The title 'The Colliers Procession at Hawarden Wakes', could apply to any of Sir John's coal works and maybe relates to the opening of Woods mine around that date. A note of direction advises that, 'the procession is to attend the Undertaker, to make a beginning in a great design, which is by opening a level to be driven one mile and three quarters in length and eighty yards deep, in order to lay dry a body of coal for future ages: and without which, probably in a few years, the Processioners will want employment and the public coals'. It suggests the exhaustion of coal near the surface and the need to go deeper. It shows that there was the means and ability to drive a level at some distance. The procession is made up of various groups each distinguished by 'Colours of cockades' representing 'the several employment and daily wages'. The first group, numbering 26, wearing white cockades, were 'Boys. Gin lads, horse drivers, and of various employments, at about 6*d.* per day.' The second, numbering 42, wore green and represented Engineers, smiths, carpenters, sawyers, basket makers, bankmen and labourers of all denominations above ground, at about 16*d.* per day each. 'A horse got and bred underground sixteen hands high, two years old, to represent twenty of those animals, which from their situation cannot conveniently attend the procession; at about 2/6*d.* each.' The 42 underground labourers of all denominations wore red, and were paid 18*d.* per day, as were the 68 cutters wearing blue. The 10 underground stewards and reeves received the same wage and were distinguished by red and blue cockades and their black wands. The wages of the 'Stewards and accountants of the works with white wands, at various salaries', were not revealed, but there was no mistaking the superiority of these six officials with their blue and silver fringed cockades. The daily pay was estimated at £16 and yearly total, with salaries, about £4,500. 'The Director of the new undertaking with a cockade of all the fore going colours, signifying how much their future employment depends on his success: carrying the iron centre whereon the Arch is to be turn'd, followed by four others with tools and implements for sinking which closes the procession'. The Director was probably Aaron Roberts, junior of Hawarden, who in December 1771, was appointed by Sir John, as inspector of his collieries of Sandycroft, Mancot, the Woods, and Pontyplasmaen.[12]

Some of the Staffordshire coalmasters failed in their enterprises. George Sparrow at Sandycroft, and Madame Haytrel, the widow of George Haytrel, at a pit near the Boar's Head, Ewloe, in 1738. Maybe this made her vindictive and led to her reporting the Rector and Sir John to the authorities after seeing them kneeling on the lawn of the Stag's Head drinking the Health of the Pretender in 1745. After the failure of Sparrow in 1737 Mr Gartside of Chester took over his lease, followed ten years later by John Stubbs of Beckbury, a few miles from Coalbrookdale. In 1750 Sir John leased his coal in the townships of Pentrobin and Bannel for 30 years to Walter

An early collier.

Stubbs. In 1750 Stubbs was granted the right 'to level the ground and lay rails from any coal pits in that part of Sir John's Lordship'. The contemplated tram road was to run from Sandycroft old colliery, near Lloyd's Hill, past the lead smelting works at Pentrobin, northwards along Moor Lane, Hawarden to the river at Sandycroft. The lease of Lloyd's Hills terminated in 1763, and was taken up by 'Read and others'. The Sandycroft Colliery was to the left-hand side, towards the later site of Drury Brickworks, and was working continuously from 1753. Mr George Berks managed the colliery for Stubbs and Sir John and in 1768 they opened the small mines of Woods, probably having two pits, near Sandycroft, which worked from 1771–80. Sir John Glynne died in 1777 and the estates coal interests were judiciously managed after his death, particularly by his daughter-in-law Dame Mary Glynne. Sandycroft worked from 1753 until after 1793, Woods between 1771–80, and Mancot from 1752 to 1758. Between 1755 and 1760 the annual production of the district was about 10,000 tons per annum and by 1775 it had probably reached a maximum of nearly 20,000 tons. Among the buyers of the 1,339 tons sold by sea from Sandycroft Colliery in 1757 there were several with Irish names. The production at Sandycroft Colliery rose significantly from 361 tons in 1757 to 4,837 tons in 1766 and continued to rise so that by 1778 they exceeded 12,000 tons. The increased sales probably reflect the land sales to the pottery and firebrick works which in 1784 numbered fourteen.[13] Little Mountain was another colliery, which was controlled by Sir John Glynne and probably worked with Lloyd Hill's and Sandycroft with the involvement of Stubbs and Berks until it came under the control of Thomas Botfield in 1790. Botfield of Dawley, Salop, received the lease of the coal in the townships of Pentrobin and Bannel, from Dame Mary Glynne, as well as those in Mancot, and in the words of Rawson 'became the great coalmaster of the whole district'.

Thomas and his brother Beriah Botfield, were Shropshire ironmasters who had control of the coalmines in Mancot and Sandycroft (Buckley) in the last decade at the end of the eighteenth century. More significantly these years marked the beginning of the industrial age in the Buckley area. Botfield, like Stubbs, and Hope before him, were responsible for the laying down of tram or railroads, first of wood and then of iron, to carry their coals to the ships on the river. But it was the partnership, begun in 1792, between William Hancock II and William and John Rigby and their association with Jonathan Catherall II which laid the foundations of industrial development in the region. The Catheralls, Hancocks, and Rigbys were to dominate the industry in the area for the first half of the nineteenth century and beyond. Coal was essential to their business interests in potteries, brickworks, lead smelting, iron founding and ship building.

To ensure that they could compete and find profitable markets for their goods it was essential that they had an adequate supply of coal and good access to their markets by road, rail and sea. Equally important

An early colliery showing a horse-gin. I. Tenen A History of England, *pt IV, p. 475 (Macmillan & Co. Ltd).*

was a good relationship with those who owned the mineral rights in order to obtain on reasonable terms clay, coal, and the right of passage over the railroads charged at a competitive tonnage rate. There is a plenitude of leases made in the nineteenth century to Buckley industrialists. These are divided into three. The minerals in the south-eastern side of Buckley were owned by the Glynne family as lords of the manor of Hawarden, those in the south-west by the Davies Cooke family of Gwysaney, lords of the manor of Ewloe and, in the townships of Argoed and Bistre, by the lords of Mold. The Hawarden and Mold lordships previously belonging to the Stanley family were sold under pressure after the execution of the seventh earl of Derby in 1651 during the Civil War. The lordship of Mold was then bought by three Cromwellian supporters, Sir John Trevor, Andrew Ellis, and Charles Twisleton. They were known collectively as the lords of Mold. Their interest in the lead mines in the parish of Mold made them fortunes to which was added those of coal royalties. The reports of their agents throw some light on mining in Buckley and Argoed in the nineteenth century.

Our survey of the coal mines in the Buckley area will look at groups of collieries associated with the following: those leased and owned by the Rigby-Hancock partnership, later the Hancock Company; collieries leased by the lords of Mold; the Gwysaney estate; the Hawarden estate; those worked by George Watkinson & Sons and taken over in the twentieth century by John Summers & Sons, known after 1920 as the Buckley Collieries. Other collieries will also be discussed.

The chief coal seams were 'Main coal, the most important seam, by reason of its quality, thickness and persistence. The Hollin probably ranks next to the Main in importance. The Brassy is a good house coal, used as a steam-coal, and at Buckley as a coking coal. The Rough was a very good steam-coal at Little Mountain. The Main is a good steam-coal everywhere, and is regarded as a good house-coal at Aston Hall; also as a coking coal in the Buckley district. The Yard coal is a very good house and gas coal in the Buckley District. Premier is a good house, steam, and coking coal'.[14]

If the use of coal became more widespread in the eighteenth century, by the beginning of the nineteenth century it was essential for the steam engine and advancement in engineering. By the end of the 1820s steam revolutionised transport. The steam packet took the mail from Holyhead to Ireland. Twenty years later trains replaced coaches for travellers. The railway age had arrived to transport Buckley Coal to Connah's Quay, Queensferry, Chester and by ship to Dublin. The local Firebrick works sold their products in these places and whatever surplus coal there was. In the years after 1790 the cousins Jonathan Catherall II and William Hancock II invested in collieries to feed their steam engines, kilns and under floor flues for drying their clay goods. Brickworks and collieries were situated side by side; industry was wedded to geology, clay to coal, joined together by a railroad built by Rigby and Hancock in the 1790s.

1. Lexham Green Colliery Company (Old Coppa), acquired by Jonathan Catherall II in 1798. Five years later he was seeking, on behalf of his partners in the Ewloe Colliery, permission from the Gwysaney estate to mine the coal under the Common Land, with the option to extend it to mining under enclosed lands. We don't know if this ever took place.[15] It was connected to Hancock's siding by private tramroad.

Hancock & Rigby, arriving at Lane End in 1792, immediately took over the late Botfield lease of coals in the townships of Bannel and Pentrobin from the Hawarden Estate and began a profitable connection which ended in 1933. Their partnership as brickmakers, ironfounders, coal owners, and smelters gave them superiority over Jonathan Catherall II, which was emphasised by control of the railroad to the river. In 1815 Rigby & Hancock acquired a lease to extract beds of coal on the Aston estate of Dundas at Ewloe and in 1829 gained access to beds of coal in Northop parish.[16] The nature of the agreement made between the Lane End partners and the Hawarden estate is seen in a memorandum of 1832.

> Offer to Messrs Rigby & Hancock of Leases of Coal, Brick, Clay & Railway belonging to Sir S. R. Glynne Bart. Lease of Coals in Pentrobin, Bannel, Ewloe & Shotton for 21 years, power received by Sir Stephen Glynne to take possession of them at the end of 7 or 14 years upon giving six months notice. Received rent of £150 per annum to be paid quarterly when the Royalty of 1/7th of the Main Coal & 1/8th of other coals does not amount to that sum. Hawarden Castle Garden etc. to be supplied with Coal gratis. Lessees to bind themselves to search for coal in any part of the devised lands where it is expected there may be any. Right of Railway to the River upon the old term for 21 years excepting that any thing not the produce of Sir Stephen Glynne's Land shall be paid for

Coppa Colliery photograph 1976. [Buckley Library]

after the rate of 2d. per ton less an addition to the assured rent. Lease of Clay for 21 years upon payment of £150 per annum instead of £100. In all other respects the Covenants of the old lease to be introduced into the new one.

Here are some of the collieries in the area, some of them leased to Hancock and Rigby.

2. Little Mountain, Drury. Number 7 pit of this colliery was later known as 'the strip and at it'. In 1750 it was worked by Sir John Glynne and Mr George Berks; between 1777–90 by Stubbs, Berks and Co.; from 1801 by Rigby and Hancock; and from 1864 by Thomas Rose and partners. In 1865 John Bates Gregory was the manager. In 1873 it was worked by the Little Mountain Coal, Iron & Clay Co.Ltd and from 1882–86 by Hawarden Collieries Co. Ltd after which it was closed.[17] The colliery eventually grew to consist of eight shafts. Hollin Coal was reached at 180 ft., Main Coal at 380 ft. Soon after 1801 Hancock and Rigby provided it with a rail outlet to the River Dee via the Buckley Horse Tramroads. The Buckley Railway opened in 1866, bisected the colliery.

3. Sandycroft Colliery.

4. Lloyd's Hill.

5. Woods Colliery.

6. Mount Pleasant.

Collieries numbered 3, 4, 5, 6 previously, were leased in the eighteenth century. Main, Hollin, Rough, King, and Brassy Coal were worked.

In 1737 Mr John Lloyd of Ewloe leased the Colliery to Mr James Garside of Chester. In 1747 it was leased to Mr Walter Stubbs of Beckbury, Salop, who used a Fire Engine. Later in 1763 leased to 'Read and others'. There were at least six pits and two Fire Engines between 1752–71. They supplied the Pentrobin Smelting House (1751–1810), owned by Mr Richardson of Chester, with coal. In *c*.1886 the proprietor of Mount Pleasant was Messrs J. B. Gregory & Co. The collieries and brickworks employed about 450 men. Modern methods were pioneered including electric lighting. On the death of Gregory in 1891 the Standard Buff and Glazed Brick Co. was formed, later the Standard Buckley Ltd. The Colliery closure was announced in May 1931.

The employees who work underground at the Mount Pleasant Colliery have received a weeks notice to finish work, This small colliery is under the management of Mr Thomas Jones of Bromfield Hall, Mold, a well known mining expert in Flintshire. The reason this colliery is compelled to close down is owing to water trouble, and not because there is a shortage of coal. Under the existing economic circumstances it is felt that it would not be remunerative proposition to put in a new plant to deal with the water trouble.'[18] It was proposed in May 1930 to reopen Drury Colliery closed for a number of years. The newspaper reported 'we understand the winding, ventilating, and pumping will be done by electrical power now being taken to this district by the North Wales Power Co. Ltd. Captain Leonard Newtown, a mining engineer, who has returned from India, is interested in the concern.[19]

Mount Pleasant Colliery including sidings c.1881. [FRO PH 11/211]

7. Cheapside Colliery. Opened *c.*1849 and abandoned in 1876 mined the Main and Brassy coals eastward from their outcrops, and a little farther to the east, the Ewloe Cross pits of the Ewloe Hall Colliery were sunk.

8. Ewloe Hall Colliery. Worked at different times. The mining engineer, Henry Beckett, gave a report in 1843, which shows the difficulties in the coal trade at this time.

'The proceedings in this Colliery are temporarily suspended in consequence of the depressed state of trade, and a ruinous competition, which appears to be one of the clashing interest caused by the County Election.' Beckett reported that:

> the Hollin Coal workings were principally in the lands belonging to Admiral Dundas, the eastern boundary being the Ewloe fault and the one on the west extended 'to the 'old deads', terminating in the ancient excavations. A shaft had been sunk, but there appears to be a perfect labyrinth of faults. Nearly the whole of the operations have been exploratory and no quantities of coal gottten can be given with accuracy. I cannot learn that there is any immediate probability of the Ewloe Hall Colliery being recommenced. The Lessees naturally finding that the less distance they are from the River and therefore the less cost in carriage; so much more able are they to compete with the other companies and their erections are therefore confined to the Mare Hey and Lodgecroft collieries.[20]

In 1861 Edward Parry was mentioned as manager. The colliery had closed by 1879.

9. Smalley's Colliery, Liverpool Road. Probably mined by the Smalley & Williamson, Brickworks, who operated until 1842.[21]

10. Nant Mawr. In the township of Bistre. John Leland mentions mining in this area in his itinerary of 1536. In the Commonwealth period the mines were leased by Robert Coytmor of Caernarfon, who lived at Plas Onn, Nercwys. He complained that the mines had been destroyed by the enemy and he had to pay for their repair in 1657.[22] Nant Mawr fell under the jurisdiction of the lords of Mold. Odd scraps of information show the continuity of working throughout the nineteenth century. The output between June 1837 and June 1838 was 17,941 tons. Between January and June 1853 4,823 tons were produced, of which 4,080 tons of Hollin and Brassy coal was used in the brick works and pottery: presumably Hancock's.[23] Hancock & Co. were operating there between 1854–56, Nant Mawr Coal Co 1860–64, and Padeswood United Coal & Cannel Co.Ltd 1871–86.[24] In February 1859 Robert Williams in the mineral report stated 'Mr A. C. King has commenced operations, the loading or foundation of the Pumping Engine has been laid, and a second for the Winding Engine.[25] Four years later in 1863 the position had changed when J. Tolson White reported on the collieries in the lordship of Mold.

> The Nant Coal Company, limited, was formed 1st January 1861, with a capital of £39,000.
> The coal field granted by the Lords of Mold, consists of 1stly, Bistree Estate, originally leased 2 or 3 years since to Mr May, for a term of 23 years, at 1/9th royalty, and £100 dead rent; it was purchased by consent from his mortgagees. 2ndly, Nant Mawr Estate, at £20 dead rent, and 1/9th royalty; and 3rdly, of Bryn Faigas Estate, which is let upon a take note of £150 dead rent, and 1/8th royalty: altogether 360 acres. A lease of the Bryn Fygas

Old coal banks at Nant Mawr.
[Buckley Library]

Estate has been promised, and should be completed. Three beds of coal were worked by the old Nant Mawr Company (who sold to this company) to the following extent, viz.; - The Hollin Coal – 13a. 0r. 0p.. The Brassey Coal — 5a. 0r. 0p. The Main Coal — 17a. 0r 0p. The new company have not followed the old workings, but they have sunk the shafts 17 yards deeper, and then cut across a throw down cast to the south, and have driven about 77 yards SSW in the main coal to Padeswood Station. They have a pumping engine of 50 horse power and have got machinery ready and sufficiently powerful for drawing coal at the rate of 2,000 tons a week.

However Tolson White expressed some concern and went on to say:

> Though this plant has been placed upon the estate of the Lords of Mold, I am of opinion that the shafts would have been much better situate upon the Carreyg Lwydd Estate, also under lease to this company, through which the Chester and Mold Railway passes at the dip end of the coal field. I made an underground inspection, and found they were not commencing upon the best principles. The shafts were too small for drawing coal and adequate ventilation. The roads intended for inclines to be worked with ropes were not driven straight, and the posts proposed to be left, too narrow to support the permanent ways.

White concluded:

> … there is a fine coal field to be worked. The main seam is 9 feet 6 inches thick at 220 yards deep, and well situated close to the railway running between Chester and Mold. Other valuable working seams of coal have been found here. Under proper management this ought to be made a productive colliery.[26]

White's misgivings were confirmed when the liquidators were instructed in February 1867 to wind up the company with the speculation in the *Chester Courant* of new lessors. 'The area of land connected with the Colliery amounts to 50 acres containing the famous North Wales Steam and Domestic Coals. It is contiguous to the well-known and extensive Buckley Brick and Tile Industries'.[27] In 1902 G.Watkinson & Sons were reported to be 'filing returns for their Nant Mawr Colliery'.

11. Upper Nant Mawr Colliery. Tolson White reported in 1863. 'This is a small colliery worked by Robert Williams and Co., who have been "hunting for coal" for 8 or 9 years, amongst old workings of the Maur coal, 8 feet thick, 60 yards deep, without any written agreement. They have made returns of gettings, which Mr Davies checks with their books. The last year's half rent is £56. The royalty is computed at 1/8th, and there is no dead rent agreed for'.[28]

12. Padeswood Colliery. Known locally as 'the hop, skip and jump'. Worked from 1865 by William Fidler & Co., in 1871 by A. C. King. The Padeswood United Coal & Cannel Co. Ltd acquired the mining rights to the Nant Mawr Colliery. In April 1875 Padeswood Hall Colliery Co. was registered on a lease from William Hancock. In May 1895 the *Chester Chronicle* reported its closure appreciating that 'This has been a very valuable mine and a large quantity of cannel has been raised. The exhaustion of the seams is the cause of the stoppage'. The colliery appeared to have continued working until 1901 when it was abandoned and the plant and machinery auctioned the following year. In 1934 J. B. Gregory was anxious to restart the site. Nothing came of it.

13. Wind Mill Colliery. Tolson White reported in 1863: 'This is a small grant to Mr King, who has sunk 23 yards and found a coal 6 feet 8 inches thick, including 2 feet of cannel. I had no opportunity of minutely inspecting this coal, as the engine was removed for repairs; but I believe the discovery of cannel coal in this district an important accession to the value of the minerals'.

14. Spon Green Colliery. We have mentioned previously D. Walker's survey of Thomas Symmer Champneys' estate in the parish of Mold. His client was one of the lords of Mold as a descendant of Andrew Ellis and married in 1792 Margaret, daughter of Sir Roger Mostyn. His share in the lordship was later sold to Lord Mostyn. The report of 1791 as well as describing the steam engines at Spon Colliery goes on to say:

> The Colliery is about 8 miles from Chester principally down hill. A great part of the Coals are carried there and deemed much preferable to any other coals which come to that City. As this Estate is capable of great Improvement and the Mines therein likely to produce considerably more than they have hitherto done, would advise it by no means to be sold. The present Rents are near £1400 pr annm. And therefore sufficient Security for £20,000 if wanted.[29]

Walker was correct in his judgement as Tolson White's report confirmed seventy years later and emphasises the Hancock's great demand for coal. In 1821 the Spon estate was in the occupation of Mr Randle Hancock.[30]

> This is an old colliery, leased to Messrs Hancock and Shepherd for 21 years from 1858. 163 acres are leased, but only six or eight acres of the main coal, 7 feet 9 inches thick, remain to be worked. It lies 130 yards deep, and is worked as a convenient addition to large fire brick works in the neighbourhood, belonging to Messrs. Hancock & Co. They are drawing 250 tons per week, the whole of which is consumed at the brick works at 6s. 4d. per ton for large coal, 4s. 2d. for small. The royalty is $^{1}/_{10th}$. The sleeping rent £50. Besides the main coal, there are lying above it the "Two Yard Seams," 3 feet thick, $52^{1}/_{2}$ yards deep. It has been extensively worked, though little information exists as the exact position of the old workings; 10 or 12 acres have been gotten under the present, but none since Christmas 1862. There is also "The Brassey Coal," 75 yards deep. About $2^{1}/_{2}$ acres have been worked, but it was unprofitable, and abandoned in Midsummer 1861, because the coal was tender and unmarketable. The lease is a grant of all the minerals. Mr Hancock has made borings at the bottom of No. 6 shaft, 60 yards deep to the depth of 162 yards below the main coal, in search of cannel coal, recently found, of very valuable quality, usually lying from 80 to 90 yards below the main coal. Mr Hancock has spent £260 in prosecuting these borings, and announced his intention of abandoning the search without assistance from the Lords of Mold.[31]

15. Pentrobin Colliery. Situated to the east of Hancock's Lane End Works. In 1860 it was worked by H. Fenton & Co., William Tudor was the Engineer, with a shaft named after him. After 1869 it was linked with the Aston Hall Colliery Co. and closed by 1899.[32]

16. Aston Hall Colliery.[33] Situated on the Dundas estate. Worked in 1865 by the Aston Hall Coal Co. with two main shafts — Main Coal Pit and the Rough Coal Pit. Purchased by W. E. Gladstone in 1869. It was reported in 1871 'The men are now getting the five feet and three feet seams, both excellent coal, a good deal of the steam qualities being sent for the use of the Holyhead steam vessels.' In 1872 the Aston Hall Colliery Company Railway opened, connecting the colliery with the LNWR. W. E. Gladstone, at the time Prime Minister, was involved in the wage dispute of 1874, interviewing the strikers, who accepted a wage reduction of 10%. After 1878 the enterprise was designated the Aston Hall Coal and Brick Co. Mr Mayhew and the Hawarden estate were involved in the company, after 1883. It became a large and profitable brick and coal company employing over a thousand men and boys. Closure came in 1909.

Aston Hall Colliery. [FRO 28/N/117]

Old Aston Hall Colliery Office, watercolour.
[FRO PR/F/1541]

17. Lane End, affectionately known as 'the Dumpling'. It was short lived, sinking operations began in 1889 and closure occurred in the spring of 1903. There was a small railway laid down by H. Croom Johnson, which ran from Knowl Lane siding to the colliery. A short account of the colliery was given in *St Matthew's Parish Magazine* for April 1903.

The Lane End Colliery started in the beginning of 1890. Up to the year 1895 it was under the management of Mr Joseph Newton, when Mr James Hampson became manager of both Lane End and Aston Hall Collieries. On and off, some 300 men and boys have had regular employment at the Colliery, and an average of about £400 per week has been paid in wages. The Colliery has been noted for the amicable and peaceful working between the men, managers, and employers. It was the property of the Right Hon. H. J. Gladstone, and Messrs H. N. Gladstone and Horace Mayhew, under a lease from the Trustees of the Hawarden Estate. Mr Mayhew has been the managing partner.

The Gladstone brothers generously subscribed to requests for financial assistance from their sister Mrs Mary Drew towards the restoration of St Matthew's Church, which took place during the life of the colliery. The colliery site was later quarried away by Hancock's Lane End Brickworks and may have been used by them in the mid 1920s as a drift mine.[34]

Various mining activities were carried out from early times in the township of Argoed, which fell within the area of the lords of Mold. Part of Argoed Township became with the addition of the township of Bistre a new ecclesiastical district separated from Mold. There were a number of pits in the township using either the name Argoed or designated otherwise.

17. The Argoed Hall Colliery Co. Operated by Hampton & Company in the 1830s had two main shafts. It was subject to flooding and was closed by 1840 after a major disaster at the colliery.[35]

Chester Chronicle, 12th May 1837 — Awful calamity — thirty-one lives lost Mold, Wednesday, May 10th. This town and its neighbourhood have been thrown into a state of the most distressing excitement by an accident which happened today at Argoed Colliery, belonging to Messrs Hampton and Company, by which it is feared that twenty-eight colliers, consisting of men and boys have lost their lives. From enquiries made on the spot, it appears that during last week an increased quantity of water had appeared in the underground

'Dumpling' Colliery, Lane End, c.1900.
[FRO PH 11/256]

workings to the north, and which was supposed to issue out of some old workings, or 'deads', on the rise of the bed of coal. As the pumping engine had been able to cope with it, it was not supposed to be dangerous, but on the workmen going down this morning the pit on the east, it was found that the water had increased so materially that the underground agent, upon coming on the spot about nine o'clock, gave immediate orders to the men to leave off work and proceed to the surface. The order had scarcely been given before the roaring of torrents of water was heard, and the men to the number of eighteen, by dint of hard running, got to the mouth of the pit and made their escape to the surface. The water was in the meantime running past them knee deep, and with great impetuosity, to the engine pit, which is on a lower level of coal. There are extensive workings connected with the engine pit to the west, and the men employed there, to the number of thirty, not being warned of the imminent danger, had (with two exceptions) no opportunity of attempting to escape before the water had risen too high to enable them to reach the pit. The two men who escaped were near the pit, and climbed up the pumps beyond the reach of the water, while the remaining twenty-eight were too far off to render escape possible. The engine was immediately set to pump on its full stretch, but the water is gaining fearfully upon it and by the last soundings it had reached from twelve to fifteen yards up the pit. The colliery bank had in the meantime presented the most heartrending scenes, by the parents, wives, children and other relations of the poor fellows, giving vent to their grief and lamentations, and others again in the midst of their tears, clinging to the last ray of hope. It is quite uncertain how long it may be before the bodies are extricated, as it will depend upon the time which the engine will take in clearing the working of water. Little hopes are entertained that any of the men will survive, for if not destroyed by the water, the foul air will so speedily accumulate, owing to the derangement in the ventilation caused by the rising of the water, that there would not be a sufficiency of oxygen to sustain human life for ten minutes. About ten of the men were married with families of children.' A week later the same newspaper announced 'Miraculous to relate, ten individuals have been brought up by the most strenuous exertions of the sympathizing neighbours who had the inexpressible pleasure of discovering them still alive, after being confined three days and two nights in the pit.

The thirty –one lives lost reported on 12 May, was reduced by the rescue of ten colliers, five boys and teenagers and ten men.

An inquest held on 15 May recorded:

The Jury found 'that the deceased came to their deaths on the twelfth or thirteenth of May, in the underground workings of the Argoed Colliery, owing to the accumulation of foul air in the said colliery, from the rising of water, which accidentally broke into the colliery on the 10th of the same month.' The Foreman added that the Jury acquitted the agents and proprietors of the colliery of any blame or neglect, connected with the breaking in of the water.[36]

On subsequent days the remainder of the bodies of the victims were brought to the

Argoed Collery disaster, 1837.
[FRO D/DM/22/1]

ACCIDENT

AT ARGOED HALL COLLIERY, NEAR MOLD, FLINTSHIRE.

AT A PUBLIC MEETING,

Held at the Black Lion Inn, at Mold, this 16th day of May, 1837,

JOHN WYNNE EYTON, ESQ., OF LEESWOOD HALL, IN THE CHAIR.

WHEREAS, it appears to this Meeting, that an accident dreadfully fatal in its consequences, occurred at the Argoed Hall Colliery, near to this Town, on Wednesday morning last, the 10th instant, by which awful calamity twenty-one lives were lost, eight widows left desolate, and about thirty children left orphans.

FIRST—IT WAS RESOLVED UNANIMOUSLY,

That this Meeting deeply deploring so great a loss of human life, and compassionately sympathising with the widows and relatives of the deceased, is of opinion that a PUBLIC SUBSCRIPTION should be entered into for the purpose of raising a sum of Money for their relief, and also for rewarding the meritorious conduct of the several labourers who assisted in extricating the sufferers; and that the Fund so raised be entrusted to a Committee of Management, consisting of JOHN WYNNE EYTON, Esq., Chairman; the Rev. C. B. CLOUGH, Vicar of Mold, Colonel PHILIPS, Hon. Major NAPIER, WILSON JONES, Esq., M. P., EDWARD PEMBERTON, Esq., REV. Mr. BROWNE, T. T. MATHER, Esq., C. B. T. ROPER, Esq., Mr. CHARLES H. INGLEBY, Mr. THOMAS WHITLEY, of Broncoed, and all Subscribers of £5 and upwards, any three of whom shall be competent to act.

2nd—That Messrs. DOUGLAS, SMALLEY, and Co. of the Holywell and Mold Bank, be requested to act as general Treasurers; and that the Bankers at Chester, Wrexham, Denbigh. Oswestry, Liverpool, Manchester, Wolverhampton, Carmarthen, and Messrs. MASTERMAN, PETERS and Co., London, be also invited to open Books of Subscriptions at their respective establishments.

3rd—That the foregoing resolutions be published in the Chester, Carnarvon, Bangor, Liverpool, Manchester, Wolverhampton, Stafford, and Carmarthen, provincial journals, and also in the Times, Morning Chronicle, and the Record, London papers; that copies of the same be distributed by circular under the direction of the managing committee; that this meeting cannot separate without expressing its satisfaction, that it has been shewn by the evidence upon the coroner's inquest, that no blame is imputable to any person connected with the work, but that this sad catastrophe was purely and wholly accidental.

4th.—That this meeting do appoint a scientific person conversant with coal mining, to attend the inquisition of the Coroner, upon the bodies yet expected shortly to be found; and that the thanks of the meeting are justly due and hereby given to all the colliers, miners and others, who so nobly exerted themselves on this melancholy occasion, in rescuing their fellow-labourers and companions from destruction. This meeting also most highly appreciates the landable zeal of those in the neighbourhood, who displayed such a manifest anxiety in behalf of their fellow-creatures by the gratuitous use of their horses, carts, &c. &c., in furthering the general exertions of all.

5th.—That the warm thanks of the meeting be given to the Medical gentlemen for their prompt and efficient assistance rendered to the individuals raised from the workings.

6th.—That Mr. THOMAS WHITLEY, of Broncoed, be requested to act as Honorary Secretary, and to render his services in promoting the general views of the meeting.

JOHN WYNNE EYTON, CHAIRMAN.

The Chairman having vacated his seat, it was resolved by acclamation that the thanks of this meeting be given him for his conduct in the Chair.

THOMAS WHITLEY, HON. SECRETARY

Mold, 16th May, 1837.

surface bringing the total to twenty-one. Among them were the father and brother of the writer Daniel Owen who used this tragedy in his novel *Rhys Lewis*.

A year later at a meeting of the subscribers to the Argoed Colliery Fund on 28 May 1838 the members were piously informed that 'The Committee have the satisfaction to report that the sum subscribed amounted to £888 0s. 1d.; that thus through the aid of the public, under the blessing of Providence, the Committee have been enabled 'to visit the fatherless and widows in their affliction' — to soothe the sorrows — and to alleviate the sufferings of EIGHTEEN poor families by administering permanently to their wants according to their several necessities.'[37] The tragedy of the Argoed disaster would live forever in the minds of the victims and their families as a continual reminder of the colliers' enemies of flood water and foul air.

18. The Argoed Colliery Company.[38] The colliery was situated to the south west of the South Colliery, near the present Southdown School. The company had been mining there from at least 1808. By 1828 the owners Messrs Rigby & Hancock were working two pits which increased to five by 1839.

19. The Aberllanerch Colliery, or Buckley Colliery, *c.*1820–43, situated near Aberllannerch Farm. The colliery was operated from the 1820s to 1840s, under the chairmanship of P. Davies-Cooke, Gwysaney. The company leased General Gascoyne's lands in Argoed. Some of the company's resolutions at their meeting in September 1834 make interesting reading. The committee agreed to sell Mr Catherall's coal for 5s. a ton. They discussed the terms offered to them by Captain Dundas for their coal traffic to travel along his railway for 7d. per ton, including wharfage, but accepted a proposal from Mr Smalley who offered 6d. a ton. They agreed with Mr Catherall to make a railway from his brickwork to Buckley Colliery.[39]

20. The Argoed Colliery Company Ltd, 1863. Worked from various pits situated in the vicinity of Aberllanerch, South Buckley, and The Square. A report in the *Chester Chronicle* gives the prospectus of the Company and details of the available coal:

> This Company is formed for the purpose of working the Cannel and other valuable seams of Coal, Iron, Stone, Fire Clay, and other minerals lying under upwards of 220 acres of proved mineral ground, held by the lessee under agreements for leases for 21 years, and upon very favourable royalties, and for the distillation of oil from the Cannel Coal. The property is situate in the townships of Bistre and Argoed, near Mold, Flintshire, and is distant about 800 yards from the Buckley and Connah's Quay Railway, to which line it is intended to construct a branch over Buckley Common, which can be done at a very small outlay, thus giving railway communication with the Rivers Dee and Mersey and the principal coal markets, and bringing the colliery within 5 miles by railway of the shipping port of Connah's Quay. The demand for coals for shipping, is so great as to exceed the supply by thousands of tons weekly.' The prospectus listed the thickness of the seams of coal and their depth; Hollin 6 feet thick, 40 yards in depth; Brassey 4 feet thick at a depth of 60 yards; Main 11 feet depth 100 yards down; Yard 3 feet thick 140 yards in depth; and what they considered as the prize, a seam of Cannel 2 feet 2 inches, with 5 feet of bituminous attached and conveniently worked at a depth of 20 yards, by sinking a pit on the outcrop of the coal seam at the extreme eastern boundary of the estate. It added that 'There is a splendid bed of fire-clay sixteen feet thick, underlying, it is believed, the greater portion of the estate.'[40]

The optimistic forecast dangled before the investors was not realised. There were legal proceedings over the patent rights for the distillation of oil from Cannel, an uncertainty of trade, financial difficulties, and the eventual fall in the price of Cannel by the discovery of oil in the United States. In 1866 the company was taken over by

21. The South Buckley Coal and Firebrick Company. Incorporated in February 1866, it was a business venture by speculators from Manchester and Rochdale. It was not successful for they encountered difficulties in getting the coal due to faulting and previous workings, problems exacerbated by falling price and the depressed coal trade of the mid '70s. They sold up to William Nuttall & Co, who were known as

22. The Main Coal & Cannel Company Limited, 1876. They met with the same difficulties as their predecessors as well as experiencing working conditions aggravated by breaches in mine safety regulations. In 1876 a collier was killed in a gas explosion due to naked lights being used. The company was wound up on 13 March 1878 bringing unemployment to about 200 colliers. The company was dissolved in 1886 in the meantime being bought by an enterprising group of local men with little capital and management experience. John Rowlands, James Brannan, and Thomas Roberts were fortunate in the interest taken in the company by David Evans from Liverpool who bought them out in 1880. A builder by trade, Evans was keen to develop the clays under the Hollin and Brassey Coal and for this purpose erected drying sheds and kilns. To carry out his designs he went into partnership in March 1881 with Robert Rossborough of Southport and Charles Holland a Liverpool merchant.

23. The North and South Buckley Colliery Brick & Tile Co. Ltd. This was the name they gave to the company in 1881. But it was unable to steer through the stormy industrial seas of the early 1880s. Beset by depression and fall in prices the employers found it unprofitable to pay the wages given when their returns were higher. Their colliers resented a 10% wage reduction and the ton being reckoned at 21 *cwt* instead of 20 *cwt* a ton. However, a compromise was reached, and they avoided strike action, which brought Watkinson's collieries to a standstill. Against this background the partners lost heart and the company was dissolved in 1891.

24. The South Buckley Rock Brick Co. Ltd. Incorporated in 1889, it bought the assets of the North and South and was the most profitable and successful of the foregoing companies because, although it mined what was left of the coal reserves, it concentrated on brick manufacturing of a high quality.[41] At the end they mixed the Brassey fire-clay with the Brassey coal to fire the bricks. Coal mining was abandoned in 1909.

25. The West Buckley Colliery Co., Alltami, 1870–1920. This was a small colliery, having two shafts and a drift[42] and was connected to the South Buckley Colliery and Brickworks. The West Buckley was developed in 1870 by John Lassey and five partners on the estate of General Gascoyne. Lassey, a Yorkshire mining engineer from Halifax, married Catherine Hewitt, licensee of the Black Horse Public House. Probably through his wife's family he became a shareholder in the Buckley Colliery Company. In 1875 the West Buckley Colliery was renamed the North Buckley Colliery. Lassey failed in this venture and returned to Yorkshire. The colliery's fortunes were then tied up with the companies previously discussed.[43] In 1898 the West Buckley was taken over as a private venture by Joseph Ellis, a mining engineer from Drury. His hope of making money from the coal was obviously regarded with some scepticism by the locals who dubbed the colliery 'the Klondike'. Unfortunately Ellis suffered a fatal accident in the mine in 1903 and died on his way to hospital. William Hopwood, a talented but litigious local mining engineer, continued the quest for coal begun by Ellis. The colliery supplied Yard Coal and fire-clay to the South Buckley Brickworks which closed in 1915. By 1920 the West Buckley's coal was exhausted and the colliery wound up.

George Watkinson and Sons, Buckley Collieries, 1870–1920

This firm dominated the coal industry in Buckley for almost fifty years. They brought to Buckley Yorkshire vigour, shrewdness, stubbornness, determination, and capital made in the woollen industry of Halifax. The architect of their success in Buckley was John Watkinson (1845–1907), the fourth son of George Watkinson, a successful woolstapler who by the 1860s was developing colliery interests in South Wales. John Watkinson's obituary[44] explains his arrival in Buckley and his influence on the community:

> After finishing his education he was sent by his father to Buckley to manage and develop the colliery business taken over by Messrs George Watkinson and Sons from a Mr John Williams, by whom the two then existing pits had been worked down to only some eighty yards. The combination of abundant capital with the go-ahead policy and shrewd direction of Mr John Watkinson put new vitality into the industry, and thorough working of the then existing coal pits was followed by the establishment of prosperous new pits until ultimately the control of about a thousand men made the firm the largest employers of labour in Flintshire.
>
> On coming to Buckley first, Mr Watkinson's methods as an employer and his association with the unpopular side in politics made him the mark of openly avowed hostility from which personal violence was feared. A Parliamentary election, in which the Liberal candidate was Lord Richard Grosvenor and the Conservative Mr P. P. Pennant, happening simultaneously with a labour dispute, the elated state of public feeling placed Mr Watkinson (a supporter of the Conservative candidate), in peril of bodily injury, if not of losing life itself. The culminating point of some riotous conduct was an ugly scene following an incident when the masterful young colliery proprietor had been pelted with clods. He was strongly advised not to again venture into those quarters with the enraged multitude, but characteristically, brushing aside the promptings of timidity, he did again expose himself, and the threatened molestation by the angry crowd was only frustrated by the ruse of smuggling Mr Watkinson into Mr John Dunn's trap, while his coachman fought his way through a big crowd who were clamouring to smash the carriage.
>
> Of the big output of the Watkinson Collieries, the bulk becomes steamship fuel (for which the Buckley coal

is well adapted), and one of the best markets has been the L. and N. W. Coys mail and passenger steamboats between Holyhead and Dublin.

By the wisely directed use of capital to develop industry Mr Watkinson was a real benefactor to Buckley, and to men of such sound commercial habits as Mr John Watkinson, Mr Charles Davison, Mr Parry, the Hancocks and the Catheralls, the town of Buckley owes not only its tangible wealth, but the thrifty, business interests of its prosperous population. In addition to his large capital in colliery enterprise, Mr Watkinson had invested in Flintshire lead mining and was principally interested in W.M. & C.Q. railway and other commercial concerns.

Next to being a colliery proprietor, Mr Watkinson was best known in role of magistrate. His common sense business habit of going direct to the pith of a thing proved a serviceable qualification on the bench, and plausible fairy tales were unlikely to succeed with him. But somewhat lacking in the qualities of calm judicial detachment and long suffering patience he was not exactly the ideal presiding magistrate.

Admirable though the frankness of the obituarist was we will look more closely at John Watkinson's relations with his workers when we consider industrial relations at the end of the review of collieries.

The Watkinson Colliery interests in Buckley were[45] founded on their acquisition from the Buckley Colliery Company in 1872 of three collieries — the Willow, Oak, and Elm and the lease of coal from the Gwysaney estate. They soon added to this in 1873 by an additional five hundred acres of lease coal from the neighbouring Clough and Bankes estates in Northop, to which they added in 1884, lease of coal from the Howard lands in Sychdyn and the old Catherall lands at the Trap from Gwysaney. In the 1890s they increased their holdings by the acquisition of the Ash and the development of Mountain Colliery in 1897. At the turn of the century they acquired control of other small brick and colliery works in an attempt to stifle competition.

26. Willow Colliery. The first Watkinson acquired from the Buckley Colliery Company. It was probably worked as a drift mine in the 1860s and by 1878 the new proprietor had worked it out. George Lewis recorded '1901, May 8, the Willow colliery started to work for the second time. There were only a few men engaged and they were searching for Hollin coal', and fifty years later: '1952, Feb. 11. To-day men started with a bulldozer to fill the Willow Pits and the Oak pits for the Castle firm'.

27. Oak Colliery. Worked in the 1860s by the Buckley Coal Co. and bought by Watkinson from the Buckley Colliery Company in 1872. Between 1890 and 1912 the Hollin Coal was worked from its outcrop.

28. Ash Colliery. Working between 1856 and 1872 when Watkinson's bought it from the Buckley Colliery Company. Reopened in 1894 when the Main Coal was worked from its outcrop. George Lewis recorded its demise: '1913, Aug. 30, Sat. The Ash Drift near Alltami closed down.'

29. Maesygrug Colliery. An old pit in Northop parish close to Watkinson's other concerns in the Buckley area. The *Chester Chronicle* announced in January 1807: 'The Public are respectively informed that these works being now completed and opened may rely on a constant supply of any quantity of Main coal at 5*d.* per *cwt.* — one ton of which is esteemed equivalent to one ton and a quarter of any coal in the country. A good sound road is making from the turnpike across Soughton Common to the Colliery'. Fifteen months later the same paper advertised the undertaking as 'land 69 acres, plus several holdings, rent £62 annually together with royalties of coal now working under lease granted to Messrs Oakley & Coy'. It was one of those collieries acquired by Watkinson in 1872. It produced excellent Main and Hollin Coal but the Colliery was heavily watered and ceased working about 1898. George Lewis noted: '1913 Nov. 29. Pumping began at Maesygrug old pit in order to restart it'. Hopwood spoke of post-war activity before the Colliery was sold to John Summers & Sons in 1920.

This particular coal mine came to life, probably for the third time, c.1918-1920, when two 'Lancashire' boilers were installed for laying dry the shaft. The winding engine, housed in a corrugated iron building, had been retrieved from the old Lane End (Dumpling) colliery. The shaft had been used as a refuse pit by local farmers for many years, and some 15 yards of animal bones were cleared out. New wooden guides were put in to serve the single cage, the second winding rope running in the upcast shaft with a heavy balance weight attached. It was intended to work the Wall & Bench and Premier seams below the old workings and run the water off to no. 3 Elm pit whose workings were already 160 yards below. Unfortunately, when the cross measure drift from Maesygrug shaft was well advanced, the 1921 coal strike began, and the pit was allowed to drown for the last time.[46]

30. The Elm Colliery. The most ambitious of the Watkinson enterprises. It was begun in 1876 when number one and number two pits were sunk to a depth of 180 yards to work the Main and Hollin coal. A ready market was found at Holyhead to fuel the cross-channel steamers. The colliery was developed further in 1894 when a third shaft was sunk. Hopwood recounted that it was 'finished at 16 feet in diameter inside the brickwork and 340 yards deep to the Premier seam. This was, by far, the largest and deepest pit in the Buckley area. The No. 2 pit (upcast) was also deepened to the same depth. The Premier being a good coking coal, a battery of coke ovens was built on the northern side of the shaft.[47]

31. The Mountain Colliery, 1897. Hopwood described the operation of this colliery in conjunction with the Elm. 'The Mountain colliery shafts were sunk on to the roadways already driven from Elm No. 1 pit, which by this time had advanced two miles southward, in the Main coal seam at a depth of 140 yards. The Mountain colliery completed the extraction of this area of coal and also pushed out main roadways to the west and south. In addition to a good area of Hollin and Main coals worked, the Mountain also worked very large areas of Wall & Bench and Premier seams underlying the Main seam which had been extracted by old collieries in the Spon Green and Padeswood districts'.[48]

Watkinson is reputed to have employed a thousand men from the Buckley community and this probably influenced the outcome of a complaint to the Parish Council in June 1896. A meeting was held at the Town Hall, Buckley to discuss the alleged encroachment by Watkinson's Buckley Colliery Company in setting up of Mountain Colliery. The following year Flintshire County Council wrote to the Committee requesting them 'to remind the District Council that George Watkinson & Sons have appropriated a portion of Common Land for the purpose of carrying on the Mountain Colliery, and that the Council seek compensation for trespass, say, at the rate of 10s. per acre *per annum*.' No further action was taken.

The death of John Watkinson in 1907, the First World War, and an attractive offer from John Summers & Sons in 1920 led to the transfer of ownership. The steel makers had already guaranteed a supply of refractory goods for their furnaces by the take-over of the Castle Works in 1916 and now they added adequate coal resources. A report of 1923 on the Buckley collieries sums up the position. The company purchased in January 1920 made losses for the first three years. There were five pits working — numbers one and three Elm pits used for winding coal, and number two pit for ventilation. No. 1 Mountain for winding coal and No. 2 for ventilation. The two pits at Maesygrug were reported as standing full of water and their reopening was not recommended. Coal production during the best period nearly twenty years ago was 230,000 tons per annum and in 1923 the output was 130,000 tons. This was expected to increase considerably by the working of new areas at Elm and Mountain Collieries and a new colliery at Bannel, averaging 222,050 tons per annum for sixteen years with estimated net profit of £217,857.[49]

32. Bannel Colliery, 1923. This colliery was developed as a drift. Bought by the new company from a local prospector with the hope of reaching Main coal, after expenditure in the region of £30,000 it was abandoned in 1926. Water was encountered in the modern workings and it was realised that the Main coal had been worked out.

The closure of Bannel was the prelude to the last act in the long history of coal mining in the Buckley area. After the uncertainty at the end of the 1926 strike, the industry never recovered and rumours began to circulate. For example, in June 1928 the local press reported that 'the employees working in the Buckley Mountain Colliery have been put on fourteen days notice. We understand that it is the intention of the owners to close this pit

Above and left: Elm Colliery lamp and lamp tally c.1920s.
[Buckley Society Archive]

Elm Colliery surface workers 1911.
[Buckley Society Archive]

'A' Team, Elm Colliery Rescue Brigade,
with W. C. A. Collin (Colliery Manager).
[Buckley Library]

Mountain Colliery, c.1900.
[Buckley Society Archive]

down. If such a drastic step is taken approximately 200 workmen will be thrown out of work. The whole of the plant has been converted from steam to electricity at great expense with the power generated at the Hawarden Bridge Ironworks.' The colliery ceased production in 1930 and was dismantled. George Lewis recorded the events. '1928, June 9, Sat. 200 colliers finished at the Mountain Colliery.' '1929, Sept. 21, Sat. The Mountain Colliery finished working and they started to dismantle it on Monday'. '1947, June 5, Thurs. The Castle Firm started to take Mountain Colliery dirt heap away. The dirt heap was about 17 yards high and covered about 2 acres'.

The Elm Colliery closed in 1934. The process took three years and was reported in the newspapers.

> May 22, 1931. Last weekend about 100 men finished work at the Elm Colliery. These included 20 surface workers, electricians, etc. On Friday further notices were issued that the remainder of employees would cease to work in a fortnights time. Mr Spencer Summers, in a speech in the Albert Hall Buckley, said there would be work at these collieries for two or three years for a number of men getting the pillar coal from around the shafts.

In August 1933, the chimney was demolished by steeplejacks from Smethwick, having been disused since the introduction of electricity. A fortnight later Mr Thomas Jones of Brunswick Road recounted how his father had built the demolished chimney in 1886. It was 42 yards in height, contained 120,000 bricks, with 50 tons of material in the foundation and 100 tons of mortar. The structure was built in 22 working days for the sum of £40, the contract figure. There were 3 bricksetters and a youth on the job. The bricksetters wages were 5d. per hour or 4s. a day. The same year this team built seven chimneys, two of which were still standing in 1933 at the Buckley Standard Sanitary Pipe Works. In May 1934, the colliery closed when 150 men were unemployed. John Summers & Sons found it more economical to buy its coal from the modernised Llay Main Colliery.

Demolition of Elm Colliery chimney, September 1933. [FRO PH 11/182]

Coal and the Community

Wherever coal was the chief industry in a community in the nineteenth and twentieth centuries it meant that periodic mass unemployment was inevitable. This was the situation in the Buckley area and continued until the collieries closed there.

Mass unemployment was brought about by the economics of the coal industry. Coal fuelled the Industrial Revolution in Great Britain and abroad. The total annual production rose from an average of 56 million tons in 1845–9 to 180 million tons in 1890–4,[50] a period during which the industry was at its height in Buckley.

Production followed the demand of the market place and was subject to competition in price. The cost of production was reflected in the selling price. The price of coal was subject to fluctuation, which determined the wages paid to the collier. The coal owner had to sell his coal at a profit to cover his overheads and give a return on invested capital. It could rise to a high price and within a short time fall dramatically. The peaks and troughs occurred at regular intervals during the nineteenth century and were unpredictable. When they came they caused great hardship in communities where the colliery was often the only employer.

Wages were paid by the employer who felt justified, with little notice, in regulating them particularly during times of depression in trade when they were reduced. The story of industrial relations in the coal industry is an account of the struggle between collier and coal owner usually fought over the issue of the reduction in wages. If the collier withdrew his labour and went on strike or was locked out by the employer he invariably lost and had to return to work empty handed. There were a number of major examples of these conflicts in Buckley; always occurring at times of depression, which followed years of prosperity.

The colliers wanted a regular working week — not short time and days 'playing'. A fair wage rate to support a family, which was not subject to the Tommy Shop or a cut for the publican. He looked for some relief against sickness, unemployment or funeral expenses. He sought protection against dangerous working conditions — flooding, gas, bad ventilation, explosion and roof falls.

The vulnerability of the collier during these conflicts was because he was never able to negotiate from a position of strength. This strength only came gradually when government intervention promoted parliamentary legislation to give mine workers the right to belong to trade unions and promoted Acts concerned with safety. Negotiation became more common towards the end of the nineteenth century through conciliation and arbitration between employers and the workers representatives in the trade unions. Some success was achieved at the beginning of the twentieth century. In 1908, the Mining Act limited underground shifts to eight hours and in 1912 guaranteed a minimum wage.

The struggle was long and hard and lasted virtually to the end of the coal industry in Buckley in the 1930s. In the early years very often violence was not far below the surface. Starving men were desperately concerned for the welfare of their families. In Buckley the collieries were the chief employers. The other subsidiary industries, the brickyards and potteries, depended on coal and suffered a knock-on effect whenever there was a stoppage of production. As we have seen after the eighteen sixties the influence of non-conformity exercised some restraint on the workers with the chapel vestry as a training ground for the trade union leadership.

The most important event in the struggle between labour and capital in the first part of the nineteenth century was the Repeal of the Combination Acts in 1824–25 which gave workers the power of collective action and the right to withhold labour. This led to the formation of trade unions with the miners from Flintshire belonging to the Friendly Association Coal Miners Union Society in Lancashire. Local magistrates were afraid of riot and mob rule and in March 1826 two troops of the Royal Maylor Cavalry were rushed into Mold, and the local yeomanry remained on duty twelve days because of the turbulence of the colliers.[51] On Christmas Day 1830, Sir Stephen Glynne of Hawarden Castle, a local magistrate, despatched a courier to Chester Castle urgently soliciting the assistance of troops, the conduct of the people having been violent to the extreme.[52] This was the first great strike in North Wales on a large scale, which won an advance in wages for the men of Hawarden parish. There was further trouble in July 1831 when a gang of colliers from Holywell came to Mold 'and forcibly took away from their Employ a Body of Colliers working peaceably and paraded them thro' the Town to send them to their native County Anglesey'.[53] The Mold area developed a reputation and it was reported in 1835 that 'the system of combination and striking for wages has prevailed so extensively in the neighbouring collieries as to have called for a permanent station of military at Mold, distant about six miles from Flint'.[54] In spite of the fears of the authorities the trade unions were distinctly conservative in their procedure and demands cautiously avoiding falling foul of the law. Non-conformists who did not approve of swearing oaths of secrecy, which the members had to take, or their meeting in public houses, boycotted them. There is no doubt of the squalor and misery of the colliers often aggravated by such disasters as the one that occurred at Argoed in 1837.[55] Ways of improving their standard of life began to be recognised by Parliament. The first Mines Act of 1842 prohibited employment underground of women and girls and boys under the age of 10 years (increased to 12 in 1860). Acts concerned with safety were implemented in the 1850s and continued to the end of the century. Royal Commissions reporting in the 1840s highlighted the plight of the young in the mines and the inadequacy of educational provision.[56] By the 1840s the collier settlements in the outlying townships of Mold and Hawarden parishes were experiencing the influences of control provided by the Primitive Methodists.

There were long periods of depression in the coal industry. From 1834 onwards, during the 'Cruel Forties' and the slump of 1847, which followed the financial crisis. Even in these years, as in 1844, the Union of Miners of Great Britain and Ireland held the allegiance of 534 members from Flintshire. This faith in the cause of trade unionism still prevailed in the 1860s when lodges of the North Staffordshire and North Wales Amalgamated Miners Association were established in Flintshire. In the 1850s there was a rising coal market, a shortage of skilled labour in Flintshire and wage rises up to 20%. There was a successful strike at Great

Oaks Colliery in December 1862 against a new system of coal getting with support from the colliers of Ash and Ewloe Hall.[57]

The union movement in North Wales and Staffordshire was consumed with quarrels and thus enfeebled was unable to resist wage reductions imposed by the coal owners in a falling market. The conduct of trade unions was still regarded with suspicion as Rogers reports on the remarks made by Mr J. Scott Bankes of nearby Sychdyn, as Chairman of the Flintshire Quarter Sessions, in January 1866:

> He deplored the unrest between Capital and Labour. Persons calling themselves philanthropists were teaching the working classes that they were independent. He was 'proud of the working classes, and desired their welfare, but there was a degree or scale in which all men were placed by Providence, and if they attempted to put themselves out of that scale they should be doing that which was wrong, and that which was unbecoming their station. The Trade Union were a curse to the country ... He had no hesitation in saying that Trade Combination of all kinds were bad ....[58]

It is doubtful if this sanctimonious paternalistic advice reached the colliers but the owners certainly endorsed his views when they imposed a 10% reduction in wages in the summer of 1867 and went further by charging the ringleaders of a strike at Ewloe Hall at Hawarden with leaving their work without giving fourteen day's notice. They were ably defended by W. P. Roberts who 'asserted that the miners were willing to work out their notices, on condition that attention be given to the defective winding machinery and that the rope be fixed to the satisfaction of Mr Higson, the Miners' Inspector.' The owners at once stated they did not want to press the case. If the men returned to work for the time being that would be the end of the matter. The promise had already been given by the astute lawyer and the ringleaders were released.[59]

The decade of the 1870s was one of mixed fortunes in the industry, which had increased considerably in Buckley since 1860. There were troughs in 1869, 1879, and 1886 and peaks in 1865, 1873, and 1882. Buckley men left the National Association of Miners to join the Amalgamated Association of Miners the body to support them in the forth-coming troubles. These events were fully reported in the *Chester Chronicle*. At the end of December 1869 the colliers met in the Royal Oak in Buckley addressed by the union Agent, Mr R. Lewis of Wigan, who pointed out the benefits of membership in the light of gaining a rise of 10% in their wages and expressing the object 'of the movement was to do justice to the masters and the men'.[60] The agent's plea was successful and a lodge was established which met at the Blue Bell. Three years later they showed their strength in a traditional Whitsuntide procession:

> The colliers and Brickmakers of Buckley and District mustered to the number of 2,000 for the purpose of showing that union is strength and induce others to join the United Miners Association. About 9 a.m. both men and boys formed a procession and marched to Mold headed by the Buckley Brass band playing 'Put me in my little bed'. During the afternoon they returned to Buckley headed by the Longton flag of the Association and the band of the Hawarden Volunteers playing the 'Red, White and Blue' being preceded at some distance by the Rhosllanerchrugog and N. Wales officials. It was remarked by many that the youthful colliers seemed to enjoy better health than the brickmakers. In the evening the procession reformed and proceeded to a piece of open ground known as the Mountain where they were addressed on their objects.

A further demonstration of 500 colliers from the district took place in Mold in October. This meeting in connection with the Amalgamated Association of Miners showed that a spirit of goodwill existed with the attendance of Sir Robert Cunliffe, MP for Flintshire, Mr Jacob Frost of Oaks Colliery and the union agent Mr W. Brown, of Hanley Staffordshire. Three years later the period of prosperity was over. Wages were reduced by 10% by the summer of 1877 and in March 1878 the Main Coal and Cannel Company was in liquidation and strike action resorted to in the Buckley collieries.

Worse was to come. Between August 1884 and January 1885 Watkinson's colliers at the Elm and Maesygrug were out on strike. It was the most momentous strike ever to take place in Buckley. The hardship and bitterness it caused was to linger in the memory of mining folk for generations. It was an example of the destructive nature of antagonism between capital and labour and the foolishness of refusing to accept arbitration.[61]

There was nothing new in the circumstances which led to strike action. It was the usual issue over wages.

Colliers in Buckley were faced with a reduction of 10% in wages. There were complaints about the prospects of an enforced wage rate based upon a reckoning of 21cwt. to the ton in place of the 20cwt. By August the situation was critical. The workers gave notice to strike on the 26th and John Watkinson retaliated immediately by threatening to terminate all contracts after 14 days. The *Chester Chronicle* reported the workers' grievances:

> It is alleged by the men that during the last few months the managers, have from one week to another without notice, violated all the systems of working that have governed the district for the last eleven or twelve years; and they declare that in consequence of having had their tasks doubled, and in some cases trebled, they are unable to earn sufficient wages to maintain themselves let alone providing for their families. A struggle is anticipated, as these colliers are members of the Lancashire and North Wales Federation, and it has been understood for some time that arrangements were being made for a long stand out.[62]

The newspaper was correct in reporting active union preparation. What made the strike effective and different was the influence of Edward Jones, secretary of the Buckley Lodge, appointed agent of the Miners Association in Flintshire with a promise of full support from members in North Wales and Lancashire. For the past four or five months he had held meetings and recruited a membership of 300 members from Watkinson's Pits. Jones had local knowledge having lived in Bistre and worked previously at the Elm.

John Watkinson disliked Edward Jones. Watkinson was a right wing Conservative, a churchman, and an arrogant, overbearing businessman who resented being presented with the facts of the miners' situation dressed up in the working class rhetoric of the Primitive Methodists of which Jones was a member. Throughout the dispute he refused to meet any deputation of which Jones was a member; it was enough for Watkinson to be confronted by the reports Jones published in the press from time to time. Watkinson's intransigence was the chief reason why the strike dragged on for so long.

Messham unearthed several other issues relating to the strike, which throws a curious light on the relations between colliers and underground management. One of the most interesting is the complaint made to John Watkinson by John Wright as early as June. He writes to Watkinson as a friend and trusted workman at the Elm for fourteen years. As a trade unionist and chapel man he is well acquainted with the men's grievances. Wright points out the way in which officials behaved to the men. Exercising authority in a tyrannous manner, compelling them to accept rates for different tasks without notice given, forcing them to work a nine-hour day. Wright denounced the nepotism practised by the underground manager Isaac Hopwood and the conduct of some of his relatives to whom he had given underground responsibility. He writes a forthright but polite letter to his employer in the Buckley idiom:

> Sir,
> I now write a few lines to you to tell you that I am sorry to see you robbed in the way that you are for there is Isaac Hopwood and all his family esplecly John Jones with a moleskin jacket on and nothing to do and the pit is full of gaffers coming bullying over men from morning to night they are all uncles and aunts in that pit esplecly all the gaffers and chaple men they are sitting down at a hole at the shaft on a Monday morning tell dinner time talking about the sarmons and after that they go around the places and them that does not belong to the chapels as to suffer to help them that does there is one boss coming and ordering one thing and another ordering another thing there is no less than £20 a week going for gaffers that is not wanted for they are only in the road.[63]

By the beginning of October Edward Jones was frustrated by Watkinson's stubbornness and in his 'second report' on the strike wrote:

> We appeal to our friends and neighbours to assist us, and to let John Watkinson and his Managers know that WE ARE CHRISTIANS in a Christian Country, and we demand to be treated as such.
> We at these two pits can challenge any other two pits in the United Kingdom to produce such a number of preachers of the Gospel, deacons and class leaders, members of religious bodies, Sunday School teachers and scholars, and is it reasonable that two pit crews of the mentioned classes of men should stay away from their work for nine weeks, and resolve to stay another nine weeks for a trifle?[64]

Six weeks later the strike was biting harder with no sign of ending. Jones reported that the total amount of relief received over 12 weeks was £265 18s. 6d. distributed amongst about 300 of the most needy. He continued: 'We pray earnestly for a little assistance; as our rents are now standing, cold weather is setting in, and with aching hearts we can see our wives and little ones becoming ill clad and shoeless and wanting for food. We have above 600 workmen affected by this Strike, which means at least 2,000 persons thrown upon the goodwill of their fellow-workmen and the public'.[65] The strike dragged on until the end of January 1885. A score of men drifted back on 24 November. Violent protest erupted at a General Election meeting in December when the mob failed to lynch Watkinson who made his escape. As stubborn as ever, he refused to meet the union deputation. The colliers and their families went from door to door begging at Christmas time. John Scott Bankes of Soughton Hall, a neighbour of Watkinson, but a Liberal in politics, appealed for arbitration in October and January, but failed to touch his heart. A deputation of colliers met Watkinson on the 24 January. He made no concessions. Five days later the strike was over. The *Flintshire Observer* noted that the men had returned to work on the master's terms. The *Mining Journal* put it more bluntly: 'the strike had ended in total surrender'.[66]

The six months strike destroyed the credibility of the union in North Wales and was later bitterly attacked by David Gough. 'What, he asked, had the men of Elm Colliery, Buckley received from Lancashire? When they applied for assistance, the men of Elm Colliery had been told they were out of benefit, and they had 'to fight alone, to sing in the streets, unsupported, until they were famished and driven to surrender to the starvation terms of their employers, and to submit to their being victimised'.[67] In 1892 the men joined the Denbighshire and Flintshire Miners' Federation and became part of the newly formed Miners' Federation of Great Britain (MFGB).

Once again the movement in prices and wages plagued the stability in industrial relations. Between 1888 and 1890 wage rates were increased by 40%. The return of falling prices in 1891 continued and in June 1893 the employers presented a formal demand for a 25% reduction in wages and the new national union, the MFGB resolved to resist the proposed reductions and the great lockout of 1893 began in the last week in July. The Union attracted less than 30% membership in North Wales and the Flintshire men wanted to stay in work and refused to follow the MFGB or the North Wales Miners' Council. Eventually the Buckley Colliers organised by Edward Peters left the pits in the last week of August 1893. This time the Colliers of Buckley were part of a national stoppage. The new Federation was fighting for two important principles. First, the right of miners to control the selling price of coal and second the right to a minimum wage.

The *County Herald* reported in the middle of September that 'Everything almost is at a standstill for want of coal. The men hold mass meetings in this district with no practical result, while hundreds of men and boys are rambling about, and things look as dark as they can possibly can'. In October the brickworks were almost at a standstill, the *Chronicle* reported, and added, 'we are told that people are begging for food especially some of the lads and the way the poor fellows devour what is given to them makes one realise the reality of the want of food and nourishment'. However, the *County Herald* informed its readers on 6 October under the heading 'Termination of Strike' '… the colliers in this district have returned to work. The Mount Pleasant Colliery commenced on Monday, Sandycroft on Tuesday and Watkinson's Elm Collieries commenced on Wednesday. The only colliery not working at present in the immediate

Coal picking 1911 coal strike.
[Buckley Library]

Miners gather outside the Parish Room, Lane End, during the 1912 coal strike. [Buckley Library]

neighbourhood is the Lane End Colliery. All the others have returned at the old rate of wages'. Some colliers did not return to work. The Relief Committee was still distributing money and the brickworks were still at a standstill for coal as reported by the *County Herald* on 20 October. A week later a mass meeting of colliers was held at the Central Hall, Buckley, under the chairmanship of the Reverend Joseph Davies, who spoke on 'Mining Royalties'; Mr Edward Peters, the miners' agent followed him, when the assembly was addressed by Mr T. Glover, St Helens 'who strongly advocated the MFGB as the greatest protection the working collier can have'.

The lock-out was ended by the intervention the Prime Minister W. E. Gladstone, more radical at the end of his career, who invited both sides to a conference which took place on 17 November, under the chairmanship of Lord Rosebery, the Foreign Secretary. Once again the union had lost to the employers who reasserted the principle that wages must follow prices. But this was the first time a government had intervened to end a strike. The issue of the minimum wage was merely postponed until the great dispute of 1912.[68]

The next major national dispute was the 1912 Coal Strike. Despite fluctuations in trade, as in 1904 when Colliers worked for only three or four days, the Union's position was strengthened. The North Wales Miners' Association was ably led by Edward Hughes, its agent and financial secretary for over twenty years, from 1898 onwards. There were several improvements brought about by the great reforming Liberal government elected in 1906 but more significant was the increase in Labour Party representation in the House of Commons greatly dependent on the miners' vote. This was reflected in the report of Edward Hughes to the North Wales Association for 1912. He argued that the Liberal government's programme of social reform — Old Age Pensions, Eight Hours Act for Miners, Amendments to the Workmens' Compensation Act and the Minimum Wage Act — had been greatly influenced by the increased number of Labour members of Parliament. He went further and stated that 'It is essential that the workers should recognise that unless they are represented by their own class they can expect only milk and water legislation … there is only one real remedy, viz. the Nationalisation of Mines for the people, and not for the benefit of a few share-holders'.[69]

The 1912 National Coal Strike began in March 1912 and lasted for six weeks. It was terminated by Government intervention and resulted in a new Minimum Wages Act. Amongst the million miners involved were those from Buckley. The prospects for them were reported to be more optimistic than had been in the past. The *County Herald* declared at the beginning of the strike:

At Buckley the greater part of the population, which is chiefly dependent upon collieries and brickworks, is

Picking coal at Knowle Lane Brickworks during the coal strike of 1912. [Buckley Society Archive]

unemployed; but generally speaking, the pinch here will not be felt for some time, as many are wholly or partially the owners of their dwellings, and others having savings in co-operative societies, banks, home-purchase societies etc. which they can fall back on in time of need.[70]

The newspaper was perhaps a little more realistic a week later reporting of the coal strike in Flintshire 'the position grows desperate, the service of trains has been still further reduced, midnight marauders have stolen pigeons, poultry and rabbits. Many tons of potatoes stored under earth in fields have disappeared.'[71] There was more goodwill shown on this occasion than previously. 'An illustration of the prosperity of Buckley due to the generosity of the owners of the coal pits (did they mean clay pits? — the School Log Books report parents and children picking coal in the clayholes) 1912 in allowing the coal to be mined free of cost is reflected in the negative answer given to the schoolmaster of the Buckley schools each morning last week by scholars to the query whether any scholar had come to school without breakfast. Coal has been sold in large quantities by the miners and thousands of tons of fairly good coal are being got each week in this way, and bust scenes have been witnessed.[72]

Further anxiety was felt by the people of Buckley a year later when in May 1913 Watkinson's gave their underground and surface workers at the Elm, Ash and Mountain Collieries fourteen days notice to terminate their contracts. The *County Herald* commented: 'About 800 men are affected. This is a blow to the Buckley district, which, now that brick making has greatly declined, practically depends upon the coal mining industries for its existence'.[73]

But in reality, it was the coal mining industry which was in decline in Buckley rather than brick making. Edward Hughes' son, Hugh Hughes, an unsuccessful Labour candidate in the 1918 General Election, recognised 'that it was impossible for North Wales owners to pay anything like a living wage to the miners, because of the geological and geographical conditions of the coalfield'. By the end of the lock-out of 1921 union funds were exhausted having spent large sums in benefit, strike and lock-out pay.[74]

The three months coal strike of 1921 was the beginning of the end for the industry in Buckley. It could not survive the new post war economic climate. Exports were down by 30% and Industrial Production by 18%. The government decontrolled the mines at the end of March and gave the owners the opportunity to demand cuts in wages of over 40%. The age, exhaustion and geological difficulties of the Buckley pits meant a severe contraction of the Industry in the district.[75]

The spring of 1921 witnessed as great a pantomime as ever seen in Buckley. It was as if the safe had been left open and the workers were permitted to help themselves. It provided a surrealist scenario, the last dance of the swan, a busman's holiday for the striking colliers, fully dramatised in the local press. The *Chester Chronicle* reported three week's frenetic activity:

Picking coal at Etna Clay Hole during the 1921 coal strike.
[Buckley Library]

Many of the miners are now getting coal in the disused clayholes around Buckley. Day and night shifts are being worked by some of the gangs who are working as partners. In the clayhole near the Silica Works, Drury Lane, the coal runs to nearly 5ft. thick…In the Mount clayhole the men have drilled underneath and propped the roof up in real mining fashion; candles and bike lamps being used when they work. The owners of these clay holes allow the men to get these seams of coal free. During last week a grand seam was discovered in Old Ewloe Works clayhole near to Buckley Church …The different gangs have their own piles of coal which are placed in rotation on the top. Two or three hundred tons are placed in heaps along each side of the roadway. Nearly everybody in the district has turned temporary miner, and tradesmen of all crafts are trying their hand. In most places the men are working in three shifts so as not to lose the places after opening them out.[76]

This capitalistic enterprise by the Buckley colliers did not amuse their union bosses:

Differences of opinion have occurred at Buckley between the officials of the North Wales Miner's Federation and the local miners who are working day and night in hundreds getting the outcrop seams of coal in the old clay holes and sending it away in hundreds of tons every week. The coal is leaving Buckley, by motor transport and railway wagons, to Liverpool, Birkenhead, Wallasey, Bangor and most of North Wales towns along the coast, and as far as Shrewsbury. The coal is sold wholesale at £2 and £2.10s per ton, and some of the men have made good money, and up to the present no one has sought outdoor relief from Buckley…A resolution was passed to cease selling the coal for industrial purposes. The men were given until twelve o'clock on Saturday to sell their heaps of coal, which would amount to a few hundred tons in the various places. Some of the men who had done well out of the outcrop seams showed much resentment all through the meeting and arguments followed for and against the Federation interfering.[77]

By 1921 the North Wales Miners' Association had reached a peak membership of 16,000 through the leadership of Edward Hughes and his son Hugh Hughes. But there was an uncertainty, volatility and restlessness about these post-war years. An indicator was a succession of Coalition, Conservative, Labour and Conservative administrations within the usual septennial period allotted for government. In 1925 the Conservatives under Baldwin were back in power faced with a million unemployed. Competition from foreign exports led the Prime Minister to pronounce in July that 'all the workers of this country have got to take a reduction in wages to help put industry on its feet'. The mineworkers' leaders had heard this all too often and were determined to resist.

By 1925 there was European competition from Poland and the coal producing region of the Rühr. The coal owners sought to use their usual remedy of lower wages and longer hours. A lock-out looked imminent until at the end of July the government agreed to bring in a subsidy for nine months. Desperately seeking a way out and playing for time the government appointed a royal commission to propose ways of raising productivity. The government feared an escalation of strike action with support from the railway and transport unions. Haunted by the sceptre of socialist revolution and fear of 'reds under the bed' they prepared emergency measures. The Samuel Commission, when it reported in March 1926, was favourable towards reform in the coal industry advocating such measures as the nationalization of royalties; amalgamation of smaller pits; better working conditions such as pithead baths — and an immediate

Picking coal at Knowle Hill during the 1926 coal strike.
[Buckley Society Archive]

reduction in wages. This last recommendation was too bitter a pill for the miners to swallow. They jibbed at once again becoming the industrial scapegoats and coined their battle cry 'not a penny off the pay, not a minute off the day'. They were locked out on 1 May. The trade union conference planned for a national strike on 3 May which began at midnight and lasted until 12 May.

The embittered miners stayed out for six months, rejecting government attempts at compromise. Defeated by starvation they went back to work having gained nothing and succumbing to longer hours, lower wages, and district agreements.[78]

That summer and autumn of the miners' strike in Buckley was bravely and cheerfully faced. The men kept themselves busy attending to the business of the strike by holding mass meetings. In May one was held in a field behind the Albert Hall. A week later in June a bellman paraded the streets announcing that Miss Ellen Wilkinson, M.P. was to speak. In the end she didn't come, 'having been called to London where she was doing noble work to relieve distress and suffering amongst the poor, caused through the present industrial trouble'. Nevertheless the Tivoli had the basement floor filled to hear the miners' delegates and local dignitaries.[79]

The Sunday school belonging to the United Methodist Church in Buckley was completely renovated by workers thrown idle and the house adjoining the schoolroom converted into four classrooms. Local tradesmen and business people also gave their assistance and lent horses, carts, and motor vehicles.[80] Expressions of goodwill continued and local events connected with the stoppage were reported, as on 18 June:

> The local miners were all paid 8s. each on Saturday from the national funds that have been subscribed to from all parts of the world. We understand over 700 miners at the Elm and Mountain Colliery received 8s. each.
>
> The Elm and Mountain Lodges Committee have organised a great Gala day and Sports to take place on the Buckley Cricket ground on Saturday next, on the same field a 'Pit Ponies Derby' will be held together with a tug-of-war, flat racing, throwing the cricket ball, musical chairs (mounted), etc. Offers have been made to Buckley Lodges from wealthy people living in other parts of the country that they would be willing to take children belonging to miners with large families and feed and cloth the same as long as the miners' lock-out lasts. Several families have been approached to let one of their children go, but none are willing so far.[81]

As the stoppage continued through the summer dances were held to raise funds for relief with the Buckley Imperial Jazz Band under the direction of Mr Arthur Roberts giving their services free. The proposals suggested by the bishops and Free Church leaders, as a basis of settlement for the dispute, when put to a mass meeting of miners on the Common, were approved.[82] New terms for a resumption of work at Buckley collieries were posted up but rejected 'for it means eight hours and a reduction of 13% of the wages of the piece workers'.[83] On the same day, 17 September, the headmaster of St Matthew's Boys School noted, 'although it is 20 weeks since the commencement of the coal strike, all the boys are well clothed and apparently well fed'. This was an improvement on a previous entry of 21 June which recorded, 'a number of boys have been away this week owing to the fact that they had no boots, due to the continued coal strike'.[84]

BUCKLEY COLLIERIES

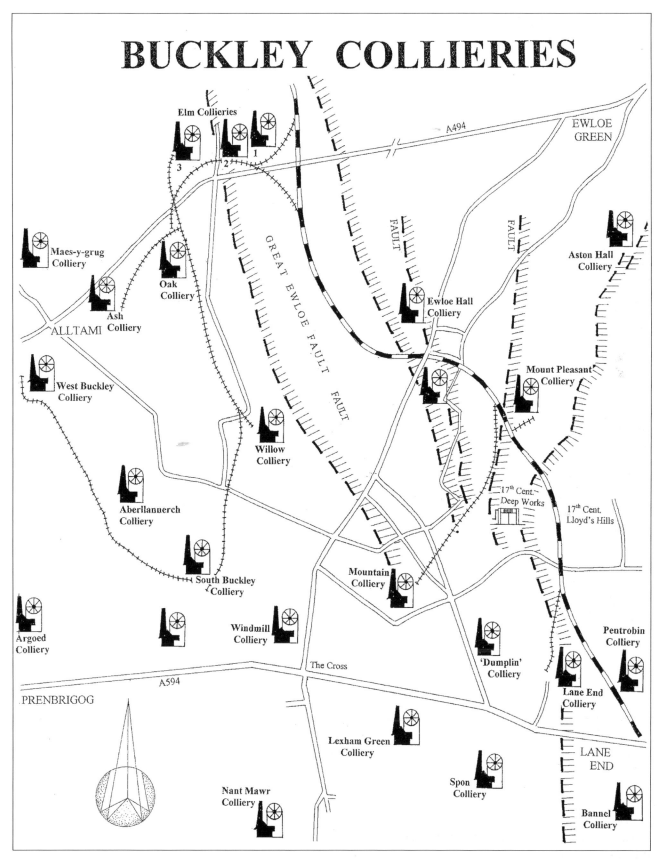

Buckley Collieries. [K. Lloyd Grfiffiths]

The last recorded incident concerned the enterprise of a number of local miners and occurred at the beginning of October:

> Considerable damage has been caused to the bye road locally known as Army Lane, through the outcrop of coal operations which have been going on just behind the old Salvation Army Building and Gladstone Villa, Lane End. For several weeks a fairly good quality of coal was found in one of the gardens about 300 feet deep. Owners of ground nearby sank miniature shafts and for weeks five of these small outcrop mines have been raising hundreds of tons of splendid coal. The five mines are in close proximity to each other, two being on one side of the roadway and three on the other. Just before noon on Sunday there was quite a commotion in the locality for the main road way between the mines and the railway around the garden suddenly collapsed and the subsidence created a large crevice in the road.[85]

A list of Collieries mentioned in the text.
1. Lexham Green.
2. Little Mountain.
3. Sandycroft.
4. Lloyd Hills.
5. Woods.
6. Mount Pleasant.
7. Cheapside.
8. Ewloe Hall.
9. Smalley's.
10. Nant Mawr.
11. Upper Nant Mawr.
12. Padeswood.
13. Wind Mill.
14. Spon Green.
15. Pentrobin.
16. Aston Hall.
17. Lane End (Dumpling).
18. Argoed Hall, 1808.
19. Aberllanerch, or Buckley Colliery.
20. Argoed, 1863.
21. South Buckley, 1866.
22. Main Coal and Cannel Company.
23. North and South Buckley.
24. South Buckley, 1889.
25. West Buckley.
26. Willow.
27. Oak.
28. Ash.
29. Maesygrug.
30. Elm
31. Mountain.
32. Bannel.

Notes

1. A. B. Searle, *Ceramic Industries Pocket Book,* 1920, p. 212.

2. To be found in FRO under 'What the eye does not see, the heart does not grieve. The investigation of an environmental problem: abandoned coalmining shafts in Clwyd County with special reference to Buckley Urban District Council'. B.Ed. degree essay, Univ. Wales, Bangor, 1974.

3. K. Lloyd Gruffydd, three articles: 'Medieval Coalmining in Flintshire', *Buckley 1*; 'Coalmining in Flintshire in the Sixteenth Century', *Buckley 2.* 'The Flintshire Coalfield in the Sixteenth and Seventeenth Centuries', *Buckley 3.*

4. Summarised from K. Lloyd Gruffydd, 'The Development of the Coal Industry in Flintshire to 1740', pp. 59–60.

5. ibid.

6. ibid, p.22.

7. R. Rees Rawson, 'The Coal-Mining Industry of the Hawarden District on the eve of the Industrial Revolution', in *Archaeologia Cambrensis,* vol.xcvi., Part ii, 1941.

8. J. N. Rhodes, 'Early Steam Engines in Flintshire', *Transactions of the Newcomen Society,* vol. xli, p. 217.

9. FRO D/KK/267, Survey of Thomas Symmer Champneys' Estate in the Parish of Mold, 3 Dec. 1791.

10. FRO D/DM/809/97, Edwin Rogers Diary, 1847–92.

11. Found in a typed copy at the back of W. Bell Jones' copy of Rawson's article, see fn. 7.

12. Hawarden Deeds, 1534, op cit.

13. Rawson, op cit p. 128.

14. C. B. Wedd and W. B. R. King, *The Geology of the Country around Flint, Hawarden, and Caergwrle,* (HMSO: 1924).

15. J. E. Messham, 'Thomas Cropper's 'Jonathan Catherall', Part II; How he became a businessman', *Buckley 24,* p.19.

16. H. Morris-Jones, 'The Hancock Family Industrial Entrepreneurs', *Buckley 21,* pp. 3–10.

17. Harold Gregory, 'The Little Mountain Colliery, Buckley', *Flintshire Historical Society Publications,* vol. 23, p. 86.

18. *Mold, Deeside and Buckley Leader* 8/5/1931.

19. Ibid, 16/5/1930.

20. FRO D/BC/589, Henry Beckett, Wolverhampton, 1/8/1843, Ewloe Hall Colliery Report no.2.

21. Connolly. op cit p145.

22. KLG thesis. p. 70

23. FRO, Trevalyn mss, D/TR/110 & 113.

24. Bradley, op cit, p. 347.

25. FRO, D/M/5227.

26. FRO, D/M/5218.

27. *Chester Courant,* 13/2/1867.

28. FRO, D/M/5218.

29. FRO, D/KK/267.

30. *Chester Chronicle,* 6/4/1821.

31. FRO, D/M/5218.

32. Connolly, op cit p. 163.

33. For a detailed account see T. W. Pritchard, *A History of the Old Parish of Hawarden* (Wrexham: Bridge Books, 2002) p. 75.

34. Bradley, op cit, p. 298.

35. K. Lloyd Gruffydd, 'The Argoed Hall Colliery Disaster of 1837', *Ystrad Alun 2.* This is an excellent article. I limit my account to quoting the report in the *Chester Chronicle* 12/5/1837, which KLG does not quote directly.

36. *Chester Chronicle,* 19/5/1837.

37. FRO, D/GW/637.

38. For collieries listed 19 to 24 see B. D. Hodnett, 'Coalmining and Brickmaking in the South Buckley Area', *Buckley 25.*

39. FRO, D/GW/630.

40. *Chester Chronicle,* 28/11/1863.

41. See no. 15 under brickworks.

42. Brian D. Hodnett, 'The 'Klondike' or the West Buckley Colliery', *Buckley 23,* Bradley, op cit, p. 416.

43. See collieries listed 23 and 24.

44. *Chester Chronicle,* 1/6/1907.

45. For Watkinson's colliery interests in Buckley see: Thomas J. Hopwood, 'A Brief History of Buckley Collieries under the Ownership of George Watkinson & Sons Ltd. And the Buckley Colliery Co. Ltd.' *Buckley 7,* and J. E. Messham, 'Conflict at Buckley Collieries. The Strike at the Elm and Maesygrug, 1884-5', *Flintshire Historical Society Transactions,* vol. 33, pp. 151 ff.

46. Hopwood, ibid, p. 20.

47. ibid.

48. ibid

49. FRO, D/DM/355/15.

50. K. Theodore Hoppen, 'The Mid-Victorian generation, 1846–1886', *The New Oxford History of England* (Oxford: Clarendon Press 1998), p.287.

51. Emlyn Rogers, 'Labour Struggles in Flintshire, 1830–1850, Part I', *Flintshire Historical Society Publications,* vol.14, p.47.

52. ibid, p. 48.

53. ibid, p. 58.

54. Rogers, ibid, quoting Report of Commissioners appointed to enquire into Municipal Corporations of England and Wales, 1835,

App. 1, p. 2682 in *FHSP,* vol. 15 p. 102.

55. See above.

56. See Report of Children and Young Persons in Mines and Mineral Works of North Wales, Herbert Jones, 1842, xvi, and Report of Commissioners of Inquiry into the State of Education in Wales, 1846–7.

57. Emlyn Rogers, 'The History of Trade Unionism in the Coal Mining Industry of North Wales', *Denbighshire Historical Society Transactions,* vol. 17, p.151–2.

58. Rogers, DHST, vol. 18, p. 124, quoting *Wrexham Advertiser,* 12/1/1867.

59. Ibid, p.120.

60. *Chester Chronicle,* 1/1/1870.

61. J. E. Messham, *FHSJ,* vol 33, op cit.

62. *Chester Chronicle,* 16/8/1884.

63. FRO, D/DM/809/105, quoted by Messham, op cit p. 162.

64. ibid.

65. ibid, 19/11/1884.

66. Messham, op cit, p. 186.

67. Rogers, op cit, *DHST,* vol. 21 p. 90f.

68. J. E. Williams, 'The Miners' Lockout of 1893', *Study of Labour History Bulletin,* no. 24, 1972.

69. FRO, D/BP/1016-7

70. *County Herald,* 8/3/1912.

71. *County Herald,* 15/3/1912

72. *County Herald,* 29/3/1912.

73. *County Herald,* 9/5/1913.

74. Sally Venn, 'Labour Politics in North East Wales. A Study of the North Wales Miners Association from 1898–1947', M. A. Dissertation, Univ. of Wales, Bangor, 1994, Sally Venn.

75. For the background to the 1921 Lockout see: C. J. Wrigley (edt.) *A History of British Industrial Relations,* vol. II, 1914–1939, ch. 2 'The Trade Unions between the Wars', Chris Wrigley pp. 71–129, (Harvester Press: 1987).

76. *Chester Chronicle,* 16/4/ and 7/5/1921 quoted by Andrew Connolly, op cit, pp. 71–2.

77. *County Herald,* 135/1921.

78. A. J. P. Taylor, *English History, 1914-1945,* The Oxford History of England, (Oxford: Clarendon Press, 1965) pp 240-8.

79. *Mold, Deeside, & Buckley Leader,* 28/5/ & 4/6/1926.

80. ibid, 18/6/1926.

81. ibid.

82. ibid, 13/8/1926.

83. ibid, 17/9/1926.

84. FRO, E/LB/11/3.

85. *Mold, Deeside, & Buckley Leader,* 8/10/1926.

Chapter 6
Brickworks and Railways

If the seeds of Buckley's growth were sown in the boulder clay of the pottery industry in the seventeenth and eighteenth centuries its blossoming took place in the clay seams worked in the fire-clay quarries for the next two hundred years. Millions of tons of clay goods were sent all over the world to build towns, lay sewage systems, make railway embankments, bridges and tunnels, drain agricultural land and equip dairies. Specially developed products were used in the emerging chemical industry; pots made for lead and glass works, and furnace linings for steel works.

Brickmasters and coal owners thrived on an inexhaustible supply and ample variety of clay and coal, which sustained them for a hundred and fifty years. There was an army of colliers and clay workers toiling in the pit, quarry, brick shed and kiln.

Transport was the lifeline to the market place. Not until tramways and railroads were made to the River Dee at Queensferry and Connah's Quay did the industry really develop. Success for new brickworks depended on connection to the national system and horses were harnessed to haul trucks to sidings.

First we will look at where the fire-clay was available, its special properties and the processes involved in the manufacture of clay goods. The potter's clay was easily won, being found on the surface of Buckley Mountain, having been deposited there as boulder clay during the retreating glacial period. The first bricks were made of this clay according to the same manual processes employed in pottery making.

Further advance in the clay industry was made with the potter's realisation that there were other clays below the boulder clay, which could be used for manufacturing bricks and refractory (heat resisting) goods. These were the fire-clays, which in Buckley form the highest part of the Middle Coal measures. This appearance of both coal and fire-clay together revolutionised the industry. Coal was the ideal agent to burn the fire-clay because it possessed the capability of reaching higher temperatures of between 1100–1500 degrees centigrade. Its first recorded use for this purpose in Flintshire was in 1640. The first mention of a brick kiln is in Mynydd Isa in 1668.[1] Bricks were used in the construction of residences for both the gentry and for humble cottages.

The Buckley fire-clays occur in three areas. The main outcrop is a quarter of a mile wide extending in a line southwards from Castle Brickworks. Another important outcrop is to the east and south for about a mile from Ewloe Hall to Lane End, Buckley. A third, unworked, followed the course of Alltami Brook. These three outcrops have a combined area of between 300 to 400 acres.[2] The various seams of clay are exposed in the several quarries, or clay holes as they are known locally, of the brickworks (most of them are now either in-filled or flooded), where there are as many as thirty different varieties.[3] These are seen in the sequence exposed in the quarries of the main outcrop from Castlebrick Works. In descending order they are:

6. Purple shaly clay, pale-green clayey shales,

5. Sandstone, fine-grained, usually yellowish-white, but rather felspathic and pinkish in some of the higher beds, forming a well-marked bed and weathering with a purplish-brown crust, with subordinate beds of shale and fine-grained white siliceous clunch. This passes down into

4. Siliceous clay or silt rock, greenish-white, very fine-grained and sporadically developed-on, or sometimes mixed with

3. Mottled purple clay, usually split up by a bed of white siliceous clunch. This clay is termed 'Blue.'

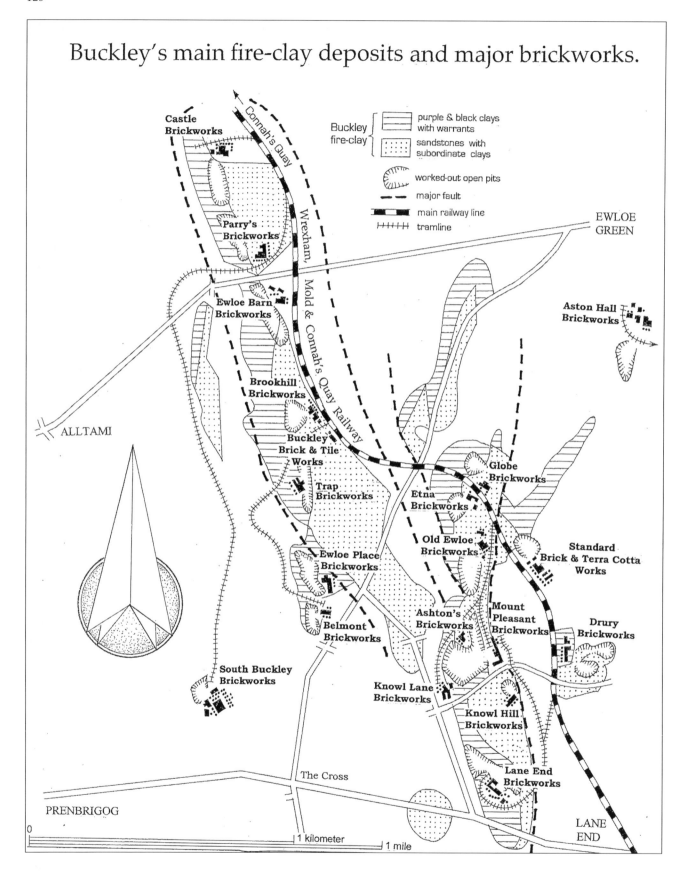

Buckley's main fire-clay deposits and major brickworks.

Buckley fire-clay {
- purple & black clays with warrants
- sandstones with subordinate clays

- worked-out open pits
- major fault
- main railway line
- tramline

Castle Brickworks

Connah's Quay

Wrexham, Mold & Connah's Quay Railway

Parry's Brickworks

EWLOE GREEN

Ewloe Barn Brickworks

Aston Hall Brickworks

ALLTAMI

Brookhill Brickworks

Buckley Brick & Tile Works

Trap Brickworks

Globe Brickworks

Etna Brickworks

Old Ewloe Brickworks

Standard Brick & Terra Cotta Works

Ewloe Place Brickworks

Ashton's Brickworks

Mount Pleasant Brickworks

Drury Brickworks

Belmont Brickworks

South Buckley Brickworks

Knowl Lane Brickworks

Knowl Hill Brickworks

The Cross

Lane End Brickworks

PRENBRIGOG

0   1 kilometer   1 mile

LANE END

2. Shaly clay, dark-grey or black, sometimes with thin coal seams; replaced northward almost entirely by red- and grey-blotched warrant and quartzitic sandstone.

1. Coal, thin, becoming a mere streak of carbonaceous shale towards the north.[4]

Buckley firebricks are of two kinds, the reddish-blue purple or 'brindled' brick and the 'white brick'. The 'white' brick is made chiefly from black clay. The brindled is made from blends of the more siliceous beds with purple clay. This is called 'clunch' to denote a stiff clay.[5]

The special properties of the fire-clays governed the great variety of manufactured products in Buckley — especially because they are used to make both refractory and non-refractory products. The refractory goods produced during the long life of the industry included acid and fireproof goods, fire bricks, furnace linings, crucibles, retorts, glass-melting pots. Paving, ridge tiles and common bricks were also made. The growth of the industry in the mid nineteenth century depended on the special qualities of Buckley brick to withstand abrasion and pressure and for this reason large quantities were used for building tunnels and bridges. Acid resisting goods were supplied for the chemical, cement and glass industries. The non-refractory goods produced from fire-clay were sanitary ware, acid proof ware, salt glazed pipes and tiles. The durable glaze of these products was only obtained by firing at high temperatures, which were unobtainable for non-refractory clays.[6]

The brick making processes

For centuries the brick making industry was controlled by parliamentary legislation. An Act of 1478 stated that 'the earth, whereof any such tiles shall be made, shall be digged and cast up before November 1, next before they shall be made; and stirred and turned before February 1, next following; and wrought before March 1, next after; and the same earth, before it be put to making of tile, shall be truly wrought and tried from stones'.[7] Legislation in 1777 stipulated the size of bricks. 'All bricks made for sale, when burned, be not less than eight inches and an half long, two inches and an half thick, and four inches wide; and all pantiles, not less than thirteen inches and an half wide, and half an inch thick'.[8] The 1478 legislation describes the seasonal nature of brickmaking with its various processes of clay getting, weathering, turning over, tempering and moulding.

The late Dennis Griffiths has given us an account of brickmaking in Buckley going back to the late eighteenth century. He describes early brickmaking as seasonal with bricks made outdoors, the clay being dug from shallow pits, mixed with water in heaps of blunged material. For tiles and ridge tiles, the best clays would be selected, and after water had been added and the clay had mellowed by exposure to the atmosphere over a period of weeks, more water would be added. The clay was then tempered to the best degree of stiffness for moulding by the bare feet of men and boys treading on it. So was derived the word treading. Mixing pits would hold about twenty or thirty tons of clay after grinding by rollers. Treading was not abolished until the 1920s–1930s.

After the clay was tempered it was wheeled on barrows along a plank to the moulder's bench. Here the bricks were hand-moulded in open wooden moulds, a barrow load being sufficient to make fifty 9 x 4.5 x 3 inch bricks. After the moulder had filled the mould with clay rolled into a sanded clod, he dipped it into the water box on the bench, so that the clod would leave the mould cleanly, and finally he would scrape surplus clay from the top of the mould with a wooden stroker. It was then that the brick runner, usually a boy not more than fourteen years old, would carry it away and lay it on the grass to dry. Then he would go back to the bench with the mould, the brickmaker having meanwhile cut and sanded his clod and watered his mould to receive it. In his day's work a boy would run about twelve miles and carry more than eight tons of bricks, afterwards helping to dress the bricks and stack them when dry.

The same process of moulding was applied to larger articles, such as bearers, blocks and large tiles, but these were dressed more carefully, either on the floor, or on benches to secure the correct shape. After the goods had been dressed, they were built into clamp kilns, the dried bricks forming the walls in which fire ports were left, and small coal mixed in the layers of the bricks, the whole top of the kiln being roofed over with the final setting of bricks. Brickmakers were skilled in the best methods of clamp kiln formations. The kiln would be lit with branches of trees, the coal ignited and the bricks burned to a proper degree of hardness.

Clayhole men, with the assistance of labourers, did the clay getting. They worked the clay from open faces until, at twenty or thirty yards deep, the black clay measures were reached. Great care had to be taken to drain the water and not to excavate seams lower than the black clay in order to avoid too large a proportion of ironstone. Drainage until the 1930s was by the 'bucket' type pump. Electrically operated ones gradually replaced these steam driven pumps. Hancock's Lane End Works bucket pump, fixed in 1853, worked satisfactorily until new plant was introduced in 1934.

From the nineteenth century onwards machinery was very gradually introduced. Soon after 1815 Jonathan Catherall II began to use the Yorkshire Horse for mixing clay.[9] This comprised a circular trough in the floor of the shed into which was fed clay which had passed through crushing rollers. Water was added and the clay passed through a spiked rotating arm driven by steam engine. The name 'horse' was presumably used because earlier versions used a horse to provide the power. Eventually other machinery made some of the processes easier; for example, clay rollers were bought to crush lumps of clay before being fed into grinding pans to sieve powdered clay ready for the next process of mixing clay in the pugging mill. The pugging mill replaced the manual process formerly done by the treading boys. However, it took some time before machine-made bricks were manufactured. It wasn't until October 1875 that the cautious Buckley brickmasters agreed to test the suitability of their clays to be manufactured into bricks by machine when they sent a sample to the Saltney Solid Brick Company. The subsequent report read that 'having passed once through two pairs of rollers, the brick produced was in fact little worse than when it came out of the machine'. But it wasn't until 1894 that the first brickmaking machine, on the wire-cut system, was first installed in a Buckley brickworks. This was only successful after trial and error and the adaptation of the machine by Jonathan Rowland of Buckley Foundry, who designed and made a machine with a much longer barrel to suit the more rock bearing, refractory fire-clay of Buckley which needed a longer mixing process. It was not many months before each of the Buckley works gave him an order for a similar machine. These continued working until the Second World War, but the accepted method was to use wirecut bricks and hand press them, as with tiles, both for paving and chemical use.[10] Bricks were made of various sizes, shapes and types, sometimes known by their market — London, Irish, etc. There were groups of special hand-moulded lines: ridge tiles, floor tiles, block bearers, wall copings, furnace doors, dog and pig troughs, chimney pots, etc. Most of the processes were team efforts in the quarry, shed and kiln, which engendered a strong sense of loyalty and comradeship in the work force as it did in the collieries.

The growth and development of Brickworks, 1790–2003

1. The early period, 1790–1860. Characterised by the development of markets and establishment of communications.
2. The middle period, 1860–1920. Marked by the opening of the Buckley Railway and its incorporation in the Wrexham, Mold, Connah's Quay Railway, the arrival of new brickmakers, the expansion of trade, the alliance of the Buckley Brickmasters, industrial unrest, and closures.
3. Years of uncertainty, 1920–45. Mergers, the strengthening of the industry by John Summers and Sons.
4. The last phase, 1945–2003. Revival, mergers, modernisation, closure.

Twenty-one brickworks are named in the review. They are discussed in chronological order.

1. The early period, 1790–1860

The Catherall family were the pioneers of the Buckley Firebrick Industry. Grandfather Jonathan Catherall I, (1699–1761), as a potter and manufacturer of clay goods, saw its potential. Grandson Jonathan Catherall II (1761–1833) doggedly demonstrated the possibilities of large scale manufacture, the availability of markets for a variety of products and the importance of marketing and a personal acquaintance with the client.

Four brickworks were opened by the 1790s; one of which remained in production until the 1970s and another was the last survivor of the industry, closing in 2005.

The first known firebrick works in Buckley is the **Trap Works (site one)**, which was first worked by Jonathan Catherall I. Although there is no factual evidence the date given is traditionally 1737. The date the River Dee Canal was first used. From 1771–92, the Trap was successfully run by Jonathan Catherall II and his mother Martha (d.1792). On her death the Trap was taken over by the heir, John Catherall, and continued working until his death in 1805. Inconveniently it was left to his nine children in equal shares, which were not consolidated until 1842 when they acquired by Cynric Lloyd of Pontruffydd Hall, near Bodfari. After thus being alienated from the Catherall family Jonathan II's descendants gradually gained repossession in a somewhat round about way.

Jonathan Catherall II (1761–1833) from T.Cropper Buckley and District.

The ownership of Jonathan Catherall II's interests in the Trap and Ewloe Place brickworks in the second half of the nineteenth century was influenced by the marital relationship of William Catherall (1798–1875), the heir of Jonathan Catherall II, and William Shepherd (d.1866).

William Shepherd was an enterprising, self-made man, who bought out his employer at the Trap, Cynric Lloyd, in the 1850s. In 1854 William Catherall was in financial difficulties and assigned his lease in Ewloe Place brickworks to William Shepherd. When the lease came up for renewal in 1863, William Catherall assigned it between William Shepherd, William Roberts Catherall, his natural son, and his half-brother, Timothy Catherall. Shepherd's daughter, Mary, married in 1848 William Catherall Roberts, (1827–1902), the illegitimate son of William Catherall. Another Shepherd daughter, Sarah, married Timothy Catherall in 1854. On the death of William Shepherd in 1866 the Trap Works was sold by auction and bought by William Catherall Roberts. As his brother Timothy died in 1876, he was left sole proprietor of the Ewloe Place works and in 1895 the business became Catherall and Company Ltd.

The second Catherall Works was **Ewloe Place (site two)**, opened by Jonathan Catherall II in 1793. It was adjacent to the Trap Works and its clay hole is known as the Trap Pool. Jonathan II was succeeded by his son William Catherall (1798–1875), the father of William Catherall Roberts, who in turn was followed by his son William Catherall Shepherd, (1871–1938). The Ewloe Place Works closed in 1914.

The Lane End Works (site three), was opened by William Hancock II (1762–1832), in partnership with William Rigby, Iron Founder of Hawarden. Hancock was a cousin to Jonathan Catherall II. The Rigby-Hancock partnership was a masterstroke in entrepreneurship and laid the foundation of an enterprise which dominated and led the clay industry in Buckley until its closure in 2005. Judiciously making use of leases of clay, coal and a railroad from the Glynne Estate, other leases from the Lords of Mold and Dundas of Aston Hall, they launched a frontal assault on the Buckley Coal and Firebrick Industries. During the course of its existence the Lane End Works continued to expand and was the largest in Buckley.[11] The firm bought land from the Mold Enclosure Commissioners in 1800 and built a Pottery at Daisy Hill adjacent to their brickworks. They had interests in local collieries and the Buckley Smelt, nearby. The Rigby Hancock partnership was dissolved in 1817. Four William Hancocks followed each other as head of the firm until the family connection ceased in 1933.

Trap Works. The Pool and Hope Anchor.
[Buckley Library]

Hancock's Lane End, c.1905.
Postcard [Buckley Library]

The opening of **Knowl Lane Works (site four)**[12] was due to the enterprise of William Leach, the nephew of Thomas Jones of Farm Stile. Here seventeen acres of land between Church Road, Knowl Lane, and Mount Pleasant Farm was proved to be in a prime position in the clay beds. Six kilns were working there in 1815. By 1822 the Works was leased to Mather Parkes & Co. who owned it for nearly twenty years until it was sold to Richard Ashton, a Liverpool merchant.

In 1842 William Hancock & Co. opened **Mount Pleasant Brickworks (site five)** which was developed to become a good-sized yard with nine kilns.

John Smalley and William and Mary Williamson established brickmaking at **Old Ewloe Works (site six)** in 1818. The Works was sold to William Pownall in 1842, who, in turn, sold it to Charles Davison in November 1843 for £900. At that time it was described as 'a Firebrick and Tile Manufactory with six kilns capable of burning 800 bricks each.' Charles Davison was a merchant who lived at Shotton Cottage. Before he died about 1850 he opened another brick works close by in 1847, which was known as **Ewloe Barn, (site seven)**. The Old Ewloe Works was linked to the River by the Aston Hall tramway, but Ewloe Barn was too far away for such a connection.

Another newcomer by 1850 was John Royle and Sons who opened **Etna Brickworks (site eight)**. This too was linked to the tramway.

The early development of the industry is shown in advertisements in the *Chester Chronicle*. The great step forward took place in the 1790s. Hancock announced on Boxing Day 1794.

It having hitherto been the practice of manufacturing of Fire Brick and Tile in a few Summer months only – the Public have been at a loss the major part of the year to get supplied, to obviate which Messrs Hancock and Company have at a considerable expense erected sheds of a peculiar construction, by means of which they will be able to manufacture their products in all seasons. Any demands for any of the above articles will be speedily supplied on very reasonable terms. Messrs Hancock & Co. can particularly recommend them as they are manufactured in the neatest manner, and the material is ground exceedingly fine by means of a new steam engine – Common & Key Bricks, 9" to 12" tiles, Malt or Kiln Blocks, Ridge tiles, upon a new plan and exceedingly durable, coping for walls, etc., and any other articles in the trade made in any form or dimension according to order on ten days notice.

Hancock's new methods increased production by the use of steam power,

Old Ewloe Fire-brick and Tile Works letterhead.
[Buckley Society Archive]

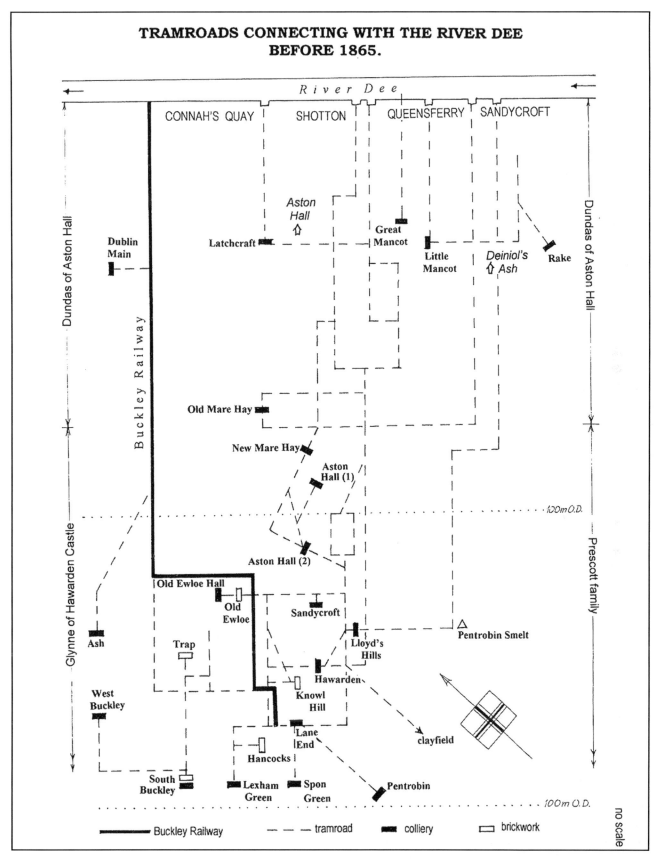

Sandycroft and Aston Tramways[K. Lloyd Gruffydd]

Etna Brickworks 'Davison's Top Yard'. [Buckley Library]

drying sheds, the ability to manufacture all the year round, and meet orders promptly as well as supplying a great variety of products.

Catherall's followed suit by leasing a Works which was advertised in 1810 as having:

> … a right of rail and road to the River Dee with twenty five acres of land, three cottages for workmen, a stable and workshop, average profits £600 a year; and that by erecting a steam engine to grind the clay considerable expense might be saved. There are nine kilns, three clay mills, and three sheds with flues under to dry the articles in the wet seasons.[13]

Good communications were absolutely necessary for the development of the industry. The railroad became the handmaid to the brick kiln. It was to this problem that Rigby and Hancock addressed themselves. Before the growth of national railways in the 1840s, in the absence of local canals, the quickest means of transport was by the nearest navigable river. The Dee channel made in 1737 was only a few miles down hill, with a full load, from the Buckley clay field. By the middle of the eighteenth century wooden tramroads with horse drawn trucks trundled their way to the river. Cargoes of coal were carried from Sandycroft Colliery, Lloyd's Hill, via Moor Lane Hawarden, to the loading point on the River known as Sandycroft Mark, This was under an agreement between Sir John Glynne, John Dutton and Walter Stubbs.[14] This colliery, with others, was leased by the Glynne estate to Rigby and Hancock, together with the first tramroad, named Sandycroft number one. They immediately began to lay a more durable system built of iron, Sandycroft Rail Road number two, which ran for the length of 4¹/₂ miles to the riverside at Sandycroft Wharf, passing through Glynne property virtually the whole of its route. This railroad was in operation until about 1840.

Another route to the river was through the lands of the Dundas family, heirs to the Whitleys, of Aston Hall. This northerly approach to the river at Queensferry was more direct. An iron railroad, the Aston Tramroad, was built in stages. Stage one was the work of Leach and Company in 1799 and ran for 1¹/₄ miles. Willett reported that they built:

> … an iron railway through the Aston Estate, down to the River for the discharge of their Collieries, and these works together generally employed four hundred and fifty men, and raised annually 72,000 tons of coals, by means of twelve Steam Engines, from seven horse power, to sixty horse power.[15]

Leach & Co added another length after 1809 to Higgins Croft. Eventually Hancock & Co. completed the tramroad link between Buckley and Queensferry by connecting it to the sections laid down by Leach & Co. Hancock & Co. operated this tramroad as the Buckley Railway Company from about 1840 until it ceased to work on 9 August 1869. By the late 1860s it only carried the traffic of those who refused to patronise the new Buckley Railway opened in 1862.

With the growth in the number of collieries and brickworks each was dependent on gaining access to the Dundas and Glynne Tramroads. This was done by means of horse drawn tramways to the junction with the main tramroad and this principle of making sidings to the main route became the basis of the early Buckley transport system.

Bentley described the way in which the Aston Tramroad was linked to Buckley brickworks and collieries:

Large exchange and marshalling sidings were constructed. Branches proceeded across Bunker's Hill to the Mount Pleasant brickworks and along the Tram Road to serve Catherall's and other brickworks and collieries. Another branched off to the Lane End Collieries, and another to the chain of Little Mountain Collieries, whilst the main road proceeded under a curved tunnel into Lane End brickworks. Branches went to Spon Green, Lexham Green and to Hancock's Pottery on Daisy Hill.

A tavern with associations with the tramway was the Grandstand, Burntwood, which was demolished as recently as 1969. The tramline from the Mountain over Drury Lane met the tramway from Knowle Hill near the tavern before proceeding down the Dinghouse Wood to Aston Hall. A door in the inn was adjacent to the line and this provided an easy means whereby colliers and carters could obtain drink unnoticed before rejoining their loads. It was nicknamed Tram Door'.[16]

A third route to the river was by cart from Buckley to Connah's Quay. This route was unsuitable; it broke the coal and was not good for the carriage of earthenware.

Most of the Buckley brick and coal masters resented their dependence on the owners of the railroads to whom they had to pay tonnage and wharfage charges. One master in particular, Charles Davison, reacted to the actions of Admiral Dundas and proceeded against him.[17] This quarrel led to proposals for a new railway to Connah's Quay, which no longer relied on access to the river through Dundas land.

The value of the Aston tramroad to the brickmakers in the period up to 1860 is seen by an examination of a statement of account of the brick and coal tonnage on the tramroad for six years from 1850–6. It shows that it was used by all the brickworks.[18] The low figures shown for Catherall's suggest that they were using more than one transport route. As would be expected, Hancock's were the chief users. Over the six year period their figure for coal was 117,493 tons. This figure is made up from their brickworks at Lane End, 113,372 tons and Mount Pleasant (over three years) 12,661 tons. No figures for other coal proprietors are given. Hancock's would have consumed a considerable amount of their coal to fire their kilns. Hancock's other competitors amongst the brickmakers were Ashton & Co. at 71,948 tons, and Davison & Co. 38,612 tons. This figure would account for carriage from Old Ewloe only. William Shepherd manager of

The remains of Buckley's tramways. Investigations by James Bentley. [Buckley Library]

Ewloe Barn had no access to the Aston tramroad and carted his goods to his own wharf at Queensferry. In 1858 the tonnage was 12,084 tons,[19] which places Davison's next to Hancock's in the figures we have available to assess the production figures of the Buckley brickmakers at the end of the period up to 1860. The total for Royle & Son was 18,687.

Surviving accounts for Catherall's show that they exported large quantities of earthenware, firebricks, slop bricks, kiln tiles, pottery etc all around the Welsh Coast and across to Ireland.[20] A letter from the Railway Office, Conway, 27 August 1845, to Catheralls, shows the briskness of the trade as a result of the building of the Chester to Holyhead railway. 'We are wanting some 90,000 Blue Metal Bricks on our Railway Contract here. Could you let me have a vessel load immediately'.[21] Another order, in September 1848, from Morfa Copper Works, Anglesey, requested : 'We will thank you to load the 'Hafod', for Captain Green, with a cargo of 30,000 of your large size fire bricks for delivery at the Rose Copper Works'.

There is no doubt that the Buckley coal and brick industry was spared the severity of the years of depression experienced in the trade by the demands of the railway contractors. The coal fired the kilns, which produced millions of blue bricks used in the construction of bridges, culverts, stations, etc. in England, Wales and Ireland. Dennis Griffiths reckoned that 'in the ten years between 1841–51 the traffic from Buckley increased 250%: bricks, coal and pottery being carried in proportions 60% bricks and pottery and 40% coal. At this time there were some 250 little ships of 50 to 80 tons register regularly trading from Queensferry for North and South Wales, London and Ireland, with Buckley goods. About two and a half

million Buckley handmade blue brindled bricks were used in the building of Britannia and Tubular Bridges by Robert Stephenson at Menai to carry the Railway to Holyhead. Buckley brick, number 18 was selected, from 48 in tests to reveal a crushing strength of 2130.3% lbs. per square inch. The backing of the walls were built with firebrick from Buckley'.[22]

In 1852 Hancock's announced that they 'feel desirous of acquainting the public generally that with the increased space and facilities which they now possess, they can supply much larger quantities than heretofore of all bricks, tiles etc.'[23] The growth in business was reflected by the fact that Hancock's had branches for their coal and brick trade at

Britannia Tubular Bridge over the Menai Straits, 1849 Lithograph by George Hawkins.

Queensferry, Chester and Liverpool. By the end of the nineteenth century they were trading with firms in New Orleans, New York, and Galveston, Texas. Company records show that goods were sent as far as Canada, British Guyana, New Foundland, Las Palmas, Manilla, Australia, Palestine, Peru, Brazil, India, China and Japan.

2. The Middle Period 1860–1920: Railways

The Buckley Railway, 1860. Its incorporation in the Wrexham, Mold & Connah's Quay Railway, 1873

The growing dissatisfaction with the monopoly of Hancock and Dundas in the running of the Aston tramroad led to the formation of a strong lobby for the building of a new railway link between Buckley and the port of Connah's Quay.

The lobby achieved its purpose and a Parliamentary Bill for the Buckley & Connah's Quay Railway with power to join the Chester and Holyhead Line was submitted in November 1859 and received the Royal Assent on 14 June 1860. The railway was opened on 7 June 1862. The prospectus rehearsed in a succinct and persuasive manner the cost, purpose and advantage of the new railway taking the opportunity to undermine the Aston tramroad:

The object of this Company is to establish a railway communication between Buckley, an important district for the manufacture of Bricks, Tiles, &c., where there is an extensive Coal-field, and Connah's Quay, the best shipping place on the river Dee.

The present mode of transit is by carts to the Queen's Ferry Station on the Chester Holyhead Railway, and by a common and very defective Tramway, worked by horses, to a shipping place on the river Dee, above the Queen's Ferry.

The advantages offered by a Railway from Buckley to Connah's Quay are acknowledged by all the Brickmasters and Colliery proprietors (excepting, of course, the firm interested in the existing Tramway), and the scheme will have their entire support. They are prepared to subscribe largely, and are ready, in addition, if required, to enter into an arrangement to send their traffic along the line for a term of years, thus not only giving the best evidence of their confidence in the soundness of the undertaking, but establishing it as an investment.

A careful survey has been made of the line. It will be of the easiest description, no expensive works being required on any part of it. The main line will be about four miles, and the branches into the different Brickyards and Collieries about a mile in length.

No difficulties are anticipated with the landowners.

The estimated cost, including Parliamentary expenses of the line, with the necessary sidings and plant, is £28,000.

That this line would be the means of rapidly increasing the Coal trade in its vicinity, and of developing the resources of an important mineral district, no one can doubt; the facilities and advantages afforded by a communication with the Chester and Holyhead Railway, and also of shipping at the best shipping place on the river Dee, being obvious.

Returns have been carefully prepared showing the existing traffic of the district, from the brickworks, potteries, and collieries, whose support can be relied upon; upwards of 70,000 tons are now annually exported, the whole of this would be sent along the proposed line.

Estimates have also been prepared, with the assistance of the brickmasters and colliery proprietors, of the increased traffic from existing works that would undoubtedly be created by the formation of this railway. The collieries alone would be enabled to export 70,000 additional tons annually, and from the Brickworks and Potteries there would be annual increase of 20,000 tons at least.

The promoters have entirely omitted from their calculations any anticipated revenue from collieries and works which would certainly be opened after the formation of the railway. They have confined their estimates entirely to the present produce of existing works, and to what they are capable of producing, if they are possessed of the advantages of railway communication.

The chief mode of transit at present from the brickworks and potteries is by the very defective tramway of Messrs. Dundas and Hancock, which has the disadvantage of having its shipping stage two miles higher up the river, thus causing a delay of twenty-four hours, as laden vessels starting from this Quay are not able to proceed beyond Connah's Quay in one tide. The rates for the use of this tramway, coupled with the cost of haulage and wharfage, average $4^1/2d.$ per ton per mile; the charge for the use of the proposed Railway, together with haulage and wharfage, would be 3d. per ton per mile. Assuming that the annual traffic would be 100,000 tons only. This at 3d. per ton per mile would produce a revenue of £5,000, from which must be deducted a sum of £1,936 for expenses of management, engines, gatekeepers, breaksmen, station-men, maintenance of way, renewals and all other expenses — thus leaving a net revenue of £3,064, which gives a dividend of nearly 11 per cent.

The promoters believe that the superiority of this Line would ultimately secure to it the entire trade of the district, and this would, of course, materially increase the dividend above mentioned. Applications for further particulars and shares may be made to Mr Roberts, Solicitor, Mold.[24]

Davison's were not slow to follow up the propaganda of the prospectus with a panegyric advertisement published for two successive weeks shortly after the opening of the railway:

Messrs. Charles Davison & Co., Firebrick & Tile Manufacturers, Buckley Mountain, have the pleasure to inform their friends that both their works at Buckley are now in direct communication with the LNWR by means of the Buckley & Connah's Quay Railway just opened. It enables goods to be delivered direct from the Works to various stations and sidings and renders loading and unloading from carts and tram-wagons un-necessary…Connah's Quay is three miles nearer Holyhead than Dundas' Sidings where the bulk of bricks sent

ANNO VICESIMO TERTIO

VICTORIÆ REGINÆ.

•••

Cap. lxxxix.

An Act for making a Railway from *Buckley* to *Connah's Quay* in the County of *Flint*, and for other Purposes.   [14th *June* 1860.]

WHEREAS the making of Railways from *Buckley* to *Connah's Quay* adjoining the River *Dee* in the County of *Flint*, and also to connect with the *Chester and Holyhead* Railway in the Parish of *Northop*, would be of public and local Advantage: And whereas the Persons herein-after named, with others, are willing, at their own Expense, to carry such Undertaking into execution, but the same cannot be effected without the Authority of Parliament: May it therefore please Your Majesty that it may be enacted; and be it enacted by the Queen's most Excellent Majesty, by and with the Advice and Consent of the Lords Spiritual and Temporal, and Commons, in this present Parliament assembled, and by the Authority of the same, as follows:

I. "The Companies Clauses Consolidation Act, 1845," "The Lands 8 & Clauses Consolidation Act, 1845," and "The Railways Clauses Con- cc. solidation Act, 1845," (save so far as any of the Clauses and Provisions and thereof respectively are expressly excepted or varied by this Act,) shall be incorporated with and form Part of this Act.
     [*Local.*]   13 Y   II. The

Title page. The Buckley Railway Act 1860.

by rail is usually loaded…In future Connah's Quay will be used as a shipping port instead of Queens Ferry-its superiority over other places on the Dee is well known and needs no comment.

Packing for Shipping. Bricks and tiles will be put into boxes on wheels at the Works, placed on the top of a railway truck and lowered by a crane into the hold of a vessel, thus entirely preventing the snipping and breakage unavoidably caused by four or five handlings.

These facilities cannot be offered by any other manufacturer as none of the other firms have availed themselves of the facilities of the new railway…[25]

Two significant points emerge from Davison's announcement. The first is that contrary to claims made in the prospectus there was no support initially for the new Railway from the local businessmen. No doubt this would soon follow under the influence of P. B. Davies-Cooke who invested £8,000 in the project and as chief landowner controlled the clay leases. The prospectus was correct in its anticipation of new works after the formation of the railway and within the next five years brickworks opened and the Watkinsons from Halifax acquired considerable colliery interests in the Buckley area. The second point concerns the use made by Davison of shipping boxes for conveying and loading their produce. This was an important feature of the Buckley trade in clay goods. George Lewis described them:

For shipment at Connah's Quay each works owned its own railway trucks, called 'shippers'. These trucks had only ends and no sides, and were fitted with tramway lines of the same gauge as the tramway along which the horses brought the goods in the small, sideless trucks, known as shipping boxes, which were pushed straight onto the railway trucks instead of having to be unloaded. At the four top corners of the ends of the shipping boxes were eyelets into which sling hooks could be fixed, and the box was then lifted and lowered into the hold of the vessel to be unloaded by men sent from the brickworks (known as shippers or stowers) who knew how to stack the bricks correctly in the ship.[26]

The Buckley & Connah's Quay Railway was soon to be part of the Wrexham, Mold & Connah's Quay Railway (WMCQR), the first sod of which was cut by Catherine Gladstone at Wrexham on 22 October 1862. After uncertainty about the suitability of the temporary Buckley station, the line from Wrexham to Connah's Quay came into being with a trial run on 30 April 1866. The *Chester Chronicle* reported:

On Monday last directors and friends of this undertaking had a trip to Buckley and Connah's Quay previous to the formal opening of the line for passenger traffic. On the following day between 600–700 persons availed themselves of the opportunity of having a trip gratis and soon after 10 am the train started, calling at the different stations on the line which were decorated with flags and banners etc. After enjoying themselves the train returned after 2 pm bringing a great number of people from Connah's Quay, Buckley and neighbourhood.

However, the next day, passenger traffic was limited to the Wrexham–Buckley stretch with the line from Buckley–Connah's Quay confined to goods carriage. This is not surprising because this latter stretch had its inadequacies. It could be the euphemistic statement of the Prospectus should have been a warning when it stated 'the line will be of the easiest description, no expensive works being required on it'. But what could you expect on a budget of less than £30,000.

Boyd is extremely critical of the very primitive and basic condition of the Buckley Railway and calls it 'a strange line', 'a most idiosyncratic institution'. Its limitations were all too apparent particularly in its lack of resources. The rolling stock consisted of two locomotives and two-brake vans, and it owned no wagons. The company had no buildings, warehouses, goods sheds, nor stations; there was a small office on the dockside at Connah's Quay.[27] Boyd's description of the route from Buckley Junction is fascinating for the picture it gives of the intensity of industrial development and its variety:

> Buckley itself was approaching, unmistakable for its clusters of brick ovens, open-sided buildings, stacks of finished bricks, pipes, and all manner of associated clayware; and many of these buildings, as the railway drew nearer them could be seen hanging precariously on the cliffs above deep claypits.

Shipping wagon and shipping box.
Drawing by Ken Lloyd Gruffydd.

From the bowels of such buildings emerged inclined tramways which fell, cable-operated, into the same pits to spew out in all directions on the floor of the excavation. Mixed in amongst this anthill of chimneys, ovens, kilns, waterlogged lagoons of former pits, domestic dwellings and chapels, the Buckley line found its way; branches and sidings made junction with it at a score of trans-shipment platforms, each having a separate identity. And as if variety thereby was insufficient, here and there a coalmine with its winding gear loomed tall among the chimneys of the clay-linked businesses.[28]

The Port of Connah's Quay

This is at the head of the Dee Channel of 1737 which was made to give a sufficient draught of water to take sailing vessels to the Port of Chester. Connah's Quay had the advantage over creeks lower down the river because of the depth of water and its approach on one tide. In 1784 Thomas Pennant noted its development: 'of late years a very handsome pier has been built by the River Dee Company, jutting into the channel for the protection of ships bound to and from Chester under which they take shelter in bad weather or adverse winds'.[29]

The growth of the Port at Connah's Quay was stimulated by the building of the Wepre Iron Road in 1799 to Dublin Main Colliery at Northop Hall, and the arrival of the Chester–Holyhead railway in 1848. In 1865 the WMCQR began to develop docks, wharves and railway sidings and goods were also transferred onto the Chester & Holyhead Railway. Twenty years later the WMCQR was conveying 640,000 tons of coal annually of which 100,000 tons was shipped from the port and the rest consumed locally. For this trade Watkinson's were providing 150,000 tons of coal annually. The port shipped firebricks to Liverpool to be stored before being exported all over the world.

Connah's Quay had its limitations. Berthing space was limited, there was great deal of delay. Goods could only be loaded when the tide was right, and the capacity was limited to vessels of about 600 tons. In 1881, 135 ships called there and discharged 25,000 tons, or about 185 tons per ship.[30]

A number of Buckley brickmasters were quick to take advantage of ship building opportunities provided by Ferguson, McCallum & Baird. Charles Davison & Co. owned 15 sailing vessels. In 1864 William Shepherd bought a 72-ton schooner named after him. Gibson's had a vessel aptly called *Problem*, in collision in 1868, damaging the *Earnest* at a cost of 37s. In the following year Captain John Owen of the *Problem* was accused of 'grossly misconducting himself by leaving the vessel for three weeks in Liverpool Docks and going drinking' and as a result he was discharged. The *Problem*, a schooner, cost £569, and was judged to be 'earning a good return and proving a great convenience and assistance'.[31]

Hancock's had a number of vessels launched at Connah's Quay in the 1860s, all of them in some style. The *Mary Caroline*, a schooner of 150 tons, was described as:

one of the finest specimens of modern build, and there is every probability that she was one of the fastest clippers which the River Dee can boast of. Captain James Coppack commands her. The launch was performed by Mrs Hancock. Through the liberality of the respected owner, five shillings was given to every vessel in the harbour, and the workmen with others, numbering about 70, were treated to dinner at the Ship Inn.[32]

Another vessel, the *Florence Emily*, followed in April 1865, and a year later the Padeswood of 160 tons. An example of the close connection between William Hancock and the Glynne estate was seen in July 1867 with the launch of two ships, *Mary and Gertrude* and the *Glynne*. 'The ceremony of christening was ably and graciously performed by the Misses Glynne and Sir Stephen Glynne, landlord of the extensive works of W. Hancock & Co. after whom the vessels were called. A large party numbering 200 sat down in a spacious marquee erected in the grounds of the Ship Inn to a substantial dinner liberally given by Mr Hancock and served up in Captain Coppack's best style'.

Expansion in the 1860s

The hopes of the railway promoters were more than fulfilled in the decade which followed by the establishment of ten brickworks and the development of George Watkinson's & Sons colliery interests.

In 1861 Edward Parry (1806–73) established a brickworks, **Ewloe Barn (site nine)** across the road from Davison's works of the same name, on sixteen acres leased from the Gwysaney estate. It developed by 1912 to comprise 11 kilns. Edward Parry, born in Ireland, gained experience as a young man in Buckley as manager of a colliery and brickworks. He was much respected in the community as a Wesleyan Methodist serving the cause as a lay preacher. When he died, the business was managed by his sons, George, Thomas, and Robert Parry. George played a prominent part in the affairs of Buckley Urban District Council. In 1923 George's son, George Edward Armstrong Parry, along with Arthur Davies of Oaks Farm, were co-managers.

Drury, Sandycroft Brickworks (site ten) was established sometime in the 1860s. In the 1870s it was known as the Sandycroft Colliery, Brick, Tile and Pottery Co., at the time it was taken over by Samuel Ward. In 1878 the firm advertised blue and white firebricks and buff facing bricks. From 1889–1901 the owners were John and Charles Wycherley and Samuel Higginbottom. Charles Wycherley took control in 1901 and closed the colliery while retaining the brickworks. In 1913 it was known as Drury Lane Brick and Tile Co.

Knowl Hill (site eleven) or Hancock's **New Mount Brickworks**, as it was also known, was built about 1864. There is some mystery about its duration as a brickworks because of its irregular working life. George Lewis was of the opinion 'that it was constructed with ultra modern features which would have created serious unemployment problems in the local industry'. In 1895 the *Chester Chronicle* speculated that Hancock's erected the works under some pressure from the landowner Sir Stephen Glynne (d.1874), who thought 'that it was desirable for Mr Hancock to erect new works and unless he was prepared to do so he would have to consider letting the land for this purpose to some other firm'. Hancock admitted that he erected the new works to stifle competition; the decision turned out to be short sighted and for twenty five years the works stood idle until, in 1889, a tramway was constructed and the buildings repaired with the intention of extracting new light

Connah' Quay Wharf.
[FRO PH/15/51]

Buckley Railways & Brickworks in the nineteenth century from Buckley Society Magazine drawn by Ken Lloyd Gruffydd.

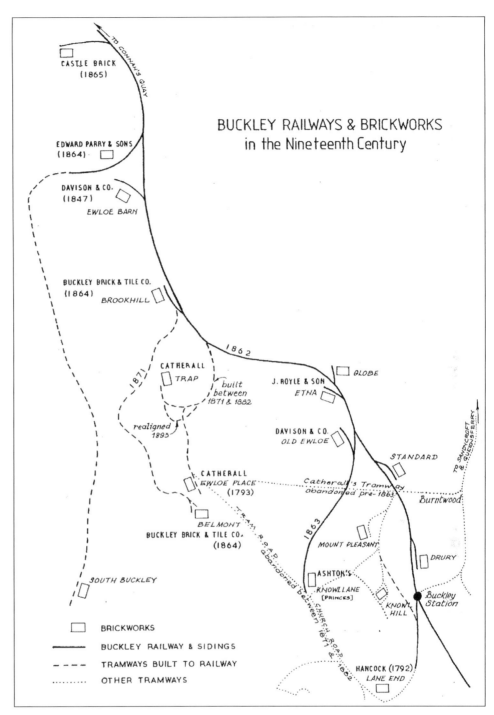

BUCKLEY RAILWAYS & BRICKWORKS
in the Nineteenth Century

clay.[32] Nothing came of this and the buildings were used by a local farmer for stalling his animals. The 1881 OS map shows two long sheds with 3 kilns on either side. It had a very tall chimney, 225 feet high which was built by Buckley craftsmen, members of the Humphreys family. The distinctive brickwork had four spirals of white bricks snaking their way to the top which gave it the colloquial name of 'Candy stick chimney'. The top was crowned with a large overhanging coping. Here, it was said, that on completion of the chimney, members of the Buckley Town Band were hoisted to the brim to perform a celebratory piece.[34] It was demolished in 1941 as a hazard to aircraft and a landmark to the enemy.

Brookhill (site twelve) and Belmont (site thirteen) were part of the Buckley Brick and Tile Co. Ltd. This company was started in 1863 and incorporated in 1865, with the amalgamation of Buckley Draining Pipe Works with the new enterprise at Brookhill.

The Upper Works, Brookhill, was built alongside the Buckley railway, with road access through the Trap Works. Belmont, the Lower Works, was about a mile south west and was connected to Brookhill in 1871 by Meakin's tramway which ran via the Willow Colliery. Meakin was responsible for building the plant for the new works with both eventually using seven kilns. Belmont had two chimneys, but Brookhill's first chimney was blown down in the gales of December 1866. It was 105 feet high and was toppled at 1 a.m. one Friday completely destroying the offices and stabling adjoining. There was a house under the same roof as the office where a carter with his wife and three children lived. They escaped without injury.

Edward Parry Junior was appointed manager but was soon replaced by John Merriman Gibson in June 1867. His influence was to dominate the Buckley Brick and Tile Co. for the next sixty years so that the works was known locally as 'Gibson's'. Born in Hexham, Gibson first served as a regular soldier before coming to the Company as its representative. His background as a soldier led him to form the 1st Flintshire Volunteer Royal Engineers in which he held the rank of major. Its headquarters were in Buckley. Conservative in politics, he met with the approval and support of John Watkinson the local coal magnate. Life was not easy in the brick trade, as we shall see later, and both Brookhill and Belmont had their disadvantages. Brookhill suffered from a shortage of water in dry seasons when it had to be carried in casks by tramway from its sister works. The access to Belmont was not easy but its closure in 1912 came as a result of the exhaustion of its clay supply.

Railway sidings Drury Brickworks.[Buckley Society Archive David Jagger Collection]

The company manufactured a wide range of goods: facing bricks, boiler blocks, flue covers, tiles for paving and roofing, maltkilns, bacteria beds, finials, and terra cotta of various hues, troughing and chimney pots. They marketed a pressed 'metalline' brick tested for crushing strain which was not broken until a pressure of 569 tons per square feet; as well as the famous brand of acid resisting clay goods, 'Gibsonite'.[35]

Castle Fire Brick Co. Ltd (site fourteen) was established in 1865 by George Herbert Alletson (1841–1922), of Boughton Grange, Chester. The company was incorporated in 1875, with six of the seven directors of Irish origin. The object of the company was to acquire and work the Castle Fire Brickworks, Plas Bellin Colliery and Northop Hall Colliery. The Wepre tramway had been taken over by the recently arrived Buckley–Connah's Quay Railway.[36] The refractory goods produced at Castle Fire Brick throughout the nineteenth century were similar to the other Buckley manufactures.[37]

South Buckley Coal and Firebrick Co. Ltd (site fifteen)[38] was built in 1866 with a capital of £5,000 when entrepreneurs from Rochdale and Manchester developed new brickworks on a colliery site. In July 1881 it was sold to the newly incorporated North and South Buckley Colliery, Brick and Tile Co. Ltd. The new owners improved the site considerably and a large brickworks with 17 round kilns is shown on OS 1899 and 26 on OS 1912. The fire-clay was mined at the adjacent colliery. The South Buckley Rock Brick Co., under which title, it is later recorded, achieved some success at the London Building Exhibition of 1892 when the *Clay Worker Journal* remarked:

> The South Buckley Rock Brick Co. has just produced a new manufacture. They now produce coloured glazed bricks of all tints, which have been very successful. The glaze is so thoroughly burnt that it becomes part of the brick itself. Specimens of these glazed bricks were the chief feature of their exhibit.[39]

With the closure of the colliery in 1909, the clay was obtained from the north site and renamed the West Buckley Colliery.

The Buckley Brick and Tile Co. Group of workers from Brookhill 1884. John Philip Gibson and John Merriman Gibson are standing at the extreme left and right of the main group. [FRO PH 11/213]

Dennis Griffiths described their manufacturing method:

Their process was dry-pan grinding, the clay passing through fine sieves of the piano-wire type. The works had an up to date mixing shop, where the various constituents for glazing or annealing the bricks were carefully weighed and mixed prior to the sides and edges of the bricks being dipped into the liquid 'slip' of cream constituency. The bricks were of a light buff variety, similar to those of the Aston Hall type, largely used in Southport and Llandrindod Wells.

Until the last few years, South Buckley bricks were of the biscuit type. The process was for the bricks to be burnt in kilns to a low temperature, just sufficient to harden them and extract a sufficient shrinkage, or contraction, for the glaze to harden. Many bricks were also salt glazed in brown and other colours. South Buckley enjoyed a large trade with a national reputation. It was a big blow to the industry when South Buckley closed in 1914.[40]

Aston Hall Colliery & Brick Works Co. Ltd (site sixteen). Between 1866–68 the brickworks was leased to Kershaw & Co. The site was developed further in 1869 to work the fire-clay below the coal, and when large sheds were erected and the capacity of two of the kilns increased to a capability of 25,000 bricks each. The 1881 OS map showed two oblong kilns and an aerial photograph of 1923, three oblong kilns and nine round kilns. In 1869 W. E. Gladstone purchased the Aston Hall Estate from the Dundas Trustees. Amongst its assets was the potential for mining coal and extracting clay. This was recognised by the *Mining Journal* in December 1871 when they commented that the resources of coal and clay were of 'excellent quality'.[41]

In 1878 a new company was formed with Alexander Ward as manager. It produced the well-regarded Aston buff bricks described as 'a beautiful rich coloured yellowish brick', being noted 'for retaining their original colour and for not vegetating as is the case with soft, common bricks. The electric light has been placed

Belmont. The sister works of the Buckley Brick and Tile Co. The Clayhole, 1894. [FRO PH 11/215]

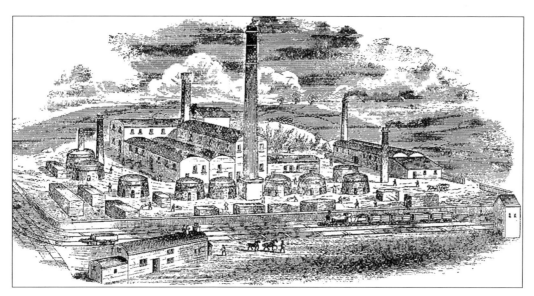

The Castle Fire Brick Co. c.1900.
[FRO D/DM/355/18]

throughout the works, and manufacture now goes on day and night'.[42] At the turn of the century they produced mostly buff bricks and floor tiles. The colliery closed in 1909 depriving the brickworks of its source of clay and brought working on the site to an end.

Thomas Jones, Pentre (site seventeen). James Bentley describes it as 'a small family brickworks employing two or three workers with two round kilns. It was situated at the rear of Pentrobin Methodist Chapel, Burntwood. It was in use for about twenty years from about 1870'. Andrew Connolly designates it as Charles Jones, Brickworks, and states that 'Charles Jones owned the land, the adjacent house and built the small brickworks which had two kilns. On the Land Valuation Map of 1912 it was described as the 'site of an old brickworks' in the occupation of Charles Jones. Brickworks was established c 1879 and lasted until 1905. Charles Jones was the manager of Sandycroft Brickworks in 1889'.[43]

Globe Brickworks (site eighteen). Very little is known about this brickworks. It appears to have been of very modest size and was working in 1878 when Mr Joseph Griffiths was manager. It was leased by Charles Davison & Co in 1891. By 1904 the clay supplies were diminishing rapidly and it was closed by 1911. An attempt to continue work on the site was made, as George Lewis, noted:

> 1911 April 24 Mon. Work began at the Globe brickyard making Staffordshire Ware and a number of Staffordshire men and women have been employed there.
> 1916 May 22 Mon. They began to pull down the Globe brickyard.[44]

Standard Brick and Terra Cotta Co. Ltd (site nineteen) was established on a former site in 1886 by J. B. Gregory and T. Kenyon to utilise the underclass of Mount Pleasant Colliery. The OS Map of 1912 shows ten round and four oblong kilns and an aerial photograph of 1935, thirteen round kilns and four oblong kilns. The output in 1907 was 50,000 bricks per week, of which 20,000 were buff and 30,000 salt glazed or enamelled, and a wide range of ornamental tiles, paving, ridge tiles finials, garden edging, statuettes, vases and terra cotta.

In the twentieth century it became the **Standard Pipe Works**, of which more later.

Brickmasters and workers. Industrial relations

The growth in the industry in the 1860s led to the formation of the Buckley Brick and Tile Manufacturers Association in the 1870s[45] and abortive attempts by the workforce to establish a trades union. The years of boom of the 1860s were being submerged by depression in the 1870s. The closely associated coal and brick industries in Buckley were interdependent and both felt the affect of high wages when the price of products began to fluctuate and fall.

The Brickmasters Association consisted of representatives of seven of the main brick manufacturers — Wm. Hancock & Co., Chas. Davison & Co., Catherall & Company, Richard Ashton & Co., Edward Parry & Co., Buckley Brick & Tile Co., Castle Fire Brick Co. Although not members of the Association of Colliery Proprietors their interests were taken into account when necessary.

Their main strategy was expressed in a resolution of May 1870: 'that owing to the ruinous competition that has lately existed in the brick trade, all the Manufacturers agree to sell at uniform prices & terms which they respectively agree to'. To ensure that there was no confusion or disagreement about terms of sale and prices, printed circulars were distributed to customers giving the prices and sizes of Buckley fire-clay goods, which were revised whenever necessary.[46] The manufacturers treated with abhorrence any attempt by members to undercut agreed prices. Freight charges were fixed and the Association negotiated terms with and made complaints to the railway company about the methods of operating the WMCQ line.[47]

In April 1875 hours of working were mutually agreed to by employers when:

The Buckley Brick & Tile Company complained that Charles's Davison's day workmen were allowed to leave off work at five o'clock daily. It was decided that from the March Mold Fair until the October Mold Fair the hours worked by all the day workmen would be from six a.m. until five-thirty p.m. with half an hour for breakfast and one hour for dinner. On a Saturday there would be half an hour for dinner and the men would leave off work at three thirty p.m.

In July 1875 the Association united to reduce the wages of all their workers by 10% and repeated the exercise in September 1877 which was followed by a strike at Catherall's Ewloe Place. But union power in the Buckley industry remained weak probably on account of the comparatively small work force.

The Brickmasters Association was dissolved in November 1880 following a stormy meeting at the Black Lion in Mold. The proceedings of the meeting have not come to light. There is however no doubt that the Association brought a lasting uniformity to the Buckley clay industry by the adoption of standard practices and a united lobby to deal with the railway company.

The work force was in a more vulnerable position lacking bargaining powers in a market ruled by supply and demand with wages following prices. Strikes and stoppages were not uncommon. Strikes were not undertaken lightly because the workers lacked resources to maintain themselves in time of industrial action as in November 1845 when it was reported that at Buckley 'These extensive Brickworks are silent in consequence of the men holding out 'on strike' for an increase in wages. About 400 hands are now out of work, and most of whom are miserably poor, and have large families to maintain'.[48]

Earlier in the nineteenth century it was not unknown for colliers in the Denbighshire and Flintshire coalfield to become violent, as in the winter of 1830, or in the Mold riots of 1869. Two unusual incidents took place in the Buckley district in 1842, both involving men from Rigby & Hancock's, some were from the brickworks, the remainder were colliers. In April 1842 colliers gave rough justice to the agent from Lane End Colliery who failed to persuade them to adopt a larger sieve for the coal:

Mr Staley after vainly attempting to pacify them tried to pass through the mob to mount his horse, when he was violently seized and carried towards the railway formed for carrying coals to the River Dee at Queensferry. Here he was thrust into the bottom of a railway wagon and conveyed very much bruised along the line towards the river, the men on the way telling him he had not long to live, as they intended to drown him in the Dee. On arriving they stated that his life would be spared but only on condition of banishment to England. He was then placed in the ferry boat; the colliers threatening revenge if he ever dared to return.[49]

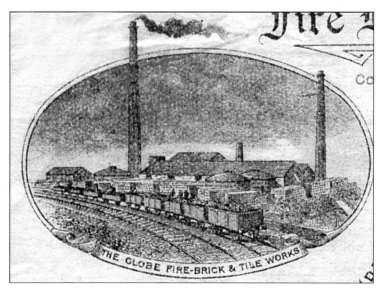

The Globe Fire-brick and Tile Works c.1900 letterhead [Buckley Society Archive]

Buckley Railway with view of Standard Pipe Works and Mount Pleasant Colliery 1957. [Buckley Society Archive]

A week later brickworkers attacked the property of Sir Stephen Glynne, Hancock's landlord, in a demonstration against supposed trade competition. It was reported that:

On Monday night a number of men and boys at least two hundred, stating themselves to be from Messrs Rigby and Hancock Brickworks, assembled in a field adjoining the dwelling-house of Mr Joseph Higgs, agent to Sir Stephen Glynne, but on finding that Mr Higgs was not at home, they prowled around the premises for a considerable time and after some of them had made an ineffectual attempt to force open the doors into the yard, they marched off and proceeded to near the village of Broughton where Mr Higgs had erected some buildings for the purpose of manufacturing tiles or draining shells for the use of the tenants on Sir Stephen's estates, which they quickly demolished, scattering the materials in all directions. It appears by a written document left on Mr Higgs premises, they had taken umbrage at his erecting these buildings and threatening if he persisted in going on with the works as he proposed, they would again visit him.[50]

In the 1870s there was no violence shown by the brickworkers . The pattern was reduction of wages by employers, reluctant strike action by the workforce, and a period of stand off, great misery of dependants, unsuccessful attempts to form a union and a return to work with nothing gained. In January 1874 it was announced that:

A notice of reduction of wages of 10% of kiln burners, and brick and tile makers was served last week upon the men employed in these Industries in the neighbourhood of Buckley. We hear it is likely however that they will not accept it, and that a strike will take place which will cause a great deal of hardship, and result in unemployment and a decrease in trade in the district.[51]

A month later there was an attempt at arbitration:

A meeting was convened by Mr Bell of Chester to arrange a meeting between masters and men to attempt to avoid a strike in the trade. They met at the Ship Inn at 5.30 pm and among the Masters were Messrs Hancock, Parry, Catherall, Davison, etc. and they occupied the parlour, and the men were in the room below. Mr Bell arbitrated between the two parties, but the Masters for three reasons refused to agree to withdraw their demand for a cut in wages. The first was the recent rise in the cost of coal, secondly the lower demands for goods and their lack of competitiveness because their prices were far too high. The Workers accused the employers of demanding higher prices for their goods, and denied that the prices of coal were higher. The meeting ended by the men refusing to work only at the present rates'.[52] Within a week the strike was over. 'It was at length agreed that the men resume work at the prices they left off at for a certain length of time, and at the expiration of that period, if the price of their goods did not increase they would suffer no reduction. It was also agreed that in future all disputes should be settled by arbitration, and not by strikes.[53]

In November 1877 the Brickmasters Association gave notice to their workers of a 10% wage reduction, the workers offered to take 5%. There was no agreement and all works were closed by strike action but after a week 'the men called it off as they see nothing but starvation facing them and their families. They have now gone to work at the full reduction demanded by their employers'.[54]

A year later the industry was again hit by a slump in trade and the men refused to accept a wage reduction with inevitable strike action. This time the men were out from the middle of December 1878 until February 1879. Serious efforts were made to reduce the hardship experienced by the workers and their families. A committee was organised to care for the starving with William Catherall as chairman supported by schoolmasters, doctors, and ministers of religion. Several hundred tickets were issued for soup and bread and fifteen tons of coal. Again the men returned to work empty handed. In 1880 there was another dispute with the workers being offered a 5% reduction. The brickmasters on this occasion were not unanimous, the first hint of the break up of their association. Hotheads sent to all employers a threatening letter enclosed with a drawing of skull and cross bones with a coffin.

Sir Stephen Glynne, Bart.(1807–74)
[FRO 28/B/21[

In 1879 a union was organised, known, during its brief life, as the Buckley Brickmakers Union. If a stoppage occurred either in the coal or brick industry there was hardship when scenes like those in 1893 were experienced. 'The Coal Strike in this area is making very slow progress to a settlement. The brickworks are now almost all at a standstill and the begging of food, especially by young lads, has been quite a common event, and the way the poor fellows devour what is given to them shows the reality of their wants.'[55]

During the brickworks strike of 1885 it was reported in the School Log Book 'many boys absent during the week picking blackberries. A strike amongst the brick makers, which is likely to affect school fees, commenced this week'.[56]

Indeed in 1875 the Inspector of Factories complained that a large number of children were employed at Ashton & Co. He regretted to say that the school attendance regulations had been entirely disregarded. A custom intensely disliked by the school authorities led to the following resolution in 1901.

That children whose parents want them to leave school before 12 o'clock for the purpose of taking dinners to the works for their parents or for others requiring their services — must present to the Head Teacher of their Department a written request to that effect, signed by the parent and by a foreman at the works or by a member of the School Board, and that such children shall be allowed to go out at 11.35.[57]

For some children the works was too close, too familiar and too tempting as a playground as in April 1890 when two young boys were hurt at Ashton's brickworks:

It appears they were in company with other boys playing in the dinner hour with the clay hole wagons, when one of these wagons overpowered them down an incline. It is a very common thing in all the brickworks for young persons to congregate together and play in dangerous places and with dangerous tools. When will the workmen come to think it is their duty to stop them?[58]

Severe frost continuing for any length of time could disrupt production and cause stoppage. In March 1855 the season was particularly cruel when it was reported:

Numbers of families having been in a state of extreme destitution, the Reverend Mr Wilkinson and others have done much to aid them. Admiral Dundas having been acquainted with the stoppage kindly sent £5, a seasonal and welcome donation. Such acts of charity cannot be too highly commended and do much to promote a kindly feeling between the rich and poor.

The same thing happened in 1873 and in the severe winters of the 1890s. In January 1893 it was noted that 'men are seen daily wandering about in large groups and while this weather continues they are hopeless of finding employment'. Two years later it was reported that 'Great distress is to be found in Buckley. Extreme poverty and starvation have been greatly exaggerated by the extremely cold weather over the last few weeks so much so that the Brickworks have had to close down causing severe unemployment'.

But good times were shared in this close-knit community as in October 1878 when:

> The proprietors of the new Globe Firebrick Works gave a supper of roast beef and plum pudding to the men and boys in their employ at the house of the Manager, Mr Joseph Griffiths. Twenty men and four boys partook of the excellent repast provided. After supper the Manager gave to each man and boy a piece of silver in lieu of beer, the firm being unwilling to encourage drinking. Songs were sung and votes of thanks were given to the firm for their kindness also to Mrs Griffiths who kindly prepared the supper. We are glad that this new company has set such a good example to the old firms and hope the latter will do likewise.[59]

New Railways

In twenty years, two new railways were opened on the south-eastern side of Buckley, both with the intent of serving the brick and coal industries. The first, the Aston Hall Colliery Railway, was opened on 16 August 1872. A single-line railway, it connected the colliery with the Chester and Holyhead portion of the LNWR and ran for about three miles, via Aston Bank, to Queensferry. It lasted as long as the colliery which was closed in 1909. The second line, the Hawarden Loop, is still in existence, outlasting the Buckley Railway, (absorbed by the Great Central Railway Co. in 1905 and closed in July 1965). It ran from Buckley Junction via Hawarden, Shotton High Level, with a branch to Connah's Quay, before which the railway crossed the Dee over Hawarden Bridge, opened in August 1889. This connected the WMCQ to Sir Edward Watkin's Manchester, Sheffield & Lincolnshire Railway. The advantages were described:

> The Hawarden branch or loop will doubtless afford more acceptable accommodation to the great brick, tile and drain manufacturers of the Buckley district, which will thus gain a direct outlet to the Manchester and Liverpool markets. Mr Gladstone has for many years advocated the establishment of a more direct route from the mineral districts of North Wales to the manufacturing centres of Lancashire and Yorkshire'.[60]

Over 300,000 Buckley bricks were used in the cutting near Shotton.

In spite of the benefits to passengers provided by the Hawarden Loop line, there was no lasting change for those who wished to travel from the Old Buckley Station.

The Buckley Railway was never a route for passengers. A passenger service introduced in October 1893 was short lived and withdrawn in 1895 and the Old Station closed in 1901. A petition of 1000 signatures to the LNWR asking them to run a branch line to the centre of Buckley from the Padeswood and Buckley station went unheeded. At a public meeting in the Black Horse clubroom in the 1890s, Mr George Armstrong Parry had said:

> The Manchester, Sheffield, and Lincolnshire Railway had in contemplation the making of a new station, which would lie somewhere between Mr Charles Aston's Shop at Lane End and Buckley Church; and the proposed scheme was to continue this line on through Buckley along to Alltami, on to New Brighton, thence to Mold thereby opening up the whole district through to Manchester, Chester, Wrexham and Mold, and eventually Birkenhead and Liverpool.[61]

Unbeknown to the enthusiasts, the railway was facing a new competitor, motor transport. In a few years the more flexible trolley bus would rival the train especially for short journeys, and the motorised wagon become the vehicle for clay goods.

3. Years of uncertainty 1900–45. Mergers, John Summers & Sons.

The years 1900–14 saw the closure of Buckley brickworks, half the existing number disappeared, each of the main works suffered. Hancock's lost Knowl Hill in 1900. The old works started by William Leach at Knowl Lane and successfully run for sixty years by Ashton and the Prince brothers closed in 1902. Thomas Jones' small Pentre Works went in 1903, as did Aston Hall in 1909, followed two years later by the Globe. Belmont in the Gibson domain and Etna were finished by 1913. The year the Great War began saw the disappearance of Catherall's Ewloe Place and South Buckley. For young men clay was replaced by khaki, the quarries by the trenches.

Contrary to this trend a new brickworks was started by John Jones and Henry Lamb, both of Daisy Hill, in 1911, on land leased from the Hawarden Estate. As the name suggests it was conveniently situated near Buckley Junction railway station. It was sometimes known as 'Jack Cheshire's' after the manager. It was sold in 1919 to Captain Frederick Jones of Moreton and renamed the **Buckley Junction Metallic Brick Co. (site twenty).**

Before the end of the Great War another trend was seen to follow that of the closures, this was merger, a process which reshaped the management of the Clay Industry throughout the twentieth century. The arrival of John Summers & Sons, iron and steel makers, at Shotton in 1896 was to have a tremendous beneficial effect on the Buckley brick industry and for a while its ailing collieries. In 1916 they took over the Castle Fire Brick works which became an important subsidiary. In the next thirty years the Castle-Summers combination absorbed Catherall's Trap Works in 1936, Gibson's Brookhill in 1940, and Parry's Ewloe Barn in 1944. Mount Pleasant closed in 1931, Hancock's Lane End went out of the family in 1933, purchased by Mr Fred Jones, Davison's at Old Ewloe and Ewloe Barn were taken over shortly after the Great War by General Refractories of Sheffield. Mr George Oates of Halifax bought the Standard, only Drury retained its independence.

When questioned in November 1917 by the Local Government Board about new housing the Buckley Urban District Council replied:

> The nature of the industries of the district itself makes the Council hesitate to embark upon serious expenditure. The local Industries comprise Coal Mining and Brick Making but it is stated by persons who are qualified to speak upon the matter that the coal and clay can only be got by greatly increased expenditure. Should anything happen to both these industries the population of the town would depend entirely upon the industries of the neighbouring districts,' concluding, 'it would be unfair to burden the town with any Housing Scheme unless the Council were satisfied that the population is likely to be permanent.[62]

A reply to government in 1933 noted the changes: 'The Coal Mining industry is unfortunately not in a flourishing condition, but the Brick and Pipe Manufacturing can be regarded as being fairly progressive'. Asked about prospects of further development they replied: 'The present conditions would appear to indicate that this District is likely to develop more residentially than otherwise'.[63]

However the post war decade witnessed industrial disputes. In July 1921 a strike took place over the reduction of wages signalling that the brief boom period was over. A strike three years later lasted from July into August. A newspaper report shows that the Buckley Firebrick Masters Association must have continued to exist in an *ad hoc* way. The workers refused their offer protesting that their wages were below those recommended by the Whitley Council rate. The employers knowing this refused to go to arbitration. Eight works were idle — Parry's, Gibson's, Catherall's, Hancock's and Castle. Unlike the nineteenth century the workers now belonged to three different unions who co-operated to organise their members. Sensibly 'engine drivers at the various works are being allowed to remain on duty to keep the water down in the clay holes by pumping so that a commencement can be made as soon as the dispute is settled'. The Minister of Labour, Mr J. Whitley, appealed for arbitration because of the house building programme.

Buckley Junction Station opened 1890.
[Buckley Library]

Between five and six hundred men were affected. It was fifty years since a strike of any length by the brickworkers had taken place.[64]

What was new between the wars was the **Elm Brickworks (site twenty-one)** opened near the Castle Works, with which it was run, by the Castle Summers Company. A full report of the works presented in April 1930 shows the state of the Buckley industry. It begins with a description of Castle Fire Brick Works:

The beds of clay in these works are about 80 feet in depth, in a sequence of seams: purple clay, silica rock, green shale, shaly sandstone, white clay, and strong blue clay.

The clays are not specially weathered, but by the method of working the lower blue clay, the upper strata are brought down as a fall and weather where they lie for some time, in some cases for nine to twelve months.

The material is hauled to the grinding plant (where the harder portions are crushed in a stone breaker), passes to a grinding mill and is reduced to a powder, passing through perforated plates in the pan bottom. It is then elevated and screened, the coarse material passing back to the grinding mill for further treatment. The finely ground clay is then ready for tempering in the various mixers, where it is prepared for use in the moulding sheds.

The greater part of the firebricks made are hand moulded, and the bricks dried on floors which are heated by hot air flues passing under them. The clay for common bricks is ground in the same manner, but the bricks are made by machines, into either pressed or wirecut varieties.

The clays for special fire-clay goods, after grinding, are allowed to mature, after being watered, for 24 hours or more before being tempered. The moulding of these goods is a slower process than the hand moulded brick making, the goods often having to remain in the sheds for some weeks drying before removal to the kilns. The kilns used for fire-clay goods are of the ordinary beehive type, and contain 35/40 tons of goods. The firing is slow and the period of burning occupies about 96 hours, and the goods are burned at a temperature of about 1,400 degrees Centigrade. The bricks soften at about 1,700 degrees Centigrade, and only crack slightly at a pressure of 3,890 lbs. to the square inch. For the last 10/12 hours burning, as little air as possible is admitted to the kilns in order to set up a reducing action, which gives the brick its characteristic colour and adds to its mechanical strength.

The Castle works also manufactured building bricks. The output was two

Knowle Hill from Lodge Road, Drury, 1988. [Buckley Library]

and a half to three million firebricks and silica bricks, and three to three and a half million building bricks per annum. The report continued:

In 1925 a new brick works was erected by the Company, situated about half a mile south of the old works, to manufacture Building Bricks from Pit Shale, of which large supplies were available adjoining the site.

The plant was brought into operation in August 1925, and in 1926 a second kiln was added, giving the works a capacity of from 230 to 240 thousand bricks per week.

The material is brought from the shale dumps to a Blackett Conveyor, by which it is brought to the mill house, and is fed into a pair of crushing rolls, which deal with the harder portions, it then passes through a heavy grinding mill 10ft. diameter, the rolls of which weigh three and a half tons each. It then passes through grids at the bottom of the pan, and is elevated to an upper floor where it is screened by means of a "Hummer" Vibrating Screen, the rough material passing back to the pan.

The ground shale is then led down to the brick making machine constructed by Bradley & Craven Ltd., Wakefield. This machine moulds and presses the bricks, and has a capacity of 2,200 per hour. The bricks are carried by means of electric trucks direct to the Kilns, drying sheds not being required in this process.

The Kilns are each 180 feet long, divided into thirty chambers and contain approximately 190,000 bricks. These Kilns are continuous and are of the Belgian type.

The time occupied by the bricks in the kiln is about 12 days, and they are burned to a temperature of about 1,100 degrees centigrade to 1,200 degrees.

The bricks are removed from the kilns by electric trucks and are then loaded into railway wagons or motors as required by means of an electric overhead runway.

The bricks are used extensively for housing schemes in various parts of the country, and owing to the process of manufacture are of a very durable character, being practically unaffected by either acid or freezing tests, and they also withstand a very high crushing strain. The output is approximately 12 million bricks per annum.[65]

Further mechanisation took place after the Second World War.

We hear something about a number of the Buckley brickworks through two reports published in 1920 and 1932. At Lane End in 1920 it was recorded that the clay beds were worked by driving shallow dip-headings into the blue or black clay at intervals when the separating pillars were blown out. The clays were not weathered but sorted and ground, under edge-runners, passed between rollers, blended and pugged with water, and hand-moulded. The wares produced consisted chiefly of acid-resisting goods made mainly from the outcrop portion of the blue fire-clay. Two types of firebricks were produced — blue or 'brindled' and white made chiefly from the black clay. The firebricks were used as building bricks also, especially in the construction of railway stations and bridges.[66]

At Ewloe Barn in 1920 it was stated that: 'The blue and white firebrick made here are termed 'Davison' brand. The chief output consists of acid-resisting goods. The brand registered as 'Obsidianite' is both acid and fire-proof, and is used in the construction of Glover and Gay-Lussac towers etc. and in electrolytic and chemical works. Fire-resisting goods are termed 'Adamantine', and are made from blends of raw material such as the yellow sandstone, purple clay beneath cover, black clay and selected warrant, and some siliceous beds in the purple clay. In the works, drying grinding pans, rollers and tempering pugs are employed, as well as the treading.'[67]

The method of production at Gibson's Brookhill was described in 1920:

Ordinary 'brindled' or 'blue' Buckley firebricks are made of mixtures of two-thirds brown rock and one third Blue Clay, but in the large blocks these proportions are reversed. White bricks are made from the Black Clay. The white Silica-rock is added in small proportions to raise the silica percentage. Little time is permitted for weathering, as the clays are used up as quickly as they can be dug. Acid-resisting goods, termed 'Metallic', form the chief part of the output. Fire-resisting goods are the 'brindled' ('Gibsonite') or white varieties.[68]

It was reported of Parry's Ewloe Barn in 1932 that 'they produce blue engineering bricks, firebricks, bearers, tiles, boiler seating, blocks, tiles and acid resisting bricks. About 40 men are employed'.[69] The same clay was found here as at Davison's two works close by. They specialised in acid and fireproof bricks with the brand names of Dragon and Acido which they advertised in their catalogue:

We have the choice of ten distinct clays, varying in their contents of Silica and Alumina. 'Dragon' Brand Firebricks are pressed by hand in specially constructed presses, which results in the brick being of uniform size and shape. They are dried in sheds, which have specially heated floors. The burning or firing of the material is conducted in a round kiln of special design to the correct temperature, which is controlled by the use of thermoscope bars. 'Dragon' brand firebricks are not affected by the action of pot-ash salts, sulphur, lime, etc. at any temperature up to 3,000 degrees Fahr. They are admittedly the best brick in the market for use in Furnaces where crushed Sugar Cane is used as Fuel and consequently large quantities are shipped to Demerara, Cuba, and other countries for this purpose.

Of interest to Engineers, Surveyors, the 'ACIDO' vitrified bricks are the best on the market for bridges, arches, foundations, lining of reservoirs, and all engineering work which requires a strong non-absorbent brick.[71]

At Drury Brickworks, where the workforce numbered twenty-seven, sand-faced, rustic facing, sewer, and engineering bricks were made.

The Buckley Junction Metallic Brick Co. extended the Works in 1932 and of which it was reported:

They manufacture a very good quality of sand-faced bricks. There are three brands of facing bricks produced at these Works and they are known in the trade as 'Jacobean', 'Mulstone Grey' and 'City Rustic'. There is a big demand for these bricks and they are used to face some of the best buildings in this country. About 25% of their output is used in Government undertakings. The number of men employed is about 70, but this number will be increased when the extension now proceeding is completed. It is interesting to note that this firm was recently awarded the First Diploma for general excellence for the Building Trades Exhibition.[70]

By 1932 the clay industry was recovering and coming out of the Depression; it was expanding, making use of technical developments, able to provide for the needs of a variety of industries at home and abroad, and producing a range of attractive bricks for the growing house building programmes in the private and public sectors.

Another advance between the wars was the growing use of motorised transport. Previously the transport of goods to their port of destination was shared between the horse and the railway. Where the railway failed to reach, horse drawn transport provided the link particularly from the brickworks to the sidings. It was the huge Irish bred shire horses who brought the laden shipping boxes to the sidings. You can see them on an early advertisement of Castle Fire Brick and in a few surviving photographs.

Brian Lewis remembers that they were kept in the stables at Ewloe Wood. Shoeing was carried out at the works by the blacksmith, who was, incidentally, deaf and dumb. The manager of the old works, David Hughes, communicated with him via the manual alphabet for the deaf and he always completed his tasks faultlessly. Their groom, Hughie Hume, would give the horses a 'start' with a pivoted lever placed under the back wheel of the rear wagon, whereupon, at a command from Hughie, the horses would take the strain and, once mobile, it was then merely a question of setting the points correctly as the wagons made their way down the incline to the Connah's Quay line. The horses were harnessed to the side of the front wagon by a chain and bridle in the manner of barge horses. Subsequently, a large Fordson tractor succeeded the horses. This was fitted with large steel buffers, front and back, and Hughie would drive at the wagons to effect the same movement as he had done with his horses. It was always a dramatic sight.

Horses featured at other brickworks in Buckley and it is hard to forget the two-wheeled tipping carts, pulled by one horse, with the driver elevated directly behind his horse, (on dark November days, like a page in a medieval book of hours!) as they plodded their way back to Aberllannerch, the home of Fred Thompson, who owned them. These horses carried slack from the Buckley Colliery Company for firing the kilns at Davison's Old Ewloe Brickworks.

Castle Fire Brick Co. had early petrol wagons and later their fleet of wagons were either Bedfords or Commers. But Castle Fire Brick Co. was most noted in the area for its Sentinel steam wagons. It was these that were used for their ability to carry a load of bricks equivalent to the capacity of railway trucks. With a trailer they weighed 22 tons, that is, with a 7 ton payload on the back and 7 tons on the trailer. They were garaged at the Top Yard in the care of the manager, Sydney Jones. The drivers and firemen were very skilled and had a hot and uncomfortable life, but of great mechanical interest. The heat from the boiler was not unpleasant in the winter months, but, to make the cab bearable in summer, the wagons were fitted with

Ewloe Barn Firebrick and Tile Works, c.1900. FRO D/DM/267

side-louvres to ventilate them. However, should there be heavy rain, the louvres, substituted for the half-opening windscreen which, when the vehicle was in motion did a much more effective job. The drivers and firemen were given extra payment for getting up steam and cleaning the copper pipes from and to the boiler and traction at the beginning and end of each day.

Sentinel waggons were made at the Sentinel Works in Shrewsbury. They were bought by Castle Fire Brick between 1927 and 1937 and sold in the mid 1950s. The earlier ones had solid tyres, the later ones pneumatic. The early 1920s Sentinel wagons were used for local delivery, but in the 1930s, wagons with a trailer used to ply between Buckley and London. The agent, Messrs Sharpless & Co., builders merchants at Northwood, distributed hundreds of thousands of Castle's rustic bricks, which were popular in the area as a change from the buff-coloured London bricks. These great orange waggons, with their aprons inscribed with the firm's name 'Castle' in large gold letters became almost an ikon of Buckley on the long route to London through Whitchurch.[72]

4. The Last Phase, 1945–2003. Revival, mergers, modernisation, closure.

War and peace: the industry 1935–60
A Castle Fire Brick Co. report dated 17 March 1945 gives us an understanding of the lost years of the Second World War. The prospect for recovery by the industry after the war and Castle Fire Brick's future were reviewed by the company secretary in a report of the progress of the company over the past ten years. War time working in the industry had led to a reduction in output although there had been a demand for bricks at the beginning of the war for shelters and other buildings which meant the temporary recall of labour from the services. More goods with a higher alumina content had been produced for ladle linings and other products. Improvements had been made at Brookhill with the introduction of machinery, a policy to make use of inferior clays for building bricks, and reduce the quantity of overburden. The works were to be used for the production 'of large quantities of special lining material for cement kilns'. Although the price of bricks during the war had risen 50%, the cost of fuel and wages had risen by almost 100%. However, plans were made for expansion, in the light of the need for reconstruction of the industry in the post war period and the anticipation of a period of prosperity as a result of a government house building programme. To prepare for this land was leased from the Gwysaney Estate and twenty acres of land purchased which had been leased previously to the Buckley Colliery Company. There was confidence of a return to full output with the deficiency in the labour force being remedied by Italians. The plans for the erection of a new brick making plant at the new Buckley works were being advanced with the main items of machinery already purchased capable of producing 700,000 bricks per week.[73]

In the meantime discussions were already taking place within the community about the revival of the clay industry. The question of the reinstatement of men returning from war service was discussed. It was reckoned that John Summers expected the return of 1800 men. The 274 Buckley personnel of Vickers-Armstrong in Broughton would have to be deployed, and a place found for between 70–80 Italian prisoners of war. Standard expected a return of 28 men, Buckley Junction Metallic Brick Co. 30 and Castle Fire Brick 100. By November 1947 a sign of recovery and reconstruction was that over 800 men were directly employed in the Buckley clay industry. The annual wage bill was calculated to be about £250,000–£300,000, producing 40,000–50,000 tons of refractory clay goods, with a capacity about one third more. Additionally, about 20–25 million building bricks were produced per annum, with a capacity nearly double that figure. The fuel consumption at the refractories works was about 20,000 tons per annum and for building brickworks about 8,000 tons per annum.[74]

A public conference was held in June 1945 to discuss the revival of the industry chaired by Dennis Griffiths. They reached the obvious conclusions of the benefit of a strong house building policy, controlling wages, recruiting labour, and ensuring that the Dee was a worthy outlet for Irish trade. Buckley Urban District Council wanted the town designated as a 'Development Area' arguing that the district was a pocket of unemployment and depression between the wars. In January 1946, a joint approach was made by Flintshire County Council, Buckley Urban District and Industrialists to the North Wales Post War Development Committee pointing out the strength of the clay industry:

It is considered that the main industry of Buckley in the future is likely to be brick manufacturing. The clay of the area makes excellent engineering bricks and good class earthenware pipes for use in house drainage, as well as agricultural drainage pipes, excellent rustic bricks, and rustic multicoloured bricks'.

They also thought that 'It may be possible, by the mixture of chert with some of the local clay, to make good class pottery'.

Dennis Griffiths wrote a well argued letter on behalf of William Hancock & Co. to the Clerk of Buckley U.D.C. in support of shipping from Connah's Quay to Ireland and the Isle of Man.

Although during the War period, shipments have dwindled to a very low tonnage, we consider that provided adequate facilities exist at Connah's Quay, a revival of trade from that Port my be expected. Diversion of shipments from the Dee to Mersey Ports has necessarily taken place of late years, when smaller lots have been ordered and more frequent sailings are available from Liverpool and Birkenhead.
Firebricks, flooring and ridge tiles are the chief items of export so far as concerns Hancock's and Buckley Junction Metallic Co Ltd. had a very substantial Facing brick trade to Northern Ireland and Eire. The revival of both trades is largely dependent upon Port services.
In the huge decline of Export trade from the Buckley Firebrick Firms, (whose combined shipments from Connah's Quay in 1898 totalled 54,626 tons falling to 4,670 tons in 1922, dwindling to 5,344 tons in 1925, maintaining a tonnage of from 3,000–5,000 annually until the outbreak of War in 1939,) the condition of the River Dee and the unsatisfactory Dock facilities and services played a big part. Improvement of these services is bound to stimulate increased trade with us.[75]

A horse drawing shipping boxes at the Willow, lead by Alex Hughes c.1925. [FRO PH 11/355]

In a talk to the Buckley Firebrick Manufactures Association in 1950, Dennis Griffiths was optimistic about the future, asserting that 'in every branch, Welsh Claygoods Industries regard future prospects with confidence. Ample clay reserves exist for centuries, at present rate of extraction:

Castle Fire Brick lorry on new Queensferry road bridge, 1926
[FRO PH 51/23]

Below: Castle Fire Brick Steam Waggon
[DM/6114 J. B. Lewis]

conditions of employment have improved tremendously during the last decade, and should lead to better recruitment to the Industry'.[76]

The 1960s witnessed a further rationalisation of the industry. Again Castle-Summers Company were the major instrument of merger taking in Buckley Junction and Lane End in 1956. The modernisation of Lane End doubled the output of the famous Jacobean bricks. The Buckley Junction site was closed and the workforce moved to Lane End. The *Chester Chronicle* reported in February 1959: 'There will be no redundancies, about forty men are affected, the manufacture of the celebrated 'Jacobean' and 'City' facing bricks is to be transferred, the decision has been prompted by the need for urgent and extensive repairs to the kilns and buildings'. The company's rationalisation was carried further by the closure of the old Gibson Works at Brookhill in 1961 and Parry's Ewloe Barn in 1962.

The Standard Pipe Works, taken over by Hepworth Iron Co. after the Second World War, prospered for twenty years having been modernised in the 1950s. At the end of its life the company was trading as the North Western Ceramic Pipe Co. In 1966 there were 90 employees but only 65 remained at its closure in September 1969; the reason given was the shortage of skilled labour.[77]

In spite of rationalisation, further closures took place. The 1970s were the beginning of the final chapter in the story of the Buckley clay industry. The national economic climate was unfavourable after devaluation of sterling in 1967, a huge balance of payments deficit, wage inflation, and a steel industry under threat.

The Buckley industry was continuing to modernise. G. R. Stein Refractories at Davison's Works at Old Ewloe and Ewloe Barn continued to produce high grade refractory bricks. By the 1970s lorries had replaced rail for transporting clay goods and propane gas delivered by tanker from Shell was used instead of coal. There were 88 employed before Ewloe Barn closed in 1977 because of a drastic reduction in orders.[78]

Drury was one of the success

Castle Fire Brick top-yard c. 1960
[Buckley Society Archive]

stories of post war industry in Buckley. Dennis Griffiths visited the works in 1948 and made a report presumably on behalf of Hancock's. He reported that the plant was capable of making 3,000 bricks an hour. The capacity of the six kilns totalled 96,000 although two were 'in a very bad state', two 'needed to be recased and crowned' and of the six, four 'could be expected to last up to eight years.' He concluded that '… there is ample room for development, the sheds are brick built and have recently been recovered. The site is good, and modernly equipped, the works could be improved to a profitable basis'.[79] Griffiths' assessment was correct and Drury continued another thirty years. They were taken over by Shone's Builders in the 1960s. It was noticed in 1977, that: 'In 1973, 27 men were employed, producing 2,000,000 bricks per week. Some years ago, before modernisation of the plant, 49 men, working two shifts, produced far less. The bricks are fired by coal, brought in by road from the Point of Ayr Colliery. These are the only brickworks in Buckley still using this fuel. In recent years the works have been extensively mechanised'.[80] In 1978 Drury was closed and demolished.

The final act in the life of the Buckley clay goods industry came, when, ironically, the Castle-Summers Brickworks Empire was taken over. Early in 1972 Butterley Building Materials Ltd of Ripley, Derbyshire, a Hanson Trust Co., purchased the brickmaking and refractory interests of the British Steel Corporation-Castle Brick Co. (what we have called Castle-Summers). Butterley quickly dispensed with Castle Fire Brick and Castle Elm Works and concentrated their attention on Catherall's Trap Works and Hancock's Lane End. These, the oldest of the Buckley brickworks, were brought together in their final hour and run as one enterprise.

Lane End was the source of clay where it was dug, primarily crushed and brought to the Trap by road transport. There it was stocked in bins before being loaded by a mechanical shovel into hoppers to obtain the prescribed mix. From thence it was carried by elevators to the screening room before being made into bricks. The bricks were piled in quantities of 250 on steel pallets and taken by platform truck to the dryers. After this process, forklift trucks conveyed them to the kilns where they were off loaded by hand and set in the kilns. The total firing period was approximately six days with a cooling time of three days and a kiln cycle of a fortnight.[81]

The Butterley Catherall catalogue of 1976 advertised a variety of goods — Metalline (heat and acid resisting bricks and shapes), Castle brand ladle bricks, 'Parry Blue' shapes, blue brindle etc. Butterley ceased production at Catherall's sometime in the 1980s. The oldest firebrick works in Buckley was abandoned after a working life of nearly 250 years.

Lane End was the sole survivor. In 1977 it was reported that the quarry had large reserves of fire-clay and described the effects of modernisation:

Oil is used for fuel and this is brought in by tankers from Ellesmere Port. Today very sophisticated machinery has replaced hand methods. 'Versatran' setting is part of this. The bricks, which are handled here, are green, repressed wire cuts sanded on all six faces. As the bricks are very soft they have to be handled very carefully even though a setting rate of 6,000 per hour is required. The bricks are fed to 'Versatran' on a conveyor, which fills a spreader mechanism. When the spreader is full it opens out, pitching the bricks as required in the stack. 'Versatran' picks the bricks up ten at a time and sets a course. After each course the pallet is lowered allowing 'Versatran' to set the course in the same height but with the bricks turned through 90 degrees. 'Versatran' handles a load of 93 lbs, and in an eight hour shift moves 190 tons of bricks, replacing five men. It is largely by using the latest techniques that this industry remains viable. The 65 employees live fairly locally, use car, bus and train to and from home and work. Markets are

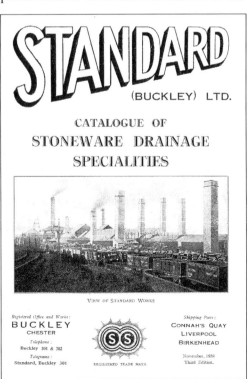

Standard Pipe Works, 1938 catalogue. [FRO D/DM/288/3]

throughout North Wales, Lancashire and north east counties. The products are all delivered by road.[82]

It is interesting to read the description of the visit made by the Buckley Society to the Lane End Works in February 2003 a few days before it closed. The process of brickmaking hadn't changed over the 211 years since first undertaken on the site but the machinery and techniques had. The style of working from the time when clamp bricks had been made seasonally on the Common or by chapel members after work, to build their new holy places, was revolutionised. I wonder what Enoch Hughes would have said. He who was reputed to have sanded, rolled and moulded 10,500 bricks in one day on Buckley Common.[83]

Hancock's railway wagons. [FRO PH 11/114. By kind permission of Mr Platt]

In her report, Mrs Carol Shone noticed three large stock bins of Buckley blue clay and the process in two Incla pans for crushing, blending, grinding and screening before being conveyed to a vacuum chamber to be pugged by the extraction of the air. The clay was then compressed and fed to a cutter which sliced 22 bricks at a time with a capacity of 8,000 bricks an hour. Which just shows how awesome was the achievement of Enoch Hughes! The bricks were taken in parcels of 388 to the drying sheds. The seven dryers supplied the exhaust heat from the kilns, controlled by conical devices, nicknamed 'daleks', which blasted air at a temperature between forty to eighty degrees centigrade for a week, on up to 24,000 bricks. The bricks were then ready for firing in ten kilns of different capacities. Kiln one held 50,000 and kiln nine 72,000 bricks. Finally the bricks were sorted, packed and despatched. A thousand Jacobean bricks cost about £400.[84]

Many reasons have been advanced for the decline of the clay industry in Buckley. Bentley attributed it to the general world trade recession in the late 1960s and 1970s, the rapid reduction of Buckley clay in economical workable supply, the inability to keep up with competitive techniques of production and alternative supplies of refractory materials.[85] In 1977, Richards attributed the contraction of the industry in Flintshire to exhaustion of clay, lack of capital and the inability to compete with brick manufactures elsewhere.[86]

The local direction of men like Jonathan Catherall, William Hancock, Charles Davison, Richard Ashton, Edward Parry, John Gibson, the Prince and Hurlbutt brothers and others had long gone. Their heritage and memory in the making of Buckley is recorded on the sign which greets travellers to the 'Historic Brickmaking Town'.

A list of Brickworks

The entrance to Lane End Brickworks 2004. [Buckley Society Archive]

Site one: Catherall & Co. Ltd., Trap Works.
Site two: Catherall & Co. Ltd., Ewloe Place.
Site three: William Hancock & Co. Ltd., Lane End
Site four: Knowl Lane.
Site six: Charles Davison & Co., Ltd., Old Ewloe Works.
Site seven: Ewloe Barn.
Site eight: Etna.
Site nine: Parry's Ewloe Barn.
Site ten: Drury, Sandycroft Brickworks.
Site eleven: William Hancock & Co. Ltd., Knowle Hill.

Lane End Pit, 1999.
[Buckley Society Archive]

Site twelve: Brookhill.
Site thirteen: Belmont.
Site fourteen: Castle Fire Brick Co. Ltd.,
Site fifteen: South Buckley Coal and Firebrick Co. Ltd.
Site sixteen: Aston Hall Colliery & Brick Works Co. Ltd.
Site seventeen: Thomas Jones, Pentre.
Site eighteen: Globe.
Site nineteen: Standard Brick and Terra Cotta Co. Ltd.
Site twenty: Buckley Junction Metallic Brick Co.
Site twenty-one: Castle Elm Works.

Notes

1. K. Lloyd Gruffydd, 'The development of the Coal Industry in Flintshire to 1740'. p 112, MA Thesis ,1981, University of Wales, Bangor.
2. P. S. Richards, ' Brick Manufacturing in Flintshire', *Industrial Archaeology*, vol. 12n no. 3, 1977.
3. T. M. Thomas, *The mineral wealth of Wales and its exploitation*, (Oliver & Boyd: 1961).
4. *Mineral Resources of Great Britain*, vol. xiv, (HMSO: 1920), Refractory Materials, Fire-clays.
5. ibid, p. 170.
6. Thomas, op cit, pp. 135–5.
7. 17 Ed4 c4, see also Richard Burns, *The Justice of the Peace and Parish Officer*, (London) 20th ed., 1805, vol. I, p. 327.
8. 17 Geo3 3c42. ibid, p. 342.
9. Thomas Cropper, *Buckley & District*, (Buckley 1923), p. 66.
10. Based on FRO D/DG/48.
11. In the OS Map of 1912, shows 14 round kilns and 5 chimneys.
12. See Bryn Ellis, 'Knowl Lane Brickworks c.1794–1902', *Buckley* 13.
13. *Chester Chronicle*, 9 February 1810.
14. Frances Green, *Calendar of Deeds & Documents* Vol. III, The Hawarden Deeds, (Aberystwyth: The National Library of Wales), No. 1327. Dec. 2, 1751.
15. James Bentley, 'Old Buckley Tramways'. *Buckley*, No.1.
16. Richard Willett, *A Memoir of Hawarden Parish*, (Chester: 1822), p. 105.
17. James I. C. Boyd, *The Wrexham, Mold & Connah's Quay Railway*, (The Oakwood Press, 1991) p 24
18. FRO D/HC/A/25.
19. Boyd, op cit, p. 28.
20. See chapter on Potteries.
21. FRO D/DM/809/12.

22. FRO D/DG/48.

23. *Chester Chronicle*, 24 April 1852.

24. FRO D/BC/6/2.

25. *Chester Chronicle* 28 June 1862, quoted in Boyd, op cit, p. 64,

26. George Lewis, 'The Buckley Clay Industries', *Buckley*, No.1.

27. Boyd, op cit, pp. 66–67.

28. ibid, p. 71.

29. Thomas Pennant, *Tours in Wales*, (London: 1778) p. 88.

30. Boyd, op cit, p. 169.

31. FRO D/DM/417/1.

32. *Chester Chronicle*, 26 Feb. 1864.

33. *Chester Chronicle*, 22 June 1895.

34. *Chester Chronicle*, 15 March 1941

35. See articles by Bryn Ellis: 'Buckley Brick & Tile Company: the first ten years'. *Buckley* 8; 'Buckley Brick and Tile Company: the Middle Years, 1882–1908', *Buckley* 9; 'Buckley Brick & Tile Company: the Final Years, 1911–1940'. *Buckley* 10.

36. *Chester Courant*, 4 Aug. 1875.

37. J. B. Lewis, 'A note on the history of the Castle Fire Brick Company, Northop, and on related Brick and Coal Entrepreneurs', *Buckley*, No.6.

38. See B. D. Hodnett, 'Coalmining and Brickmaking in the South Buckley area'. *Buckley* 25.

39. Andrew Connolly, *Life in the Victorian brickyards of Flintshire and Denbighshire* (Gwasg Carreg Gwalch: Llanrwst, 2003), p. 164.

40. Based on FRO D/DG/28.

41. See T. W. Pritchard, *A History of the Old Parish of Hawarden*, (Wrexham: Bridge Books 2002) pp. 74–6.

42. See Connolly, op cit, p. 134.

43. ibid, pp. 151

44. ibid, pp. 1412–3.

45. See FRO D/DM/809/36 for the first meeting, 16–17 May 1870 and D/DG/26, The Minute Book of the reformed Association, from Jan. 1875 to 1880, also, Sheila Lyons, 'The Organization of the Buckley Brick Industry in the second half of the nineteenth century'. *Buckley*, no.11.

46. See for example FRO D/DM/809/36.

47. Boyd, op cit, p. 164.

48. *Chester Chronicle*, 28 Nov. 1845.

49. *Chester Chronicle*, 29 April 1842.

50. *Chester Chronicle*, 6 May 1842.

51. *Chester Chronicle*, 24 Jan 1874.

52. *Chester Chronicle*, 21 Feb 1874.

53. *Chester Chronicle*, 28 Feb 1874.

54. *Chester Chronicle*, 17 & 24 Nov & 1 Dec 1877.

55. *Chester Chronicle*, 7 Oct. 1893.

56. FRO E/LB/3, 11 Sept. 1885.

57. FRO E/LB/5/6, Bistre Board School, 8 Feb. 1901.

58. *Chester Chronicle*, 19 April 1890.

59. *Wrexham Advertiser*, 5 Oct. 1878.

60. *Chester Chronicle*, 8 Sept. 1888.

61. *County Herald*, Dec. 1890.

62. FRO, Buckley Urban District Council Minutes, 1917.

63. ibid, March 1933.

64. *Mold, Deeside & Buckley Leader*, 8 Aug. 1924.

65. FRO, D/DM/355/18.

66. Op cit, HMSO Special Report, 1920.

67. ibid.

68. ibid.

69 'Report on Planning of the County of Flint under Town and Country Planning Act', 1932, p. 54.

70. FRO D/DG/43.

71. op cit, 1932 Report, p. 54.

72. Information from Mr J. B. Lewis who adds, according to records kindly supplied by Mr Justin Goold of Bath; Castle Fire Brick Co. Ltd appear to have owned eight Sentinel waggons and three trailers, of these three have survived.

73. FRO D/DM/355/18, date of Report 17 March 1945.

74. FRO D/DG/48, figures provided by Dennis Griffiths

75. For much of the above discussion see FRO UD/A/1/50–1.

76. FRO D/DG/48.

77. Connolly, op cit, pp. 149–151.

78. Richards, op cit, p. 231. Old Ewloe closed in 1973.

79. FRO D/DG/48.

80. Richards, op cit, pp.233–4
81. FRO D/DM/1011/2.
82. Richards, op cit, p. 233.
83. FRO D/DG/48.
84. Carol Shone, 'From Hancock's to Hanson's: Closure of Buckley's last Brickworks', *Buckley*, No. 28.
85. James Bentley, Refractory Goods, FRO BP 1367.
86. Richards, op cit, p. 236.

Chapter 7
Small industries before 1945

Nothing can compete with the length of time and magnitude of the coal and clay industries in Buckley but there are some small businesses which should be mentioned. The post 1945 industries, which replaced clay manufacturing, are dealt with in chapter sixteen.

Buckley Mills

Water mills existed in the three lordships of Hawarden, Mold, and Ewloe from well before the thirteenth century. The plateau formation of Buckley was unsuitable for waterpower but within the first years of the nineteenth century there was a windmill towering majestically over the Higher Common. By the beginning of the 'Hungry Forties' there was another corn mill at the Lane End powered by steam.

These early years of the industrial revolution were marked by bad harvests, fluctuations in trade, high prices and a scarcity of cereals. In 1795 troops were summoned to Mold to quell food riots, and unrest occurred on occasions until the middle of the nineteenth century. Corn Laws controlled the import of cheap foreign grain and the poor often went hungry in the years of trade depression. In such circumstances the miller was an important member of the community. To meet these needs a windmill was erected near the Cross in the direction of the new road leading to King's Ferry.

The windmills in Buckley were of the tower-type introduced by the Dutch when they were draining the Fens in the seventeenth century. The sails of the tower-mill were carried on the cap, or top of the mill, only the cap was turned by the wind thus saving considerable effort, avoiding the use of large timbers, and allowing the tower to be built of stone or brick to give it strength and stability.

Charles Duckworth provided the evidence we have for Buckley mills; he was, however, unable to come to a firm conclusion on their position and he couldn't decide whether there were two or three mills.[1] The evidence Duckworth presented was based entirely on advertisements in the Chester newspapers, and a brief reference to Cropper.[2] I think that it is possible by looking at the total evidence Cropper presents, in conjunction with the newspaper advertisements quoted by Duckworth, to reach the conclusion that there was a windmill in Mill Lane by 1802 and that in 1837 a corn steam mill was erected at Lane End.

Cropper states that William Leach and Samuel Beavan built a windmill on land, later to be called Mill Lane, purchased from the Mold Enclosure Commissioners in 1795. In 1802

The Old Windmill, Mill Lane.
[FRO PH/11/350]

Jonathan Catherall was working the mill. Cropper cites items of expenditure spent by Catherall in that year on its maintenance including the purchase of rollers from John Wilkinson, the Bersham ironmaster who had opened the Smelt in Buckley. The first of the newspaper advertisements relating to the windmill appeared in April 1809. This gives Samuel Beavan as the owner of the premises, and another of February 1818, refers the reader to apply to William Leach of Ewloe, and Samuel Higginson of Barrow, for particulars. Both these advertisements give the position of the windmill as adjoining 'the main turnpike road' (1809), and 'on the highway between Chester and Mold' (1818). Cropper says 'the mill house in Mill Lane was in its day an old tavern, held by the Higginsons', although he doesn't give a date. Advertisements for 1811 and 1818, mention a house, garden, and stable. An advertisement for 1837 describes the premises as:

> a well accommodated Windmill situated on Buckley Mountain, with house adjoining now used as a Public House, and known by the name of the Mill Tavern with a good garden and stabling for 8 horses, carthouse, drying kilns, warehouse, pigsties etc, and in the occupation of Thomas Higginson. The Mill contains one pair French Stones, and three pairs of Grey Stones, and is capable of performing more than an ordinary quantity of work.[3]

In the 1870s the windmill was in the occupation of James Clarke, miller.

Duckworth says that the *Chester Chronicle*, 26 May 1837, tells of a new Mill at Lane End and quotes the advertisement:

> A fine corn Steam Mill erected on the premises of Mr. Swettenham at Buckley Mountain. The admirable machinery for which has been manufactured by Messrs Rigby of Hawarden, and commencing work on Wednesday last. It is the first Corn Steam Mill in the County of Flintshire.

Swettenham was a Wesleyan who took his religion seriously as a notice in the newspaper, twelve years earlier in December 1825, made clear — 'Wanted a Journeyman Windmiller, he must be a single man and a member of the Methodist Society, he will not be required to work on the Sabbath day. Apply to Mr. W. Swettenham, Buckley Mill, Flintshire.'[4]

Swettenham died about 1848 and his premises, described as, a 'Corn grist mill, steam engine, machinery, and building', was bought by William Hancock for £630. Sometime later, the building, described as a 'Provision Warehouse, Steam Flour Mill, Lane End, Buckley' was occupied by Ishmael Roberts, 'wholesale and retail miller, tea dealer, and grocer'. It was situated adjoining the site of the Palace cinema and Lane End post office, although it is strange that Cropper doesn't mention it.

There is no reference to the site of this Buckley Mill. There are no reports of food riots in Buckley. It is evident that there was a close-knit group of businessmen emerging in Buckley with names such as Catherall, Hancock, Rigby, Leach, and for a brief spell John Wilkinson and his associates.

The Buckley Smelt and Foundry

Richard Willett records an eighteenth century Smelting-house in Pentrobin,[5] where more than 10,000 tons of ore were smelted in twenty years:[6]

In the year 1751, Mr Richardson, of Chester, erected a Smelting-house in Pentrobin, of a conical form, where Lead continued to be smelted under the agency of Mr Joseph Berks, during his

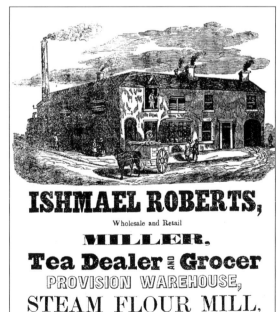

ISHMAEL ROBERTS,
Wholesale and Retail
MILLER,
Tea Dealer and Grocer
PROVISION WAREHOUSE,
STEAM FLOUR MILL,
LANE END,
BUCKLEY.

Nineteenth century Steam Flour Mill Lane End.
[FRO D/DM/263]

time, and that of his son Richard Richardson, Esq. of Capenhurst, in Cheshire, till the year 1810, when the Building was entirely taken down.

Cropper mentions the Smelt in his survey of Buckley and district place-names:

The Buckley Smelt and Foundry, with Foundry Cottages. [Buckley Archive]

John Wilkinson, the great eighteenth-century ironmaster, who owned a score of ironworks, collieries, lead mines, etc., in different parts of the country, built the Smelt about the year 1797. Its purpose was the smelting of lead brought down from his Llyn-y-Pandy lead mines, beyond Mold. He it was who owned the Maes-y-grug Colliery, Alltami, long before Messrs. Watkinson reopened it.[7]

The export abroad of smelted lead from Flintshire was seriously affected by the outbreak of the Napoleonic Wars and after Wilkinson's death in 1808 his estate went into Chancery. By 1832 Llyn-y-Pandy was in possession of 'William Jones, Lead Merchant, now bankrupt', when it was sold to Hancock's.[8] The long advertisement announcing its sale, describes it as a compact, well-equipped lead-smelting works, standing within two acres of land, comprising four furnaces, three slag hearths, engine house and engine, bins, coal shed, office, smith's shop, and every other convenience for the smelting trade. Also six dwelling houses and gardens for workmen, about half a mile of rail road, forty rail wagons, weighing machines, tools and the necessary implements.

This was an ideal addition for Hancock's for the maintenance of their brick, pottery, colliery, and railroad interests. They retained ownership of the Smelt until 1933. During their hundred years of ownership they let the works. From about the year 1870 until 1913, The Foundry, as it was now described, was worked by the talented Buckley engineer Jonathan Rowlands. He made and designed machinery and was known as the 'Buckley Pioneer'. Many of the local brickmakers used him for his skills in designing, and casting machinery; Rowlands provided the Lane End brickworks with a brickmaking machine, which they failed to obtain elsewhere.

From 1913–40 the Foundry was worked by Charles and Laurence Beavan who specialised in forging, brickmaking machinery and colliery plant, supplying customers throughout the United Kingdom and Ireland. Hancock's disposed of the works to Buckley Foundry in 1933. It was managed by Mr Robert Fox who was succeeded by Mr Goodwin. After the Second World War the foundry business was transferred to modern buildings in the adjacent yard by the Buckley Foundry (Chester) Ltd who specialised in grey iron castings for various engineering works throughout the country.

The late George Lloyd described the Smelt before its demolition:

This unique conical brick structure is situated about 400 yards east of the Buckley Cross Roads and is a land mark in the surrounding countryside. It is 40' 0" internal diameter at the base, approximately 60' 0" high, with an opening at the top of about 15' 0" diameter. The walls, for half the height, are of 18" brickwork with an internal offset of 4.5" to the top. This top circle of brickwork is capped with heavy cast-iron segmental plates.[10]

Dennis Griffiths added the information that the peculiar shape of the building was best suited to emit the fumes of lead smelting, and that it gave partial protection both to the men and to the smelting hearths they tended. It was built with some 130,000 hand-made slob-bricks, made from surface clay in the old Buckley fashion before machinery was introduced.[11]

The demolition of the Smelt marked the disappearance of an important example of Buckley's industrial archaeology.

Gregorys Limited, Mineral Water Manufacturers

The *'Pop' Alley Bottle and the 'Pop' Cart* was Harold Gregory's title for his story of the family's aerated water works which was in existence from about 1888 until around 1942. These were the vintage years of the mineral water trade, when children were free to roam the countryside in the long summer holidays, and every improvised picnic included a bottle of fizzy pop and jam butties, to take to the Common or clay hole.

It was the provision of a regular water supply to Buckley from Moel Fama and the Clwydian Range in the 1880s, which ensured the prosperity of the new venture begun by Mr John Bates Gregory (1847–91). A Lancastrian from West Leigh he came to Buckley in 1872 as manager of Little Mountain Colliery and in 1886 became proprietor of Mount Pleasant Collieries employing 450 men. He was a man of some drive and initiative who helped to secure the Act for the Buckley gas undertaking and assisted in obtaining the water supply and once that was achieved he began manufacturing mineral waters. On his premature death in 1891 his widow, Mrs Ellen Kenyon Gregory, with the assistance of various members of the family, continued trading under the name of 'E. K. Gregory, Buckley'.

The family lived for three generations at Cold Arbour House, Buckley, and established their business next to Lane End School. The proximity of the works to the school was on occasions a cause of complaint:

Advert for Gregorys Mineral Waters, 1906, in Souvenir Programme – Grand Bazaar St Matthew's School. [Buckley Society Archive]

1908 May 11. The Mistress wrote to the Manager of the Ginger Beer Works re-smoke nuisance from the works.

1916 September 28. The smoke was so very bad to day that the mistress had to send a final notice to Mr Gregory that she would have to complain to the Authorities. The teacher could not actually see the children at the back of their classes for the smoke.

1925 September 17. The girls at the Pickle Works were sitting outside peeling onions and the smell is so strong in school that we are all feeling quite sleepy.[12]

The business was in the charge of Henry Kenyon Gregory (1871–1927), who came home in 1913 to manage the works. He was employed from 1921 onwards as assistant manager at Messrs Hancock's. Like all the Gregorys he played a prominent part in community affairs as member of the Buckley UDC, overseer for Buckley for the Hawarden Board of Guardians, and a playing member of Buckley Cricket Club. After his death in 1927 Harold Gregory carried on the business until its sale by the family in 1942.

The firm managed to survive the restrictions and shortage of labour of the First World War. One of the main ingredients 'carbonic acid gas,' was unobtainable and instead special soda cake from the Munitions Factory, Queensferry, and bicarbonate of soda from Messrs Brunner Mond & Co., Northwich, were used as substitutes.

When peace came in 1918 horse transport was replaced by steam and internal combustion engines for delivery over a large area. The works were improved by investing in bottle-making machines, the use of a new type of bottle stoppers, additional storage, and the erection of a wooden building for the manufacture

Girls of Gregory's pickling onions c.1938. [Buckley Society Archive]

of pickles. Gregorys now specialised in 'Piccalilli' and sauces. They had acted for many years as an agency for the supply of malt and pure distilled vinegar. Improvements were made in the 1930s by the purchase of a Morris Commercial lorry, the reordering of the works, and the erection of a second storey for an office and storage area.

The Second World War imposed severe restrictions on the manufacture of mineral waters and Gregory's was taken over in 1942/3 by a London firm for the manufacture of pickles. They later finished production at Buckley and the works was closed down for several years. In 1962/3 the building and works were demolished and the site developed as a petrol filling and service station. Buckley lost one of its most colourful industries.[13]

Padeswood Hall Demonstration Centre

The Padeswood Hall Estate was in the hands of the Hancock family for about ninety years until they sold it to Flintshire County Council in 1919. The purchase price of £1,100 bought the hall and 100 acres of land.

The new owners began to develop the newly acquired estate as an agricultural education centre. Padeswood they regarded as ideal for the introduction of short-term residential courses in a variety of subjects. Nine residential students were housed and others attended on a daily basis. The County Council paid the fees of students to undertake courses in further education. They had reciprocal arrangements for scholarships with Denbighshire for entrance to Llysfasi. Flintshire County Council worked closely with the University College of North Wales, Bangor, in the provision of agricultural education. A horticultural superintendent was appointed in 1920 and full-time courses began at Padeswood in 1928.

The Padeswood Hall Horticultural Demonstration Centre, as it was known, was officially opened by Earl de la Warr, Parliamentary Secretary to the Ministry of Agriculture and Fisheries, in July 1930. The Centre attracted widespread attention in North Wales and the north-west of England and proved a popular place for visitors in the 1930s.

The prospectus described the objects of the centre as:

… designed to provide instruction in the science and practice of Horticulture, Poultry-Husbandry and Beekeeping to young men and women who intend taking up one of these industries as their future education or desire to take courses at the Centre as a preliminary to more advanced instruction at a College. It is also designed as a Demonstration Centre to persons interested in the above-mentioned subjects.

About 35 acres of land were attached to the Centre: 10 acres devoted to horticulture, 5 acres to intensive poulty keeping, while the remainder was let as accommodation land, and used as a range for poultry. The horticultural department had two acres devoted to ornamental and glasshouse work, with 8 acres cultivated with field crops. Two acres were allocated to arable fruit culture with apples intermixed with black currants. A variety of manurial and other experiments were carried out.

The horticultural superintendent, Harry L. Jones, presented quarterly reports to Flintshire Education Authority.[14] In September 1934, for example, he reported 'new greenhouses in course of construction — tomato crop suffered very severely from shortage of water —

Advert for Gregorys Pickle, 1908, Hawarden Parish Church Booklet. [Buckley Society Archive]

Padeswood Hall Demonstration Centre. Prospectus 1930. [FRO]

Glass houses Padeswood Hall Demonstration Centre. Prospectus 1930. [FRO]

spring cabbages, broccolis gave an excellent return — black currants excellent crop. Visitors have been numerous since July 1st 312 visitors, quite a number from Lancashire and Cheshire — bees have done very well — they are at present on the moors — 15 varieties of old apples to send to the apple conference held at the Crystal Palace. The Poultry Instructor reported that the total number of eggs produced from April 1st to August 31st as 24,725 as compared with 17,798 last year — they were breeding Rhode Island Reds ... Buff Plymouth Rocks. The fees charged to resident students £10 per course.'[15]

Padeswood prospered during the high summers of the 1930s but failed to cope with the stringent conditions imposed by the Second World War. The cellars at the hall were overrun by rats, the roof leaked, and the heating was inadequate. Fifty-one turkeys were reared for Christmas 1940 but there was a shortage of feeding stuffs. Heavy snow in the severe winter of 1940 damaged the glasshouses, and thousands of cauliflower, broccoli and cabbage were killed outright. The poultry were devastated, several three-month-old chicks were frozen to death and many lost their toes as a result of frostbite. Things improved gradually but by 1943 production and harvesting was strained by labour shortages and in his report for November 1943 the superintendent stated that 'I should like to put on record the assistance I have obtained from the Buckley St Matthew's School. The boys sent by the Headmaster enabled us to get our potatoes and apple crop under cover'.

Efforts were being made before the war to replace the Agricultural Demonstration Centre at Padeswood. By the end of the war the building was condemned and Flintshire Education Committee was making plans to develop land at Celyn Farm, Northop. When the Centre closed at the end of the war F. L. Smith (Tunnel Cement) purchased it. Cabbages were replaced by cement and a new industry came to Padeswood.[16]

Notes

1. See Charles Duckworth, 'Buckley and its Windmills', *Buckley* 9, and George I. Hawkes, 'A Ewloe Manor Windmill in 1571', *Buckley*, 24.
2. This reference by Duckworth is misquoted. He gives 1902 instead of 1802, see Cropper, op cit, p. 63. He fails to read Cropper's evidence on p. 119.
3. The advertisements mention, for 1809 'two machines', and for 1818 'two dressing machines'.
4. *Chester Chronicle*, 16/12/1825.
5. Richard Willett, *A Memoir of Hawarden Parish* (Chester: 1822), p. 107.
6. A. H. Dodd, *The Industrial Revolution in North Wales* (University of Wales Press, Cardiff, 2nd edition, 1951), p. 171.
7. Cropper, op cit, p. 16.
8. Pigot's *Directory of North Wales*, 1835, lists 'Hancock, William, Thomas and Samuel, smelters and lead merchants'.
9. See *Chester Chronicle*,10/2/1832.
10. George Lloyd, 'The Smelt at Buckley', *Flintshire Historical Society Publications*, vol. 19, p.91.
11. FRO D/DG/48.
12. Entries from Buckley Lane End School log book, FRO.
13. The above account relies on Harold G. Gregory, 'The 'Pop' Alley Bottle and the 'Pop' Cart', *Buckley* 1, and H. G. G's notes in FRO D/NT 73 and 77.
14. These are to be found in FRO FC/2 for the appropriate years.
15. FRO/FC/2/35 P. 522F.
16. For an account of Castle Cement see chapter 16.

Chapter 8
Nonconformist Churches

This section deals with the history of religious bodies in the area. There was no Nonconformist presence recognised by law in Buckley before the year 1785. For hundreds of years religious provision in the area had been made from the large Anglican parishes of Mold and Hawarden. By the beginning of the nineteenth century energetic incumbents recognised the need to build churches in outlying industrial townships. George Neville, Rector of Hawarden, was first to act in 1822 when he built St Matthew's Buckley, to serve the townships of Ewloe Town, Bannel and Pentrobin. He was followed in 1842 by Charles Butler Clough, Vicar of Mold, who created the new parish of Emmanuel, Bistre. Both enterprises needed approval from diocesan bishops, government grants, lay patronage and substantial endowments. Roman Catholicism arrived relatively late on the scene and was viewed with hostility by evangelical Protestants as papist, ritualistic and foreign. Anglicanism in Wales as part of the Church Established, dominated by the gentry and, for the most part Tory in politics, was alienated from the Welsh people over a number of issues such as education controversies and tithe wars. It succeeded in uniting nonconformist bodies in a campaign for the disestablishment and disendowment of the Welsh Church, which came into operation in 1920. Nonconformists found political expression for their views in support for Liberal governments. W. E. Gladstone patronised both Anglicans (his son-in-law was Canon Drew) and nonconformists. He attended churches, spoke in chapels and was entertained by the Town Band.

The first decade of the twentieth century is an ideal time to show the relative strengths of all the religious bodies. By this time many had reached their peak of membership, their building programmes were completed, religious revivals were nearly over, and the decline, which came after the First World War, was not much in evidence. The figures are based on statistics provided by the Royal Commission on the Church of England and other Religious Bodies in Wales and Monmouthshire 1905/06. The Nonconformist statistical entries for Buckley shows their strength.

Sittings in Chapel	3,505
Sittings in School Room	1,610
Number of Communicants	791
Number of Adherents	2,909
Teachers and Scholars	1,887

The numbers for the various denominations were

Sittings in Chapel	550 (Cong)	1015 (PM)	460 (WM)	500 (MNC)	370 (B)	500 (CM/Pres)	SalA (110)
"" School Rm	300 "	560 "	200 "	350 "	100 "	160 "	nil
No. Comm.	250 "	184 "	52 "	89 "	23 "	138 "	50
No. Adherents	550 "	814 "	315 "	650 "	200 "	280 "	100
Teachers & Sch	291 "	558 "	318 "	352 "	120 "	210 "	38

Anglican	Emmanuel	St Matthew's	Total
Accommodation	538	560	1,098
Communicants	237	551	788
Teachers and Scholars	180	397	577

You will notice that in some instances the number of adherents, that is, those who were not members of the denomination but merely went to listen, outnumbered the number of sitting places.

The number of sittings in places of worship were almost 3.5 to 1 in favour of Nonconformists.

The number of communicants almost equal 791 Non.con. 788 Anglican.

Teachers & Scholars 1,887 Non.con. 577 Anglican.

The population figures 1901 Census: Buckley 2,949, Bistre 4,070, total 7,019.

The population figure for Flintshire was 81,700 communicants: Non-con 14,016 Anglican 11,621.

There are no figures for Roman Catholics. They would not number more than forty.

The Nonconformist places of worship were:

Congregationalist (Cong.) St John's: Methodists, The Square (Wes.); Brunswick (Wes.); Mold Road (Welsh Wes.); Tabernacle (Prim. Meth.); Alltami (Prim. Meth.); Drury (Prim. Meth.); Bistre, Providence and Pentrobin, Bethesda (Methodist New Connexion); Nant Mawr and Daisy Hill (Baptist); Mold Road (Cal. Meth.); Zion (English Presb.); Salvation Army.

The value given for the religious buildings, including schoolrooms, belonging to thirteen Nonconformist churches was £17,920. The Salvation Army did not give a valuation for their Barracks. The figure for St Matthew's Church, £14,000, is the amount spent on the church building between 1892–1906. I have valued Emmanuel Bistre as £4,500. This figure was arrived at by taking into account that St Ethelwold's Church Shotton opened in 1904 at a cost £7,000. There is no figure for the Church of Our Lady of the Rosary, Daisy Hill. I have given an estimate of £850. This sum of £37,270 represents a considerable investment by the community in the bricks and mortar of religious life over a period of not more than seventy years. An account of these buildings will follow in the chapter.[1]

We begin with a review of nonconformity in the area over the last two hundred years or so in an attempt to explain the influence of such a rich variety of religious experience which has in many ways given Buckley its own distinctive character.

There are many questions to ask. Here are a few to begin with. What made Nonconformity different from the Established Church of England? What did Nonconformists in Buckley have in common? In what ways did they differ? How did Nonconformists express their unity in public witness to their faith? What determined the nature of Nonconformist places of worship?

In the nineteenth century Welsh working class communities developed their own religious organisations and were independent of the class above them. They built their own chapels, supported their own ministry with a great deal of lay participation. It was said by George Osborne Morgan that 'every small farmer, small tradesman and the whole of the labouring population went to chapel'. It was from this class that they found their preachers.

Nonconformist bodies were united in their demand for liberty of conscience. Baptists, Independents (Congregationalists) and English Presbyterians were heirs of the seventeenth century Puritan tradition. In the nineteenth century the Primitive and other Methodist bodies fashioned democratic institutions of government and worship. Nonconformity grew in strength because it was flexible and able to adapt to the needs of large numbers of immigrants who flooded into newly industrialised areas. In the first half of the nineteenth century, Wales was in reality a frontier society and newly gathered religious groups often met together in barns, private dwellings or public houses before they were able to build their own places of worship. In Buckley members often made the bricks for these after their day's toil. All this they were able to do without reference to the complicated procedures and regulations demanded by the Established Church.

By the middle of the nineteenth century it was apparent that Nonconformists outnumbered Anglicans in Wales as revealed in the 1851 Religious Census. Furthermore the 1847 Education Commissioners had goaded Nonconformity into a united front whose report by an Anglican inspectorate completely alienated them. They invoked the fury of Nonconformist Wales by alleging that sexual morality was low, drunkenness rife and prayer meetings the opportunity for young people to misbehave. An example of the evidence given is that of the Anglican curate of Buckley, H. P. Ffoulkes, who reported 'that the state of morals is degraded in respect of drunkenness, profanity, dishonesty, and incontinence; that the latter vice is increasing so rapidly as to render it difficult to find a cottage where some female of the family has not been *enceinte* before marriage.'[2]

Whatever the criticism the Nonconformists began to shape and transform Welsh communities through the influence of their places of worship. Their chapel worship provided effective preaching, evangelical, revivalist and radical in tone, which gave their members a sense of assurance and confidence. Sunday schools for adults as well as children provided a system of elementary education and an access to popular religious literature. Buckley Congregational Church had a library of 350 volumes and Tabernacle Primitive Methodist Church one of 100 volumes. Prayer meetings, missionary meetings and the use of the chapels for choir practice, gave the members an active weekday routine which was an alternative to the public house culture. The togetherness experienced at the coal seam, clay hole and pottery shed was repeated in the chapel with opportunities for self-expression, self-improvement and experience of leadership through the offices of deacon, lay preacher, schoolteacher, choir member, etc.

Religion to some extent was connected to popular entertainment. Society became more civilised when self-improvement, domestic piety, thrift and chapel going became a matter of pride and a badge of respect. To some extent temperance triumphed over drunkenness and immorality was banished in a tightly-knit, rigorous, inquisitive society. The busy Nonconformist community expressed a distinctive sense of unity with its revivalism, prayer meetings, hymn singing, Sunday schools, temperance demonstrations, Band of Hope processions, joint choirs for oratorios and brass bands.

All these activities produced a folk culture with a strong religious fervour, which lasted a hundred and fifty years and prepared the ground for trade unionism and local government politics as the twentieth century dawned.

It was the piety and resolution of Jonathan Catherall II that established religion in Buckley. He was not alone in his endeavour for there were other Christians dwelling on Buckley Mountain at this time intent on the same purpose. These events took place in the 1780s. Willett describes the situation on the Mountain:

> This manufactory has occasioned a great population in the neighbourhood, and the situation being nearly three miles distant from the parish Church, ignorance and irreligion must have continued the necessary consequence, had it not been for the unshaken perseverance of Sectaries. These men, to their credit be it spoken, arrested the vicious and intemperate career of the young, the ignorant, and the licentious, of this distant quarter of the parish, and rendered them more correct in their principles, and more orderly in their conduct; and this tribute of applause, truth and justice requires to be acknowledged.[3]

Richard Willett was headmaster of the old Grammar School, Hawarden, and a friend of Jonathan Catherall. They later collaborated as members of the British and Foreign Bible Society.

Jonathan Catherall II, as we have seen, was a man of some standing in the industrial life of Buckley and was a person of great integrity. To his biographer, Thomas Cropper, he was something of a hero, and it may be said that Cropper had got to know his subject well. He says:

> I have practically 'lived' my subject during the time this chapter was in course of preparation, and from the available material to which I have had access, consisting of letters, some items of dairy records, and the reputation handed down through the medium of aged people, together with the fruits of his work, still apparent, his character has taken quite definite shape in my mind. He was of a gentle, refined, benign, and lovable disposition — a benevolent, philanthropic, nature's gentleman … . It may confidently be asserted that there is scarcely a place of worship in the district whose founders were not in some sense inspired by the personality or through the labours of the subject of this sketch.[4]

Jonathan Catherall II died in 1833 and Cropper is therefore speaking of his influence on the religious life in Buckley during the formative period of about fifty years from the mid 1780s. This began with his religious conversion. Cropper gives an account of this but mentions no specific date. He says 'The family was accustomed to attend the services of Hawarden Church, and so it transpired that on one occasion Mr Catherall casually attended a Dissenting open-air preaching meeting at Hawarden Cross and was converted to the Nonconformist faith.'[5] Charles Duckworth was of the opinion that the preacher at the Cross was a Wesleyan Methodist from Chester, a schoolmaster by the name of John Sellers, whose hostile reception is

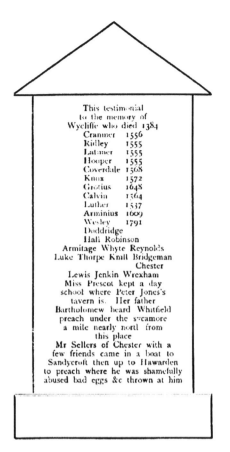

An inscription on a stone in the Congregational Graveyard, Buckley.
From T. Cropper, Buckley and Distirict.

The text within the image reads:

This testimonial
to the memory of
Wycliffe who died 1384
Cranmer 1556
Ridley 1555
Latimer 1555
Hooper 1555
Coverdale 1568
Knox 1572
Grotius 1648
Calvin 1564
Luther 1537
Arminius 1609
Wesley 1791
Doddridge
Hall Robinson
Armitage Whyte Reynolds
Luke Thorpe Knill Bridgeman
Chester
Lewis Jenkin Wrexham
Miss Prescot kept a day
school where Peter Jones's
tavern is. Her father
Bartholomew heard Whitfield
preach under the sycamore
a mile nearly north from
this place
Mr Sellers of Chester with a
few friends came in a boat to
Sandycroft then up to Hawarden
to preach where he was shamefully
abused bad eggs &c thrown at him

cited on the Catherall memorial in the Congregational burial ground.[6]

Jonathan Catherall's conversion to the Nonconformist branch of the Church took place sometime before 1788, when he was about twenty-seven years of age. No date has survived for this event but it was before the beginning of January 1788 because Cropper relates that Jonathan was accused by his brother Joseph when the latter was brought before the justices for a breach of the peace when under the influence of drink. Jonathan said 'he told the Justice that I did give to and keep in the house Dissenting preachers to injury of my relations. Which assertion caused the Justice to speak disrespectfully of my mother and me.'[7] Which branch of Nonconformity was responsible for his conversion? No satisfactory answer can be given to this question. The opinion of Charles Duckworth that he was converted by the Methodist schoolmaster John Sellers, cannot be fully substantiated. What is certain is the total allegiance of Jonathan Catherall to the Nonconformist cause and the pattern of subsequent events reveal that he supported the causes of the Independents, Wesleyan Methodists and Calvinistic Methodists not only in Buckley, but also throughout Flintshire. In this sense he may be seen as the founding father of Nonconformity in Buckley in the formative years of its planting.

The business interests of the young man took him to many parts of Wales where he experienced the religious revival that was taking place primarily amongst the Baptists and Independents. Chester was the place where the Catherall firm did its banking and used the post office to receive its mail orders. The Nonconformist life of the city gave him many contacts and influenced his religious progress and probably gave him his conversion experience. What the young man first encountered was a flourishing Wesleyan Methodist church, the Octagon, built in 1756, and the Meeting House in Common Hall Street in which Baptists, Methodists and Independents worshipped together until the new Independent Church in Queen Street was opened in 1778.[8] Catherall therefore experienced the goodwill which existed between the various Nonconformist churches and what is more shared the enthusiasm of their members some of whom played an important part in his religious development. For example John Sellers, three years older than Catherall, was a Methodist local preacher and class leader. He died aged 32 years in 1790. Of greater influence were the Independent minister of Queen Street, the Reverend William Armitage, and most importantly two of the deacons, John Ellis (a vintner) and Thomas Jones (a cutler). Catherall was beginning to find his feet in business and had the full support of his mother in his determination 'to be of service to the cause of Christ' and both these deacons encouraged the young man in his missionary endeavour to build an Independent church in Flintshire, at Holywell.

The new Independent chapel in Chester was described as 'new and neat' and Catherall wanted the same for Holywell where he worshipped on alternate Sundays going to Chester on the other. Messham sees Thomas Jones as a father figure to Catherall and experienced enough to give him sound advice on the building of the chapel in Holywell. It cost Catherall £474 2s. 6d. and the trust deed is dated 31 August 1789 with Thomas Jones and John Ellis named as trustees.[9] Thomas Pennant noted in his history of the parish published in 1796 that 'in the town are three places of worship besides the church, two for the Roman Catholics, and one for dissenters. The last was built on my ground, by lease dated April 16, 1788, and is maintained by voluntary contributions.'[10]

Holywell was seen as an important place to foster the revival of the Independents in Flintshire. The town, the fastest growing place in North Wales, in the vanguard of the industrial revolution with its numerous metal and textile works set along the Holywell stream was seeing a population explosion. It was an important market for Catherall and he probably felt grateful to the Nonconformists there for nurturing his faith and giving him the opportunity to express his new-found zeal.

How and why did the Methodists establish themselves in Buckley before the Independents? The obvious explanation is that there were other Buckley folk who worshipped with the Wesleyan Methodists in Chester and by 1785 felt confident enough in their numbers, strength of fellowship and commitment to pursue the course of seeking licences in the Bishop of Chester's court for permission to worship in their own places. The first licence issued on 10 August 1785 gave permission for worship at a house, which became known as Buckley Mountain Chapel, later changed to Buckley Mount Chapel, supported by John Sellers, Ithel Davies and Thomas Astbury yeoman farmer of Daisy Hill. This was the parent body of what later became Brunswick chapel in the 1860s. The second licence, granted the following day, gave permission for the use of the home of Jeremiah Hayes, a brick-built house, to be used as meeting place for public worship. John Sellers again signed the licence with other signatories. This building was situated on the topside of the Middle Common, off the Alltami Road just beyond Cheshire's Lane near to Hawkesbury. It was the parent body of what in 1834 became the Square chapel. Both these causes were served from St John's Methodist circuit, Chester.

We know that the Methodists made a great impression on Jonathan Catherall because he recorded the missionary activity of their preacher, John Sellers, on the stone erected in the Congregational burial ground. In 1785 Catherall was only 24 years of age and not quite established in his business. The major point, however, is that Jonathan and his mother had joined the Independent cause and worshipped alternately in Holywell and Chester and did not feel the necessity to licence their home for worship in spite of the reproof they received from the Justices in January 1788.

By 1792 circumstances were changing for Jonathan Catherall. He suffered a serious illness, his mother was infirm and at the end of the year he married Catherine Jones, the daughter of the Reverend William Jones, Vicar of Llannor and Denio, Pwlhelli. Catherine transferred her membership to the Independent chapel in Holywell. Before his marriage and probably for the sake of his ageing mother Catherall decided to establish an Independent cause in Buckley. He recorded in his personal memorandum, 'April 24 1792. While Mr and Mrs Clegg were at our house, my mother and they agreed to have preaching by the Oswestry students in the shed by Whitleys, where it was continued every other Sabbath while my mother was alive'. Jonathan Catherall now followed the course of the Buckley Methodists and initiated proceedings for the granting by the Bishop of Chester of two licences for permission to use two separate places for public worship. These were granted shortly afterwards on 21 June 1792. The applicants were Catherall's old mentors, the minister and members of Queen Street Chapel, Chester. The first made it possible for the house of Jonathan Catherall II, 'being in Ewloe,' to be used for public worship and the second allowed a warehouse on Buckley Mountain occupied by Robert Whitley, to be used for the same purpose. These two places of worship were adequately serviced by the students and teachers of the Independent Academy at Wrexham, which had recently removed from Oswestry under the direction of Mr Jenkin Lewis. In the meantime, following the death of his mother in October 1793, Catherall took the opportunity of purchasing land from the Mold Enclosure Commissioners on which he built a house. This marked the beginning of a small estate which eventually extended to forty five acres concentrated on what became Hawkesbury Place and stretched along the Argoed side of Mill Lane, from the Mold to Chester road at Buckley Cross and across the road from Hawkesbury.

Hawkesbury Place, the house that Catherall had completed by 1801, was probably named after the Home Secretary of the day, Lord Hawkesbury, a noted anti-Catholic. Catherall was granted a licence to permit public worship there at the Quarter Sessions on 8 October 1801.

Catherine Jones. From T. Cropper Buckley and District.

The Pottery Shed in which the Oswestry
students began to preach in 1792.
From T. Cropper Buckley and District.

It has been suggested that the newly appointed minister at Holywell, the Reverend David Jones, also served at Hawkesbury.[12] He became a good friend of Catherall's and was a regular correspondent. Before his ordination, Jones was a maker of wooden domestic dishes and utensils. His ministry was fruitful and active both as a hymn writer and founder of chapels.[13]

Catherall suffered the loss of his wife Catherine in 1807. She was buried in the burial ground of the Queen Street Chapel, Chester. In 1808 he built an Independent chapel in New Street, Mold and, as was his custom, he chose the minister and paid him a basic salary of £30 a year.

In 1811 Catherall purchased a field of eleven acres from Mr Edmund Lloyd, landlord of the Duke of York public house, on which he built an Independent place of worship which was first known as Buckley Mountain Chapel. It was the first purpose built place of worship in Buckley.

The church was opened on the Tuesday of the first week in October 1811, when the Reverend William Browne, pastor of Chester Street Independent Church, Wrexham, officiated. The church was on the side of the Common and approached by a narrow country lane. It was a small building, sixteen yards long by six yards wide, and was neatly finished with what Catherall described as 'pretty' ceilings and a 'uniform' interior with a coloured-glass window. On the left hand side of the entrance 'a staircase from the place where the coal was stored led to the roof and on the right hand side of the entrance there was a high-backed pew that filled the corner, its occupants being entirely hidden from view. The building was heated by a stove and lit by ten tallow candles.'[14] Three years later in a letter to his friend Mr Foster, Catherall writes of the progress of the chapel, its minister and speaks about its enlargement and the provision of a bell:

> My children are indefatigable in the school; the children are numerous. We cannot leave them remain in the chapel during the service for want of more room. The attendance is regular every Sabbath. The chapel is so neatly finished that I cannot think of destroying the uniformity of it inside … We want more walls to hang lessons on, Lancashire's plan, which I wish to adopt.[15] Mr Powell has been ordained when I was from home. He regularly attends, and though he looks so despicable in and out of the pulpit, the people hear him attentively, like him much, are going to make a collection for him … I bought a bell in Cork for £12, but as there is one steeple near the house I cannot think of having a second.[16]

On the drawing of Buckley Mountain Congregational Church in Cropper's *Buckley and District* there is a small bell-cote, which appears to be built on the gable end of the 1814 enlargement. However, there was a campanile in the grounds of Hawkesbury Place, a description of which appears in Cropper:

> The tower was put up in the garden of the late Mr Catherall. The Congregationalists were anxious that the building should be as handsome as possible, and wished it to have a tower, but the rector of that period, thinking that the chapel with a tower might rival the church with a tower, objected. The law was on his side, and the authorities decided that the meeting-house, as it was termed, should not have a tower. Mr Catherall resented this attitude, and as a protest erected the tower. Of course, no parish authorities could prevent him from doing this and consequently the tower stood as a monument.[17]

The establishment of a Sunday school was an integral part of the provision of religious instruction and the natural corollary to a place of worship, as was the setting up of a day school, when the same or adjacent premises could be used. Catherall started both day and Sunday schools in Buckley a decade in advance of those of St Matthew's. In these endeavours he looked to help from his enthusiastic teenage children, particularly Martha and Catherine, together with William. They were all that were left to the grieving

Buckley Mountain Congregational Church 1811. From T. Cropper Buckley and District.

widower after the death of Catherine in January 1807. Their success was both a matter of consolation and pride. Shepherd records:

We do not know definitely when the Sunday school was actually begun. But apparently by 1810 it was a thriving institution as an old handbill suggests which states 'a sermon will be preached for the benefit of the Sunday School instituted on Buckley Mountain on Sunday 18th day of November, 1810, by the Rev. Mr Braithwaite. As the Sunday school is large and there are upwards of fifty children taught gratis on the week days, it has involved the Managers in considerable expense; they now solicit the help of all who are friends of the institution and that of a generous public.'[18] Cropper adds 'In the year 1813 Mr Catherall purchased Frog Hall and also opened a day school there, in which for a period his two young daughters taught the youth of the neighbourhood.'[19]

In 1818 tragedy struck and Martha and Catherine died within two days of each other aged respectively 24 and 23 years. They contracted fever whilst nursing a sick person in Smelt Cottage and were laid to rest beside their mother in Chester. One cannot imagine the grief of Jonathan Catherall but he kept the faith. Ironically the last addition he made to the Buckley Mountain Congregational Church was a burial ground situated between the chapel and Hawkesbury and two years before he died he placed his own monument 'Erected A.D. 1831 by Jonathan Catherall in the LXX year of his age. A Nonconformist.'

Jonathan Catherall's pride in being a Nonconformist was more than justified and his contribution to the cause in Buckley immense. As with most pioneers, he had his faults, but they were those of the age he lived in. He was paternalistic and owned the chapels he built. He was despotic and appointed, paid and controlled the ministers. His relationship with his only surviving child William was uneasy and unpredictable. At his death he had failed to surrender the chapel into the hands of the members and thus deprived them of a responsibility, which was theirs by right. He triumphed over much adversity. In his early life he was opposed by jealous siblings, dogged by ill-health in a business which demanded constant travelling over rough roads, met with hostility from the Established Church, and experienced the heart-rending early loss of friends and family. He was a true pilgrim in Bunyan's sense and with assurance and faith overcame hardship and danger. His death in 1833 marked the end of the first phase of the establishment of a number of Nonconformist causes in Buckley and the building of their places of worship.

The Nonconformist places of worship built in the life of Jonathan Catherall II are described in the following account which provides a list of them, a brief description of the first chapels erected, and some background information about their particular religious traditions. The first is the Independents, or Congregationalists, whose origin went back to the seventeenth century, Jonathan Catherall's denomination. All the members and none but the members have a

The Tower in the grounds of Hawkesbury. Drawing by K.Lloyd Gruffydd in Buckley Society Magazine 24.

Brunswick Methodist Church Banner 1927, group includes Samuel Collins, Edward Edwards and Leonard Edwards. [Buckley Society Archive]

voice in the management of their affairs. They are thoroughly Calvinistic, Evangelical and Protestant in doctrine and are linked to other churches.

We have given a description of their first building above and seen that the initial establishment of the cause took place in dwelling houses which received successive licences either from the Bishop of Chester or the magistrates in Quarter Session, two in 1792 and another in 1801. The first church as such, Buckley Mountain, was built in 1811, enlarged in 1814 with a burial ground added in 1822.

The Methodists in Buckley received their first licences in 1785 when John Wesley was still alive. The denomination with its various branches of Wesleyan Methodism, Methodist New Connexion, Primitive Methodism and United Methodism was the strongest in Buckley. Its intentions and organisation appealed to the growing working class communities in Buckley with the opportunities it gave for the involvement of the laity. John Wesley (1703–91) was the founder of the Methodist movement, which was a major influence in the religious revival in the eighteenth century. Wesley's professed object was 'to promote as far as I am able vital practical religion and by the grace of God to beget, preserve, and increase the life of God in the souls of men'. When he died in 1791 the movement had become a separate denomination from the Church of England. Its doctrine differed from the Calvinistic Methodists who believed in predestination.

John Wesley and his followers believed that the sovereignty of God does not exclude free will. They held that Jesus died for all and the offer of salvation is open to everyone who will accept it. This is known as the Arminian view. A feature of Methodism is its ecclesiastical organisation. Local groups are divided into 'Societies', which are subdivided into 'Classes'. A class was a small unit under the leadership of a class leader, which met together weekly for fellowship and pastoral care. Membership of the class was a condition of membership of the society. This is no longer compulsory. Societies are grouped together in a circuit. The superintendent of each circuit is responsible for making the preaching plan. Quarterly meetings of societies in the circuit are held to enquire into the spiritual and temporal state of each society. The annual Methodist Conference consists of delegates and is the legislative body responsible for the definition and interpretation of doctrine.

The first Wesleyan Methodist church was the Buckley Mountain Chapel. Its founders were Thomas Astbury, a yeoman farmer, and Ithel Davies. In 1818 land was purchased at Daisy Hill for the building of a chapel with its name later changed to Buckley Mount Chapel. The site was later known as Chapel Walks.

The next Methodist church was Bethesda, Pentrobin. It was not Wesleyan but belonged to a group which had seceded from the parent body in 1797 following the expulsion of its founder Alexander Kilham when the Conference refused to allow lay representation. They were known as the Methodist New Connexion. It was part of the St John's Chester circuit. The members first met in an old barn known as Newton's Barn in Burntwood in 1820. Their membership of twenty was recorded as part of the John Street Methodist circuit in 1803/4. Two classes were in operation. The first, under the leadership of Thomas Astbury of Buckley Mountain Chapel, had sixteen members and the second, under Samuel Hughes, had a membership of ten. A year later the Pentrobin members became part of the Methodist New Connexion circuit at Pepper Street, Chester. Their first small chapel was built by the members 'after the normal days work was over', and was ready in 1823.

In 1834 the Calvinistic Methodist Church, Bethel, was built in Mold Road. Welsh Calvinistic Methodism was not as strong as Wesleyan Methodism in Buckley and district probably because it was more prone to the influences of the English border. This denomination was established in Wales through the revivalist preaching of Howel Harris and Daniel Rowland. Separation from the Anglican Church in Wales began in 1795 as a result of persecution. In 1811 they began to ordain their own ministers. Like the Methodists it is connexional in organisation. Local churches report to their district meeting, which in turn reports to the Presbytery, which is a monthly meeting of a group of districts. The Presbyteries then appoint delegates to the Association, which are the main legislative courts of the church. There are three Associations and they meet together in a General Assembly. They differ from the Wesleyan Methodists in believing the Calvinistic doctrine of predestination.

Bethesda, Pentrobin, Methodist New Connexion Chapel.
[Buckley Society Archive]

Jonathan Catherall II was sympathetic to the Calvinistic Methodists with their Presbyterian roots and his acquaintance with them on his business travels in Wales and he encouraged them by giving them permission in 1816 to use his schoolroom at Frog Hall for Sunday services. He showed further goodwill with a lease for a thousand years at a pound a week and ,on the death of his daughters, presented them with the land on which the building stood on condition that the school continued. The day school closed in 1836. They had first come together in Buckley in 1813 when they met to hold Welsh services in the Drummer public house (later the White Lion) where they started a Sunday school. Their first members were Ithel Hill, a cooper, Robert Jones, David Evans, Ephraim Hopwood and others who joined them from Mold. They built their first chapel on the same site in 1834 when the school at Frog Hall was converted into a chapel and schoolroom.

In 1834 the Wesleyan Methodist cause which had first received its licence to worship in the dwelling house of Jeremiah Hayes on the Middle Common opened their first specially designed place of worship, the Buckley Square Chapel. The members yearned to settle in a permanent place after meeting in a number of private houses and, in 1832, they bought a piece of land on Mold Road and built their chapel. It cost £170 and, as was the custom in Buckley, the members who were able, namely Isles Jones, Robert Hanmer and Robert Wynne made the bricks by hand when their day's work was complete. An Indenture dated August

1834 gives the names and occupations of the first trustees, which illustrates the working class membership of the movement in Buckley and the gathered nature of its support. John Jones, Bistre, collier; Richard Rowland, Bistre, collier; Robert Price, Ewloe, potter; William Bellis, Argoed, collier; Joshua Sharratt, Ewloe, potter; Edward Parry, Bistre, brickworks manager; Robert Wynne, Argoed, brickworks manager; John Griffiths, Bistre, brick burner; and William Wilson, late of the Crown Inn Denbigh, Superintendent Preacher of the Wesleyan Connexion.

The second phase of Nonconformist development began in the late 1830s and lasted until the end of the 1870s. It was a growth which belonged primarily to the Primitive Methodist cause with a secondary expansion of the Wesleyan Methodists at Brunswick and the introduction of the Methodist New Connexion cause at Providence, Bistre. The sole exception to this pattern was the establishment of English Presbyterians in Brunswick Road in 1869. Although this was really an off-shoot of the Welsh Calvinistic Methodists in Mold Road.

Bethel, Calvinistic Methodist Church, Welsh, Mold Road.
[Buckley Society Archive]

The Square Wesleyan Methodist Church.[Buckley Society Archive]

Another feature of this period was the rapid growth in population, which brought in a migrant community with a high birth rate, a factor which rapidly increased Sunday school numbers and necessitated either the enlargement of the first chapel buildings or their replacement.

It was an exciting and formative period in the religious life of Buckley with what appears to be ceaseless activity as the following number of new buildings and causes suggests. Alltami Primitive Methodist Chapel built in 1836 was enlarged in 1866. Mill Lane Primitive Methodist Chapel built in 1841 was replaced by Tabernacle Chapel, the most splendidly conceived of all the Buckley chapels. Providence Methodist New Connexion established in 1842 found its eventual home in an enlarged place of worship in 1878–9. The old Wesleyan Methodist cause at Brunswick had its building replaced by a new one in 1867. At Drury Lane another cause of the Primitive Methodists was begun from Ewloe over a shop in 1872 which moved to a new chapel in 1880. The Congregationalists faced by growing numbers built a new church in 1873, capable of seating a congregation of 600 and changed its name from Buckley Mountain Chapel to St John's. Another feature of this period was the accommodation made for Sunday schools in the respective building programmes.

In 1842 the Anglicans created a new ecclesiastical district, later the parish of Bistre, by the separation of the townships of Argoed and Bistre from the parish of Mold.

The opening up of the Buckley coalfield and the multiplication of brick and tile manufactories to furnish the materials for new towns and railway construction transformed the outlying townships of Mold (Bistre and Argoed) and Hawarden (Ewloe and Pentrobin), which turned the area into a frontier zone. An immigrant population of agricultural labourers who had left the land for the coal seam and clay hole clustered in new settlements around their mines and works. In the uncertain climate of change uprooted families needed a sense of security and identification. This was difficult to find in a boom and slump economy and the dangerous environment in which they worked. Pit villages in the 1830s and 1840s were described as by turns idle, deceitful, ignorant, vicious, drunken, shameless, irreligious, and dangerous.[20] A situation witnessed to in Buckley by Willett in 1822 and Ffoulkes in 1847.[21] It is not surprising that social control broke down when injury, sickness, poverty, destitution, homelessness and death were regular visitors. The old restraints exercised by the Established Church were too far away and the working class divorced from the leadership of clergy and magistrates apart from appearing before them on the bench charged with vagrancy, poaching and riot.

How were they to find a remedy for these ills? The answer lay in religion. A new religion brought to them by men and women who had shared their experiences. In this way Primitive Methodism was introduced into their lives bringing salvation and hope. Missionaries came to them from Cheshire and Staffordshire with a Christian message to which they could relate. Missionaries who were to improve the conditions of life of their poverty stricken brothers and sisters. The movement began on 31 May 1807 on the slopes of Mow Cop, a thousand feet above the plains of Cheshire and Staffordshire. This large open-air religious gathering was known as a 'camp meeting' and provided a heady mixture of revivalist preaching, extempore prayer, hymn singing and the opportunity for relaxation and a picnic. It was a formula, which became a ritual for the Primitive Methodists who applied it wherever they went. 'Primitive Methodism was born in the workaday circumstances of middle England, on the borders of Cheshire and Staffordshire where agriculture and industry (coal mining, metal working, and above all potters) were carried on in close

Commemorative plate: '1807 Primitive Methodist Centenary 1907'. Wood & Sons (Burslem), Staffordshire ware.

proximity with one another'.[22] The founders of the movement were Hugh Bourne, from an agricultural background, and William Clowes, a potter. They were influenced by the American evangelist, Lorenzo Dow.

Revivalist preaching had a powerful effect. Its end result was aimed at conversion. The poor were preached to by the poor, the working class preacher had an extempore conversational style, which cajoled, persuaded, and wooed his hearers by anecdotes, and parables of experience. He gave them a vision of a new Jerusalem in which they shared a place of glory in this life and the next. The Biblical epic was transformed and related in contemporary terms. The message was alive and God's Holy Spirit possessed them and filled them with new life. They were converted and in Christian terms experienced new birth, sanctification, revelation, perfection and assurance. They were born again and could bear Christian witness in their own society. They were given new goals, which aimed at self-improvement, education, and respectability. The women became good housewives, the men were given a democratic opportunity for self-expression in their religious meetings and had a renewed confidence. The chapel community exercised its own control and organisational discipline.

Besides preaching there were scripture readings, lengthy prayers and hymn singing which, in larger congregations, was choir-led with instrumental accompaniment. Later it was led by an organ. A 'prayer meeting' in which members could participate usually followed the evening service and demonstrated their enthusiasm and personal witness.

The Love Feast and Sacrament of Holy Communion was regularly celebrated by the congregation. It was the sharing of bread and water, drunk from a two-handled mug which was passed amongst the members with the opportunity for prayer and song interspersed by personal witness and praise. Hugh Bourne printed his own hymnbook which was revised in 1887 and 1912.

The Primitive Methodists were whole-hearted supporters of the Temperance and Band of Hope movements and most of their local preachers and ministers were total abstainers. They shared their pattern of worship and involvement in the Temperance and Sunday school movements with all Nonconformists and the assessment made of their influence may be applied to them all:

> They were a people caught between a passing traditional order and a developing society. Primitive Methodism helped them to make the transition from the Old World to the New. Becoming a Primitive Methodist meant affirming that one's soul was important, but also to other members of the society. Ordinary working-class people were bound together in a fellowship in which each was given responsibility and opportunities. A person's opinions counted, his health and his material welfare mattered, his spiritual odyssey during life and his triumph at death would be recorded. Intimate love feasts as well as giant camp meetings brought spiritual drama and song and colour into lives that were otherwise drab. Above all, the Primitive Methodist experience was one of participation in a community of the people's own making, not something bestowed or imposed by their betters.[23]

We will now review the chapel buildings of the second phase. The first is Alltami Primitive Methodist Chapel. The cause came from Chester in the summer of 1836 and started in characteristic fashion by the holding of a camp meeting in a field belonging to Griffiths' farm at Bryn-y-Baal, conducted by Henry Brining. This attracted a membership which continued to meet at Kitty Howell's cottage and at a place in Alltami called Old Taylor's. The first members were Joseph Arrowsmith, Hannah Stanley, John Evans, Samuel Stanley, Mrs Evans, Mary Lamb, Robert Lamb and Robert Roberts.

Two years later the first Primitive Methodist chapel in North Wales was built in Alltami. It was remembered that:

> They ventured to build with empty pockets but with overflowing hearts. Stones were hewn and carried in carts from the surroundings. Sand and lime were at hand and so building operations were commenced by these enthusiastic workers. Their daring adventure has been amply rewarded. The old chapel was a low building. The entrance faced the road within a paving between the road and the chapel. There was a step down into the Chapel on to a grey tiled floor and facing you was the pulpit. The edifice was lit by tallow candles and heated by a small coal stove. There was no musical instrument of any description and it was sometime after the present Chapel was built before hymns were accompanied.[24]

In 1866 a sanctuary was added, and in 1879 the church was extended and opened as a schoolroom to accommodate the increasing number of Sunday school scholars. The career of the Reverend Joseph Davies began at Alltami. He kept a shop in New Brighton before ordination and is remembered for his contribution towards the enlargement of the church in 1866. 'He was musical and organised a children's choir which visited neighbouring towns to raise funds. Travelling conditions were poor, farmer's carts were used to carry the children over bad roads and very often they arrived home at two or three o'clock in the morning after awaiting the Ferry (at Queensferry) and a suitable tide before they could cross'. The Alltami members in turn were responsible for the introduction of Primitive Methodism to Buckley, Penyffordd and Mold.

In 1825 the Primitive Methodist magazine instructed its readers in the basic requirements of their religious buildings. They were modest:

> A central aisle leading from door to pulpit is recommended with short forms on either side of the pulpit facing inwards. Chapels wider than seven yards ought to have two aisles. Pulpits should be at least one yard square and a yard deep, with a Bible board at least two feet long, and inclined slightly towards the preacher. Much emphasis is laid on adequate ventilation by means of window casements. Windows behind the pulpit are condemned.

As the nineteenth century advanced these basic modest proposals were ignored as the movement grew. We see this in the design of the new chapel at Tabernacle in the 1870s. The original cause met on the site of Mr Williams' timber yard in Lane End. Services continued there for twelve months with occasional meetings held in the house of Edward Jones, Smelt Yard, and later in the old Duke of York public house. By 1841 they established their first chapel in Mill Lane, when the members made the bricks from clay dug from the ground on which the chapel stood. A day school for boys was opened in 1843, a Sunday school formed about 1850, and the chapel enlarged in 1863. Ten years later, land was purchased in Padeswood Road on which to build a new chapel. It was an ambitious project which demonstrated how far the fortunes of the Primitive Methodists had advanced over thirty-five years:

> The plan is a parallelogram the inside measurements being 62 feet by 44 feet. It will have galleries on three sides and the fourth will be for the organ and choir. There will also be four large classrooms and vestry with access from the chapel and from without. The principal entrance will look on to the main road, and will have two doorways leading into a vestibule

Alltami Primitive Methodist Church.
[Buckley Society Archive]

Alltami Primitive Methodist Church interior.
[Buckley Society Archive]

paved with encaustic tiles, from which staircases leading to the galleries will spring, and where also the doors open into the ground floor of the Chapel. There will be seating accommodation for 700 persons, and the seats and fittings will be of pitch pine. The ceiling will be cut into sixteen panels of various shapes, deeply grooved and moulded relieved with perforated borders and ornamental centrepieces. The front elevation will comprise a central façade of two wings, the centre pediments with large cornices, and the wings with plinths and copings. The walls will be of brick and the dressings of stourton stone. The building will be heated by Whitakers' Hot Air System. The contractors are Messrs J. & T. Woods of Hooton, and the architect Mr Richard Owens of Breck Rd. Liverpool and the cost will be about £2,000.[25]

The Trustees Minute Book gives some insight into various aspects of the venture. The architect chosen was Mr Richard Owens of Liverpool. He was the most prolific chapel-builder in Wales, where he was called the 'arch-architect,' and drew up plans for some three hundred place of worship in the principality.[26] The trustees went over to Liverpool to inspect 'the new Chapel in Everton and resolved to build a similar one at Buckley'. They agreed to engage Owens as architect and pay him £60 total 'being for plans and designs, letting and superintending the work, journey &c' and 'that a chapel be built to hold 700 persons after the model of the Everton Chapel'. Seven tradesmen were appointed to act as a building committee.

Once again the principle of self-help was used to advantage when the members persuaded the tenant of the field where the chapel was to be built to allow them have a portion of land on which to make bricks and get the well prepared and the water available for making bricks as early as possible. Mr Thomas Jones gave an estimate for 200,000 bricks at fourteen shillings per thousand, which were to be inspected when burnt by Samuel Kendrick and Joseph Peters.

The foundation stone was laid in April 1875 when a procession marched from Mill Lane Chapel to the new site led by the minister, local preachers, class leaders and members together with other Nonconformist ministers and their congregations. It was resolved that all 'Pay at the door one shilling and that the children have an orange and a bun'.

Although members of Tabernacle needed a large building to accommodate increasing numbers, they over-stretched themselves and it took 44 years to pay off the debt. Every effort was made to raise money. Mrs Catherine Gladstone was approached to open the bazaar. Money was borrowed from those willing and able to lend it. In 1886 it was decided that in order to get £100 off the debt 'we endeavour to get 100 people to collect £1 each'. Modest pew rents brought in an income probably sufficient enough to pay the chapel cleaner. It was agreed 'that the pews in the bottom in the middle line up to the rise be 9*d.* per sitting, also the side pews at 9*d.* each, the pews all round the gallery 9*d.* each, second row at 7*d.* each, all the remainder pews be 6*d.*'[27]

It was the ubiquitous Reverend Joseph Davies who opened the Primitive Methodist church in Drury Lane in February 1882. It was reported in the *Chronicle* that 'it was finally opened' and somewhat

Tabernacle Primitive Methodist Church.
[Buckley Society Archive]

Drury Lane Primitive Methodist Church interior.
[Buckley Library]

mysteriously two years later 'the services in connection with the reopening of the chapel' had commenced and 'the collections were in aid of the renovation fund.'[28] It has been said that that Joseph Davies, a Congregationalist, built the church in 1880 'which was taken over by the Primitive Methodists'. This circumstance was not unusual in the long career of Joseph Davies who retained close contact, after he joined the Congregationalists, with the church in which he was nurtured. Certainly Davies would have admired the musical tradition which grew up in Drury Lane where there was an orchestra of sixteen led by Thomas Griffiths of Ledsham House. The church prospered under the leadership of John Millington.

The Methodist New Connexion cause, in what later became Providence Chapel, came into being about 1842. John Lee is said to have joined them at Lane End as a Sunday school teacher in 1842. The Reverend John Williams reminiscing in 1885 said that he remembered during the thirty-five years he had been connected with the cause different kinds of buildings used, from a dilapidated barn to the present handsome temple. But it was William Hughes who was really the founder of the cause in Buckley. This is evident from the return he made for the Religious Census in 1851:

> Bistree Chapel. New Connexion.
> Erected 1850
> Space: free 80; other 60; standing 34 ft by 18 ft
> Present: aft. 20; even. 50.
> Remarks: I built this Chapel and allows the same to be used free of any charge.
> William Hughes. Owner
> Timber Merchant.

William Hughes in his will dated 6 February 1862, made two years before his death, said: 'I do will and bequeath the Chapel which I have erected near my large house to the use of the Methodist New Connexion, free of all incumbrances for ever, and pray God that it may be a blessing to the neighbourhood'. This did not please his relatives who unsuccessfully contested the case.

The history of the development of the cause is related in the *Chronicle* in 1878:

> It is but a little over twenty years since the Methodist New Connexion friends first made a move towards the building of a place of Worship in the populous and neglected district of Bistre. The person whose name stands out amongst the rest is the late William Hughes, and he built the first House. That building was subsequently enlarged, and now is the present chapel, and this has become too small to afford the necessary conveniences to the Congregation worshipping therein.[29]

The original chapel was enlarged in 1872 at a cost of £132 but this did not satisfy the needs of the Trustee body set up that year. This was composed of a cross section of people: John Williams (builder & contractor), Lane End; Thomas Williams (grocer), Lane End; William Peters (collier), Megs Lane; Hugh Hodge (farmer), Mostyn; Henry Luke Estob (gentleman), Hawarden; Edward Roberts (cordwainer), Wepre; Joseph Hall (painter), Flint; and Joseph Grime (cordwainer), Flint.

The *Chronicle* gave further information:

> It was finally decided in 1876 to build a new and larger Chapel and a parcel of land was purchased from Elizabeth Ratcliffe of Hawarden including cottages and other buildings on the site for £140. They decided to pull down two cottages, which were side by side with the original chapel (now the Sunday school). The new chapel

Providence Bistre Methodist New Connexion Church.
[Buckley Society Archive]

Bistre methodist Chapel.
[Buckley Society Archive]

was created with its rear in line with the side of the old chapel. Behind the pulpit was a stained or painted window set in a three sectioned folding screen fitted on wheels on a short track. The screen when pushed back opened up the Sunday school and the entire pulpit and communion area thus making it possible for the enlarged congregations to be in front of and behind the preacher.

Providence was opened on 10 May 1879. The cost was in the region of £1,000 and provided a chapel capable of seating 270, that is £3.70 per sitting place, a reasonable return on their money. The architect was John Williams from Lane End. The former chapel became a schoolroom able to provide for 150 scholars. Four years later the debt stood at £650. It was an unpropitious time in which to consider such a venture but the members reaffirmed the faith that had led them to choose the name Providence. During the winter of 1878–9 a long and severe spell of frost was experienced, which forced the brickworks to close.

In 1871, the first Wesleyan Methodist cause in Buckley licensed in 1785 and later established as Mount Chapel became known as Brunswick. Like other Nonconformist places in the area it had outgrown its old premises. The 1851 Religious Census is the first to provide us with reliable information.

BUCKLEY CHAPEL. WESLEYAN METHODIST.
Erected before 1800.
Space: free 100; other 75.
Present: morn. 120 + 80 scholars; no aft. Sermon; even. 119.

Edward Denvers. Mill Lane Chapel.

Lead Works, Buckley.

The history of the cause was given in the *Chronicle* when the foundation stone for a new chapel was laid on 1 August 1867:

For some seventy years past a congregation of Wesleyans has assembled in the old chapel at Buckley, a small confined and uncomfortable erection and they have at length decided to build a new one. The project has been under discussion for some years and preparations for building commenced on Thursday afternoon last when it was arranged that the foundation stone should be laid by Mr Thomas Hazeldine of Runcorn. The new chapel is to be situated on land given for the purpose by Mr Craven. Its dimensions will be 56 ft by 36 ft and is calculated to seat 300 persons. That will be sufficient for present requirements, and should the congregation materially increase, galleries can be added in perfect harmony with the design. The style will be modified Gothic, the architect being Mr Krolow of this City (Chester). The total cost is estimated at about £600, and towards this sum £400 has been obtained either in cash or promises while a bazaar is projected for next week, and by that means the building cost is hoped to be completed. The proceedings commenced on Thursday last with a procession of School children to the site of the stone laying where a considerable number of spectators were already assembled. After Mr Hazeldine had performed the ceremony 'the proceedings terminated in the evening with a Tea meeting held in a wooden structure erected for the purpose. A Public Meeting was held afterwards'.[30]

The new building was first referred to as 'Brunswick Chapel' on the occasion of the anniversary services in May 1871.

Thomas Cropper's impressions of his visit to Brunswick is given in his chapter Sunday evening in the churches of Buckley and district where he remarks that the 'fairly large building would have accommodated the congregations of several others I had experience of in addition to its own' and led him to reflect 'upon all this surplus emptiness'.[31]

The touching manner in which the congregation greeted their new minister in 1873 demonstrated their affection and zeal. The Sunday school children walked in procession with numerous banners from the old chapel towards Hope Station on the way there they met their new minister and his wife and accompanied them all the way to the Manse with the singing of hymns. On arrival, a public meeting was held when Mr John Lamb presented the new minister, Mr Jeffries, 'with Dr Smith's *Dictionary of the Bible* in three large volumes, as a token of esteem for his interest in the younger people since he came to them five months ago'.

The occasion was marred by the funeral of Mr Edward Parry on the same day. His obituary spoke of the great loss his death was to Buckley:

Edward Parry was born in Ireland in 1806 his father being in the service of the Bishop of Rapho, with whom young Parry became a favourite. When quite a lad his father returned to Buckley, and unfortunately he died soon after returning, and having kept school at Dodleston for sometime. He then became a clerk at one of the Buckley Collieries. Mr Parry then undertook the management of brickworks, which he brought up to a state of prosperity. He added to this and whilst conducting the brickworks he started at Ewloe Hall a Colliery which for many years was of great benefit to the district because of the number of men that he employed. Subsequently he started a large brickworks of his own, which he left to his family in a very prosperous condition.

Mr Parry was a member of the Mount Wesleyan Methodist Chapel and held all the offices that a layman could possibly hold. He did good services to the Buckley and Mold Wesleyan Methodist Circuit, and whilst circuit steward, he was frequently out of pocket from £30 to £40 at a time.[32]

In 1890/1 a Sunday school was built at Chapel Walks.

In 1869 an English Presbyterian Congregation and a Sunday school was formed in Buckley by two of the brethren from Bethel Calvinistic Methodist Church. For seven years

Above and right: Brunswick Wesleyan Methodist Church with locally made font.
[Buckley Society Archive]

they met together in private dwellings using Bethel for special occasions. The two founders were Thomas Williams, Bryn Teg, and Richard Roberts, of Nant Mawr. Both men served the church in Buckley with dedication and distinction. Thomas Williams was born in Machynlleth and became a successful tea merchant in Bolton where he founded the Welsh Calvinistic Church. He came to reside at Llong and later moved to Bryn Teg and became a member of Bethel. He was much respected for his deep spirituality. His companion Richard Roberts of Nant Mawr was a good musician and an advocate of the Temperance movement. He lives in the memory of Buckley folk as one of the instigators of the Jubilee.

The new church, Zion, was opened on 11 June 1876 when an account appeared in the *Wrexham Advertiser*:

> The opening service of the new English Calvinistic Methodist Chapel was held on Sunday last when the Reverend John Ffoulkes of Liverpool officiated. The chapel is a very neat and well-furnished edifice accommodating 200 persons. On the first Sunday it was filled to overflowing and the collections realised a pretty liberal sum of £23. Before the opening day the friends had succeeded in paying off £400. There remains a debt of less than £400 which it is hoped will be reduced at least to £300 before the opening services are concluded.[33]

In 1851, the Trustees of the Congregational church paid the late Jonathan Catherall's son, William, a nominal sum to obtain possession of the church, burial ground, manse and schoolroom. It was the year of the Religious Census and the return for this church shows a healthy membership although the concluding remark about evening services is at first a little puzzling.

> INDEPENDENTS, BUCKLEY.
> Erected 1810.
> Space: free 200; other 100.
> Present: morn. 208; aft. 260 + 140 scholars; even. 180.
> Average: general congregation 280 ; scholars 180.
> Remarks: Services in the evening at the neighbouring Chapels.
> John Griffiths. Minister.

Griffiths was a much-respected minister noted as a good theologian and a supporter of the foreign missions of the church. His influence was such that 60 or 70 people attended the Monday prayer meeting. The education of all age groups and music in worship was encouraged. Griffiths won the support of William Catherall who was keen to see that his workmen received a basic education. To this end the brick maker built a schoolroom to accommodate a growing Sunday school and induced the minister's son, Robert, to open a day school for boys and girls at a salary of £40 a year. His sister later succeeded him. J. R. Griffiths recorded: 'went to Miss Griffith's school. At first she held the school in an upstairs room of their Manse, then in a new portion built on the end of Tom Catherall's School, which afterwards was the site of the present Sunday school'.

Towards the end of his ministry John Griffiths was in failing health and the life of the church began to suffer. Eventually a young and vigorous successor was chosen who impressed the members with the power of his preaching. Thus the Reverend E. Ambrose Jones came to Buckley in 1870. The old building was unable to cope with the people who flocked to hear his eloquence. Obviously a new church was needed and the minister took the lead in the design and choice of architect. Anticipating a greater harvest of souls, the architect, the Reverend Thomas Thomas of

Zion English Presbyterian Church.
[Buckley Society Archive]

Glandŵr, designed a building to accommodate 600 adherents. Thomas came up with a fairly modest design not quite what the *Builder Magazine* dubbed his 'Landore Lombardic', although the edifice almost matched his criteria of having a squared plan which made it 'easier to preach in, and gave good oratorical space'.[34] The foundation stone-laying ceremony took place in June 1872. A report in the *Chronicle* suggests Jonathan Catherall's old chapel had for a long time been inadequate and that another place had been used in conjunction with the Buckley Mountain Chapel. The new church now became known as St John's:

> On Saturday last the foundation stone of a new Congregational church was laid by Robert Sinclair, Esq., of London, a member of the executive of the Congregational Union of England and Wales. For many years the congregation has been worshipping in a chapel at the bottom of Mill Lane and between that and the church which was built at the expense of Mr Catherall of Hawkesbury.

St John's Congregational Church 1873.
[Buckley Library]

> In front there is a cold, wet and bleak common land, and the houses are very sparse in the district. The old chapel has more the appearance of a dwelling house than a place of worship, and was fitly designated during the afternoon of Saturday by the Reverend G. W. Galloway as a barn. The pulpit is placed near the entrance, and the pews are in the fashion of olden times, more like boxes than seats. On the wall to the left of the entrance there is a white marble slab erected in the memory of Lt-Colonel T. Jones of the Fourth King's Own Regiment, who served in the Peninsular War, and commanded it in the American War of 1814 and was mortally wounded in the attack on New Orleans in 1815. Underneath, there is another slab in memory of Jonathan Catherall. Attached to the chapel is a graveyard, half-an-acre or thereabouts, and in it is a prominent ruin of what was intended, we should imagine to form part of an obelisk, to be a monument in honour of Nonconformity. Several large stones are lying about, on one of which is carved the initials 'J.C.' and some feet away lies a stone intended, we should imagine, to form part of the obelisk. On two faces of it there are inscriptions, the pedigree of the Catherall family, and on the other the names of Wycliffe, Cranmer, Ridley, Latimer, Hooper, Coverdale, Knox, Grotius, Calvin, Luther, Arminius, Wesley, Doddridge, Hall, Robinson, Armitage, Whyte, Reynolds, Luke, Thorpe, Knill, Bridgeman — Chester, Lewis Jenkins — Wrexham and Miss Prescott. The graveyard is not yet filled, and the centre of it is the site chosen for the new chapel which is designed by the Reverend Thomas Thomas of Glandŵr a gentleman who is the architect of a number of Congregational chapels in Wales, and whose style has been named the Glandŵr style. Over all the dimensions of the new chapel are 54 ft x 43 ft, there is a spacious gallery, and the new chapel should seat 500. Mr John Williams builder of Buckley has undertaken the contract for the sum of £1300.

> The friends had been requested to meet at 2 o'clock at the chapel but, by that time, only a score of children were present and it was not until half past two that a respectable number came together. They were formed into a procession, the children of the Sunday school, and the day schools at the head with banners and flags, and were marched to Lane End to meet the gentleman from London, and from Warren Hall who came to participate in the ceremony. It was not until half past three that the procession returned, and a large crowd assembled in front of the platform erected close to the front of the chapel. The Reverend E. Ambrose Jones opened the proceedings. William Catherall, senior, of Hawkesbury Place, presented Mr Sinclair with a beautiful silver trowel. Miss Pattie Shepherd presented Mr Sinclair with a mahogany mallet with which he laid the foundation stone'.[36]

The date was 11 June 1872.

The third phase of church building in Buckley began in the last decade of the nineteenth century when the Baptists and Roman Catholics opened places of worship in the town. The two Anglican parishes of Bistre and Buckley added four mission churches on the edges of their ecclesiastical districts at Lane End,

Mynydd Isa, Pentre and Ewloe. Likewise the Presbyterians opened a new chapel at Ewloe Green and the Reverend Joseph Davies founded a Congregational church at Mynydd Isa in 1912. In a district which was obviously over-saturated with competing denominations, the Salvation Army made only a tentative beginning. A Wesleyan Methodist church for Welsh speakers in Mold Road barely survived a decade.

In these twenty or so years before the First World War, the strength of Nonconformity was at its height. As a group of diverse causes it found its unity in promoting through the agency of the Liberals a Parliamentary Bill for the Disestablishment and Disendowment of the Anglican Church in Wales. The Buckley Nonconformists received the support and patronage of the Protestant Liberal Member of Parliament for the County of Flintshire, Samuel Smith. Its confidence was reinforced by anti-Catholic demonstrations and frequent processions of Orangemen who conveniently arrived from Liverpool by train. There were hordes of children to march in demonstration carrying Temperance and Sunday school banners singing gospel hymns. Buckley Common, the new Central Hall or Tabernacle Chapel readily welcomed these gatherings which were more acceptable than those of unemployed brickworkers and colliers.

The Baptist cause dating from the seventeenth century was late to take root in Buckley. Anne Price, an old lady of strong convictions, invited fellow Baptists to worship in her house in Daisy Hill. The following year, 1876, they moved to a little house in Lane End, and opened a mission room there. They found a good friend in the Reverend Gethin Davies, Principal of the Baptist College, Llangollen. He came over in July 1877 to preach at an open-air meeting at the Lane End. Gethin Davies was to play an important role in their eventual success in establishing a cause. At this stage efforts were being made to raise funds for the building of a permanent chapel. Tabernacle members lent their chapel for a series of concerts. In February 1883 new members attended a service on the banks of the river Alyn 'at which the Ordinance of Baptism by immersion was administered on two persons by the Reverend J. Davies, Brymbo, although the weather was very bad, a large company witnessed and took part'. But in spite of this encouragement the cause was faltering and would have become extinct had it not been for the intervention of the Llangollen Principal. He described how, in the summer of 1888, 'he happened to be passing through Buckley and found a feeble few gathered together to worship God in their little mission room at Lane End. The little band being as it were at the last gasp for breath. Strife without and strife within had done their dire work'. One of the difficulties arose because the local Welsh Baptist Association had failed to find for them English speaking preachers. Immediately Gethin Davies introduced them to a rich benefactor Alderman Richard Cory of Cardiff, who promised three hundred pounds towards a new building on condition that the chapel was free from debt and guaranteed the pastor's salary for twelve months.

The new church, Ebenezer, was opened at Daisy Hill six months later in April 1889. It was described as being in the gothic style and the architect named as J. G. Owen of Liverpool. Its dimensions were 56ft long, 31ft wide and 20ft 6ins high, was built in red brick, the front of Ruabon buff bricks, the windows filled with red cathedral glass, the roof of best Caernarfon slates, and the baptistery lined with white glazed tiles.

In May 1890 it was announced that:

Mr Cory is so well satisfied with the success of the Baptist Mission Chapel at Buckley that he wants another establishing at Nant Mawr. For this purpose he offers to invest one thousand pounds if the small sum of only two hundred pounds can be raised by the end of June. The Reverend Doctor Davies of Llangollen has taken up the matter and will see that it is carried through.

Both Alderman Richard Cory and Principal Davies were present when the new chapel was opened on 9 September 1890. The chapel, named Bethel, stood at the junction of Stanley Road, Well Street, and Nant Mawr Road. Two years later the two churches found it necessary to share the same minister and by 1914 Nant Mawr closed and the congregation returned to

Ebenezer Baptist Church 1889.
[Buckley Society Archive]

Ebenezer. The disused chapel was sold, became a wholesale salt warehouse and, becoming derelict, was demolished during the Second World War.

The Salvation Army was founded by William and Catherine Booth as the East London Christian Mission in 1865. In 1878 it adopted the name Salvation Army and by 1884 had over 600 missions in Britain and the Empire. Its members were essentially working class, recruited by William Booth to fight a war against the evils of Victorian Society, and easily recognisable through their distinctive uniforms. Each mission had its headquarters from which members moved out into the community to preach salvation and condemn drink, gambling, domestic violence and prostitution. They offered salvation and new life through conversion, and faith, through prayer and Bible classes. They provided food and shelter for the destitute and home visits brought hope to abused women and children. Their battle plan was to confront all classes in British Society with the good news of the gospel. Their appeal was the methods they used. Men and women Salvationists worked side by side, they preached, played in brass bands, on tambourine and drums, and sang their hymns to tunes from the music halls. The 'Hallelujah Lasses' with their distinctive Quaker bonnets won the respect of all sorts and conditions of humanity.

In October 1881 a meeting was held in the Buckley National Schools to consider evangelistic services during the winter in co-operation with other denominations when reservations were made by the more 'puritanical' speakers 'of any attempt which might be made to introduce scarlet uniforms or any other similar display of military uniforms'.[37] By 1882 the Army was working in Mold and held discussions with the trustees of Tabernacle Chapel with a view to taking over the old Mill Lane Chapel. These fell through. In January 1890 headlines in the *Chronicle* heralded 'The Army is come'. The report explained:

> On Sunday last the Salvation Army opened a Barracks at the Lane End in the old Wesleyan Chapel vacated by the Baptists in 1889. The attack was conducted by Captain Emily Ford and Lieutenant Jones. There was a band in attendance. They had a large audience three times on the Sunday. Evening meetings in the week have been full.'[38] A month later a monster meeting met in the Congregational Schoolroom when an interesting lecture was delivered on the slums of London. The excitement was very high and it is hoped that much good will come out of it.[39]

In May the newspaper announced 'Salvation Army to quit,' having been ordered by their superiors to withdraw from Buckley. On a Saturday evening in June they held 'an open-air meeting from the Cross to the Post Office and gathered quite a crowd of people to listen to their speaking, singing, and music', but there was no reprieve, and their effects were auctioned in January 1891. They came back in November 1893 when a bulletin announced 'the Salvation Army again commenced operations at their old barracks and the place is crowded at almost every service'. Here they remained until around 1914 when they moved into the Welsh Wesleyan Chapel in Mold Road continuing there until the 1930s by which time the corps had declined. Their numbers in 1905 were on the low side in comparison with other bodies having a 100 adherents and 38 members in the Sunday school. In August 1907, General Booth came to Mold and Buckley. The *County Herald* reported 'the veteran leader of the Salvation Army commenced his North Wales motor campaign at Buckley on Thursday morning last week. He arrived at the Tabernacle Primitive Methodist Chapel shortly before eleven o'clock accompanied by a muster of

Salvation Army Membership Certificate.
[By courtesy of Mr Wilfred Owens; Buckley Society Archive]

principal officers and on alighting from his motor car was heartily cheered by a large crowd'.

There is little information on the Wesleyan Methodists attempt to establish a Welsh speaking cause at Mold Road apart from this quotation:

The first sermon in connection with this cause was preached by the Reverend T. O. Jones on September 18th 1894, in the old English Wesleyan Chapel. At the close of the service eleven expressed their desire to join. Services were held there for a few weeks and afterwards at the house of Mr E. Pritchard, where they continued until a new schoolroom was built in 1895. The school is yet in its infancy.[40]

The chapel was said to have been built in 1900. The statistics for 1905 reveal that their modest building was valued at £190, the least for all the places of worship in the district, as was the membership of five communicants, thirty five adherents, and twenty three in the Sunday school. It could not sustain itself and around 1914 the Salvation Army began to occupy the building.

The English Presbyterians were more successful. The *Chronicle* in January 1903 reported in glowing terms:

The Ewloe Green Presbyterians opened their new Chapel, which will seat 250 worshippers opposite to the old chapel. The contractors are Messrs Wright's of Kelsall and the price was £1250. We would describe it as a positive step and the new chapel is a superlative building. The Presbyterians built their first chapel in 1860 and their second chapel in 1890. This is their third building'. The 1905 statistics gave the Chapel seating as 230, Schoolroom, 150, Communicants 67, adherents 200, Sunday school 132, and the value of the buildings £1,900.[41]

St John's Congregational Church had a mission room at the Trap in the 1880s. The Reverend H. Elvet Lewis remembered it for 'the surprising homeliness of the services in the Cottage' which lived in his memory still. He spoke about such men as Tom Cropper, who used to get through the Sunday school window to practise on the harmonium. It was still going strong in 1888 when it was in the charge of Charles Gerrard, Ewloe Green. There appears to be no further record of the mission.

In 1934 the Congregational minister, the Reverend Keyworthy Lloyd-Williams, was requested by the Moderator of the Congregational Union of England and Wales to visit and supervise the Village Temple, Mynydd Isa. An account of the foundation of the church is given in the *County Herald* for March 1912:

Mynydd Isa Temple, a well equipped and comfortable corrugated iron building, lined with wood inside, which has been erected at the entrance to Rhos Lane, Mynydd Isa, to meet the religious needs of the growing population in this village, was opened on Sunday last. The new place of worship is intended to be Nonconformist, but undenominational. At the morning and evening service the Reverend W. Thomas of Gwersyllt, was the preacher, and in the afternoon the Reverend R. Fletcher of Buckley officiated. Sacred solos were pleasingly rendered by Miss Kate Peters, of Buckley, at the afternoon service, as a prelude to the opening services on Saturday evening. On one evening during the present week it is hoped to secure the services as preacher of the Reverend Stanley Rogers, Liverpool.

We are informed that the prime mover in the erection of the new chapel is the Reverend Joseph Davies of Buckley, whilst an active and sympathetic interest in the movement has been evinced by Mr James Peters, Buckley, and Mr John Roberts, Mynydd Isa. The new edifice is to be known as 'The Temple'. It is hoped to secure the hearty co-operation and assistance of ministers and friends of Nonconformity at Mold, Buckley, and neighbouring places.

It is now time to see what the various

The Village Temple Mynydd Isa, 1912.
[Buckley Library]

The interior of the Village Temple Mynydd Isa
[Buckley Library]

Nonconformist traditions in Buckley had in common, how they witnessed to their faith through joint witness and shared activities. We begin by looking at the Sunday school movement one of the most influential vehicles of the Protestant evangelical revival in the nineteenth century.

Robert Raikes (1735–1811), an evangelical printer from Gloucester, founded Sunday schools in England in 1781. His philanthropic concern was for children, to improve their lot by removing them on a Sunday from the corrupting influence of feckless parents, and teaching them to read the gospels and better themselves. Teachers from the same working class background gave them instruction in reading from a large range of biblical texts instilling in them self discipline, good manners, and an avoidance of the corrupting habits of swearing, alcohol, and gambling.

The Reverend Thomas Charles (1755–1814), although not the founder of the Sunday school movement in Wales, became its most important advocate and organiser and used it to advance probably more than any other institution the Welsh evangelical revival. He continued the work of the Reverend Griffith Jones (1684–1761) of Llanddowror, and Madam Bridget Bevan (1698–1779), through the Circulating Schools. Charles trained a succession of groups of travelling teachers who remained for a period of sixth months and taught pupils of all ages to read the Welsh Bible. His innovation was the decision that such schools should continue meeting on Sunday. Realising the opportunities available Charles showed his genius by developing them as agencies for evangelism. From the time he became a Methodist in Bala in 1784 until his death thirty years later he threw all his energy into organising the Sunday school movement in Wales. He provided reading matter which included a Biblical dictionary, *Geiriadwr Ysgeythyrol*, and a manual for catechists, *Yr Hyfforddwr*, and published in 1813 'Rules' for the conduct of Sunday schools. Many of his ideas are contained in a letter he wrote in 1808 outlining the beneficial aspects of Sunday schools: 'the useful practices of learning chapters out of the Bible, and being catechised publicly,' and making progress 'in learning their own native language, and in acquaintance with the word of God.' Noticing the improvement in the behaviour of the scholars he observed that 'Their usual mode of profaning the sabbath, in meetings

for play and amusement, or in public ale-houses for drinking, and its usual concomitants of idle sports, and at last quarrels, have been forsaken: and the sabbaths are spent together in the schools, or in some religious exercise, of either reading, or hearing the word preached, or in praying together.' 'We have also this year held associations of different schools meeting in some central places, to be publicly catechised together.' 'Though the Sunday Schools have done, and are doing immense good in different parts of our country, yet I find that thousands are perishing for lack of knowledge. Though we have prevailed with many old people to attend these schools, and hundreds have learnt to read at an advanced age, yet these are but few compared to the many thousands who continue ignorant and negligent'. 'I shall conclude by adding that many children and also grown persons, have manifested a serious concern for their souls as the effect of the

The Reverend Thomas Charles (1755-1814) Welsh Methodist Divine influential in Sunday School Movement. From a painting in the Bible Society House.

instruction they have received in the Sunday Schools, and some hundreds in different parts of the country have joined religious societies'.[42]

Thus the Sunday School became the handmaid of Nonconformist churches acting as preparatory schools to instil the basic principles of the faith and make ready its scholars for the strong meat of the eloquent expositions of the preacher.

Who belonged to the Sunday schools in Buckley? The evidence is found in the Education Commissioners' Report of 1847. Figures are given for four religious denominations: the Independents at Buckley Mountain, Calvinistic Methodists at Mold Road and Mynydd Isa, Wesleyan Methodists at Chapel Walks and the Square, and the Anglican Church at St Matthew's. We see that the Welsh and English languages are used in instruction by the Calvinistic Methodists, all the other churches teach through the medium of English. The numbers of Nonconformists taught in Sunday school are children under 15 years of age, 415; persons over the age of 15 years, 217; a total of 632. Of this number 467 are able to read and 216 of them attended a day school. Of the Wesleyan Methodists 66 members of the Sunday school did not attend worship in chapel. The figures for St Matthew's reveal that 183 children attended Sunday school and no persons over the age of 15 years, 33 were able to read and the majority went to church.

The Commissioners' Report in its evidence for the township of Bistre throws further light on both day and Sunday school attendance and stresses the indifference of parents as being the greatest obstacle to education. It stated that '700 children are of an age to receive instruction. The means available for education are very inadequate'. It also spoke about the Nonconformist interest in the provision of day school and Sunday school education:

> The Buckley Union Schools are so called because the principal Dissenters in the neighbourhood have united to support them. It is stated by Mr Catherall, the principal promoter, that no efficient school can be maintained in this place without Government assistance; that the children remain uneducated, because their parents, being poor and ill-educated, cannot be induced to make the smallest sacrifice for the sake of education; that even when the children are of an age to be sent to work it is impossible to induce them to attend even a Sunday school, or a place of worship on Sunday: that he himself has offered to raise the wages of youths engaged in his works 1s. per week, and to give them a reward of 1s. every time they attend a Sunday school; but although they have never received any kind of instruction they refuse compliance. It is stated that the promoters are anxious to establish the schools upon the British and Foreign system, that £70 could be raised by local contributions for the creation of school-rooms, but that, at present, a site cannot be obtained.'[42]

The Commissioners further revealed that the Boys section of the Buckley Union School met in the Primitive Methodist Chapel in Mill Lane and the Girls section in a room belonging to the Independent Chapel. A factor which made the Sunday school vitally important in the nurturing of the Faith was the inadequacy of the day schools and the short time pupils attended them. 'It is stated that the children are employed as early as nine years of age in the coal pits, and at eleven years old in the brick-work, where they earn from 6*d*. to 9*d*. per day'.

The number of those who belonged to the Sunday schools in 1905 had significantly increased. Out of a total membership of 1707, 585 were over the age of fifteen years, that is, almost a third of the members. In other words it was not unusual for children, parents and grandparents to attend Sunday school!

In 1905 every chapel, apart from the Welsh Wesleyan Chapel in Mold Road and the Salvation Army meeting place, had a school room adjoining. The total number of sittings available in the schoolrooms was 1610, adequate enough if one surmises that there would be absentees. In the three phases of chapel building we discussed earlier, provision was eventually made for schoolrooms, and the practice continued well into the twentieth century of building new ones and adapting some of them as a place of worship.

The primary purpose of the Sunday school was to give grounding in the faith through the teaching of Scripture and the fundamental truths of Christianity. The 1847 Report suggested that this was achieved in four ways: scripture committed to memory; catechism or religious formulary memorised by repetition or through the exercise of a school theme, *Pwngc Ysgol*; the use of the hymnal; the final method was the teaching of 'Scripture Geography'. Obviously the emotional and mental experience of the Sunday school improved the scholars' quality of life. The teacher became a surrogate parent and helped children to accept

St John's Congregational Church Sunday School.
[Buckley Society Archive]

authority and develop habits of industry and punctuality. Friendships were cultivated which lasted a lifetime and a sense of mutual welfare developed.

Joseph Griffiths looked back with affection to the early days of the Sunday school in the Independent chapel:

I have been told ours was the first Sunday school in the neighbourhood. I remember it nearly sixty years ago when I was a little boy it used to commence at nine o'clock in the morning and conclude at eleven or a quarter past. Often, before Sunday school, a prayer meeting was held for the teachers and after school a Bible Class for them and the elder scholars met. Then again, at one thirty until two thirty, at this time the scholars were marched to one place in the Chapel and the teachers sat with them to keep order.

In the autumn there was a novelty in our school, which was not found in any other. About two o'clock Mr Catherall might have been seen wending his way towards the school with a large market basket on his arm filled with apples which he distributed to the scholars not as prizes but a gift to all those present. Oh if you could have seen the beaming faces of the children and heard their excited cries at the sight of the apples. We had a very large school as long as the apple season lasted.

There were no six, seven, and eight standard girls and boys classes in those days, only the first, second, and third class. The first taught the ABC, the second from a book of short words and sentences such as dog, cat, and 'feed my lambs', 'Jesus wept', and the third class for those who could read the Testament. It was not unusual to see men of thirty or forty years of age in the ABC class and several of them before they died could read the Bible fluently, and took great pleasure in doing so.[44]

Nonconformist Sunday schools came together on frequent occasions. A great deal of goodwill existed between them, they were always willing to support one another by attending each other's choral performances and chapel anniversary. They would find room for a Nonconformist congregation when it was trying to establish itself. In the summer the large number of scholars belonging to the Sunday school association would meet together in the open air to hold the festival. The Reverend Joseph Davies, brought up in Alltami as a Primitive Methodist and later ordained as a Congregational minister, is an excellent example of the good works which could be performed in the name of true religion. He even went as far as arranging that the Buckley Nonconformists should be together on the 'Day of Judgement' by providing them with a public cemetery!

The Temperance movement was the first great cause, which united Buckley Nonconformists. Nonconformists regarded the demon drink as the destroyer of health, family and livelihood, to be avoided

and, if possible, removed. But public houses were an essential part of community life. The Primitive Methodists first met in a room of the Duke of York, whilst bull baiting took place nearby. Colliers met in the clubroom of the Black Horse where the first meeting to form a Trade Union in Buckley was held. The Royal Oak, Lane End was the headquarters and clubroom of the Bannel Friendly Society. It was nicknamed the 'War Office' because of frequent fighting. The Oil-Man Inn at Spon

Cemetery House nonconformist burial ground presented by
the Reverend Joseph Davies c1890. [FRO PH/11/373]

Green lost its licence for fighting and gambling on the premises. Cropper listed twenty-one public houses in existence about 1860.[45]

By the 1830s total abstinence from alcoholic drink was being promoted in the country at large by the Temperance movement. A festival of teetotallers was held in Buckley and Hawarden in May 1836, which claimed seventy converts. They walked in procession, attended a place of worship, had tea and converts signed the pledge. The festival was still continuing in 1851 a report of which shows the strength of the movement and its leadership in Buckley with great support from the chapel authorities:

On Tuesday the 3rd June the Teetotallers of Buckley held their Annual Demonstration in favour of entire abstinence principles. At one o'clock they assembled at the entrance to the village, and upwards of 500 formed themselves into a procession, which was interspersed with numerous flags and banners bearing suitable emblems and mottoes. Two first-rate choirs of singers accompanied them, all pledged teetotallers, whose delightful harmony added largely to the pleasure of the day's proceedings. After perambulating the greater part of Buckley, they held their first meeting at the Independent Chapel on Buckley Mountain, after which they adjourned for tea which was provided in the Calvinistic Methodist Chapel where upwards of 600 took tea, after which the procession reformed again and marched to Buckley Mountain where an outdoor meeting was held. Mr Davies, the Secretary of the Society, moved that five pounds of the proceeds of the tea be set apart for the building of a new Temperance Hall in Buckley. The building is planned to hold one thousand persons and many have promised to give bricks, etc.. The fruits of Teetotalism are a large increase in the various religious societies, chapels better attended, Sabbath schools full, more domestic comfort and the people better clad.[46]

The Temperance movement had been strengthened in 1847 by the formation of the Band of Hope. The organisation was concerned with all kinds of temperance work among children of both sexes, between the ages of six and twelve. It was itself undenominational but very Protestant in spirit. The Sunday schools became strongholds for the Band of Hope and the place where the children heard their first Temperance lecture and signed the pledge.

Its success was due to its ability to present a programme, which mixed education with recreational activity. The usual meeting began and finished with a simple form of worship, a prayer and a hymn. A lecture given by an adult gave them instruction on temperance and then the children would sing and recite. They would be given the opportunity to sign the pledge promising to abstain from alcohol and, in some instances, tobacco. Music played an important role and members were encouraged to play a musical instrument, choirs were formed, concerts given and competitions arranged.[47]

Another teetotal organisation in the crusade against drink was the Blue Ribbon Army. It originated in the United States and was brought to Britain in 1877. By the end of the 1880s over a million people in Britain had signed the pledge. The missions were the opportunity for a mass release of emotion and gave the audience both a psychological cleansing and an enjoyable evening's entertainment with hymn and choral singing.[48]

There are several newspaper accounts of temperance activities in Buckley.

1875 January 19. On Monday evening last the Band of Hope members walked in procession through the village of Buckley with their regalia and flags each wearing a Temperance and Band of Hope Medal. The singing children attracted a great crowd to inspect them. They held a meeting at Bistre Chapel. Recitations and dialogues by the children were said and speeches made by the older members of the society.[49]

1882 November 4. An interesting entertainment was held at the Bistre Methodist Chapel on Monday evening in which the choir under Mr Edward Wainwright took part. The entertainment took the form of a burlesque entitled 'King Alcohol' in which Mr Edward Wainwright as 'Total Abstainer' makes 'King Alcohol' disappear with the 'Temperance magic wand.[50]

In February 1883 a meeting was held in Providence Chapel to inaugurate the Blue Ribbon Army when a lecture was given on the subject of drunkenness when three members were invested with the blue ribbon and seventy two members joined.

1900 July 7. Unique Temperance Proceedings. The Temperance stalwarts of the town of Buckley made a good bid on Tuesday evening last in which they succeeded in attracting large crowds to their open-air meeting. First of all they sent a bellman in a conveyance containing large sized posters with the following inscription:
'Wine is a mocker; strong drink is raging, and whosoever takes therof is deceived thereby and is not wise.'
'The man who helps to make your son a drunkard is not your friend.'
'Jesus Christ is the best master and friend, and the Devil is a Bad un.'
'O Lord save Buckley from the midnight Public House.'[51]

1903 June Teetotalism. The Reverend Joseph Davies a leading teetotaller of Buckley arranged a display of seven figures in his parlour window for everyone to see as they passed each representing barrels labelled as follows: Gin, Ale, Porter, Rum, Whisky, Brandy, & old Tam. Each barrel held a flowerpot, and above them was a poster with the following inscription: 'Use barrels to hold flowers, and they will do you no harm. Use barrels to enrich the brewers and public houses, and as quickly as they can they will pass you, body and soul, to take your turn numbered among the hopeless, helpless class of the wrecked and ruined.' — Druid's Loyal Perseverance Lodge, headquarters the old Cross-Keys Inn, Lane End, Buckley.

Emmanuel Church Bistre held an inaugural meeting to form a Band of Hope in February 1890. It was reported at the end of March of an increase of membership at Lane End to 47 and at Bistre to 118.

Another method in the pursuit of temperance was the establishment of places where cocoa and coffee were the only beverages available. In 1881 two cocoa houses were opened in Buckley. The first, the Urn Cocoa House, was opened by Lieutenant J. M. Gibson when it was reported that 'quite a rush was made for refreshments, which were of first rate quality and gave universal satisfaction. The cups and saucers used were purchased in Staffordshire and have the Urn Cocoa House branded on them and are very handsome'. The second, the Newcastle Cocoa House, was opened by Henry Hurlbutt of Shotton and managed by W. Iball, under the directorate of the committee of the Reading Room.[52]

Whatever the success of these two cocoa rooms they were followed in 1890 by the opening of a Temperance Hotel, the Cosy Coffee Palace and Commercial Hotel, a new building erected near Buckley Post Office. A coffee supper was given to the workmen of Mr Robert Davies the contractor and other friends in one of the spacious rooms. After supper the Reverend Joseph Davies gave an address. The Cosy was built to attract visitors, with stabling and good accommodation, and became the headquarters of the Buckley Liberal Association and the tent room of the Rechabites.[53]

The annual Buckley Jubilee held on the second Tuesday in July is a demonstration of Christian witness and the symbol of unity and co-operation between the churches in the district. For many years it was confined to the Nonconformist churches until the Anglicans first walked in 1933 and the Roman Catholics in 1970. The Jubilee was born as a result of the co-operation between Nonconformist Sunday schools and Band of Hope branches and gradually assumed the form it has now. The story began in the winter of 1856 when three outstanding Nonconformists organised a concert in the Welsh Calvinistic chapel. They brought together over a hundred children, about forty from each of their three chapels, all of whom had signed the

Members of the Band of Hope with the Reverend Joseph Davies (middle row second from right) at the Buckley Jubilee 1890 seated in the Temperance Tent. [FRO PH/11/248]

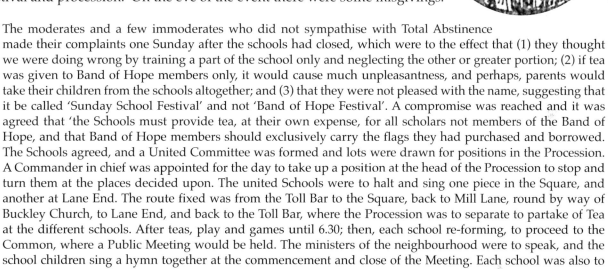

Edward Davies, one of the founders of the Buckley Jubilee 1857. Buckley Sunday Schools Centenary Jubilee 1857–1956. booklet.

Band of Hope pledge and rehearsed them in the singing of temperance and sacred songs. The concert was a great success and showed the good which could arise from such co-operation. Instead of a concert, a Band of Hope procession was planned. The three organisers were Edward Davies, a tailor, Secretary of the local Temperance Society, a Primitive Methodist and member of the Mill Lane Chapel; Richard Roberts, conductor of the Buckley Temperance Choir, a member of the Welsh Calvinist Church and a founder of the English Cause at Zion; and Joseph Griffiths, a member of the Congregationalist church. Nearly fifty years later Joseph Griffiths related the circumstances surrounding the first festival and procession. On the eve of the event there were some misgivings:

> The moderates and a few immoderates who did not sympathise with Total Abstinence made their complaints one Sunday after the schools had closed, which were to the effect that (1) they thought we were doing wrong by training a part of the school only and neglecting the other or greater portion; (2) if tea was given to Band of Hope members only, it would cause much unpleasantness, and, perhaps, parents would take their children from the schools altogether; and (3) that they were not pleased with the name, suggesting that it be called 'Sunday School Festival' and not 'Band of Hope Festival'. A compromise was reached and it was agreed that 'the Schools must provide tea, at their own expense, for all scholars not members of the Band of Hope, and that Band of Hope members should exclusively carry the flags they had purchased and borrowed. The Schools agreed, and a United Committee was formed and lots were drawn for positions in the Procession. A Commander in chief was appointed for the day to take up a position at the head of the Procession to stop and turn them at the places decided upon. The united Schools were to halt and sing one piece in the Square, and another at Lane End. The route fixed was from the Toll Bar to the Square, back to Mill Lane, round by way of Buckley Church, to Lane End, and back to the Toll Bar, where the Procession was to separate to partake of Tea at the different schools. After teas, play and games until 6.30; then, each school re-forming, to proceed to the Common, where a Public Meeting would be held. The ministers of the neighbourhood were to speak, and the school children sing a hymn together at the commencement and close of the Meeting. Each school was also to give an anthem.[54]

Thus from 1857 onwards the pattern was set for the day's procedure and the Jubilee put into the hands of a committee of Nonconformists representing the Sunday schools rather than the Band of Hope. The report of the Jubilee for 1887 describes the introduction of brass bands into the procession when opposition to the belief that musical instruments were the work of the devil was overcome. It comments on the conditions encountered by the procession. 'In spite of clouds of dust blowing from the dry roads the proceedings were carried out with as much enthusiasm as ever', and adds, 'The Penyffordd Brass Band was waiting for the Congregationalists at the bottom of Church Road, and from there conducted them to their own place of worship for tea, playing some very beautiful music under the leadership of Sgt W. Griffiths. We hope the splendid music provided by Mr Griffith for the Congregationalists will be the means of introducing Band Music played before the general procession in the future'.[55] But it took another ten years for brass bands to be accepted when in 1897 the Engineers played for the Congregationalist Sunday school and the Buckley Town Band for the Square Wesleyans. The new Sunday school Union Committee in 1902 offered a prize for the best suggestion for improving the Jubilee. The prize was won by the Reverend Joseph Davies who suggested a brass band and march contest and a Jubilee Queen but these ideas when tried failed to attract enough entrants. Over the years the banners of the Band of Hope were replaced by those of the Sunday schools and the singing of hymns in the procession by the music of brass bands. Until 1933 the Anglican scholars from Emmanuel and St Matthew's Churches held their own teas and sports on Jubilee Day. In 1890, for example, the Bistre and Lane End Sunday school children had tea in the National Schools and then marched up the Square to a field lent by Mr Edward Jones, Bistre Farm, 'where the children were amused with racing and various games'. The report continued:

Two of the founders of the Buckley Jubilee 1857 Joseph Griffiths (far left) and Richard Roberts (left). Buckley Sunday Schools Centenary Jubilee 1857–1956 booklet.

It was the unanimous opinion that this was the largest Sunday school gathering that had ever been brought together in connection with Bistre Church, about 450 teachers and scholars, and for this very reason it is to be regretted that the amusements in the field came to a premature end owing to the stubbornness of the older scholars and visitors in not giving way to the Vicar's sensible suggestion that the objectionable game, 'kiss in the ring' should be given up, and that they should amuse themselves in a more becoming manner.[56]

St Matthew's arranged things differently when on Jubilee day 1897 the Sunday school scholars had tea at the vicarage in the company of Mr and Mrs W. E. Gladstone.

On the occasion of the 62nd Jubilee Procession in 1917 it was reported that 'Cinematograph operators were busy taking pictures'.In 1933 the churches joined the procession and St Matthew's Bugle Band joined with the Buckley Royal Town Band and the Salvation Army Band. In the same year the Buckley Toc H group collected money 'to provide necessitous children with new clothes for Jubilee Day. As a result fourteen families received assistance'.

Every effort was made to make the centenary celebration of the Jubilee in July 1956 memorable when a week of events was organised. They began at St John's Congregation on Sunday in the presence of members and officials of the churches and 800 people when a commemorative tablet was unveiled and dedicated in memory of the founders, Joseph Griffiths, Edward Davies and Richard Roberts:

> On Tuesday for the highlight of the week's events, the Jubilee centenary procession the population of the town was more than doubled as something more than 6,000 visitors and former residents poured in from surrounding districts and from places hundreds of miles apart.
>
> Over 8,000 people lined the streets as 4,000 Sunday school children and church members marched in the two-mile procession for four miles round the town. Police were drafted in from outside districts to control the traffic. In perfect weather, with four bands to set the tempo, the giant cavalcade made a brave and stirring sight. Up Stanley Road and Lane End, in seemingly never-ending array, the representatives of sixteen churches and Sunday schools stepped out with banners aloft. In their wake came horse drawn and motorised vehicles, beautifully decorated with many mounted tableaux with religious themes. It was the custom for the local businesses to provide their lorries for this event. The ever faithful Buckley Town Band led the Procession, and the other bands were Llay Welfare Silver Band, Caergwrle Boy's Brigade Band and Chester Salvation Army Band.[57]

1970 saw the symbolic ending of religious prejudices with the welcoming of the Roman Catholic Church Our Lady of the Rosary, a significant expression of Christian unity, which re-emphasised the purpose of the Jubilee.

As well as Sunday schools, Temperance and the Jubilee, Nonconformists in Buckley shared other things in common. There were elements in their pattern of worship, such as the prayer meeting and the use of lay preachers, which they inherited from their Puritan background and the evangelical revival. Choirs developed from the musical accompaniment to worship the ability of which was often proved in competition or the joining together to perform oratorio. They shared in common the practice of lining-out in the singing of hymns many new ones which were introduced as American gospel, temperance mission, or from the evangelistic leaders General Booth and Messrs Moody and Sankey. The haunting melodies of

Royal Buckley Town Band in Jubilee Procession 1990. [Buckley Society Archive]

the Welsh revivalist hymns were equally appealing and contagious when sung in the *Cymanfa Ganu*.

Prayer meetings were held on weekdays and sometimes following the Sunday service in an 'after-meeting', when converts were welcomed, and others could gain the experience of praying aloud spontaneously. Joseph Griffiths remembered the prayer meetings at the Congregationalist church in the middle of the nineteenth century.

Prayer Meeting was held every Monday, the first Monday in every month being a Missionary Prayer Meeting. Society Meeting was held on Wednesday night in summer at 7 o'clock and in winter at 6. 30 pm. From the formation of the Church until about two years ago Prayer Meetings and Society Meetings were held on those nights until we gave up the Society Meeting for the young men's improvement class.

Although our Church was much smaller then, (pre 1873), it was no uncommon thing to see sixty or seventy people at the Prayer Meeting. I only wish you could have heard the old people pray it would have astonished you: such earnestness, fluency and power, with hand uplifted their faces shining, the love that was in their hearts' blessing and praising the God that had been so good to them.[58]

His grandson Dennis Griffiths gave a more humorous account of such meetings as he remembered them in the First World War:

These men had no doubt about a clear personal understanding existing between them and their Maker, and addressed Him in prayer as if He were their next-door neighbour.

One of them was a cattle-dealer whose quaint style was particularly memorable. I remember him praying 'Thou knows Lord that at the Fair to-day, a man tried to do me a dirty trick by selling me a cow that wasn't worth half the price he asked for it. That's not right Lord, Thou knows it isn't.' He paused, 'So I didn't buy it,' he concluded.

Another devout shopkeeper prayed to the Lord to bless the colliers at the 'Dumpling' Pit. 'And remind them, Lord,' he said, 'they haven't paid me for their picks and shovels.'[59]

Sunday was precious to them and such was their influence that the Buckley Urban District Council resolved in 1909 that four of its members should join with those appointed by the Free Church Council to interview police authorities as to Sabbath observance.[60]

The Nonconformist lay preachers were the backbone of their churches and an influence in the work place. An appreciation of their dedication is to be found in the minutes of Buckley and Mold circuit of

The Salvation Army Band marching in Jubilee Procession 1956. [Buckley Society Archive]

Four Jubilee Processions:

Right: St John's c.1930 [Buckley Society Archive].

Below, left: Procession marching in thunder storm Mold Road 1965 [Buckley Society Archive].

Below, right: Members of the Church of Our Lady take part for the first time in 1970 [Church Archive]

St Matthew's c.1940 . [Buckley Society Archive]

Methodist lay preachers. Here is an example of their ministry at the beginning of the twentieth century:

> Brother E. H. Davies (died 1945) was converted in Brunswick Wesleyan Chapel in January 1896 during a ten day Mission conducted by Mr W. Bibby, evangelist, Liverpool. Brother Davies was especially gifted, not only as a preacher, but also as an elocutionist and Gospel soloist. He had a deep sense of humour with exceptional disposition. It was usual in those days for young beginners to take as many as nine or ten Sundays in one Quarter, having only one minister. Though he worked nights in the Mine he never failed his planned appointments.
>
> William Hewitt (died 1948), of Penymynydd, was a Lay Preacher for forty-five years. It was said of him, 'Often did he deplore his lack of education that when an evening school class was opened in 1907 at Penymynydd he was one of the first to enrol. He followed his father down the pit. As a result of an accident he left the pit to become a roadman. He knew his Bible, his complete Library, and what an inspiration it was to catch that radiant smile of his, the sure and certain evidence of a deep and abiding joy within'.
>
> In 1948 Charles Duckworth gave this appreciation of Percy Peters: He was a member of the cause at Bistre all his life following in the footsteps of his forebears who had been choirmasters, preachers, etc., from the inception of the Church. He gave his life to this work without stint of his time and energy. In turn he was Sunday school Superintendent, Secretary, Junior Department Leader and Teacher. In 1926 he felt called to take up the great work of preaching the Gospel. He served the cause of the Methodist Local Preacher's Mutual Aid Association helping the aged preachers. Up to the time of his death he held the position of Choir Master at Bistre, a position which his grandfather the late Thomas Wainwright held many years before when the Choir was well known for the high standard of its choral work. Music to him was one of the highest and noblest things in life. Just before he died he was elected to the Buckley Urban District Council. He was keenly interested in National and International Affairs and was disturbed by the events which led up to the war and the insecurity which followed, but his faith was such that he looked beyond the disturbed present and saw that in the years to come following hard work and earnest prayer the big day would come when mankind would listen to the voice of the Prince of Peace.[61]

The great Buckley choral tradition dates back to the middle of the nineteenth century, originating in the various churches it became a regular feature both as an expression of religious devotion and solemn entertainment. The Jubilee programme of 1902 spoke lovingly of its development. 'Old inhabitants will speak with pride of the days of their youth when choirs existed which could sing Handel's big choruses. In those days of expensive music with no Tonic Sol-Fa, and four staff notations, this was a worthy feat. The musical standard to day is at high water level, as evidenced by recent successful performances of the great oratorios'. These words were written by Joseph Griffiths who left an account of his musical experiences at the Congregational Church, during the formative years of the making of a musical tradition:

> I was told by the old people that William and John Shepherd played clarinets, Peter Williams a serpent, Edward Price a bassoon, and someone else a viol. I heard Isaac Hopwood recount at our choir supper that he was the first, through his home lesson to introduce the tonic sol-fa system into this neighbourhood. That may be true in its present form. But many years before Mr Hopwood was born, and long before Mr Curwen, the founder of the Sol fa method as it now stands altered the system, there was a man called Thomas Mather who taught the singing in the old chapel here from those syllables fa sol la. He now lies in our stable and his head stone or rather brick stone is outside by the heating apparatus.
>
> When I formed the church choir singing was at very low ebb indeed. We had no kind of instrument and our good old friend and deacon used at that time to start the singing but he had such a tremulous voice that we were not certain for a few notes that he had begun. Eventually he persuaded his son Robert Price to replace him and asked me to instruct the singing. About 1862 I thought that if we could obtain a Harmonium it would make the singing more agreeable. When I mentioned the matter I met with opposition but I persevered, begged the money and we bought one for fourteen pounds. We were the talk of the country. We were so proud and stuck up that we must have a machine to worship God with. One old Primitive Methodist who is now in heaven said that when that harmonium came over the Chester bridge the devil came with it.[62]

In 1902 Joseph Griffiths heard of the availability of a good pipe organ through his son John Robert Grifiths, Mus. Bac., who was an organist in London. Its purchase was described to the Church Commission in 1907 by the Buckley minister Thomas Mardy Rees:

The organ in the church, formerly at Grafton Square, London is considered to be about the most powerful in North Wales outside the Cathedral. In Buckley all denominations join during the winter to prepare an oratorio, including the Church of England, or some other important piece of music for a first class concert which is held annually in May. During my residence in Buckley the following oratorios have been performed with unique success: *The Messiah, Judas Maccabaeus, Elijah* and *The Banner of St George*.

At this time Thomas Cropper was responsible for organising an orchestra of three violins, two cornets and a bass viol, for the chapel services, in addition to the organ. The Cropper family were gifted instrumentalists and took a leading part in the musical life of Buckley.

Other churches, too, developed their musical traditions. Cropper singled out Providence, the Bistre United Methodist Chapel, for praise:

> I invariably think of Bistre Chapel in terms of music from recollections of the line of Wainwrights and the choir. I recall the closing years of Edward Wainwright's charge of the choir. He was a man after my own heart, full of enthusiasm, as well as natural ability. In addition to the choir he organised a fife band, and the effects of the electricity he infused in those days, a generation or more ago are still felt in the place.[63]

Wainwright was conducting the Providence Choir in the 1880s. In January 1886 they performed the sacred cantata *The Pilgrim Fathers* of which the *Chronicle* remarked: 'Apart from the merits of the cantata's music, is its interest to all nonconformists as a sketch of persecuted people leaving their homes and country in search of a land where freedom to worship could be theirs'. In April 1884 a service of song was performed by the choir at Brunswick Wesleyan Methodist Chapel entitled *The People's William*, based on the life of the Rt Hon. W. E. Gladstone, in aid of the Sunday school fund, unfortunately there was a small audience. In the following year the Trustees ruled 'that the Glee party practise nothing but sacred music in the chapel '. In March 1881 a Welsh Eisteddfod was held at the Tabernacle chapel when the young minister, Elfed, the Reverend Howell E. Lewis presided.

Another stalwart who encouraged and promoted music in worship in the district's chapels was the Reverend Joseph Davies. He formed a choir to raise money to pay for the extension of Alltami Chapel in 1866, and arranged concerts for the opening of Drury Lane Chapel in the 1870s and the Village Temple at Mynydd Isa in 1912. He was a popular chairman at many fund raising concerts in Buckley, 'presiding at the Band of Hope or singing for the gospel Temperance Society at Zion' and composing both words and music to several hymns, including 'Jesus the Promised Saviour dear' which is sung annually as 'The Alltami Carol' at the chapel.[64]

Tabernacle chapel with its seating capacity for over seven hundred people was the ideal venue for joint choir oratorio and fund raising concerts. In October 1899 the 'Concert of the season' was billed there given 'by the renowned Royal Welsh Ladies Choir, conductor Madam Clara Novello Davies' admission to which cost between five shillings for reserved seats to one shilling for a seat at the back with the plan for seating and arrangements for booking at the Cosy.[65] The customary way to celebrate the Sunday school anniversary at Tabernacle at the beginning of the nineteenth century was by singing either or a part or the whole of the standard oratorios with *Messiah, The Creation*, and *Elijah* being performed on different occasions.

The Buckley Choral Society is said to have begun in 1891 in a room in St Matthew's school where they held their rehearsal. However, other dates have been given. There was a great deal of talent available in Buckley as is seen by the various concerts arranged in the 1890s one of which was held in the Central Hall in February 1892. It was described as 'a Choral Festival sustained by the united choirs of the various Nonconformist chapels when the chair was taken by the Reverend Joseph Davies'.[66] In December 1893 a choir of 70 voices and an orchestra of 30 conducted by Thomas Cropper held the first of a series of concerts at the Central Hall Buckley.[67] It appears that in the winter of 1899 the Mold School Board set up an evening class for music under the tuition of Wilfred Jones of Wrexham who trained a choir, which gave a notable performance the following summer. It would undoubtedly be made up of many of the members of the Nonconformist choirs who came together for this occasion and remained to form the Buckley Choral Society. This account was given in the *Chronicle*:

St John's Congregational Church Organ installed 1902.
[Buckley Society Archive, Shepherd]

The local committee set up to manage the class were fortunate in getting the services of Mr Wilfred Jones of Wrexham, a conductor of considerable repute, and members joining have exceeded expectations. It started in October last and has continued weekly down to the Festival, the attendance averaging one hundred per meeting, in fact there are one hundred and fifty names on the book. We may remark that this is not a singing class everybody being presupposed to have a knowledge of music in staff notation or tonic solfa. A small fee is charged members to cover expenses and we understand this has been sufficient to defray the expenses of the preliminary rehearsals.

The work chosen is Handel's *Messiah* and it seemed open to question whether this exacting work was not a bit too ambitious to begin with. From the first meeting doubts were set at rest as to the ultimate issue. When the time arrived for the performance it was decided to have it done in a worthy manner with principal artistes of high rank in their profession, and also a professional orchestra and the guarantors include such names as Lady Penrhyn, Miss Helen Gladstone, Samuel Smith M P, the Rt. Hon. H. Gladstone, J. Watkinson, P. B. D. Cooke, H. Hurlbutt, Horace Mayhew, G. A. Parry, F. L. Hancock and most other principal residents in the neighbourhood. A grand Marquee capable of seating three thousand people was erected on Reney's field, Main Street, with a platform for two hundred reserved seats immediately in front of the orchestra with the bulk of the audience behind and the transept on either side of the stage which was filled with spyrea, geranium and a variety of greenhouse plants.

The artists came from Hanley, Liverpool, St Paul's Cathedral and Westminster Abbey. The harmonium was played by the sister of the curate of Buckley, Miss Kitcat.

The Choral Society flourished until the First World War with a chorus and orchestra numbering about a hundred with a repertoire made up of oratorios and other works by the early and modern masters.

One of Buckley's outstanding musicians, Mr Tom Roberts, was responsible for the revival of the Choral Society in 1925. It had a membership again around the hundred mark. With Tom Roberts as conductor, its first performance was given in the spring of 1926. For their first concert, a performance of Handel's *Samson*, the orchestra was chiefly composed of members from the Liverpool Philharmonic. The venue for this and succeeding performances was the Tivoli when the profits were shared between the local Nursing Fund, the Buckley Ambulance Fund and the Chester Royal Infirmary. By 1931 membership of the Choral Society had risen to 180. One of the soloists in 1931 was Isobel Baillie, soprano, but there was a great deal of outstanding local talent, amongst whom were Katie Peters and Hilda Roberts. Tom Roberts, Head Teacher of Buckley Board School, and later Deputy Director of Education for Flintshire, was a superb musician, regular accompanist at the National Eisteddfod, Conductor of the Choral Society, and organist of Tabernacle Chapel. No doubt through the influence of Tom Roberts, the Flintshire Education Authority arranged musical recitals in the Tabernacle schoolroom, frequent visitors were the Bangor Trio, and the highlight was the visit of the oboist Leon Goosens and the Carter Trio in 1946.

Mr J. B. Lewis has contributed the following note on Mr Tom Roberts:

Tom Roberts was both Headmaster of The Buckley Board School and Custom House Lane School, Connah's Quay, and Organist of the Tabernacle Methodist Chapel, Buckley. He married Miss Ethel Reney, daughter of James Reney.

He was an outstanding musician and an accompanist of remarkable technical confidence and sensitivity. His services were required not only weekly at the chapel, but as accompanist at the International and National Eisteddfodau of Wales; he had a particular musical 'rapport' with the mellifluous Welsh Tenor from Trelogan,

Interior of former Tabernacle Chapel.
[Buckley Society Archive]

David Lloyd.

It was widely known that the Soprano, Dame Isobel Baillie would only agree to sing in this area if Tom Roberts were her accompanist. This was also the case with such celebrities as Thomas Allen, Owen Brannigan, Jennifer Vivien and Peter Pears, who sang from time to time in the Tabernacle.

He attracted a choir at the Tabernacle of a constant and remarkably high musical proficiency under the baton of David Hayes. Together they performed most of the well-known oratorios in the religious musical repertoire. Many Buckley people were to learn to sight-read and develop a deep love of music under their auspices over a period of 40 years or more.

The choir often augmented the Chester choirs, in the Cathedral there, at concerts under the baton of Dr J. Rowland Middleton, the Cathedral Organist. (Many of the Buckley singers had been taught music by Dr Middleton, when he was organist at Mold Parish Church and Music Master at the Alun Grammar School.) Tom Roberts frequently played piano duets with Sir Geoffrey Summers, a pianist of 'concert' standard, at his home Craig-y-Castell, near Dyserth.

The Buckley Choral Society, under Tom Roberts' baton and with the outstandingly gifted accompanists, Miss Gwyneth Jones and Raymond Reney Roberts (his son, who had read music at Oxford), created a vibrant, satisfying and unforgettable musical culture in Buckley during the middle years of the last century. Many will recollect Buckley Choral Society's production of Edward German's Merrie England in the hall of the recently built Elfed School.

Those who were fortunate to have heard him play, would agree, that when Tom Roberts sat at the Tabernacle organ, so sure was his touch, that there would ensue a faultless performance that was a delight and a joy.

The Choral Society ceased to function around 1956 when it moved from the Tabernacle schoolroom to the Elfed School. It was revived at St Matthew's Church in 1979 and gave a series of oratorios over the next ten years: *Messiah, Samson, Elijah, The Creation, the Bartered Bride, Trial by Jury*, and *Merrie England*. They were performed in May and December either at St Matthew's, Emmanuel or Elfed School.[67]

List of Religious Buildings

For this list I have relied to a great extent on Charles Duckworth,[68] particularly for the establishment in Buckley of the Nonconformist churches and the buildings they used over the years. I have made additions to Duckworth's list by the inclusion of the buildings of other religious denominations and supplemented his information given in 1985.

1. Brunswick Methodist Wesleyan, English. The oldest cause in Buckley. First mentioned in 1785 when a licence to permit public worship was received from the Bishop of Chester, for meeting places described as 'Buckley Mountain' and the 'Mount'. The date of the first church was 1803 in Chapel Walk. Later church built 1867 in Brunswick Road. Sunday School built in 1890 at Chapel Walk. The church building was demolished in 1972.

2. Square Methodist Wesleyan, English. The second oldest cause in Buckley also received its licence from the Bishop of Chester in 1785. The date of the first church 1834 in Mold Road, building restored in 1884. Sunday School sites on Mold Road. The Church closed in the 1990s, and members became part of Buckley Cross Methodist Church in the Tabernacle Sunday School erected in 1936.

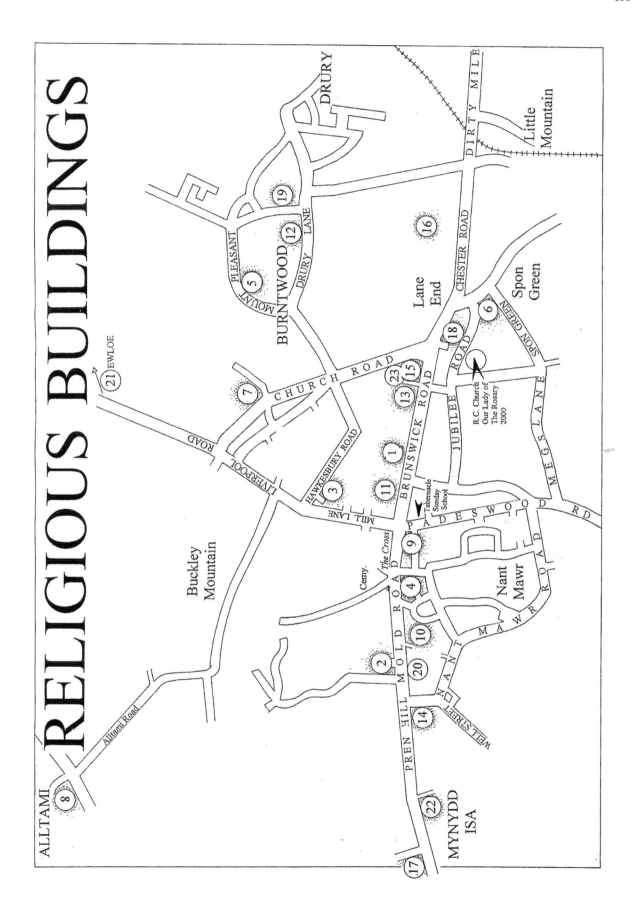

RELIGIOUS BUILDINGS

3. Buckley Mountain, St John's Congregational. First mentioned in 1792 as an Independent cause when a Licence for worship was received from the Bishop of Chester. The first church on the present site was built in 1811, enlarged in 1814, and replaced in 1873, by a church which was by this time known as St John's Congregational. In the meantime the English Presbyterians from Zion joined with St John's to become part of the **United Reformed Church** and a new church was opened on this site in c.2000. The old Sunday School building was demolished.

4. Mold Road Calvinistic Methodist Welsh Bethel. First mentioned in 1794. The first church dates from 1819 in premises used by Jonathan Catherall as a school-room. This was replaced in 1878 by a building designed by the architect Richard Owens.

5. Pentrobin Methodist New Connexion Bethesda. First mentioned in 1803–4 and until 1835 was part of the St John's Chester Circuit. The Methodist Cause here, over the years, belonged to the New Connexion. The first Church is dated 1823 and a later building 1878. Sunday school sites are at Pentrobin and Burntwood.

6. Providence Bistre Methodist New Connexion. First mentioned 1842. Enlarged 1872. Later chapels 1878–9.

7. St Matthew's Church in Wales, Parish Church of Buckley. The church was opened in 1822 and completely renovated between 1897–1905.

8. Alltami Primitive Methodist. First mentioned in 1836 with the first church in 1838, extended in 1866 and in 1879. Now called **Bryn Methodist Church**.

9. Tabernacle Primitive Methodist. The first church was established in Mill Lane in 1841. In 1876 a new church was built in Padeswood Road and in 1936 a new Sunday School was built opposite. This substantial building replaced the church of 1876, which was demolished. It is now used by the amalgamated congregations from the Square (see 2 above) and Tabernacle, and is known as **Buckley Cross Methodist Church** from March 1994.

10. Emmanuel Church in Wales, Parish Church of Bistre. Opened in 1842. Designed by John Lloyd. Renovated in 1881 by W. H. Spaull.

11. Brunswick Road English Presbyterian, Zion. Founded in 1869 by members from Bethel (see 4 above). The church was built in 1876 in Brunswick Road. It was demolished in the 1990s. Members from Zion joined with those of St John's to establish the United Reformed Church in Buckley.

12. Drury Lane Primitive Methodist. Founded 1872. New chapel opened c.1882 and extended 1957.

13. Daisy Hill Baptist English Ebenezer. First mentioned in 1877. Date of the first church 1889.

14. Nant Mawr Baptist, Bethel. First mentioned 1890, closed by 1913. In 1919 the building was used as a warehouse for salt. Demolished in the 1940s.

15. Daisy Hill Roman Catholic, Our Lady of the Rosary. The first congregation met in Mill House, Mill Lane in the 1880s. The church was opened in 1893 and in use until 2000 when it was replaced by an exciting modern church on a new site consecrated in 2000.

16. Lane End Barracks Salvation Army. First mentioned in 1881. Met in the old Wesleyan Church and then moved to Welsh Wesleyan Church in Mold Road c.1914–1930s.

17. Mynydd Isa St Cecilia Church in Wales Mission. Opened in 1892.

18. Lane End All Saints' Church in Wales Mission. First church built in 1881 replaced in 1892 by a church on a different site.

19. Pentre Good Shepherd Church in Wales Mission. Built in 1900 as a gift by Mrs Harry Drew.

20. Mold Road Methodist Wesleyan, Welsh. Opened for a short time before 1914 as a Methodist church before it became the home of the Salvation Army (see 16 above).

21. Ewloe St Davids' Church in Wales Mission. Opened during the incumbency of Vicar Dampier sometime in the 1890s and closed before 1914.

22. Mynydd Isa Village Temple. Opened by the Reverend Joseph Davies in 1912 and until the 1930s was under no recognised denominational jurisdiction until it came under the supervision of St John's Congregational Church, Buckley.

23. Bible Christian Church. Meets in the former Roman Catholic Church building on Daisy Hill.

The late James Bentley painted a series of pictures to illustrate the theme of 'Old Buckley Days and Ways'. They were first exhibited in Buckley Library in 19179. Some of these are reproduced here by kind permission of Mrs Margaret Bentley. They are chosen to represent many of the themes in the chapters of this book and in order to pay tribute to James Berntley's knowledge and devotion to his adopted town.

James Bentley based his paintings on the rcollections of Charles Connah of Drury and immoralise life in Buckley. They reflect the variety and intimacy of work and play in the community and the afectionate way the scenes are captured by the artist.

New Fangled Monster!
A Sentinel wagon belonging to Castle
Fire-brick Company at Lane End.

The Potter's Stall.

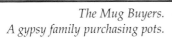

The Mug Buyers.
A gypsy family purchasing pots.

The Sleeper.
Closing your eyes during the sermon in chapel.

The Pig Killer. Slaughtering the commoners' pig.

Playtime at St Matthew's School.

Emptying the Privies.
The arrival of the night-soil cart, 'the golden dream-boat', to empty the closets.

'How art thou, awd 'un?'
Meeting up on Jubilee day.

The illustrations represent different periods of pottery making in Buckley, the varieties of pottery made, and examples of the methods used by the potters. Most of the objects pictured were are to be found in Buckley Library and are in the care of Flintshire Museums Service (FMS). Some are on loan from the National Museums, Liverpool (NML). Some of the examples shown here are in the Bentley Collection (BC), and are reproduced by kind permission of Mrs Margaret Bentley. Some of the examples of Powell's pottery are reproduced by kind permission of Mr Paul Davies (PDPC0.

I am indebted to Deborah Snow, Principal Museums Officer for Flitnshire County Council, and Christine Longworth, Curator of British and European Antiquities, National Museums, Liverpool, for their kind assistance.

Early Buckley Pottery (Brookhill Pottery)

Slip-decorated dish, c.1640–70. White slip over a red earthenware body with sgraffito bird design. NML.

Press-moulded dish, c.16901720. Brown slip-trailed lines joggled on a yellow slip base. NML.

Chamber pot, c.1640–1670. FMS.

Black-wag tyg with multiple ornate handles. NML.

Domestic Ware

Collander, yellow glaze. Nineteenth century. FMS.

Ham pan mug for soaking hams. Nineteenth century. FMS

Jug, black glaze. Nineteenth century. FMS.

Commemorative teapot (left) from Ebenezer Baptist Chapel, 1889. FMS. Buckley ware teapot c.1880, attributed to Powell's Pottery. FMS>

Hayes Pottery

Jug c.1890. FMS.

Tobacco jar 'John Hayes 1870', sgraffito ware. FMS>

Pair of candlesticks, sgraffito ware. FMS.

Powell's Pottery

Blue glazed jar. FMS BC.

Teapot stand. FMS.

Hat pin holder. FMS.

Green glazed decorated
vase. PDPC.

Lustre ware jug. PDPC.

Rustic ware, 1870–1950.
Flowerpot with scraffito inscription. FMS; tobacco jar
FMS; self-watering plant pot, 1910 souvenir. FMS.

Local Artists

Dennis Griffiths (pantomime set behind). By
Thomas Dempster Jones.

Coal pickers Standard Clay Hole. By John Whormsley.

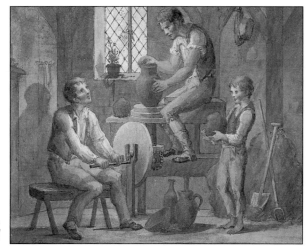

Buckley Potters at Work, 1823. Watercolour by Lady Delamere.
[By permission of Sir William Gladstone, Bart, KG.]

Etna Quarry before landfill. By Joe Chesters.

Breezy day on the Strip. By Joe Chesters.

'And Jim Bentley trod this way'. By Joe Chesters.

Southfields pool mid 1980s. By Joe Chesters.

Top o' the Strip – hands off. By Joe Chesters.

Members and Officers of Buckley Town Council, Centenary Year, 1997.
Back row: Clls H. D. Hutchinson; J. Glendenning; H. Roberts; G. D. Williams; D. Messham; W. A.
Roberts; K. Glendenning; A. Woolley; J. F. Thornton; K. Hegarty; A. M. Jones; J. Connah.
Front row: Cllrs T. H. Peacock; G. Brocklebank (Secretary); D. Salusbury (Town Clerk & Finance
Officer); R. G. Hampson (Town Mayor); K. Iball (Deputy Town Mayor); J. R. Kennett-Orpwood; H. I.
Jones. Inset: Cllr N. Phillips.

The Royal Buckley Town Band at the Welsh Regional Championships, Brangwyn Hall, Swansea, 2006.
Back row: Jonathan Moss; Andrew Letman; Dave Brooks; Ivor Jones; Stephen Pugh Jones; Glyn Smith; John Wynne; Simon
Moss; Christina Turner; Terry Malone; Jim Tunney; Amy Butler; Emma Butler; Howell Griffiths; Dave Davies (Musical
Director). Bottom left: Caroline Prince, Andrew Roxton; Miln Robinson; Stephen Griffiths; Darren Booth; Paul Copper (guest
Conductor). Bottom right: Christine Smith; Colin Smith; Carolyn Smith. Inset: Pedr Roberts (left); Wilf Wilcock (right).

*The Elfed High School Wind Orchestra, 2002.
Conductor Barry Smallwood. Mr Kevin
Grandfield (Headteacher) front left behind
keyboard.*

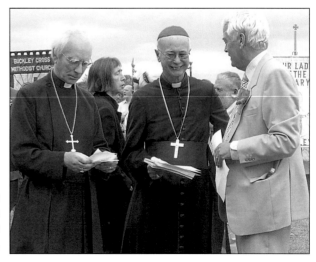

*The Buckley Society Committee, June 2006.
Back row: Phil Hodges; Emrys Williams; Don
Donnell; Mervyn Ffoulkes. Front row: Paul Davies;
Carol Shone; Ken Lloyd Griffiths; Brian Hodnett.*

*The Buckley Jubilee, 2006. The service on the Common. The
Bishop of St Asaph, The Right Reverend John Davies; the Bishop
of Wrexham, the Right Reverend Edward Regan;
Mr David Anglesea (Secretary).*

Notes

1. *The Royal Commission on the Church of England and other Religious Bodies in Wales and Monmouthshire*, 1906, vol vi, p.138.

2. *Reports of the Commissioners of Inquiry into the State of Education in Wales*, Part III, North Wales, 1847, p. 94.

3. Richard Willett, *A Memoir of Hawarden Parish* (Chester: 1822), p. 124.

4. Thomas Cropper, *Buckley and District* (Buckley 1923), pp.71–2.

5. ibid, p. 73.

6. ibid, p. 70.

7. ibid, p. 73.

8. F. C. Brotherton, *Early Methodism in and around Chester* (Chester:1903).

9. J. E. Meesham, 'Thomas Croppers's 'Jonathan Catherall'. Part II The Builder of Chapels'. *Buckley* 25.

10. Thomas Pennant,*The History of the Parishes of Whiteford and Holywell*, (London; 1796) p. 244.

11. Later the Hope and Anchor.

12. Messham, op cit.

13. *Dictionary of Welsh Biography Down to 1940* (Blackwell: Oxford), 1959, under David Jones (1770–1831) p. 451.

14. Robert Shepherd, *A History of St John's Congregational Church, 1792–1947*.

15. Probably Bell and Lancaster teaching method.

16. Cropper, op cit, p. 86.

17. ibid, p87, quoted in *The Sunday Companion,* 14 September 1901.

18. Shepherd, op cit, p. 20.

19. Cropper, op cit, p. 89.

20. *Disciplines of Faith. Studies in Religion, Politics, and Patriarchy*, ed. Tim Obelkevick, *et al* (1987) see p. 326 chapter 'Primitive Methodism in the Northern Coalfields' Robert Colls (Routledge & Kegan Paul London 1987).

21. See footnotes 2 and 3 above.

22. Geoffrey Milburn, *Exploring Methodism: Primitive Methodism*, p. 7 (Epworth 2002)

23. Julia Stewart Werner, *The Primitive Methodist Connexion: its background and early history* (Madison: Univ. of Wisconsin Press 1984), Pt 1, pp. 175–6, quoted by Geoffrey Milburn, op cit (22).

24. FRO N/36/16

25. *Chester Chronicle*, 1/5/1875.

26. Anthony Jones, *Welsh Chapels*, (Alan Sutton) and National Museums and Galleries of Wales, 1996, p. 98

27. FRO N/10/17 Minute Book Tabernacle Chapel, 1873–1907.

28. *Chester Chronicle*, 13/2/1882, 14/6/1884, Davies was ordained a Congregational minister in 1878.

29. *Chester Chronicle,* 3/8/1878.

30. ibid, 3/8/1867.

31. Op cit, p. 233.

32. *Chester Chronicle*, 30/8/1873.

33. *Wrexham Advertiser*, 24/6/1876.

34. Anthony Jones, op cit, p. 91.

35. Cropper, op cit, p.70.

36. Account in *Chester Chronicle*, June 1872.

37. *Chester Chronicle*, 22/10/1881.

38. ibid, 25/1/1890.

39. ibid, 22/2/1890.

40. Official Programme, Buckley Jubilee, 8 July 1902.

41. Statistics under Hawarden in *Royal Commission* 1906, see fn 1.

42. Letter addressed by Thomas Charles in 1808 to the daughter of Alderman Lea, London. Quoted in R. M. Jones and Gwyn Davies, *The Christian Heritage of Welsh Education*, (Evangelical Press of Wales, 1986) p. 66f.

43. Education Commissioners, 1847, op cit, p. 103.

44. Joseph Griffiths, one of the founders of the Buckley Jubilee.

45. Cropper, op cit, p. 130.

46. *Chester Chronicle*, 14/6/1851.

47. Lilian Lewis Shiman, 'The Band of Hope Movement: Respectable Recreation for Working Class Children', *Victorian Studies*, vol. xviii, no. 1, 1973.

48. Lilian Lewis Shiman, *Crusade against drink in Victorian England*, pp. 109–21 (MacMillan, 1988).

49. *Wrexham Advertiser*, 19/1/1875.

50. *Chester Chronicle*, 4/11/1882.

51. ibid, 7/7/1900.

52. ibid, 12/3, 23/4, 11/6/1881.

53. *Chester Chronicle* 4/10//1890, *County Herald*, 3/10/1890.

54. Official Programme, Buckley Jubilee Day Festival, 8/7/1902.

55. See Charles Duckworth, 'The Buckley Jubilee', *Buckley*, no. 3 quoting *Chester Chronicle* July 1887.

56. *B istre Parish Magazine*, 1890.

57. FRO D/DM/686/8.

58. FRO D/DG/53.

59. Dennis Griffiths, *Out of this Clay* (Gee: Denbigh 1960), pp. 113–4.

60. FRO UD/A/1/6.

61. FRO N /10 /34.

62. FRO D/DG/53.

63. Cropper op cit p. 238.

64. Nigel Lemon, 'The Reverend Joseph Davies of Buckley', *Buckley* 29, p. 11.

65. FRO D/DM/111/8.

66. *Chester Chronicle*, Feb. 1892.

67. ibid 30/12/1893 and Charles Duckworth, 'The Buckley Choral Society', *Buckley*, 1.

68. Charles Duckworth, 'The development of Non-Conformity in Buckley since the Eighteenth Century', *Buckley*, 10.

Chapter 9
St Matthew's Parish Church, Buckley

Evangelical fervour, missionary zeal, the elimination of lawlessness, the eradication of immorality, the provision of education for the children of the labouring poor was the crusade of Anglican clergy and gentry in the years that followed the victory at Waterloo in 1815. In this they were abetted by repressive parliamentary legislation against radicalism and the grant of a million pounds for the building of churches. The Rector of Hawarden, the Honourable the Reverend George Neville, brother-in-law to the widowed Lady Mary Glynne of Hawarden Castle, and related by marriage to the Tory politicians, the Pitts and the Grenvilles, threw his considerable energy into reforming the miserable lives of his parishioners. Coming to Hawarden in 1813 he was supported by his wife Charlotte and her sister-in-law Lady Glynne in closing public houses and opening day schools in the parish. By 1817 plans were being made to build schools and erect a church in the most notorious part of the parish. These endeavours were completed over the next years by a series of events that were well-reported in the local press and by the actors themselves. They were enacted with great pomp and splendour as befitted the Church Triumphant announcing its victory and progress over the sectaries by the sound of the trumpet, a corps of cavalry, a band of music, robed clergy, and thunder from the pulpit.

The first act took place in September 1817 at a service in Hawarden Parish Church with the object of raising money for the erection of a National School in Buckley. The preacher was the Bishop of St Asaph, John Luxmoore, who appealed for 'assisting so great a good work forward', giving 'in illustration of the necessity of the National School that within a short distance of Hawarden there was no less than 1200 persons whose offspring experience all the melancholy evils of ignorance and lack of religion', and emphasising that 'it was the great object to attempt the amelioration of their hapless condition'.[1]

This necessity for school and church, religion and education was repeated later by the local newspaper:

> Within the last few years this district has risen from the obscurity of a wasteland to a place even of commercial notoriety from the extensive coal works which it contains, and the manufacture of firebricks and earthenware etc. which is carried on there. The population of the parish has had an extraordinary increase within the last few years. In consequence of which and the distance from the parish church the worthy rector the Hon. and Rev. George Neville actuated by feelings

The Revd and Hon. George Neville, Rector of Hawarden 1813–34, Master of Magdalene College Cambridge, Dean of Windsor, builder of St Matthew's Church and Schools 1819–2. [By kind permission of the Master and Fellows of Magdalene College, Cambridge]

197

The Hon. Mary Lady Glynne, (née Neville) 1784–1854. [Hawarden Castle]

highly creditable to himself and advantageous to the parish formed the laudable resolution of providing his parishioners with a suitable place of worship.[2]

By the spring of 1819 schools for boys and girls had been opened for the education of nearly three hundred children and 'a curate's dwelling house with every requisite accommodation was erected on the Buckley Mountain.' The sum expended on these buildings exceeded £1200 and the newspaper reported 'that the remaining sum in hand will hardly pay for the foundations of the church which will form a principal feature of the moral improvement and civilisation of this extensive and hitherto inaccessible district.'[3] The Rector reported subsequently that 'Her late Majesty Queen Charlotte honoured these undertakings with her Patronage', and that, 'two acres of land were given by Bryan Cooke, Esq. the Lord of the Manor' and a grant of £4,000 was made by His Majesty's Commissioners for building churches which sum covered all the expenses incurred in erecting the new church on Buckley Mountain: an acre of land for the site was contributed by the Trustees of Sir Stephen Glynne, a minor.' Rector Neville used all his influence and connections in raising subscriptions of £1,967 12s. 7d. headed by £200 from the Prince Regent and £25 from Prince Leopold and £21 from the Chancellor of the Exchequer and donations from five bishops, several members of the peerage and many others.

An account of the laying of the foundation stone on 14 December 1821 is to be found in the Common Place book of Henry Neville:[4]

The first stone was laid with much ceremony. The morning was ushered in at Hawarden with ringing of bells & soon after eleven o'clock the procession moved to Buckley in the following order: Trumpeter, Advanced Guard of Hawarden Yeomanry Cavalry with the Standard, Band of Musick, Architect with plan of intended Church, two gentlemen, Miss Boydell & Barker Registrar of ye Ecclesiastical Court, Rev. Hugh Jones & Rev.Henry Jones Surrogates of the Peculiar, Church Wardens, Rector's carriage, Detachment of Cavalry, Clerk of the work carrying a large flag with the new Church painted on it by Lady Charlotte Neville, Lady Glynne's carriage, Sir Stephen & Mr Henry Glynne wearing the Uniform of the Corps — Detachment of Cavalry.

On arriving on the ground the procession was formed on foot headed by four hundred children of Mr Neville's & Lady Glynne's National Schools and proceeded into the area of ye new Church, the rector attended by the officers of the Ecclesiastical Court, the Honble Lady Glynne & several of ye neighbouring Gentry, took his station on a platform at the east end of the intended building when the ceremony of laying the stone was performed by Sir Stephen Glynne & his brother previous to which the 100th Psalm was sung by the children, after the stone was properly adjusted the Rector offered up a prayer in a most feeling & impressive manner. At the end of this prayer the 84th Psalm was sung & the Rector concluded the ceremony with an energetic Address, to which, as far as we could collect, he commenced by reminding the numerous assemblage of persons around him that, however curiosity or the love of novelty might have brought them together, he thought it was his duty to tell them that it was more important solemnity which they had just witnessed no less a one than the public commencement of a building destined for the Service of Almighty God:- and perhaps, he observed, it may not have struck you, who are inhabitants of this district, that by your assembling here today you are identifying yourselves as members of the future congregation which will, I trust, assemble weekly within these sacred walls & may you never desert that Church in which you have formed to yourselves a peculiar interest by witnessing the laying of its Altar Stone … Church Bells will, however be necessary to perfect this undertaking, & for those we must look at home, so much having been done for us at a distance … if by contributing to these bells, you may be the humble means, under Divine Providence, of their calling a Sabbath breaker to Church & thereby bringing a sinner to repentance. Before I take my leave of you, I would wish to impress upon your minds, that however anxious I may appear to compleat this Earthly Temple, my sole object is, that with God's blessing on it, this Church may be an instrument in His hands of drawing my parishioners of this distant district, (who have been so long wandering as sheep without a shepherd), nearer to the great Shepherd of their souls; nearer to the future inheritance of the Temple not made with hands eternal in the Heavens!

The proceedings concluded in Buckley and the procession moved to Hawarden where the Dowager Lady Glynne entertained her guests at the Castle. Toasts were drunk to the success of the enterprise and the Rector, after returning thanks for the good wishes of the company concluded by observing that, although he considered the new Church as his own child, yet he earnestly exhorted all his parishioners not to forget the Mother Church at Hawarden.[5]

St Matthew's Church under construction.
[FRO PR/F/107]

The Church was built within the short space of nine months and dedicated to St Matthew near the festival day of the Saint on 25 September 1822. Buckley was the first of a number of Churches built under the patronage of the Glynne/Gladstone families and with Shotton destined to become a Parish Church separated from the mother parish of Hawarden. The others are St Mary's, Broughton (1824), St John Baptist, Pentrobin (1843), St Bartholomew, Sealand (1867), St Ethelwold, Shotton (1902), St Francis, Sandycroft (1912) and the Church of the Holy Spirit, Ewloe (1938).[6]

An account of the consecration was given by Richard Willett an eyewitness to the event.[7] The act of consecration of the church and churchyard was performed by the Bishop of Chester, in whose diocese the Parish of Hawarden was then situated, and the sermon was preached by Dr Gardener, Pebendary of Lichfield. The Bishop was attended by his chaplains and registrar, the Rector of Hawarden by his surrogates and the officers of the Ecclesiastical Court of the Peculiar and Exempt Jurisdiction of Hawarden. The Rector used the occasion to declare the rights of his Ecclesiastical Court for the continued exercise of the jurisdiction of his peculiar. Once again there was a large concourse of two thousand people gathered to greet the procession of clergy, members of the Glynne family, and court officials who were ceremoniously escorted from the Cross Keys, Lane End by the Hawarden Troop of mounted cavalry.

After the solemn services were concluded the Duchess of Marlborough, Mr and Lady Caroline Pennant, Mr and Mrs Pennant of Downing and a large party dined with Lady Glynne at Hawarden Castle; the Rector entertained the Bishop of Chester, Lord Kenyon, Lord Padstock and the Clergy at the Rectory and the Troop of Yeomanry Cavalry at the Glynne Arms.

Present at the consecration was Lord Kenyon, one of the

The Glynne children at Audley End (L–R: Catherine, Mary, Stephen and Henry), by Henry Edridge, 1816. [Hawarden Castle] Stephen was the last Glynne baronet of Hawarden. Henry became rector of Hawarden with the care of Buckley. Catherine married W. E. Gladstone and they were the parents of Mary Drew.

Rector Henry Glynne, (1834–72). [B. Jones deposit, FRO D/DM/592]

Parliamentary Commissioners for building churches. The architect was John Oates (d.1831) of Halifax who next designed the church at Broughton opened two years later. The contractors were Messrs B. J. & J.Howell of Dewsbury.

George Neville wrote a description shortly before he left Hawarden to become Dean of Windsor:[8]

The interior of the Church presents one broad space without aisles, and is very light, but devoid of ornament. The timbers of the roof are exposed. Over the west door is a gallery in which there is a large grinding organ under it on one side is the Ordinary's seat, and on the other side a pew for the Churchwardens.

The Chancel opens to the body of the Church by a pointed arch, and contains the altar table, which is approached by three steps. Its furniture is of handsome crimson cloth, the gift of the Honble Catherine Neville in 1825.

The east window has some ancient painted glass purchased at Norwich and presented to the Church by the present Rector. The subject is Daniel in the Lions' Den, being the saint to whom the Parish Church is dedicated. The pulpit and reading desk are placed on each side of the chancel aisle. The former is approached from the vestry. There is a small pew in the chancel appropriated to the Glynne family.

The Church is sixty-eight feet long by forty-four feet wide and is divided into three aisles. There are sixty-eight pews, which contain three hundred and six sittings; also benches for one hundred and six persons and two hundred and eighty school children. Seven hundred and six persons can consequently be accommodated on the floor: in the event of more sittings being required, two side galleries might easily be added.

The underwritten inscription is cut out upon a large stone in the wall under the east chancel window:

This stone was laid
By
Stephen Richard Glynne Patron
and
Henry Glynne his brother
George Neville Rector and Ordinary
John Husband BA Curate
Hugh Jones MA
Henry Jones MA Surrogates
Francis George Barker Registrar
William Walley and John Catherall Churchwardens
Peter Reynolds and Richard Roberts Sidesmen
John Oates Architect
December 14 1821

The general effect of the exterior of the Church is handsome, especially the tower, yet the architecture, in its detail, will not stand the test of some criticism. The walls are of fine hewn stone drawn from a quarry in the neighbourhood. A small addition to the east end of the main fabric forms the chancel having the vestry on one side, and the baptistery on the other. The church is lighted on either side by five windows each of two lights, between which on the outside are slender buttresses surmounted by short pinnacles. The east end of the chancel has a window of five lights dissimilar to those in the body. The east gable is flanked by octagonal turrets. The tower is ninety feet ten inches high to the top of the pinnacles. It has three stories, and the summit is finished by a pierced battlement with pinnacles at the angles, each crowned with a finial. The lower story forms the entrance to the church, having doorways on the south and east sides, and a window of two lights on the west. The next story has on each front a window of two lights and a clock, which was purchased by subscription in 1827. The belfry contains four large windows of three lights divided by a transom. There is only one bell, which was purchased at Downham Market in Norfolk, and is distinguished for its deep sonorous sound.

George Neville engaged the assistance of curates who were resident in the newly built house. John Husband (1820–5) was the first resident in the parish before the church was built. Samuel Gilbert Compton (1825–39) remained during the first years of Henry Glynne as Rector of Hawarden. Parochial work in Buckley was hard and at first unrewarding as George Neville recorded in 1835.

Thirteen years have elapsed since this church was completed. Acts of Parliament have subsequently passed contributing much to remove difficulties with which the writer of these pages had to contend when the building of a Church on Buckley Mountain was first entertained. Never however can he forget the successful termination of all his labours or the sensation, which filled his heart on witnessing the solemn consecration of this church to the public service of Almighty God.

Although experience may have proved that many sanguine hopes are yet unrealised that the morals of the inhabitants have not actually improved, nor the services been attended as well as we anticipated yet the delightful fact that a temple is now established for ages yet to come in which the knowledge of a God and Saviour can be faithfully proclaimed to every inhabitant of this hitherto benighted district.

There are neat gates to the churchyard and a wall round it. A strong prejudice prevailed against being interred here. One old woman objected because part of the site had been used as a kiln and the best of the soil appropriated to making bricks![9]

The second phase in the life of St Matthew's was marked by the long curacy of Henry Powell Ffoulkes (1840–57). His devoted and energetic ministry of seventeen years shaped forever the pattern of worship in the parish and began a tradition which has lasted until this day. His priestly vocation inspired his parishioners who said of him, 'The first man who worked among us was Mr Ffoulkes'. He overcame the difficulties and prejudices he first encountered by daily prayer, frequent celebrations of the service of Holy Communion, choral services, house to house visitations, communicant, Bible and other classes which soon won the rough hearts of his people.

Ffoulkes came to Buckley as young man aged twenty-five years having served a brief curacy at Halkyn. He studied the Welsh language under the Revd John Williams (Ab Ithel), the incumbent at Nerquis. Educated at Balliol College Oxford and graduating in 1837, he fell under the spell of the Oxford Movement and was influenced at his college by two Tractarian fellows, Frederick Oakley and William George Ward, ardent followers of John Henry Newman. He brought these ideas with him to Buckley and sought to emulate in a modest fashion the liturgical and ritualistic ideas, which Oakley took with him to Margaret Street Chapel in London. The young curate found support for his ideas from his patron Sir Stephen Glynne, a distinguished ecclesiologist and High Church Tory, and his like-minded brother Henry, the Rector. Another ally and sympathiser was J. E. Troughton, curate at Pentrobin (1843–64) who was responsible for adorning St John Baptist Church with frescoes and stained glass.

Liturgical innovations and ritualistic tendencies were introduced at St Matthew's by means of reordering the interior and the introduction of church furniture with the purpose of bringing the beauty of holiness to worship. This was done in an inexpensive and modest manner. The only surviving record of payment is a sum of £533 spent on alterations and improvements in 1845 when the architect was James Harrison of Chester.

Ffoulkes began his work of reordering the church immediately upon his arrival. He introduced two choir stalls, which he placed on either side at the East End of the nave below the steps at the entrance to the chancel. The singers were brought there from the West End gallery and to mark their new status were robed in surplices. In 1843 he turned his attention to the chancel. Candlesticks were placed upon the altar designed especially by William Butterfield. The stained glass depicting Daniel in the Lions' Den, which Neville had purchased in Norwich, was replaced by a window showing the crucified Christ in the centre light, with the two thieves, soldiers and spectators on either side. In the 1870s Archdeacon Thomas noted 'The sacrarium contains a credence and a sedile; and the east window, a perpendicular of five lights, is filled with stained glass in dark but fading colours.' On each side of this window the Ten Commandments were displayed on wood. The next year Ffoulkes brought into the church a font, which he found in the rectory garden in Hawarden. It was richly carved on the panels of the bowl with the heraldry of the Stanley family once possessed of the lordship of Hawarden. Although the church was designed to have a baptistery at the south-east end, the font was now installed under the west end gallery, at the entrance from the porch into the nave, thus symbolizing that baptism was the gateway to salvation. In 1852 a second-hand keyboard was purchased by Sir Stephen Glynne and Mr Ffoulkes which was set up in the south-east corner of the nave near the choir. Two colliers, self-taught musicians, led the choir. Daily services were established and it not infrequently happened that, when there were mining accidents, many of those who escaped injury would go to church in their working clothes to return thanks for their preservation.

In 1849 St Matthew's school was transferred from the parsonage to a new site adjoining the north side of the churchyard given by Sir Stephen Glynne. It was opened on Easter Tuesday and the newspaper report shows the influence Ffoulkes was exerting in Buckley. At the service conducted by the Bishop 'Gregorian chants were sung to Venite & Psalms, one harmonised by Tallis to the Benedicite and the anthem by Boyce. On leaving the Church a procession was formed.. the choir in surplices, clergy in surplices, the Te Deum was sung down the road to the schools.' The reporter commented:

The manner in which the Godly order of the Church is observed at all religious celebrations within the parish of Hawarden is deserving of commendation on this gratifying occasion. The singing and chanting were admirably effective and the services were conducted with impressive solemnity. The restorations and improvements which have lately been affected at St Matthew's are in the best ecclesiastical taste, and the schools of a character well adapted to that prevailing spirit of true Churchmanship which finds a genial home at Hawarden.[10]

W. E. Gladstone observed the young man's capacities and offered him preferment in Liverpool but Henry Glynne took steps to retain him. After Ffoulkes left the parish in 1857 for a living in Montgomeryshire, Bishop Short recognised his worth and made him Archdeacon of Montgomery in 1861.

Four curates followed in succession until Buckley was created a separate parish in 1874, two years after the death of Rector Glynne. One of them, Charles Bellairs (1861–7), was described as 'gentlemanlike, 42 & above, 6 feet high & in all ways well suited to Buckley & a good practical Parish Priest & used to deal with the rougher people.'[11]

In November 1865 a new pipe organ built by Gray and Davison of Chester and bought by public subscription was installed. To mark the occasion two special sermons were preached by the Rev W. Lyttelton and Archdeacon Ffoulkes.

William Fox Whitbread Tore was appointed curate in 1873 and became the first vicar of Buckley the following year and was formally instituted on the 1 May 1875. The new parish was created by an Order in Council on 12 December 1874 and a full description of boundaries published in the *London Gazette* three days later. Wholly created out of the mother parish of Hawarden it comprised the township of Ewloe Wood and parts of Ewloe Town and Pentrobin. It was endowed with £400 per annum. The right of patronage was at first vested in Sir Stephen Richard Glynne, his heirs and successors and passed immediately to W. H. Gladstone eldest son of W. E. Gladstone in which family it remained until the disestablishment of the Welsh Church in 1920. The male Glynne line died out with the deaths of Henry Glynne (1872) and his brother Stephen (1874).

The Anglican Church in the district thus assumed the boundaries and identity it still possesses in the parishes of Emmanuel Bistre and St Matthew's Buckley which twenty-five years later became an Urban District Council.

The Census of 1871 gives some idea of the delineation of the new parish. The enumerator noted:

The Township of Ewloe Wood is … an agricultural, mining and manufacturing district. There are 4 potteries & 1 Colliery within it. It includes the parts known as Buckley Mountain Altamay; Pinfold Lane; Ewloe Barn; Ferry Road; Ewloe Green; Stamford Way; Vinegar Hill; Foreign Parts; Brook Hill & Sea View. The Houses are chiefly scattered, and only a few have names which causes some inconvenience to the Enumerator.' There were 125 inhabited houses, 314 males, and 287 females.

The Township of Ewloe Town. The inhabitants are principally engaged in agriculture, mining and manufactures, The manufactures carried on are firebricks, tiles and coarse earthenware. The Township has increased so much during the last ten years, that it is physically impossible for the Enumerator to perform his task in the time allowed him. It occupied three days in delivering the schedules and two days or twenty-five hours in collecting them.' There were 319 inhabited houses, 857 males, and 723 females.

The part of Pentrobin in Buckley in 1881 was Church Road, Barracks, Lane End, Primrose Terrace, Blue Bell Inn (Lord St), the Bull Inn, the Feather's Inn, Knowl Hill, Johnson's Row, Prince of Wales Inn, Bannel Lane. There were 162 inhabited houses, 430 males, and 384 females.

The Reverend William Dampier, vicar of Buckley (1885–97).

Torre was incumbent until 1885. In 1875 he requested G. A. Bell of Chester to report on the state of the fabric and drainage prior to the repair and cleaning of the church. Torre began to keep the large book known as Buckley Parish Records in which Canon Harry Drew noted as 'apparently started by the Rev. W. F. Torre, but I found very little recorded when I came into the Parish in 1897.' What was there was derived from the *London Gazette*, Willett's *Memoir of Hawarden Parish* and the names of seven choir men, twelve choir boys and the twenty-six male members of the Bible Class for the information of his successor William Dampier.

Dampier was vicar for twelve years (1885–97), a period which was marked by the building of two mission churches. The first at Pentre, the Mission Room of the Good Shepherd, was opened on 29 November 1893. It was built of wood and measured 24ft 6ins by 13ft 6ins. For the occasion 'the surpliced choir of St Matthew's headed by Mr Swinnerton, licensed lay reader, walked in procession from a tent in an adjoining field. On arriving at the west door a halt was made whilst the vicar offered an appropriate prayer, after which a key was handed to Mr Swinnerton, who unlocked the door and proceeded up the aisle, the choir and the clergy following. The harmonium was played by Mr Hughes, a professor of music. The service was held in the evening when the vicar preached to an overflowing congregation. The room will seat one hundred persons. Great praise is due to Mr R. D. Davies, contractor of Buckley, who carried out the erection in an efficient manner.'[12]

The Bishop of St Asaph opened the second Mission Room of St David's at the other end of the parish at Ewloe Green on the 4 March 1894.[13] It was larger than Pentre Mission and had a chancel at the east end. Squire Cooke gave the ground on which it was built. Ewloe Mission was closed in 1906 and the Church of the Good Shepherd replaced by a new building at Drury clad with corrugated metal sheets and was the gift of Mrs Drew in 1899.

The churchyard at St Matthew's was extended eastwards, drained, levelled and bounded on the south side by a stone wall. The gift of the Trustees of W. H. Gladstone, it was consecrated by the Bishop of St Asaph in October 1893.

Inserted in the Parish Book is a memoir written by the Rev. Oswald Stent in the 1940s, lay reader under the Revd William Dampier 1894–5. It gives a vivid picture of church life in Buckley in the 1890s:

I saw an Advertisement 'Junior Lay Reader wanted immediately, Vicar of St Matthew's Buckley'. I answered it, and within a week I got a wire 'Come at once. Expenses paid; Dampier'. I left Salisbury by an early train on June 23rd 1894 and arrived at Buckley Town at about 5 o'clock, and was met by William Swinnerton, the Senior Lay Reader. On my way to the vicarage he gave me one piece of advice 'Don't take the Vicar seriously, and then you will get on with him'. Mr Dampier was standing at Vicarage door. A short, thick, well built man of anything between 50 and 60 years, sporting a heavy moustache and wearing a golf cap, Norfolk jacket, plus fours, stockings and walking shoes, blunt in manner, and unconventional in speech. Soon we were sitting down to tea, with his sister who kept house for him, for he was a bachelor. Swinnerton also lived at the vicarage. Not a word was said about my duties the following day, a Sunday. Swinnerton accompanied me to my room and told me that I would have to take the Services at Ewloe Green the following day, a Mission Church which had only been built a week or two, and they were a Children's Service at 10.30, and then return to St Matthew's to serve the vicar at the mid-day celebration, Sunday School at 2.30, go anywhere I was invited to Tea, and finally take full Evensong at 6.30.

Swinnerton called me at 7 o'clock and I went to the 8 a.m. Service at which there were about twelve communicants, eight were men. The only ceremonial was Lights and the Eastward position. After breakfast I left

Mr & Mrs W. E. Gladstone in a carriage.

for Ewloe Green. When I reached the Mission Church I found just the congregation I had expected, about a dozen little people who were too young to go to the parish church, and four or five old people too infirm to walk more than a short distance for worship. Tom Wynne was seated at the American organ, and we were soon ready to start, when the tinkling of the bell suddenly stopped, and a Carriage and Pair was heard at the Church, and the caretaker ran into the vestry and with bated breath announced that Mr and Mrs Gladstone were coming into Church. I went forward to meet them, and asked whether they had not made a mistake Mr Gladstone replied "No" and brushed passed me with his friends accompanying him into one of the front seats. What was I to do, a mere youth and not yet nineteen years of age! I decided to hold the Children's Service exactly as I had been told, except that I offered the authorised prayer for the Duchess of York (Queen Mary) and her infant son (Edward). The previous week the Liberal Government had been defeated by a vote in the House on the Home Rule question, Mr Gladstone had left London with some members of the Cabinet. That weekend Hawarden was swarming with members of the Press and public and in order to escape them Mr Gladstone had gone to the Church where he would be least expected. After the Service I hurried back to Buckley and was in time to assist the Vicar. When I told him about my experience he simply laughed and said "Serve you right". The Sunday school in the afternoon and Evensong at night were uneventful. We had about forty children at Sunday school and about fifty to sixty people attended in the evening,

After I had been at Buckley a day or two the Vicar had a talk with Swinnerton and me about our work. We breakfasted at 8 am, and went to Church for Matins at 9am, and he suggested that we should read the lessons alternate weeks. From 9.30 am to 11 am. there was to be silence in the Study and this time was to be given up to reading and study. From 11am to 12 noon we attended to correspondence and discussed parochial questions. After lunch we were to visit, Swinnerton being in charge of Pentre and the Town, and I in charge of Buckley Common and Ewloe Green. I was also responsible for editing the Parish Magazine. The Vicar rarely visited. He insisted upon our going away from the Parish on Mondays, and sometimes he accompanied us, and was profuse in his hospitality. We could never get him to visit our Mission Churches. St Matthew's was the place for them to attend for Baptisms, Churchings and Holy Communion. We were very happy in our relationship with our Vicar. He was a strange mixture of a man of God and a man of the world. Mr Dampier had been nurtured in the early Tractarian atmosphere. He always followed us when we read the lessons from his Greek Testament.

The Vicar persuaded me to join the 1st Flintshire Royal Engineers, and, in my first summer, I went into camp at Henley on Thames, and I would have gone to Aldershot the second year had I not left Buckley for Oxford University. Of Miss Dampier the Vicar's sister I cannot speak too highly. She was the essence of kindness and consideration and we were well looked after.

Other incidents I can recall of our work at Ewloe Green was that Mr and Mrs Gladstone, after their retirement from public life, frequently called upon old parishioners they knew, and on one occasion I accompanied him to the dying bed of one who had been in the service of his parents, and I heard him read to her the 23rd Psalm and offer the Lord's Prayer. On another occasion we were together at a Bazaar, which Mrs Gladstone opened, and in the course of the afternoon she asked me to see that her purse was not lost, and then forgot she had entrusted it to my keeping!

Towards the end of 1894 Dampier asked the Bishop to ordain Swinnerton in deacon's orders. Upon the Bishop's refusal, Swinnerton resigned, married Miss Dampier, and was accepted for ordination by the Bishop of Zululand where he served with the SPG Mission. Stent was more fortunate in that, after some persuasion, the Bishop formally licensed him as a lay reader on condition that he proceeded as soon as possible to Oxford to study for the ministry. Dampier introduced him to the Principal of St Edmund Hall, which Stent entered in the Michaelmas Term 1895. Stent had a great affection for the vicar and came back to assist him during the long vacation in 1896. After graduating Stent was ordained in the diocese of Bristol and after curacies he served in New Zealand for twenty years returning to the parish of Gusage in Sarum diocese in 1929. By the time Stent revisited Buckley in 1902, Dampier had moved to the living of Nailstone in the diocese of Ripon.

There is some mystery about his departure. The question is, did he move on his own accord or was he 'nudged out' by persons of influence? These are the circumstances.[14]

W. E. Gladstone was out of office in 1894 and spending most of his time in Hawarden where he and Catherine were increasingly dependent upon their children, particularly their daughters Mary and Helen. In December 1896 Mary's husband, Harry Drew, gave up the librarianship at St Deiniol's. Mary Drew's correspondence with her brothers, Henry and Herbert, make it quite clear what was in their thoughts. On 10 December she wrote to her brother Henry, saying that her husband was looking for a living, which would fulfil two conditions: nearness to her parents for MD and pastoral work for HD, adding that a place like Buckley appeals to Harry specially, but if it turns out impossible to remove Dampier, HD has a sense of having some gift of organisation such as a large parish demands. By the end of January HD had been approached about Birmingham and St Albans, and Mary wrote to her brother Herbert, 'now as to Buckley & if we were to go there I shall try with all my might to put my heart into it, & shall be helped by feeling Harry will make its wilderness blossom as a rose.'

In the meantime W. E. Gladstone wrote to the Bishop of St Asaph on 4 January 1897 saying:

I believe that our neighbour Mr Dampier of Buckley, has appealed to your Lordship to remove him on some early opportunity from Buckley to a less rough and laborious country living. I need hardly say that this was not done upon instigation from us; indeed it was, I believe, without the knowledge of any one in this house'. Mr Gladstone then explained that his son-in-law was looking for employment which 'should be so near as not to remove our daughter, his wife, beyond the circle of constant domestic intercourse. At our time of life, my wife would feel her removal very seriously.'[15] Mr Drew, I may say, is a person really and deservedly in request ...we feel certain that his qualifications for Buckley would be, not good only, but exceptional.

On the last day of January, Mary wrote to Herbert: 'no words can express the relief of Buckley being settled ... we must be hooked on somehow to the telephone ... bicycles will come in very useful, & we must be geniuses and make the house, Church and garden a little less repellent.'

On 27 February the *Chronicle* announced that Dampier had accepted the Crown living of Nailstone, near Nuneaton: and a month later that Harry Drew had been appointed his successor. He was inducted to the living on 30 April and Mr and Mrs Gladstone were at Divine Service when he preached his first sermon as vicar. The effect of these events on his predecessor was recorded by George Lewis who noted in his diary:

1907 Sept 22 Sun Mr Dampier preached at St Matthew's for the first time since he went away. He was vexed when he had to leave. I stood with him in the aisle after the Service. When he had had a good look at the Church he said, 'I will forgive now. I see that the Lord called me away so that the church could be rebuilt; a thing which I could never have done.'

Harry Drew became a legendary figure in the parishes of Buckley and Hawarden. He possessed great qualities, which inspired his parishioners and endeared him to all age groups of Church people and Nonconformists alike. Revered and respected for his personal holiness as a parish priest and dedication as a pastor, he possessed an ability to get things done and had a practical vision of a social nature which was valued in a working class community in the process of finding its new identity as an Urban District Council. He came to Buckley at the age of 41 years, virtually unknown, and never having been in charge of a parish. Arriving in Hawarden as a humble curate in 1883 he surprised everyone by eventually taking as his wife Mary, the daughter of W. E. Gladstone, ten years his senior. It was to prove a happy marriage and an ideal partnership of two people, not only married to each other but to the parishes they served. At Oxford, Drew fell under the influence of Charles Gore, three years his senior, who became his mentor and directed him to the diocese of St Asaph for his ordination and the parish of Hawarden for his title. Gore was a High Churchman and one of the charismatic figures in the Church of England, who had a 'concern to bring Catholic principles to bear on social problems.'

The Gladstone Family at Hawarden. Seated William and Catherine Gladstone, in front of Catherine 'Dossie' Drew.
Back row L–R: The Revd Stephen, child and wife Annie, Mary and Harry Drew, Herbert Gladstone (holding dog), Helen Gladstone.

The family quickly settled down at Buckley vicarage, as Mary Drew noted in her letters to her brothers: 'we are snug & so happy & the servants are angels.' They felt at home in the industrial landscape. Mary noted in October, 'such a glorious Tuneresque evening: the sun is an angry red glow burnishing everything into wild beauty even Buckley chimneys!' She reported to Henry in May 1898, 'HD is giving £550 his first year to the Church & Schools.' From the beginning there are detailed records of what was done. A pragmatic programme of innovation to do what was necessary and to introduce new ideas for improvements to the churches, schools, the vicarage, beauty in worship, efficiency in parochial administration, better living conditions and facilities for leisure and recreation for their poor parishioners. An example is Harry Drew's summary of the first year at Buckley:

> The Rev H.Drew read himself in as Vicar on May 2nd. On June 20th Special Services to Commemorate the Diamond Jubilee of the Queen; among the worshippers in the morning being the Rt. Hon W. E. Gladstone. This Summer the flagstaff was erected on the Church Tower, & the Clock repaired (£17.10s) by Messrs Joyce of Whitchurch, also the Tower roof was releaded, Three windows of rolled Cathedral Glass were put in the Church Tower in place of dilapidated ones, the levelling of the Churchyard graves was begun, On Christmas Day, the Parish Church Choir wore Cassocks for the first time with their surplices (the gift of Mrs Gladstone) The "Buckley Church Improvement Fund" was started with a gift of £100 from Mr Gladstone. The Lane End Sunday school was reopened after being closed for 3 or 4 years. The Rev W. de Winton Kitcat, (Christchurch, Oxford), was ordained deacon & licensed to Buckley in September. The Vicarage had £600 spent on it in improvements during the summer: Buckley was formed into an Urban District in October this year. The Timber Porch to the Vicarage was built in December & was the gift of Mrs Gladstone.[16]

The lasting achievements of Harry Drew at Buckley may be considered under four main headings. First: the reconstruction of church buildings at St Matthew's and the Church of the Good Shepherd. Second: parochial work. Third: care for church schools at St Matthew's and Lane End. Fourth: contribution to community life. To understand the complexity of his life, it must be realized that these areas of activity continually overlapped each other and brought him into contact with all members of the local population. There was always the need for explanation, public approval, ability to deal with controversy, and the necessity of finding a great deal of

The Reverend Canon Harry Drew, vicar of Buckley (1897–1905).

money to finance these schemes. In this he was totally supported by the dynamic energy of his wife, Mary, and the goodwill of the members of the Gladstone family. For the first three years of their life at Buckley they were involved in the last illnesses of the Gladstone parents, William (died 19 May 1898) and Catherine (died 14 June 1900).

First. Church reconstruction was a major undertaking from 1897 to 1905. It was not done for the sake of replacing what was considered to be an ugly building but out of necessity. What was replaced and added was to the glory of God, of the highest quality of craftsmanship, and under the expert guidance of the architects Douglas and Minshull of Chester. The major part of

The Vicarage, Buckley. [FRO PH/11/226]

the work was instigated as a result of two reports by the architects dated 11 April and 5 December 1900.

Harry Drew set the ball rolling in 1898 by paying for the building of clergy and choir vestries and five windows on the south wall of the nave were reglazed. Opportunity was used to renew and repair the old fabric and make significant additions to the building as a memorial to William and Catherine Gladstone. It was announced at the Easter Vestry meeting on 16 April 1900 that Mrs Drew and her sister Miss Helen Gladstone offered the gift of £1,000 for the erection of a chancel to be a memorial to their father. Harry Drew then brought before the meeting the desirability of carrying out much needed work on the church and reminded them of Mr Gladstone's gift of £100 in October 1897 to inaugurate an improvement fund. The sum in hand was now £900. He also spoke of the visit of Sir Arthur Blomfield[17] in 1897 and his written advice and opinion and then read the report of the architects upon the condition of the fabric and advising the carrying out in sections of certain additions and alterations. The Vestry agreed to seek a faculty for the erection of a memorial chancel with a heating apparatus chamber, alterations to the roof, the reseating of the nave, the conversion of the present porch (connected with the nave by an open arch) into a baptistery and the erection of a new porch outside the existing one.[18]

On further investigation it was realized that the tower was of poor construction and in an unsatisfactory condition. As a result of this development the whole matter was presented in the *Parish Magazine* for January 1901.

Mrs Drew has for some time felt desirous of offering to be responsible for the Baptistery, as a memorial to her mother, thus connecting Mr & Mrs Gladstone specially with the East and West ends the Alpha and Omega of the building.

Mary Drew expressed her thoughts to Henry about her mother:

… her connections with Buckley and her mother's (Lady Glynne who built the church in 1822) were so peculiar in their intimacy & interest, & then later on her devotion to it through and because of us as to make a permanent memorial there specially fitting … the poor old ugly cheap building will become a worthy place of worship & I hope be rather more inspiring to the people of Buckley.[19]

Drew concluded his remarks to the Vestry by saying that:

In considering what should be done at the base of the Tower in carrying out this memorial it was necessary to make a thorough examination of the Tower throughout, not only on account of the Baptistery Memorial to Mrs Gladstone, but for the safety of the Tower itself, that it should be dealt with thoroughly and without delay from

Arrival of new bells and rebuilding of the church tower, 1902.
[FRO PH/11/44]

top to bottom. With regard to this upper portion, the Vicar's announcement was that Mrs Drew and himself had offered to the Building Committee to guarantee whatever was necessary for placing the Tower in a thoroughly sound and satisfactory condition, as advised by the Architects, and that they desired to include in this offer a Peal of Bells (if found feasible), which might be put in connection the Church Clock, and mark the Quarters as well as the Hours ... Meanwhile the four pinnacles and parapet are to be taken down at once as a precautionary measure.[20]

The new chancel was consecrated by the Bishop of St Asaph on 24 July 1901 and a year later he returned to dedicate the baptistery with its new font; the tower, new clock, and peal of eight bells and the porch. The font was a memorial to Joseph Tyson headmaster of St Matthew's for over thirty years. Harry Drew gave the clock with its Cambridge chimes, made by Smiths of Derby and designed by Lord Grimthorpe who provided the specifications for the peal of eight bells to the founders John Taylor & Sons, Loughborough. They were the gift of Mrs Drew who raised the money required for the building of the porch by the sale of a small volume of John Ruskin's Letters.

A description of the baptistery, the walls of which were decorated in 1903, appeared in *The Builder*, in October 1905.

Portland stone and black marble have been used for the pavement, and St Bees stone for the font; over this is suspended, an octagonal oak cover carved and traceried, having as a background a stained-glass window by Mr H. Holiday.

Above the wood panelling, stained green, the surface of wall and ceiling has been treated in colour, wax medium being employed. The scheme of decoration has reference, in the lower and upper parts respectively, to the initiatory and complementary rites of baptism, and confirmation. Surmounting the dado, the emblem of the net enclosing enfolded fishes is introduced as a band with a label bearing a text, and rising from this are stems and leafage, interspersed with the dove and crown and sacred monograms, leading and growing into frieze containing medallions, with angels supporting shields charged with symbols of the seven-fold endowment enumerated in the confirmation office.

The decoration was executed by the late Mr W. F. Lodge, of West Hampstead, from the designs of the architects, Messrs Douglas & Minshull, Chester, from whose coloured drawing, exhibited in this year's Royal Academy, our illustration is reproduced.[21]

St Matthew's Church reached its completed state when the east and west ends were joined by a new nave consecrated on 11 January 1905 a few days before the Drews left for Hawarden for Harry Drew to become rector of the parish. The nave is impressive and a great improvement on the austere barn-like character of the original building. It gave the church a more spacious feeling and certain uniqueness with a half-timbered clerestory and timber arcades with decorated panels below the clerestory given as a memorial to Harry Drew who died in 1910. The nave is linked with the

Memorial Baptistery, The Builder, October 1906.

chancel and baptistery by arts and crafts furnishings and decoration. On the panels angels bear shields with emblems depicting the eight Beatitudes. More angels with instruments of music represent the worship of heaven.[22]

Once again the implementation of work on the nave was dependent upon the generosity of the vicar and his wife and the consent of the Vestry. Drew put the matter before them with another proposal for a new organ and used his characteristic powers of persuasion to show them the advantages of both proposals. He told them an offer had

The restored nave. [FRO PH/11/33]

recently been made to give half the cost of a new organ on condition that the parishioners will themselves raise the other half, suggesting, 'It just wants a systematic plan of weekly contribution, steadily carried on for six months.' The nave he said was deteriorating and a faulty roof had caused both north and south walls to bulge considerably. By building new walls outside the existing ones they would gain 120 sittings. He reassured them that Mrs Drew and himself would make themselves jointly responsible for the cost of the new nave and its fittings upon the 'condition that the parishioners would willingly consent to the abolition of the existing pew rent.'

Mary Drew related to her brother Henry what happened after the vicar had made these proposals.

He then left, & a new chairman was elected, & a discussion ensued, with the result that in an hours time, a messenger was sent over to say they undertook the organ job, & accepted the Nave offer, & begged we wd. come over for a moment. I was in my dressing gown & had to put a skirt and cloak on over it & we went across and they expressed their appreciation.[23]

Excellent new windows were installed during this period the work of Henry Holiday a stained-glass artist of the pre-Raphaelite and art nouveau schools. He was also a friend of W. E. Gladstone and had met Mary Drew from the 1870s onwards staying on occasions at Hawarden and attending Gladstone's funeral in 1898. Not surprisingly the family asked him to design memorial windows. The five-light window in the memorial chancel depicting the crucifixion was dedicated to Henry Powell Ffoulkes; that on the north-east side depicting Righteousness and Truth was given in memory of Mr and Mrs Gladstone by Henry Holiday and his wife; that on the south east depicting Faith and Love in memory of W. E. Gladstone was given by his daughter Agnes Wickham, the wife of the Dean of Lincoln, who also provided the Baptistery window depicting

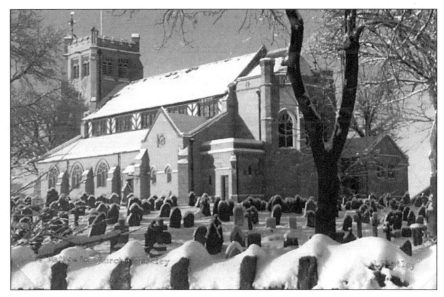

The restored church seen in snow, 1998.
[Buckley Library]

Angels with children in memory of her mother. A final window by the artist depicting the Good Shepherd carrying a lamb in his arms and surrounded by his flock was given in memory of Harry Drew by his wife and daughter in 1910.

The tin tabernacle, the Church of the Good Shepherd, was replaced by a building of brick and dedicated on 27 January 1900. It was built on the road leading from the Parrot Inn to the Pentre on a plot of land given by Mrs Lloyd of Drury. The building cost £327 16s. and was paid for by Mrs Drew. The parishioners furnished it at a cost of £137. Present at the opening were Mrs W. H. Gladstone, and Lady Frederick Cavendish. Evensong was held on Thursdays and a voluntary choir, Women's Sewing Meeting and a Night School for young men were begun.

Harry and Mary Drew made substantial donations to pay for the work of the reconstruction and adornment of St Matthew's Church and from 1897 to 1905 contributed over £11,000 towards the church, schools and vicarage with another £7,000 from other sources. It was obviously easier to pay for things themselves. Mary complained in 1901 that 'we have to spend our whole life begging or subscribing. We shall have to appeal to landowners, employers of labour & scratch up all the shillings and pence from working people. We have had to use the £6,000 father unexpectedly left in 1898. I won't say that some of the things we have spent it on (like the Peal of Bells & the Big Ben Clock) were necessaries as it took several surgical operations to get £5 out of those who make their money out of the parish.'

Detailed statistics relating to the parish were recorded in The Official Parochial Register.[24] Attendance at the church schools averaged over 600, Sunday schools 350, Bible classes 100, district visitors 5, choir 24 males, baptisms 60, church accommodation 110 assigned, 160 free, the number increased to 400 when the new nave was finished; communicants averaged 250; the parish magazine distribution was 500; attendance at the church institute was 35, the reading room 39 and St Matthew's summer recreation society 150, both male and female. Canon Henry Scott Holland of St Paul's, a noted theologian and preacher, spoke to 300 at the Men's Service in August 1899 on 'Training and self-discipline.' Scott Holland had known Mary Drew since 1876 and he was the godfather of Dossie Drew. He preached the sermon at Harry Drew's funeral. Mary published a selection of his letters to her in 1919.[25] St Matthew's bell ringers were formed in 1904 and joined the North Wales Association of Church Bellringers.

The third area of parish life where Harry Drew made a lasting contribution was church schools. When he was appointed vicar, he found the school buildings condemned by the education authorities, and, most dangerously, threatened with absorption into the local School Board. In 1897 the number of scholars on the register for the Elementary Schools in the district was 1,428 (Buckley National Schools, 637; Ewloe Green British School, 107; Bistre Board Schools, 429; Bistre National Schools, 255). The National Schools, (Church Schools) and Voluntary aided, thus educated 62% of the children in the Anglican parishes of Bistre and Buckley, although some Nonconformists sent their children to these schools. Drew was responsible for the schools at St Matthew's and Lane End and it took four years to get them in a state of repair which

Above & left: The Mission Church of the Good Shepherd, Drury, exterior and interior.
[Buckley Library]

was acceptable to the secular authorities. The estimated expenditure of £3,456 was met by a voluntary rate for two years contributed by the Buckley church people and the payment of nearly a third of the cost, £1,070, given by Harry Drew. In August 1899 St Matthew's Schools were reopened after two large new classrooms were added to the boys' and girls' departments and two years later the Lane End Infants Department was enlarged by the addition of a classroom, when the editor of the *Parish Magazine* wrote, 'The people of Buckley might congratulate themselves on the possession of School Buildings in first rate order, and thoroughly well equipped.' The fact that this work had been completed may have given the Anglican church people in Buckley some small satisfaction in light of the crisis brought about in Wales in 1902 by the passing of the Education Act. School Boards were abolished and authority was given to local committees. This posed the threat that the distinction between board and voluntary schools would end. All schools would be financed from the rates, giving the local education authority the right of inspection in voluntary schools and the power to appoint two out of six managers. In Parliament the Welsh Liberal MPs revolted against the act and encouraged the Liberal dominated local authorities to ignore the act. The Welsh revolt, in which Lloyd George took the leading role, led to sustained confusion, great uncertainty for the future, and the threat of the confiscation of the church schools. Wales at the time was in the passion of a great

religious revival and the old fears, which were all too often expressed against Roman Catholics, and High Church Anglicans in anti-ritualistic demonstrations in Buckley must have divided the community. There were a number of children of nonconformists being educated in Church schools in Buckley. An entry in the St Matthew's School Log Book explained the action taken by Drew:

A. G. Edwards, Bishop of St Asaph (left) and his political adversary Lloyd George with Winston Churchill at the National Eisteddfod Llangollen 1908.

Leaflets were issued by the Vicar to all nonconformist parents giving them the option of withdrawing their children from Catechism & Prayer Book Lessons. These were sent to 146 Nonconformist homes, and 19 availed themselves of the offer — the remaining 127 preferring their children to be taught Prayer Book and Catechism as heretofore. In all, 33 children out of about 250 Nonconformist children are thus partially withdrawn; it takes away all ground for suspicion. Certainly the air is perfectly clear.[26]

The final area for appraisal is Drew's contribution to public life. He was a man of his time, the kind of parish priest who fervently believed that the church and its gospel must advance social welfare and social justice. The church was a brotherhood transcending all human distinctiveness, the eucharist the sacrament of fraternity and Christians must be prepared to make sacrifices and use their wealth for the benefit of society. All this he practised in partnership with his wife. It was chiefly her wealth and inheritance as a daughter of a Prime Minister which was spent for the benefit of Buckley and he would have approved.

In August 1902 a newspaper article discussed, 'the progress of Buckley. How the Rev. H. Drew has improved the Parish.' The writer began by remarking that 'the district realised when Mr Drew set to work, a new spirit was in its midst.' After a detailed list of improvements to the church, vicarage and schools he noticed that through his influence an ambulance van had been provided for the district out of funds raised by the Cycle Carnival Committee to provide transport to Mold Hospital for those injured in the local collieries and brick works. Previously Mrs Drew initiated the employment of a parish nurse making herself responsible for her payment for the first year. He continued:

In the social work of the district the Rev H. Drew has taken a keen interest and has done much to ventilate the lighting question in Buckley by arranging with the Gas Company to light Church Road on the incandescent system and last winter saw the principal streets of Buckley lighted by the same method. A short time ago Mrs Drew presented to the Urban Council a new watering cart. Recreation clubs have been organised, and in the winter there were social evenings for the young men of the district at Pentre and Lane End schools, and at the vicarage. During the last two years the vicarage field has been entirely relaid, and has been converted into tennis, croquet bowls and quoiting ground. The offer of Mr Herbert Gladstone M.P. and of Mr and Mrs Drew lately in connection with the free library offer of Mr Carnegie is too fresh in the minds of our readers to require an extended reference. If the Urban Council had accepted a site at Lane End, offered by the Hawarden Trustees, there would have been £800 forthcoming towards the erection of an adjoining institute.

The background to the idea for an Institute is to be found in the correspondence between Mary Drew and her brother Herbert Gladstone. In the spring of 1901 a performance of *Elijah* took place and Mary reported that 'no event in Buckley has ever before happened which brought such a fellow feeling, such community of interest between Church & Chapel. The orchestra engaged from Halles band at Manchester & the Liverpool Philharmonic, were astonished by the performances & declared the singing of the chorus beat anything they had played for in Liverpool & Manchester.' It was compared most favourably to the Leeds Festival and from this grew the idea of building a suitable concert room to hold from 1500 to 2,000 people. For the fulfilment of this idea Mary Drew solicited the help of Herbert Gladstone who had been the force behind the building of Hawarden Institute. She suggested that with Buckley coal and oil dividends bringing in so much he could afford to write a fat cheque. He responded by sending £500 towards the building of an Institute.[27] Harry and Mary Drew took the idea a stage further in 1902 when Andrew Carnegie offered to give a Free Library to the Urban District Council by suggesting a site offered by the Hawarden Estate, off Church Road, opposite Lane End Colliery, on which to build both Institute and Library, next to each other. They argued that Buckley was the predominant partner of the two parishes in the Urban District and must always of necessity be so. The 'junior partner' has the two existing Public Buildings (Council Chambers and Bank) within its borders. It would not be reasonable to expect the 'senior partner' to place itself at a distinct disadvantage with regard to a boon it has worked so hard to procure for the district generally. There is justice in the old saying that 'those who pay the piper have a right to call the tune.'[28]

Against this it was stated, 'that as nonconformists were in a majority their interests must prevail & they must have the chief voice in the Free Library's government, therefore the site on the Mold Road must be chosen', adding rather pointedly that, 'it was hoped the Gladstone family would imitate their father's broad mindedness & take no heed of its not being in their parish.'[29]

In June 1904 Harry Drew was appointed Rector of Hawarden in succession to his brother-in-law Stephen Gladstone where he was inducted on 21 December — the Drew family staying on at Buckley Vicarage until they left for Hawarden on 15 January 1905. Here again the rectory and the schools had to be put in order but Mary was happy and wrote to her brother Henry, 'I can hardly tell you how deeply I feel the sacred privilege & honour of going to Hawarden, I trust & pray that H. & I may not disappoint your hopes & confidence as to guarding this inheritance.'

Other preferment was offered to Harry Drew. He accepted a Canonry at St Asaph in 1903 but in the same year declined the benefices of St James's, Plymouth, and St Alban's, Birmingham, as ten years before he refused the vicarage of St Margaret's, Anfield, Liverpool, and five years later, in 1908, the suffragan Bishopric of Ipswich. He remained at Hawarden and died after a short illness at the age of 54 years a few days after Easter on 31 March 1910. He was deeply mourned, no more than at Buckley, where a window and the clerestory decoration were given by the parishioners to his memory. G. W. E. Russell wrote a memorial volume.[30] It contains a description of his Buckley Ministry and tributes contributed by amongst others Thomas Cropper. Mary Drew made regular visits to Buckley, as did Dossie. When Mrs Drew died on New Years Day 1927 on a visit to Hawarden Castle the ringers of St Matthew's rang a quarter peal in her honour on the bells she had proudly and generously donated.

Douglas Raymond Pelly succeeded Harry Drew and was Inducted on 18 February 1905. He was directed to Buckley by both Edward Isaac, Curate in Charge from 1867–71 and the Bishop of Mashonaland in Southern Africa. Pelly had a varied career in Africa. He trained catechists and during the Matabele and Mashona Wars served as chaplain to the Rhodesian Horse. In 1897 he became the first Principal of the Industrial School and native training centre in the diocese. After bouts of fever he returned to England and worked in Worcester diocese. He remained at Buckley until 1912 and introduced a Nursing Association in 1905 and a branch of the Church of England Men's Society in 1906. A company of the Church Lads' Brigade was established and the Mothers' Union branch revived in 1909. Mr and Mrs Pelly gave a stained glass window in 1907 and a window by C. Ford Whitcombe was given in 1909 to the memory of Elizabeth Annie Jacobs headmistress of St Matthew's Girls' School. 1910 witnessed the decorative work on the clerestory and the introduction of the last of the Henry Holiday windows in memory of Canon Drew. Pelly left in 1912.

The Reverend D. R. Pelly, vicar of Buckley (1905-12). [Eric Hayes]

Gilbert Heaton was Instituted on 19 May 1912. One of the first things he did was to introduce vestments in 1913 which were presented by the Vicar and Mrs Heaton, and Mrs Pelly and the Communicants Guild. The Great War devastated the young men of the parish and the names of 32 of the fallen are remembered, including Lieutenant Frederick Birks, VC, MM. During the war the north-east corner of the nave was converted into a side chapel and after the Armistice a memorial calvary was erected by the lych gate and dedicated on Palm Sunday, 1921.

When the peace came the parish received the gift of a wooden hut from Mr Henry Gladstone and his wife, which served the purpose of a church hall and meeting place. They opened it when Colonel and Mrs Parish (Dossie) and their two little boys accompanied them. Gilbert Heaton conducted outdoor services during Lent of 1921 with the choir visiting in turn each of the outlying districts of the parish.

Daniel Saunders Rees followed Gilbert Heaton in 1922. He had as his assistant priest 1926–32 the local boy and war hero Horace Enfield Simmons MC, DFC, who died suddenly at Owston, Yorkshire in November 1935. Saunders Rees went to Hawarden in 1936.

The ministry of William John Rees, his successor from 1936 to 1949, spanned the Second World War. He commenced the practice of a daily eucharist and reserved the Blessed Sacrament and after the war promoted a drama group.

J. T. James came as vicar in 1949 and reopened the Mothers' Union branch the following year. In 1953 he saw the dedication of a window in memory of the fallen of the parish in the two World Wars bequeathed by Esther Dutton. The window is by Harry J. Stammers with the main subject taken from 'Pilgrims Progress' showing Christian walking through the Valley of the Shadow of Death, with the flames of Hell rising from one side, and the bottomless pit on the other.

When St Matthew's School closed in 1963 a window was given by teachers and scholars to commemorate the church schools of the parish. It was designed by

St Matthew's Church Lads' Brigade with the Revd H. E. Simmons c.1930. [Buckley Archive]

with Auntie Queenie?

Dedication of window to commemorate the Church Schools 1967. Clergy L–R: Canon Arthur Roberts; Canon E. Clwyd Jones (vicar); Canon W. J. Rees, (former vicar); Canon T. P. Davies; and the Reverend J. T James (former vicar). [By courtesy of Mrs E. C. Jones]

Sir William Gladstone, Bart., KG, with the builders Wilf and Ken Jones at the laying of the foundation stone for the Church Hall. [By courtesy of Mrs E. C. Jones]

H. P. Thomas and H. Martin at Celtic Studios in 1967 and represents Christian teaching and those involved in teaching at St Matthew's during the 144 years of the life of the school. The window was dedicated soon after the arrival of Ernest Clwyd Jones as vicar. During his time the new vicarage was built on the site of the old school and blessed in 1968. A further benefit to the parish was the opening of a new church hall with the Gladstone family generously contributing. The new ecumenical spirit of the age was demonstrated in 1973 by the inaugural service of the Buckley and District Council of Churches.

Edward Glyn Price, Vicar 1976–91
John Hay, Vicar 1991–96
John Tudor Hughes, Vicar 1996–2004
Alan Michael Tiltman, Vicar 2004

Notes

1. *Chester Chronicle*, 17/9/1817.
2. *Chester Chronicle*, 4/10/1822.
3. *Chester Chronicle*, 18/3/1819.
4. FRO Glynne/Gladstone (hereafter G/G ms) 106.
5. ibid.
6. T. W. Pritchard, *History of the Old Parish of Hawarden* (Wrexham: Bridge Books, 2000), passim.
7. Richard Willett, *A Memoir of Hawarden Parish* (Chester:1822).
8. FRO D/BJ/445, *c*.1835.
9. The site is referred to as 'marlfields' in the deed of consecration.
10. *Chester Courant*, 18/4/1849.
11. FRO G/G/ MS Henry Glynne to Sir Stephen Glynne 4/9/1861.
12. *Chester Chronicle*, 2/12/1893.
13. *Chester Chronicle*, 10/3//1894.

14. FRO G/G/ ms.

15. G. W. E. Russell, *Harry Drew: a memorial sketch* (London:1911), p.69.

16. FRO P/11/1/50.

17. FRO P/11/1/78.

18. ibid.

19. FRO GG, ms 849.

20. *Buckley Parish Magazine,* January 1901.

21. *The Builder,* January 1901.

22. J. Clifford Jones, *Buckley Parish Church,* 1822–1972 (Gee: Denbigh, 1974), pp. 50–1.

23. FRO GG ms 849 Mary Drew to Henry Gladstone, 13/1/04.

24. FRO P/11/1/50.

25. S. Ollard, ed., *A forty year's friendship. Letters from the late Henry Scott Holland to Mrs Drew* (Nisbet: London, 1919).

26. FRO E/LB/11/4 21/11/1902.

27. FRO GG ms 949 21/6/1901, and others not dated.

28. ibid.

29. ibid.

30. Russell, op cit.

Chapter 10
Emmanuel Parish Church, Bistre

In 1825 Charles Butler Clough became vicar of Mold at the age of 32 years. He was young, experienced, well educated and a member of an old Denbighshire gentry family. Born in 1793 he lived through the Napoleonic Wars and witnessed first hand, as curate of Mold since 1816, a tremendous growth in population in this newly industrialised area. The extensive parish of Mold of over 18,000 acres and sixteen townships was experiencing unprecedented upheaval from the demands made for lead, coal, and clay which lay within its borders. The town of Mold was forced to cope with cotton spinning, lead smelting and coal mining. All of these industries were subject to a boom and slump economy. In the hungry years it was difficult to raise the parish rate to provide relief for the poor unemployed. It demanded vigilance to maintain law and order and control the hordes of workers who flooded in from the rural areas of North Wales and Ireland to settle in the vicinity. As an earnest young clergyman he felt a sense of mission and preached the same. 'Ministers should be, above all, sincere, zealous and diligent, not content with the regular public performance of our duty, but from house to house, rebuking, reproving, exhorting, going about like our blessed Saviour doing good, with a view to the universal diffusion of peace and good will.'[1]

A further challenge to the Anglican Church came from the religious revival which had begun in its midst but frustrated with the lack of recognition and support began to act independently. Wesleyan, Calvinistic, and Primitive Methodists, and old Independents built their own conventicles in the new workers' settlements. The Bishop of St Asaph supported the young Vicar of Mold in his mission to build new churches in the outlying areas of his vast parish. In 1834 Bishop Carey established the Diocesan Church Building Society and gave generous financial support. Clough, a member of the Society, set an example by immediately setting about the task of providing churches and schools for newly created parishes with their own resident clergyman in the outlying districts of the mother parish. Christ Church, Pontblyddyn, in the coal-mining area of Leeswood was the first in 1836, followed by Holy Trinity, Gwernaffield, in 1838, for lead miners. Finally in 1842 Clough turned his attention to the coal-mining, pottery and brick making townships of Bistre and Argoed in the north east part of the old parish of Mold.

The church was built in 1841–2 and dedicated to Emmanuel and the district was constituted a parish by an Order in Council, dated 23 May 1844. It received a Parliamentary grant of £200 and £250 from both the Incorporated Church Building Commissioners and the Diocesan Church Building Society. There was a parsonage house with two and a half acres of glebe purchased from a grant made by the Governors of Queen Anne's Bounty who gave a like sum.

The Venerable Charles Butler Clough Vicar of Mold and Archdeacon of St Asaph. Founder of Bistre Church. [FRO PR/C/48]

It was not an easy task for Clough to build churches and establish endowments to support resident clergyman. In 1847 it was reported:

Township of Bistre — The population of this township is 1325, consisting for the most part of potters, brick makers and colliers. It is estimated that there are, within a distance of two miles, 700 children of an age to receive instruction. The means available for education are very inadequate. The local contributions for the support of the Church school do not exceed £5. The surplus expenditure is defrayed at private cost of the vicar of Mold.[2]

The accuracy of this was substantiated by the new Bishop of St Asaph Thomas Vowler Short, who visited the church in the same year, five years after its consecration:

I preached there August 22 1847. In the year 1841 a Church (with schools for 200 boys & girls) was built in this coal & brick district containing 660 sittings 2/3 free (440). Glebe house small built 1843, a garden bought and a field. The population is abt. 2,200. Extremely poor with scarcely a resident landlord among them. The Church is better attended than could have been expected, the district having 8 sectarian Chapels, & two other denominations meeting in rooms with it. To the endowment the Vicar of Mold gave up, the Tithe rent charge the value of which is £32, a field £4, fees etc £10.[3]

Clough's choice for architect was John Lloyd from Mold who was commissioned by him to build Christ Church, Pontblyddyn (1836), St Mark's, Connah's Quay (1837), Holy Trinity, Gwernaffield (1838), Emmanuel, Bistre 1841–2 and Christ Church, Llanfynydd 1842–3. Four out of the five eventually required reconstruction. Good Hart Rendel noted, after the church had been improved that: 'This church is said to be 'on the model of Casterton church in Westmoreland'. It seems odd that anyone having seen anything like it should want another.' Archdeacon Thomas noted in 1874 'that it lies north and south instead of east and west. It consists of a broad nave with a small sacrarium, and has at the north end a gallery (which forms by the space beneath it an ante-chapel), and externally a battlemented tower, the base of which forms the entrance. The roof is open and of very wide span; the windows lancets; some of the seats in the gallery and those in the middle of the church are open benches and free, the sides being occupied by pews, the rents of which were originally intended to improve the stipend.'

The church was consecrated on 25 October 1842. The *Chester Chronicle* gave a long account:

The commodious new building was consecrated for divine worship by the Lord Bishop of St Asaph. The day proved unfavourable owing to the heavy rain, which continued incessantly throughout the day and prevented most of the surrounding gentry from attending. However most of the neighbouring clergy braved the elements to observe the solemn consecration of the church and burial ground. In the evening at 6.30 p.m. prayers were read by the Rev. Edward Jones, the newly appointed minister of the place, and an excellent sermon was preached by the Rev. C. B. Clough Vicar of Mold from Matthew 11 v.5 'And the poor have the gospel preached to them.' The expense of building the church and schools may be estimated at the sum of £1,700, most part of which sum is from voluntary contributions. We have also been informed that his Lordship, finding the great benefit that is likely to result from Church building, and owing to the low state of funds belonging to the diocese of St Asaph Church Building Society has intimated to the Treasurer, the Rev. C. B. Clough of his intention to give £500 to the Society in addition to his £100 per annum subscription.

Emmanuel Church Bistre. [Buckley Society Archive]

Emmanuel Church Bistre.
[Buckley Society Archive]

The first vicar was Edward Jones M.A., Jesus College, Oxford, formerly a schoolmaster. He was ordained in 1840. He served the parish faithfully for thirty-three years until his death in 1876. A clock in the tower and a brass mural tablet in church were given to his memory. The Religious Census of 1851 revealed that the Calvinistic Methodists were the strongest denomination in Bistre followed by the Wesleyan Methodists with the Anglicans in third place. Their average attendance on a Sunday morning was seventy plus sixty scholars and a hundred plus forty five in the evening. Although attendance was sometimes affected 'in consequence of the bad road in this mountain district & the distances that many of the scholars have to come.'[4]

Edward Jones was succeeded as vicar by John Michael Evans, (1876–89). During his incumbency the church was restored and a new vicarage built. A letter in the *Chester Chronicle* in 1873 advised the provision of a new parsonage house. The writer, C. B. Clough, stated that he had been a magistrate at the time of the Mold Riots in 1869 when he saw 'Mold Station covered with the blood of Soldiers and the Police'. He warned the readers that 'There is a large population gathering round the new works and railways and to keep this increasing district in order it is necessary and important to have clergy residing in this spot. There is a piece of land which if not purchased for a vicarage will probably have the effect of driving Mr Jones' successor away from the neighbourhood. I trust the funds will be made available to assist this purchase.'[5] The architect for the new vicarage in 1883 was C. A. Ewing of Chester. It was enlarged in 1908 'making sanitary improvements and building stables'. A new vicarage was built in 1984. A newspaper report gives an account of the improvements, which were made to the church building in 1881:

This church was re-opened, after restoration, on Tuesday September 20, through the indefatigable exertions of the Vicar, the Rev. J. M. Edwards. The church, which was erected some fifty years ago, has been restored and although the main structure was sound and good the interior arrangements were most deplorable. There were some ten boxes (pews) on each side of the church. The rest of the floor was covered with dirty-coloured fire bricks and some loose forms, which were generally arranged in two squares round two stoves with iron pipes running straight up through the roof which is an ordinary Queen post, and the beam roof, open to the ridge and boarded. The timber of which the roof was formed had not even the rough slabs taken off. The restoration consists in cleaning, painting, and decorating the roof timbers: the introduction of a new stone arch into the sacrarium, the walls of which have been raised, the east window being also bodily raised, so that instead of being level with the table it is now some three feet above it, and filled with a stained glass memorial window by Ballantyne, the gift of the Pemberton family of Plas Issa. The subject is our Lord's Agony in the Garden. The last bay at the east end of the church is raised two steps, and

Bistre Vicarage built 1883.[Buckley Library]

The interior post 1881.
[Buckley Society Archive]

divided from the rest of the church by an open screen, behind which, in the centre are the choir stalls and reading desks, the organ chamber on the north and the vestry on the south. The seats are open and arranged in two blocks, accommodating 320 persons. The heating is by two of Porritt's apparatuses below the ground. The aisles, chancel and sacrarium are laid with tiles from Mr J. C. Edward's Penybont works Ruabon. The pulpit is of stone, and with the other furniture was supplied by Messrs Jones and Willis of Birmingham. The work, which has cost about £700, was carried out by Mr John Williams, builder of Buckley from the plans and under the direction of Mr W.H.Spaull of Oswestry.[6]

In 1926 the exterior of the church was thoroughly restored and the interior cleaned and decorated. A lych gate, the gift of the Edwards family Holly Bank, was dedicated in September 1922 and a new vestry in April 1935. A new burial ground situated between the vicarage and Nant Mawr was provided in 1890 and an adjoining field for its extension purchased in 1927.

Over the years a number of stained glass windows were introduced into the church:

1881 east window, three lights, by James Ballantine, Edinburgh, representing the Agony in Gethsemane to Edward and Mary Pemberton, Plas Isa.
Nave south, 1889, one light, by Baillie and Lutwyche. London, representing the Good Shepherd, to Vicar John Michael Evans. Erected by public subscription.
Nave north, 1912, one light, by Jones & Willis, London, Birmingham and Liverpool, subject Christ the Light of the World, to Edward Jones.
Nave north, 1923, one light, by James Powell & Sons, London, subject Nunc dimittis, to J. & M. Edwards.
Nave north, 1930, one light, by Alfred Ernest Child, Dublin, subject the Angel of Peace, to John (d.1927) and Mary Jones (d.1917).
Nave south, 1950, one light, by Trena Mary Cox, Chester, Nativity scenes, to E. H. Jones
Nave south, 1957, one light, by Trena Mary Cox, Chester, Childhood Scenes, to J. H. Hughes.
Nave north, 1953, one light, by Shrigley & Hunt, Lancaster, the standing figure of Christ with choir boys below, to Canon A. W. Rees.
Two windows, nave north, 1966, one light, by Shrigley & Hunt, Lancaster, designed by Mr.J.Fisher, formerly of Hough Green, Chester. One inscribed 'The gift of H.S.Collins, in memory of his wife Caroline, and his sister Hilda, 1965.' Subject, 'suffer the little children to come unto me.' The second inscribed 'In memory of Florence Catherall. The gift of her husband and children, 1966.' Subject, 'the Resurrection.'[7]

In 1932 a set of three painted and gilded panels with scenes of the Annunciation, Nativity and Visitation, a triptych, forming

Peter Jones the Parish Clerk and Sexton of Bistre with his family. [Buckley Library]

*The Reverend Canon A. W. Rees, vicar
of Bistre (1924–53).*
[Buckley Society Archive]

an altarpiece, were given by the Rev. O. E. Gittins in memory of his parents who lived at the Mount. They are carved in golden pine and were executed by the Art and Book Company. The newspaper described them:

The centre panel representing the Nativity, is reminiscent of Fra Angelico's painting of this scene, the thatched roof and the natural positions of the ox and ass being characteristic of his picture. On the left there is the Annunciation, which once again brings Fra Angelico's work to mind, the arched background, with the Holy Ghost in attendance, together with the rainbow hued wings of the angel being features of the famous fifteenth century artist. The third panel is of the Visitation, and the graceful positions of the figures closely resemble Andrea Della Robbia's work of this subject.[8]

To mark the centenary celebrations in 1942 a processional cross in silver was given by the Sunday School, silver communion vessels by the parishioners and two altar books one by Mrs J.Dawson, Spon Farm and the other anonymously.

Mission Church, All Saint's, Lane End

The first church at Lane End was built in 1881 and opened in June of that year. It was moved shortly afterwards in 1884 when the *Chronicle* remarked in July, 'That it had become necessary to enlarge the building in so short a time after its first erection proves that the mission work has not been in vain.' In February 1892 it was decided to build a new church at Lane End, 'the Vicar, The Reverend H. T. Hughes, taking the responsibility of building a small church at Mynydd Isa. The Vicar said that he had been very fortunate in obtaining a grant of £50 from the Curates' Aid Society towards the stipend for a second curate for the Parish.' Mrs Catherine Gladstone supported these efforts in a letter published in the Bistre *Parish Magazine* in June 1892. She wrote, 'We are greatly interested in the case of that very poor but interesting place Bistre (so near Hawarden), and can safely recommend it to the support of friends. Two Mission Rooms are, in fact, called for urgently and needed for the working class. Will you help our friends at Bistre, a mining district, however small a donation? A real work is doing, but Mission Rooms are called loudly for. Catherine Gladstone.'

The foundation stone for Lane End was laid with great ceremony in September 1892.

At 3 o'clock a procession was formed at Bistre Church consisting of the Flintshire Volunteers Brass Band and the Buckley Town Brass Band, the choir and clergy plus Church friends. They marched along the main street singing

'Onward Christian Soldiers'. Lady Cunliffe, wife of the Conservative candidate for the Flintshire Constituency laid the foundation stone. The Contractors were Messrs Davies and Beavan and the building was in Ruabon red brick.

The foundation stone for St Cecilia's, Mynydd Isa, was laid on 22 October, 1892 by Mrs Henry Raikes. Both Churches were built with some alacrity and they were opened before

The Mission Church of All Saints, Lane End.
[Buckley Society Archive]

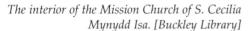

The Mission Church of S. Cecilia Mynydd Isa.
[Buckley Library]

The interior of the Mission Church of S. Cecilia
Mynydd Isa. [Buckley Library]

the end of the year on the same day, 20 December.

At Lane End on All Saints' day 1935, an oak screen, made by Mr Robert Davies and his sons, in memory of the late Mrs Eleanor Davies (d.1933) was dedicated by the Vicar. In July 1936 a panelled oak reredos was dedicated by the Vicar. This too was made by Robert Davies and sons and was erected by the family of Miss Fanny Elizabeth Hughes (d.1932), Liverpool House. It was said of her that 'she was kind and generous to the poor and did much to alleviate their suffering and poverty. She did much for the church and started the Boy Scout movement in the parish.' Improvements were made to All Saints' in 1939 when Robert Davies and sons built a new vestry. In 1945 a new organ supplied by Rushworth and Draper was installed.

A source of information for details of Sunday worship and parochial organizations is the Bistre *Parish Magazine*.[9] Entries begin in 1876 and show how influential the local church was in providing elementary education and the means of improving the lives of the poor. The Sunday school library in 1876 had grown to 150 volumes. Religious and devotional instruction was given by the means of Cottage Lectures during the winter months. The talent that many possessed for music and drama found an outlet in frequent amateur concerts and pantomimes performed in the local schools and churches. Choral singing and brass bands were a means of bringing together people of different religious traditions. A Church Lads' Brigade was set up with the support of Major Gibson in 1892 with a further intention of forming a gymnastic club. Boy Scouts and a branch of the Girls' Friendly Society over the years gave further encouragement to young people. A recreation ground and bowling green met the needs of all age groups together with a tennis club. The church choir ran its own cricket club in the 1900s. A church guild was active in the 1930s and 1940s promoting monthly socials and running its own drama section. Tea was served to children on the vicarage lawn on Jubilee day followed by games in the vicarage field whilst adults resorted to the schoolroom for tea and afterwards dancing on the lawn.

Vicars of Bistre
The Rev. Edward Jones, M.A. Priest in charge 1842–44. Vicar, 1844–76.
The Rev. John Michael Evans, B.A., 1876–89.
The Rev. Hugh Trevor Hughes, M.A., 1889–97.
The Rev. John George, B.A., 1897–1904.
The Rev. Owen David Williams, M.A., 1904–07.
The Rev. Lewis Hugh Oswald Price, M.A., 1907–10.

The Rev. John Edward Morgan, B.A., 1910–24.
The Rev. A. W. Rees, M.A., 1924–53.
The Rev. John Roberts, B.A., 1954–66.
The Rev. Ogwen Lloyd Williams, B.A., 1966–80.
The Rev. Gwynn Rees Jones, B.A., 1980–89.
The Rev. Jason Robert Kennett-Orpwood, Dip. Theol., 1989–2000.
The Rev. Martyn William Hill, B.Sc., Ph.D., 2000–05.
The Rev. Martin John Batchelor, B.Sc. 2006.

Notes

1. M. V. J. Seaborne, 'Charles Butler Clough, 1793–1859. Church Building in Victorian Wales', *National Library of Wales Journal*, vol. 29, 1998, Pt. Summer p. 283.

2. *Reports of The Commissioners of Inquiry into the State of Education in Wales*, Pt III, North Wales, 1847, p. 103.

3. National Library of Wales, SA/MB/26.

4. Religious Census, 1851.

5. FRO D/DM/434/191, quoted by Charles Duckworth.

6. In Archdeacon D. R. Thomas, Manuscript Books, NLW SA/DR/51 re-opening of Bistre Parish Church 1881.

7. M. V. J. Seaborne, *Victorian and Later Stained Glass in Flintshire Churches*, 1996, and correspondence with the author.

8. FRO Bistre *Parish Magazine*, P/5/1/49, Sept. 1932.

9. ibid.

Chapter 11
The Roman Catholic Church of Our Lady of the Rosary, Buckley[1]

The permanent presence of the Roman Catholics in Buckley became a reality when the Bishop of Shrewsbury dedicated a Church to Our Lady of the Rosary on 6 April 1893. They had gained a foothold in a community which was not always welcoming. Their little flock was gathered together and had found shelter after much support from the religious orders which had established themselves in North Wales in the second half of the nineteenth century. The old Catholic families in the parish of Mold, the Roberts of Plas Ucha and Giffards of Nerquis Hall had kept the faith alive until the Catholic Hierarchy were forced to take action by the growth in population and influx of the Irish into the new industrialised areas. The Catholic population of Mold numbered 100 in 1847, the Religious Census of 1851 recorded the presence of 133+41 scholars at the Sunday morning Mass, a figure which rose to 300 in 1853. In 1840 Pope Gregory divided England into eight vicariates of which Wales and Hereford were one. In 1850 the six northern counties of Wales became part of the diocese of Shrewsbury under the jurisdiction of Bishop J. T. Brown. Because of the shortage of British born priests the Bishop used the Italian Capuchin Franciscan fathers newly arrived at Pantasaph in the 1850s. Later the Fathers from St Francis Friary, Chester, replaced them. In 1871 No. 4 Ffordd Ffain, Mold was designated as a Chapel and the foundation stone of St David's School was laid.

It was to the French Jesuit seminarians that Buckley Catholics looked for the foundation of their church. Seeking refuge from anti-clerical persecution, the Jesuit Fathers with their student priests, had arrived from Lyons in France in 1881. They found ample and suitable accommodation in the recently-closed new gaol in Bryn Coch, which housed staff and students, numbering 86 on their arrival. Their potential for pastoral and missionary activity was recognised by Bishop Knight of Shrewsbury, who welcomed them into his diocese and encouraged them to care for his little flock in nearby Buckley. We hear of some of them at this time; for example, in 1882, 'Annie Brennan of Buckley, one of a family of at least seven children began work at St David's school as a monitoress. She stayed at the school for only five months. We next hear of her marriage to William Williams, also of Buckley, when she was twenty-two. Fr. Lynch officiated, and the young couple set up home in Victoria Terrace, Buckley. On their marriage they joined a wide group of relations in Mold and Buckley, to which they eventually added at least five children of their own, many more of whose descendants are still members of St David's parish to-day.'[2] Another was

St David's College Mold. [Mold in Old Photographs, *p.34]*

Mr Jaconelli, 'Pippin', an Italian, mentioned in the diary of George Lewis as living in Coppa View, also known as Lodging House Lane. He allowed vagrants to sleep there. Another colourful character was called 'La Douche'. He had a band organ with a monkey and was distinguished by his old khaki overcoat, which was too big for him.

The Jesuits left an interesting account of their activities, which covers the formative period of twenty-seven years. This was added to by Father Pochard.

This little mission was established in 1881, when two fathers from St David's College, Mold, assembled the Catholics of Buckley, on Sundays to the number of 80 persons, in an old mill in order that they might be able to receive some instructions. This place is now known as Mill House in Mill Lane. It was closed in 1884 when the greater part of the people, owing to want of work went away. It was reopened January 1888, at which date & up to 1893, there were about 90 Catholics. Out of these 39 were assembled on Sundays in a poor and dilapidated room again for instructions. This room was one of the bedrooms in the lodging house on Daisy Hill. Services were held too sometime in the Drill Hall by kind permission of Major Gibson, in spite of Protestant opposition.

During these periods from 1881 to 1884 and from 1888 to 1893 Mass was celebrated 3 or 4 times in the year. During the year 1892, Mass was celebrated regularly every month. In 1893 the new Church of Our Lady was opened. Up to that time, with the leave of the Rector of St David's Church, Mold, various priests from St David's College had occasionally said Mass and heard confession at Buckley and had also several times, attended for Baptism or Extreme Unction. Two students also belonging to the College at Mold, not yet priests, would see the people at their home and assemble them on Sundays for instruction and catechism.

Now follows a short summary of the work done by the French Jesuits of Mold belonging to two French Priories, first Paris and then, later, Lyons Province. The names which remained in the memory of the Catholics of Buckley, are Rev. Father Chauvin, who later was stationed at St Leonard's-on-Sea. The Rev. Father Lucas who, with two other fathers, gave lectures on the Catholic faith in the Central Hall, but the people of Buckley did not give them a fair chance. Another priest still remembered by the congregation is Father Louis Hinault who worked with great energy to keep and increase the faith of the congregation.

For sometime when the Jesuits had left Mold Mass was said by the Rector of St David's or his assistants amongst whom we can name Father Nightingale, to-day Rector of St Mary's Wrexham and Vicar General of Minevia Diocese.

The College of St David's, Bryn Coch, Mold, was sold to the Sisters of Our Lady of Refuge, Caen, France, for a new intended foundation and their Chaplain went every Sunday to say Mass in the Church at Buckley. Father Rooney and Father Pierre (since gone to New Orleans) were the last two to serve at Buckley before I came to Mold.

In January 1908 Rev. Father Pochard chaplain of the Sisters of Our Lady of Refuge at Troy House Monmouth was sent to the Sisters in Mold. By a mistake of the Superiors Rev. Father Boissel had been sent from France at the same time for the same post. As he was already an old man, it was agreed that, pending a settlement by the authorities, Father Pochard should take charge of Buckley on Sundays. By arrangement with Wm. H. Hughes, cab proprietor, a closed carriage came every Sunday from St David's to Our Lady of the Rosary in the morning and took him back in the evening after Benediction. Mr & Mrs McEvoy acted as sacristan and his wife did all the washing of Church linen, for which work they received only a nominal salary. They also gave breakfast to all who fasted before Mass and travelled a long distance to receive Holy Communion. Mr & Mrs Williams, General Merchant, Main Road, received the priest for luncheon and he stayed there till, Benediction. In my diary I find that the average attendance for the first Sundays was 20 to 25. The collection for the whole Sunday was eight shillings of which five shillings went to pay the cab and two shillings to the organist. The organist Mr W. Roberts had been in charge of the organ for many years already before I came to Buckley for the first time, and it is now about 20 years since he started his work in the Church of Our Lady of the Rosary. His devotion to our little Church far from decreasing has tied

Father Pochard. [Parish Archive]

him to us by solid bonds of affection. Proud of his small choir and absolutely disinterested on the question of his fees, he has done a great deal for our mission and deserves the gratitude of the congregation. Apart from Holy Mass and Confessions, the first Sacrament administered by Father Pochard was the Extreme Unction and Viaticum to Mr J. Croxford, Red House, Hawarden. Mr Croxford recovered and enjoys good health at the present time.

On Monday 30 March, a letter from his Lordship Bishop Francis Mostyn of Menevia appointed Father J. J. Pochard as a resident priest at Our Lady of the Rosary, Buckley. The new mission is founded.[3]

Mr William Roberts, the church organist mentioned in the above account, was a versatile musician. A report in the local newspaper in 1906 describes him thus, 'a young musical composer, the cornetist of the Royal Buckley Town Band, has just completed a new Benediction Service of his own composition for the choir at Buckley of which he is the Director. This young composer has made a reputation as an excellent accompanist.'[4] He was still playing at the end of 1932.

The controversy referred to in the account given above concerning the lectures given by Father Lucas occurred in the years 1896 and 1897. It began with a reply given by Father Lucas of the Jesuit College of St Beuno at Tremeirchion to an extreme Protestant pamphlet, *The Claims of Rome*, published by Mr Samuel Smith, Member of Parliament for Flintshire. Father Lucas expressed his views publicly at a meeting held in the Central Hall Buckley in December 1896. This gesture aroused the antagonism of some of the local nonconformist ministers, the Rev. Jonathan Edwards, Congregationalist, and the Rev. J. Idloes Edwards, Presbyterian, who retaliated by arranging a series of meetings in February with the Rev. Alexander Rogers of the Protestant Alliance as the main speaker. Two lectures were organised, one for children and one for adults. For the first of these the Central Hall was unable to hold the eight hundred people who clamoured to get in to share in the controversy, banter and excitement aroused by the prospect of revelations about the papists. Father Lucas attended accompanied by other Jesuit priests, the meeting was very lively and it was reported that, 'The lectures were illustrated by one of the finest magic lanterns in existence.'[5]

At the end of April Father Lucas again hired the Central Hall to give two addresses in reply,'on certain points of Roman Catholic Faith and Justice, in the hope of modifying to some extent the impression produced in February by the Rev.Alexander Rogers.' Again there was much enthusiasm and it was reported that the crowded audience opened the proceedings by singing with extraordinary zest the hymn 'Crown Him Lord of all'![6]

The Bishop had been warned of opposition in 1893 by one of the students at the Jesuit College, Mold, in answer to a questionnaire he circulated asking for comments on the state of Catholicism in North Wales and its future prospect. The student made several important points. He observed that, 'the loss of faith for Catholics (Irish) coming to Wales seems to be chiefly, even perhaps exclusively attributed to the want of priests and schools,' and 'However useful, or even necessary the use of the Welsh language may be for the Conversion of Wales, I do not think it is so necessary that this work could not be begun by English speaking priests or missionaries.' As for Buckley, 'we have no Welsh-speaking Catholics, but we have sometimes to deal with the Welsh people. The Welsh members of the Church seem, in general, to be better disposed towards the Catholics than the English Churchman. This sympathy is not perhaps altogether disinterested, but they feel necessary to make common cause with the Catholics against the Dissenters. Thus Welsh Churchmen would willingly attend Catholic services in a Catholic Church; but Dissenters, and especially Welsh Calvinistic Methodists, would not. At Buckley, many Churchmen asked for tickets for the opening of our little Church; but I do not think any Dissenters did. This, however, may be peculiar to Buckley, where a great antagonism reigns between Dissenters and Churchmen.'[7]

It was members from outside Buckley who provided the initiative for the building of the Church. Mr James Banks, chairman of the building committee was a native of Liverpool, the Secretary, Mr H. Parsons, hailed from Warwick and Mr Michael Kelly came from Ireland. In 1892 they received the blessing of the Bishop of Shrewsbury, Edmund Knight, to go ahead with their fund raising for the building. He wrote to them in December 1892 commending 'The efforts made by yourself and your fellow workers to provide for the spiritual needs of our little outlying flock of Buckley are worthy of all praise. Those who hold as I do that a working congregation like yours with limited means and numbers, which has done so much in the first instance for itself, has earned thereby a right to ask the help of others, will not I hope refuse the assistance you need to complete your good work.'[8]

The main subscribers were: £10 each — the Bishop of Shrewsbury, J. M. Villefraches, Mr & Mrs J. Banks, Mr & Mrs W. Williams; £5 each — The Duke of Norfolk, the Duke of Westminster, the Marquis of Bute and J. Parry, Esq. Major J.M. Gibson gave £1. Somehow £300 was raised and a piece of land on Daisy Hill formerly the site of Hancock's Pottery was bought and in February 1894, a piece of land adjacent of twenty yards in length was purchased for £140 on which to build a presbytery.

The opening of the first (1893–2000) Church of Our Lady of the Rosary on 8 April was reported in the press:

A new Catholic Chapel was opened at Daisy Hill, Buckley, on Thursday. Formerly the Roman Catholics of the district, who number about fifty or sixty, were accustomed to worship in a room at Daisy Hill, but this was found extremely inconvenient, and, for a long period, a desire had existed in the minds of those who attended it to have a better place of worship provided. With this object in view a working committee was formed eight or nine months ago, and, through their zealous efforts, a good sum was raised in response to an appeal for subscriptions, whilst a proportion came from the proceeds of a drawing (raffle). A site at Daisy Hill was acquired, and a chapel capable of seating about 180 people was erected. The building, which is a brick one, presents rather a plain appearance as regards the exterior, but the inside is nicely and comfortably fitted up.

The opening services were initiated by a solemn High Mass at eleven o'clock, at which the Rev. Francis Lynch, rector, Mold, officiated, there being also present the Lord Bishop of Shrewsbury, Dr Knight, and others. The Bishop at the close delivered a most appropriate address, and referred to the erection of the chapel, thanking all the subscribers, Protestants and Catholics alike. There was a large congregation. At four o'clock the Bishop gave the solemn benediction of the Blessed Sacrament, and a sermon was preached by Canon Henry Hopkins. The musical part of the services, including a special mass by Gounod was ably executed by the choir of St David's College, Mold. Subscriptions are still asked for on defraying the existing debt.[9]

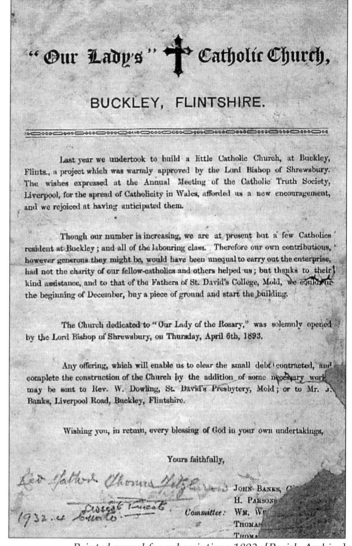

Printed appeal for subscriptions 1893. [Parish Archive]

The interior of the church was at first big enough to accommodate only fifty or sixty parishioners. More space was provided when Father Pochard moved the altar against the wall of the sanctuary which was framed by a plasterwork arch and which had on either side niches containing the statues of the Sacred Heart of Jesus and Our Lady of Lourdes. The walls of the sanctuary were decorated with a repeat pattern of *fleur de lys*. At either side of the altar were two doors with curtains which led to the sacristy and confessional. The original altar was more decorative, made of marble with four pillars at the front. On the altar was an ornate tabernacle with a painting above of the Madonna and Holy Child. In front of the altar were rails and a raised floor in the sanctuary, which was tiled and carpeted. The main floor area was made of wooden blocks.

Renovation work on the church was contemplated in 1927 and a fund-raising ball was held in the Albert

Above:The interior of the church in the 1920s. [Parish Archive]

Left; The church of Our Lady of the Rosary opened in 1893.
[Buckley Society Archive]

Right: Ceramic plaque of Virginand Child in the
style of brothers Della Robbia. [Parish Archive]

Hall 'in aid of the renovation fund and was well patronised by a large company which included distinguished visitors from London and Paris, and several local gentry. Mr Hitchcock was MC and splendid music was supplied by the augmented Buckley String Band under the direction of Mr Will Roberts. The clergymen present included Father Pochard, Buckley and Father Kelly, Connah's Quay.'[10]

The church was heated by gas and electric light was installed in 1932. Further improvements were carried out the following year to mark the Holy Year decreed by the Pope when an entrance porch was added, a confessional box installed and a new tabernacle purchased. Above the front doors was placed a ceramic plaque to provide an object of devotion for the faithful. It depicts the Virgin Mary, kneeling, and the infant Jesus, and is bordered by flowers, cherubs, a wreath and cornucopia in the style of the brothers Della Robbia and was probably made in Italy in the 1890s. At the altar end of the church the statue of Our Lady Immaculate was replaced in 1943 by one of Our Lady of Lourdes and in the 1950s the statue of the Sacred Heart of Jesus was replaced by another and a new tabernacle purchased in 1957. A new set of Stations of the Cross, hand-carved in Italy, were blessed by Bishop Petit in 1962. Three years later a new altar was dedicated to the memory of four altar boys killed in the Second World War. A new entrance door was fitted in 1981. In December 1991 a new celebrant's chair with matching stools and a credence table were dedicated to the memory of Canon Fitzharris. Voluntary labour was used when the block flooring was re-laid in 1953 and for the major extension two years later which gave the church interior an extra ten feet in length. The original sacristy became the sanctuary and a new sacristy was built. Some of the original benches were still in use in 1999.

The pattern of the social and pastoral life of the parish over the last hundred years may be seen through the notice book, October 1931 to May 1989, used by the officiating priest at Mass. Other sources witness to a faithful congregation worshipping regularly on a Sunday with a daily Mass, and weekday evening service. The instruction of children in the catechism, a concern that they receive a good Catholic primary and secondary education and participate in the life and worship of the parish as altar boys and members of the choir, is evident. Opportunity for Catholic families to meet at dances, whist drives, outings, pilgrimages and processions is chronicled. There are the usual Catholic organisations. With the growth in the population of Buckley the numbers of Catholics increased and the need for extended church buildings became apparent. It was not until after the Second Vatican Council, which met in Rome between 1962-5, that radical changes were seen in church life in Buckley and these were slowly implemented over a period of twenty years and had an impact on all Christians in the area. There were major reforms in the liturgy. The language used was the vernacular, there were alternative choices in the eucharistic prayers, and baptism, marriage and burial liturgies were revised. The emphasis was on lay participation in liturgical worship and pastoral work with women sharing equally in the lay ministries. The faithful were described as 'the people of God'. Vatican Two declared a positive role for the Catholic Church in the development of relations with other Christian bodies with emphasis placed on them working together in the community enjoying a fruitful dialogue and establishing bonds of friendship.

There are the usual Catholic organisations: the Union of Catholic Mothers, the Knights of St Columba, and a CAFOD Group. From time to time there were youth groups. Annual events in the past life of the parish included a parish ball in January, a St Patrick's Day dinner dance in March, a Corpus Christi Procession at the convent in Hawarden usually in May.

The notice book has many items of a particularly Catholic flavour.

> 1933 'Money for confessional stolen. In process of being built. Confessional completed more donations needed to pay off the debt of £12.' 'Corpus Christi-Procession at Hawarden Convent. Children should wear white and be modestly dressed. Silk rosettes will be available for one penny,'
> 1938 'Second Sunday after Pentecost – Confraternity of men – special intention for Employment.'
> 1963 'Fourteen babies available for adoption anyone interested?'
> 1967 Letter from Irish Embassy, London.'Don't go home.'
> 1968 'Outdoor Mass celebrating 75 years. Choir from Liverpool to lead singing.' 'Crowning of Our Lady's Statue by one of the children. Response to a suggestion by parishioners last year. Please come along with the children. One of the Broughton children will crown the Statue.'
> 1972 'Reminder about Irish coins in the collection, sweets in church, late coming and saying Amen before Communion.' 'Knights of St Columba Buckley Catholic families took in Belfast Catholic and Protestant children.'
> 1978 'Ray Shaw asks for Green Shield Stamps to send people to Lourdes.'

As a result of the Second Vatican Council new ministries were established under the leadership of Father Fitzharris in the late 1960s and 1970s. Women became readers from 1970 and 'extraordinary ministers' from 1973 to assist at Mass and take the Sacrament to the sick. The laity gave instruction to children who did not attend Catholic schools.

A week after the Church was opened in April 1893 the secretary, Mr H. Parsons, wrote to the Bishop of Shrewsbury to thank him for his support for the Buckley Catholics and stated, 'There remains something for us to do & that is to provide a Catholic School at Buckley for our children, this work is almost as necessary as the other.'[11] This intention was never realised, probably because of the proximity of Catholic schools in Mold, Saltney, Shotton, and Flint, and the poverty of the working class parish of Buckley. Hope of the building of a school in Buckley was never abandoned and as late as 1969 a piece of land near Lyme Grove was bought as the site of a new primary school but falling numbers in St David's School, Mold, influenced the decision not to proceed.

It was a hardship for children to attend Roman Catholic day schools out of the parish. In the early days children walked to Mold after attending the eight o'clock Mass, but their parents were reminded in 1932 'that children who attend non-Catholic schools must not attend scripture or religious education lessons.' And the following year were 'encouraged to send their children to Catholic schools … grants for fares were available thro' the Catholic Educational Council.' In the 1950s travelling expenses could be claimed from the Flintshire Education Authorities as a refund at the end of term. In the 1960s fund raising events were held to meet the cost of providing special buses to Catholic schools. In large families bus fare could cause great hardship.

The 1944 Education Act threatened the existence of Catholic schools because of the cost of bringing them up to the required standard. Bishop Petit regarded the provision of secondary education as a priority and persuaded the government minister, George Tomlinson, to sanction the building of the Blessed Richard Gwyn Secondary School at Flint. The school officially opened in October 1954. There was a long and acrimonious dispute between the Bishop and Dr Hadyn Williams, Director of Education for Flintshire, often conducted openly in the local press, about the attendance of children from Buckley at Roman Catholic schools in Flint and Shotton. When a new county primary school,

Father Fitzharris with the altar boys, 1952. [Parish Archive]

Southdown, was opened to replace the one at Bistre, the Catholics failed to buy the old school which they planned to reopen for their own use.

The bitterness and religious divisions expressed at the Central Hall in the late 1890s when members of the Protestant Alliance publicly attacked Catholic teaching was expunged in 1970 when the parishioners of Our Lady of the Rosary walked together with members of all religious denominations in the Buckley Jubilee procession. The desire expressed at the Vatican Council for understanding, friendship, dialogue, and a recognition of other Christian churches was being seen in the most traditional way in Buckley. In 1968 Father Fitzharris urged his parishioners to take part in the interdenominational service held at St Matthew's during the week in January to mark Christian unity. It was a complete reversal of policy for until then Catholics had been forcibly forbidden to join other Christians in worship. In 1933 the priest Dr Crowley announced his prohibition on two occasions. He reminded parishioners 'not to attend services by non-Catholic ministers re British Legion meetings. This would involve breaking of the first commandment,' observing that 'a united service is to be held in this town.' He pronounced that 'Catholics were not to attend under any circumstances. You can do no better than to attend the evening services and obtain the blessing of our Eucharistic Lord in your own Church.' The children were discouraged by being told in 1934 that for Jubilee day 'we have been especially asked by the parish priest at Mold to point out that it will not be fair to Mold School if children from Buckley take the day off school on Tuesday, Catholic children get more holidays than Protestant children as they get Holy days of Obligation and a certain number of attendances have to be made.' As late as 1952, Father Schwarz put it bluntly when he said 'the procession is regarded by the people as a symbol of Christian unity and consequently Catholics may not have anything to do with it.'

On Jubilee Tuesday afternoon in July 1970, members young and old made their debut in style. Some hundred Catholic children dressed either in Biblical costume or their Sunday best marched in the procession when it was reported that, 'A small milestone nestles near the base of

Civic Sunday 6 July 1958. L–R: Rev. Thomas Fitzharris, Rt. Rev. J. Petit, Bishop of Menevia, Councillor R. B. Faulkener, Rev. J. Hannigan, (later Bishop of Wrexham), Rev. Cyril Schwarz. [Parish Archive]

Our Lady of the Rosary Catholic Church. Its significance was never more symbolic than the moment that Buckley's 114th Jubilee passed by and another milestone in Christian unity was reached with the inclusion of every place of worship in Buckley.'[12] The following year the Roman Catholics were invited to head the procession. In 1984 Father Fitzharris advised his flock, 'This year the Jubilee will be televised. The T.V. people hope to concentrate on the Catholic Church. Please children wear white and the boys wear sashes.'

During the Second World War a considerable number of evacuees, 650 from Birkenhead in 1939 and 229 from London in 1944, came to Buckley. Many of these were Catholics and found a welcome from the local Church and schools in the area. A few evacuees preferred to remain, as did some prisoners of war ,many of whom were Roman Catholics — a phenomenon which was experienced throughout the Roman Catholic diocese of Menevia with a predominance of Polish and Italian men who married local girls. There was a significant increase in the Catholic population of Buckley in the second half of the twentieth century when it grew from 500 in 1965 to 1,000 in 1995. The concentration of industry in the area always attracted immigrant labour. In the nineteenth century Irish labourers found work in the collieries. A nearby district at Northop Hall was known as 'little Dublin'. The clay industry absorbed many others and at the end of the Second World War there was a fear that local men would be denied employment because of the large number of Italians at the brick works. Italian prisoners of war had been brought to work in the clay industry and in 1951 as a response to an advertisement in the Sicilian press, some Italian families settled in the area and met together at the Catholic churches in Buckley and Mold and the Garibaldi Club.

Improved facilities for parish meetings and social events were badly needed for an increased congregation. The use of the Presbytery or a hired hall for such purposes was no longer feasible and the parishioners sought to provide one themselves. It was 'a do it yourself effort'. They bought from Kinmel Camp an ex-army medical centre housed in a wooden hut built on brick foundations with a brick entrance hall at a cost of £600. Canon Fitzharris lent the money to the hall committee who undertook the responsibility for dismantling the hut and its transport to Daisy Hill. It wasn't realised until the hut arrived in Buckley that there would be extra costs for the foundations, sewerage, electricity and a roof in spite of some voluntary labour and donation of materials. However, there was plenty of goodwill and friends who were able to attract sufficient funding for the £20,000 required for financing the project. The Welsh Office provided 50%, Alyn and Deeside Council 25% and the parishioners the remaining 25%. Funding was given with the understanding that the hall was used for community use. The work to reconstruct the building was undertaken by the Knights of St Columba and other parishioners. Ron Perry supplied the roof and the brickwork and local firms the plumbing, lighting and flooring. The Hall was opened on 22 May 1982 by Barry Jones, M.P. and soon proved its worth as a community centre as the venue for dance and craft classes, bingo, line dancing, meetings of church groups, fund raising events, fairs, private parties, and private hire by local groups and individuals.

By the 1990s it was obvious that a crisis was looming because of the age of church buildings and that a great step forward was needed. Within a hundred years the parish had outgrown its church and both the presbytery and community centre were inadequate to meet the contemporary needs and satisfy new health and safety legislation. The church roof leaked, the walls were damp and the windows rotten. The community centre was in a state of decay and too small to meet existing demands, the parish house needed modernising and parking facilities were inadequate and the busy highway a hazard. A new vision was required and the project to go into the new millennium with a new church and community hall was conceived.

A scheme was proposed towards the end of the 1990s under the direction of the parish priest, Father Adrian Morrin, working with Development and Business Committees. It matured after a process of consultation between parishioners, the Bishop of Wrexham and the Diocesan Trustees. In December 1996 Bishop Edwin Reegan of Wrexham Diocese gave consent to a new church, parish house and community centre at Spon Green on a site acquired by the parish in 1960.

The community hall was designed to provide two or three function rooms, access for the disabled, with scope for a broad range of users to include self-help groups, pensioner activities, the unemployed, nursery and crèche facilities, youth groups, badminton and table tennis provisions.

A three or four bedroomed house was to be built for the parish priest, deacon or lay administrator.

Canon Fitzharris with Community Centre Committee, 1981. L–R Back row: Barry Smallwood, Keith Jones, Vincent Brennan, Roy Edwards, Terry Loftus, Jim Tunney. Front row: Margaret Tunney, Eileen Roberts, Ann Jones, Canon Fitzharris, Pat Tyrell. [Parish Archive]

A design for the church was arrived at after a lengthy consultation with the parishioners under the guidance of Dom Robin Gibbons. Three architects submitted proposals taking into account spiritual and community needs and these were considered by parishioners who answered a questionnaire designed to reflect their ideas, which were considered by the building committee. Eventually the diocesan trustees appointed the firm of Pozzoni as architects.

In February 1999 the firm of Anwyl developers began the construction work in Jubilee Road. On 17 April Bishop Reegan laid the foundation stone with its inscription in Welsh and English and the church was officially opened on 4 December 1999.

The congregation came to say goodbye to the old church of Our Lady of the Rosary on Friday 3 December. It was reported 'around 250 people gathered for the celebration of the final closing Mass, and the torch light procession that followed to the new church.' At the end of the Mass 'with lights switched out and faces glowing in candlelight, the doors of the old church were locked behind us. Fr Adrian carried the Blessed Sacrament and the altar servers led the way to the new church. This was the culmination of a vision, a dream come true, exceeding all of our greatest expectations. The congregation flowed into the semicircular church and the pews were almost full and we continued our songs of praise to the Lord and our thanksgiving that so much had been achieved. On Saturday, following a crowded first mass, the church was open for friends, neighbours and other Christian communities.'[12]

Fr Morrin published a special newsletter to commemorate the opening and one of the entries was written by Sophie Kelly aged 8. It said:

My great grandfather, Thomas Kelly, was one of the people who got together with others, and saved for a church in Buckley. He lived in the Parrot Inn in Drury, after arriving from County Mayo in Ireland. He had to get up very early on Sunday mornings and walk to Mold. This was very difficult with a large family. In 1893, the church was built and the foundation stone with his name on it can still be seen. I often look at it. Earlier this year, I was there when Bishop Edwin laid the foundation stone for our new church. Our old church will sadly be knocked down. I wonder what is to happen to the old foundation stone?

In the newsletter Fr Morrin described the new building as 'A church designed for today with echoes of the past.' He described the impressive façade of the fan-shaped gable, with the unusual window in the shape of an elongated hexagon. He spoke of the building materials used.

There are many features included to give interest to the exterior, brick octagon corners have been added to allow the angles of the fan to be worked in Buckley brick using fawn coloured Jacobean bricks, concrete blocks in interlacing band echo the design of the old church with its yellow banding of South Buckley bricks. Hard roof tiles in blue imitate the Welsh slate, which is used in the floor of the baptistery. The surrounding gardens are landscaped and edged in Jacobean blocks to provide ample secure parking areas.

Some of the furnishings came from the old church others were introduced. The Stations of the Cross, the Tabernacle, the statue of Our Lady of Lourdes, the altar chairs in memory of Canon Thomas Fitzharris, the altar

Exterior and interior of the new church building of Our Lady of the Rosary, 2000. [Buckley Society Archive]

stone he carried with him to North Africa, in the Second World War and the memorial altar to four altar servers who died in the conflict are symbols of the continuity of worship from the beginning of the church in Buckley. The new altar also has a sense of continuity, renewal and future offering, representing as it does the Sacrificial Block Altar of Judaism, the twelve tribes of Israel and the twelve Apostles. The Ambo, the Altar of the Word, where the Gospel is proclaimed and the scriptures read, has four stones on each face representing the four evangelists, is a reminder of the good news for the people of God.

The church was consecrated by Bishop Edwin Reegan on the eve of Pentecost, 2000.

Parish Priests

Jean Jacques Marie Pochard, 1907–29
James Mulroy, 1929–31
Wilfred Brodie, 1931–32
David Crowley, 1932–36
Thomas Fitzharris, 1936–39. Served as Curate.
F. James Furniss, 1944–52
Cyril Schwarz, 1952–57
Thomas Fitzharris, 1957–88
James Durkin, 1988–96
Adrian Morrin, 1996–

Notes

1. I am grateful for assistance in preparing this chapter from Mrs Kathryn Byrne, archivist of Wrexham Diocese; Father Adrian Morrin, parish priest of Buckley; and Ann Tansley who kindly put at my disposal a great deal of material. Any mistakes are mine.
2. Margaret Joy, *A History of St David's Roman Catholic Parish, Church and School* (Mold, 1992).
3. Wrexham Diocesan Archive. The account is not signed but I think it is probably written by Father J. J. Pochard, parish priest of Buckley, 1907–c.1930. Francis Mostyn was Bishop of Minevia 1898–1921, when he was translated to become Archbishop of Cardiff, although he continued to administer the Diocese of Minevia until Francis John Vaughan was appointed bishop in 1926.
4. *County Herald*, 20/11/1906.
5. *Chester Chronicle*, 20/2/1897.
6. *Chester Chronicle*, 1/5/1897.
7. Wrexham Diocesan Archive. Response to questionnaire from the bishop, 1893.

8. Wrexham Diocesan Archive, Birkenhead, 2/12/1892.
9. *Chester Chronicle*, 8/4/1893.
10. *Mold, Deeside and Buckley Leader*, 9/12/1927.
11. Wrexham Diocesan Archive, Buckley, 17/4/1893.
12. *Buckley Gazette*, 17/7/1970.
13. 'Wrexham People', *Wrexham Diocesan Newspaper*, 12/1/2000.

Chapter 12
Going to School

Not until the end of the nineteenth century was education in Britain compulsory and free of any charge on parents. The majority of schools were 'elementary' schools, where pupils generally received their entire education before leaving to enter the work force. The state provision for secondary education in Wales did not come into being until after the implementation of the recommendations of the Aberdare Commission in the 1890s, and then it was of a voluntary nature and mostly fee paying. The possibility of obtaining entrance into a university was about four in every thousand. The school leaving age, when education became compulsory, was thirteen years of age for pupils of both sexes:[1] although it was still possible until the First World War to leave school earlier, to enter into paid employment, by passing what was called the Labour examination.

The history of education in Buckley up to the Butler Education Act of 1944 falls into four main periods. The first period from the beginning of the nineteenth century ended in 1847 by the publication of the controversial *Report into the State of Education in Wales*. The second phase lasted from 1847 to 1902 and was marked by two important Education Acts. W. E. Forster introduced the first of these in 1870. This Act established important principles, which were to have an enduring effect on National education. It provided for a dual system. The Voluntary Schools, most of them established by the Church of England, were to receive state aid towards the running of the schools.[2] They were allowed to manage their own affairs, and provide denominational religious teaching, on condition that they were open to regular government inspection. Most importantly, elected School Boards, mostly in Wales, subject to the control of nonconformists, were permitted to provide schools by a levy on the rates, and to enforce compulsory attendance. Denominational instruction in these schools was forbidden. These schools were known as Board Schools. Such a school was opened in Bistre in 1877. The second Act, introduced in 1902 by A. J. Balfour, was of a controversial nature in Wales. It led to a revolt by the Welsh Nonconformists and at one time threatened the existence of Church schools in the urban district. The dispute was caused by Nonconformists objecting to paying for denominational religious instruction on the rates. School Boards were abolished and counties and county boroughs became the authorities for elementary, secondary and technical education. The third period lasted from 1902 to the Butler Act of 1944. In 1918, H. A. L. Fisher's Education Act made schooling compulsory and free to 14 years of age. Although stringent economic cuts were introduced during the years of depression, in the 1920s and 30s, Flintshire Education Authority was responsible for an increased range of services and a widening of educational opportunities. The fourth and last period in this survey is after 1944 until the closure of the old primary schools and their replacement by the existing schools. A great deal of very varied information from local schools is available through entries in logbooks which the head teacher was compelled to keep on a weekly basis from 1863 onwards. These are often amusing, eccentric, informative and at times libellous!

The first period, 1800–47

In this first period of fifty years, both Nonconformists and Anglicans founded schools in the area. The first society, the British and Foreign School Society, was established in 1808. It was originally called the Lancasterian Society, after its Quaker founder, Joseph Lancaster. In 1811 the Church of England set up an

educational society with the rather forbidding title, The National Society for Promoting the Education of the Poor in the Principles of the Established Church. The teachers were to be practising Anglicans; the syllabus included compulsory study of the Anglican liturgy and catechism. The first period ended in 1847 in a major national row between Anglicans and Nonconformists. It led to open hostility between them and eventually led to the disestablishment of the Anglican Church in Wales. The Report revealed how inadequate the schools were of both Societies and led to Government intervention into education.

Religion was the spur to both societies for the establishment of schools for the poor. Grammar schools had been established by rich benefactors from the time of the Tudors in the sixteenth century. George Ledsham of Farm Stile, Ewloe, a noted lawyer and steward of the Inner Temple, London, endowed Hawarden Grammar School, in 1606. This provided secondary education for fee-payers and scholarship boys until its closure in 1893. The new County School for boys and girls replaced it in 1896, and some provision was made for free places by means of scholarships, although most pupils paid fees until 1944.[3] If you wished to attend the school at the beginning of the nineteenth century your parents would have to pay the necessary fees. It was advertised in 1815:

> At the above school young gentlemen are boarded and very carefully instructed in all branches of learning at 26 guineas per annum with one guinea entrance fee. French and German charged extra. Many young gentlemen have received silver medals and books from the school.

Amongst these prize winners were a Boydell, Hancock, and Rigby, sons of local industrialists.[4]

In our earlier review of the establishment of religion in Buckley at the end of the eighteenth century we have seen the influence of key figures. Griffiths Jones and his Circulating Schools were continued by Thomas Charles of Bala with the important addition of Sunday schools and the Catechetical Method of teaching the fundamental truths of Christianity to the Welsh people in their own language. Although, it is probable, that in Bistre only, the early Calvinistic Methodists taught through the medium of Welsh. But the Welsh nonconformist influence remained. Jonathan Catherall II encouraged Independents of his own persuasion to worship, by building a chapel in 1811, which was used as a Sunday school, and supporting Calvinistic Methodists by enabling them to do likewise. The Anglican key figures, in stark contrast, were Rector Neville of Hawarden, and his nephews, Sir Stephen Glynne and Henry Glynne, both High Churchmen, and strong supporters of the National Society. Of more evangelical churchmanship was Archdeacon Charles Butler Clough of Mold who established that tradition in the church and school in Bistre.

It was the nonconformist Jonathan Catherall II (1761–1833) who was credited with opening the first school in Buckley. At an early age, his daughters, Martha (b.1794) and Francis (b.1795), became dedicated to teaching. By 1813 their father writing to a friend proudly stated, 'my girls have a Sabbath School, eighty children we had lately'. A year later Catherall wrote 'my children are indefatigable in the school; the children are numerous. We want more walls to hang lessons on, on Lancashire's plan [Joseph Lancaster],

Bistre National School. [Buckley Library]

which I hope to adopt.'[5] In 1814 the British and Foreign School Society was formally established to promote the Lancasterian system of education. Catherall was a strong supporter of the Society and made a fund raising tour on their behalf. The Independent chapel was enlarged around this time, and it is probable that the minister appointed by Catherall also taught a day school in the chapel. In the same year, 1813, Cropper informs us:

> Catherall purchased Frog Hall, and also opened a day school there, in which for a period his two young daughters taught the youth of the neighbourhood. This venture had a double purpose — on Sundays they were freely lent to the Welsh Methodist friends who had just commenced to hold cottage services in the vicinity.[6]

Cropper came to the conclusion that the Welsh Calvinistic Methodist chapel in Mold Road was built on the site of Frog Hall. In September 1818 tragedy struck and both Catherall's daughters died of fever. Two months later Frog Hall, with its chapel and schoolhouse, was leased to the Calvinistic Methodists. We have no evidence that day schools continued in either the Independent or Calvinistic Methodist chapels in the 1820s or 1830s but Sunday schools were probably continued.

Hugh Owen, an Anglesey born civil servant in the Poor Law Commission, generated a revival in enthusiasm for the provision of day school education for nonconformists in Wales. In August 1843 he addressed a 'Letter to the Welsh People' on day schools. He advised that British Schools should be established in every district in Wales, run by a committee whose members were to be chosen from among the various religious denominations in the district. Owen advocated that grants be provided by the government, that school buildings should be built to a certain size, and teachers well-trained.

However, some Nonconformists in many parts of Wales, had earlier anticipated Owen's concerns. Alarmed by the threat of the government to give power to Anglicans in the education of children in workhouses and factories, they decided to make their own provisions. In February 1843 the Nonconformist bodies of Buckley and district came together to make their arrangements. This was a momentous event in the history of education in the area. It was recorded in a report in Welsh in May 1843 by Hugh Jones.[7]

Hugh Jones was a Calvinistic Methodist. He was concerned that apart from a dame school in Nant Mawr the only other schools available for the children of Nonconformists were those established by the Anglicans at Buckley and Bistre. Attendance at these schools obliged them to receive full-time instruction in the Church catechism and attend Anglican worship in the parish church in order to qualify for admission. Hugh Jones proposed more satisfactory alternative proposals:

> When the religious denominations of the district realised that their young members were attending a place of worship without parental supervision it was considered an oppression, an obstacle to religious freedom. The matter was unanimously resolved when the Wesleyans, the Old and New Connexions, Independents, Calvinistic and Primitive Methodists, set up a communal school whereby members were educated together but worshipped separately on the Sabbath.
>
> Now we have two schools, one for boys which is being held in the Primitive Methodist chapel and supervised by a headmaster of the Independents' cause; another for girls occupying the Independents' Schoolroom and run by a lady of the New Connexion. There is hardly three months since these schools were opened and already the boys attending number 95 and the girls 85.
>
> The master's salary is £45, mistress £20 p.a. All children contribute 1d. a week for their tuition but if

orphaned no payment is expected. Numerous individuals have promised annual sums towards the cause if the money from fees proves to be insufficient.

The master and mistress begin and end each day with a prayer and a hymn. One man from each of the denominations involved in the venture is allowed to question the children for an hour once a month i.e. girls from 2 p.m. to 3 p.m., boys, from 3 p.m. to 4 p.m.

The master teaches his pupils to read, write, grammar, arithmetic, geography, history, etc. Likewise the mistress with the girls, who also coaches them in the art of needlework. To date all is well, both tutors giving satisfactory service to the community in providing the youth with sound beneficial education that includes instruction in the scriptures.

13 May 1843 Hugh Jones. Buckley.

N.B. Regarding religious education, no form of catechism is practised in these schools, only the expounding of gospel principles. Questions are asked solely on the Divine Revelation of God's word.[8]

School numbers increased over the next three years from 180 to 222, of whom 40 were fatherless and received free education. At the beginning of March the scholars walked in procession from the Primitive Methodist chapel in Mill Lane to the Wesleyan Methodist chapel at the Square. Here they were examined in geography, grammar, scripture, history and the elements of religion, together with spelling and mental arithmetic. It was reported 'that they gave general satisfaction especially the girls, and they reflected honour on the master and mistress who have been amongst them for only five months.' It was said 'the institution was principally supported by private subscription and the children pay a trifling sum, but it scarcely supplies them with books.' After the examination over four hundred people were provided with tea and the 'children also regaled'. Ministers from the Wesleyan, Methodist New Connexion, and the Independent churches were present.[9]

Within six years of Jonathan Catherall building the first Nonconformist church in Buckley, the rector of Hawarden made plans to provide a school and church in this remote district of his parish. With pious ostentation, in 1817, the Honourable and Reverend George Neville exerted himself to solicit aid from his wealthy aristocratic relatives and friends for this purpose. The response was overwhelming. The Prince Regent, later George IV, his son-in-law Prince Leopold, the Chancellor of the Exchequer, the Duke of Devonshire, five lord bishops, a marquis, earls, lords, viscounts and over 170 other benefactors presented the rector with nearly two thousand pounds. This generous sum included a collection made at a church service in September 1817 when the Bishop of St Asaph launched the appeal for subscriptions with an eloquent sermon. To illustrate the necessity of a school the Bishop stated:

> That within a short distance of Hawarden there was no less than 1200 persons whose offspring experience all the melancholy evils of ignorance and lack of religion. It was the great object to attempt the amelioration of their hapless condition.[10]

It was as if the Bishop was appealing to the nobility and gentry assembled to make a subscription to bring religion to a foreign country, to bring treasure from the old world to the new, echoing the words of Jonathan Catherall: 'There is the same need of Divine teaching and ministerial labours amongst the refined English and the rude Welsh as there is amongst the wild Indians.'[11]

The execution of Rector Neville's plans was well described by Richard Willett.

> … the Rector, Mr Neville, with a laudable and unremitting zeal for our Church Establishment, and to extend and render permanent its effective influence throughout his jurisdiction, projected the erection of a new Church in the midst of this populous district, and as preparatory to its success the erection of two

The Honourable and Reverend George Neville. [B. Jones deposit, FRO D/DM/592].

Richard Willett (1761–1829) [FRO PR/C/45]

Schools, the one for boys, and the other for girls. A large and commodious House was expeditiously finished, which comprehends a Clergymen's residence, with every requisite accommodation, and two large School rooms each capable of containing, one hundred and fifty children at least. The Girls School was opened upon the first day of January 1819, and the Boy's School upon the tenth day of February following. At these Schools proper Instructors regularly attend, and every encouragement is given by the Rector, and the Honourable Lady Glynne, to foster the growth, and forward the ends of this infant charity'.[12]

Mr Davies-Cooke of Gwysaney, lord of the manor of Ewloe, gave the site of three acres for the triple purpose of parsonage, schools, and church.

With much pomp and ceremony the foundation stone of the church was laid on 14 December 1821 and consecrated and dedicated to St Matthew on 25 September 1822.

Therefore within the space of a decade the moral and spiritual lives of the people of Buckley were provided with a choice of a place of worship and their children rescued from a life of ignorance and given some educational opportunity. The landscape announced the change. Catherall's bell tower at Hawkesbury stared through the smoke of potteries and brickworks across to Neville's church tower.

Rector Neville was an excellent administrator and made good use of the experience gained through the establishment of a school at Hawarden. We may assume that he introduced the same methods of teaching and rules of conduct for children to the new schools in Buckley.

'Rules to be observed by parents whose children are admitted into Lady Glynne and Mr Neville's Schools in the parish of Hawarden, which are recommended to be pasted up in some conspicuous place in each Parent's House'. There were ten rules, the chief of which instructed parents to send their children at 8.30 a.m. and 1.30 p.m. on weekdays with Saturday as a holiday, and half an hour before church on Sundays, 'and that they say their prayers before they go out in the morning, and when they go to bed at night, and also, that they say grace before and after meat.' Unless the parents gave a satisfactory account for absence, children would be expelled. Parents were instructed to send their children to school well washed and combed, with their clothes clean and mended. Parental care at home was advocated where children were to be called upon to repeat the catechism and to read the holy scripture especially on Sunday. They were not to suffer their children to swear, quarrel or use bad language, and were to freely submit their children to the discipline of the school. All children resident in the parish, on application, were eligible for admission. The four quarter days of the year were specified as the only days for entrance. Regulations for the distribution of rewards were announced with the rules. These consisted entirely of gifts of clothing dependent upon attendance and punctuality earned during the four quarters of the year. The maximum reward for a boy was, 'a Jacket, a pair of Trowsers, [sic] a Hat, and a Pair of Stockings', and for a girl, 'a Cloak, a Frock, a Pair of Shoes, and a Bonnet'. The rewards were distributed on New Year's Day from which the quarters of the year were counted.[13] St Matthew's schools were conducted by the method advocated by Andrew Bell an Anglican clergyman, whose ideas were adopted by the National Society. The basic principle of Bell's method was that the older children taught the younger.

In 1840 Rector Henry Glynne erected a purpose built school for the education of infants. The plaque on the front of the building was inscribed.

Erected……..AD MDCCCXL
Henry Glynne
Rector & Ordinary
Even a child is known by his doings
Whether his work be pure and whether
it be right.

Henry Glynne (1810–72) was the younger brother of Sir Stephen Glynne (1807–74), 9th Baronet, of Hawarden Castle; their sister, Catherine, married W. E. Gladstone in 1839. Henry Glynne succeeded George Neville, his uncle, as rector of Hawarden in 1834. The Glynne brothers were deeply attached to one another, corresponded regularly, and shared High Anglican and ecclesiological ideas. Henry Glynne appointed men of the same churchmanship to be curates in charge of Buckley. They worked very closely with him in the development of Church schools. For example Henry Walford Bellairs, M.A. curate of Buckley, 1839–40, left to become one of the newly appointed Her Majesty's Inspectors of Schools. He may have introduced Henry Glynne to the work of the Home and Colonial Infant School Society (1836) which was more progressive in its methods than Andrew Bell. Henry Powell Ffoulkes, who spent seventeen years as curate in Buckley, and gave outstanding service, succeeded Bellairs.

In 1843 another church with a school attached to it was built in the township of Pentrobin which was divided between the ecclesiastical district of Buckley and the parish of Hawarden.[14]

The vicar of Mold, later archdeacon of St Asaph, Charles Butler Clough, during his long incumbency, made provision for schools and churches in the outlying districts of his extensive parish. In 1842 he built a church and school at Bistre.

A small plot of land was bought from three local farmers in 1841 to be used as a site for a school 'for the education of the children of the labouring, manufacturing, and other poorer classes in the townships of Bistre and Argoed, in the parish of Mold, which said school should be always conducted upon the principles of the Incorporated National Society for promoting the Education of the Poor in the Principles of the Established Church'.[15] The architect was John Lloyd who on more than one occasion received the patronage of Clough. The plans show a simple building divided into two large classrooms each 30 ft x 20 ft for boys and girls with outside offices and separate playgrounds. The front elevation is plain but not unpleasant.

In spite of this local activity in the building of new schools it was generally agreed that the educational opportunity in Wales was inadequate. A view which was expressed by the National Society in 1845. This prompted William Williams, a Welshman and Member of Parliament for Coventry, to press for an inquiry to be made into the state of education in the principality. J. P. Kay Shuttleworth, Secretary of the Committee of Council on Education, gave careful instructions to the three commissioners appointed to make the inquiry: J. C. Symons, R. R. W. Lingen and H. Vaughan Johnson. He told them that the purpose was 'to direct an inquiry to be made into the state of education in the Principality of Wales, especially into the means afforded to the labouring classes of acquiring a knowledge of the English language'. They were cautioned, 'Your success will in a great degree depend on your own courtesy and discretion in the prosecution of your inquiry.'

They were asked to report on all matters relating to the school's foundation, building, teachers, scholars and the curriculum:

… the subjects professed to be taught, the time allotted to each, the books used, whether the children are instructed in the Welsh language, or in the English, or in both, whether in each case in the grammar or not, the

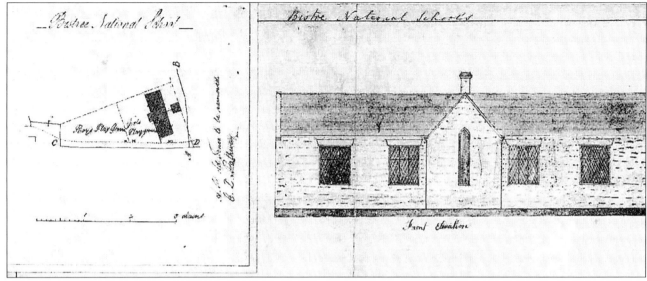

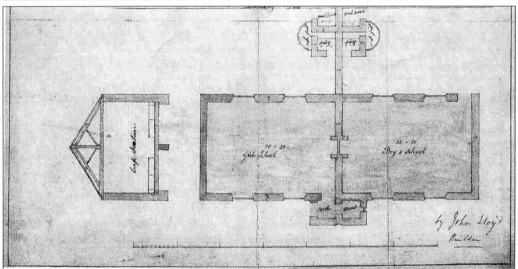

Bistre National School Plans 1840s. [John Lloyd. FRO E/SBO/5/1]

actual condition of their instruction on all subjects professed to be taught.

Whenever you have means to form a just estimate of the qualifications and attainments of the master, it should be so stated as not to operate as a discouragement to humble but deserving men, who may have had few opportunities of education.

You will also be enabled to form some estimate of the general state of intelligence and information of the poorer classes in Wales and of the influence which an improved education might be expected to produce, on the general condition of society, and its moral and religious progress.[16]

The long and detailed report of the commissioners was published in 1847. The response of the Welsh people to the report was one of immediate condemnation. They were appalled at the ignorance and lack of sympathy of the commissioners towards the Welsh nation, their religion, customs and moral state. They perceived it as an act of treachery, as *Brad y Llyfrau Gleision* (Treachery of the Blue Books). They could not stomach the implications of the commissioners that the nation was degenerate in religion and morality. The commissioners showed a total disregard for, and understanding of Nonconformism and the Welsh language, the main pillars of a distinctive Welsh society. This attitude roused the Welsh to express their indignation at being governed by Anglican gentry and having the religion and education of the Established Church enforced upon their children in the schools. They demanded the right of individual families to educate their children in institutions which reflected their own religious views. They responded to the accusations of law-breaking, prostitution, and the number of children born out of wedlock, by pointing out that the figures were all lower in Wales than in England.

Whatever may be said about the insensitivity of the commissioners and their assistants it must be said that Welsh people gave some of the evidence on which the report was based to the commissioners. Evidence was quoted as given by the curate of Buckley, the Reverend H. Powell Ffoulkes, for St Matthew's, and Mr Catherall, for the Buckley Union Schools. But whatever its drawbacks the report is of great importance for the detailed picture it gives of Welsh society in the middle of the nineteenth century. It helps us to understand the divisions and hostility, which were to plague religious and public life in Wales for the next hundred years. It showed the inequalities existing in educational opportunities, the general inadequacy of teacher training, poor teaching in the classroom, lack of resources, and the problems of language communication between teachers and pupils. For an understanding of the development of the provision of education in Buckley the report is the first detailed survey we have, and no matter its flaws, is a good starting point.

The report gives an account of the state of education in all the schools existing in Buckley in 1847. It is not proposed to quote the long report in full but to look at it comparatively by discussing various issues.[17]

The reports for Buckley and Bistre gave some insight into the social conditions prevailing in the communities. Evidence for Buckley district was given by the Reverend H. Powell Ffoulkes who stated:

> The inhabitants are for the most part employed as potters, brickmakers, and colliers. It is stated that the children are employed as early as nine years of age in the coal-pits, and at eleven years old in the brick-works, where they earn from 6*d*. to 9*d*. per day. It appears from the statements of the Rev. J. P. Ffoulkes, the officiating minister, that there are about 300 children between the ages of 3 and 12 years who attend no school; that the state of morals is degraded in respect of drunkenness, profanity, dishonesty, and incontinence; that the later vice is increasing so rapidly as to render it difficult to find a cottage where some female member of the family has not been *enceinte* before marriage.

The Assistant Commissioner, John James, reporting on Bistre township found that 'It is estimated that there are, within a distance of two miles, 700 children of an age to receive instruction. The means available for education are very inadequate'.

Commenting on the Buckley Union schools, he said that the schools:

> … are so called because the principal Dissenters in the neighbourhood have united to support them. At present £75 is promised to the teachers, which is to be raised in part by the payments of the children, the school being available for members of every denomination. It is stated by Mr Catherall, the principal promoter, that no efficient school can be maintained in this place without government assistance; that the children remain uneducated, because their parents being poor and ill-educated cannot be induced to make the smallest sacrifice for the sake of education; that when the children are of an age to be sent to work it is impossible to induce them to attend even a Sunday-school, or a place of worship on Sunday; that he himself has offered to raise the wages of youths engaged in his works 1*s*. per week, and to give them a reward of 1*s*. every time they attend a Sunday-school; but although they have never received any kind of instruction they refuse compliance. It is stated that the promoters are anxious to establish the schools upon the British and Foreign system;[18] that £70 could be raised by local contributions for the erection of school-rooms, but that at present a site cannot be obtained.

The report referred to the state of the school buildings. Those belonging to St Matthew's were described 'as built for the purpose', likewise Bistre Church school. The Buckley Union schools set up by the Nonconformist churches did not have a purpose built school. It was suggested that one could be built from local contributions, at a cost of £70, 'but that at present a site cannot be obtained'. Instead, the boys' school met in the newly opened Primitive Methodist chapel in Mill Lane, and the girls were taught 'in a room belonging to the Independent chapel'.

The number of teachers and scholars varied from school to school. At St Matthew's there were 58 boys, 62 girls, with 8 employed as monitors. They were taught in separate rooms. The boys by a master aged 38 years of age, trained at Westminster. This was Joseph Ellis, head teacher from 1836–64, of whom it was said:

Lane End School. Drawing by J. Clifford Jones [Buckley Society Magazine, 1]

… his manner towards the scholars is calculated to secure respect, and to stimulate their intellects; and they appear to hold him in high respect. His manner of teaching the Church Catechism was so elaborate and uncommon as to form a feature in the character of the school. He teaches arithmetic without any book; and employs a species of mental exercise in Addition, Subtraction, Multiplication, and Division which is calculated to prove of great assistance to the children in working sums.

The subjects taught were reading, writing, arithmetic, English grammar, geography, history and music, the scriptures and Church catechism. The fees, 1*d.* per week. The salary of the master £50; of the mistress £30. The mistress, aged 20 years of age, was trained at Warrington. 'She appeared anxious to do her best. Her control over the school was imperfect. Her pupils are taught needlework every afternoon'.

Of the infant school at Lane End, opened by Henry Glynne in 1841, it was stated that 'the premises and furniture are suitable, and in good repair'. 'The mistress received some preparation for her present employment at Warrington, in 1840. There are 48 scholars who paid a fee of 1*d.* per week. The mistress was paid £30 and taught the infants 'the Scriptures, the Lord's Prayer, the Creed, and the Ten Commandments, reading, the tables, &c'.

At the Buckley Union school 130 boys were taught with 12 employed as monitors. The master was paid £50. The curriculum was 'the Bible, reading, writing, arithmetic, English grammar, geography and history'. 'But all pupils were very ignorant of these several subjects. They all speak English, but with a strong provincial dialect. The Master has never been trained to teach, but endeavours to imitate the British system.[19] He takes great pains to interest his pupils, and to keep their attention alive. The school is held in part of a chapel very inconvenient for the purpose. It contains but one small desk'.

At the same school 48 girls were taught the scriptures, reading, writing, and arithmetic, for which the fees were 1*d.* and 2*d.* per week. 'The mistress was formerly a dressmaker, and is competent to give instruction in needlework, which is regularly taught. She has not been trained to conduct a school, and has received very little education'.

The Bistre Church school was not as well provided for as its sister school in Buckley, and was described as:

A school for boys and girls, taught separately by a master and a mistress, in a school built for the purpose. Number of boys, 47; girls, 62; number employed as monitors 8. Subjects taught – reading, writing, and arithmetic, the Scriptures and Church Catechism. Fees, 1d. per week; total income of master £16; of mistress, £18.

John James, the Assistant Commissioner, was not impressed, and reported:

The children appeared dirty and ragged, and were very disorderly. The master is 58 years of age, and although he has never received any kind of training, has been a teacher for 30 years. He is an ignorant man, and appears to neglect the school.

The mistress is 24 years of age, and has been a teacher for about two years. She has not been trained; she occasionally spoke English ungrammatically. Both schoolrooms were dirty.

Whatever we may think of the commissioners there is no denying the lamentable state of education in Buckley and Bistre. Improvements were to come slowly and it wasn't until thirty years later that nonconformists in Buckley had their first purpose built school.

The Right Reverend Thomas Vowler Short,
Bishop of St Asaph (1846–70). [FRO PR/C/36]

The year 1847 was a turning point in Welsh education. This was most apparent in the Anglican diocese of St Asaph, through the leadership of Bishop Thomas Vowler Short. The years of his episcopate, 1846–70, mark the beginning of the next major phase, which lasted until 1902. In these years a new St Matthew's School was completed in 1849, a feeder infants' school opened in Church Road in 1857, and Board Schools for infants and boys and girls opened in Bistre in 1877. Before we look in detail at the building of these schools, a brief look at the effect of Bishop Short's work in the diocese will help to put into context the major advances in education in this second phase. One of Bishop Short's lieutenants was the Reverend Henry Powell Ffoulkes, curate of Buckley until 1857, and from 1861 archdeacon of Montgomery, who served as an influential member of the diocesan committee for education.[20]

After the calamitous publication of the Commissioners Report in 1847, Short, who regarded himself as an educationalist, was determined to remedy some of the shortcomings. He went as a member of a deputation of the National Society's Welsh Education Committee, together with Bishop Connop Thirlwall of St David's diocese (an Englishman who had learnt Welsh), and Sir Thomas Phillips, a barrister, to lobby Earl Grey, the Lord President of the Council. They impressed upon Grey the need for the moral and social regeneration of the people of Wales through a state supervised system of education. They requested two things from Grey. Firstly the government's assistance in creating a professional teacher training structure within the principality, with state funding for training, and grants towards salaries, and secondly, the appointment of two inspectors 'acquainted with the Welsh tongue' to 'superintend' the establishment and growth of the new structure in Wales.

Short was a practical, vigorous, and determined man who took pride in devising and implementing a whole range of educational reforms within his diocese. His aim was to make immediate improvement by bringing together teachers from all schools for three weeks in the summer where they would receive instruction and be provided with teaching aids. As a Bishop he promoted literacy and understanding particularly in the religious instruction of children in whatever was their mother tongue. Here are a few examples of his methods.[21] Bishop Short was determined to make clear his strategy for the improvement of education in his diocese and to this end he circulated a letter to the clergy in the diocese explaining his experimental methods. These methods concentrated on the instructions he gave to teachers in the Church schools. He recommended they use 'some Elementary books, in which the Welsh and English languages are printed on opposite pages'. He suggested that dictation be used to help the pupils learn English, 'by dictating sentences in Welsh, to the children, who would be required to write them down on their slates individually in English of their own'. He stressed that 'One great object which must be kept constantly in view is the improvement of the present race of School Masters and Mistresses. It is indeed of the utmost importance that a superior race of Teachers should be prepared for the rising generation.' He saw as 'the most obvious evil at present existing in our schools is this, that the little children are not taught in an intelligent manner. They learn by rote and do not comprehend what they learn-and this is an evil which might easily be remedied in existing schools, and among existing Teachers'. In order to instil these basic ideas and explore others he arranged for a clergyman from each local group of parishes, the rural deanery, to be a member of the Diocesan Board of Education.

It was through the members of the Board that Short circulated his ideas. They met in consultation for two days in the spring and then returned to their locality to impart their methods and ideas. The next stage of instruction took place in the 'Harvest meeting' of schoolmasters who met for three weeks in August and September. In 1852, they met at Caernarfon in the North Wales Training College for Teachers. The Masters were requested to carry with them 'a Bible and Prayer Book, any Book on Geography or Grammar which

North Wales Training College for Teachers (later St Mary's College, Bangor). [National Library of Wales, St Asaph MS, Bishop Short's Book]

they are in the habit of using, and any work on Arithmetic or Mathematics which they possess and approve of. Forty-two masters of National Schools from various parts of North Wales attended together with the assistant secretaries for the several rural deaneries, Mold deanery being represented by the Reverend H. P. Ffoulkes. Year by year Bishop Short persevered in his crusade to improve the standard of education in the diocesan schools which continually increased under his guidance and personal generosity. His was always the first and largest benefaction in the building of schools and churches. By 1866 there were two hundred and twenty eight church schools in two hundred and four parishes and the 'character of the education was also pronounced to be generally very greatly improved, owing to the great increase in the proportion of schools under certificated teachers'. Bishop Short's efforts were beginning to bear fruit. Throughout his educational work in the diocese he made best use of the resources offered by voluntary support from the National Society and State aid from the government. How did this effect education in Buckley?

There were significant developments in the ecclesiastical district of St Matthew's, Buckley. The first of these is seen in the opening of new schools. In 1849, St Matthew's school was transferred from the parsonage, across the road, to new buildings on a site conveyed to the parish by Sir Stephen Glynne. For this a government grant of over £600 was obtained and another £1,000 raised by subscriptions given by members of the Glynne family. A large quantity of building material and its cartage was supplied by manufacturers and farmers of the parish, in generous support of a scheme to increase educational opportunities for the 700 children in the district under 14 years of age. The opening of the new schools was reported as a demonstration of ecclesiastical exuberance much as it had been for the new church and schools in the 1820s:

The formal opening of the school at Buckley Mountain was celebrated by a religious festival on Easter Tuesday. The new school is on the north west side of the church and is in the Elizabethan style and were designed by the Reverend H. Rose, Rector of Brington in Northants. The size of the rooms are 43 ft. x 21 ft. and are divided by sliding doors all dark stained and varnished with the open roofing of the same material There is a classroom 20 ft. square and recess in each school holding a small gallery for writing and simultaneous instruction. The front is laid out with gravel walks with a border having a handsome entrance gate. The building is of brick, with stone mullions, and caps to chimney-lanterns acts as a ventilator and bell turret. A teacher's house is built in corresponding style adjoining the ample playground with good garden etc.

St Matthew's School for Boys and Girls, 1849–1963. Drawing by J. Clifford Jones. [Buckley Society Magazine, 1]

The Bishop of Chester robed in the new classroom with ten of his clergy attending the opening, and then, proceeded to the church, the 'Churchwardens with white wands, the boy and men choristers in surplices and the clergy in surplices. The Bishop followed by clergy in gowns and hoods.'

The Bishop celebrated at the service of the Holy Communion. A feature of the service was the music. The canticles and psalm were sung to Gregorian chants, one harmonised by Thomas Tallis to the Benedicite. The anthem by William Boyce was 'Wherewith shall a young man cleanse his way'. The old hundredth psalm was sung before the Communion Service and joined in by the congregation most heartily. The Bishop preached from *Proverbs* xxii v.6, 'Train up a child in the way he should go: and when he is old, he will not depart from it'. The newspaper report continued:

> On leaving the Church a procession was formed as follows. The verger, the churchwardens of Buckley and Hawarden, workmen engaged on the schools, the members of the boys school with flags, by two, and the girls in similar formation, the choir in surplices, clergy in surplices, the bishop, and again clergy in gowns with hoods, the parish clerk of St Matthew's and the clerk of Hawarden, followed by the congregation.
>
> The Te Deum was sung down the road to the schools to the chant commonly called Tallis. In the school a beautiful scriptural and appropriate form of prayer for the occasion beginning with chanting psalm 127, 'Except the Lord build the house, they labour in vain that build it', after which the bishop pronounced the Blessing.
>
> The children went down to the old school to fetch their plates and cups and returned preceded by a band who kindly gave their services for the occasion. About 200 children dined off roast beef and plum pudding, and as soon as they finished their meal and retired, the company, the choir, the teachers, the workmen etc. sat down to the repast after which the band played several airs and the choir sang several songs and glees amongst which was the 'Song for the times' which was much admired and repeated.[22]

The Glynne brothers, rector Henry, and squire Sir Stephen, initiated the building of St Matthew's infants school, completed in 1857. Sir Stephen Glynne gave the site, in Church Road. James Harrison of Chester was the architect.[23] His plans for the school survive and show a simple, small but attractive school and house for the mistress.[24] But for some reason it was not used as a school until 1874, when the log book commences. The decision to do so was taken by the Reverend Stephen Gladstone who reordered school accommodation in the light of government requirements. Instead, Harrison's building was used as a reading and recreation room. The building was subject to alteration in 1891 when a new classroom for infants was built. The galleries were taken down in 1898 and replaced with desks, the school enlarged and the large porch added. A screen was put in the main room in August 1909.[25] Although alterations were to take place *c.*1900 to the Anglican schools in Buckley parish they were to be the last built there.

From 1863 onwards we are provided with a day-to-day account of school life in Buckley from the information recorded in school logbooks. They make fascinating reading and provide a lively commentary on changes in education, the attitudes of head teachers, the comments of Her Majesty's Inspectorate, and the progress and behaviour of generations of scholars and anxious parents.[26] The logbook was regarded as 'A Diary which should be a bare record of the events which constitute the history of the school'. It was meant to contain details of schoolbooks, apparatus, and lessons, HMI reports, the visit of managers, absence, illness or failure on the part of any of the school staff, or any special circumstances. It was

St Matthew's Infants School, architect James Harrison, Chester. Drawing by J. Clifford Jones. [Buckley Society Magazine, 1]

not meant to contain essays but to collect items of experience. 'A teacher who performs this duty simply, regularly, and with discrimination will find it a powerful help in mastering his profession, as well as an honourable monument to his labours'.

The first major event described is the introduction of the Revised Code in 1863. It was the work of Robert Lowe. The code was the assessment upon which grants to elementary schools were to be paid. It laid down the 'standards' which had to be attained in the government-established curriculum. Scholars were subject to examination by government inspectors in various subjects at six levels and if successful qualified for a government grant. Attendance was also taken into consideration when making the grant. This system was heartily disliked and became known as 'payment by results'. Lowe the author of the Act declared that education 'if it is not cheap, it shall be efficient; if it is not efficient, it shall be cheap'. Apart from religious instruction the rest of the curriculum taught was to be controlled by the Revised Code — reading, writing, arithmetic, English grammar, poetry, geography, history and music. No grant was paid unless the Department of Education recognised the teacher, unless the inspectors considered the school building satisfactory, and unless the school taught sewing to the girls. This accounts for the rather paternalistic entries in the logbook of St Matthew's girls in the 1860s.

In July 1864 they 'sent the needlework for the Castle', and in 1865 excelled themselves by 'finishing 3 nightshirts and 3 pairs of sheets for the Parsonage' and 'Miss Gladstone's sewing'.

The Act discontinued paying fees to the head teacher for the instruction of pupil teachers. Pupil teachers were introduced in 1847. They had to be over 13 years of age and serve a five-year apprenticeship to teaching in schools, and were paid £10 rising by annual increments to £20. They would be dismissed if they failed to pass the annual examinations. Gradually school boards developed pupil-teaching centres and after 1902 it became more common to send boys and girls to secondary schools before apprenticeship.

There are many references to pupil teachers in the Buckley school logbooks. They were poorly paid, required to do other things besides teaching in the days before school caretakers, such as lighting the school fire, many of them struggled in their attempt to learn and teach at the same time. Such were the pressures that some attempted to earn money elsewhere. For example in 1876 Thomas Connah was absent from Bistre National School on account of his working in the churchyard grave digging, an occupation which was taken up by his successor in 1882. The action of William Jones was more positive, when it was recorded that he 'did not turn up, appears to have run away to America'.

In 1864 a reading room was opened and evening schools were held for many years providing instruction in the 3 Rs. Mr Gladstone gave a lecture in the school in 1864, and in 1866 a Mr Sutton gave a lecture and 'experimentation' on electricity when it was said that 'some children were very much afraid'.

The 1870 Education Act gave Nonconformists an excellent opportunity to build their own schools. William Catherall had shown the same faithfulness to the Nonconformist cause, as his father Jonathan Catherall II (d.1833). He was heir to this tradition and a natural leader as a Congregationalist and one of the principal firebrick manufacturers. As vice chairman of the Mold School Board, Catherall was determined that his native district should have its own school. In this enterprise he was well supported by the local Nonconformist ministers and his fellow Congregationalist Joseph Griffiths, who acted as secretary.

There is a silence about the continuation of the Buckley Union School after the Commissioners' Report of 1847. In 1871 it was reported that a few boys from St Matthew's had gone to a school started in the old Wesleyan Chapel (in Mill Lane), and in January 1872 two boys who left to go to the Independent chapel were readmitted. Notes of other schools are given in school logbooks. For example in 1874 boys from Mr Whalmsley's school were readmitted to St Matthew's. It was noted in the logbook of Bistre National School in 1875 'that thirteen new scholars were admitted from Miss Higgins school', and in 1877 'Thos Catherall, Main Street, having again commenced to keep school, several children have gone to him'.

The foundation stone for the new Board Schools in Padeswood Road was laid on 11 October 1876. It was made up of separate departments for boys, girls and infants, and was opened on 3 December 1877. The first headmaster, appointed in 1877, was Thomas Jones who served the school faithfully until 1913 and laid the foundations of a sound scholastic tradition.

The Board School met the needs of the nonconformists of the district and fulfilled the intentions of its architect W. E. Forster, M.P. and vice-president of the Board of Education and a member of W. E. Gladstone's

first Liberal government. The result was the Education Act of 1870 in which Forster's twin aims were 'to cover the country with good schools' and 'to get the parents to send the children to school. Where provision of schools was not satisfactory he intended to fill up gaps with non-sectarian schools publicly financed and managed.' They were built and managed by school boards, the members of which were elected. The school boards had the right to enforce the attendance of all children between five and twelve years. Forster's Act was carried a stage further by Lord Sandon's Act of 1876. His Act forbade employers to hire children over ten, and allowed that children under fourteen could be employed if they held a labour certificate issued by a school inspector. Average scholars could apply for their certificate when they had achieved a specific standard of work. In March 1875 three boys were admitted to St Matthew's 'as half timers. They are to work at Mr Catherall's brickworks in the morning and come to school in the afternoon'. In May two brickwork manufacturers were fined for employing two boys under thirteen years of age full time.

In the first years of its existence the board school was well nurtured under the watchful eyes of William Catherall and Joseph Griffiths. They no doubt channelled the future of its proteges and found suitable employment for them in the local brickworks and collieries. By the beginning of February 1878, eight weeks after opening, it was reported that the attendance was 'little more than 300'. Three weeks later the number increased to 460, (175 infants, 135 girls, and 150 boys). Prominent members of the school board were the Reverend J. D. Thomas, Congregational minister; the Reverend J. M. Evans, vicar of Bistre; the Reverend Samuel Norman, Wesleyan; and Messrs John Lamb, Robert Griffiths, Thomas Edwards, Dr MacMillan, Joseph Griffiths (Secretary), Thomas Jones (Headmaster) and William Catherall (Chairman). The committee were deeply concerned about the children's welfare and made every effort to help their parents, many of whom were affected by hard winters when some of them were laid off from the brickworks because of frost and others on short time in the collieries. A practicable way of alleviating hardship was by the formation of a children's clothing club, in which the children saved money to buy new clothes, and the awarding of a sum 'of fifteen pounds to be given as bonuses to the children for good and regular attendance — viz 2/6d. per scholar who has not been absent for more than ten times during the year'. The collection of school fees was a problem. In May 1879 the headmaster reported 'that during the hard and distressing winter many children have had their fees remitted as it was realised their parents could not afford them'.[27]

Rector Henry Glynne died suddenly in 1872 and Sir Stephen Glynne appointed his nephew in his place. The new Rector, Stephen Gladstone, was the second son of the Prime Minister W. E. Gladstone, and to meet the demands of the 1870 Education Act began reorganising schools and building new ones. He set about rationalising the church schools in Buckley. St Matthew's infants was reopened as a school and the numbers limited to 75 with other children under seven years attending the school at Lane End. In May 1874 Gladstone issued a 'Copy of the Rules & Regulations of the schools, which have lately been printed'. They set out the hours of the school day: three hours in the morning and two and a half in the afternoon. School holidays were a week at Christmas and Easter and four weeks at harvest time. The rules dealt very strictly with the payment of school fees. 'Payment for each child, to be paid in advance, is 3d. per week. In the case of children of the same family, the oldest pays 3d. and the rest 2d. each'. Another rule stipulated that 'scholars are expected to provide their own slates, pencils, copy books, drawing books, exercise and home lesson book'. Parents were held responsible for sending children regularly to school clean, tidy and in good

The Reverend Stephen Gladstone, Rector of Hawarden (1872–1904), in charge of Buckley until 1874.

time with their home lessons prepared. They were to help the teachers 'by carefully watching the conduct of the children when at home, and assisting to train them in habits of truth, honesty, kindness, good manners, and to send them to Sunday school'.

The payment of school fees was a necessary and vital part of the school economy and there is frequent reference to them until they were finally abolished in 1891. In 1873 Mrs Gladstone paid the fees of four children 'their mother being ill'. In July 1877 it was noted at Lane End infants that 'Margaret Jones left this week parents too poor to pay for her. Others unable to come because their parents are out of work and cannot afford to pay for them'.

Some parents tried to dodge paying fees by removing their children to another school and in many cases parents were prosecuted. In 1887 children were taken from Bistre National School, 'Two boys left the school for the Board School owing to non-payment of a standing bill for school fees'.

It is notable that when the school fees were abolished in 1891 some schools introduced savings schemes; the vicar, the Reverend W. Dampier, started one at St Matthew's, and a penny bank was set up at Bistre National School.

Gradually attendance officers began to enforce the regular presence at school of all children of required age, up to eleven years in 1893, twelve in 1899 and fourteen in 1918. Sometimes poor attendance was seasonal as in September 1882 'owing to gleaning and many boys having gone to Mold with the 'Blue Ribbon Army' (a temperance organisation). Absence at other times was 'owing to illness, and want of shoes,' in the winter of 1885, and in 1893 due 'to sickness and picking coal'. But there were other reasons. 'A number of boys were late and overslept owing to staying out too late at night at the hobby horses' in July 1920. Conditions during the great coal strike in the summer of 1926 made the absence of some children unavoidable when some 'had no boots'. By contrast, in the same year, two boys at St Matthew's, Edward Bellis and Walter Jones were presented with watches, for eight years perfect attendance.

In the nineteenth century school attendance was often interrupted by epidemics. Children were debarred from school if there was a case of smallpox in the family. In the summer of 1871 several boys were absent from St Matthew's and a girl was told to 'remain away a little while until her sister recovered'. Two children died of scarlet fever in 1880 when Bistre Board infants was closed in April, and at St Matthew's, infant scholars returned late to school in January 1888, because 'fever is still prevalent in some parts of Buckley. Mr Jones, the organist sent some oranges to be distributed among the children'. In May measles devastated the Board School with as many as 250-260 of the three departments away'. The Infants' department at Bistre National school was closed for six weeks in the winter of 1907–8 because of an epidemic of whooping cough. All the schools suffered in the Influenza pandemic in 1918–9 with a few fatalities.

Over the years children met with accidents, some of them fatal. In 1889 'the Revd W. Dampier cautioned the boys against the habit of riding on the trucks on the line, James Shone having had his arm cut off in jumping from one last night'. In June 1898 John Rob Croft, a Standard 1 boy of St Matthew's 'got his leg drawn into a wheel at Sandycroft Colliery on Tuesday at noon. He died in Mold Cottage Hospital at 9.30 the same evening'. In 1902 'Charles and William Dolby were sent home as their brother, an infant, was killed at the Church Road, siding gates on his way to school'. Another St Matthew's Standard 2 boy, John Morris Jones, 'was killed by a traction engine on Wednesday evening. He was riding under the waggon and fell off under the wheel, being killed instantaneously'. The report concluded rather despairingly that 'the boys have many times been cautioned about this'. Some schoolboys did possess courage and resource. This was shown in 1920 when the vicar of St Matthew's 'presented a framed testimonial from the Royal Humane Society to Dennis Hobson for saving the life of Dennis Jones in September 1919 in Catherall's Clay Pit'.

Due to large classes and pressure on teachers to prepare for inspection a regime of discipline was enforced which may seem harsh by to-day's standards.

The first examples are from St Matthew's schools in 1863–5:

Some little children naughty in Church made them stand on the form for an hour, punished a girl for blotting her copy book, caned a girl for losing her place in reading, ordered the late comers should sweep the school, two boys fighting after school flogged them severely, but few boys attended church gave them 40 lines, punished a girl for refusing to sweep, gave Margaret Teggin 50 lines to write on her slate for pulling the brush lead off purposely.

In the 1880s, infants at St Matthew's were 'put into the dark space under the gallery where the school cleaning utensils were kept'. There was more drastic punishment for truancy. In 1879 it was recorded at the Board School 'The attendance very much improved this week owing to action of the Board sending away a boy on the Training ship 'Clio' for irregular attendance. Many come to School since, who often absconded themselves'.

HMIs were quick to report any irregularity in punishment and recorded their views in the logbook. At Bistre National School in 1882, there is a severe criticism of the head master, Mr Cockcroft:

Both tone & order were indifferent, and it is with grave hesitation that I recommend a grant for Discipline: in my opinion the master is a bad disciplinarian: when I entered school just after nine a.m. my ears were saluted with a series of whacks and my eyes were grieved with the sight of a row of writhing hands and faces; upon enquiry I found that the master had beaten the poor little things with a formidable piece of wood, because they were about a minute late for school: he did not stop as a just and human man would do, to enquire the cause of their unpunctuality: once before I have had occasion to speak to him for beating a child in my presence: I thus fully draw this painful subject to the managers attention that they put an immediate stop to the Masters' unreasonable and cruel treatment of the scholars treatment that does not secure either tone or good order in his school.

Cockcroft wrote a rebuttal of the Inspector's comments. He left the following April.

Until compulsory education parents could withdraw their children if they wished. In 1863 Samuel Griffiths was withdrawn to tend his mother's cow. Another girl left to look after the geese and Thomas Doughty, a more enterprising boy, was withdrawn to manage a co-operative store in 1864. In 1874 Jones the shoemaker took away his children from Bistre National School, 'on account of the Master having corrected one of them for disobedience'. In 1902, the mother of Jabez and Gerald Jones removed them from the same school 'at Gerald being told that his face was rather dirty'.

There were rare compensations. Jubilee day, the visit of a circus, the opening of a new chapel, Mold Fair, or the visit of the school photographer. In August 1863 the children of St Matthew's couldn't hide their excitement. 'School rather unruly chattering about the tea tomorrow – tea given to all the scholars and teachers in the Parish by Sir S. R. Glynne at the Castle'. It was the custom of St Matthew's boys to go to April Hill to gather daffodils, primroses, and moss to decorate the church for the Easter festival. In 1874 the girls left school early to go to Hawarden to see a 'Panorama on Dr Livingstone's travels'. With the advent of the

Bistre National School Group, c.1913. [Joe Chesters Collection, Buckley Library]

The Tyson family, c.1883. Three headmasters of St Matthews – James Tyson (1901–40), extreme left next to Joseph Tyson (1870–1901), and extreme right Joseph Ellis (1849–64).
[FRO PH 11/25]

motor bus school excursions usually visited the local beauty spots. The seaside being the territory for the Sunday school treat. In August 1923 older scholars from Bistre Council School were taken 'by charabancs to Mold accompanied by teachers, to visit the Arts and Crafts Exhibition organised by the National Eisteddfod'.

Educational progress was made during this period — 1847–1902 — through the dedication of teaching staffs during the final decades of the nineteenth century. At St Matthew's school the headship became a family affair. Joseph Ellis was head from 1836–64. His niece Sarah Price married Joseph Tyson, head 1871–1901, and their son James Tyson was head from 1901–40. Such continuity left its mark for good on the school. At Bistre Board School they were blessed with a succession of excellent headmasters who again provided continuity — Thomas Jones 1877–1913, Thomas Roberts 1913–29, and Glyn Williams 1929–54. It was said of Thomas Jones, certificated teacher of the 1st Class, that the tone of his school was 'simply excellent' and that the 'Master is evidently most anxious to do his work thoroughly well'. A reputation he maintained for thirty-six years.

One difficulty experienced by school inspectors and head teachers alike was the Buckley dialect. Dennis Griffiths made the point that Buckley:

… had grown from a small village to a town of about 6,000 inhabitants. In this conglomerate of people from many counties, distinct characteristics had emerged, and a local dialect comprising some of the many different contributing forms of speech of Staffordshire, Cheshire, Lancashire, with others combining with that of the early English settlers here and of the neighbouring Welsh folk, became the language generally spoken by Buckley people.[28] Griffiths' defined the Buckley dialect as its 'influence in broadening vowel sounds, and the flattening of diphthongs into long vowels. This peculiar mixture, he says, follows no fixed rules.[29]

The Commissioners of 1847 had spotted this: 'All the children (of Buckley) speak English, but with a strong provincial dialect which it would be as difficult to correct as it would be to teach English to Welsh children'.

The inspectors over the years had observed that in some ways Buckley children were different, although they found it difficult to say why. In 1869 the inspector said of St Matthew's boys 'taking into consideration the rough neighbourhood from which the boys come, I consider this school to be very efficient. They display a good deal of intelligence & have a very fair knowledge of words'. The impression made by the girls two years later was not as favourable. 'The girls are making satisfactory progress. They are still a little dull but this may be owing to the locality and not to any fault in the teaching'. The government report of 1876 remarked of St Matthew's that 'the spelling throughout is very defective: this is probably owing in part to the very peculiar pronunciation in vogue in this locality'. The Inspector of Bistre National School in 1879 was more hopeful when he wrote that 'The reading of the upper standard should receive greater attention. The Buckley dialect is, no doubt, a difficult one to contend with; but, I think, if the Master or a Manager read by way of example for them that even the reading of Buckley children would be improved'. Things didn't improve and Thomas Jones wrote despairingly in 1885 that 'Spelling requires as much attention as all other subjects put together. Provincialism is so strong and so peculiar that it is almost an impossibility to cure it'. The dialect persisted in school until the outbreak of the Second World War as Mr Derek Owen observed. 'I returned briefly to St Matthew's to help out in July 1947, and what struck me most about this return was that the dialect had disappeared from the schoolyard in such a short time. To speak any other way in my day as a pupil was heresy'.

By the end of the nineteenth century the Buckley schools could no longer cope with the rising birth rate, the extended school life of the pupil brought about by compulsory education, two increases in the higher school leaving age, and the creation of standard 7 in 1882. It so happened that the oldest buildings, those of the St Matthew's schools, were in the major growth area in what was to become a new urban district in 1897. What made the problem more difficult was the voluntary foundation of these schools. Any cost of enlargement was the responsibility of their managers. Furthermore the money had to be found in a political climate which was antagonistic towards the sectarian education provided by the representatives of the Established Church. It says much for the determination, perseverance, and generosity of the vicar, Canon Harry Drew, that he carried through a successful building programme, a great deal of which was paid for by his wife and himself.

The building programme of Harry Drew was undertaken from the beginning of his incumbency in 1897. Most of the work was completed by August 1899 with other minor additions made by 1903. The major work was at St Matthew's boys' and girls' schools. Necessary work was done at Lane End infants when in 1901 a new classroom was provided. The building of a head teacher's house for St Matthew's schools and the enlargement of a classroom at St Matthew's infants were paid for by private gifts.

Alfred George Edwards, Bishop of St Asaph, reopened the newly renovated St Matthew's schools on 26 August 1899. The newspapers gave a full account of the history of the undertaking. Harry Drew reported that additional accommodation was needed because of the demands of the Education Department. In response he called a meeting of ratepayers in July 1897 to consider the matter. They concluded that a sum of around £600 would meet the cost to provide educational facilities for every child in the ecclesiastical parish of Buckley and proposed to raise this sum by means of a voluntary rate of 1s. and donations. Drew continued by recounting that in the middle of their preparations to meet this demand:

… something like a bombshell fell into their midst, in the shape of an intimation that the Education Department were suggesting to the Local Government Board that as Buckley and Bistre were being formed into an urban district, they should also be united for educational purposes. This meant that, though Buckley was prepared to provide all educational facilities for its children, it was about to be put under a board rate. The late Mr Gladstone took special interest in the subject. He felt that the suggestion of pushing the parish into a board district when it was prepared to do its duty was contravening the spirit and the intention of the Education Act of 1870, and he went personally into it and wrote the Duke of Devonshire a letter stating that he felt that it was a matter which required his personal examination. Within about ten

St Matthew's School House, 1906.
[Buckley Society Magazine]

days of sending the letter, they received a formal communication from the Education Department that there would be no change in the educational position of the parish. That was the last great service Mr Gladstone did for Buckley parish and it was a solid and sober fact that they would not be as they were today if he had not taken up the cudgels on their behalf.[30]

The interior of the schools was thoroughly renovated and all fittings and desks renewed. The major work was the addition of two classrooms, both measuring 21 ft x 20 ft, at each end of the building, making its total length 126 ft. The infant school was similarly enlarged. Other improvements included the enlargement of the cloakrooms, new outbuildings and drainage systems to four schools etc.[31] The Hawarden trustees gave land valued at £59 10s. which enabled the playgrounds to be extended.

The important achievement was that extra 126 school places had been created — from 497 to 623. But in reality this was not enough. Even in 1899 there were 639 children on the school register, although this was made feasible by an average attendance of 511. Over the next ten years these figures were to rise to registrations of 721 and average attendance of 662, thus far outstripping the increased capacity by at least an extra classroom.[32]

The work completed in August 1899 cost £1,518 19s. 11d. This included a donation of £325 by Harry Drew, £200 from Messrs Watkinson and Sons; grants of £50 from the National Society and £85 from the diocese, £26 5s. from the late Mr Gladstone and the proceeds from a voluntary rate of 1s., levied twice.

At the end of the ceremonies the vicarage grounds were thrown open from five to eight o'clock, and the band of the 1st Flintshire Royal Engineer Volunteers and the Royal Buckley Town Band played airs and selections. Dancing took place from six to eight o'clock.[33]

The Education Act of 1902 marked the beginning of a new phase in elementary education which was to last until the Butler Act of 1944. The Act brought about a complete reorganisation of Education. School boards were abolished, counties and county boroughs becoming the authorities for elementary, secondary and technical education; the current expenses from voluntary schools were met from the rates; undenominational teaching in 'provided' (ex-board) schools remained. The schools governed by the local authorities were widely known as council schools, and the church, or voluntary schools, as aided schools. In Wales the nonconformists objected most strongly to the Act refusing to administer it for awhile on the grounds that they objected to paying for sectarian education out of the rates. By the Act the local authorities had to help maintain the church schools and were responsible for paying teacher's salaries and helping to keep the buildings in good repair. The church schools, however, were allowed to give their own religious teaching, and appoint the majority of the managers. On the other hand local authority inspectors were permitted to enter voluntary schools and report to the education committee.

The revolt of the Welsh Nonconformists lasted three years. The Welsh local authorities refused to administer the Act and threatened to confiscate Church schools and bring them into the state system. In the end a compromise was reached with the establishment of a Welsh department of the Board of Education and in 1907 the Act became fully effective in Wales.

The architect of the 1902 Act, often called the Balfour Act, was Robert Morant, a civil servant. He introduced an elementary school code which brought forth advances in education. He wrote: 'The purpose of the Public Elementary School is to form and strengthen the character and to develop the intelligence of the children entrusted to it, and to make the best use of the school years available, in assisting both girls and boys, according to their different needs, to fit themselves, practically as well as intellectually, for the work of life'.[34] Morant followed this up by issuing a Blue Book, a handbook of suggestions for teachers in public elementary schools. This made clear 'that uniformity of practice throughout such schools was not desirable, but rather that each teacher should think for himself and work at his own methods according to the schools' conditions and requirements. Above all the teacher should know and sympathize with the children he was teaching. The entire process of education was viewed as a 'partnership for the acquisition of knowledge'. Facts were not to be dealt with in isolation but in relation to the total experience of the child.

The 1902 code led to an expansion in the school curriculum. In addition to the basic subjects there was special provision for handicrafts, observation lessons and nature study, including the teaching of gardening; geography, history, music, hygiene and physical training, together with cookery, laundry work, housewifery, and moral instruction given both directly and indirectly, besides providing for the teaching of special subjects suited to the particular locality.

It is against this detailed background to the new code that we may appreciate the significant developments which took place in the Buckley elementary schools during this phase and the dedication of some remarkable teachers.

This 'partnership for the acquisition of knowledge', the physical, intellectual, and moral development of the child was a continuing dialogue between the L.E.A. inspectors, the statuary provisions made by the local education committee, and the methods employed by the school staff. The logbooks give ample evidence of this.

In June 1908 Flintshire County Council decided to appoint a medical officer of health to carry out the work of medical inspection of school children. The schools received his first report in 1910 when the teachers' attention was drawn specifically to insufficient feeding, ventilation and cleanliness of schools. In November 1913 the County made arrangements for a school dental service. This was a mobile service operating from nine centres at which the dentist would be located for several weeks, moving from place to place, with his 'portable apparatus'. Buckley was one of the centres. It was proposed to make a charge of 1s. per child per annum for extractions, fillings, or any other work.[35]

Organised games were allowed in school hours from 1901. In many cases physical training replaced the drill, marching, and the use of dumb bells. In 1888, Vicar Dampier had presented St Matthew's Infants 'with 40 pairs of musical dumb bells for the use of class I and II for their drill'. St Matthew's boys quickly took advantage of organised games and 'a lesson on Football was given to the first class on 27 September 1901 by W. Lindop' and on 1 November there was an 'Inter Football Match between the Lane End and Pentre boys on Thursday afternoon at 4.20, with Lane End the winners'. Other lessons were delayed because of bad weather for a month until the eve of a game between the school team and Buckley Athletic Club. In May 1902 the school cricket club came into being. To the delight of all Buckley schoolboys they were to continue. In the 1930s some of the boys received the honour of playing for their country. In 1931 Raymond Dunn from St Matthew's represented the Welsh schoolboys at soccer against the three home nations, and Alyn Hughes played against England in 1936. Swimming became popular in the 1930s and children attended classes at the new public baths. There were keen sporting rivalries between all Buckley schools in local and county competitions throughout these years.

In July 1908, gardening was another school subject promoted by the county council by means of a government grant. They left its introduction to the discretion of the managers. In June 1909, with this in mind, William Davies, head of Bistre Church School, paid a visit to Northop 'to see the scholars at work gardening'. Impressed, he returned to Bistre, gave each child a few potatoes to plant and arranged classes on Tuesday and Friday afternoons from then onwards. For this action he was complimented by the HMI in September 1910, who noted that 'a plot of ground contiguous to the school, has been given to the boys for gardening, which affords an excellent training for hand & eye under more natural conditions than those which prevail in the classroom'. James Tyson, head of St Matthew's, sought higher advice, and received a parcel of botanical specimens from the director of the Royal Kew Gardens. He employed his boys in maintaining the school grounds and flowerbeds.

With the school leaving age at 13 years, to be raised to 14 years in 1918, it was recognised that senior elementary pupils should receive instruction in domestic subjects. From 1908 onwards boys and girls were sent from their Buckley schools in selected numbers. The Bistre children attended a centre in

St Matthew's Football Team, 1933.
[FRO PH/11/446]

*William Davies, Head of Bistre Church
School and church organist.*
[Buckley Library]

Mold and those from Buckley went to Hawarden. The subjects taught were cookery, handicraft, and woodwork. In 1913 it was reported from the manual training centre in Hawarden that the:

… classes are drawn from Buckley, Ewloe Green and Hawarden and although the boys have very much in common with Shotton boys, I think circumstances or environment affect them not a little, as they are somewhat more boisterous for one thing: only once however was horseplay attempted. There are some exceedingly bright boys in all the classes. When dealing with the growing tree, where grown and from whence shipped, the knowledge of chemistry, geography, and history acquired in school is given free play.[36]

In 1922 a centre for instruction was established in Mill Lane for groups of senior Buckley elementary boys and girls who received instruction in domestic and manual training subjects. In 1937 this building was considered unsuitable after a survey undertaken on behalf of the Board of Education:

The room here is most unsatisfactory, being dark and dirty with a low ceiling. No painting or distempering has been done during 16 years the room has been used as a Centre so its condition may be imagined. As a site has been acquired for a Central School, Domestic Science and Handicraft rooms could be erected in advance of the rest of the School for the present Domestic Science room in Buckley is equally as unsuitable as the Handicraft Room.[37]

The County Council, however, sought to make improvements to its schools in Buckley in spite of economic difficulties. Here are two examples taken from the reports of Bistre Council school. The first was reported by Lewis Thomas, the school correspondent in 1923. The school numbers were beginning to diminish and the number of children registered in the three departments were 137 boys, 161 girls, and 101 infants. Some improvements had been made to the building by adding a porch and inserting a door to give the girls direct access from the school yard to their classroom. This arrangement was sufficient to create space enough for a classroom accommodating 40 pupils. Large windows were inserted to provide more daylight and the surface of the playgrounds improved. It was noted that 'in some of the rooms in the permanent premises the floors are very thin and shaky'.

The HMI's report in 1941 on the girls' department shows the teachers doing excellent work in premises which had been little changed in sixty-four years:

This department, one of three opened in 1877, on the same site, contains four class rooms, three being formed by the partitioning of the main room. The accommodation in all four classrooms is restricted, and there is neither corridor nor teachers' room. A new block of water-flushed lavatories was erected some four years ago; and at an earlier date the lighting in two rooms was improved by increasing window space. The ventilation cannot be considered satisfactory. Heating is by hot water pipes and open fires. Electric light and running water are laid on. A field opposite the school owned by the Authority is used for organised games. Playground space is seriously restricted. The staff consists of a head teacher, appointed in 1911, and three uncertificated assistants, and one supplementary assistant.

On the day of the inspection there were 109 pupils on books. There were 115 pupils on the register ten years ago, so the decrease has been small, in spite of the fact that the migration from the town on account of the closing of certain local industries has tended to reduce the population.

The teaching throughout the school is sound and thorough. Good methods are in use in the lower classes where the foundational work is well laid. Further up the school the introduction of modern methods in some activities has been successfully accomplished, though often carried out in the face of many difficulties inherent in an old and unsatisfactory building. These difficulties have not been made any lighter by the absence of trained certificated teachers among the assistant staff. The interest of the head teacher has especially been centred

The staff of Buckley Board Infants School, 1920s. Back L–R: Florrie Jones, Freda Silver. Front: ? Millington, Emma Evans, Gwen Lewis. [Buckley Society Archive]

around the physical welfare of the girls. Outdoor games, country dancing, swimming, instruction in hygiene and in first aid have been prominent features of the work, and the School has won in competition more than the normal share of County trophies for athletics of various types. An excellent tone prevails within and without the school; and the turnout of the girls is commendable. It is obvious that the co-operation of the parents has contributed largely to the achievement of this result.

The head teacher [Mabel E. Ollive, from 1911–41] resigns her appointment at the end of the present term on her approaching marriage. She has maintained a tradition of sound work and hard play: her deep concern in all that affects the welfare of the pupils and her tact in directing and encouraging the efforts of her staff have been unremitting. Signed P.A. Lewis, HMI, June 27 1941.

St Matthew's Schools, in spite of the programme of enlargement and renovation, were, as we have seen, unable to cope with the growth of numbers, especially with the raising of the school leaving age to 14 years. Opportunity arose for them to remedy the situation after the First World War when former army huts from Kinmel Camp were being disposed of. One of these was called 'the Gladstone hut' and was given as a memorial by Henry Gladstone and his wife in 1920.

The school report, dated 12 April 1923, recorded that 'The girls have been fortunate in securing the sole use of a hut measuring about 40 feet by 20 feet and equipped to accommodate a large class of senior pupils'. A few weeks later it was noted in the logbook: '1923 May 11th The Hd Teacher & Mr W. E. Roberts visited Kinmel Camp on Tuesday to inspect the Army Huts. They purchased one to supply extra accommodation'. This was soon delivered to the boys' department and by the beginning of July classes were being held there. 'July 6 Classes have been taken in the Hut (oral lessons) during the week. The boys have creosoted the Hut this week & and are commencing painting the windows. The hut was erected in the field near the boys' playground.'

Mr Derek Owens, a pupil at St Matthew's from 1931 onwards, remembers being taught there:

For Standard 4 we moved to a hut in the yard and the formidable Miss Edith Jones. We learned a lot from her, because inattention was not possible. She could hear the faintest whisper from the other end of the room even with her back turned. However I always looked forward to Friday afternoon, for after playtime she would read Rudyard Kipling's stories to us. Also in the hut was Standard 5, the 'scholarship class' taught by Mr Bob Peters. Last thing every Friday afternoon we had a fifty word-spelling test – very different from the Kipling stories! I well remember the Friday before we sat the scholarship examination we had a bumper test of 250 words.

In February 1929 during an exceptionally cold spell, the ink was frozen in the girls' hut, and they took it in turns to have drill and games there. Forty of the elder girls were taken for a sharp walk around the Common and two classes were sent for half an hour to the Reservoir on the Common for sliding.

There were plenty of interesting diversions created by imaginative teachers and they were given more scope by the introduction of extra curricula activities and visits to the local cinema.

At the end of the First World War the Welsh Department of Education promoted improvements of musical education under the guidance of the National Council of Music. Outstanding in the memories of North Wales scholars in the late 1920s and 30s were the visits of the Bangor Trio. The logbook of Bistre Council School noted '1929 May 7 Standards 5-7 were taken from School at 10.20 to a Concert organised by the Bangor Trio at the Palace Cinema, and was quite successful.'

Music was fostered through the inspiration of Mr Tom Roberts, head teacher, 1913–29, who made an outstanding contribution as an accompanist in Buckley. When he left the school he was presented with a mahogany music cabinet. In July 1933 the school choir won the Buckley Co-operative Society's shield for juvenile choirs with the test piece *Nymphs and Shepherds* by Purcell. The school built up a reputation for excellence. In December 1936, the HMI took some of the school's musical instruments to an exhibition in South Wales and in April 1937 a party of boys accompanied him to Colwyn Bay Central School to give a percussion band demonstration to Denbighshire teachers, the chief inspector and HMIs. On 1 May 1944 the school was closed for a one-day music course. Amongst those present was Mr Tom Roberts, who by this time was Assistant Director of Education for Flintshire.

In February 1933, during the Depression, soup was supplied for a halfpenny to children of unemployed men. Fifty-three girls from St Matthew's received nourishment by this means.

From 1934 onwards each child was able to buy milk at the cost of a halfpenny a day supplied through the Flintshire Farmers Milk Marketing Scheme. Mr Derek Owens remembered with affection:

> Our head master was Mr Tyson, affectionately known by the boys as 'Jimmy'. He was kindly man and respected by us, perhaps because of the stick, which I personally experienced often for being late. I can still see him clearly in my mind's eye, and remember being fascinated by his beautiful gold watch chain. In cold weather he would allow us to put our milk bottles inside the big fireguard so that the chill would be off the milk by playtime. On Friday afternoon he also took us in music lessons where we learnt all the old folk songs. If we were prepared to sing a solo, we were allowed to go home early.

It was not until September 1942 that a school meals service was operating at Bistre Council School when '147 availed themselves of the opportunity to partake of mid day meal'.

Before we leave this review of elementary education in Buckley, we may see the way in which a high standard of education was give to Buckley children in the period up to the Second World War by examining the career of Miss Emily Jones, head teacher of St Matthew's Girls, 1907–38.

Mr Tom Roberts Head Teacher Bistre Council School (1913–29), later Deputy Director of Education for Flintshire. A distinguished musician.
[Buckley Society Archive]

The love and devotion which Emily Jones had for St Matthew's school grew in intensity over the sixty-three years she was acquainted with it as scholar and teacher. Entering the infant school at the age of four in 1875, she eventually retired at the age of sixty-seven in 1938. For the thirty-one years she was head mistress of the girl's school it might as well be said that she was married to her profession. She belonged to that era in which married women had to retire if they entered into what were seen as the bonds of matrimony. But she achieved great satisfaction from the host of young girls whose lives she shaped by her motherly care, enthusiastic teaching, and exacting standards. They were her girls and she sent them into life when the time came inspired by her curious and inquisitive quest for knowledge. By her teaching their intelligence was well tried, and their spirits enlivened by a sense of justice and patriotism. When the time came for them to leave school they were well equipped to be good housewives. None could forget her expression of praise; 'I am an excellent Buckley Brick'. She was the potter who fashioned them as perfectly as possible during the long school years. She was their surrogate parent. This claim is made on the evidence of the girls' school logbook.

Emily Jones succeeded Annie Jacobs who died suddenly in 1907. After a formative period of teaching in Bangor and London, Miss Jones returned to St Matthew's a few months before Miss Jacobs died. She was appointed head mistress in October. Miss Emily Jones began teaching at St Matthew's as a pupil teacher under Mr Joseph Tyson, and was appointed by Mr James Tyson, who succeeded his father in 1901 and remained until he retired in 1940.

She soon began to make her mark. After a visit lasting over three days in February 1912, Mr W. Williams HMI wrote the following report:

> This department has an elevating tone: the demeanour of the Girls and their neat personal appearance reflect

great credit upon the Head Mistress. Much originality has been shown in devising, and carrying out, a scheme of work containing a course of simple practical lessons in Combined Domestic subjects, using merely the open fire and a couple of gas jets. Directions are given as to the proper arrangement of the table, at which the children sometimes sit down to partake of the food they have cooked and the teacher takes the opportunity of instructing the pupils as to their behaviour. The whole proceeding from beginning to end cannot fail to exercise a salutary influence over the girls. A large doll, whose pretty cot consists of a large banana box tastefully decorated by the pupils themselves, is used to illustrate the points raised in the lesson on 'Nursing and Minding the baby'. About 37 very clear drawings in connection with this course have been prepared by the Teacher. At the time of inspection a demonstration lesson in working flannels, linen, and calico was given; the utensils were of the simple and inexpensive kind used in the homes of the scholars. All the Domestic Exercises are correlated with each other subject as Arithmetic, Composition, Drawing, Hygiene and Reading, in a manner beneficial to the general educational efficiency of the school. I have no doubt but that this Domestic Course properly handled will prove not only intellectually stimulating, but also practically very useful to the scholars.

Mr James Tyson, Headmaster St Matthew's School (1901–40). [FRO PH/11/21]

In connection with the History instruction of the younger scholars, the children were dressed up to represent the historical characters. The subject of the lesson taken at the inspection visit, was 'Caractacus captured and afterwards appearing as a prisoner before the Roman Emperor'. The episode was dramatised and the pupils had been trained to speak their parts in a natural tone of voice and in a manner which was in keeping with the spirit of the lesson. There is a healthy desire to work hard in the school, which is conducted with much skill and enterprise.

Year after year there were glowing reports. Amongst the HMI's comment in 1920 were:

The scheme of instruction mapped out for this department is one of the most comprehensive courses in the county. The course has a strong domestic bias, as well as sound literary side.

Hand and eye work enters into the instruction in the form of cardboard modelling, paper folding, modelling with plasticene, brushwork, the making of a baby's bath, all of which add interest and attractiveness to the ordinary methods of teaching and training girls.

The scope of the instruction and the methods employed generally deserve the highest commendation. The Head Teacher is enterprising and resourceful and determined to keep abreast of modern requirements.

Her patriotism was shown on numerous occasions. In the observance of Empire Day, on 24 May, Queen Victoria's birthday. In 1909, the girls, wearing coloured bonnets, formed the Union Jack and marching in single file, saluted the flag, the Union Jack, sang the Welsh national anthem in Welsh and English, and recited Rudyard Kipling's *Lest we forget*. For the celebration of St David's day, mention was made of David Lloyd George, and the vicar kindly lent his toy Red Dragon! In 1918 the implications of the Royal Assent being given to the Act to grant votes for women was explained to the girls. The girls were taught how to make porridge to encourage them to eat it during the winter months. In 1927, during school hours, she took the elder girls to her house at 3.30 p m to listen 'to a wireless lecture on cutting out.' The patterns of a girls school outfit were laid on a table and the girls followed the instructions given. She had taken them a few weeks earlier 'to look over two of the finished Council Houses at Belmont'. She described 5 February 1932 as a red-letter day, with the entry in the logbook: 'The School Library was started to day. The new books were bought with the 5% bonus granted by the LEA, on the amount of savings last year. The second-hand books were begged from friends'.

Nothing was too much trouble for Emily Jones if it benefited her girls. In 1930 two girls were encouraged to paint designs suitable for a cup, which were sent 'to the Josiah Wedgwood pottery as ideas of a clean, cheery, and free design '. In response 'the Company unexpectedly translated the designs in blue enamel on to china cups and sent a cup and saucer for each designer'. In 1935 she entered the girls' compositions (essays) into a competition organised by Cadbury's with each of the seventeen entrants receiving 'a half pound box of Princess Elizabeth chocolates'. A more arduous exercise was her efforts to provide the girls with crepe-rubber plimsolls from Woolworth's for folk dancing and physical training. The shoes were reduced to sixpence a pair. To collect 98 pairs she went to Chester and all over North Wales, and Lewis stores Liverpool, on shopping expeditions which lasted from September 1934 to March 1935.

The standard of elementary education had advanced a long way since the beginning of the nineteenth century. It was to be reshaped after the Butler Act of 1944 when new primary and secondary schools were built to mark the next step forward. That story is told later in the book.

Notes

1. Lord Sandon's Act (1876) and A. J. Mundella's Act (1880) made elementary education compulsory; in 1891 it was made virtually free.
2. Annual government grants had been given to build schools from 1833 onwards to both Anglicans and Nonconformists.
3. T. W. Pritchard, *A History of the Old Parish of Hawarden*, p. 116f.
4. *Chester Chronicle*, 6/1/1815.
5. Cropper, pp. 86–7. Joseph Lancaster (1778–1838), a Quaker, pioneer educationalist. At his schools at Borough Road, London, he developed a system of education based on the monitorial system of instructing classes. Teachers taught older children (monitors) who then passed on their knowledge to the other pupils. It was an effective and cheap method of instruction. Lancaster imparted non-doctrinal, unsectarian teaching of religion — no creeds — the holy scriptures were the only textbook. This was favoured by nonconformists and sponsored by the British Schools Society founded 1808. After 1833 they received government grants. At first they had few purpose built schools and met in chapel buildings.
6. Cropper, p. 89.
7. Quoted from K. Lloyd Gruffydd, 'The Establishment of full-time Education for Buckley's Nonconformist children', *Buckley*, 6.
8. ibid, a translation of H. Jones 'Hanes ysgol yr undeb yn Buckley', *Y Drysorfa*, cxlviii, (1843), p. 177.
9. *Chester Chronicle*, 13/3/1846.
10. *Chester Chronicle*, 19/9/1817.
11. Cropper, p. 88.
12. Richard Willett, *A Memoir of Hawarden Parish* (Chester, 1822), pp. 122–32.
13. FRO D/DM/1079.
14. Pritchard, op cit, p.167.
15. This was reciting the usual formula.
16. *Instructions Committee of Council on Education*, October 1st, 1846. J. P. Kay Shuttleworth, Secretary.
17. The report is to be found in *The Reports of the Commissioners of Enquiry into State Education in North Wales*, 1847, Part III, pp.94–5, 103–4, 226. It is reproduced by J. Clifford Jones in, 'A history of the Schools and Education in Buckley', *Flintshire Historical Society Publications*, vol. 15.
18. See fn 5.
19. See fn 5.
20. For Short's reputation as a builder of schools see D. R. Thomas, op cit, vol. 1, p. 175 and p. 190.
21. These examples are taken from Bishop Short's Ms Book St Asaph Coll., Nat. Lib. Wales.
22. *Chester Courant*, 18/4/1849.
23. He did work at St Deiniol's Church, Hawarden, and designed the church and school of the Holy Epiphany, Saltney, for the Glynnes in 1855.
24. FRO E/SB/11/9-11.
25. 1910 school room, approx. 50 ft x 20 ft; classroom, 24 ft x 20 ft: 1924, rm 1. 20 ft x 20 ft, rm 2 30 ft x 20 ft. babies room 24 ft x 20 ft.
26. The account below depends on extracts from the 18 logbooks of Buckley and Bistre schools in the FRO.
27. For information on the School Board see *Chester Chronicle*, 12/2/1878, 9/3/1878. 25/7/1881, 7/10/1882.
28. Dennis Griffiths, *Out of this Clay* (Gee and Son Ltd, Denbigh, 1960).
29. ibid, p. 33, and following and Dennis Griffiths, *Talk of my Town*, 1969.
30. *County Herald*, 1/9/1899.
31. St M's — boys, girls, and infants, and Lane End.

32. FRO P/11/1/50.
33. *Chester Chronicle*, 2/9/1899.
34. Quoted in H. C. Barnard, *A History of English Education from 1760* (Univ. London Press, 1947), p.217.
35. FRO FC/2/14.
36. FRO FC/2/14 Report, 30 July 1913.
37. FRO FC/2/38 Building sub committee, 14 July 1937.

Chapter 13
Buckley Town, 1897–1950s

Introduction

This section outlines the main themes of life in Buckley in the twentieth century, from the time it became 'Buckley Town' in 1897, a much friendlier civic description than that of urban district council. Having discussed the major themes of the early history of our area, its industry, religion and education, we begin to explore how Buckley was affected by the major events which challenged the nation: Buckley in the years of war and peace. A feature of the period was its patriotism. The nation witnessed the last brilliant display of imperialism and empire when Britain occupied a position on the world stage as a major power. The Buckley Volunteers took part in a colonial war, fighting against the Boers in South Africa at the beginning of the period. In the First World War, the Great War of 1914–18, over 600 men from the district saw military service in all the main theatres of war — the Western Front, Gallipoli, and Palestine. Of these, over 140 were killed and others were injured.[1] In the Second World War, which began just over twenty years later, in 1939, it was the turn of the next generation to make the supreme sacrifice. These deaths scarred the memory of the community and brought a burden of grief and hardship which was added to the suffering experienced in the Great Depression of the late 1920s and early 1930s.

Events like the Gold and Diamond Jubilees of Queen Victoria, the coronations of Edward VII, George V, George VI, and the Silver Jubilee of George V, were occasions of carefully planned celebrations in which the whole community rejoiced. Imperial pageantry evoked the spirit of patriotism and brought colour and romance to lighten the drabness of existence.

The people of Buckley knew how to occupy their leisure time, which is also described in this section. Between the wars the general population became hooked on a new drug, the cinema, which guaranteed a quick escape route into fantasy. Hollywood brought a new culture to Buckley, which the people re-cycled to their own advantage. The Buckley pantomime was born. The town produced its own glamour, burlesque and starlets of all ages. It was the town's week of celebration, pride and opportunity to raise money for hospitals. The pantomime joined the Jubilee as an annual ritual, giving Buckley its unique identity. Football and cricket teams played their part in bringing a sense of pride and belonging to both participants and spectators.

Local government, the role Buckley Urban District played in creating the infra-

The Co-operative Society Main Street Buckley c.1910. [Buckley Society Archive]

BUCKLEY is a large and extensive village composed of portions of the townships of Buckley, Bistre, and Argoed, in Mold parish, and Pentrobin and Ewloe, in Hawarden parish. It is situated about 3½ miles from Mold, 2½ from Hawarden, 6 miles from Flint, and is a station on the Wrexham, Mold, and Connah's Quay railway. The principal business here is the manufacture of fire-bricks, tiles, drain-pipes, chimney tops, troughs, and almost any kind of clay goods. Many of the works being very extensive, and having an unlimited supply of clay, they are able to produce very large quantities of goods. Buckley is famed for its Crown earthenware, which are of a special class of pottery ware. The above, with the coal mines in the district, affords employment to a large and increasing population.

Post Office, Joseph Catherall, postmaster. Letters are delivered at 7 a.m., and despatched at 7-30 p.m.

Parish Church (St. Emanuel), Rev. J. M. Evans, rector
St. Matthew's Church, Rev. Wm. Dampier, vicar
Mission Church, Rev. J. M. Evans
Baptist Chapel (English), Rev. D. Davies
Calvinistic Methodist (Welsh), Rev. G. Jones
Congregational Chapel
Methodist Chapel, Bistre
Presbyterian Chapel, Rev. W. Hobley
Primitive Methodist Chapel (Tabernacle)
Wesleyan Chapel (English), The Square
Board School (Boys), Thomas Jones, master
Ditto (Girls), Mrs. M. Jones, mistress
Infant School, Miss Ashton, mistress
National School, Mr. Hixton, master
Buckley Institute and Reading Room, Lane End
Buckley Liberal Association, E. Roberts, secretary
Police Station, Sergt. Thomas Jones
Buckley Station, John Newnes, station-master

PRIVATE RESIDENTS.

Dampier Rev. Wm. Vicarage
Davies Rev. D. South Villas
—— Rev. Joseph, c.c. Daylight villas
Evans Rev. J. M. Rectory
Gregory Mr. John B. Aber house
Hobley Rev. William
Jenkinson Rev. Geo. The Manse
Jones Rev. Geo. Bistre cottage
Low Dr. Ll. M. Roseneath
Wainwright Mr. John
Williams Dr. J. Main st

TRADERS AND OTHERS.

Ashton Richard & Co. brick & tile manufacturers
Aston Charles, butcher
Aston Elizabeth, *Blue Bell Tavern*
Beavan William, *Feathers Tavern*
Beck Joseph, *Rose and Thistle*, blacksmith
Birkhill Joseph, hairdresser
Birks Robert, shopkeeper
Brassan James, general dealer, Main st [Lane end
Brookfield Charles, *Bull Tavern*,

Buckley Brick & Tile Co. Limited, Jhn. M. Gibson, secretary (postal address—Buckley, via Chester), *See advertisement, page 128*
Castle Fire Brick Co. Limited, G. H. Alletson, manager.
Catherwall & Co. fire brick & tile manufacturers, Postal address, Buckley *via* Chester. Telegraphic address—Fire Brick, Buckley—*See advertisement, p.126*
—— Joseph, ironmonger and stationer, Post office

BUCKLEY—Continued.

Clarke John, draper, Manchester house [st
Connor George, accountant, Main
Cropper Thomas, bookseller, newsagent, Lane end
Co-operative Stores, Geo. Barlow, manager
Davies John, draper and tailor
—— John, butcher
—— R. D. builder, contractor, timber merchant, undertaker, wheelwright, steam sawmill owner, Main st.—*see advertisement page 9* end
—— William, general dealer, Lane
Davison Charles & Co. fire, brick and tile manufacturers, Ewloe and Old Ewloe
Edwards E. boot and shoe maker
—— Edward, butcher
—— John, grocer, Main st
—— John Jones, grocer and draper, Bee hive
—— W. grocer, Mill lane
Ellis Latham, grocer, Bannel
—— Thomas, *Ship Tavern*
Fox John, tailor
German S. M. shopkeeper
Gittins John, *Black Horse Hotel* (tourist, family, commercial, and posting house), Main st
Gregory J. B. & Co. colliery proprietors
Griffiths James, baker
—— Joseph, grocer and baker, Daisy hill [Main st
—— Lydia, draper and grocer,
—— William, *Cross Keys Tavern*
Hancocks W. & Co. fire brick, tile, and pottery manufacturers
Hawkins Arthur, butcher, Main st
Hewitt Robert, *Albion Tavern*
Hughes Elizabeth, dressmaker, Daisy hill
—— Henry grocer, Liverpool house
—— Owen, general draper, outfitter, and house furnisher, Lane end.— *see advertisement, page 124*

Hughes William, *Black Lion Tavern*
Jones Edward and Alfred, earthenware manufacturers, Alltami pottery
—— Edwin, butcher, Main st
—— Griffith, boot and shoe maker
—— J. B. draper and outfitter, Lane end
—— Jabez, *Lion Tavern*
—— John, grocer, Main st
—— John, grocer and tobacconist, Main st
—— Richard, boot and shoe maker, Main st
—— Samuel, *Blue Anchor Tavern*
—— Thomas, grocer, Main st
—— William, refreshment rooms, Main st
—— William, painter, Lamb lane
—— William, draper and tailor, The Cross
Lamb Benjamin, draper, and boot and shoe dealer, Lane end
—— John, Prince of Wales tavern
Lewin G. & Co., grocers, corn and flour dealers, Lane end
Lewis Edward, shopkeeper, Main st
Lindop Thomas, grocer, Lane end
Miles F. tobacconist and dealer in patent medicines, Medical hall
Millington Thos. tailor, Daisy hill
Morton G. & W. boot and shoe manufacturers
Nixon Robert, *Cross Keys Tavern*, Lane end
North and South Buckley Brick and Tile Company, C. Benbow, manager
Owens Alfred, butcher, Main st
Paddon A. draper, outfitter, milliner and dressmaker, Lane end
Parry Edward & Sons, fire, brick, and tile manufacturers,
Parry John, boot and shoe maker, Lane end
Peake M. E. draper, Main st
Peake Mary, draper, dressmaker, Main rd [st
Peters Elizabeth, greengrocer, Main

Peters John, shopkeeper, Lane end
Powell I. & W. earthenware manufacturers (by new patent machinery), Ewloe pottery ; residence, Gwysaney view
Roberts Henry & Son, grocers and tea merchants
—— Joseph, grocer, Main st
—— Thomas, draper, milliner, Main st
—— William, tailor, Main st
Rogers John, butcher, Lane end
Rowlands Brothers, engineers, iron and brassfounders
—— Edward, grocer and china dealer, Daisy hill
—— Robert, grocer, Mill lane
Sandycroft Brick, Tile, and Colliery Company [lane
Sharratt J. furniture dealer, Lamb
—— Moses, earthenware manufacturer
Shone John, carrier, Lane end
Snath Thomas, fancy repository, stationer, agent to the Prudential Insurance Company
Swires J. clogger, Mill lane
Farrar John, *Wellington Inn*
Taylor Charles, earthenware manufacturer, Alltami
Watkinson George & Sons, colliery proprietors
Williams Mrs. —, *Glynne Arms*
—— Catherine, grocer, Daisy hill
—— Elizabeth, boot and shoe depôt, and fancy goods warehouse
—— John, brick and tile manufacturer, builder, contractor, timber merchant, undertaker and joiner ; and at Connahs Quay—*see advertisement, page 9*
—— R. & P. grocers, Old Stores
—— T. tea merchant, Brynteg
—— Thomas, grocer, Lane end
—— W. grocer, Main st
—— W. *Crown Inn* [end
Wright James, shopkeeper, Lane
Wynne Mary, milliner, dressmaker, Daisy hill

PUBLIC BUILDINGS:—Central Hall.
    Council Chambers, High Street, and Padeswood.
    Free Public Library.

RAILWAYS:—It has a station on the Chester and Denbigh line of the London & North Western Railway, and another on the Great Central Railway.

SITUATION:—In the south east of Flintshire, 2 miles east of Mold, and 11 miles north of Wrexham.

TRADE:—Mining and the manufacture of bricks tiles and coarse earthenware.

URBAN DISTRICT COUNCIL:—
    Clerk:—J. Griffiths.
    Collector & Surveyor:—E. Astbury.
    Medical Officer:—Dr. Fraser.

Albion Inn, Main st
Anglesea J, carriage proprietor, The Cross
Anglesea T, fish frier, Chester rd
Aston C. butcher, Chester rd
Barker R. chemist, the Cross
Beattie R J, boot maker, Lane Ends, Church rd
Beavan Bros., engineers, The Foundry
Beckett T & H. grocers, Chester rd
Bells Stores Ltd., grocers, Chester rd
Bellis T E. high class tailor, Lane End
Bishop's Drapery, Hosiery, Millinery & Art Needlework Stores, Lane. End. Agent for the Yorkshire Dye Works
Black Horse Hotel — J Gittins
Black Lion Inn, Main st—F Hughes
Blue Anchor, The Square
Blue Bell Inn, Chester rd
Booth W. baker, Daisy Hill
British Petroleum Co., Church rd
Buckley Brick & Tile Co., Ltd.
Buckley Collieries—G Watkinson and Son
Buckley Co-operative Stores Ltd, grocers and provision mchts. Main st
Buckley Gas Co. Ltd., Mount Pleasant
Buckley Meat Co., Chester rd
Bull Inn. Lane End—R Griffiths
BURKHILL G H, hairdresser, tobacconist, and newsagent, Main st
Burkhill W, hairdresser, Chester rd
Burrows P. fruiterer, 104 Mold rd
Castle Brick Works, Northop—J H Allettson
Catherall J. pork butcher, Church rd
Catheral & Co. Ltd. brick and tile manfrs
Catheral J. general hardware dlr, Post Office Shop
Chesters R. librarian and curator, Free Library
Chingwin R. painter, Lambs Lane
Coles J & M. drapers, Main st
Coles M. draper, Main st
Connah R. general dealer, Main st
Cosy Temperance Hotel—E Roberts, proprietor
Cropper and Jones. booksellers, printers, stationers,
Cross Keys Inn. Chester rd
Crown Vaults, Chester rd
Davies J. butcher, Lane End
Davies J R. confectioner & tobacconist, 96 High st
Davies R & J. undertakers, Daisy Hill
Davies R. builder & contractor, Chester rd
Davies T, grocer provision merchant, Lane End
Davies W, coal merchant, Church rd
Davies W, glass and china dealer, Sheffield House
Davison & Co. Ltd. Brick Works
Drury Lane Brick & Tile Co.
Edwards, boot & shoe manfrs. Chester rd
Edwards G M, polisher, painter, glazier and paper-hanger. Windmill rd. All work punctually attended to. A choice stock of wall papers to select from

Edwards J. smith, The Wilton
Edwards Mrs T, draper, Lane End
Edwards Mrs., butcher, Main st
Edwards Mrs, draper, Lane End
Edwards S, smith, Stanley rd
Ellis J, butcher, Brunswick rd
Everall A, grocer, Chester rd
Ewloe Place Co-operative Society
Feathers Inn, Brook st
Fletcher J, general smith, Main st
Flintshire Haulage Co.
Ffoulkes P. ladies' & gent's clothier, Main st
Fox W, tailor and draper, Mill Lane
Fraser D, surgeon, Roseneath Cottage
Free Library, Main st
Glynne Arms Inn, Drury Lane
Grandstand Inn, Pentre—J H Catherall
Gregory E K. mineral water manfr
Gregory S, coal merchant, Coldarbor
Grey J, grocer, Altamri
Griffith Mrs, confectioner, Liverpool Road Post Office
Griffiths F, stationer, Main st & Chester rd
Hallam G A. grocer, High st
Hancock and Co. brick works, Main st
Hare & Hounds, Pentre
Hawarden & District Waterworks Co., Main st
Hayes Bros. builders, Main st
Hayes H. potters
Higgins S, grocer, etc., Main st
Hill Thomas. British and foreign fruiterer, and confectioner, tobacconist & general dealer in smallwares, The Cross
Hope & Anchor, Ewloe Place
Hopwood T, grocer, Main st
Horse & Jockey, Church rd
Hughes F, grocer & butcher, Ewloe Place
Hughes M, provision dealer, Stanley rd
Hughes Mrs., registry office for servants, Stanley rd
Hughes O, draper, the Exchange Drapery Establishment
Hughes S. greengrocer, Chester rd
Hughes S, grocer, Church rd
Hughes S J, grocer, Main st
Hughes W. grocer, New Stores
Hunters (The Teamen) Ltd., Chester rd
Iredale J. confectioner, Chester rd
Jenkins D. watchmaker, Lane End
Johnson Mrs., confectioner, Brunswick rd
Johnson W E. boot maker, Brunswick rd
Jones E P, grocer, Main st
Jones J. butcher, Mold rd
Jones J. grocer, Deva House
Jones J, ironmonger, Washington House
Jones R, boot maker, Main st
Jones T, boot and shoe maker, The Square

Jones T, grocer and provision mcht. Main st
Jones T C, draper and outfitter, The Cross
Jones T P, clothier and outfitter, The Cross
Jones W, solicitor. Brunswick rd
Kelly M, family grocer, etc., Main rd
Lamb J & Son. Art Pottery Works. Church rd
Lamb J, grocer, Brook st
Lewis A J, plumber & painter. Mill Lane
Lewis B, solicitor
Lewis H, picture framer. Chester rd
Lewis Mrs. tobacconist & hairdresser. Church rd
Lewis W, draper, Main st
Lloyds Bank, Ltd, Main st
McLean Dr. J. surgeon. Daylight Villas
Manning H, pork butcher. Main st
Messham Mrs, grocer, Mill Lane
Middleton W. grocer. 111 Mold rd
Millington T. tailor. Rose Mount. off Brook st
MOLE MRS G, grocer & tobacconist. 84 Brunswick rd
Moore S, cycle agent. Drury Lane
Morris W P, solicitor. Main st
Morton G and W, boot and shoe manfrs, Main rd
Nant Inn. Padeswood—W T Jones
North Central Waggon Co., Church rd
Old Cross Keys. — G Griffiths
Owen T. emigration agent. Padeswood rd
Owens W. cycle repairer, Lane End
Pantin F, hairdresser. Chester rd
Parrott Inn, Drury Lane
Parry E & Sons. Ltd., Brick Works
Peters J. baker & confectioner. London House. High street
Peters J. butcher. Market Hall
Peters Mrs, grocer, Brook st
PETERS PRICE, wholesale and retail butcher, Main st (opposite Bistre Church), and "Altami"
Peters R. hairdresser, Main st
Phillips T, grocer, Windmill rd
Powell I, earthenware maker
Price J, builder. Tre Cross—see advt
Price G, hairdresser, Chester rd

Prince of Wales Inn, Brook st
Ratcliffe E, butter, eggs and poultry dealer Mill Lane. Tel. Add. "Ratcliffe, Buckley." Tel No 1x2
Richardson W G, watchmaker and cycle agent, Main street
Roberts J & L. drapers & outfitters. Chester rd
Roberts Miss, confectioner. Main st
Roberts Mrs, grocer, Brook st
Rogers J, butcher, Chester rd
Roberts R. picture framer. Chester rd
Roberts T. draper, Main st
Rose & Thistle, Spongreen
Rowlands J, boot and shoe maker, Main st
Rowlands R. butcher, High st
Rowlett W, boot & shoe manfr, Church rd
Salter H. hairdresser, The Square
Shepherd Miss. dressmaker, Central Hall
Ship Inn, Main st
Shone W, coal merchant, Church rd
Silver P. furniture dealer, Main st
Sims L E, photographer, The Studio
South Buckley Rock Brick Co.,
Standard Brick Co.
Stevenson W H. cycle agent. Central Hall
Swire J, clogger, Mill rd
Taaffe J & E. cycle agents. Chester rd
Tavern (The) Alltami—Mrs. M. Hewitt
Taylor Bros. potters, Alltami
The Urban District Council of Buckley—E Astbury surveyor, inspector, etc., Main st
WAINWRIGHT MRS, milliner & dressmaker. All orders promptly attended to on the shortest notice
Wellington Inn. The Square—W Jones
West Buckley Colliery Co. Altami
White Lion Inn, Main st
Wilcock W H. fruiterer. High st
Wilcock W, general dlr, Main st
Williams & Hughes, surgeons, Main st
Williams E. butcher. Brunswick rd
Williams E and E, boot and shoe establishment.
Williams Ralph, grocer, butcher, provision merchant, corn & flour dealer, Central Supply Stores, Brunswick rd. Tel. No. 2x1.
Williams R O, confectioner, The Cross
Williams R & P, bakers, grocers & provision merchants, Old Stores. Try William's 1s. 6d. tea, None Better
Williams W, general dlr, Main st
Wilson Mrs., draper, Drury Lane Post Office
Wright C, grocer, Chester rd

Facing and above: Bennett's Business Directory for Buckley, 1913–14.

Roberts T, grocer, Shop Longoes
Thomas Miss, grocer and refreshment rooms
Williams G R, butcher, and at Holyhead market on Saturdays. Noted for the finest quality of home-killed meat & prime Welsh lamb
Williams R, tailor, Shop Tyngongl
Williams Mrs M (C.T.C.), Tyn Berllan. Good accommodation for motorists, cyclists and commercials. Luncheons & teas provided. Bed & breakfast. Own produce. Garage

—o—

BUCKLEY, an urban district, civil and ecclesiastic parish, is in the Mold county court area of Flintshire, 2 miles E. of Mold. The acreage of the urban district is 2,034 with a population of 7,000. It has a post, money order and telegraph office under Chester and a telephone call office in the Chester area. The nearest stations are Buckley Junction on the L.N.E.R., and Padeswood on the L.M. & S.R. The chief public buildings are the Council Chambers, High st, the Tivoli, the Public Free Library and Public Baths. The chief industries are the manufacture of bricks and pottery.
Early Closing Day, Wednesday.

Albert Hall (T E P Hibbert), billiards and dancing
Anglesea J, furniture dealer, Brunswick rd
Arrowsmith N, confectioner, Brunswick rd
Astbury K, ladies' hairdresser, Chester rd
Aston C, butcher, Chester rd
Aston Mrs, confectioner, 179 Mold rd
Avenue Nurseries, T Hibbert, propr
Bailey H, draper, P.O., Drury Lane
Balshaw Alfred, baker, grocer and confectioner, Church rd. Cakes a speciality
Barker R, chemist, The Cross
Bartley C, grocer & confectioner, Nant Mawr rd
Bartley W, butcher, Nant Mawr rd
Beattie R J, bootmaker, Lane End
Beavan Bros (L. Beavan, propr.), engineers, iron & brass founders, Buckley Ironworks. Telegrams: Foundry, Buckley. Tel. 45
Beavan B, The Ark fish & chip saloon, Liverpool rd
Beavan J, bootmaker, Chester rd, for sound repairs with best leather and materials only, at keen competitive prices
Bellis J, confectioner, Mold rd
Bellis R L, optician, Brunswick rd
Bellis T E, ironmonger, Mill lane
Bellis T E, tailor, Lane End
Bellis W, motor bus propr, Church rd
Bells Stores Ltd, grocers, Chester rd
Bistre Parish Room, Chester rd
Bistre National School — Headmaster (boys), W Davies ; Headmistress (girls), Miss E Hughes
Bistre Working Men's Social Club, Mold rd
Black Horse Hotel—R A Smith
Black Lion Inn, Mold rd—D G Bennett
Blue Anchor, The Square
Blue Bell Inn, Chester rd
Booth G H, painter & general dealer, 14 Mill Lane
Booth W, baker, Brunswick rd
Brady J, bootmaker, Lane End
Bryan G, fruiterer & greengrocer, Lane End
Buckley Brick & Tile Co, Ltd

Buckley Co-operative Stores Ltd, grocers and provision merchants, Brunswick st and Drury lane
Buckley Council School—Headmaster (boys), Glyn Williams ; Headmistress (girls) Miss Olive ; Headmistress (infants) Miss Evans
Buckley Ex-Service Men's Memorial Institute, Church rd
Buckley Gas Co, Ltd, Mount Pleasant
Buckley Junction Metallic Brick Co, Ltd
Buckley Meat Co, Lane End
Buckley St. Matthew's Church of England School —Headmaster (boys) Jas Tyson ; Headmistress (girls), Miss M Emily Jones ; Headmistress (infants), Miss Dorothy Griffiths
Buckley St. Matthew's Lane End Infants School— Headmistress, Miss C Hewitt
Bull Inn, Lane End—R Davidson
Burkhill Mrs, tobacconist, Mold rd
Burkhill W, hairdresser, Chester rd
Burrows P, hardware dealer, 104 Mold rd
Castle Brick Works, Northop—J H Allettson
Catherall E, confectioner, 45 Chester rd
Chirgwin R, painter, Brunswick rd
Clarke A, confectioner, 20 Chester rd
Clive Arms, Drury lane
Coles J & M, drapers, Brunswick rd
Connah C, haulage contractor, Drury Lane
Connah F, confectioner, Brunswick rd
Connah Mrs, confectioner, 95 Brunswick rd
Cosy Temperance Hotel—E Roberts, propr
Croose Mrs, grocer, 81 Mold rd
Cropper & Son, printers and booksellers, Lane End Post Office
Cross Keys Inn, Chester rd—W Nickson
Crown Vaults, Chester rd
Cunnah Mrs, draper, Brunswick rd
Davies A, confectioner, Brook st
Davies A E & Son, machine joinery works, Liverpool rd. Builders and property repairers—see advt
Davies Bros, grocers, The Cross
Davies C H, dentist, Chester rd
Davies E & M, fancy dealers, Chester rd
Davies J H, painter, Chester rd
Davies L, baker & confectioner, Hygienic Bakery, 96 Brunswick rd
Davies Miss, confectioner, Brunswick rd
Davies R D & Son, joiners and undertakers, 96 Brunswick rd
Davies R W, hairdresser, 11 Brunswick rd
Davies W, fruiterer, The Cross
Davison & Co, Ltd, Brick Works
Dobson J B, surgeon, Brunswick rd
Dolby A H, fish frier, Church rd

Above, facing and p.266, Bennett's Business Directory, Buckley, 1936.

Drury Brickworks Ltd, Drury

Duckworth E & C, hardware dealers, Brunswick rd

Dunn P Ll, family butcher, Church rd and Liverpool rd. Only prime English meat sold. Brawns and pressed beef of best quality

Dyment Mrs S & Sons, chandlers and oil merchants, 11 Church rd. Agents for Carr's polishes, full stock carried

Edge W H, butcher, Brunswick rd

Edwards Mrs, confectioner, Chester rd

Edwards A, butcher, Mold rd

Edwards E A, smith, The Common

Edwards J, grocer, Windmill rd

Edwards J, haulier, 5 Ffrith Houses

Edwards Miss, confectioner, Chester rd

Edwards Mrs T, fancy draper, etc, 30 Chester rd

Edwards R, grocer and confectioner, Mold rd

Edwards T, drapery stores, Lane End

Ellis Bros, haulage contractors and motor charabanc proprietors, 22 Mold rd. Cars and buses for hire. Depot for Portland cement, cinders, brickbats, etc. Tel. 66 Buckley

Ellis J, garage, Mill Lane

Ellis Miss, domestic agency, Brunswick rd

Ellis Miss, general stores, 22 Mold rd

Evans A, chemist, Chester rd

Ewloe Co-operaive Society, Liverpool rd

Feathers Inn, Brook st

Fennah Mrs, confectioner, Mill Lane

Fletcher C, smith, Liverpool rd

Flintshire Haulage Co, Drury. W Wilson, propr.

Foster K, haulage contractor

Francis W E, butcher, Brook st

Fraser D, surgeon, Hillside, Padeswood rd

Free Library, Mold rd, R J Williamson, librarian

Glynne Arms Inn, Drury Lane

Goulding Mrs, Registry Office, Brunswick rd

Gould W & E, grocers, etc

Grandstand Inn, Pentre

Grass J, clogger, Mold rd

Gregorys Ltd, Aerated Water Works

Griffin Inn—John Condon

Griffiths F, stationer and wholesale tobacconist, The Cross

Griffiths Jas, baker, Brunswick rd

Griffiths J R, music teacher, Mold rd

Griffiths F, grocer, Pentre

Griffiths Miss Helena, A.L.C.M., music teacher, Mill lane

Griffiths' Stores, grocers, Brunswick rd

Hancock & Co, Ltd, brick works, Chester rd

Hare & Hounds, Pentre

Harrop M B, chemist, 112 Brunswick rd

Harrop W, chemist, Lane End

Hawarden & District Waterworks Co, Brunswick rd

Hayes Bros, builders, Main st

Hayes H, joiner, Mill Lane

Hayes Misses E & C, confectioners, Centra Cafe

Hayes H, potters

Hereford M R, surgeon, Chalfont

Herford Miss, M.B., B.S. (Lond.), Mill lane

Hewitt G E, confectioner, Mold rd

Hibbert T, builder, Mold rd

Higgins O, grocer, Lane End

Higgins S, grocer, etc, Mold rd

Hill A, fish frier, The Cross

Hill A, ironmonger, 20 Mold rd

Hill J, fish fryer, Brunswick rd

Hodgson F, painter, Church rd

Hope & Anchor, Ewloe Place

Horse & Jockey, Church rd

Hughes A, coal merchant

Hughes Dan, butcher, Stanley rd

Hughes F, general dealer, Mill lane

Hughes F, grocer & butcher, Ewloe Place

Hughes J H & M, haulage contractors and charabanc proprietors, Lane End. Steam and petrol haulage. Tel. 39

Hughes J A, confectioner, Chester rd

Hughes Mrs, registry office for servants, Stanley rd

Hughes S, newsagent, Lane End

Hughes S J, grocer, Brunswick rd

Hughes W C, dep. clerk to U.D.C.

Hughes & Parker, drapers, 10 Church rd

Hughes & Williams, confectioners, Lane End

Humphreys E, newsagent, The Square

Humphreys, grocery stores, Brunswick rd

Hunters (The Teamen) Ltd, Chester rd

Iball F S, seedsman & florist, 151a Brunswick rd

Iball Mrs, grocer, Drury lane

Iredale J, confectioner, Chester rd

James R W, bootmaker, 9 Brunswick rd

Jenkins D, watchmaker, Windmill rd

Jenkinson R, motor car propr, 6 Padeswood rd

Johnson W E, draper, Lane End

Jones A, photographer, 22 Brunswick rd

Jones C H, undertaker, Spon Green

Jones E, grocer, Market Hall

Jones F Banister, sanitary inspector

Jones F Ll, solicitor & clerk to U.D.C., The Cross

Jones H, fish frier, Brunswick rd

Jones H Trevor, builders' ironmonger, timber merchant, and dealer in oils, paints & colours, Chester rd

Jones J, grocer, Deva House

Jones J, ironmonger, Washington House

Jones J & M E, drapers & grocers, P O, The Square

Jones Miss D, florist, Lane End

Jones Price, Ewloe Potteries

Jones R, draper, 113 Mold rd

Jones R E, fish frier, The Square

Jones Thomas (A Iball, propr). High-class draper & outfitter, complete house furnisher, valet service, Fern Leigh, Brunswick rd

Jones T, boot & shoe maker, The Square

Jones T C, draper and outfitter, The Cross

Jones T L, grocer, Mold rd

Jones , coal merchants and carriage proprietors

Kelsall C, outfitter, The Cross

Kendrick L, coal merchant The Common

Lamb E & M E, confectioners, Church rd

Lamb J, confectioner, 56 Mold rd

Lamb J & Son, Art Pottery Works, Church rd

Langford W, grocer, Brunswick rd

Lewis A J, plumber and painter, Mynyddsa

Lewis E, fruiterer, Mold rd

Lloyds Bank, Ltd, The Cross

Lloyd Bros, coal merchants, Mill Lane

Lloyd, Jones & Lloyd, kiln builders, Chester rd

Lloyd Jones (Buckley) Ltd, builders, Mold rd
Marshall A, optician, Brunswick rd
Masheder T, baker, Chester rd
Mesham A, fish frier, Brook st
Meesham A G, boot stores, Mold rd
Meesham Hugh, boot repairer, Drury
Melia's Grocery Stores, Chester rd
Messham Mrs, grocer, Mill Lane
Messham R, collector to Buckley U.D.C. & Public Baths Committee.   Tel 23
Metcalfe G P, radio stores, Mold rd
Midland Bank Ltd
Millington E, music teacher, Padeswood rd
Ministry of Labour Employment Exchange, Liverpool rd
Mole E, boot stores, The Cross
Mole R G, motor garage, Brunswick rd
Morris Llewellyn, grocer, Mold rd
Mount Pleasant Colliery Co, Ltd
Nant Inn, Padeswood—W T Jones
National Provincial Bank, Ltd, Brunswick rd
Old Cross Keys—H Griffiths
Owen Mrs C Thursby, resident Spirella Corsetiere, 122 Mold rd.   Unbreakable and rustless corsets.   Twelve months Boning Guarantee
Owens W, cycle repairer, Lane End
Panton F, hairdresser, The Square
Parker R, draper, Church rd
Parrott Inn, Drury Lane
Parry E & Sons, Ltd, Brick Works
Parry J S & F J, corn merchants, Little Mountain
Parry Mrs T, grocer, Liverpool rd
Parry T E, builder and contractor, Liverpool rd
Peacock's Stores, 9 Mold st
Peters G, pork butcher, 133 Brunswick rd
Peters J, butcher, Market Hall
Peters J, coal merchant, Mynyddisa
Peters J, grocer, 11 Brunswick rd
Paters J, surgeon
Peters Mrs, baby linen depot, The Cross
Peters Mrs, grocer, Brook st
Peters Mrs, tobacconist, Chester rd
Peters P, butcher, 72 Mold rd
Peters R, confectioner, Chester rd
Peters R, Fried Fish Saloon, Brunswick rd
Peters R, hairdresser, Mold rd
Peters S, butcher, Lane End
Phillips J, fruiterer, Mill Lane
Phillips J, tobacconist & confectioner, Lane End
Picture Palace—Cropper & Sons, proprs
Pied Bull Inn, Chester rd
Powell I & W, art pottery manfrs
Quinn's, fruiterers, Brunswick rd
Ratcliffe J, poulterer, Mill Lane
Ratcliff & Fenner, builders, Mill lane
Red Lion Inn, Liverpool rd, Miss Price
Reeve G & Son, dealers in animal products, Nant Mawr.   Bones and fat collected regularly
Reeves Mrs, confectioner, Post Office, Liverpool rd
Rhosesmor Sand and Gravel Co
Richardson W G, watchmaker and cycle agent, Brunswick rd
Roberts', drapers & outfitters, Chester rd
Roberts Mrs, grocer, Brook st

Roberts Mrs, registry office, Chester rd
Roberts P, hairdresser, Brook st
Roberts R, fish frier, 78 Brunswick rd
Roberts, T, hardware stores, 28 Mold rd
Roberts, butcher, Lane End
Robinson I & Son, plumbers and heating specialists, Codsall House, Mill Lane. Sanitary work a speciality.   Tel: 91 Buckley
Rogers J, butcher, Chester rd
Rogers J, butcher, Lane End
Rogers James, grocer, etc, Lane End Stores
Rose & Thistle Inn, Spongreen.   Joseph Peters
Rowlands J & Son, boot repairers, Brunswick rd
Rowlands A, fish and chip shop
Rowlands Mrs, confectioner, Mill Lane
Rowlands R, butcher, Mold rd
Ship Inn, Brunswick rd
Shone Bros, haulage contractors, Church rd
Shone Mrs, confectioner, Chester rd
Shone Harold, stationer, Post Office
Shone James & Sons, coal and coke merchants, and general haulage contractors Knowle Lane.   Haulage undertaken for long or short distances.   Tel 82
Shone K & W, builders & contractors, Church rd
Smith D, greengrocer, Church rd
Standard (Buckley) Ltd, stoneware, pipe m'facturers
Stanley's, Willow Garage
Stevenson W H, cycle agent, Brunswick rd
Suranyi Irma, A R C M, music teacher, Brunswick rd
Swire J S, clogger, Mill rd
Tavern (The) Alltami—N Edwards
Taylor Miss, ladies' hairdresser, Brunswick rd
Thomas C, confectioner, Brunswick rd
Thomas R, confectioner, Brunswick rd
Thomas & Son, coal merchants, Drury Lane
Thompson J, haulage contractor
Threadgold H, bootmaker, Brunswick rd
Tivoli (The)—R Rowlands, director
Tudor A, confectioner, Liverpool rd
Tudor E, grocer and confectioner, Padeswood.   Our teas are specially blended to suit the water of the district
Wainwright James, coal merchant, Church st
Wainwright S, confectioner & tea merchant, Drury Lane
Wainwright W, fruiterer, Chester rd
Ward S Lisle, surgeon, Mold rd
Wellington Social Working Men's Club, Mold rd
White Lion Inn, Mold rd
Wilcock C, wireless depot, Brunswick rd
Wilcock T, confectioner & tobacconist, Brunswick rd
Williams E, butcher, The Cross
Williams H, fruiterer, The Cross
Williams Miss N, ladies' hairdresser, Lane End
Williams R O, confectioner, The Cross
Williams W & Son, metal and general merchants
Williams & Davies (The Misses), confectioners, Central Cafe, Brunswick rd
Willow Pottery Co
Wood E H, confectioner, 26 Brook st
Working Men s Club, Brook st
Young Miss, confectioner, 9 Brunswick rd

R. Williams, Central Supply Stores Brunswick Road, c.1910. [Buckley Society Archive]

structure, to shape the modern urban environment, will be the first theme to be discussed after a brief look at the nature of the community in 1901.

The community in 1901

The census figures for 1901 give the population for Buckley Urban District Council as 5,780 persons living in 1,271 dwellings. By 1911 the population was 6,333 persons, and 1,387 dwellings. In 1931 the population was 6,726, and 1,607 dwellings. In 1951 the population was 7,697 and the dwellings 2,101. Thus, in the first half of the twentieth century, there was a slow increase in population and new available houses.

Other information is given in trade directories. For example, *Sutton's Directory* of 1889–90, shows that Buckley was already an embryo town, before receiving its Urban District status in 1897. In 1889 the town was well serviced by over 65 shop keepers, 16 licensed premises, a post office, a police station, an institute and reading room at Lane End, as well as the places of worship, schools and industries we described in previous chapters. By 1901, the Urban District Council was beginning to develop an infra-structure which included public buildings. The 1901 census lists about 80 shops and *Bennett's Business Directory*, 1913–14, here displayed, shows more than 100 shops, with the addition of professional persons and other services. About 20 public houses are named. The growth of a more sophisticated society with developing technology is reflected by an expansion in goods and services listed in *Bennett's Business Directory* for 1936. The number of shops has increased to over 170 and public houses to 24. Leisure facilities included in the directory are the Albert Hall for billiards, and dancing, and the Palace and Tivoli for cinema and other entertainment.

Buckley Urban District Council

Buckley was formally identified as a community by the creation of Buckley Urban District Council in 1897. The year that celebrated sixty years of the reign of Queen Victoria marked the beginning of a new era in the making of Buckley. Throughout the nineteenth century, the frontier community developed its own character and institutions. A variety of buildings sprang up to mark the planting of religious denominations, schools, and shops to serve a growing population of those labouring in potteries, brickyards and collieries. The establishment of the Urban District Council was a step forward. It acknowledged a growing confidence in an emergent working class community to manage its own affairs. The extension of the franchise, the establishment of county councils, and a Liberal dominance in Wales, conferred new opportunities and statutory powers for those seeking to improve their community.

There was plenty to be done. The Urban District Council was the vehicle ordained to bring order out of chaos; charged to enforce a whole catalogue of parliamentary legislation. To improve health, roads, sewerage, lighting and housing. To establish an efficient local government machine by the appointment of statutory executive officers — town clerk, medical officer of health, inspector of nuisances, surveyor, etc. The elected body to enhance social and cultural advance by the provision of a library and other social amenities. In a word, the chief function of the Urban District Council was to make a community infrastructure, the bones and limbs of the body politic.

This new devolution of power to an elected assembly was bound to cause difficulties, made up as it was of differing religious and political views and called upon to create a new political and social unit out of townships which had previously been attached to separate parishes. The parochialism engendered by

Andrew Carnegie, philanthropist and benefactor of Buckley Free Library. Taken from a sketch of him at the opening of St Deiniol's Library 1902.
[St Deiniol's Library]

centuries of suspicion between the parishioners of Hawarden and Mold was an impediment which had to be expunged. It is this background which marks the early years of the Buckley Urban Distinct Council and provides an interesting episode in the making of Buckley.

In November 1895 an inquiry by Flintshire County Council about the setting up of an urban district council revealed divisions of opinion between its future senators. Major John Merriman Gibson, a churchman and brickworks manager from the Hawarden townships, was against the establishment of the new body. He 'said that the traders and a great many of the people of Ewloe Wood, Ewloe Town, and Pentrobin felt that it was not fair that they should become part and parcel of this urban district. Where would all the money be spent? In the Bistre portion. Where would the money come from?'[2] Gibson was supported by John Watkinson, another churchman, and a powerful colliery employer, who 'urging similar objections, said his works were rated at over £2,000 per annum, but if his works were taken in he might probably be rated at four times that amount'.[3]

George Alletson, yet another brickworks owner, aired the same objection, alleging that the 'promoters of the scheme were attempting to get a large amount of rateable value they were not entitled to'.[4] George Armstrong Parry, a member of Flintshire County Council, gave evidence in favour of the scheme, saying that the recent county council election in the area had been fought entirely upon this question, and his majority had increased from 49 to 128. 'If an urban district council was formed they would have greater power in their hands. They were now paying rates and receiving nothing for them, whereas they wanted lighting, drainage etc.' Parry was supported by Edward Peters, the local miners' agent, a nonconformist from Bistre, who 'testified to the favour with which the proposal was received amongst the working men of the district. In his opinion Buckley was fifty years behind the times owing to their present divided state and there existed a great need to reform'.[5]

The establishment of Buckley District Council as 'a new Urban Sanitary District' was confirmed by Order of the Local Government Board on 21 September 1897. It comprised the townships of Ewloe Wood, Ewloe Town, Penrobin, Bannel, Argoed and Bistre. There was no doubt about an imbalance of the constituent parts. The Hawarden portion had a population of 2,750, a rateable value of £11,500, and acreage of 1,260, The Mold portion a population of 3,850, a rateable value of £1,082, and acreage of 795.[6] By 1947 the total acreage had increased to 2,667. The first election took place on 3 November 1897. There were 28 candidates for 15 seats. George Armstrong Parry headed the poll and was elected Chairman at the first meeting in the Board School, Bistre. George H. Simon was the first Clerk (1897–1902) and Richard Astbury the Sanitary Inspector. His

THIS STONE IS TO COMMEMORATE THE FACT THAT THIS LIBRARY WAS BUILT WITH FUNDS MUNIFICENTLY PROVIDED BY MR ANDREW CARNEGIE.

THIS STONE IS TO COMMEMORATE THE FACT, THAT THE SITE ON WHICH THIS BUILDING STANDS, WAS PROVIDED AS A FREE GIFT, BY MR ROBERT GRIFFITHS, AND MR THOMAS GRIFFITHS, OF CHESTER.

Plaques outside the Library commemorating the gift of land by Robert Griffiths and Thomas Griffiths and the Library by Andrew Carnegie. [Buckley Archive]

duties were formidable, charged with the task of creating the infra-structure.

The Council set about its task with zeal establishing public facilities, and in many ways the years up to the First World War were the golden age of the new Buckley community. It cut its teeth on an issue which became a 'test piece' and a trial of strength between Bistre and Buckley. This was fought out on the issue of the building of a new Free Library, the gift of Andrew Carnegie.

Andrew Carnegie (1835–1918), the Scottish-born American industrialist and philanthropist, was born in Dunfermline, the son of a weaver. His father emigrated to Pittsburgh and Andrew, by his business acumen, after a humble beginning, controlled the largest iron and steel works in America. He retired in 1901 as a multi-millionaire and devoted his life and fortune to philanthropy giving away over 70 million pounds. Experiencing kindness as a young man, by a bibliophile who gave him access to his library, Carnegie decided to promote the building of public libraries throughout the United States and Britain, and Buckley became one of his benefactions. He was a friend of W. E. Gladstone and was present at the opening of St Deiniol's Library, Hawarden, in October 1902. On this occasion he spoke with some emotion expressing the view that 'Mr Gladstone was one of the three or four men who made me better'.

'Spy' caricature of the Right Honourable Herbert Gladstone, Vanity Fair.

It was through Gladstone's daughter, Mary Drew, that approaches were made to Carnegie about the prospect of the gift of a Free Public Library to the new Urban District Council. Her solicitations were successful and the gift was announced in the newspaper in March 1902. Mary and her husband Harry Drew, vicar of the Parish of Buckley, together with Herbert Gladstone, MP, offered, in addition to Carnegie's gift of a library, to build an institute, but only on condition that both buildings should be built on Hawarden Estate land in the old Hawarden area of the new Urban District.[7] A few weeks later, at the beginning of May, it was announced that another site had been offered by Messrs Griffiths, corn factors of Chester. This was next to the new Council Chambers and situated in the old Mold area of the Urban District Council.

A decision, therefore, had to be made where Carnegie's library was to be built. It was left to the Council to accept the gift and choose the site. Was it to be in Gladstone territory in the old Hawarden area enhanced by the extra gift of an institute in the parish where Gladstone's son-in-law was the Anglican vicar? Was it to be on the site offered by the Nonconformist Griffiths brothers in the old Mold area in Bistre?

There was a further complication, which involved Councillor William Hopwood an influential Buckley mining engineer. 'Soon after the formation of an Urban District Council Mr William Hopwood was persuaded by Mrs Drew to read a paper introducing the provisions of educational facilities to the locality. Mrs Drew got the autobiographical paper to Mr Carnegie whose offer to finance a Library totalled £1,400'.[8] But it so happened that the person the Griffiths brothers approached with their offer of the Bistre site, worth between £500 to £600, was Hopwood. We shall see, when the time came to decide about the site, how ingeniously Hopwood was able to resolve this dilemma.

Mary and Harry Drew began their campaign in June 1901 to get the Carnegie library and the Gladstone institute, built in Buckley. Their attempts are revealed in correspondence with Herbert Gladstone. The idea was Mary Drew's. She was excited by the recent performance in Buckley of the oratorio *Elijah* and wrote ecstatically to Herbert that 'no event in Buckley has ever before happened which brought such a fellow feeling, such community of interest between Church and Chapel. The orchestra, engaged from Halle's Band at Manchester, the Liverpool Philharmonic, were astonished by the performance'.[9] She then revealed to her

The Carnegie Free Library and Swimming Baths. [Buckley Society Archive]

brother Herbert 'the brilliant idea of combining an Institute for future musical performances etc., and a Library built on a site at the bottom of Church Road, near Lane End, convenient for Buckley Junction Station. The Concert Room, (Institute), to hold from 1,500 to 2,000, is to be of iron'. Mary Drew suggested that Herbert, as an influential layman, write a letter to the principal employers and owners in Buckley sketching out the scheme and appealing for subscriptions. The following March, Harry Drew wrote to his brother-in-law, Herbert Gladstone, informing him that the 'The cat is out of the bag as to the Institute and Library Scheme & folk here are greatly excited and interested'.[10] He reiterated this view a month later, in writing to Herbert, informing him 'our parishioners are very keen on this site (i.e. in Church Road) & don't at all want it to be in Bistre Parish'. He told Herbert that the Council want him to meet a deputation and concluded, 'If the worst comes to the worst I could either separate the two and have the Institute in Buckley on our site and let them have the Library in the other parish if need be'.

Harry Drew met the Council deputation in April. In the same month he declared his hand publicly in the *Buckley Parish Magazine* where he expressed his strong views in such a manner that probably antagonised the Bistre people. He wrote:

> We desire to give a word of warning at this moment before any irrevocable mistake has been made, and to ask that certain things may not be forgotten. (1) Every man would like the lamp post, so to speak, to be exactly opposite his own door, but let him be thankful that the light has been brought within his reach, though it be opposite his neighbour's door instead of his own. (2) Let us be grateful for the fine and central site offered by the Hawarden Estate, representing upwards of £200. No one else could or would offer such a site. (3) There are two parishes of this Urban area. Buckley is the 'predominant partner', and must always of necessity be so. The "junior partner" has the two existing Public Buildings (Council Chamber and Bank) within its borders. It would not be reasonable to expect the "senior partner" to place itself at a distinct advantage with regard to a boon it has worked so hard to procure for the district generally. (4) There is justice in the old saying that "those who pay the piper have a right to call the tune.[11]

The decision on where to site the Library was made in July at two meetings of the Council. Both were reported in the local press. I quote the first report in full for the understanding it gives of the division which existed between the old Mold and Hawarden portions of the Urban District. It is also a demonstration of political skill and astuteness by William Hopwood, worthy of W. E. Gladstone himself:

THE PROPOSED FREE LIBRARY. THE QUESTION OF A SITE. INTERESTING ADDRESS BY MR HOPWOOD

The promotion of a Free Library and Reading Room at Buckley is resolving itself into a much-debated question of the choice of a site.

The subject came forward at last week's meeting of the Urban Council. It appeared that three sites had up to that time been offered and there was much divergence of opinion regarding the particular site, which ought to be selected.

The deputation from the Council appointed to meet the Rev. Harry Drew on the question reported that the interview took place on 6th May, when Mr. Drew gave them to understand that the site offered by the Hawarden Estate trustees could only be in the position already offered.

The Chairman (Mr G. A. Parry) explained to the members that the day following the interview he received a letter from Mr Drew, making clear the position of things in the event of the acceptance of the site offered by the Hawarden Estate trustees and of the gifts offered by Mr Herbert Gladstone and the Rev. Harry and Mrs Drew. The Chairman read this letter to the members. He might explain that Mr Drew, in the course of a conversation, had stated that neither an Institute nor Free Library would be erected on the site mentioned unless it was found that the land was absolutely safe to build upon.

Mr W. Hopwood, at this point, rose and addressed the meeting as follows:— Mr Chairman, as one of the original promoters of the Free Library and Institute scheme for Buckley, I feel that the Council ought now to decide the question of site. Before discussing the merits or demerits of the various sites offered or applied for, I think we should enquire into the circumstances, which induced our forefathers to settle in the Buckley (Mold) portion of our area. Prior to the year 1796 (or just over a 100 years ago) a very large portion of our present Urban area, of both Mold and Hawarden parishes, was open common or wasteland, with a very poor and scanty population. Although Hawarden contained the whole of our renowned Buckley fire-clay, and two thirds of our coal deposit, yet the few landed proprietors who owned our Buckley (Hawarden) area declined to sell any freehold land or build houses for those pioneers who worked in the then budding brick and coal industries of our district, leaving them no alternative but to squat on the common. In the year 1792 an Act of Parliament was passed granting the allotment for sale of the waste land in Mold Parish, and in the year 1796 the appointed commissioners divided the common in Buckley (Mold), selling the larger portion at a cheap rate, to these squatters. We can imagine the feelings of relief and freedom this Act brought to the great grand fathers of some of us who now sit around this table, and the chagrin to-day of others of us whose forefathers did not avail themselves of this privilege, but remained "squatters" on the common in Buckley (Hawarden), and whose enclosures and dwellings to-day have been confiscated. It took but a short time after the sale to enclose the whole of our Buckley (Mold) area, hence the reason of our town being situate chiefly in the Mold Parish. Nearly 100 years elapsed between what I may call the emancipation of the squatters in Buckley (Mold) and the advent of the present liberal trustees of the Hawarden Estate, who now readily offer similar privileges in the Hawarden portion of our area. No doubt had this been offered one hundred years earlier our town would have been differently situated than it is to day, for at that time there was scarcely one house built on our present Main Street. It is therefore our duty to make the very best of the situation in which we find ourselves and to try to do things in that unbiased spirit, which will deal fairly and benefit the greatest number. We ought therefore to choose a site irrespective of mineral wealth, rateable value, or ecclesiastical areas, which is at once safe, central, and convenient for the bulk of the people.

Hopwood then went on to review the merits of the three sites offered. The first, offered by Mr Catherall, the Post Office and Hopwood himself, situated in the centre of the field at the end of Park Road he considered was not suitable because of liability to subsidence and lack of frontage on the Main Street. Hopwood dwelt at length on the second site

… that offered by the trustees of the Hawarden Estate, situated in the field opposite Lane End Colliery, with a frontage on Church Road. This is the most convenient site that the trustees have available. Unfortunately this site, besides being far from central, is absolutely unsafe for the erection thereon of such a building, since four seams of coal have been recently worked away from under it, which will result in considerable subsidence for many years to come. I am exceedingly sorry for this, since this site was offered through the instrumentality of Mrs Drew, who has done so much to promote the scheme, not only in using her influence with Mr Carnegie, but also with her brother (the Right Hon. Herbert J. Gladstone, MP), who, as an employer in our area, offers £500 if conditionally situated, which also applies to a further £800 offered or guaranteed by Mr. and Mrs Drew themselves. Let us hope that the same broad principles which guided their late noble and revered father, whose parish was the world and parishioners humanity at large, will also guide them

*The Cross c.1990 with the North Wales and
Chester Bank (now Lloyd's Bank).
[Buckley Library]*

in subscribing to one central Institute and Library for Buckley, wherever situated.

After this diplomatic tribute, Hopwood outlined the benefits of the third site offered by Messrs Griffiths Bros., of Queen's Wharf, Chester:

> This site is not more than 200 yards from the centre of the population and is absolutely safe from subsidence due to mining operations, no coal having been, or likely to be, ever worked from under it. This site also possesses one other great advantage over those before mentioned, viz., the house already erected in connection with the Council Chambers will serve a double purpose and obviate the necessity of building a caretaker's or librarian's house in connection with the Library and the Institute, and the £10 now paid to the caretaker will supplement the 1*d*. rate in supporting the Free Library. Altogether the value of this site may be estimated at £1,100 or thereabouts, and as this institution will come under control of the Council, it cannot well be better placed for that purpose.

Before he concluded Hopwood tentatively sought to promote the facilities of the proposed institute advocating that:

> If a site could be procured at the very centre of our area, i.e., at a spot near the cross roads on the Common, or another site on our Main Street, anywhere between the Cross and Brunswick Chapel, I would willingly fall in and contribute towards the purchase of the same. Coupled with this Free Library and Reading Room there should be an Institute, having billiards, bath, and technical classrooms; and the technical apparatus belonging to the Council, now housed in the Board Schools, should be transferred to these rooms.

Hopwood was supported by a Mr John Jones, formerly of Buckley, now of the Victoria Hotel, Mold, who introduced a partisan element into the discussion declaring that 'inasmuch as there was a majority of Nonconformists in the district, that Nonconformists should have a great voice in the government of this proposed institution'.

Mr Lamb spoke in favour of finding a site near Brunswick Chapel. The Clerk, Captain T. M. Keane, said he had written to Mr Hancock upon this matter, and he had also seen that gentleman. Mr Hancock said he had no land which he could offer as a site for a free library, and that he did not think it would be any use of a deputation waiting upon him. The members agreed to meet in two weeks, the understanding being that the choice of a site would then be finally agreed upon.

At the meeting held a fortnight later[14] the Council formally accepted Carnegie's offer to finance the library, adopted the Free Libraries Act, and chose the Council Chamber site offered by the Griffiths brothers. The Chairman of the Council, G. A. Parry, spoke in favour of the motion by Mr Hayes of accepting the Gladstone offer to provide a dual site for institute and library remarking that:

> … he had seen the difficulty of pleasing everybody in Buckley on the question. He had seriously considered whether they would have to put the Free Library on wheels and take it round to everybody's house. An amendment in favour of the Council Chamber site was moved by Mr John Jones who believed that when they had electric trams in the district, the route would pass the Council Chambers. The motion was carried by 8 votes in favour and 5 against.

Disappointed by the decision Mary Drew wrote a despairing letter to Herbert Gladstone:

> It is, all a crushing blow about the Free Library and Institute, but it is just what I feared from its being their Vicar, instead of an Employer like you, having to take the initiative in the matter. When a man is a Parson however fair & liberal his action it is tarred with the Church brush. The Non Cons here therefore think if our site is adopted it will imply more or less Church government.[15]

She bemoaned the effort of raising money and said that they had used:

> … the £6,000 father unexpectedly left us in 1898 … but I don't mean this for a grumble, simply a statement of fact'. She returned to the same theme six months later when she was trying to eradicate a debt of £900 on St

Matthew's Church tower, lamenting, 'what can we do. It takes a surgical operation to get 5s. out of people like the Watkinson's and Hancock's. The Free Library to be built in Bistre, well out of reach of our parish, will I hope be a success as far as it goes for that parish. Relegating your gift of £500 to the far off future is unsatisfactory, furthermore, man may not wish to lay himself open to perpetual snubs, but may prefer a quiet life and to leave the people just drinking and fighting.[16]

In June 1903 the Urban District Council resolved that the library be called the Carnegie Public Library, with the motto, 'Who gives the best to man, gives most to God'.

The Library was formally opened by Mr Samuel Smith, Liberal Member of Parliament for Flintshire (of professed Nonconformist, anti-ritualistic, and anti-Catholic sympathies), when it was reported:

> Wednesday last was a red-letter day in the history of Buckley the occasion being the opening of the magnificent new Free Library amid a Public Demonstration worthy of such an auspicious occasion.
>
> The building is an imposing structure built of red brick with stone facings. A large balcony is erected over the main entrance, while the interior contains a reference room, reading room, lending room and a large room upstairs in which it is proposed to start technical classes. At the rear is a large plot of land on which it is proposed to form a bowling green in the immediate future. The architects were Messrs Davies & Sons of Chester and the contractor Mr. Robert Peters of Buckley.
>
> The building was commenced in October 1903 and finished in April this year and is lighted throughout with incandescent gas. The balance of the money will go towards buying books and furniture. At the opening there were about 200 volumes and the chief contributors consisted of Mr Samuel Smith MP, Major Gibson, Mrs Drew, and the local Co-operative Societies.

The Library was in charge of a management committee consisting of nine members of the Council and nine co-opted members. Before opening, advice was sought from the Chief Librarian of Chester, Mr Ernest Caddie. An account of the running of the Library will be given later.

Buckley Town Centre

From the year 1892 onwards there was an attempt to create public facilities commensurate with the anticipated status of a town shortly to be announced. The drive to create a town centre came from shopkeepers, County and District Councillors, and the dedication of individuals. The Reverend Joseph Davies, the ubiquitous Congregational minister, was the most outstanding, extending his building activities, from the opening of chapels and a cemetery, to the promotion of both market and meeting halls. Canon Harry Drew and Mary Drew, during their short stay in Buckley (1897–1904), won the respect and admiration of the local community for their hard work in attempting to improve living conditions and social opportunities. The Drews and Davies had a capacity for getting things done and shared an aptitude for publicity.

The Reverend Joseph Davies was at the height of his powers when elected a member of Flintshire County Council in 1889. In the following year, as if to thank the electorate, he purchased two acres of land to establish a Nonconformist burial ground in Bistre, complete with caretaker's house and small chapel. He had by this time been a generous benefactor to the Alltami Primitive Methodists and was later to assist those at Drury, as well as opening places of worship for Congregationalists at Rivertown, Shotton, and the Village Temple, Mynydd Isa. Beside his interest in building chapels he was musical. He sang, conducted choirs, wrote hymns and was a popular chairman at chapel concerts. His religious fervour was combined with a strong social conscience and he was not afraid to promote the temperance cause or oppose any issue which he regarded as unjust. An example of this was his confrontation with Major Gibson and the Buckley Engineers when he forcibly removed a fencing they had erected on Buckley Common.

In 1891 Joseph Davies set on foot the building of a meeting hall. The circumstances were explained in the local press in October:

> The public having failed to take up shares in the Public Hall Company, Mr Joseph Davies and others are in negotiations with Mr R. Davies, builder to have a hall built on the garden plot of land attached to Windsor Cottage, the property of Mr R. D. Davies. It will be at the centre of the town and might be fitly called the Central Hall.[17]

Lane End Post Office. [Buckley Library]

It was opened in February 1892 when the local newspaper remarked that the event 'was an opportunity for a number of old friends to meet with the Reverend H. Elvet Lewis', and went on to describe the building:

The Public Hall is built by the Reverend Joseph Davies, CC, at his own expense and will seat between six hundred and seven hundred persons. It is nicely arranged with one floor on an elevation over shops, which take up the front half of the building. It is well lighted with gas, and is pleasant to sing, speak, or listen in. Messrs Davies brothers were the contractors, and the Reverend Joseph Davies was his own architect, and purposed letting the Hall to the trustees of the Public Cemetery for a small rent, the profits made to go towards the cemetery funds.[18]

The following year Davies offered each friendly society the use of the Hall for club purposes and use as a committee room.[19] The Central Hall was sited where the Tivoli now stands. Davies regarded it as a business proposition. Three shops occupied its frontage: Mr W. H. Stevenson, cycles; Mr Ffoulkes, sweets and tobacco; Miss Shepherd, clothing. The Central Hall was used for religious meetings, concerts, musical performances and political gatherings and was later rented by William Wilcox as a cinema. It was demolished in 1927 and replaced by the Tivoli.

In August 1892, the Davies brothers built a Market Hall for the Reverend Joseph Davies. He became the proprietor of Buckley's first supermarket which housed sixteen stall holders! Buckley Town Band, under the leadership of Mr James Griffiths, attended the opening on a Friday evening. They played in front of the building at the front entrance on the main road. The local press left this description:

The Hall is in the form of an angle and when lit up with gas presents an attractive site. The stalls are put up well and permanently. The floor is paved with Buckley tiles. We trust that his undertaking will receive the support from the neighbourhood it deserves, as the object is to benefit the working class of Buckley. It is intended that it shall be opened every Friday and Saturday from 10 am to 10 pm.

At the opening the local Traders had a variety of merchandise to offer their customers. The sixteen stalls are listed in the newspaper report.[20] Amongst the items sold were fish, meat, green grocery, sweets, clothing, crockery, and a shoemaker had a stall.

As a sign of confidence in the anticipated prosperity of the new shopping area an impressive Bank was built in 1893 on the corner the Cross and described as 'a structure worthy of its position. It will replace the branch now carried on by Williams' old Bank in the Post Office Building.[21]

An attempt was made in 1894 to attract the farming community to do business in Buckley by the establishment of a smithfield. At the beginning of May, Mr A. Sandbach of Connah's Quay opened his new smithfield when it was reported that 'there was a large attendance of buyers from Chester, Flint, Mold, Liverpool and Connah's Quay. There

Police Station, Council Chamber and Free Library.
[Buckley Library]

was not much stock to offer, but what there was ran very high. Sheep made 10*d*. and beef over 7*d*. per *lb*. Horses also fetched very high prices'. Sales of fat and store stock were held fortnightly.[22]

The National Telephone Company opened the Buckley Telephone Exchange at New Row, Daisy Hill, on 25 March 1896, in a building rented from Frederick Leigh Hancock. In 1912 it was taken over by the General Post Office, with Margaret Ellen Johnson (née Ball) as operator/caretaker at weekends, a position she held until the opening of the automatic exchange in 1936.[23]

In 1902 a newspaper report stated that the first post office was opened in the 1840s at a house adjoining the Horse and Jockey public house, in Knowle Lane, kept by Mrs Lloyd. Letters had to be called for. It was later sited in Jonathan Sharrat's Cottage, opposite the Lane End Infants School. Not until the 1860s was it removed to Mill Lane, from where letters were delivered. The account concluded 'There are now three Post Offices and one more sanctioned, two deliveries of mail and three despatches'.[24] Was the newspaper report announcing the opening of Thomas Cropper's Post Office at Lane End? The post was taken to Chester each evening in a horse van by Mr Mountford who also kept a grocer's shop in Brunswick Road next to Arthur Jones, the photographer's shop.

It was decided to build Council Chambers as soon as possible after the first meeting of the new Urban District Council in November 1897. In 1899 Mr J. H. Davies, the Chester architect, furnished plans to provide a building suitable for a magistrates room, council chambers and a caretaker's house. It was agreed with Messrs Griffiths Brothers of Chester, to purchase the site at a cost of £275. For this purpose the Council borrowed £1,500. The Council Chambers were let to the magistrates at 20 guineas, much to their satisfaction:

> Buckley— New Court Room. The Buckley Petty Sessions were for the first time held at the Urban Council Buildings on Monday. Mr Henry Hurlbutt, who presided, said that on behalf of himself and his brother magistrates he wished to indicate the extreme pleasure and satisfaction they felt in finding themselves in that splendidly appointed and comfortable Court House.

Other improvements were made with the building of a brick urinal and the opening of a bowling green in August 1908. The Council recommended that £30 be spent on the preparation of the Green. Twelve pairs of woods and six pairs of jacks were ordered at the catalogue price of 12*s*. per pair for the woods and jacks at 2*s*. 6*d*. each. The high point of the opening ceremony was a match arranged between members of the Council and a team selected from St Matthew's Bowling Club. Care was taken that notice boards were obtained warning that bad language, gambling, and spitting on the green would not be allowed. At the opening of the Bistre Avenue Bowling Green in 1913 the Baptist Minister the Revd Thomas Roberts remarked that 'Ministers could do more good by playing a game of bowls with the men of their flock than by preaching'.

Gradually and modestly a community identity was beginning to emerge in Buckley. The work of the Urban District Council during its existence of nearly eighty years is well documented in its voluminous minute books.[25] Below are a few examples of its work during that period.

Health facilities

One of its primary functions was the enforcement of public health legislation. Dr David Fraser, the first Medical Officer of Health, was appointed in March 1898 and served in that capacity until he retired in 1949. As such he gave an annual report which estimated the population, numbered the births of males and females, the number and causes of death, the hospital facilities available to the district, and the number and condition of houses. He prompted the establishment of baby clinics. At the end of the First World War in 1918–19 he had to cope with the influenza pandemic and was responsible for the reception and care of evacuees during the Second World War. Dr Fraser's Report for May 1901, for example, called attention to the houses by Hancock's Works in Lane End, 'to which there were no back doors and no yard except to one house & that typhoid fever had occurred there'. In 1908, his report mentioned cases of typhoid at Aberdovey Terrace. On his advice the Council resolved that the doctor purchase bedclothes and destroy the old ones.

The Urban District never had its own hospital and Buckley has always looked to its neighbours for this provision. In the early nineteenth century, local patients sought treatment in Liverpool or Chester. Mold

Dr David Fraser (1870–1956) Medical Officer of Health for 51 years. [Buckley Town Council]

hospital was available at the end of the century. In a heavily industrialised community accidents at work were treated on the spot and patients conveyed by work mates to be nursed at home. Local government authorities were empowered to combine to provide hospitals. In this way Buckley entered into agreement with Hawarden to build a smallpox hospital at Dobshill in 1903, to house twelve beds. The editor of the *Buckley Parish Magazine* noted in April of that year, 'The isolation Hospital for this dreaded disease is now a conspicuous if not exactly picturesque object between St John's Church (Pentrobin) and Buckley Junction Station'. He went on to complain 'that we have in our midst a 'common lodging house', or what is in some places called a 'doss house'. It behoves those in authority to see that the utmost vigilance is exercised as to cleanliness in such places'. Unfortunately the new hospital didn't last very long as the diary of George Lewis recorded: '1907, March 19, Tuesday. A fire broke out at the fever hospital, Dob's Hill, and burnt it to the ground.' Buckley U.D.C. declined to join in the proposed funding scheme for the new isolation hospital. Instead they used the hospitals at Mold, Chester and elsewhere.[26]

The necessity of providing arrangements for victims of accidents to be conveyed to hospital in an emergency was recorded by George Lewis:

1901, April 17, Wednesday. A man was seriously injured at the Mountain Colliery at 11 pm. There was no stretcher and no ambulance available. One man went to the Lane End Colliery for a stretcher while another went to Shone's for a trap. We took him to Mold Cottage Hospital. When we were going down the Wylfa Hill, we had to pull him out of the trap to allow his feet to go down first, for the blood was smothering him. We did the same thing again going up Mold Town. If a man was killed or hurt he was usually taken home in a shandry between two bales of straw.

It was incidents like this, which prompted the purchase of a horse-drawn ambulance in February 1902. This was a community effort organised by the Buckley Cycle Carnival Committee, under the presidency of Canon Harry Drew, and assisted by 'the firms of the District who made up the balance of over £60 in proportion to the number of men they respectively employed'. The van, harness and whip were handed over at a ceremony in the new Council buildings. 'There was a large attendance and the van was escorted from Buckley Junction Station by a torch light procession, in which the Buckley Band and the Buckley Engineers Bands took part'.

This horse-drawn ambulance was in use for twenty-five years until it was replaced by a motor ambulance in June 1927. It was described as 'in every way up to date; beautifully cushioned, highly sprung, and containing the latest patent stretchers for giving patients comfort whilst transit is being made from the place of accident to the hospital'.[27]

It was long recognised that the district would benefit by the employment of a trained nurse, able to visit patients at home and give assistance to mothers in childbirth. Any form of elementary health care would have to be arranged and paid for on a voluntary basis. Industries were usually under contract to local doctors to provide medical attention at work and the benefit or friendly societies paid time off for sickness if the patient was a subscriber.

From the 1890s funds to pay for the services of a district nurse were raised in the Buckley/Bistre areas. In 1894 it was reported that 'several energetic young ladies, chiefly from the Congregational Chapel' held a supper to raise funds. This was supplemented 'by holding public sewing meetings every Wednesday afternoon in the ante room of the Central Hall Buckley, kindly lent by the Reverend Joseph Davies, for this deserving object'.[28] In December 1895, a bazaar lasting two days raised £45 towards the payment of a district nurse. The instigators were the Miss Catherall, Prenbrigog, and the Miss Gibson, Brookhill, which enabled the committee to continue the nurse's services over the winter months.[29] By 1900 a district nurse was recruited on what proved to be a permanent basis. The news was welcomed in Bistre:

> We are all delighted with the announcement that a Trained Nurse to attend the sick in cases of fever, serious illness, or accident is about to take up her residence in a central position within the Urban District. Her services have been secured by Mrs Drew for six months to commence with, for which period Mrs Drew has most generously taken upon herself the responsibility for providing the necessary funds to pay the salary and rent of a house. Should the experiment turn out a success, it is to be hoped that the matter will be taken up by rich and poor, employers and employed throughout the district. It must be clearly understood that the tentative engagement of a nurse, although for the benefit of the town and neighbourhood, is strictly private in its inception. Mrs Drew, while anxious to make the benefits as extensive as possible, thinks the whole of the two parishes, too large a field. Its boundaries as far as Bistre Parish is concerned lie within the limits of the Urban District.[30]

A progress report in June 1901 stated that:

> An effort is being made by Mrs Drew to raise £10 to provide Nurse Smith with a serviceable bicycle so that she may get about with as little fatigue as possible among sick cases. During the past seven months Nurse Smith has paid 462 visits to sick cases requiring attention. In addition she has paid 177 visits to cases not requiring her attention, and 415 general visits making a total of 1054 visits.[31]

The nursing service had advanced when, in 1918, the duties of the Bistre parish nurse were outlined in the annual report:

> Number of visits paid 1,555; patients, 96; maternity patients, 58; nights on duty 26. Since June, of last year, the nurse has been doing health visiting in the district, under the Flintshire County Council. She has visited 59 babies, and paid 218 visits.[32]

In February 1925 the vicar of Buckley, the Reverend D. Saunders Rees, invited all female subscribers of the St Matthew's Nursing Association to a social gathering held in the Church Hut to meet the newly appointed Nurse Hobson. The vicar mentioned that the services of the nurse were available to any one who subscribed the sum of 1s. 3d. per quarter and for this small amount all the members in any household had a claim to the nurse's assistance. He added that 'the Nursing Association was undenominational and was open to Church or Chapel folk alike. Nurse Hobson had come to Buckley with a fine reputation for she was fully qualified in all branches of the work and also a Church Army trained nurse'.[33]

In November 1926, the vicar of Bistre, A. W. Rees, and the Revd D. Saunders Rees, as Chairman of their respective parochial nursing associations, issued a joint-statement. In it they announced that they had unanimously decided to discontinue the association because of the progress 'made within the last 20 years by infant welfare centres with their attendant instructions to mothers', adding, that 'the question of nursing should no longer be left to philanthropic bodies, but it is time that the powers vested in the Ministry of Health should be put into operation.' Concluding that 'although they could still carry on, the committee feel that at the present moment they touch only a minority of the inhabitants of Buckley'.[34]

It was obviously proving difficult to raise funds on a voluntary basis and patients could no longer afford the basic subscription in the economic climate of the colliers strike and early signs of the great trade depression. But there must have been a demand that the service be continued.

The Flintshire County Nursing Association, in existence by 1899, was the co-ordinating body to which the district nursing associations were affiliated. Between the wars it was patronised by the Summers family, Lord and Lady Gladstone and other local gentry, who were the backbone of the organisation through their garden parties and other financial help. It was through this body that a district nursing association was reformed at Buckley in 1938 and obtained the excellent services of Nurse Florence Dyke, SRN, QN. She was soon faced, at the outbreak of the war, by an influx of evacuees from Birkenhead. A local baby clinic met weekly on Monday afternoon in the Welsh Calvinistic Methodist Chapel Sunday school building. Miss Gittins was the Chairman and Mrs George Lewis the Secretary. The report of the Buckley Nursing

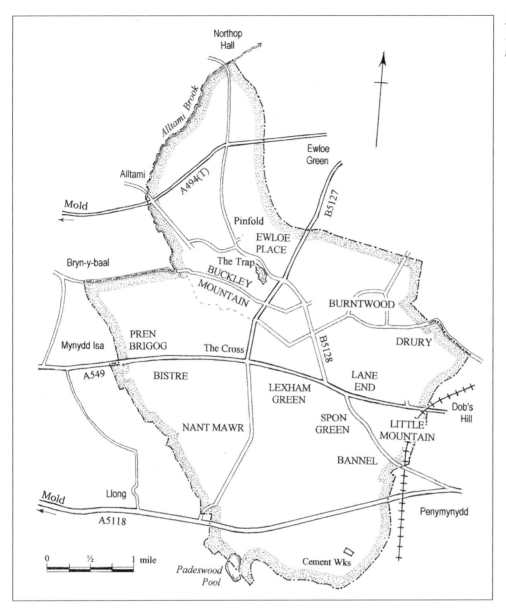

Map of Buckley Urban District.
[K. Lloyd Gruffydd]

Association for 1945 shows that it was financed by subscriptions of £273 10s. 8d. and £90 13s. from the works etc. The total income was £584 2s. 3d. and an additional £32 9s. 1d. profit from the dance.

> Nurse Dyke stated that during last year she had attended 146 new cases and paid 3,286 visits to patients in their homes, an increase of 305 visits on the previous year. The Secretary reported that Fearon had presented a bed rest to the Association, and the W.V.S. six hot water bottles.[35]

Gradually, between the wars, statutory health services were introduced. The Flintshire Education Authority provided health and dental care in eight elementary schools and a Child Welfare Centre catered for mothers and children. An attempt was being made to eradicate the dreaded scourge of tuberculosis, which thrived on malnutrition. This *ad hoc* system of health care was to continue until the introduction of the National Health Service in 1948.

Roads

Until 1897 maintenance of the roads was divided between the Hope and Hawarden Highways Board and the Mold Highways Board. They had inherited the care of the roads from the ecclesiastical parishes of Mold and Hawarden. In the eighteenth century independent authorities, turnpike trusts, had built and maintained new roads, charging a toll for their use. Turnpike roads from Chester to Northop, and from Mold to Chester and Wrexham, skirted the edges of Buckley Mountain. By the 1820s there were stretches of turnpike roads with tollgates from the Mold/Chester Road near Pentre Bridge to the Buckley Windmill, and from thence over Buckley Mountain and ending at Ewloe Green. It was generally agreed that the by-roads across the Mountain were in a bad condition. In 1861 the census enumerator complained that 'the Byways leading from Buckley Mountain, past Ewloe Barn to Pentre Moch are indescribably bad'. In 1874 the *Wrexham Advertiser* told its readers what to expect:

> If one took a stroll through the townships of Bistre and Buckley, one would see something rather shocking. Much has been said in our columns about this subject — about the sanitary state of this place. The road leading from Mold to the Lane End is the main sewer; stagnant matter in the ditches is an abomination for all travellers that way. The state of the road itself is really bad — it may be scraped occasionally, and the day we used it, it looked as though it had not been attended to for months past'.[36]

There was no improvement by 1883, and the ratepayers sent a petition to the chairman of the Mold Board 'complaining of the high rates of the township (Bistre) and nothing in return for the same. Several persons said that a local board should be formed in the township so that they could be sure of the roads being kept in better repair'.[37] The repair of roads was one of the first concerns of the new Urban District Council and they resolved to take over 'the roads leading from Alltami to Cross Roads, Buckley and also the branch road leading to Pinfold Lane'. To do this they proposed seeking the consent of the lord of the manor and his possible help. In May 1898 the sanitary inspector reported a great number of ditches alongside most roads as a nuisance. In some cases liquid manure ran on to the highway and rubbish choked the ditches. The Inspector requested the Council to serve notices on owners or occupiers to clean the ditches within ten days. Gradually some sort of order was established. The lord of the manor, P. B. Davies Cooke, agreed in August 1898 to hand over all the Mountain roads, and the Council employed three men on their roads. In 1906 the Gladstone Trustees made a new road 30-feet wide through Burntwood. It was not until 1911 that the Council finally faced the task of regularising the names of roads and numbering houses. For example, they decided that the road 'from the Bank to our boundary be called Mold Road; the road from the Bank to the Church Road, be called Brunswick road; from Church Road to our boundary, be called Chester Road; from Lane End to Liverpool Road, be called Church Road,' and so on. All streets were to be numbered, even, on the right side, and uneven, on the left.[38] It was the duty of Flintshire County Council to classify roads.[39]

Lighting
Buckley was well behind other towns in North Wales in lighting its streets. Attempts had been made before 1897 to introduce street lighting. The decision in these years had to be made by Bistre and Buckley as separate parishes. Both were handicapped in reaching a decision because the ratepayers could not agree which streets to light, and the farmers with their labourers voted against proposals from which they would fail to benefit. In February 1898 the Lighting Committee was asked to approach the gas company for an estimate of the cost of lighting the whole district, although priority was to be given to certain roads and streets. The Council then resolved that

Gas lamp at Lane End c.1926. [Buckley Library]

the cheapest and most efficient way to introduce gas lighting was to purchase the Buckley gas works outright. In April 1900 the gas company offered to sell their works to the Council for £475. The Council turned their offer down. In the meantime the vicar, Harry Drew, helped his parishioners see the light by providing 'eighteen Welsbach incandescent lamps' in Church Road in September 1900. This independent action prompted the Council to come to an arrangement with the gas company to light their streets. 'The lamps to be lit from dusk to 11 o'clock every night during the season except 35 nights allowance for the moon'. George Lewis chronicled the event: '1901, Oct. 2, Wed. The Streets of Buckley were lit by gas for the first time.'

The lamplighter became a familiar figure on the streets of Buckley. In March 1911 there were nine applicants for the post. Two were appointed for the Nant Mawr District. John Iball was responsible for 9 lamps at 4s. 6d. per week, and James Bryan for 10 lamps at 5s. per week. William Jones was appointed for Drury. In 1931, street lamps were still being lit by gas, for example, in Padeswood Road where Jos Edwards was the lamplighter. The North Wales Power Company brought the first supply of electricity to Buckley in December 1927, although it took some time before the illumination of the streets by gas was replaced by electricity. George Lewis wrote in his diary: '1933, Feb. 27, Mon. They put electric poles from the Cross Roads to Buckley Church for the first time.'

The gas works, on Mount Pleasant road, continued to play an important part in the life of the community. From 1900 to 1939 it was managed by Frederick Gittins, and then, when he retired, by his son Rupert Gittins. It was taken over during the war by Cambrian Holdings, Sandycroft. It became a sight in Buckley to see the money from the meters taken to the bank: it was no Wells Fargo. There were none of the precautions of Securicor to protect the takings. 'A horse-drawn cart was hired from Spon Green to convey money collected from the slot–meters to the bank, and this long after motor transport was available — much to the amusement of visitors to the district. Due to the heaviness of imperial coinage in the 1930s they progressed to the hiring of a car.'[40]

Water supply

Piping water into the area solved the problem of supplying Buckley with sufficient water for domestic and industrial purposes. The major problem was the situation of Buckley on a plateau. The Mold inspector advised in 1881 that the system of gravitation was the best and cheapest way, this was the method adopted by the new company, who brought their water from Moel Fammau and built a storage reservoir at Penbrigog. It was begun in 1886 and designed to hold four months supply for the whole district, allowing twenty gallons per head for the entire population. Before the construction of the reservoir the inhabitants of the Hawarden area of Buckley had received their water supply from deep wells or draw wells, six to eleven feet deep, which in some instances were affected by mine workings. Some inhabitants on Buckley Mountain had bought their water from a pauper named Tommy Leach, a water carrier. In 1893, the Hawarden and District Waterworks assumed responsibility for supplying an area which included Mold and Buckley.[41]

Scavenging and sewerage

It took over thirty years for Buckley Urban District to provide adequate sewerage arrangements. Before a scheme was carried out in 1929 the conditions which prevailed were primitive. It was the legendary era of the 'Golden Dream Boat', the local nickname of the night soil cart. In the 1920s the Council were responsible for emptying 1,350 closets, the drains in the town were, in the majority of cases, open ditches, and pollution was taking place in three of the brooks in the town. Scavenging and sewerage arrangements in the Urban District for the first thirty years of the twentieth century were dependent upon horse and cart. Running costs were minimal compared with the enormity of the problem. For example when the horse was changed in June 1916 a special deputation from the Council chose an animal which 'the owner had agreed to sell for £45 and to include the horse collar and the loan of his Lurry [sic], Cart and Gears free for one month and also to lend the stable free for one month'. The deputation and the Surveyor were despatched to the Royal Show in Manchester with a view to purchasing a Lurry [sic] and cart. A man was appointed to follow the horse and paid 27s. per week. The Council protected their investment with the resolution 'that the horse should have 5lb of oats per day in addition to the food which was now being supplied by Messrs G.

Amos Tarran's Cottage.
[Peter Hayes, FRO P/11/194]

Long Row. [Buckley Archive]

Watkinson & Sons.'[42]

The outbreak of the first First World War delayed the implementation of the first sewerage scheme, shortage of funds led to further postponement. In March 1930 Mr James Tyson opened the new sewerage works[43] and progress was made in connecting old and new housing. The sewerage scheme was in two parts and cost £1,500. It was reported in 1933 that 'Within the past eighteen months, over 450 houses have been connected to the main sewer and water closets constructed. When this work is being done other improvements have been effected — i.e. sinks, water-pipes, water laid on from the water company, yards provided, ash-pits abolished and ash-bins provided'.[44]

Housing
These few remarks do not attempt to provide a full account of housing in Buckley but a brief indication only of major trends until 1945.

The responsibility of Buckley Urban District Council for the maintenance of housing in its area increased after the First World War. Government legislation gave it powers to build council houses, demolish and replace slum dwellings and subsidise the building of houses in the private sector.

The housing stock in the area was not of a high rateable value. Housing accommodation in 1917 was given as 1,498 dwelling houses: 1,259 of rateable value of less than £10, 99 between £10–£12, 115 over £12 and under £20, and £25 with a rateable value over £20. Of this total 100 houses did not comply with the legislation of 1909 and 50 were to be condemned. The Council estimated that provision should be made for the erection of 100 houses at the close of the War. They were guarded in over reaching themselves, holding the view that the future of the brick and coal industry was uncertain and that it was 'unfair to burden the Town with any housing scheme unless the Council were satisfied that the population is likely to be permanent'.[45] This was an average of 4.47 persons per dwelling.

The majority of accommodation was for the working classes. There were no gentry houses and farmhouses would be more substantial than workers' dwellings, as would the vicarages at Buckley and Bistre, and maybe one or two manses for ministers. Amongst employers of labour Catherall, Gibson and Parry resided in the district, whereas Watkinson lived in Northop, and Hancock either at Padeswood or Hawarden.

The valuation return, made for the Inland Revenue, after Lloyd George's Finance Act in 1910, gives a detailed assessment of property in Buckley (Hawarden) and Buckley (Mold).[46] It shows a district of small properties. In Buckley (Hawarden), in Ewloe Town and Pentrobin, W. G. C. Gladstone is the chief landowner. In Ewloe Wood P. T. Davies-Cooke, as lord of the manor, owns the most land. In Buckley (Mold) there is no outstanding landowner. The Gascoyne Estate has shrunk to just over 100 acres of land. But the majority of properties are small cottages and gardens, some of them from the first settlement in the eighteenth century. A few are houses built by the Catherall's and Hancock's close to their works. The majority are divided between owner-occupiers and tenants.

The census taken in the Urban District in 1901 gave a population of 6,228 living in 1,378 houses; 2,454 persons lived in Buckley, in 537 houses, of which 251 had fewer than 5 rooms; and 3,774 in Bistre, in 841 houses, of which 476 had fewer than 5 rooms.

The major area of population for the Urban District was in Bistre. The boundary is the long strip of houses and shops, the 'Roadway' which stretched from Daisy Hill, Brunswick Road into Mold Road. Southwards of this line were the early mining communities of Nant Mawr and Spon Green. The roadway was made up of groups of small blocks and terraces of brick houses interspersed with shops. Most of these were described in the valuation of 1912 as cottages and gardens, as were the early developments in the Nant Mawr, Spon Green and the Square areas.

Many of these dwellings housed the tenants of local persons who had invested their savings and profits as tradesman in property. Prominent among these were: John J. Edwards, Holly Bank; James Brookfield; Thomas Rowlands; William Williams, Marine Stores; John Jones, Washington House; John Jones, Deva House; Daniel Hughes; Margaret Taylor; Sarah Hopwood; and others. The Buckley Lodge of the Oddfellows owned nine houses in Brook Street in Pentrobin. Most of the families were tenants with the remainder owner-occupiers.

The correspondent for the *Wrexham Advertiser* writing in February 1875 was particularly critical of the condition of housing in Buckley when he wrote that:

> The state of a large portion of the houses in this locality is appalling. The walls are so thin that the wind blows right through them. On a wet and rainy day, in not more than one hour the rain breaks in and runs about the room in streams. What aggravates the situation is the fact that the houses are only one storey high, and the inhabitants have to paddle through the water from morning to night. The rooms in the house consist of a kitchen, bedroom, and pantry. How closely the beds are packed together may be imagined from the size of the room which is twelve feet by thirteen feet. It is a scandal that Buckley should have inhabitants living under such conditions two centuries behind times. Indeed it reminds us of the mud huts in which the Romans found our ancestors living.[47]

In November 1906 the Urban District Council intervened on public health grounds to press for improvement in conditions and resolved, 'That the owners of houses in Little Mountain be written to, pointing out that the Council considered that water should be laid on to these houses, owing to the fever which had occurred there, and would like the owners to have the cistern water laid on if possible'. This was done.[48]

In 1909, the Housing Act prohibited the construction of back-to-back houses. Ten years later the post-war Housing Act gave local authorities financial assistance and responsibility to become the major suppliers of new working class and rented accommodation. Buckley Urban District Council took up the challenge and in May 1920 decided upon a new housing scheme to build two hundred houses: one hundred with parlours and one hundred without parlours.[49] People who preferred the parlour type were in the tradition of families who chose to regulate relationships with outsiders in the formal setting of the front room, in the atmosphere of the aspidistra and piano. Those who advocated the non-parlour type won the support of Raymond Unwin[50] who favoured a large living room with all the space used every day by the entire family. If the neighbours came in they met casually in the kitchen. In 1927, most of the applications for council houses[51] preferred the non-parlour design.

With the prospect of the introduction of a new sewerage scheme the Council began in 1927 to build houses. As George Lewis noted: '1927, Feb. 14, Mon. They began to build the new council houses at the Cross Roads Buckley.'

In 1933 the Council reported the progress of their building programme: 'Seventy-four houses have been erected by the Council since the year 1927 and subsidies have been paid by the Council in respect of sixty-eight erected by private enterprise.'[60]

By 1933, over 450 houses had been connected to the main sewer and the Council chose to recondition houses instead of demolishing them. This policy was soon abandoned in line with government policy and incentives. Government Housing Acts of 1930, 1933 and 1936 legislated for slum clearance. In November 1934 slum clearance took place in Mount Terrace and Hewitt's Lane. In October 1935 the Council accepted

Mill Lane Cottages, c.1990. [Buckley Library]

plans for the erection of houses without state assistance — 50 in Drury and the 30 in the Lane End District at Meg's Lane. George Lewis recorded: '1935, Dec. 18, Wed. 18 tenants were moved to the new Council Houses in Victoria Terrace from slum property in Lane End.'

In January 1937 it was decided to clear condemned houses in the following areas: Mold Road, Hewitt's Lane, Burntwood, Butcher's Row, Drury Lane, Nant Mawr, Daisy Hill, Old Parrot Cottages, Spitafield and Drury Lane. It required 68 dwellings to re-house them with a choice of two, three, four or five bed-roomed houses. The majority, forty-eight, were of three bedrooms. In June 1937 plans were laid before the Council for the erection of another 144 houses at three sites — Nant Mawr (60), Drury (36) and Coppa Fields (48) — and to serve the purposes of slum clearance (66), to abate over-crowding (43) and what were called self-supporting houses (35).[52] In spite of the war a future council house building programme was kept under review. In 1942 the District Council reported to the Welsh Board of Health survey that there were 1982 houses in the district, four had been lost through enemy action and one new house completed since the beginning of the war. There was thus a net gain in houses from 1917 to 1942 of 482, with a change in the ratio of persons per house from 4.47 to 3.48. In October 1943 the Council discussed a proposed housing scheme at Bistre. This was on a site of 17.25 acres between Bistre Church and Bistre Avenue, planned to accommodate 200 houses in blocks of sixes, fours and twos.

In spite of difficulties in the supply of materials and restrictions the ever-vigilant George Lewis recorded: '1946, May 13, Mon. They started to clear the ground in Nant Mawr to build 59 houses, which will reach to the Main Street, Buckley. Shone's, Knowl Lane, to be contracted for the Buckley Council in this matter. This was the Fraser Drive development.'

Public facilities

Although government legislation allowed the provision of public leisure facilities to be paid for out of the rates, councils were reluctant to do so, spending on average 0.5% on public libraries and around 1.2% on parks, pleasure gardens and open spaces. Buckley Urban District Council was no exception and followed the national trend in relying on philanthropic donors to provide them. It took the Urban District Council 40 years to acquire its three major public facilities — the free library, the swimming baths and the playing fields.

New Swimming Baths, Buckley.

The Swimming Baths — until the 1920s Buckley was a mining community. The collieries were the chief employers until the industry dramatically finished in 1934. It was the North Wales Miners Federation who liberally donated money from their welfare fund to build swimming baths in Buckley. This gesture was readily accepted by the Council and in 1922 they began to look for a suitable site. They chose, in July 1923, land immediately to the rear of the free library. The following May the press reported the

The Swimming Pool. [Buckley Library]

result of a meeting of the Council with a deputation from the Miners' Federation. They announced that £2,700 was to be given from the Miners' Welfare Fund and the 'remaining £1,000 to be provided by the Council out of ratepayers money'. Mr Collins, manager of the Buckley Collieries, presented the scheme to the Council, on behalf of the miners' deputation. 'He thought it more adaptable to such a place as Buckley where in the summertime a refreshing bath would stimulate morally as well as bodily, in the full sense of the word'. The welfare fund, he reported, was subscribed to by the miners at the rate of one penny per ton, for furthering the social welfare of the people'.[53] Eventually the miners' leaders generously agreed to meet the full cost of £5,000 for the construction of the swimming pool and its facilities.

The official opening ceremony by Mr Henry Neville Gladstone of Hawarden Castle, Lord Lieutenant of Flintshire, took place on 23 June, 1928. Also present were Mr Collins, head manager of the Buckley Collieries, the Chairman of the Baths Committee, members of the Miners Welfare Committee, local representatives and guests from London. Entertainment was by Chester Swimming Club who demonstrated their prowess and showed the potential of the pool with an exhibition of swimming, fancy diving, ornamental swimming and high diving. The Miners Federation then handed the premises to the Council in trust. The press gave the following account:

> The main plunge bath is 75 feet long by 30 feet wide, and is entirely of concrete construction, finished in waterproof white cement. At the deep end of the bath there is a high diving platform and two springboards. There is seating accommodation for 150 persons to watch the swimmers. There are dressing cubicles, six slipper baths and shower baths. The Jewel Filter Co. have installed a plant for the filtration of the water. The exterior of the structure is red brick, with asbestos roofing sheets laid on boards. The contractors were Messrs Hayes Bros. of Buckley. The cost of the undertaking, amounting to over £5,000 has been defrayed by the Miner's Welfare Committee. The whole of the buildings has been wired for electric lighting.[54]

The appointment, a few days earlier, of Mr Thomas Latham Catherall as supervisor, was a great success. He was the right person to introduce the swimming pool to Buckley residents and other users, which he did from 1928 until his retirement in 1965. He served the Swimming Club as coach and chairman and as a committee member of the North Wales and Welsh Amateur Swimming Association. In November 1928 the spectators gallery was improved at a cost of £45 and turnstiles introduced. Membership of the Swimming Club, under the Secretary Mr Metcalfe, quickly increased to 60. Members had the opportunity to learn to swim and to practice. Tuesdays evenings were reserved for 'gentlemen users'.

The swimming baths were an outstanding success and must have saved the lives of the more adventurous children over the years restraining them from the temptation of bathing in the clay holes of the

district. School children, in the care of teachers, were charged one penny each to use the pool. In December 1938 the Council proposed altering the baths 'with a view to facilities being provided for Physical Fitness Training at an estimated cost of £3,500.'[55]

The swimming baths were to serve the public until the beginning of the twenty-first century. In 1962, approximately half way through their life span, George Lewis noted: '1962, Apr. 28, Sat. Buckley Baths were officially reopened last night by Mr J. S. Parry Chairman of the UDC after an extensive renovation scheme costing £20,000.'

The Playing Fields — the lords of the manor, the Davies-Cooke family, of Gwysaney, Mold, were the obvious patrons to approach for land to provide a public recreation ground. In October 1904 the Council resolved to make this move 'with a view to some scheme of getting that part of the Common opposite to the Congregational

Henry Neville, Baron Gladstone of Hawarden. [St Deiniol's Library]

Chapel'.[56] Nothing came of this until 1931: the Council became possessed under a deed of gift of approximately twenty-one acres of land for Playing Fields. They stated 'that this land will, as soon as financial circumstances permit, be developed by the Council for this purpose'.

It was through the initiative of Henry Neville Gladstone, chairman of the Hawarden Embankment Trust, that in June 1933, a sum of £200 was given towards the purchase of necessary tools and materials, for the draining of part of the land for a proposed playing fields on the Common. The Council decided to spend part of this grant to purchase twenty overalls and twenty pairs of clogs for volunteers. They began to make plans:

It is proposed to level and drain nine acres of the Common, and the Surveyor has estimated it will take £100 per acre to carry out the work, so a sum of £900 is needed to complete such work. It is essential that the Common must first be levelled and drained, as a basis upon which the Committee of the Council could negotiate when making enquiries for grants from the Miners Welfare, the Carnegie Trust, and the National Playing Fields Association. The Common Land that has been given to the Urban Council is valued at £1,000.[57]

The Council decided to approach the Buckley Pantomime Company and the Buckley Choral Society for assistance in raising funds. In September the Council decided to have the work done by local unemployed. With the knowledge of the manager of the Labour Exchange the £200 from the Embankment Trustees was doled out to them in 5s. vouchers. In October it was reported that 181 unemployed men had offered their services voluntarily. To share the work it was decided that the volunteers would work in groups of twenty, a week at a time, with two shifts a day. The following week two other groups were to take their place, and so on, to give all the volunteers an opportunity. In October 1934, 42 men were working on the drainage. Further financial assistance was provided as the scheme progressed by the Miners Welfare Fund and the Hawarden Embankment Trustees. On this basis the work proceeded until July 1936. On 25 July the playground was opened by Lady Maud Ernestine Gladstone, the widow of Henry Neville, 1st Baron Gladstone, who had been ennobled in 1932. Philip T. Davies-Cooke, the lord of the manor, who had presented the land, unveiled the notice board, which carried the inscription:

Buckley Urban District Council Children's Playground. Land presented by Philip T. Davies Cooke, Esq., JP, DL, Lord of the Manor. Cost of laying out playing ground defrayed by the North Wales Committee of the Miners Welfare Fund. Opened 25th July 1936, by the Lady Gladstone of Hawarden. R. Hewitt, JP, Chairman of the Council.

The press report acknowledged the help of the various Buckley works 'who had been exceptionally good in providing material', concluding, that 'the new playing ground comprises some four acres, enclosed with iron railings. Macadam paths have been laid around the ground, and the equipment included two sets of swings, a roundabout, and a shute'.[58]

It failed to attract the local children and eventually the site ceased to be used as a playground and became the traditional setting for the Jubilee Service.

The Free Library — this description of the work of the Urban District Council began with an account of the choice of the site of the Free Library in 1902, which generated much passion in the community. Here we return to the library and examine how the Council managed the first of its public facilities.[59]

The Carnegie Free Library was opened in September 1904. The library building consisted of a reading room, book room, committee room and an upper room; there was an entrance hall and cloakrooms for men and women. The reading room, open from 9 am, was the room most used by the public. The regular readers used it as a kind of club. Most of them were elderly retired gentlemen who discovered that its friendly atmosphere gave them a certain amount of freedom. Here they could meet their former work mates, escape from the jurisdiction of their wives and daughters, and enjoy smoking their pipes or cigarettes in a place were regulations were more honoured in the breach than in the observance. Horses could be chosen, football results checked, and sensations relished with the aid of an excellent selection of national and local newspapers. The weekly and monthly illustrated magazines such as *The Strand, The Sphere, The Illustrated*

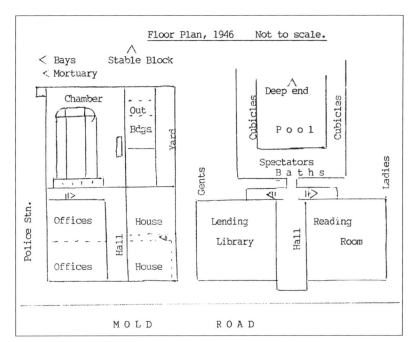

Floor Plan, 1946   Not to scale.

< Bays   Stable Block
< Mortuary

Chamber

Out
Bdgs

Yard

Deep end

P o o l

Cubicles

Cubicles

Spectators
B a t h s

Gents

Ladies

Police Stn.

Offices

House

Hall

Offices

House

Lending

Library

Hall

Reading

Room

M O L D   R O A D

Plan of Buckley Municipal Buildings, drawn by Mr Eric Hayes.

Robert James Chesters, the first Librarian of the Buckley Carnegie Library. [Buckley Library]

London News and *Titbits*, gave them the only vision of the nation and the world available to them before radio and television. Every reader over the age of sixteen years of age could borrow one book at a time from the book room which was open from 6 pm to 8 pm Mondays to Thursdays, and until 9 pm on Fridays and Saturdays. The committee room, designed for the library committee, was available to voluntary organisations. At the top of the building was an upper room: no one has ever discovered what the architect had in mind for this room. The general term 'educational purposes' probably justified its use for woodwork classes. During the Second World War it was used by the parents and teachers of evacuees as a meeting place to care for the children's clothes.

For over fifty years the library was managed on a shoestring. It was unnecessary for the librarian to have a professional qualification. What the Council wanted was someone to live in the caretaker's house next door, clean the library, hand out the books and manage the bowling green at the rear of the building during the long summer evenings. The budget in 1913–14, allocated £26 a year for payment to the librarian, £10 for the purchase of books, £10 for newspapers and periodicals and £10 for other items. From 1904 Mr R. Chesters was the first librarian. Mr R. J. Williamson succeeded him in 1916 and was librarian until he died in 1943. For many years he combined his post as librarian with his job as Council foreman in the Roads Department. Fortunately, Williamson had three daughters to assist him in cleaning the library and doing duty in the book room. The library was arranged in a very elementary way. The donor, Andrew Carnegie, made no stipulations about a catalogue system. Instead, the books were arranged on the shelves, irrespective of classification, as fiction or non-fiction, in alphabetical order. Mr William Davies, Head Master of Bistre School, and Chairman of the Library, chose the new books, with the help of Bessie Williamson the librarian's daughter. In 1931 library membership totalled 960, out of a population of 6,899. At this time the Library Committee came to an arrangement with Flintshire County Library that on the payment of £20 they were allowed to borrow 500 of their books. This increased the stock to 1,850 with issues in 1931–2 of 15,000. This agreement lasted until 1944.

When Williamson died in 1943, he was succeeded by young Miss Gwyneth Catherall. This was a very convenient appointment for the Council to make because she lived next door. Her father was Mr Thomas Latham Catherall, the Superintendent of Buckley Baths. Miss Catherall carried out the duties of librarian until 1956 when she was succeeded by Mrs B. Peters. Students receiving further education had always been able to borrow books, through the library, from the University College of Wales at Aberystwyth. Mrs Peters began for the first time, to build up a children's library. The library was reorganised and the room above used as a regular meeting place by Buckley groups.

In 1966 the Council transferred its responsibility for the management of Buckley Free Library to the Flintshire County Library Service and Clwyd County Council in 1974. Buckley Library became a branch library opened for 44 hours per week, including two evenings. In January 1977 Buckley Free Library, the Carnegie Library, was closed, and was replaced by a new building in the Precinct. Opening hours were increased to over 50 and the Library became the headquarters for the Alyn and

The Buckley Fire Brigade during the Second World War c.1940–1.
[Buckley Society Archive]

Deeside area. The Area Librarian was Mr William Walpole and Mrs Carol Shone Area Senior Assistant and eventually Community Librarian until 2000.

The Fire Service — the fear of war in 1938 and the demonstration in the Spanish Civil War of the destructive capability of Nazi air power, prompted the Urban District Council to establish a fire service in Buckley. In 1938 the Council terminated their arrangement with the Mold Joint Fire Brigade Committee whereby they paid £40 a year for the entitlement to call for the services of the brigade whenever necessary. It cost them £970 to set up their own brigade. In December 1938 they advertised for twelve men, one of whom should have mechanical experience and knowledge of driving a motor vehicle. The first recruits were trained in Chester.

This concludes the review of the first 50 years of the Urban District Council. Gradually the Community's infrastructure had been established and a sense of pride and optimism was beginning to reassert itself by the time of the outbreak of the Second World War on 3 September 1939.

Notes

1. Peter Kelsall, 'Buckley Soldiers from the Great War; Part 1.', *Buckley, 29*.
2. *Chester Chronicle*, 23/11/1895.
3. ibid.
4. ibid.
5. ibid.
6. *Buckley Parish Magazine*, March 1898.
7. *Chester Chronicle*, 8/3/1902.
8. *Chester Chronicle*, 10/9/1904.
9. FRO, Glynne/Gladstone 949 21/6/1901; FRO, GG 947 7/3/1902.
10. ibid.
11. *Buckley Parish Magazine*, April 1902.
12. *County Herald*, 11/7/1902.
13. *County Herald*, 18/7/1902
14. FRO, GG 949 14/7/1902.
15. FRO, GG 949 5/2/1903.
16. *County Herald*, October 1891
18. ibid 10/2/1892.
19. ibid 10/11/1893.

20. *County Herald*, August 1892.

21. *County Herald*, 24/3/1893.

22. *County Herald*, 11/5/1894.

23. G. Johnson, 'The Buckley Telephone Exchange, 1896-1936', *Buckley*, 29.

24. *County Herald*, 25/7/1902.

25. Deposited in FRO.

26. Pam Millington, 'A brief history of Dobshill Hospital; from its beginning in 1902 to the present day'. *Buckley*, 22.

27. *Mold, Deeside and Buckley Leader*, 17/6/1927.

28. *County Herald*, 9/11/ and 21/12/1894.

29. *Chester Chronicle*, 7/12/1895.

30. *Bistre Parish Magazine*, 1900.

31. *County Herald*, 14/6/1901.

32. *Chester Chronicle*, 23/5/1918.

33. *Mold, Deeside and Buckley Leader*, 20/2.1925.

34. *Bistre Parish Magazine*, November, 1926.

35. *Chester Chronicle*, May 12 1945, and J. B. Lewis, 'The Flintshire County Nursing Association' Ystrad Alun Summer 2000, and a personal communication.

36. *Wrexham Advertiser*, 17/1/1874.

37. *Chester Chronicle*, 6/1/1883.

38. A full list of the names and extent of the roads is given in the Urban District Council minutes, 26/9/1911.

39. FRO, D/DM/122/5 — map showing classification of roads in proposed by Flintshire County Council 1907.

40. Esther Lloyd, Charles Duckworth, K. Lloyd Gruffydd, 'A short account of bringing gas and gas lighting to Buckley up to 1950,' *Buckley*, 12, p. 42.

41. Charles Duckworth, 'Bringing Water to Buckley', *Buckley*, 20.

42. UDC Minutes, 20/6 and 28/11/1916.

43. *Mold, Deeside and Buckley Leader*, 21/3/1930.

44. UDC Minutes, 1/9/1933.

45. UDC Minutes, November 1917.

46. FRO, VR/2/13 and VR/2/16.

47. *Wrexham Advertiser*, Feb. 1875, quoted in *Buckley*, 10.

48. UDC Minutes, 11/10/1906

49. ibid, 20/4/1920.

50. Distinguished town planner. He was responsible for the munitions township at Mancot Royal in First World War.

51. ibid, 5/10/1927.

52. UDC Minutes, 27/6/1937.

53. *Mold, Deeside and Buckley Leader*, 16/5/1924.

54. ibid, 6/7/1928.

55. UDC Minutes, 13/12/1938.

56. UDC Minutes, 18/10/1904.

57. *Mold, Deeside and Buckley Leader*, 23/6/1933.

58. ibid, 31/7/1936.

59. This account relies on FRO D/DM/870/1 'History of the Public Libraries of Flintshire,' John B. Beagan, thesis for the Fellowship of the Library Association, October, 1979. And FRO D/DM/434/181 'Buckley Town Library, an account' by Mrs Bessie Jones (née Williamson), and an interview with Miss Gwyneth Catherall by Mrs Carol Shone, 25/4/1990.

Chapter 14
War and Peace, 1897–1945

1897 Queen Victoria's Jubilee

In retrospect, the celebration of Queen Victoria's reign of sixty glorious years was a turning point in the history of Buckley. During the old Queen's lifetime Buckley reached its maturity as an industrial community. Inspired by her example of family life, and moral rectitude, there was an unparalleled growth in places of public worship. The population of the United Kingdom grew dramatically, an increase reflected in the large numbers of children who were now in receipt of compulsory education. Benjamin Disraeli, William Gladstone's main political rival, had persuaded the widowed Queen to wear an imperial crown as Empress of India. The long peace after Waterloo in 1815, was now threatened by colonial wars and the ambitions of other European powers, who wanted their own empires in Africa and the Pacific. There was a price to be paid for empire. The red coats were soon to be exchanged for khaki in South Africa in 1899 and Belgium and France in 1914.

Mr W. E. Gladstone and Mrs Drew were present at the service in St Matthew's in June 1897 to celebrate her Majesty's Jubilee, when the Reverend Harry Drew preached an admirable sermon on the social and moral blessings of the Queen's reign. Religious services were held throughout Buckley. The occasion was reported in the press:

> On Sunday, the Buckley Royal Engineer Volunteers, under the command of Major Gibson, attended St Matthew's, and, at the close, the band accompanied the congregation in singing the National Anthem. On Tuesday, there were strong manifestations of loyalty displayed. The interest and enthusiasm with which the programme was carried out, and the marvellous success of the whole proceedings were unparalleled in local history. All the children on the registers of the day schools were assembled at their respective schools, where they were supplied with a capital tea and presented with medals.

The 1500 children were marched to the Common:

> On arrival on the Mountain, the Buckley division of the schools were formed on the right, and the Bistre division on the left of the Volunteers, and then were sung 'Lord of Heaven and Earth etc.', 'God bless the Prince of Wales' and 'God save the Queen'.

Tea was served, followed by children's sports, after which balloons were released and each child given a bun and an orange. By ten o'clock the celebrations had moved to the Knowle Hill where a bonfire was lit and fireworks displayed.[1]

The Boer War, (1899–1902)

Britain became involved in a war in South Africa with the Boer republics of the Transvaal and the Orange Free State, under the Presidency of Kruger. At the root of the struggle was possession of rich resources of gold and diamond mines by the Boers and the attempt by Britain to gain control of them. The progress of the war at first went badly for the British who were outmanoeuvred by the guerrilla tactics of the Boers. A feature of the war was the impression it made on British public opinion, evoking hysterical displays of patriotism. This reached its height when British troops, besieged by the Boers in two obscure settlements at

The 1st Flintshire (Buckley) Volunteers c.1900.
[Buckley Society Archive]

The 1st Flintshire (Buckley) Volunteers c.1900.
[Buckley Society Archive]

Mafeking and Ladysmith, were relieved in February and May 1900.

Men from Buckley became involved in the war as members of a volunteer force. In 1852 the volunteers had replaced the militia. The 1st Flintshire (Buckley) Engineer Volunteers had their headquarters in Mill Lane. Under the terms of the Militia Act 1852, men served for five years, and, on 'joining up,' received a cash bounty. Members had to attend an annual training camp, local drills, parades, and church parades. The Buckley Corps were commanded in the 1890s by Major Gibson, a brickworks manager. The Volunteers were in great demand to parade with their band and enliven public and festive occasions in Buckley and district.

In 1900, selected groups of Volunteers, recruited from North Wales counties, were formed into Service Detachments. Buckley men served in the 1st Service Detachment and, on arrival in South Africa, they were attached to 'A' Pontoon Troop, Royal Engineers, and were engaged in repairing the railway between Ladysmith and Standerton. They returned home in June. Other local men saw service in South Africa with other regiments.

Although the war had not ended, four men returned in July 1901, and were given a hero's welcome and each presented with a silver watch. The 1st Flintshire Volunteers were disbanded in April 1908.

It was in the years of the next generation that the blast of war was to sound, summoning them to the trenches of Flanders. Many of them had been prepared at school by daily drill exercises. Marching to the rhythms of brass bands was part of the routine of religious processions and public occasions. Many boys belonged to the recently formed troops of Scouts inspired by the example of General Robert Baden Powell, and others, as at St Matthew's, to the Church Lads' Brigade, under the vicar, Douglas Pelly.

In the run up to the First World War, Lloyd George was conducting his campaign against poverty. He was Chancellor of the Exchequer in the reforming Liberal government, in power from 1906. Its reforms benefited the working man and the elderly, by introducing sickness and unemployment provisions, old age pensions, and labour exchanges. The coal strike of 1912 and the closure of brickworks, collieries and potteries unsettled some of the young men, who were willing to travel to the dominions or the United States to find work and adventure. There was an emigration agent in Padeswood Road. In July 1907 the local newspaper reported:

During the past three months there has been a good deal of emigration from Buckley to Canada. Almost every week parties are going out, and we hear that many of the Settlers from Buckley are doing well. The emigrants from Buckley are mostly unmarried men engaged in the brick setting, joinery, and similar trades. It is worthy of remark that the Canadian journal, which is taken at the Free Library, proves exceedingly useful to those who desire information about Canada, and who have a desire to go out there. A very interesting New Zealand journal may also be perused at the Free Library.[2]

Major John Merriman Gibson. He is wearing the Volunteer Decoration.
[FRO /PH/11/191]

Many of these young men returned to Europe as members of the armed forces of their adopted countries. Great Britain entered the Great War, or the First World War, as we shall call it, on 4 August 1914. The conflict was to last until the Armistice was signed on 11 November 1918. The account of the war which follows is a summary of the main events, at home and abroad, as they relate to Buckley.

A War Diary

1914

George Lewis recorded the main events at the beginning of the War, as he saw them.

July 27 Tue War declared between Austria and Serbia.
Aug 1   Sat Germany declares war on Russia.
Aug 3   Mon German ultimatum to Belgium. British fleet mobilised.
Aug 7   Wed War begins between Great Britain and Austria-Hungary.
Aug 14 Thur Two million men ranged along 250 miles for the greatest battle in the world's history. The German right was routed with great slaughter in attempting to break down the Belgian left. Food rose in this country to excessive prices; butter 1/9d. per *lb*. sugar 6d. per *lb*.

The origins of the First World War are to be found as early as the defeat of France by Germany in 1871 and in the reaction of the other great European powers to the ambitions of the German Empire after 1871. The Great Powers divided themselves into two opposing camps. Germany, Austria-Hungary and Italy, the Triple Alliance, were ranged against France, Russia and Great Britain, the Triple Entente. The situation was aggravated by Anglo-German naval rivalry, in a race to build battleships. In the Balkans, Russian and Austrian interests were in conflict over the issue of Serbian nationalism. Turkey resented Russian threats in the region. These rivalries came to a head in the murder at Sarajevo (Bosnia) on 28 June 1914, of Franz Ferdinand, heir to the thrones of Austria-Hungary. The great powers declared war in accordance with their treaty obligations. Germany attacked France — and violated Belgian neutrality in the process. Turkey joined Germany in November 1914 and Italy joined the Allies in May 1915. Hostilities spread throughout the continent to several theatres of war in which Britain was involved.

At first, no one thought that the war would last long. It would be over by Christmas. On declaration of war Britain committed its regular army of 160,000 troops, the British Expeditionary Force, to cross the Channel and support French troops in Belgian, against the German invaders. The BEF was forced to retreat from Mons in August. In October and November the British lost 50,000 men at the First Battle of Ypres. The mobile nature of the war became static in the winter of 1914–15, when German and Allied armies faced each other in a line of trenches stretching from the Channel coast to the Swiss frontier. Britain received thousands

of Belgian refugees. On 7 August Field Marshal Lord Kitchener pointed his finger appealingly at the nation's young men with the instruction 'Your Country needs you'. By December, a million men had enlisted in the Army and the Terriorials. Kitchener's volunteers, entitled the New Army, needed months of training before they were ready to join the regulars in France or elsewhere.[3]

School log books contain entries relating

German internees arrive at Queensferry, September 1914. [FRO PH/51/96]

to the War. In 1914 the following entries occur:

Sep 4 The National Anthem was sung each day at the close of School. Special lessons have been given referring to the War.

Oct 2 A league of Young Patriots has been formed in the School, (St Matthew's). Each member is expected to do all she can to help in any way, those who are in distress in the war. They have been knitting socks for the soldiers – a parcel of 40 to be sent.

Oct 28 A parcel containing 100 pairs of socks and another containing 32 field pillows sent to Devonshire House, Piccadilly. Reply, received from Queen Mary's Lady in Waiting said, 'The Queen is much touched at the children saving their Saturday pennies to buy the wool and congratulate the Young Patriots League on their first aid being one of sacrifice. (Bistre Council, Girl's School).

Dec 17 Five Belgian Refugees visited School this afternoon – three adults and two children . The men thanked the girls for their gifts of jam. The little girls sang a Flemish song for the scholars & they in return sang the Belgian & Russian National Anthems. (St M's, Girls)

The Press reported a public meeting in support of recruiting for the army, in October, at the Picture House, Buckley.'There was a crowded audience, composed chiefly of young men. The proceedings were of a loyal and enthusiastic nature. The main speaker was the local Member of Parliament, the Liberal, J. Herbert Lewis. He also attended a concert given to raise funds for the troops, in Tabernacle, by the Buckley United Choir, composed of a hundred singers, from nearly all the places of worship. By the end of October there were 178 men engaged on active service.[4]

The original Lord Kitchener recruitment poster by Alfred Leete.

1915

Because of the need to train the volunteer recruits from Buckley many of them did not go into battle until late in 1915. The main scenes of action were the Second Battle of Ypres (April 22–May 25), when British casualties numbered 59,000, and the British attack at Loos, in September, with 50,000 casualties. In April the British and French opened a new theatre of war at Gallipoli against the Turks. The British casualties for the campaign, which lasted until the evacuation in January 1916, numbered 210,000. The public were angered by the sinking of the *Lusitania* by a U-boat in May, and the German use of mustard gas in their spring offensive.

The first recorded military death was noted by George Lewis on January 31. 'A military funeral at Bistre Church for a Canadian soldier'. This was Private R. A. Hughes of the Canadian Medical Corps, who had served in Flanders. In April 1915, Buckley was saddened and shocked by the death by a sniper's bullet, of the local 30-year old squire and Lord Lieutenant of Flintshire, W. G. C. Gladstone, who had just arrived at the front at Laviente, as an officer in the Royal Welsh Fusiliers. The first deaths in action were from the Royal Welsh: Private John Ellis was killed at Ypres on 16 May and three other privates in the regiment at the battle of Loos in September and October. Recruitment continued. By March over 130 old scholars from St Matthew's school had joined the colours. The establishment of a Red Cross Hospital at Leeswood was an outlet for public sympathy and many local women worked there on a voluntary basis. In October school children collected 650 large potatoes for the patients.

1916

The war was developing into a stalemate. There were shortages of men and ammunition. Recruitment was guaranteed by the first Conscription Bill of January 1916 when men aged between 18 and 41 years were compelled to serve. In April the Easter Rising began the Irish troubles. In May the naval battle at Jutland

was indecisive and signalled that the war had to be won on the Western Front. Lord Kitchener was drowned on the way to Russia in June when HMS *Hampshire* hit a mine. Worse was to come in July with the large-scale offensive on the western front at the battle of the Somme. It lasted from 1 July to 18 November. The casualties increased amongst the Buckley soldiers, many of them serving with the RWF. Other men perished of disease in the ill-fated campaign in Mesopatamia. They are commemorated on the Basra Memorial.

Many local women were employed in the munitions factory at Queensferry. British summertime was introduced. The penetration of Zeppelins along the south coast and as far as London, brought fear, alarm and casualties. For example, in February, the trustees of Brunswick Chapel agreed to insure the chapel against air raids and left the matter in the hands of the minister. George Lewis recorded in his diary that a bomb was found at the Compound (the munitions factory) in August, where the same month, Miss Roberts had her arm cut off. St Matthew's logbooks contain a variety of entries relating to the War:

> May 18. Each scholar has copied a letter from the blackboard today to take home asking their mother to allow them go to bed at least one hour earlier when the Summer Time Act is in force viz. 21st May.

Right: Lieutenant W. G. C. Gladstone, killed in action 1915. [FRO PH/ 28/B/6]

Far right: Lieutenant John Cragg Dunn. [Buckley Library]

Women munitions workers at the Queensferry factory. [FRO PH/51/134]

Whit Week. No holiday given this week at the request of the Board of Education in order to fall in line with the munitions workers.

June 2. This morning Mr Fred Birks, formerly of Buckley, but who came with the Anzacs from Melbourne, gave a very interesting account of his journey from Australia to Egypt, the campaign in Gallipoli and Sinai Peninsular, and his journey from Egypt to France, where the Anzacs are now.

Sept. 4. Special war lesson on the destruction of a Zeppelin in Hertfordshire on Sunday morning was given today.

Sept. 6. A bit of charred wood & damaged metal from the wrecked Zeppelin were shown to the girls.

Dec. 19. The three teachers, who have given their services to Leeswood Military Hospital during the past year, went out early this afternoon to attend an 'At home' there.

1917

In December 1916, as a result of a political crisis, Asquith was replaced as Prime Minister by Lloyd George. For civilians, 1917 was regarded as the worst year of the war. German U-boats sank one in four allied merchant ships, which caused panic and food problems for the rest of the war. Lloyd George successfully reduced the number of sinkings with the introduction of convoys. The United States came into the war in April, and Russia, on the verge of revolution, made peace with Germany in November.

On 31 July Haig launched the Third battle of Ypres, which lasted until 18 November, generally known, from its final episode, as Passchendaele, and by Lloyd George as 'The Battle of the Mud'. The British suffered casualties of 418,654, and Buckley it's greatest number of fatalities. Amongst these was Fred Birks, the Buckley hero of the First World War. He won the first Victoria Cross awarded to a Flintshire man in the war. To mark the high regard in which he was held a memorial was erected outside St Matthew's School.[5] It bears the inscription

> THIS CENOTAPH IS ERECTED BY OLD SCHOLARS
> AND FRIENDS IN PROUD REMEMBRANCE OF
> THE GREAT HONOUR HE CONFERRED ON THIS SCHOOL
> IN MEMORY OF
> LIEUT BIRKS VC; MM.
> AUST'N EXPEDITIONARY FORCE
> AN OLD SCHOLAR OF THIS SCHOOL
> WHO ON SEPTEMBER 21st 1917
> DURING THE GREAT WAR GAVE HIS LIFE
> FOR HIS KING AND COUNTRY

2nd Lieutenant Frederick Birks was born 31 August 1894 at Lane End Buckley, the third child of Samuel and Mary Birks. Educated at St Matthew's School, he was apprenticed at the annealing plant, John Summers and Sons, Steelworks, Shotton, before emigrating to Australia

Memorial to 2nd Lieutenant Fred Birks, VC, MM, in the grounds of St Matthews Church Hall. [Buckley Society Archive]

in 1914. Less than three months later, war was declared and Birks enlisted in the 1st Australian Division.[6] He was remembered with affection as a lively school boy and was the drummer in the Church Lads' Brigade. On enlisting, Birks was assigned to the 2nd Field Ambulance unit attached to the 2nd Australian Infantry Brigade. He was sent to Gallipoli and wounded there on 20 June 1915. On recovery he went to France in the Spring of 1916 and was promoted lance corporal. In July he was awarded the Military Medal 'for consistent good conduct' and bravery in the field, for action at Pozieres. When next on leave, he proudly took the medal to St Matthew's to show the staff and pupils. He was promoted corporal in August, commissioned as 2nd lieutenant on 29 April 1917, and transferred to the 6th Australian Infantry Battalion. In July, the German Army launched an offensive in its attempt to capture the Belgian ports. The British counter-attacked, supported by Australians, in what was known as the Menin Road Battle. Here Birks was killed on 21 September on the outskirts of Glencourse Wood. He was buried in the Perth Cemetery (China Wall), Zillebeke, Belgium, designed by Sir Edwin Lutyens. The citation for his award of the Victoria Cross, in the *London Gazette*, 8 November 1917, reads:

Fred Birks, VC, MM, wearing the uniform of a private in the Australian Imperial Force. [W. Alister Williams]

For most conspicuous bravery in attack when, accompanied by only a corporal, he rushed a strong point which was holding up the advance. The corporal was wounded by a bomb, but Second Lieutenant Birks went on by himself, killed the remainder of the enemy occupying the position and captured a machine gun. Shortly afterwards he organised a small party and attacked another strong point which was occupied by about twenty-five of the enemy, of whom many were killed and an officer and fifteen men captured. During the consolidation this officer did magnificent work in reorganising parties of other units, which had been disorganised during the operations. By his wonderful coolness and personal bravery Second Lieutenant Birks kept his men in splendid spirits throughout. He was killed at his post by a shell whilst endeavouring to extricate some of his men who had been buried by a shell.

The VC was presented to his brother, Sergeant Samuel Birks, RFA, by HM King George V at Buckingham Palace on 19 December 1917.[7] In his knapsack was the Bible, which the members of the vicar's Bible Class had given to him.[8]

Another much decorated Buckley First World War hero was Horace Enfield Simmons, MC, DFC, MA. Born in Buckley in 1895, he survived the war, and afterwards became an Anglican cleric. On the outbreak of war Simmons was studying classics at Durham University with the intention of taking holy orders. Volunteering, he trained as an officer, and in May 1915 was commissioned in the 5th Bn The Welsh Regiment. Whilst serving in France he was wounded three times: once at Laviente (where W. G. C. Gladstone was killed) and at the battle of the Somme in 1916. Simmons returned to the front in 1917, was gassed at Ypres, and awarded the Military Cross. The citation read, 'for conspicuous gallantry and devotion to duty during a raid on the enemy's trenches. He displayed great courage and skill in fixing a torpedo in position in the enemy's wire. He has at all times set a fine example'. After his

The grave of Lieutenant Fred Birks, VC, MM, at Perth Cemetery (China Wall). At the foot of the headstone is inscribed: 'Greater love hath no man than this that he lay down his life for his friends.' [W. Alister Williams]

A rather indistinct photograph of the Revd Horace Enfield Simmons, MC, DFC, MA, wearing all his decorations. [Buckley Society Magazine 18]

French experience Simmons transferred to the Royal Flying Corps in 1917 in which he saw service as a pilot and observer in Salonika and was mentioned in despatches. At the end of the First World War he flew with the newly formed Royal Air Force as part of the No. 47 Squadron, which was seconded to support the White Russians against the Bolsheviks. Here again his courage and devotion were marked by the award of the Distinguished Flying Cross and, from the Russians, the Cross of St George (the Russian equivalent of the Victoria Cross) and the Order of St Stanislas. The British, forced to flee by the Bolshevik Red Guards, barely escaped with their lives.

On his return, Simmons completed his theological training at Ely College, and was ordained in Birmingham Cathedral in 1923, where he served on the staff for a year. He then went to the parish of West Kirby as a curate for two years before coming to Buckley in 1926. In 1932 he was appointed to the living of Owston, Yorkshire, by the patron Captain R. Davies-Cooke of Skellow Hall. He married a Buckley girl, a daughter of Mr and Mrs Alfred Everall. No doubt his wounds, gassing and privations in Russia shortened his life. He died in his sleep on 28 November 1935 at the age of 40 years and was buried in St Matthew's Churchyard. After his death his wife entered the religious life as an Anglican Poor Clare, at St Mary's, Wantage, where she later became the Mother Superior.[9]

The Reverend Douglas Raymond Pelly, vicar of St Matthew's, Buckley, 1905–14, was an inspiration to the boys he had nurtured as members of his Bible Class and the Church Lads' Brigade. Pelly influenced Birks and Simmons and many others. He had enjoyed a life of adventure before he came to Buckley, having served in Natal as a chaplain to the Rhodesian Horse, and afterwards as the principal of the Industrial School and Native Missionary Centre in the diocese of Mashonaland. During the First World War he became an Army chaplain serving in Serbia and Salonika and may have met Horace Simmons there. Pelly was awarded the Distinguished Service Order in January 1918 'for services in the field during the past two years'.

1918.

We learn about the effects of the war on the lives of the people of Buckley in 1917 and 1918 from the local newspapers and school logbooks. The local people took every opportunity to show their kindness to the boys who were serving, by entertaining wounded soldiers as well as staff and nurses from Leeswood Hall Military Hospital. People from Bistre and Buckley provided concerts, teas, whist drives and motor transport. Cropper's Picture House, the Palace, at Lane End, was a popular venue. A number of Charlie Chaplin films were featured and live items were performed by soldiers home on leave from France. In January 1918 Drum Major Will Roberts performed on the piano,

St Matthew's Church Lads' Brigade, 1912. The Revd Pelly is seated in the centre with a young Fred Birks standing immediately behind him. [FRO PH/11/180]

accompanied by Private Elvet Rowlands on the violin. Before the war, Will Roberts was the resident pianist at the Palace. In July, a gala and dance was held on the cricket ground in aid of the Buckley Prisoners of War Fund. The programme consisted of May-pole dances by the scholars from St Matthew's Day School, a baby and pram race, tug of war and a Charlie Chaplin impersonation, with music for dancing played by the Buckley Volunteers and the Buckley Royal Town Band.

Food shortages affected morale during the final two years of the war and the government introduced rationing. The Buckley Urban District Council intervened in March 1917 to ensure a good crop of potatoes by arranging a meeting with the farmers to provide 40 additional plots for residents.[10] In April 1918 the Miners:

> ... held a meeting to protest against the attitude the local farmers are taking in regard to providing potato ground for the public and the proposed advanced price for the land. It appears the farmers only intend making one half the potato ground for the general public this year, and at the same time they propose advancing the price. As a protest against the farmers, the miners decided to stop coal supplies from the Buckley Collieries of all the farmers who insist upon the new arrangement.[11]

In June, some shops issued sugar tickets entitling customers to half-a-pound of sugar for each member of their family. The organisers of the traditional Jubilee Teas in July were informed by the Food Controller that 'if such entertainments are given the amount of food should conform strictly to the regulations laid down'. In an attempt to provide a representative membership, the Buckley UDC nominated 12 people in August — 6 from the Council, 3 members to represent Labour, 2 members to represent the coal miners, 1 from the brickworks, 2 ladies and 1 person to represent the local co-operative societies.

In February 1918 school boys absented themselves to visit Shotton for butter, and in the same month it was reported 'there was a shortage of butcher's meat of over 1500 *lbs*'. In March the Food Control Committee issued ration cards. This did not prevent the public sharing their produce. In October the children from St Matthew's gave generously when 'a vegetable collection was made for the Leeswood Military Hospital. Six sacks were filled with vegetables and a number of groceries were also brought, potatoes — 1,298; carrots 56; beetroots; parsnips etc.'

Throughout the War there was a strong British force stationed in Egypt to defend the Suez Canal and engage the Turks in Palestine. Buckley boys serving with the RWF died in this campaign which culminated in General Allenby's capture of Jerusalem on 8 December 1917, described as the Christmas present Lloyd George had requested for the British people.

They were to get very little else during 1918, until Germany collapsed in November. For the British troops it was a time for 'backs to the wall', in the face of a determined German peace offensive, *Friedensturm*, launched by General Ludendorff on 21 March. The Allies resisted and in July began to turn the tide. Germany and her allies began to weaken, the German people were starving, the arrival of the United States Army in France, the use of tanks and the growing capabilities of air power drove them back. By 9 September all of Germany's gains from her spring and summer offensive had been lost. The final weeks of the war were bitterly fought and many Buckley men were killed before the Armistice commenced at the eleventh hour of the eleventh day of the eleventh month 1918. Over 600 Buckley men served in the war and 144 died.[12]

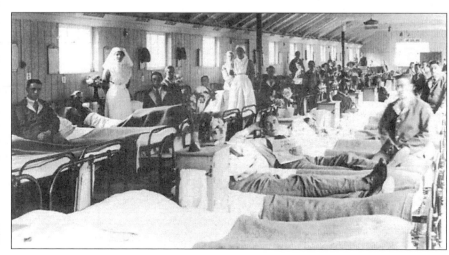

The military hospital at Leeswood.
[FRO PH/33/89]

A group of Royal Welsh Fusiliers, c.1918. [Buckley Library]

Two of these, Private Alexander Connah, Sherwood Foresters, aged 21, of Brook Street, and Private Wilfred Owens, Border Regiment, aged 20, were killed within a few hours of each other on 5/6 September and were buried at Lebucquiere Military Cemetery in the Pas de Calais, France.[12] The sad story of Wilfred Owens is recounted by himself in the many letters he wrote from the Front in the last year of his life.

He was conscripted despite the fact that the medical board acknowledged that he suffered from heart and lung problems and in the last desperate year of the War he was shipped out to France. His parents kept a motorcycle and bike shop and dealt in antique and second-hand furniture in their garage and shop at Lane End. The young soldier came from a Christian background and in his letters home wrote of the many temptations to which army life exposed him. He reassured his parents that 'I have been able to resist them and mean to be a good lad for the sake of my parents & brothers & sister'. Wilfred always expressed his gratitude for the letters and food parcels he received from Buckley, in particular he mentioned the receipt of the *Flintshire Observer, Christian Herald* and the *Motor Cycle*, which was his main interest. At one time he looked for a transfer to the Tank Corps and congratulated his father on the purchase of Harley-Davidson and Triumph motor cycles. He constantly made reference to his family and the people he knew at Lane End — Horace Beavan of the Feathers Inn, Croppers Cinema, Richardson's Coaches, Stanley Parry Corn mechant and others.

In his last letter, Private Owens excused his failure to write 'through being too busy scrapping,' remarking that 'we are expecting peace soon and all of us returning to you.' Within a week he perished of machine-gun wounds in pursuit of the retreating Germans in the attack on the Canal du Nord Line.

The *Chester Chronicle* reported spontaneous scenes in Buckley when news of the Armistice was received:

Jubilant street scenes. Buckley received the good news about 11 o'clock on Monday morning. At most of the works the news gained currency that an armistice had been signed; but although the morning papers conveyed no tidings of the good news, the telephones were busy. The children at the county school were granted a holiday, but, still, there was a feeling of doubt until the hooter at the Castle Fire Brick Works was heard, followed by the one at Catherall's works. Gibson's joined in the chorus, and then the big bell at St. Matthew's pealed forth the glad tidings.

By dinnertime everybody was convinced of the accuracy of the report and almost without exception all the employees at the local brickworks, potteries, and collieries etc. 'rang off' and marched home. The streets were soon filled with a thoroughly cosmopolitan crowd. Bunting was flying everywhere. Indeed, one wondered where all the flags came from. Children sang lustily and bands added to the harmonies. As evening drew near, the crowd became denser, and many of the shops had their windows lit with gas jets for the first time for many a month. The two picture houses had their exterior electric lamps lighted. At the Brunswick Road picture house the manager, Mr Wilcox,

Pte Wilfred Owens [Buckley Society Archive]

invited his audience to sing the National Anthem and the Marseilles. In a short speech he referred to Mr Lloyd George as the greatest man breathing, and said that had it not been for him we might have been serfs under the heel of the Prussians.

In the streets the Royal Town Band and the Volunteer Band united, and parading the principal streets, played national melodies, and the crowds who followed joined in the choruses. Not since the relief of Ladysmith and Mafeking has there been such a carnival of rejoicing in Buckley. When the band finished playing at the Cross, the people joined in singing the National Anthem and Land of My Fathers, and the bands of St Matthew's Church Lads' Brigade and the Tabernacle Boys' Brigade accompanied the celebrations.

At the Conservative Club the evening was spent in honouring the Allies in speech and song. Solos were sung by the Rev. Father Pochard (the French Roman Catholic Priest), the Rev. J. S. Richards (the Curate of Emmanuel), Mr J. Cartwright, and Mr C. Beavan. Speeches were made by Mr W. C. Colin, the Rev. Father Pochard and others.

At St. Matthew's, in the evening, a service of thanksgiving for cessation of War was largely attended, the Rev. Gilbert Heaton officiating. At the close, the organist, Mr Williams, played the 'Dead March' for the fallen, followed by the 'Hallelujah Chorus'. At most of the Nonconformist places of worship prayer meetings were held.

Much amusement was caused by a squad of airmen who paraded the streets behind one of the bugle bands. Most of the works were idle the following day through the shortage of hands.[13]

A service of thanksgiving was held at Bistre Parish Church on the following Sunday when the Church Lads' Brigade paraded at 10 o'clock and proceeded to the Council Chambers to escort the Chairman and Members of the Urban District Council to the church where the sermon was preached by the Rev. O. E. Gittins, Chaplain to the Forces, who was home on leave from Palestine.[14]

The Influenza Pandemic, 1918–9

The *Bistre Parish Magazine* in the same December issue carried the alarming report that:

> Like most other parts of the country, we might almost say of the world, our neighbourhood has been in the throes of the influenza epidemic, and the mortality has been very great. Few houses have escaped it, and the weak have fallen victim to it. The day and Sunday schools have been closed for a month.

Buckley had been affected by the epidemic since October when the *Chronicle* reported that 'the local doctors are heavily taxed in dealing with the large number of patients suffering from the disease and several of the local works greatly handicapped.'[15] The cause of death was at first given as pneumonia, so virulent and severe was the strain of the virus. Men and women in the prime of life were dead within a week. Tragically, soldiers in France suffered greatly and more people died in Europe from the pandemic than had been killed fighting. For example, Sergeant Edwin Hopwood, a teacher at Buckley Council School, died at

Buckley War Memorial to men who died 1914–18 and 1939–45 in the Garden of Remembrance, Hawkesbury.
[Buckley Society Archive]

War Memorial Plaque in Bistre Emmanuel Church. [Buckley Society Archive]

Etaples, France, on 21 October 1918. In November there was a record number of 17 burials in Bistre churchyard. In February 1919 there was another serious outbreak of influenza which was described as a more severe type than the November epidemic. Schools closed and in many instances whole families were laid up. In March the death rate was the highest for a single month in the town's history, with 22 funerals at Bistre and 12 at St Matthew's. The number of burials in Bistre churchyard from November 1918 until the end of March 1919 was 60.

Memorials to the fallen[16]

Some of these memorials originated before the end of the conflict in 1918. They exist in places of worship in the urban district area and usually commemorate the fallen of their particular denominations. Some of the memorials took the form of church furnishings, others as memorial plaques. The most inclusive memorial contains the names of 163 men, the fallen of the two World Wars, and is the Buckley War Memorial in the Garden of Remembrance at Hawkesbury, unveiled on 9 September 1951. It was Buckley's first public war memorial and took the form of a cenotaph. The land for the memorial was made available at Hawkesbury by the Buckley Young People's Cultural Association and the event organised by the Hawkesbury Management Committee in conjunction with the Buckley branch of the Royal British Legion. The secretarial duties were performed by Miss Helen Birks, the aunt of the late Lieutenant F. Birks, VC, MM. Lord Kenyon unveiled the cenotaph. The Lord Lieutenant, Brigadier H. S. K. Mainwaring, was present. Dr Bartlett, Bishop of St Asaph dedicated the memorial and with him were the Reverend D. P. Wynne Williams, curate of Bistre and the nonconformist minister the Reverend A. Newman. The band and buglers of the 4th Bn Royal Welch Fusiliers provided the music and military honours. At the end of the service there was a special peal of bells rung from St Matthew's.[17]

The English Wesleyan Church, the Square, remembered its service-men by installing a pipe organ in May 1917. The inscription stated:

War Memorial plaques in St John's URC Church. [Buckley Society Archives]

To the Glory of God, and in gratitude to those who served, fought and fell in the Great War, with the notably zealous help of young men this organ was dedicated by members and friends of the Wesleyan Church, Buckley Square, May 28 1917.

Emmanuel Parish Church, Bistre, has 69 names on the 1914–18 memorial in the church, which has the inscription 'Pro Patria Mori. To the glory of God and in Honourable Memory of the men from the Parish of Bistre who lost their lives, in the service of their country during the Great War'. An adjacent memorial commemorates and names 34 men who gave their lives in the Second World War.[18]

St Matthew's Parish Church, Buckley, has a number of gifts commemorating the fallen of both wars. In 1917 the north-east corner of the nave was converted into a side-chapel, dedicated to St George the Martyr, for the celebration of weekday communion, for private prayer and as the place of memorial. On 21 December 1919, Mrs Davies-Cooke unveiled a bronze plaque with the 41 names of the fallen associated with the church. Another 13 names of those killed during the 1939–45 were added in 1948. The War Memorial window, made by Harry J. Stammers, with the subject taken from *Pilgrim's Progress*, by John Bunyan, was given by Esther Dutton, in memory of the fallen of this parish in both World Wars. There were other gifts, which included an altar book, a copy of the Bible and book of remembrance. The chapel also contains two brass bugles given by the St Matthew's Company of the Church Lads' Brigade in memory of their fellow members who died in the wars, and the standards of the Buckley Branches of the Royal British Legion. In the chancel is a bronze plate to the memory of Horace Enfield Simmons, MC, DFC, MA, and in the ringing chamber in the bell tower a marble tablet to the memory of Lieutenant John Craig Dunn, killed 25 March, 1916. He left a diary of his life as a soldier in the First World War. He was assistant manager at Standard Pipeworks before enlisting in October 1914. Near the lych gate is a War Memorial Calvary unveiled on Palm Sunday 1921 by Colonel Maddocks, commanding officer of the Welsh Territorial Division, and dedicated by the Dean of St Asaph.[19]

On New Year's Day 1920, members of the Gladstone family came to Buckley to present a hut to the Parish of St Matthew's for use on social occasions and over-flow class-rooms for the Church schools. The party included Henry Neville Gladstone and his wife, and Colonel and Mrs Parish (Dossie Drew daughter of Harry and Mary Drew) and their two little boys. Mr and Mrs Gladstone presented £50 towards the furnishing of the hut and parishioners did the work of painting and laying a new floor.

In September 1921 the Buckley Memorial Institute was opened by Colonel T. H. Parry, MP, and an address delivered by Mr J. Herbert Lewis, MP. George Lewis recorded the event, '1921 Sep 7 Wed The ex-Servicemen's Institute was opened at the Lane End.' No longer standing, it was a wooden structure used for dances and whist drives, with a well sprung floor of maple wood.

War time experience of comradeship and military life influenced men to enlist in 1926 in a Buckley detachment to form part of the 5th Bn Royal Welch Fusiliers (Territorials).

Peacetime, November 1918–September 1939

In this comparatively short interval of peace any hopes of an age of prosperity vanished. The immense efforts of war were followed by years of economic struggle. Buckley's major industries suffered a severe setback. The coal industry died, the potteries were on their death bed, the brickworks only, made some recovery. This decline was not at first apparent but was accelerated to some extent by industrial action in the 1920s, which lurched by 1929 into a world wide depression in trade. Recovery from the trauma of unemployment was not really seen until the preparation for war in 1939.

The years of depression

The depression years in Buckley were made more intolerable by the unemployment caused by the final closure in 1934 of the collieries. Ten years previously they were the principal employers. In a shrinking economy there was nowhere else to find a job. Families had to rely on the dole, the meagre, means tested unemployment benefit, which supported a miserable existence, just above starvation level and well below the poverty line. Buckley men now looked to John Summers & Sons, steel makers of Shotton, and their local subsidiary enterprises, for employment.

Newspaper reports in May 1931 were full of gloom. In an account of the industrial outlook it was said:

The bad news of the closing down of the steel plant at Messrs J. Summers works at Shotton cast quite a gloom over Flintshire last week end and the serious announcement was followed up with quite large numbers of employees from Buckley finishing on Friday last. Amongst the number were a large percentage of staff men and Buckley in this respect was again badly hit, for quite a number from Buckley have been employed on the staff for a number of years. To add to the seriousness of the situation caused by industrial depression came a further announcement last weekend that the employees who work underground at the Mount Pleasant Colliery, Buckley, had all received a week's notice to finish work.

The report concluded that 'the industrial situation is undoubtedly very serious, and none of the inhabitants at Buckley can ever remember so many men unemployed or work so scarce.'[20]

A fortnight later it was announced that about 100 men had finished work at Elm Colliery.[21] Fortunately, however, a slight improvement at the Shotton ironworks, who were consumers of the coal, meant that the majority of those who were to finish continued working on a day to day basis.[22]

The Black Horse public house.
[Buckley Library]

Every effort was made to sell Buckley coal. An appeal appeared in the window of the Lane End post office drawing attention to the colliers' plight and asking the inhabitants of the town 'to purchase their house coal from the Buckley Collieries, Ltd, in order that the workmen may be fully employed. These collieries now have main coal to sell equal to any in north Wales and 90% of the workmen employed at these collieries are Buckley men'.[23]

In January 1932 arrangements were made to hold a series of daytime meetings and lectures for the unemployed at Buckley. One of the first of these was given Mrs Silyn Roberts, secretary of the North Wales branch of the WEA, who spoke on 'Some use to which the unemployed might put their enforced leisure'.[24]

1933 was not a good year for the unemployed and every effort was made to assist them and their dependants. The WEA continued their lectures, the Buckley branch of the Unemployed Workers' Association acquired a clubroom 'where games are played and all kinds of literature can be seen' which was opened by the Town Clerk, Mr F. Llewellyn Jones, MP. This room was used as a soup kitchen for feeding school children belonging to the unemployed. In February, at noon, over 200 were supplied with their quota of soup prepared by lady helpers on the premises of Mr R. Smith licensee of the Black Horse Hotel. The Buckley trades gave people the ingredients for the soup free.[25] By the end of March the Association was running two soup kitchens, one for each end of the town.

Another group, the Buckley Unemployed Boot Fund Committee, organised various events to raise funds for supplying the children of the unemployed in Buckley, Penymynydd, Penyffordd, Caergwrle, Ewloe Green, Mynydd Isa and Alltami with 140 pairs of boots and, during the Buckley Jubilee week, 47 pairs of rubber pumps (rubber-soled canvas shoes used for physical training) were given out to children in Buckley.[26] In June, proposals were discussed for unemployed men to voluntarily provide labour for playing fields. Means of payment was by voucher to be exchanged for goods from local traders. In September it was reported:

There is a decided improvement in the industrial position of Buckley and district, owing to the new foreign orders that have been secured by Messrs J. Summers and Sons at Hawarden Bridge Ironworks. A good number of men and youths from Buckley have been taken on during last week. Some of these men had not worked for two or three years. The local Brickworks that manufacture bricks for house building purposes are also busier than they have been for many months, and are working at high pressure in order to execute orders. There is still room for improvement at the Buckley Works, that manufacture clay goods for such purposes as fire, acid and alkali resisting purposes. Most of these works are used to do a large trade overseas, with the British Colonies, and various foreign countries, but owing to the world trade depression the overseas orders at the Buckley Fire Clay works during the last three years have not been so good. In Flintshire the industrial position appears a little brighter.

A further blow was dealt in May 1934 when John Summers announced that about 150 men at the Elm were to lose their jobs when the colliery closed down. A statement said 'that they should have closed down about six months ago, but decided to carry on to avoid the men being out of work during the winter months. Of the numerous collieries forming the Buckley group, every one has now closed'.[27]

Simultaneously with this notice of closure came some good news. It was announced that 'Messrs William Jones & Sons, 'Glendale', Buckley, kiln builders and designers, have been favoured with a contract for the design, and erecting of three large continuous oil burning eighteen chamber kilns for Iraq, where the Air Ministry have decided to erect a new brick works, capable of turning out eighty thousand bricks per day on the site of the proposed new Aerodrome and cantonment, which will be the headquarters of the Air Force.' The Castle Fire Brick Company benefited from this order by receiving from the kiln builders, contracts for various kinds of clay goods, amounting to about 1500 tons.[28]

The Buckley Standard Sanitary Pipe Works was one firm which did not suffer during the depression and kept its labour force of 130 constantly employed. They were lucky in making sanitary glazed pipes, which were used by the government for the laying of underground telephone cables. Enjoying full employment and order books the directors Messrs. W. and G. R. Oates, and the manager Mr W. Hannaby, encouraged their workmen to save money and gave them an annual share out. They made charitable donations and gave an annual Christmas party for the children of the unemployed.[29] The cheerful atmosphere of the event in 1934 was described: 'Gaily decorated with festoons, lanterns and flowers, the British Legion Institute in Church Road, presented a festive picture which was completed when 231 excited and smiling children sat down to a sumptuous spread generously provided by the Directors of Standard. This is the third year in succession in which they have shown their gracious sympathy with the unemployed'. After tea the children went to the Palace Picture House and then returned to the Institute to be entertained by the magic of Professor Dan Leno.[30]

The attendance of 150 children at the Oates Christmas party in 1936 was an indicator of the reduction in unemployment. The number of unemployed in Buckley in January 1932 was approximately 700. To help relieve the situation the Buckley Unemployed Association was formed on 5 January. As we have seen it organised lectures for men and soup kitchens for the school children. In the month of its formation a letter was written to Lord Henry Gladstone of Hawarden Castle and the Secretary of the General Unemployment Committee, Mr W. H. Bennett, Transport House, Shotton, for financial assistance. The letter spoke of the work they were doing:

We have opened a clubroom for the unemployed but we feel that having the room is not enough. We should like to form some kind of a class for handicrafts such as joinery, basket making, etc., or other useful purposes that would help us financially as well as finding something for our members to do.[31]

From this appeal eventually came the scheme which enabled some of the men to work on the UDC playground scheme. The Association used the Black Horse Hotel for recreation purposes. Although the Association might have raised morale it could do little else until the economic climate began to improve. The brick industry rallied when the country began to emerge from the Depression and government legislation to build council and private housing began to take effect. Many of the Buckley men found new work at John Summers in Shotton, which recovered its market and began to modernise. The government decided, in 1935, that an aircraft factory and housing for workers should be built at Broughton. The nearby Royal Air Force base at Sealand was also expanding.

1935 — the Silver Jubilee of King George V

National events surrounding the monarchy acted as some kind of diversion from the years of gloom brought about by the Depression. They were an occasion for national rejoicing with members of every community in the land brought together and given a role and opportunity to express their patriotism,

Above: Waiting for a match! The bonfire-beacon at Mountain Colliery to celebrate the Silver Jubilee. [FRO D/JB/115]

Right: Clock outside the Council Chambers to celebrate the Silver Jubilee of King George V 1935. [Buckley Society Archive]

loyalty, and thanksgiving, to the Crown.

The first event, in 1935, was the celebration of the Silver Jubilee of the accession of King George V. It expressed the awe and affection with which King George and Queen Mary were held in the hearts of the nation. He was seen as a plain man, full of common sense, gruff, inarticulate, but one of those who had doggedly shown courage and leadership during the Great War, even to the extent of giving up whisky for it's duration. His recent illness had brought him much sympathy and here was an occasion of thanksgiving. Bunting, brass bands, processions, commemoration mugs for children, souvenir canisters of tea for old ladies, and an ounce of tobacco for their men folk, brought 10,000 people on the Buckley Common, 3,000 more than the estimated population. The celebration was crowded with events including a football match in the morning, later in the day, English country dancing, community singing under the direction of Dennis Griffiths, a free picture show in the Palace and Tivoli, the presentation to 1,250 children of Wedgewood china mugs, tea in the schools and the Memorial Institute.

In August 1935 the memorial clock in the Council Chamber was unveiled together with the public Jubilee Clock on the outside of the building. This was followed by a civic reception to the Royal Buckley Town Band to mark their success in gaining first prize at the National Eisteddfod.

King George V died in January 1936 to be succeeded by his eldest son as King Edward VIII. His short reign was marked by the abdication crisis brought about by the government's resistance to his wish to marry Mrs Wallis Simpson, an American woman who was twice divorced. Edward was succeeded by his brother, who reigned as King George VI from December 1936.[33]

1937 the Coronation of King George VI

The Coronation took place on 12 May 1937. The new king and his family won the devotion of the nation by their ordinariness and simplicity after the uncertainty of the abdication crisis. His loyal subjects felt they could relate to the new king who shared the same values as his father and through the years of war which were soon to follow, their admiration and love for the royal family increased. The Coronation was memorable for its splendour and pageantry, every community in the land tried to surpass each other. They showed their pride in belonging to the nation state by turning out on parade to pay homage to their new monarch. A Civic Sunday was organised by the Urban Council, with a service at Bistre Church, followed by a procession led by the Royal Town Band to the new playing fields where the Chairman of the Urban District Council took the salute. What was noticeable was the parade of uniformed organisations — Church Lads' and Boys' Brigades, Girl Guides, Royal Welch Fusilier Territorials, the Women's VAD, the local constabulary, ex-servicemen, St John's Ambulance and the Fire Brigade. Community activities lasted a week and followed the same pattern as the Jubilee. In addition, there was a Coronation Queen, Miss Phyllis Lloyd, a firework display on the Common, and a bonfire on the metal bank of the Old Mountain Colliery as part of the chain of bonfires to be lighted throughout the country. Coronation week was observed as a special shopping week in Buckley with prizes awarded for the decoration and illumination of the shops.[34]

Premonitions and preparations for war

In March 1936 Germany reoccupied the Rhineland which had been a demilitarised zone since 1918. In the same month Buckley Urban District Council's representatives attended a conference in Mold to discuss air raid precautions. German troops marched into Austria in March 1938 and the *Anschluss* was proclaimed. German planes of the Condor Legion bombed civilian targets in Guernica, in the Basque country, on 27 April 1937, killing hundreds of people.[35] Hitler's intentions in Europe were becoming even more clearer to politicians like Winston Churchill. The public began to share his apprehension through the newsreels at the local cinemas. These fears were aired at a public meeting in Buckley in June 1938. The response was overwhelming as 450 people volunteered their services for the civilian body of the ARP, 180 to act as Air Raid Wardens, 24 to man air raid posts, 30 to be in attendance at rescue posts, another 70 to be available at casualty clearing stations (with 70 to follow up as decontamination parties in the event of the use of gas), 24 were ready as ambulance drivers and attendants and the same number to form a repair party. This volunteer force was to be administered by a report centre staff and clerical staff, each with 20 members; 4 storekeepers were to issue the necessary equipment. The Chief Constable, Mr Yarnell Davies, demonstrated the ARP equipment.

When war came in September 1939, air raid shelters for the public were provided. One was 200 yards from the Tabernacle Schoolroom Rest Centre, in Belmont Street, Buckley, and another 10 yards from the ex-Serviceman's Memorial Institute in Church Road. There were air raid wardens' posts based at 11a Mold Road; Holly Bank; Knowle Lane; Ewloe Place; Alltami; Nant Mawr; Dobshill Cross Roads; and the junction of Liverpool Road and Mold Road. There were two first aid parties and a dressing station at Holly Bank. The Council set up two feeding and rest centres. The decontamination squad (in case of gas attacks) was based at Manor Farm, Buckley. The Home Guard used the ex-serviceman's Memorial Institute in Church Road for training and storing their equipment.

Neville Chamberlain returned on 29 September 1938 from his meeting in Munich with Hitler holding a piece of paper, which he described as 'Peace with honour'. This did not prevent the issue of 6,000 gas masks brought from Connah's Quay which were hastily assembled and distributed from the Council Chambers. Instructions were given at the brickwoks, to the first and second house audiences at the Palace and Tivoli, spectators at football matches and to a public meeting at Tabernacle, on what to do in a gas attack.

Further plans made by Flintshire County Council on what to do in the event of an emergency were revealed on 15 May 1939. Reception areas were to be established and controlled by marshalling officers, together with distribution points and a road transport officer in charge of three motor buses and a van for the conveyance of rations. Arrangements were planned to recruit twelve members of the St Matthew's Church Lads' Brigade to act in a general capacity as messengers. A display of strength had been witnessed two days earlier when the Buckley Battery of the 69th Anti-Tank Regiment in procession with Buckley Royal Town Band, members of Buckley's Volunteer Auxiliary Defence Force (VAD) and 100 Territorial recruits, marched from their headquarters in the Mill Lane School Room. On 5 June all men aged 20 years had to register at the Labour Exchange under the Military Training Act. On 3 September 1939, Britain and France declared war on Germany. The reality of war was felt in Buckley before the declaration when George Lewis recorded '1939 Sept 1 Fri. 650 mothers and children were evacuated from Birkenhead to Buckley in a dirty and filthy condition' part of the 20,000 evacuees received in Flintshire, designated as a reception area in January 1939. The burden of finding accommodation, arrangements for schooling and their general welfare fell on the shoulders of the teaching staff of the Buckley Schools and the Medical Officer of Health for the Urban District, Dr Fraser. The events surrounding their arrival and reception were subsequently reported by the MOH who wrote:[36]

… over 500 scholars, teachers and helpers from Birkenhead arrived here on September 1st. The next day, Saturday, a further batch of 45 children under five years arrived with 50 mothers. I was at the station to receive them, and had the assistance of a local medical man, two trained nurses, and twelve VAD's. It was suggested that I examine every one of them individually. I refused to attempt such a thing. The children had been standing by since 10 am. They were tired and thirsty. It would have taken hours to have examined them individually. There were certain little troubles that had to be attended to there and then, grit in the eyes, bruises, complaints of illness, etc. While these were being attended to, the VAD's were going about among the children, giving them drink and looking for any obvious cases of scabby sores, infested heads etc. Any cases they found were sent to me, and their names taken. The Parish Room in Lane End was used as the reception depot on Saturday for the mothers and young children. There was some disappointment where mothers were billeted apart from their children. A few of these mothers and children have returned to Birkenhead.

The churches had large posters printed and signed by the local ministers welcoming the children to their churches and Sunday Schools, but nearly all the arrivals are Roman Catholics and the Memorial Institute in Lane End has been taken over by the Roman Catholic Church to minister to the great influx of their adherents and several services were held there on Sunday.[37]

I spent the next two or three days tracing them to their billets, prescribing treatment, and warning the billeting people of the possibility of infection. They, very naturally in most cases, made strenuous objections to keeping the children. And the problem arose what was to be done. I consulted the County Medical Officer of Health who advised me I had no alternative than to open a small hospital. Fortunately there was a house becoming vacant that week that was quite suitable if not absolutely ideal. Equally fortunately I heard of the wife of one of the Birkenhead teachers, who, being a trained fever nurse, was qualified to take charge. Her services were available, and I secured them. I spent a strenuous few days furnishing the hospital. The great difficulty was to obtain beds. This was overcome in some fashion, and the hospital was opened on September 8th. It was almost immediately filled and from that time until the end of October nearly constantly so, having nine or ten cases in most of the time. For the last month there have not been more than six cases in at a time. 46 patients were admitted between September 16th and December 9th. The most common cases admitted were scabies and impetigo. Suspected cases of major infection were admitted, and when confirmed, removed to St.Asaph Isolation Hospital. Of these during the period there were 40. On discharge from St. Asaph they returned to my care in Holly Bank. Those in contact with major infections, and cases of bedwetting, were admitted. The average stay in hospital was 11 days. 16 outpatients were treated.

The hospital established by Dr Fraser was Holly Bank, in Brunswick Road, the residence of Mrs W. Simmons, the widow of the late water engineer. She offered Holly Bank 'for the purposes of an evacuee hospital for the duration of the war'. Mrs Butler assisted Dr Fraser there. The Buckley people responded generously to the evacuees. They received many gifts, attended Christmas parties, and the boys took on the Buckley lads at football.

1939

Immediately after the declaration of war the British Expeditionary Force left for France. A few days later Buckley members of the Territorial Army, part of the Anti-Tank Regiment, left with their equipment. It was reported that 'the boys went away singing and were cheered on their way'. On the home front there was time for the ARP and the Local Defence Volunteers (later re-named the Home Guard) to organise. There were plenty of rumours.

1940

The winter of 1940 was one of the severest of the century as George Lewis observed: '1940 Jan 30 Tue. The worst weather this month that I can remember. Frost for 3 weeks and deep snow; hard times to live in.'

In April and May Germany increased her grip on the Continent by invading Denmark, Norway and the Low Countries. Winston Churchill replaced Neville Chamberlain as Prime Minister and ordered the evacuation from Dunkirk and Norway in June when Italy joined the Nazis and France capitulated. It was Britain's darkest hour. From August into September the Royal Air Force in the Battle of Britain successfully withstood the German air offensive.

The first fatal casualty from Buckley was in June. Fusilier Jack Baldwin stationed at a training camp was struck by lightning. In July, Sapper Frederick Newton Wilson died of wounds. Three other men were captured in the retreat from France and became prisoners of war in Germany.

On the night of 30 August, German aircraft visited Buckley on their way to Liverpool. For whatever purpose, they dropped three high explosive bombs: one in Church Road near the Workingman's Club; another in a clay hole at Hancock's Brickworks; and one in a field at the rear of the Horse and Jockey. Damage was caused to gas and water main pipes but no one was killed or injured. Incendiary bombs fell near the Mount Chimney and Pentrobin Chapel. On 1 September hundreds of small incendiaries were scattered over an area from Buckley Junction to Caer Estyn, an attack repeated before Christmas, when a cluster of bombs landed in a field on Lower Garmon, surrounding fields at Alltami, and through the roof a bungalow known as Mountain Farm.

The visit of the Heinkel He111, 29 May 1941. A Heinkel aircraft and the manufacturer's plate from the bomber that crashed at Ewloe Place. [Buckley Society Archive]

1941

Britain and the Empire now stood alone against the German might until on 12 June Hitler's armies invaded Russia and the United States of America came into the war after the Japanese attacked Pearl Harbour on 7 December. The main theatres of war were the Mediterranean and North Africa. The Germans expelled Britain from Crete in May, Tobruk surrendered to Rommel in June and the British 8th Army became engaged in a long offensive in the Western Desert. It was a bad year for morale but not patriotism. This was demonstrated by the response to special weeks organised under the direction of the National Savings Committee. In War Weapons Week in May Buckley raised £76,155, and gave the opportunity for the ARP, AFS and WVS to parade. Few casualties and no deaths on active service were announced in the local press. Names of men captured in the desert and Crete trickled through. In June, Nurse Elsie Okell was one of 13 nurses killed in an air raid on Manchester.

One British success was the sinking of the German battleship *Bismarck* in the Atlantic on 27 May after being hunted down in a dramatic search and chase operation by aircraft from the *Ark Royal* and ships of the Royal Navy. In retaliation, the Germans set out to find and attack the British ships responsible and came in search to the entrance of the port of Liverpool. An aircraft on this mission, a Heinkel He.111, was dramatically shot down by British anti-craft fire. It came down at 1.20 am, on 29 May in a field at Ewloe Place, and exploded on impact. The situation was complicated by the discharge from the aircraft of its cargo of eight high-explosive bombs. Seven had come loose and fell indiscriminately in the Buckley area after the crew had baled out. No one knows what happened to the eighth bomb. Four bombs failed to explode, three landing at Isa Farm, Bryn y Baal, and one on the Lower Common, and all had to be defused. Three bombs exploded: one on the Lower Common opposite Oakley and Ivy House and two in Bryn y Baal (one in a field at Beech Farm and the other at Bryn y Ffynnon). Damage was caused to 130 buildings, including three shop windows in Mold. Thirty people were slightly injured.[38]

An account of the reaction of the residents of the Trap to the incident showed the drama surrounding the incident. A witness recounted:

However, you ought to know about the time the war came to Buckley, and to the Trap, in particular. The ones who kept the home fires burning had grown used to lying in their beds at night and listening to the sound of German bombers droning high overhead en route for the docks and installations of Merseyside.

One night pandemonium broke loose. Many can still recall the spectacle of a blazing German bomber streaking across the skies, its crew parachuting to safety, to be later captured by the local Home Guard. The plane and its load of bombs had to come down somewhere, and perhaps it was some divine plan that it crashed and exploded on a spot where least damage and casualties would be caused. The 'happy plot' was a hollow in a field

'Warship Week', March 1942. Plaque to commemorate the adoption of HMS Foxtrot, a trawler designed for convoy escort duty. [By kind permission of Buckley Town Council]

at the Trap – opposite the Lakeside Garage, where houses have been built in later years. What pandemonium there must have been. Because of the hollow, the blast from the explosion was directed upwards, and only the roofs were blown off the houses, windows and doors removed, and electric wires demolished. Many fires were started besides the one from the plane.

The stunned Trapites were soon about, and with soot covered faces were either putting out the minor fires, finding candles to light their roofless homes, and rustling up jam butties from the meagre wartime rations, and the inevitable cup of tea boiled on the trusty old Primus stove. Spontaneous prayer meetings were held in the broken homes thanking God for their deliverance, children hiding under tables for the drone of planes still went on overhead.

Next morning came the sightseers to see the remains of the plane now guarded by the military. That night and for many nights to come, the fast recovering community was housed in a local Sunday school where extra food and blankets were soon in evidence.

The final air raid came on 22 October when four high explosive bombs were dropped, 'making very big holes'[39] in a field at Brook Farm, Bannel Lane, and alongside the Buckley–Connah's Quay Railway, between the Junction Station and Metallic Brickworks.

1942

On the 16 of February, 60,000 British troops capitulated at Singapore to experience the horrors of captivity at the hands of the Japanese. Amongst those interned were Army and RAF personnel from Buckley. British forces struggled in the desert until Montgomery arrived to give them a new spirit. North Africa was the resting-place for soldiers killed on active service, others were captured and taken to Italy. For Lance Corporal T. M. Wilcox of the 2nd Cameron Highlanders, from Meg's Lane, it turned into an adventure. He had joined the army in 1935, left for service overseas and fought in Abyssinia and North Africa. He was captured by the Italians at Benghazi and was sent to Italy until in 1943, when the Allies landed in the country, arrangements were made by the Germans to transfer all prisoners to Germany. Wilcox saw this as an opportunity to escape, and with a comrade made his way to the British lines. He was awarded the Military Medal in 1945 for bravery on the battlefield.

In January, Buckley hearts were lifted by Dennis Griffiths's third Pantomime Revue of the war, at the Tivoli, which attracted an attendance of 8,702. The object of the National Savings Drive was for naval forces, 'Warship Week', 7 to 14 March. Buckley was set the target of raising £40,000 towards a minesweeper. They passed their objective, reaching £65,332 17s. 10d. and adopted the vessel HMS *Foxtrot*. At Buckley, the Lord Lieutenant, Rear Admiral Sir Rowley Conway, took the salute for the parade, which consisted of soldiers from the RWF, 60 ATC trainees, RAF personnel from Hawarden, Girl Guides and the Church Lads' Brigade.

The loss of the Far East territories meant a rubber shortage. To remedy this the government organised another of its re-cycling events in May:

The rubber salvage week campaign began on Saturday and the competitive element between the various schools spurred on the effort. By the end of the first day, eight tons of rubber tyres had been sent to the Council yard, where they are being stored. It was an amusing sight to see the boys rolling the tyres along the streets, sometimes racing each other to the Council yard. Later in the week something like 300 heavy motor truck tyres were to be seen at the dumping ground.[40]

Buckley Jubilee Procession, 1942. Mr Harold Gregory in the procession wearing his ARP uniform. [Buckley Society Archive]

In order to supplement rationing Buckley had its fruit canning centre in Mill Lane Schoolroom, run under the direction of Mrs E. Cropper and Mrs A. Iball. In October, it was estimated that over 800 tins of peas, plums, damsons and tomatoes were canned. The victory at El Alamein in November marked what Churchill described 'as the end of the beginning'. The church bells of St Matthew's together with those of the nation rang out in celebration.

1943

The Germans VIth Army surrendered to the Russians at Stalingrad in January. The war was taken from North Africa, into Sicily and then mainland Italy. The Battle of the Atlantic against U-boats reached its height. Unlike the First World War, a number of men from Buckley joined the Royal Navy, and some were tragically lost in the cruel sea, through enemy action.

In March 10,000 people attended the pantomime, with the profit increased by the raffle of a three month old pig and a doll's house. In May it was announced that 10,159 books were collected in Buckley during the Book Salvage Campaign, of which 2,030 were sent to the troops. In July George Lewis recorded: 'July 16 Fri All iron gates and railings in Liverpool Road and Buckley and District taken for the War Effort because of shortage of iron.' Much to the anger of the local residents they remained where they were dumped to the end of the war. The National Savings campaign was directed to Wings for Victory. Buckley's target was set at £40,000, the price of two Wellington bombers — £65,006 was raised. The opening ceremony was performed by Mr George A. Griffiths, MP for Hemsworth, and Parliamentary Private Secretary in the Ministry of Pensions. Griffiths was a local boy from Drury; he became a Salvation Army Officer, but preferred being a collier. He moved to Royston, known as 'little Moscow', on the South Yorkshire coalfield. He is alleged to have been the first member to sing the 'Red Flag' on the floor of the House of Commons, following the Labour victory in the 1945 Election. Opening the event Griffiths hoisted the RAF flag above the Council Offices. Rear Admiral Conway took the salute at the march past headed by the RAF band, leading service personnel, the local voluntary defence and youth organisations.

In August the Buckley Prisoners of War Association sent eighteen parcels, consisting of 30 books and 500 cigarettes, to the prisoners in Italy and Germany and £30 from the local fund to the British Red Cross Society Parcels Depot for Prisoners of War. In December the WVS sent comforts or postal orders to the six hundred men and eighteen women from the Buckley district serving in the forces.

1944

Britain and the United States launched their armada on fortress Europe on 6 June, the D-day landings in Normandy. In Buckley the National Saving event, 'Salute the Soldier Week' was held at the same time, and raised £71,644, exceeding again the target of £40,000. The number of men killed on active service in Europe and Burma increased. Hitler hit back with frightening weapons, flying bombs and rockets, in 'the battle of London'. There was a new evacuation — nearly 1.5 million people left London before the end of July. Buckley received 77 mothers and 152 children from London in the middle of July and 100 more evacuees on 19 August. The redoubtable WVS rose to the occasion, or rather continued what they had been doing throughout the war. Their achievements were listed in December, with the headline 'The work of the WVS — 5,000 articles knitted in four years'. It stated:

During the evacuation of children from the London area the members had done much good work. They had prepared and served 1,479 meals to the two Buckley rest centres, which were kept open for one week. Again in August when another 100 evacuees arrived in the district, the WVS served 406 meals. During this period the WVS had provided 132 London evacuees with 456 garments and 58 pairs of shoes. The WVS have on their list 667 men and women in the Forces and have sent out 792 Postal Orders. Since 1940, members of the Buckley WVS have knitted 5,004 articles for members of the Forces and the WVS depot.[41]

1945

The Normandy landings in June 1944 had raised people's hopes of a speedy conclusion to the war. But Hitler did not think of surrender. The British failed to shorten the war at Arnhem in September. It was a bridge too far, and Buckley men were killed there. It was not until March 1945 that the British crossed the

Rhine. Meanwhile the situation had eased in Britain. In February the Buckley Home Guard attended 'a stand down supper' with nearly 100 members present with their officers Major J. S. Parry, and Lieutenants Edwards, Mutch, Roberts and Green.

At the end of April the first two returning prisoners of war were welcomed home by 1,500 people at the Council Chamber after being escorted from their homes by the Buckley Royal Town Band. In June the number had risen to 24 who were welcomed at a special gathering at the Albert Hall.

Eric Hayes returned to Buckley on 19 May after five years of captivity. He has told his story and this is a very brief resume.

Eric Hayes was 21 years old when war broke out. He was the son of Joshua and Annie Hayes of 84 Chester Road. He attended Hawarden County School matriculating there in 1935 when he left to work in the County Medical Office, Mold. Before the War he enlisted in the Territorial Army 279 Battery 70th Anti Tank Regiment, and was promoted lance bombardier. The battery was in camp at Trawsfynydd in August 1939 when Hayes was recalled to Buckley to mobilise for war. On 2 September he was posted to Aldershot for training and embarked for France on 28 November. At the end of April 1940 he was manning a Bren gun near Rouen. In the confusion of the rapid German advance he was taken prisoner on 20 May.

Corporal Bill Fisher (top left) wireless operator Churchill tank, 79th Armoured Division, 141st RAC posing with three tank crews across the Rhine, March 1945. [Courtesy of Bill Fisher]

It was then that he began a journey of 850 miles across Germany to Stalag XXA, at Thorn, in Poland. The prisoners were marched for a fortnight and then loaded into railway trucks for a 60-hour journey 'with no food or sanitary arrangements and very little water to drink'. Hayes was imprisoned in Poland until he was moved into Germany on the approach of the Russian Army in January 1945. From 1942 until January 1945 he worked on a farm at Gross Lunau, in the Polish Corridor, inhabited by Germans. The prisoners returned to camp every night. The farmer fed them, most of the food being home produced, and the work was healthy. Eric Hayes was on friendly terms with the farmer and his young family with whom he corresponded after the war. Some of his letters home survive and are full of gratitude for the food parcels and cigarettes received from the Red Cross.

Bombardier Eric Hayes, RA, photographed on embarkation leave November 1939. [Courtesy of Eric Hayes]

At the approach of the Red Army the prisoners were removed in the depths of winter and forced to walk back to Germany. Many didn't survive the awful trek. Eric Hayes suffered from severe frostbite and lost parts of seven fingers amputated in a POW hospital. The day after the operation the hospital was evacuated and the prisoners bundled into railway trucks and transported to Stalag Xb between Bremen and Hamburg. Here they remained for nine weeks before being liberated by the Grenadier Guards on 29 April 1945.

Eric Hayes arrived in Buckley on 19 May 1945, 'five years all but one day after I was captured'. This was a daunting experience:

> Even coming home was a funny feeling. Everyone had altered. Everything seemed different. So much had been happening that I knew nothing about the blitz, the blackouts, rationing, doodlebugs, and the concentration camps. My actual homecoming was overpowering. There seemed to be hundreds of people gathered round 84 Chester Road. Some of them I didn't recognise, but I think the whole family had come to welcome me home. It

was a relief when people began to drift away and leave me with my family. Even with them I felt awkward. After six years of all-male company and barrack-room language, I was afraid of slipping up in the presence of ladies and it was sometime before I conquered that fear.

During the early days after getting back home we really 'lived it up' meeting almost every night in the Black Lion and very often staying in the back room until well after hours or going to the dance at the Albert Hall.

Eric Hayes returned to work in Mold and was employed by the Buckley UDC, Alyn and Deeside Council, and was Clerk of Buckley Town Council in 1980. His is one experience amongst many of the Buckley prisoners of war. We salute them.[42]

Hitler killed himself in his Berlin bunker on 30 April. The Germans surrendered unconditionally to Montgomery on 4 May. Churchill announced victory in the House of Commons on the afternoon of 8 May and the nation began celebrating. Buckley gave thanks the same evening with a series of religious services in all places of worship. Soon houses and public buildings were decorated with bunting and streamers and the Royal Buckley Town Band paraded the streets with helpers collecting for the Welcome Home Fund.

The war in the Far East continued until August when the Japanese were forced into unconditional surrender by the dropping of the atomic bomb at Hiroshima on 6 August and Nagasaki on the 9th. The Emperor announced his people's submission on the 14th. Now it was the turn for VJ Celebrations:

Buckley held VJ celebrations last weekend, when schoolchildren and adults over 65 were entertained to tea. The district was divided into fourteen areas and rooms were lent, as were tables, crockery etc. by the various places of worship and other organisations. There was an abundance of eatables to which justice was done. The old people who could not attend for tea had it taken to their homes, with a gift of 2s. Concerts were organised and cinema shows were arranged for the children. Through the kindness of Mr Hanmer 800 were entertained at the Tivoli, and by Mr Jervis, another 400 were entertained at the Palace. The celebrations ended on Saturday night with a bonfire on Knowle Hill and a fireworks display, which could be seen for miles.[43]

In November the people of Buckley contributed another £61,191 13s. 10d. to National Savings, passing their target of £40,000. £368,314 5s. 10d. was raised in the six efforts organised since 1939.

Another important result was that of the Parliamentary Election held in July 1945, the first for ten years. Mr Nigel Birch was returned as Conservative member for Flintshire with a majority of 1,039 votes over Miss Eirene Jones (later Mrs White), Labour, out of a poll of 71,568. A Labour government replaced a National Coalition wartime government; Clement Attlee succeeded Winston Churchill.

The whole of Europe became engaged in reconstruction. Buckley people faced the future with some uncertainty. There was no clear way forward, the only prospect was that things would improve with the end of rationing, and the return of men and women from the forces. What was called getting back to normal. Buckley shared the hope with the rest of the nation that changes in education, a free National Health Service, and the provision of more houses, would banish poverty, unemployment, and provide more houses. It was these new social opportunities that prepared them to open a new chapter in the history of the making of their community.

Street parties in Buckley celebrate the end of the Second World War, August 1945. Party for Church Road and Daisy Hill children. [Buckley Library]

Notes

1. *Chester Chronicle*, 26/6/1897.
2. *County Herald*, 19/7/1907.
3. Diary of John Dunn, *Buckley*, 24. He enlisted in October 1914 and was killed on 25 March 1916.
4. *County Herald*, 23/10/1914.
5. When the school was demolished, the memorial was moved to the church grounds.
6. For an account of the life of Frederick Birks see, J. E. Griffiths and K. Lloyd Gruffydd, 'Second Lieutenant Frederick Birks', *Buckley*, 7.
7. From W. Alister Williams, *The VCs of Wales and the Welsh Regiments* (Bridge Books, Wrexham, 1984).
8. J. E. Griffiths, '2nd Lt Fred Birks, VC, MM: Postscript', *Buckley*, 9.
9. F. Dorber, 'Onward Christian Soldiers', *Buckley*, 18, and *Mold, Deeside and Buckley Leader*, June 1932.
10. *Chester Chronicle*, 22/3/1917.
11. *Chester Chronicle*, 4/4/1918.
12. Peter Kelsall, 'Buckley Soldiers from the Great War: Part 1,' *Buckley*, 29. See entries for Privates A. Connah and W. Owens.
13. *Chester Chronicle*, 14/11/1918.
14. *Bistre Parish Magazine*, December, 1918.
15. *Chester Chronicle*, 24/10/1918.
16. This list does not claim to be comprehensive.
17. *Mold, Deeside and Buckley Leader*, 14/9/1951.
18. Margaret Mole, 'The Memorials, Plaques and Window Commemorations of Emmanuel Church, Bistre', *Buckley*, 20.
19. J. Clifford Jones, *Buckley Parish Church, 1822–1972*, (Gee, Denbigh, 1974)
20. *Mold, Deeside and Buckley Leader*, 8/5/1931
21. ibid, 22/5/1931
22. ibid, 19/6/1931
23. ibid, 4/1931
24. ibid, 8/1/1932.
25. ibid, 24/2/1933.
26. ibid, 8/12/1933.
27. ibid, 4/5/1934.
28. ibid, 4/5/1934.
29. ibid, 15/1/1932.
30. ibid, 4/1/1935.
31. FRO D/HA/1505, January 1933.
32. Given in memory of the late Alderman Jonathan Catherall.
33. *Mold, Deeside and Buckley Leader*, 3/5/1935.
34. ibid, 15/5/1937, and the programme of the 1937 Coronation festivities, to be found in Buckley Library.
35. The Condor Legion was a unit sent by Hitler to aid Franco in the Spanish Civil War.
36. Report to the UDC 9 December 1939, supplemented by information from newspapers.
37. *Mold, Deeside and Buckley Leader*, 9/9/1939.
38. Edward Doylerush, *Fallen Eagles, A guide to Aircraft Crashes in North-East Wales*, p 48.
39. Diary of George Lewis.
40. *Chester Chronicle*, 16/5/1942.
41. ibid, 2/12/1944.
42. Eric Hayes 'About me in a nutshell', Buckley Society Multi-media Archive Team Publication, June 2005.
43. *Chester Chronicle*, 6/9/1945.

Chapter 15
Leisure Time

Leisure time was precious in a community where long hours were spent working. In Buckley the colliery, brickworks and clay hole were the work places. The workman could not desert his machine or coalface. He was enslaved and trapped for long hours. Supervised and controlled to produce as much as possible for his master, no matter the season or weather. What little time he had for himself could be used for a variety of purposes. Leisure could be spent in tending a garden, keeping a pig, going to a place of worship, roaming the countryside, tippling in the alehouse, gossiping, or attending whatever event was organised to attract him. Too often the choice was limited to either the alehouse or a place of worship.

Thomas Cropper gives a list and description of thirty[1] 'Bygone Taverns of Buckley' and makes the comment that 'the sport of those days was cock fighting, bull baiting, and all sorts of wagering. Wagers would be got up at the 'Red Cat' (Red Lion) for a race to a bush on the Pren Hill and back for the prize of a pint of ale. Close to the 'Red Cat', less than a stone's-throw farther along the road was the old Cockpit'.[2]

'Friendly Societies', Cropper recounted, 'were held at many of these old taverns. I have copies of rule-books of the Bannel Friendly Society, held at the Royal Oak; date 1836; annual meeting, first Sunday in July. The United Friendly Society, held at the Horse and Jockey; date 1844; annual meeting, second Saturday in July. The Church and King United Brethren Society, instituted 1823; annual meeting, last Saturday in June. The club dinner of these Societies was usually spread over two or three public-houses, no one place being then able to undertake the catering.'[3]

Friendly societies came into existence in the seventeenth century, and eventually, much later, became a conventional alternative to parish relief. Members paid subscriptions from which they were entitled to claim benefits in times of sickness, unemployment, and funeral expenses. Each Society contracted a local physician to provide free treatment for their members. It is not surprising that friendly societies attracted large memberships. In addition they provided an opportunity for members to meet together socially. They provided them with a convivial leisure activity. In some ways friendly societies were like the medieval guilds. They had regular meetings, annual feasts; they marched in processions carrying banners, wearing regalia and led by a band to a service in church. Attendance at fellow members' funerals was regarded as a duty. Candidates for membership would be put through an initiation ceremony, learn passwords, secret gestures, and be entitled to wear the regalia.

By 1900 a large proportion of the male population, and some females, belonged to friendly societies. They were one of the authorised institutions chosen by Lloyd George's National Insurance Act of 1911 through which members' contributions were paid. Mr W. E. Gladstone and his sons were members of the Hawarden Lodge of

Friendly Societies walking through Hawarden village, Whit Monday, 1908. [FRO PH/28/P/37]

Public Houses [Buckley Library]

The Grandstand.

The Blue Anchor.

The Cock and Hen.

The Blue Bell.

The Parrot.

White Lion.

Buckley Ladies Shepherd's Club at the Jubilee 1908. [Buckley Library]

the Loyal Order of Ancient Shepherds and Winston Churchill, one of architects of the Liberal Pensions and Insurance legislation, was a member of the Blenheim Friendly Society Lodge.

The earliest press report of a friendly society meeting in Buckley is 1835 when on 4 July 'The Bannel Friendly Society held their Annual Meeting, and after hearing Divine Worship and a sermon in Buckley Church, the members dined together'.

In the late nineteenth century, in years of depression and industrial unrest, the Buckley working men found as much solidarity in friendly societies, as in trade unions, and probably received more financial help from them. Newspaper reports show that they were particularly active in this period. For example in 1880, the Church and King United Brethren Friendly Society held their 57th Anniversary at the end of June. Ninety of their brethren walked in procession, headed by Buckley Brass Band, from their usual meeting house, the White Lion, over Buckley Common to Lane End, then along the main street to Bistre Parish Church. They returned to the White Lion for their annual dinner. It was remarked that 'the catering on this occasion was everything that could be desired. Later on there was dancing on the green which was very largely attended, and the locality provided a lively scene during both afternoon and night.' The account stated that the Society funds remained at £2,352, after £382 had been paid to sick members.[4]

Gladstone's lodge, the Loyal Order of Ancient Shepherds, had sixteen lodges in the Hawarden District with a membership of 1,474 members in 1884, of which Buckley provided 306 brethren. In June 1878 they held a united procession. Meeting on Belmont Common, they marched to St Matthew's Church for a service conducted by the vicar, and then walked to Hawarden for dinner. 'The procession was headed by two Chester brass bands and they played at night for dancing etc., at night in the Rectory grounds'.[5]

Another well-supported Buckley friendly society was the Order of Oddfellows. In 1879 it had a membership of 276, annual contributions £293, sick payments £234, assets £2,344. Membership rose in 1889 to 362 adults and 84 juveniles.

The advocates of temperance established a branch of their own society in Buckley, the Rechabites, in 1889. The instigator was the Reverend Joseph Davies. The lodges were known as 'tents' since the biblical Rechabites, as narrated in Jeremiah 35, 'had dwelt in tents'. Soon, they too, were marching in procession led by the Buckley Brass Band, from their 'tent' to the Tabernacle Chapel.

The anti-Catholic, anti-ritualistic activities of some Buckley protestants, led to the formation of a lodge of the Orange Order in Buckley. This combined its activities as a protest group with those of a friendly society. The Buckley Lodge held a 'smoking concert in the Congregational Church in 1899', and on 12 July 1900, welcomed 3,000 of their Liverpool brethren.

Before the industrial revolution the situation was different in the neighbourhood. Buckley was the outpost and frontier zone of two large parishes, Mold and Hawarden. Until the beginning of the nineteenth century they were primarily agricultural in nature. The seasons, the weather, and the agricultural calendar governed the rhythm of life in the pre-industrial community. On this yearly round the Church imposed its own calendar of religious seasons, festivals, saints, and holy days. Around these grew customs and celebrations. The annual wakes, beating of the bounds, the perambulation of the parish at Rogationtide.

The term 'wakes', is of Saxon origin, and means watching, and refers to the vigil observed by parishioners

Beating the Bounds. Painting by James Bentley. [By kind permission of Mrs M. Bentley]

at the festival of their local saint. Church ales were brewed, the church strewn with rushes and the churchyard used for a variety of activities. Here pedlars and hawkers set up booths, and parishioners indulged in sports, drinking and dancing. Hawarden wakes were kept on the Sunday following Holy Cross Day, 14 September, and subsequent days. A lawyer of the Inner Temple passing through Hawarden in 1705 stumbled upon the festivities:

We crossed the Roodee to Hawarden where there was a wake, which was very diverting to us. The country lasses were dancing in the middle of the town and seeing them so merry for a frolic, we got off our horses and danced with them two or three of the Northern Volunteers, and kissed them all round at which they were pleased. We went afterwards to a gentleman's house to drink some Welsh Ale and found it very strong.[6]

Horse racing was a feature of the Hawarden Wakes and prizes to the value of £50 and silver cups were offered.

An annual event was the defining of the parish boundaries, beating the bounds. This was important in an age when each parish was responsible for raising money to pay for a number of purposes out of the rates. These included the support of a workhouse, the relief and maintenance of orphans, destitute widows, and deserted wives. Most parishes marked their boundaries with a series of incised and numbered boundary stones. It was these that the parishioners marked in procession. To instil this knowledge the group was made up of young and old. The old men knew exactly where the boundary was and young boys had their ears tweaked to help them remember. The perambulation procession was led by a robed clergyman, who stopped at the boundary markers to recite prayers for the fruits of the earth.

The boundaries of the manor of Ewloe, for example, were 'walked over on Tuesday and Wednesday, the 15th and 16th of November 1803', by the members of the Court Leet of Bryan Cooke, lord of the manor. They followed twenty numbered stones. 'The Manor Lordship of Ewloe is limited and bounded from the Bull's foot or stone numbered 1 on Ewloe Common across the Encroachments…and so on…. to a stone numbered 20 opposite to Mr Jonathan Catherall'.[7]

Both Hawarden and Mold were notable for their wakes and fairs for the sale of animals and produce. In Mold in 1835 the market days were Wednesday and Saturday and the fairs were held on 13 February, 21 March, 12 May, 2 August and 22 November. Hawarden did not have a market place, although a market was held on Saturday, and the fairs on 1 October and 24 December for cattle.

The entries in school log books from 1863 onwards show the continuation of these attractions and the thrill experienced by generations of boys and girls as they played truant to go to the fair, the travelling menagerie or circus. The school provided a pool of labour, which could not be ignored. Their holidays in the summer were arranged to coincide with the grain harvest. When the potato crop was picked in October they absented themselves until it was gathered in. Blackberries were part of the household economy and if necessary a day off from school would be taken gather them.

In the nineteenth century leisure time was a combination of customs, traditions and activities inherited from a pre industrial age and aspirations introduced by the new industrial society. The employer to a large extent tried to control the leisure activities of his workmen. He wanted a healthy and intelligent workforce regular and reliable in the work place. Church and chapel going was encouraged. It fostered the greatest of all-Victorian virtues, self-help and self-improvement. From the 1870s onwards sport became more popular.

Cycle Club parade. [Buckley Society Magazine, 20]

It developed both for the spectator and the participant. Football and cricket clubs became associated with churches, chapels, Sunday schools and shopkeepers.

At the end of the nineteenth and beginning of the twentieth century the nation followed the example of Mr Polly and climbed on their bicycles. Buckley had its own cycling club, which flourished around 1900, with its headquarters at the Urn Cocoa Rooms. The early bicycles had solid tyres, in spite of which the members braved the stony roads, on weekly outings in the neighbourhood of Chester and North Wales. At the end of the season they were entertained in the Falcon Cocoa Rooms, Chester, by Mr John Davies, a native of Buckley, who was an architect in the city. A feature of the early twentieth century was the Cycle Carnival, which provided great fun and raised money for charitable purposes, including the horse ambulance.

Another feature of leisure in the Victorian age was its collective nature and the peculiar habit of the populace to march peacefully in processions, carrying banners and following bands. The brass band became essential to public life in Buckley. Since the 1820s five main bands, at one time or another, played a leading part by their presence on public occasions. One of these was the drum and fife band formed at Bistre Methodist New Connexion Chapel in 1881 under the leadership of the distinguished Buckley musician, Edward Wainwright.[8] Another band from a religious background, was that of the Salvation Army, which was first heard about 1890. The leading military band, that of the Buckley Engineers, which flourished from the 1880s until shortly before the First World War, came under the influence of the Griffiths' family. William Griffiths was a noted bandmaster of the Engineers under whom they won a number of prizes. Griffiths was a noted 'soprano' player and teacher of other bands along the Welsh border. Arthur Griffiths conducted the Engineers for 15 years, and played before Queen Victoria, Edward VII, and George V. 'The Slaughter house band', was the name of the Denbighshire Hussars Imperial Yeomanry band, so called from its place of rehearsal. But the band with the longest history is the Royal Buckley Town Band which claimed to go back to 1822. It was probably this band which took part in the events surrounding the opening of St Matthew's in 1822, and may have been present when the foundation stone was laid on 14 December 1821.[9] The band was restored to good order in 1853 by its leader Edward Griffith, who built up its reputation over the next fifty years. In April 1897,

The Buckley Old Town Band had the honour of playing a programme of music at Hawarden Castle at the express invitation of Mr and Mrs Gladstone. The band went by train from Buckley and marched through the Park and took up position in front of the Castle. The band having played several pieces, Mr Gladstone came out, and called one member, Mr John Jones the corresponding secretary of the Band. The Hon. Gentleman cordially shook him by the hand, and expressed his pleasure at their efficient playing, and to see it in a flourishing condition. The day renewed old associations with the band, which he had known for many years and hoped to hear again shortly.[10]

A few weeks later the band returned to Hawarden Castle and

Griffiths family brass bandsmen c.1895. William Griffiths (seated), conductor of Buckley Engineers Band. His son James and grandson John both conducted the Buckley Royal Town Band. [FRO D/DM/434/6]

Royal Buckley Town Band.

had the honour of playing before Edward, Prince of Wales (later King Edward VII), and Princess Alexandra. After this performance it became known as the Royal Buckley Town Band. Another member of the Griffiths family, James Griffiths, was a distinguished cornet player, winning the solo cornet competition at the National Eisteddfod at Llangollen in 1888. He had the honour, as trumpeter, of being chosen to precede the funeral cortege of W. E. Gladstone, as it went in solemn procession through Hawarden Park to Broughton Station in May 1898, previous to his State Funeral in Westminster Abbey. In 1923 Griffiths conducted the Royal Buckley Town Band at the National Eisteddfod held in Mold. His son John James later succeeded him as conductor.

The Royal Buckley Town Band flourishes and over the years has renewed its instruments on at least two occasions, in 1924 and 1966. Over the years it has played a leading part in the Jubilee Procession. It was not until the end of the nineteenth century that it was allowed to walk in the Jubilee because Nonconformists disliked music in worship. They felt that the 'Devil' sat on the organ seat and waved the conductor's baton.[11] Once they had got rid of these inhibitions music began to flourish in Buckley under the influence of several musical families such as Griffiths, Roberts, Hayes, Peters, Jenkinson, Smallwood, Wainwright, Cropper, Lloyd, Wilcox, Hulley, Smith and others. Soon every place of worship had its own first class choir; most of them accompanied by an orchestra.

The Anglican Church did not share the Nonconformist suspicion of musical instruments. A great promoter in the early days was Mr Ffoulkes, the curate in charge of St Matthew's. In 1851, the *Chester Courant* observed: 'We understand that satisfactory arrangements have been made for a vocal and instrumental performance of sacred music in the schoolroom belonging to the Church at Buckley Mountain. Selections will be performed from such noble oratorios as the *Creation, Messiah,* and *Elijah*'. The principal soloists were from Chester Cathedral and the Buckley Choir sang the choruses. This was one of a series of concerts organised at St Matthew's by the Reverend Henry Ffoulkes.[12]

In December 1869 a concert was organised in the Buckley National Schoolroom on behalf of the Buckley Workingmen's Institute. Those taking part were members of the Prime Minister's family and their friends and included Miss Lesley Mary Herbert, Misses Agnes and Mary Gladstone, Miss Gertrude Glynne and Mr William H. Gladstone. Mary Gladstone (later Mrs Drew) was an accomplished pianist and her brother William a gifted musician and hymn writer.[13] The first Buckley Orchestral Society was formed in 1891 and reformed in 1925.

Places of worship, public houses, friendly societies, and other groups became the centres for leisure. The church, chapel, and Sunday school had their own organisations. Groups for men and women: the prayer meeting, Bible class, choir practice, bell ringing, temperance and Band of Hope. These were the stock in trade of every religious group in Buckley until quite recently. In some ways worship was transmuted for a large majority (but not all) through these group activities into entertainment. If there was talent why should it not be displayed and everyone share the pleasure, particularly if they were spiritually uplifted? Choral singing and oratorio performance became part of the annual cycle of religious observance. Voices from different chapels were brought together for specific purposes like eisteddfodau. Soloists, conductors and organists won national reputations.

The secular influence of entertainment in Buckley began to emerge at the end of the nineteenth century. It was seen in the activities of the elementary day schools. They began to organise concerts, often to raise

Pupils from Bistre School performing at Bistre Church garden fete, 1912. [Buckley Society Archive]

money. As schools have always done they sought to give every child a part in the production, and bring every parent to the concert to dote on their offspring. The burlesque, the Japanese operetta, the pantomime, were presented in colourful productions, which made their mark and introduced a form of performance which was ideal for a community as close knit and talented as Buckley.

An example of this was the children's entertainment, given at the Central Hall in December 1906 by about eighty Band of Hope members, in connection with Emmanuel Parish Church Bistre. The account is from the *Bistre Parish Magazine*:

> The chief item on the programme was the highly amusing and clever Japanese Operetta entitled 'Princess Ju-Ju' by Clementine Ward, which, a few years ago, met with such great success at the Olympic Theatre, London. The Operetta consisted of three acts and told how a prince of royal blood narrowly escaped execution through being mistaken for an impostor, who sought the hand of the Emperor's daughter in marriage. The music, composed of solos and choruses, was quaint and fascinating, while the dialogue was lively and witty. The dresses of the principal characters were supplied by Messrs Nixon & Co., London and the entertainment was got up by the Reverend O. D. Williams and Mrs Williams, the Vicarage.

Youngsters enjoying their debut on the school stage graduated to the more sophisticated church or chapel drama group. The theatre became an essential part of entertainment and the hunger for performance found its satisfaction in the magnificent, spectacular annual pantomime revues presented from 1932 onwards by the home grown impresario Dennis Griffiths.

Much was learned from the cinema. Buckley saw its films in the Central Hall, the Palace Picture House and the Tivoli. Television is now the greatest of all leisure activities with its multitude of channels to suit all interests. Its precursor was the cinema, which influenced the masses more than any other media activity. From the opening of cinemas, or picture houses as they were then known, in the decade prior to the First World War (before 1914), a new leisure activity was available to everyone in society. It met their every need. For a few pence it provided unimaginable riches. It gave all members of society a sense of confidence and well being. They developed new identities. They shared the lives of their screen gods and goddesses. They took part in their adventures, often in exotic locations. They imitated their speech, manners, clothes, hairstyles, home furnishing, love making, habits, and conduct. They approved of, or condemned, their behaviour, and were taught the difference between right and wrong, good and evil, the meaning of social justice. The newsreels kept them in touch with the world's celebrities and political figures. It was their university of life, their source of conversation and discussion and their further education.

The cinema gave them more than the church or chapel. They had immediate salvation. Once they paid their shilling or few pence they gained admission to their own pew in their new heaven. The cinema was the dream factory, 'the opiate of the masses'. Here they felt warm, comfortable, and could laugh and cry without restraint. This was the place for courtship, it was romantic, cheap, dark, private, away from parental observation, and the oversight of the chapel deacon. Everyone was present, and everyone was alone in the darkness. No one could keep away. Every child went at least once a week, 50% of the adult population once and 25% twice a week.

Buckley cinemas

A licence was needed from the local authority to show films. Once granted it had to be renewed every year. The Cinematograph Act of 1909 laid down rigorous safety standards, which were administered by the local authority. The records of the Urban District Council provide the first information about the early Buckley cinemas and their proprietors. Thomas Cropper was probably the first cinema proprietor and manager in Buckley. His cinema known as the Picture Palace was situated together with his business premises in Lane End. Unfortunately these were destroyed by fire in February 1913. But the indomitable Cropper was not to be deterred and he rebuilt them during the First World War.

The other cinema was owned by the Buckley Picture House Limited registered on 28 January 1913, with a capital of £8,000. It was imaginatively known as the Buckley Picture House and occupied part of the Central Hall, built by the Reverend Joseph Davies. Mr H. Wilcox was the manager. In 1911, a Mr H. Hughes, submitted to the UDC plans of a picture house, and the following year Mr H. Wilcox applied for a cinematograph licence.

The years 1912–27 were those of the silent films. These were a challenge to their local promoters. The attention of the audience had to be held by music, sub-titles and novelties which included in some instances creating an atmosphere which matched the theme of the film, such as a desert oasis with its camel and palm trees. Sometimes prizes were offered in competitions relating to the subject of the film.

Thomas Cropper opened the new Palace Cinema in December 1917. The report in the *Chronicle* describes the new building:

The Palace Cinema, Lane End in the process of being demolished. [Buckley Society Archive]

The new Picture Palace at Lane End was opened on Friday evening when an excellent programme was presented to a crowded audience. The Palace, which is arranged on up to date lines as a house of entertainment, comprises a pit, balcony, and balcony circle. It provides accommodation for nearly 500 persons, with tip-up chair seating. The stage is commodious, with an anteroom on either side. The interior decorations give a pleasing effect, and the building is lit with electricity and heated with hot water apparatus. The cinema apparatus is installed in a fireproof room. The proprietors, Messrs T. Cropper and Sons, have studied the comfort of their patrons in every way, the entrances and exits, (the latter four in number), are well arranged, and no effort has been spared to make the Palace fully adapted for the purpose of a picture house.[14]

In the same building complex Cropper opened a billiard hall in May 1917. It was described as the 'New Temperance Billiard Palace', with nine full sized billiard tables. The report added that 'the game is to be played for the love of it, for there is to be no drinking, no betting, and no gambling, according to the rules'.[15] Cropper provided his own electricity generated by a national gas engine driving a dynamo. Three huge lamps illuminated the whole of the Lane End. Cropper was a great publicist and being a printer and literary minded, he issued a free monthly programme announcing 'Exclusive Star Pictures'. In the April 1921, edition the opening times were given as – 'commence nightly at 7.30, Saturdays 6 and 8. Matinee 2.30. Holidays and special occasions as announced. Prices, 5*d*., 9*d*. and 1*s*. Children's Admissions to Matinees, 2*d*., 3*d*. & 5*d*. Complete change of

Thomas Cropper (1869–1923). [T. Cropper Buckley and District]

Programme every Monday and Thursday'. Application had to be made to the UDC for a programme to be shown on Sunday and Good Friday. It was usually stipulated that a local minister of religion introduced the programme. Sunday, 3 April 1921, was designated 'Warriors Cinema Sunday', with proceeds in aid of the Earl Haig appeal, 'on behalf of Soldiers broken in the War', and Major Gibson gave a short address.

In the 1920s Mr Sinclair Ormonde was manager. He was succeeded by one of Thomas Cropper's sons, Mr Noel Cropper. The projectionist was Mr Sam Ratcliffe. Thomas Cropper died in 1923, and, a few months before, promoted one of the films shown by a press announcement, which read:

> A local film authoress – The local patrons of the Palace Picture House have had a special privilege during the first three days of this week of seeing a picture screened, the story of which was written by a Buckley lady. The notes in the current issue of the Palace programme refers to the picture as a beautiful Welsh story by a Buckley lady and a landmark among the star films of this house. The picture was Edith Nepean's Gwyneth of the Welsh Hills and refers to the gifted authoress as Miss Edith Bellis, daughter of the late Mr and Mrs John Bellis, originally of Buckley. The old mountain cottage of the family is still occupied by an aunt of Mrs Nepean. In order to infuse still more homeliness into the event complimentary tickets were sent to every local member of the family down to cousins. The authoress had promised if possible to be present at one of the houses. She wrote to Mr Cropper, the manager, offering a prize of £2 2s. and another of £1 1s. for the best critical essay of the film by patrons of the Palace. The result of the competition will be known next month. Crowded houses attended. The settings of the Welsh hills and views of mountain, lake and glen were charming. Critics agree that finer scenery has never been seen in a British production.[16]

The critics regarded the film *Gwyneth of the Welsh Hills*, produced in 1921, in the same vein as 'other Welsh films of the day', in that it 'placed heavy emphasis on religion, Celtic mysticism and ritual pastoral, forlorn romance and identity puzzles'.[17]

The script writer Edith Nepean, whom Cropper claimed was born in Buckley, gave her place of birth as Llandudno, and her father as John Bellis, a Caernarfonshire County Councillor. She moved to London, married well, and became a successful journalist and writer specialising in Welsh life. She travelled widely, in pursuit of her interest in Romany culture, in Roumania and Transylvania.

Cropper was a good showman, and knew how to attract his audiences. When D. W. Griffiths' epic *Way Down East* was shown he crammed 750 people into his cinema of 350 seats and proceeded to give them 'the full works', which included sound effects from an ice-breaking machine, used to stimulate the sounds of Lilian Gish's river ordeal.[18]

The Palace under the proprietorship of the Croppers was a lively and interesting place as his son Neil recalled:

> One cannot help remembering different characters and amusing instances. One cannot mention the Palace without the name of Mr George Powell. I think I am right in saying that he took the tickets downstairs almost throughout the period, and many will remember how he used to keep the audience in order. He was never seen without his cap, but he was always tidy and was a most loyal servant.
>
> Does someone recall telling the old gentleman to remember that the bottom step is the last and how he replied in best Buckley "I knowed that afore thou was atched, and a fine job they made o' thee when they atched thee"? And how in silent days groups would collect round someone who would be willing to read the sub-titles aloud. And what happened in the back row of the eighpennies? And the happy stout lady who was fast in her seat at the end of the show and laughed and laughed whilst the whole row of seats was dismantled to get her out'.[19]

The Croppers were a musical family and good instrumentalists. They encouraged suitable music, which was essential during the days of the silent screen. Mr Elvet Rowlands, a local man, who had been Musical Director of Lowestoft Municipal Orchestra, a fine violinist, was persuaded to take charge of the musical arrangements at the Palace. He put his talents to good use by reviving the Buckley Orchestral Society and forming the Buckley Salon Orchestra. When the Tivoli was built in 1925, it joined the Palace in producing Sunday evening charity concerts, featuring Buckley's finest soloists including Sid Peters, Arthur Messham, Billy Powell, Amos Roberts, Jimmy Downey, Sam Bentley, Winnie Spencer, and Katie Whalmsley and violinists Elvet Rowlands and Harold Shone.

The Palace Cinema was sold to Mr J. Jervis in 1936 and in the 1960s was in the ownership of Mrs E. T. Robertson. Although taken over by Wedgwood Cinemas it did not re-open. Owing to its dangerous state it was condemned by Alyn and Deeside Council and demolished in the 1970s.

More fortunate was the fate of the other Buckley cinema, the Tivoli. It was built by the Buckley Picture House Company Ltd on the site of the Central Hall.[20] The local newspaper gave an account of the opening in May 1925:

> A new theatre for Buckley. Buckley's new theatre, the Tivoli, was formally opened on Monday evening. This beautiful building, which has been erected on the site of the old Central Hall, should play a large part in the development of the district, for there is certain to be a large weekly influx of patrons from the surrounding villages.
>
> Just twelve months ago to the very day of the opening of the new theatre the old Central Hall closed down and was immediately dismantled and pulled down. The old building had for many years been used as a picture house, but the owner, Mr. Robert Rowlands, considered that the old hall had served its purpose, was antiquated in more ways than one, and totally inadequate to meet the needs of any large function, so he made up his mind to erect a building which Buckley people would be proud of, and anyone passing along Brunswick Road and seeing this imposing structure that has been erected will at once realise and admit that Buckley is now in possession of one of the largest and most elaborate places of amusement for miles around. Nothing has been spared to make the building attractive and comfortable.
>
> The interior is artistically and expensively decorated in pleasing colours. All the latest and most up to date devices in theatrical art have been introduced in making the edifice right up to date. The ornamental woodwork is of solid mahogany and the massive doors at the entrance are surrounded with large panels of stained glass, and are protected by large iron gates that open and close with a patent device. Even the name Tivoli is spelt in electric bulbs over the entrance, which flash in and out at night-time in London style. The music arrangements are in charge of Miss Suryani the well-known violinist.
>
> During the performance on Monday evening Miss Clara Hayes contributed a solo and Mr William Wilson chairman of the Buckley Urban Council in moving a vote of thanks said he would like to say a few words as a representative of the public. Mr Rowlands, the proprietor, made up his mind to provide a theatre for Buckley second to none in any way and this he had accomplished. Nearly all the work had been done by Buckley men. Mr Rowlands had spared nothing to make the place comfortable and he was sure he would supply amusements in keeping with such a beautiful place'. Mr W. C. Collin seconded the resolution. In responding Mr Rowlands said 'The building which has been designed on up to date lines contains the latest appliances and equipment, and will accommodate a foyer, which can be adapted as a lounge or waiting room, and auditorium with lavatory accommodation leading from the same. On the first floor, space has been provided for a Café with waiting room with lavatories adjoining. The balcony and staircases are constructed of reinforced concrete, no columns being used for supports, thus giving an unrestricted view from all parts of the auditorium to the stage. At the rear of the screen a stage 45 feet by 23 feet for theatrical productions, with gird roof to fly all curtains and scenery, is arranged with six male and female artiste's dressing rooms adjoining them. The main operating room is also placed behind the screen, the latest method of rear projection on a transparent screen being adopted, thus removing causes of eyestrain and rays of light in the auditorium and rendering it unnecessary for the auditorium to be in total darkness. Tip up chairs are provided for the whole of the seating, and the floors are covered with carpets and patent linoleum composition, and are warm, resilient and sound proof, and numerous exits in addition to the main entrance and exits are suitably placed so that the building, in case of fire, can be emptied in the shortest possible time. Messrs Hayes Bros. of Buckley were the general contractors for the work. The building was designed and the work supervised by Mr R. Lloyd Roberts of Mold.[21]

The Tivoli was planned as a combination of cinema and theatre. It was a more adaptable building than the Picture Palace and could accommodate more people. It gave Buckley people a choice of entertainment, provided a competitive basis for the proprietors, and gave local talent a stage upon which to perform. The building of the Tivoli began the golden age of Buckley entertainment and gave tremendous scope for imaginative and lavish productions. It became Buckley's 'West End'. It was not long before the Tivoli was used to its best advantage by local amateurs, for example in October 1925, when it was reported that:

> Music lovers of Buckley and district had a rich musical treat, when the annual concert of the season, which is organised by the Welsh Calvinistic Methodist Church, took place at the Tivoli. This was the first concert in this

magnificent building since its erection. The theatre was packed with an audience which was raised to a state of enthusiasm with the exceptionally high standard of the programme. Amongst the artists taking part were: Miss Dorothy Bennett, soprano; Mr Frank Webster, baritone, of the British National Opera; Mr John Buckley; Miss Irma Suranyi, celebrated violinist; Mr Ernest Thornley, cello soloist; and the Buckley male voice choir of 30 voices.[22]

The versatility of the building, and business acumen of the management, were demonstrated in its advertised programme for February 1926.

> This week Percy Holmshaw presents the famous London Nights Revue. Tomorrow at 2.30, every child will be given a picture book. Next week, Geo Batty presents the Royal Empire Circus. This is going to be a record breaking attraction, so book your seats in advance to make sure of the best seats. There will be every kind of circus attraction on the stage, including performing horses, ponies, dogs, and other animals, and every night there will be a bare back riding competition for local people. No entrance fee. The final will be held on Friday night. There will be a matinee on Wednesday at 3.45 and matinee on Saturday, at the usual time. Full shows are always given at matinees.

In 1927 the owners of the Tivoli, the Buckley Picture House, Ltd, were forced to raise their admission prices. The new prices for adults were dress circle, 2s. 4d.; family circle and orchestral stalls 2s.; circle, 1s. 6d.; stalls 1s. 3d.; pit 8d. Half prices for children were 1s. and 8d. The reasons given for the increase in prices were the:

> … the great difficulty in getting first class shows to think of coming to Buckley, owing to the size and population of the town. We cannot get them to entertain Buckley without guaranteeing them a salary in addition to shares of the Box Office takings. We are therefore forced to one of the three following alternatives:— revert to pictures — give a poorer type of music hall entertainment, as is usual in small towns — keep our present high class shows and raise the prices.

The situation was changed with the replacement of silent films by the 'talkies'. George Lewis noted — '1930 Mar. 15, Mon. The 'talking films' came to the Tivoli Buckley for the first time.'

In 1937 the Tivoli was taken over by the Stanley Grimshaw Theatres and then by Byrom Picture House Ltd under the proprietorship of Philip M. Hanmer. In the 1960s it became for a short while a bingo hall, but was reopened in February 1965 as, 'what is described as North Wales' grandest ballroom and entertainment centre, the Tivoli at Buckley'.[23]

The Tivoli of the 1930s had fond memories for hundreds of school children who passed with wonder and excitement through its magical doors into their special world of the Saturday matinee. Here they followed the adventures of their heroes — Flash Gordon, the Man in Black, the Iron Claw and cohorts of cowboys and indians, who thundered across the screen to the accompiament of much booing, hissing and stamping of feet. Remembered with affection was Bill Wilcox, of the Central Hall days of pictures, who kept erring customers in order with a blow from his wooden leg; Mr Brimblecombe, smoking his calabash pipe whilst taking the children's tuppences for admission to the Saturday matinee. The exhibitions of boxing given by the north Wales hero Johnnie Basham, supported by his nippers, juvenile boxers, from Wrexham.[24]

One of the tragedies of the cinema era was the fire at the Tivoli on Sunday 20 May 1945 in which Harry Goldrich, the projectionist, lost his life. The building was empty apart from Goldrich and a cleaning lady. His death took place on Whit Sunday afternoon when he was working in the winding room preparing for a film show. The fire probably resulted from a burning cigarette. Giving evidence at the inquest the cleaner, Mrs Alice Lewis, told the coroner that 'she covered her face with her coat and tried to enter, as she wanted to know whether Harry was in there or not. The flames and the smoke drove her back and there were sounds like a lot of fireworks going off. They seemed to be coming from the winding room. She had shouted Harry, but got no reply. She came down and went to another flight of stairs, but the smoke was too terrible'.

Her evidence was followed by that of Police Sergeant Ben Williams, who said,

> … that the doors of the winding room and the operating box were ablaze. He imagined he saw a boot between the two operating machines, and told his companions that he was going to attempt to get in, telling them to work on the doors with the extinguisher.
>
> He placed a handkerchief over his mouth and crawled into the operating room. He felt a man's leg and after some difficulty, being nearly overcome by the fumes, he got Goldrich outside on the staircase. The man was, in the witness's opinion, dead.

The coroner came to the verdict that death was caused from carbon monoxide poisoning from the gas given off by burning celluloid films. He commended the action of the cleaner and the police sergeant.[25]

Community leisure in the 1920s and 1930s

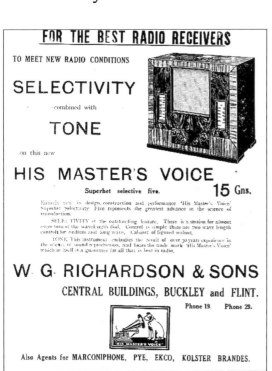

The phenomenal growth of cinema enriched rather than diminished peoples lives in Buckley between the wars. People still went out as much as possible in their leisure times. The wireless was very much in its infancy. It could be found in less than one quarter of all households in 1928, was present in over half in 1934, and was effectively universal by the late 1940s. Thus it entered peoples' homes gradually, almost stealthily. When not in use it was covered by a cloth as if it were a sleeping parrot. It was used warily and selectively, particularly when the news was grim. On the occasion when George V was seriously ill, when he addressed the nation as the 'Father of the Empire', and during the abdication crisis. There was no such thing as using wireless for background music, which came during the war, as 'music while you work'.

Wireless came of age at 11 am on 3 September 1939, when the Prime Minister broadcast to the nation and told them that they were at war with Germany. Until the Second World

1930s wireless advertisement in the 1934 pantomime programme.
[Buckley Archive]

War one did not stay at home to listen to the wireless. Leisure time was shared between visiting the cinema and loyalty to one's place of worship. Membership meant not only attending Sunday worship, but joining in denominational activities. Talents, as the gospels taught, were meant to bring forth a hundred-fold, not be buried in the garden or allotment. As in the sporting arena, there was opportunity in the religious sphere, not only of being a spectator, but also, a participant. Every place of worship encouraged its young by having football and cricket teams, and dramatic and debating societies. The love of music became a shared experience not only through singing hymns but also by the performance of oratorio. This talent, in its enthusiasm, spilt out into the community at large and entered secular entertainment in the form of local concerts, with programmes of choirs, choruses, a galaxy of local soloists, accompanied by a small orchestra of local musicians and led ultimately to the formation of a company which brought together all these skills in the presentation annually of a high class pantomime. Ballroom dancing was fashionable. Buckley used the Albert Hall as its ballroom or danced in the Parish Rooms at St Matthew's and All Saints, Lane End, and the Ex-Servicemen's Institution. There was an adequate choice of dance bands, jazz performers, and entertainers. If you didn't show any talent there was plenty of scope as an onlooker mingling in the carnival crowd. In spite of the gloom and distress of the depression years, in general, Buckley folk showed a great aptitude for enjoyment and used every opportunity to develop their sense of humour.

We now look at some of the leisure activities available to the people of Buckley in the 1920s, concluding with a list of the events arranged for Christmas 1930 and New Year 1931.

The annual carnival was the event which drew the largest crowd of Buckley folk from all backgrounds in the 1920s. The following account says a great deal about leisure in Buckley during this decade. The report is from August 1927:

The town of Buckley was *en fete* on Wednesday, the half day, on occasion of the carnival, an annual event promoted by the Ex-Servicemen's Club. This organisation can truthfully be classed as the liveliest in the locality. They have possessed for a considerable time an excellent institute which is run and managed on proper lines, and the building provides every modern facility including wireless, billiards, bagatelle, badminton, dry canteen, etc.

This year's carnival was the ninth of its kind. In previous years the proceeds, which have run about £100 from each one, have chiefly gone to Charity. Chester Infirmary has consistently benefited, and in addition a fund has been kept going all along for the purchase of a new motor ambulance for the town. This materialised early this year, when a handsome and well-appointed new motor ambulance was purchased at a cost of £450 and handed over to the care of the Buckley Council. During the coal strike carnival proceeds were distributed to destitute miners' families. This will give the outsider a fair indication of the activities and usefulness of the Buckley Ex-Servicemen's Institute, and at the same time it will be sufficient explanation for the fact that Wednesday's carnival proceeds are to be kept for the use of the Institute. The Committee has in view a scheme for the beautification of the grounds round the Institute, and this it is hoped to accomplish, by the laying out of six tennis courts.

The chairman of this year's carnival committee was Mr Harold Shone and he had two energetic secretaries in Mr Frank Kelsall and Mr Ted Lloyd, who accomplished a difficult task in a creditable manner. Entries were well up to previous years and if anything the procession was larger and certainly more varied.

King and Queen carnival in the persons of Messrs Frank Roberts and Frank Kelsall arrived in the town in state the previous Saturday, and by their riotousness immediately captured the Town and delivered it over in carnival spirit. Riding in a horse drawn landau, their majesties, escorted by courtiers and led by the town band, went through the principal streets to the Free Library. Here they were received by the 'Lord Mayor of Buckley' who was no other than Mr Joseph Tarran. Addresses of welcome were given and then speeches were delivered from the Library balcony to a large crowd beneath.

The carnival was preceded by a baby show held in the Palace Theatre during the afternoon. Local doctors and nurses were the judges. This was followed by a push ball match on the cricket field between two eight-aside teams, Brook Street v. Harlequins. A good crowd gathered round a specially enclosed pitch and thoroughly enjoyed the novel sight. During this entertainment the motley crowd of carnival competitors &c. assembled in their respective classes in another part of the cricket field, and spectators were able to inspect at leisure the ingenuity shown by entrants to capture prizes for best turn-outs, tableaux, fancy dresses, &c. In the meantime judges got busy selecting the successful participants. The judges were Messrs J. Roberts, W. C. Collin, J. S. Shone, W. Davies, W. Hannaby, W. Wilson, S. Dunn, and Father Pochard.

A little after time, the procession marshalled by Mr S. Dunn, left the cricket field for a tour of the town. The Mold Fire Brigade and Buckley Band led the way; the streets were thronged with people who were given a good laugh by the very pronounced comic element in the procession. Horace Tarran's 'Washing Day' tableaux caused great amusement, as did Professor Cocoa's 'Musical Eight' which, was composed of eight local-musicians on a motor lorry. A hit at the local Council was the appearance of two young colliers with towels round them and bearing cards 'Order of the Buckley Baths', the allusion being to the provision of baths for the colliers by the Urban Council.

A rather striking turnout was Captain Lindbergh's 'Spirit of St Louis' aeroplane which was in charge of Miss W. Astbury, Stronghill, as the American airman. A topical hit was the 'Umbrella Hay Harvest', tableaux entered by Mr Anglesea of Buckley. This depicted the gathering of the harvest with umbrellas, the reference of course being too obvious to need explanation. There were four mounted entries. Steve Donoghue was well portrayed by Lawrence Kettle, a little boy from Shotton. Emlyn Jones splendidly impersonated an Indian Girl, whilst A. Hughes, of Buckley, looked a typical Dick Turpin. There was a strong turnout of local tradesmen, motor vehicles of the BP Petrol Co. and a dairyman.

One does not pretend to mention everything and everybody here, but there were several more in the various classes who deserve praise for the originality shown. After the town had been paraded the procession returned to the cricket field where Miss Sergeant presented the prizes.

A carnival ball was held in the Institute at night and continued until 2 am. There were six fancy dress and four spot prizes.[26]

The Buckley Glee Club, 1930, conductor Harry Phillips. [FRO D/DM/434/32]

Buckley Male Voice Choir in Hawarden Park, 1934. [FRO PH/11/210]

Other group activities were enhanced by organisations formed or revived in the 1920s. One was the Buckley Glee Party, which commanded the assistance of such local stars as Miss Clara Hayes, soprano, Miss Doreen Iball, elocutionist, and Mr Tom Roberts, accompanist. The Buckley Orchestral Society was revived in 1925 under the direction of Mr William Davies and attracted a membership of around thirty members. After one of their Sunday evening concerts at the Tivoli in February 1927 a critic writing in the local press was fulsome in his praise:

Buckley is making rapid advancements in musical matters, and the tastes of vocal and orchestral musicians are catered for on elaborate lines. The present orchestral society is the finest achievement that the town has produced in a combination of wind and string instruments and the strongest so far as numbers are concerned and Mr Davies their conductor deserves complimenting as well as the Society on their success.[27]

The richness of this musical versatility and the variety of opportunities for its expression is seen in a review of events surrounding the celebration of Christmas 1930 and New Year 1931. The churches excelled at Christmas time in providing religious services and musical presentations in accord with the season. In December 1930 the *Messiah* was performed at the Tabernacle with an augmented choir and special artistes. The conductor was Mr Davies Hayes and the organist Mr Tom Roberts. After Christmas the Congregational Church presented a sacred cantata, From Manger to Cross, by John Witty. with guest principals, assisted by the Buckley orchestra, conducted by Mr Dennis Griffiths, and Mr Tom Roberts, organist. The newspaper reported that:

> The president was Mr J. R. Griffiths, Mus. Bac. of London who in his reminiscent remarks referred to his earlier associations with the church. Mr Griffiths said he felt very pleased to be amongst old friends at Buckley. There were such a number of things he felt proud of. The conductor was a nephew of his whose father died when he was 37 years of age. He thought he would be proud if he was there tonight. The organ blower was another nephew and his son was now a deacon at this church. He was also very pleased to learn of the excellent progress the Buckley Choral Society was making under the guidance of his friend Mr. Tom Roberts at the organ, whose father, Mr Edward Roberts, JP, had been a life long friend of his. He hoped that this temporary choir that had done so well there would spring up a permanent one.[28]

It was announced at the next rehearsal of the Choral Society that the committee had been very successful in securing as soloists for their annual performance, two of the finest artists in the country, Miss Isabel Bailey, soprano, and Mr. Watcyn Watcyns, bass.

The Brunswick Wesley Guild Amateur Dramatic Society presented three farces and the Tabernacle Young People's Dramatic Society gave a humorous sketch entitled the 'Headwaiter'. In a more serious vein were the meetings of mutual improvement societies at the Square Methodists, the Congregationalists, Zion, and at Alltami P.M. Church where Mr Charles Duckworth gave an address on the League of Nations. At the close all present signed the petition for disarmament. Concerts were arranged at the Congregational Church as a 'bachelor's effort', and at Tabernacle in aid of the new Sunday school building. The proceeds of a jumble sale and carol singing at the Drury Lane PM Church, which raised £20, paid the cost of installing electric light. Every Sunday school had their treats, mostly on New Year's Day. St Matthew's Church held their Annual New Year's social. Tea was followed by an entertainment, whist drive, and dance, with music provided by the Bible Class minstrel troupe and the Buckley Vaudeville dance orchestra. The orchestra played too at All Saints Choir whist drive and dance attended by 100 persons in the parish room. The Bistre Parish Church annual social gathering was held in the parish room, Lane End. 'After tea a musical programme was sustained by Mr Joseph Bartley and Mr. Robert Mountfort, who sang solos, and Master John Owen who rendered violin solos. The remainder of the evening was devoted to dancing with music supplied by the Imperial Dance Orchestra.'

Many organisations held dances. The Royal Buckley Town Band held their annual ball at the Albert Hall, where a Mistletoe Dance, took place on Christmas Eve, with music by the Palm Beach dance band. The Buckley Swimming Club used the same venue and chose the Rhyl Melody Makers to provide the music for their Invitation Ball. The Brook Street Working Men's Club entertained 130 of their members to supper and a musical entertainment at their headquarters.

For ardent supporters football matches took place. On Boxing Day Buckley Alex beat Gwersyllt by 4 goals to 3. The result was more disappointing a week later when Buckley playing at Oakenholt in a Charity cup-tie match were leading 3–1 when fog enveloped the ground and the match abandoned. A local derby was played between Buckley Amateurs and Burntwood Rovers who were opponents in the Welsh Amateur Cup. The

Buckley Olde Time Band — Len Bartlett, piano; Harold Wilcock, trumpet; Bill Holmes, accordion; Billy Harry, drums; Arthur Jones MC; Emlyn Davies, banjo.
[Buckley Society Archive]

St Matthews Drama Group c.1954. L–R: (Back row) Rupert Robinson, Mary Birtwistle, Lelia Hewitt, Helen Birks, Brenda Maloney, Frank Birtwistle; (Front row) Peter Rowlands, Enid Griffiths, Ada Roberts, Dorothy Shone, Vera Johnson.
[Buckley Society Archive]

St. John's Congregational Church performance of Royal Jester c.1930. L–R: Joseph Roberts, Connie Roberts, Dennis Griffiths, Gladys Hughes, Herbert Bellis, Gwen Price.
[By courtesy of J. B. Lewis]

match went to a replay with Burntwood the winners by 3 goals to 2.

The Christmas handicaps were played at the Palace Billiard Hall, and the Christmas competitions concluded at the Albert Hall. In the junior frames R. Jenkins beat L. Lamb and in the senior frames Horace Davies triumphed over George Booth.

Other leisure activities were successfully revived in the 1930s. To encourage gardeners and allotment holders the Buckley Allotments and Cottage Garden Association held their first annual flower and vegetable show in the Council Schools in August 1932 after a break of 26 years. The following year, Lord and Lady Gladstone accompanied by Mrs Parish, the former Miss Dorothy Drew, attended the event. The purpose of the Association was to bring neglected gardens back into cultivation. To achieve this, seeds and fertiliser were bought collectively, the unemployed offered allotments, and Mr Jones of Padeswood Hall Demonstration Centre, lectured to members in the winter months.[29]

In January 1934 St Matthew's amateur dramatic society was successfully revived,

> … after a long rest, which has really been for a few years. The last time the Society appeared was in the play 'Tilly of Bloomsbury', in the old Central Hall, before the Tivoli was built. This time they have aspired to even greater things, for they have been rehearsing for several months, R. C. Sheriff's famous war play, "Journey's End", under the tutorship of the Reverend A. H. Fox, of Broughton Church. The cast will have war equipment and other effects lent them by the C.O. at Chester Castle.[30]

The Buckley Pantomime

The Buckley Amateur Pantomime Company was the most successful of any leisure activity in the history of Buckley. The company ran from 1932 to 1959. Its longevity was due to the admirable leadership given by Mr Dennis Griffiths from 1933 until his company was disbanded twenty-six years later. The history of the company has been well described.[31]

Dennis Griffiths was invited by the committee to produce its second pantomime, *Dick Whitington and his Cat*, which opened at the Tivoli in January 1933. He had been involved for many years in producing operettas with members of the Congregational Church. He brought with him not only great experience but a team of enthusiastic performers and stage assistants.

The town was no stranger to pantomime. In January 1931 the people of Buckley were shown what a professional company could achieve when the management of the Tivoli announced the advent of 'William

De Lacey's gorgeous pantomime *Mother Hubbard'*. It was as the advanced publicity declared:

> … not the usual travelling pantomime, but a wonderful production coming direct from a season in the Opera House Coventry, where it is now playing to crowded houses'. The press enthused that 'Mr Sharples should be congratulated, for he is giving the public the very best entertainment that it is possible to secure. This visit being the outstanding event of the entertainment year will enable everyone to make arrangements for theatre parties for there is nothing like a pantomime of the year.

A statement with which the budding talent of Buckley concurred for in January 1932 the Buckley Tabernacle Amateur Operetta Society performed Clementine Ward's *Pearl the Fishermaid* in the Albert hall. It received a favourable review for what was described as 'a crowded performance on a large scale for this able company to perform , as last season they were most successful with a performance of Princess Ju-Ju in the same hall. In this their latest effort, there was a marked improvement, for the characters sang, acted and danced more naturally, and had overcome stage fright which generally causes new beginners to make blunders'.[32]

A more ambitious attempt to emulate William De Lacey's was the formation of the Buckley Amateur Pantomime Company the same year. It had as its objects 'to encourage local stage talent by voluntary tuition and training', and 'to raise funds for such local charities as may be decided upon by the committee'.[33] Their first production was *Cinderella* staged at the Tivoli, which ran for three nights in March 1932. According to the critic, writing in the local paper, it 'took very well, the Theatre being well filled with appreciative audiences'. He supplied other information. For example, that the book was by Mr John Evans of Connah's Quay, 'who was responsible for such a successful show of *Dick Whittington* at Shotton a few weeks back'. He hinted that a crisis had happened during rehearsal and the producer was replaced 'by Mr W. Barratt of Mold, whose first effort it was. I understand it was only seven weeks ago he was called in, so that in a comparatively short time he had to do what would be a strain to an experienced producer'.

No matter how well *Cinderella* was received by the local audience it met with a mixed reception from the critic 'Redcap'. He described it as a very lively and funny pantomime with some cute songs, and praised the orchestra, whose playing contributed a good deal to the success of the show. But it was the strong comedy, which 'Redcap' found was the outstanding feature with Harry Dolby and John Duffield 'being about the best pair of comedians he had seen in amateur productions in the district'. They were well supported in mirth and patter by Dick Catherall, Tom Tarran, and Albert Griffiths. But it was not ' a spectacular panto. The dresses were pretty though plain'. 'The show was a bit weak from the vocal point as all the principal female characters were taken by comparatively young girls and some of them were not equal to the vocal effects demanded from the characters they were impersonating'.[34] However, the Pantomime Committee must have taken notice of the review, for they decided in a matter of weeks to approach Dennis Griffiths to take charge of the next show. It was a decision which they never regretted.

Dennis Griffiths' first pantomime production was at the Tivoli in January 1933. For the 'book', or script, as it was known, he relied on one placed at his disposal by Mr Walter Roberts, a successful Wrexham businessman, who for thirty years produced pantomimes in the town, raising over £40,000 for the War Memorial Hospital and the Pantomime Children's Ward.[35]

Dennis Griffiths rehearsed his cast of principals for several months at the Memorial Institute and for the pantomime performances recruited a chorus of 150, with special items given by the Buckley Glee Party, members of the Royal Buckley Town Band, and the orchestra, numbering 18 players, led by Elvet Rowlands. Valuable help was received for mechanical and electrical effects and from the wardrobe mistress and her assistants. The scenery effects were made locally and painted by W. E. Roberts, drawing master, at the Buckley evening class. All the principals are listed in full in the newspaper report, as they were to be over the next twenty-six years.[36] A large book could be written from the amount of material available.[37] However we may shed new light on the motives of Dennis Griffiths and find a summary of his many productions in his own words.[38]

From his very first production Dennis Griffiths was able to build upon local talent which had emerged over the past decade and been channelled into disciplined musical productions. To this he added another essential ingredient, comedy. His own musical and dramatic talents combined with a sense of compassion

Dennis Griffiths.
[Pantomime programme]

and understanding of Buckley folk worked their magic spell and brought laughter and entertainment for a quarter of a century.

Dennis Griffiths was born in Buckley, as were six generations of the family before him. The year was 1895, and the birthplace, a cottage next door to his maternal grandfather Hill, a kiln worker. Here his father died at the age of 37 years, leaving a wife and family of five boys and three girls. The family then moved to a house with a little shop attached, on Bunker's Hill, built for his mother by much loved 'grandpa Hill'. The family worshipped in the Congregational Church where his paternal grandfather was Joseph Griffiths, senior deacon, an excellent musician, superintendent of the Sunday school, one of the three founding fathers of the Buckley Jubilee and a little forbidding to young Dennis. He attended St Matthew's school winning a scholarship to Hawarden County School where he remained four terms only because of his mother's straitened circumstances. He started work at Catherall's brickworks and rose to become work's manager at the Trap when twenty-one years of age, later moving to Hancock's. His life centred on the Congregational Church. Here he became organist, and made the best of the cultural opportunities provided through music and drama, producing his first play at the age of seventeen, and gaining a reputation as a talented actor and musician. He was well prepared, and respected by the time the Buckley Pantomime Company approached him to be their producer.

In the draft manuscript of his autobiography *Out of this Clay* Griffiths described the times in Buckley from which the Pantomime Company originated:[39]

Buckley did not escape the lean years of the late 1920–1930s. There was much suffering, a lot of it silent suffering, and many a hard working family saw its little store fritter away at a time when jobs were hard to get. Short-time working was a common expedient of firms battling for their existence. A feeling of injustice pervaded public life, and embitterment was the natural consequence.

In those days, I heard Church and Chapel going people, rage with resentment, at the treatment they received by the enforcement of the hated 'means test', by local religious leaders. Although justified by the letter of the law, it was difficult to accept when it appeared that the thrifty were penalised and the improvident aided.

I recall a Moderator of the Free Church seething with indignation in the pulpit as he condemned the South Wales colliers who gambled away a shilling a week of their meagre public allowance. Intolerance abounded, and at a period when there was an over-abundance of enforced leisure, few either knew how, or had the inclination to use it purposefully.

Even steelworkers, so much better paid than brickworkers, gladly availed themselves of any opportunity to work a day or two at a brickworks on their off-days from their regular employment. Fortunately, local brickworks were among the last industries to feel the effects of the slump, but when they did, it hit them so badly, that one firm was glad to sell its large stocks of excellent firebricks listed at 200/0 for 35/- per thousand.

Industrial depression was matched by spiritual gloom, and individual and family hardships and discontent were reflected in group and social apathy.

Yet in that period, some encouraging local

Dennis Griffiths (to the right of the central character) outside Central Hall, 1916.
[Buckley Library]

enterprises were launched. The Buckley Choral Society was revived, and apart from a break during the war it continued its successful career until a combination of unfavourable circumstances depleted its membership and it ceased to meet a year or two ago.

One very encouraging feature in local cultural activity emerged during this period. Drama, until then hardly known in Buckley, became very popular, and to a considerable extent it compensated for decreased interest in music.

I remember the first time I saw a play. I was a boy then, and the performance was in the old Central Hall. The play was called Owen Glendower and it was written by the Reverend D. W. Morgan, then minister of Zion Presbyterian Chapel in Buckley. The performance, which impressed me deeply, was by a local cast, but after Mr. Morgan left Buckley, there was hardly any drama until Buckley Drama Circle was formed in 1933. Since then it has become one of the best-known amateur drama companies in Wales.

There is a popular misconception in the minds of many who do not live in Buckley that an effort has only to be announced in Buckley for its success to be assured. The idea is summed up in a phrase one often hears, that 'everything goes in Buckley'. Much as one would like to believe it to be true, experience belies it. For one thing, in any community there is to be found only a proportion of people willing to assume responsibility, and of that proportion but few are prepared by ability or disposition to be leaders. Here, as elsewhere, it is generally the same folk who are called upon to sustain by their efforts existing organisations, religious, social, or otherwise, and their loyalties already being engaged, they cannot easily be persuaded to add to their responsibilities.[40]

For the twenty-seven years he was in charge as producer and director of the Pantomime Company, Dennis Griffiths received the loyalty of his cast, until forced to retire through ill-health in November 1959. He had summed up his thoughts on the Pantomime Company's success nearly three years before, in a talk on the BBC. This is a transcript:

I am not blessed with a good memory, but I'm sure that when we started our Pantomimes 25-years ago we had neither the idea nor the intention that in Buckley, a Flintshire town of 7,000 inhabitants, we would eventually stage the largest amateur pantomime in Great Britain — as I'm now told ours is.

Our first pantomime, in 1933, was *Dick Whittington*, produced from a borrowed script and performed by a company of over 100. All the cast, chorus, orchestra, stage staff and producer were amateurs, backed by a committee of enthusiasts all drawn from an abundance of local talent. We had no pantomime experience, although there was a rich tradition of vocal music in the area, and we had performed dramas, some operettas and an opera or two. Fortunately, we had an excellent local theatre, capable of staging big shows and seating 1,000 people, where professional pantomimes had been staged in the late twenties.

Our rehearsals were held in cold, drab rooms, when these were available, and often we had to break up into sections and practise in each other's homes. All our costumes and scenery were made locally.

I shall never forget the dress rehearsal for that first pantomime. It was dreadful; everything seemed to go wrong. Yet our opening performance went smoothly, and before the week's run had finished we were playing to packed houses, although advance bookings were less than £5. The pantomime cost less than £200 to stage and we made a profit of £178. What was far more important was the birth of the team spirit and the fund of goodwill which have sustained our activities for a quarter of a century. All our artists are still local amateurs; our scenery and lighting equipment are now hired from specialists in the theatre.

Some of our artists have been with us since we started, and appearing in almost every performance. One of them is a comedian who is normally engaged in making aircraft. He is also a Town Councillor, and as such is fair game for his partners! A schoolmaster, a painter, a local government official and a steelworker, also in the cast, are all experienced artists. Principal Boy and Principal Girl were in the chorus twenty-five years ago, and they, also have played in nearly all our pantomimes. One is a journalist, and the other a dancing teacher, who with our sequence mistress is responsible for the Ballet. Our fairy, too, has been in our pantomimes since she was five. A few years ago she had poliomyelitis, but so keen was she to maintain her unbroken pantomime record that she asked for, and obtained a walking-on part for two seasons while she was still in plaster.

Our Junior Chorus, girls under ten, have already played to over 100,000 people, and, like the Senior Chorus, who have doubled that total, they take the stage with the confidence of veterans. Bless their little hearts, how they love it!

Make no mistake about this, children are the best judges of pantomime. My most anxious hours are those when I allow the children in our choruses, to see the show for the first time, a week or so before we open. If they approve, all's well. Children like strong meat for their entertainment. What they want is plenty of monsters, demons and buffoonery, and pantomime gives full opportunity for that.

Apart from that first borrowed script, it has been my lot to write all the scripts we have used and also to produce and musically direct all our 25 pantomimes. I'm afraid this is rather unusual, but one can in this way employ dialogue, business and music best suited to performers and audiences. In pantomime, people expect something to see and something to hear, a catchy, lilting tune and popular songs. We have also an occasional song-scene for our vocalists, who have frequently sung at Welsh National Eisteddfodau. For pantomime one takes a favourite legend, uses poetry and music, dancing and comedy to adorn it, indulges in any irrelevance of time and space to satirise anything that happens about us, and most important of all, tells again the story of the pantomime. It may be the lovely, romantic Cinderella we presented last year, or the strongly contrasted Jack and the Beanstalk, with all its excitement, which I have chosen for our Silver Jubilee production. It is better to depend on the freshness and originality of an amateur show, mixing the ingredients of spectacle, comedy, music and ballet than to try and copy professional techniques, which we can never hope to do successfully.

We have our full share of problems, of course. For three successive seasons in our early years, when we ran only a week's show, we had snowfalls over four feet deep. One year, not a single vehicle was able to reach the theatre, but our audiences came, some of them walking over ten miles through the snow. Even petrol restrictions are not so great a threat to success as weather of that kind. Since then, we have always staged our pantomime in late February and March. You see, most of our audiences come by bus, train and car from surrounding towns and villages, and a few come every year from distant places, from Scotland, Ireland, London and South, from the Midlands and the North.

Our greatest problem now is that our pantomime is probably too big and runs too long for an amateur show. About 36 hours at the theatre each week for three weeks of pantomime, following three nights of intensive dress rehearsal until the early hours of the morning is hard going on top of a usual week's work, especially for volunteer staff.

But what a lot we have to be grateful for! No worries about advance bookings now! Our 20,000 seats are sold out before the pantomime opens each year. Last year's gross taking were over £5,000 and profits for several years have been about £2,000 per season. In the 600 performances by our Company over half a million people have paid over £50,000, of which over £25,000 has been given to charities.

I suppose that this is, in a way, quite an achievement. One of the aims we have realised by our gifts is the provision of a Community Centre with facilities and equipment for social and cultural activities. I like to think, however, that our pantomimes have above all given joy and happiness to laughter-loving people, and the successful careers of own young folk have been stimulated by their share in them.

Perhaps, after all, we may be forgiven the special flourishes and that extra bit of excitement, which will herald the opening night of our Silver Jubilee Pantomime in a few weeks' time.[41]

A review of the pantomimes

Dennis Griffiths was responsible for the production and musical direction of the pantomimes from 1933 until 1959. He wrote 'the book' for everyone, apart from 1933, and the titles were repeated. The list is *Dick Whittington* 1933, 1948, and 1953; *Aladdin* 1934, 1939, 1946; *Robinson Crusoe* 1935, 1943, 1951, 1958; *Cinderella* 1936, 1945, 1956; *Ali Baba* 1937, 1944, 1950, 1955; *Puss in Boots* 1938, 1959; *Babes in the Wood* 1947, 1954; *Jack and the Beanstalk* 1949, 1957.

At the beginning of the Second World War, in 1940, '41 and '42, Panto Revues replaced the fully staged pantomimes. These were sustained by the principal artists of the 1930s productions and assisted on stage by many local war-time organisations — WVS, VAD, ARP, AFS, Report Centre, St John's Ambulance Brigade, Special Decontamination Party, Boys' Brigade, St Matthew's Brownies and Girl Guides. The programme consisted of wartime songs, sketches, monologues, and included an audience guessing competition on 'amazing Buckley views'. Elvet Rowlands conducted the review orchestra.

The personnel connected with the pantomimes from 1933 onwards are well documented in the complete collection of programmes.[42] Once a member of the Buckley Pantomime Company it needed either age, ill-health or change of residence to make you quit. Consistency was the hallmark of service both on the stage and off and members often fulfilled more than one role. The best administrators and technicians were recruited to ensure the pantomime's success. All members acted in a voluntary capacity and all the considerable profits were given to charity.

Behind the scenes were the officials. For a while in the 1930s until his death in 1941 the influential F. Llewellyn Jones, former MP for Flintshire and Town Clerk of Buckley, was president. For the same period is a list of patrons headed by the philanthropic Lady Ernestine Maud Gladstone of Hawarden, together with

Principals
L–R: Top row — Dick Catherall, Frank Roberts, Harry Dolby. Middle row — Harry Phillips, Peggy Griffiths, Peggy Hughes. Bottom row: Peter Wilcock, Winnie Humphreys, Winnie Spencer. From the 1938 programme for Puss in Boots.

local clergy, ministers and businessmen. The first chairman was W. Hannaby who was succeeded by R. L. Hopwood. T. W. Owen held office as vice chairman and publicity, to be followed by Fred Dugdale who acted as treasurer, and vice chairman. H. F. Beavan was followed as secretary by Jack Kelly and then for a long spell by Miss Clara Messham.

It was a big undertaking to take over the management of a large theatre and provide the props, lighting, sound effects, and costumes for an annual spectacular and lavish new production. Year by year the pantomime was maintained by a dedicated and technically equipped staff who became thoroughly conversant with their particular role and were readily assisted by the resident stage manager of the Tivoli, A. Lewis.

Here is a list of most of the staff over the years 1933–59. Some worked together, others followed them. Electrical effects and lighting: Charles Wilcock and T. Drury. In 1934 the scenery was by Messrs H. Parker, C. Peters, and J. & T. Hughes, later stage carpentry by Cyril Peters, D. E. Davies, T. Trevor Davies, R. R. Rowlands and Messrs R. D. Davies. Stage managers: F. Dugdale, R. L. Hopwood, Alec Hughes, Vernon Hughes, O. D. Hayes and Derek Williams. Property Managers: Kingsley Hughes, K. R. Hopwood, E. Hayes, C. Griffiths, E. Hewitt and John Wainwright. Publicity was in the hands of T. Wilcock, programmes Mrs T. Wilcock, competitions Mrs R. Catherall, and the chief steward was Latham Catherall.

The search for ideas for costumes took place on visits to London and its theatres. A quest in which Mrs Lilian Wilcock was involved. Burkinshaws of Liverpool supplied some of them; a sewing party in charge of the wardrobe mistresses, Mrs R. L. Hopwood, Mrs F. Dugdale and Miss Clara Messham, made others.

The dance arrangements and teaching of the three choruses were in the hands of Miss Peggy Griffiths, a professional dancing teacher, and Mrs Peter Wilcock, ballet mistress. In the 1930s the company had the assistance of Miss Myfanwy Jones as ballet mistress. She had returned to Buckley when her mother died, to care for her father, after being a member of the Tiller Troupe and Jackson Girls for five years and danced in every Continental capital. As well as training the dancers she performed speciality items, as in the 1938 production of *Puss in Boots*. Misses Winnie Spencer, Katie Davies, Glenys Hughes and Mrs Downey provided make up. The important sequence direction was provided by Mrs Peter Wilcock.

Dennis Griffiths was the musical director who took the baton for each performance. The orchestra was both faithful and impressive. From the first pantomimes the orchestra was made up of about a dozen players. Its main strength was a violin section strengthened by cello, bass, trombone, trumpets, drums, and piano. If any other able instrumentalist was available they were added. For example E. Aubusson, on viola, became a regular after 1949. Until 1946 Elvet Rowlands was the leader, to be succeeded by L. Bartlett for two years and then by S. Hughes. Members of the Cropper family were regular players for the whole period; E. T. Cropper played the cello and N. T. the bass. David Cropper joined them in the 1950s on drums. Amongst the violinists over the period were N. Humphreys, H. Shone, H. Stanley, R. Smallwood, M. Harrop, S. Hughes, R. Hughes, P. Jenkinson, E. Maddocks, J. Huglow, Misses Bryan, Hayes, Suranyi and G. Rich. Trumpeters were J. J. Griffiths, W. Davies and R. McMahon; trombonist N. Griffiths; drums J. Ellis;

Dick Whittington, 1948. [Buckley Library]

saxophone J. Ellis; piano Latham Ellis and H. Griffiths; and organ Graham Davies. Dennis Griffiths played the piano at rehearsals but conducted the pantomime performances. There was therefore an impressive backing for the principal players on the large Tivoli stage.

Considering that the pantomimes ran for a period of twenty-seven years the principals were small in number. The main principal boys and girls were Miss Winnie Spencer, Mrs Peggy Downey (née Hughes), Miss Winnie Humphreys and Mrs Peggy Griffith, who all appeared from the

1930s to the 1950s, when they were joined by Mrs Mona Stansfield. Others who are named in the programmes supported them. A great favourite of all age groups of Buckley pantomime audiences were the dames and comedians, whose slap stick and clowning so often reduced them to tears. Harry Phillips, Jimmy Duffield and Billy Shone made their contributions in the 1930s and Frank Roberts until 1947. Reuben Dolby, Bob Pownall, Alf Bell, Billy Williams, Frank Birtwistle and the singer Peter Davies came to the fore in the 1940s and remained until the end. Providing comedy of the highest calibre for over twenty years were Dick Catherall, Peter Wilcock and Harry Dolby.

It is impossible to review and describe every pantomime in detail. In place of this, extracts from newspaper reports have been selected to give some flavour of the exciting experience of the annual Buckley pantomime.

The 1938 production of *Puss in Boots* contained dance numbers which attracted the critic and showed the strength of the musical backing when he remarked that

Doris Jones, 1939 programme for Aladdin.

The dancing displays were a triumph of effective presentation, while the song scenes were particularly charming. The Merry Widow waltz proved a charming number by Mr Dick Catherall and Miss Peggy Hughes in rich Viennese costumes with a background of juvenile spectators cunningly arranged on raised gallery-tiers of stout timber realistically painted.

In the shade of 'the old apple tree' and 'the Old Bull and Bush' were also charming numbers, in which Mr Harry Dolby was joined by Miss Winnie Humphreys in coster costumes. Mr Dolby and Miss Myfanwy Jones did the Apache dance with all the native virility which the part demanded and danced against a colourful chorus background. Three couples danced the old fashioned polka with more than Victorian vigour, while Mr Peter Wilcock and Frank Roberts brought down the house with a realistic 'bicycle made for two' in the old-time favourite 'Daisy, Daisy'.[43]

The headlines of the 1939 report read 'How they do it in Buckley, *Aladdin* merrily rolls along'. Here the critic paid tribute to the principals:

Mr Dennis Griffiths was again well served by his principals. Miss Winnie Spencer, as Principal Boy, was as gay and debonair as ever and sang most charmingly. A gracious charm radiated from her every appearance, and if I leave it at that, it is because Miss Spencer, in seven years, has exhausted my adjectives. Miss Peggy Hughes was resplendent as the Princess and gave a magnificent performance, which included some attractive dancing, and some charming singing. Miss Winnie Humphreys acted with her usual vivacity, and will shine on any stage.

Miss Doris Jones, who has been a fairy on previous occasions, makes a stage triumph of the part and can successfully overawe any Demon who treads the pantomime stage. Miss Peggy Griffiths fills the part of Mustapha with a captivating exuberance which makes her an indispensable member of the pantomime cast; while Miss Enid Griffiths, as the Child who challenges Father Time and makes him put back the clock, played with a rare skill for one of her young years.

The male cast included all the old favourites. Mr Peter Wilcock and Mr Dick Catherall — that mettlesome and inseparable pair of comedians — brought new energy to the fruity parts from which everybody would expect they had extracted all the juice in previous years. But not so; they keep up the comic element with unwearied zest by means of an inexhaustible fund of gags and sparkling fun. Mr Frank Roberts, who duplicated the parts of Father Time and Abanazar, the villain of the piece, rekindles his demonic fires and weaves those plots of evil which are never allowed to triumph in pantomime — all with his usual impressive skill.

Mr Harry Dolby repeated his stage triumphs as Demon Discontent and the Slave of the Ring; while Mr Harry Phillips, as the Gorgeous Sultan and the Slave of the Lamp plays both with suitable barbaric brilliance.[44]

March 1953, Coronation year, saw the performance of *Dick Whittington*, deliberately chosen to provide an opportunity for a display of London pageantry, and as an occasion to celebrate the twenty-first production of the Buckley Amateur Pantomime Company. Before the curtain rose for the opening evening performance

Committee
L–R: Top row — Cyril Peters (scenic effects), Charles Wilcock (lighting), O. D. Hayes (treasurer).

Middle row — Lilian Wilcock (ballet mistress), Fred Dugdale (property master), Jack Kelly (secretary).

Bottom row:R. L. Hopwood (chairman), Thomas Wilcock (publicity manager) Taken from the 1939 programme for Aladdin.

a large gold-painted key was suspended in front of the stage. The critic paid tribute, writing, that 'when the key was removed and the curtain raised, a production was presented which had the maturity which surely must be unrivalled by any other amateur company in Great Britain'. He continued by declaring that 'a nostalgic note was introduced by the appearance of four former principals. Before a back cloth on which was painted a huge birthday cake and 21 candles, ex-Principal Girls, Peggy Downey, Peggy Griffith and Winnie Humphreys with Winnie Spencer, who was principal boy for 15 years, sang with charm and much of their old verve the hit songs of yester-year'. But what stole the show for the critic was 'the junior chorus in the Charlie Chaplin dame number. Not only was it original, but it was also a timely tribute to the greatest comic artist of the present century. Angela Hopwood, Lorna Lamb, Marie Thomas and Betty Royce stepped out of the chorus to give speciality items, which showed that these youngsters possess exceptional talent. They sang and danced with the confidence of seasoned troupers and gave promise of one day emerging as principal boys and girls of future productions'. The reviewer praised 'Mona Stansfield who is in her fourth year as Principal Boy. Not only does she possess all the physical attributes for the title role but she is also an artist in her own right. She can sing and dance quite attractively, but what is more she can act. Peggy Griffith has lost none of her sparkle as soubrette. Her twinkling toes and coquettish personality were once more an outstanding feature of the show. Her cavorting reminded one of a shorter plumper edition of Betty Hutton'.[45]

The 1956 production of *Cinderella* was hailed as:

> … a show to delight the young of heart, whether they be seven or seventy. It's gay. It's colourful. It has lavish spectacle and simple charm. It is a captivating show, a bright and breezy show. It has unflagging pace and zest. It bounces along as jauntily and merrily as a rainbow coloured caravan. All along the line there is evidence of the guiding genius of Mr Dennis Griffiths. His hallmark of quality is stamped ineradicably on this splendid production. Peggy Downey, as Principal Boy (Prince Charming) and Peggy Griffith, the Principal Girl (Cinderella) both add fresh lustre to their great reputations. Brave young Margaret Bell, a former polio victim, she was in plaster for twelve months, also scores heavily in the part of Fairy Godmother, her first major role. Dick Catherall, who once again plays the Dame as in each of the previous twenty-three shows, is as funny as ever. See him as the Barber of Seville, miming to the words of 'Figaro' and sloshing lather about with joyous abandon. Equally funny as the Ugly Sisters, Sarsperella and Dandylion, are Harry and Reuben Dolby. You should see them in the Charleston.[46]

But in spite of new talent emerging from the chorus members of the cast who had been with the company were feeling the strain. Peter Wilcock made his last appearance in 1952, Dick Catherall in 1956 and Harry Dolby a year later. Symptomatic of the triumph of the new media (everyone wanted a television set in 1953 to watch the Coronation) was the introduction of humorous sketches imitating programmes seen there. Soon the public would be completely captivated and stay at home to watch it, abandoning the Tivoli and Palace. Before this could happen Dennis Griffiths was forced to retire from the Buckley Pantomime

Company. The announcement, some months after the 1959 production of *Puss in Boots*, took everyone by surprise. Fortunately Dennis Griffiths was still able to make a contribution in the public sphere and drama and theatre continued in Buckley, although in other directions.

Football

A newspaper headline in January 1890 warned its readers about a new epidemic in Buckley:

> As a result of the terrible football mania now raging in this district, some half a dozen clubs have been formed in the neighbourhood by the young people, but wherever you turn your eyes to a shop window of any significance, it is pretty well studied with notices of matches by different teams on each other's grounds.[47]

Schoolboy enthusiasm for an informal game of football was being transformed into a spectator sport on a national scale. How this happened in the late 1880s was recounted by one of these young lads:

> It was on the Middle Common, then (and probably still) called "Bell-mount", that I played my first games of Football (soccer). That was in the middle of eighteen-eighties. At that time there was no properly organised Buckley football club. We played on quite a good pitch in the middle of the Common. Our coats piled up, formed the goal posts. (We were forbidden by the Lord of the Manor, Philip Bryan Davies-Cooke, Esq., of Gwysaney Hall, to erect wooden ones, and the Lord of the Manor had a very vigilant scout, named Robins, of Alltami, a part of whose job was to see that we did not take undue liberties on the Common).
>
> At first we played with an ordinary soft India-rubber ball. But what a day that was, and how excited we were when we were presented with a real, proper-size, brand new football! The donor was a Liverpool Clergyman, surnamed Shields, who at the time was staying at the Vicarage with the Vicar, the Rev. W. F. Torre. The Rev Shields took a keen interest in our youthful aspirations, and he evidently thought we were deserving of some encouragement. How we cheered him!
>
> With a real football we now regarded ourselves as a real football club, and we called ourselves "The Bel-mount Swifts". Friendly games amongst ourselves served the purpose of enabling us to discover which members of our club were really good players and these formed the nucleus of what, later on, became the Buckley Victoria Football Club-Buckleys first organised football club. The Buckley Town Football Club was formed a little later, and in course of time became Buckley's senior club.
>
> We migrated from Bell-mount to a properly equipped football field off Mill Lane, a field adjoining the old Headquarters of the Buckley Engineer Volunteers. At our new ground we were joined by a number of players from the other local clubs, George Chesters, Tom Jones, Jack Wilcock, George Lloyd, Joe Parry, John Wood, Joe Anglesey and others, the original "Buckley Vics". In a few years they became one of the best-known football clubs in the district, and were regarded as doughty opponents by the leading clubs in North Wales. By defeating Llandudno at Holywell in 1895, they became the proud winners of the North Wales Junior Cup.[48]

By this time the most senior local football club was Buckley Town who were soon to be challenged by the greatest of all amateur football clubs in Buckley — the Engineers. For a number of seasons before the First World War they reigned supreme winning the Flintshire League in 1905 and 1907, the Welsh Amateur Cup in 1905, 1906 and again in 1910. They won the Flintshire Challenge Cup in 1909 and were runners up in the Flintshire League Charity in 1909 and 1910. The Engineers side was made up of ten colliers and a plumber.[49] As well as the big clubs there were many other amateur sides such as the

Buckley Engineers Football Team, 1907.
[Buckley Society Archive]

Buckley United Football Team, c.1920.
[Buckley Society Archive]

Below: Buckley Town Football Team, 1936/37, North Wales Amateur Cup Winners. L-R, Back Row: Heron, Catherall, Garston, Dunn. Middle Row: Messham, Williams, Bellis, Hughes, Parrish, Harvey, Bell, Millington, Tarran (Trainer), Burton (Groundsman). Front Row: Kelsall, Morris, Roberts, Arthur Jones (Sec.), Edwards, R. S. Smith, Campbell. [Courtesy of Gareth M. Davies]

Snuffs, Trap College, the Albion, Lane End Corinthians, the Square, Nant Mawr Jolly Boys and the Buckley Co-op Wednesday. A number of players turned professional such as Jabez Evans (Everton), Ginger Williams (Crystal Palace and Milwall), and Eddie Peers (Wolverhampton Wanderers).

In the 1920s a new semi-professional club was formed known as Buckley United who about 1920 defeated Wrexham in the FA Cup.[50] Many other junior clubs flourished between the wars representing the local chapels and brickworks.

Burntwood Victoria emerged as a successful side and in 1929 reached the final of the Welsh Amateur Cup, losing to Cardiff Corinthians in the final. In 1936 a senior club was formed and assumed the name Buckley Town, with their ground in a field behind the Co-operative Stores. They immediately proved themselves and won the North Wales Amateur Cup 1936/37.

After the Second World War football in Buckley was revived. Hawkesbury playing fields was the home of both of Buckley Wanderers and Buckley Rovers. The Urban District Council were excited as the rest of their supporters when the Wanderers reached the final round of the Welsh League Cup in April 1950 and

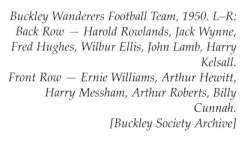

Buckley Wanderers Football Team, 1950. L–R:
Back Row — Harold Rowlands, Jack Wynne, Fred Hughes, Wilbur Ellis, John Lamb, Harry Kelsall.
Front Row — Ernie Williams, Arthur Hewitt, Harry Messham, Arthur Roberts, Billy Cunnah.
[Buckley Society Archive]

arranged whatever the result for a civic reception outside the Council Chambers. The Royal Buckley Town Band was requested to join the reception and meet the players on their return from Wrexham at the Lane End corner of Brook Street. They beat Brymbo by four goals to one. The match was played at the Racecourse, Wrexham, in front of a crowd of 3,481. The gate receipts were £191. This success was repeated on 25 April 1952 with a victory over Johnstown and once again a civic reception was arranged. They won the cup again in 1966. Buckley Rovers played in the Halkyn and District League and were champions in 1953–4. In the 1968–9 season Hawkesbury Youth Football Club won the North Wales FA Youth Cup.

Nearly forty years on, the area is represented by another team, playing under the name of Buckley Town, their headquarters is at a new ground at the Globe. The enthusiasm for soccer displayed on the Common in the 1880s is still shown by the local youth. Today they do not have to pile up their coats for goal posts but are given excellent facilities on specially prepared surfaces.

Cricket

The game of cricket arrived in Mold in 1865 when it became the headquarters of the newly established Flintshire County Cricket Club under the patronage of Sir Stephen Glynne of Hawarden Castle. It was not until 1876 that we have the first reference to a Buckley team when they are recorded as defeating Leeswood, although for many, belonging to the Club was seen perhaps as a social activity rather than a sporting pursuit. This was the view of the *Chronicle* when the newspaper observed that 'however good the financial success of the Club has been during the past season their muscular activity seems to have been very small'. However the game was spreading in Buckley with a number of small teams in existence representing Cold Arbor, Knowle and Spon Green.

Buckley Cricket Club was formed in 1889 under the guidance and leadership of two of Buckley's most influential citizens, Major J. M. Gibson, and Councillor G. A. Parry, both of them managers of brickworks. Cricket now began to prosper in Buckley and is still flourishing today. They had a home at Lane End in the ownership of Mr Lindop, an enthusiastic member. They enjoyed the support and hospitality of the Bevan family at the Feathers Inn, which served as the clubs' headquarters. They had a regular fixture list and eventually played league cricket. Their financial situation was secured by the backing of generous vice-presidents including Herbert Gladstone, the Hancock family, P. B. Davies-Cooke, J. B. Gregory and others. Under the guidance of a professional named Houseman, who had played for Derbyshire, they built up a strong team of all round cricketers. A number of outstanding cricketers emerged before the First World War. As batsmen, Robert Davies and Herbert Piercy, with a trio of devastating bowlers, Joe Peters, Bill Parry and Billy Hughes. The great all-rounders were Tom Rowlands and J. W. Williamson. In his memories of Buckley Cricket, William Lindop recalled the impact of the Reverend W. P. de Winton Kitcat, an assistant curate at St Matthew's, 1897–1903:

He came of cricketing stock, and the family name may be found in the annals of Gloucester County. He was a brilliant opening batsman, with a straight drive which was positively dangerous to the oncoming bowler, and a hitting power which was tremendous. On one occasion at Boughton Hall he opened his shoulders to lift a ball over the tall poplars and beyond the canal. As a wicketkeeper he was quite literally, of county class. He was a man of outstanding personality, with natural gifts of leadership and control.[51]

Members of Buckley Cricket Club, 1920s.
L-R: Back Row — Reg Peters, -?- , W. G. Astbury.
Front Row — Joshua Hayes, Cyril Peters.
[Courtesy of Eric Hayes, Buckley Society Archive]

He eventually left Buckley to serve in South Africa as curate of Capetown.

The long and detailed story of Buckley Cricket Club has been ably told by Dave Williamson.[52] His fascinating and enthusiastic tale recounts the drama on the field and the struggle the club has had to survive at various times in its history. Over a hundred years is a 'long innings'. Innumerable players have performed on the field at Lane End, many with distinction, all with enthusiasm and sportsmanship. Like a good five day test match or an 'Ashes' series there have been superb performances, dogged efforts and flamboyant personalities, the memories of which survive in score books or in photographs.

Like every amateur, sporting and leisure group, Buckley Cricket Club has been dependent upon a team off the field for wise counsel, fund raising, ground preparation, refreshments, and a loyal body of spectators.

Many Buckley people remember in particular the knock out competition at Lane End, which enabled the adventurous and foolhardy to tread the sacred turf and enjoy their hour of glory as the sun went down in front of excited spectators.

One of the outstanding members of the Buckley team between the wars was W. G. Astbury, with great ability as a spin bowler and batsman whom Williamson recalls:

> Wilf Astbury was a gentleman farmer who lived in a large house, Plas Ifan, at Northop Hall. His arrival at Buckley brought not only a considerable cricketing skill but also a new sense of style. This was, after all, 'The Twenties' and W. G. A. embodied all the contemporary images of that era. He was always dressed in the height of fashion and, what was equally important, sported a very long black car usually of the sporting saloon variety. His means allowed him to indulge in a rather more flamboyant lifestyle than his team-mates thus his arrival at Lane End on the afternoon of a match was an event not to be missed.[53]

He donated a silver cup for the winners of the local knockout competition. This was a much-anticipated event, which was revived in 1946 with many memorable moments as Williamson recounted:

> The Knockout treated its audiences to the usual displays of entertaining cricket and was won in that first year by Brook Street Workingmen's Club, a great deal of their success being due to the mighty hitting of a ruddy complexioned local farmer, Tom Dawson, who hit some of the longest sixes ever seen. They were a typical Knockout team having, as Webbert who was a member of the team recalls, 'Not a cricket shirt between the lot of us'.

Williamson recounts the legendary occurrence in a Knockout match between the Brook Street Club and their opponents at Pontblyddyn when Webbert opened the batting for the visitors clad in hobnailed boots on a coconut matting wicket with which he became so entangled that he fell down and uprooted both the mat and the stumps and it took twenty minutes to sort out the mess.[54]

The 'Collegians' from Ewloe Place and educated at the mythical establishment of 'The Trap College'! won the competition in the years 1947–50.[55]

Buckley Cricket Club, winners of the McAlpine Knockout Cup, 1960. L-R: Back Row — Walter Bartley, Wilson Alcock, David Rowlands, Jeff Hughes, Alan Millington. Front Row — Ken Thompson, Bill Ellis, Tom Lewis, Leslie Rowlamds, Neville Lamb. [Buckley Society Archive]

People will always use their leisure time in differing ways and this diversity continues today taking advantage of new facilities and funding arrangements. Some of these themes are discussed in the Postscript.

Notes

1. Cropper, op cit, p. 130.
2. ibid, p. 122.
3. ibid, p. 128.
4. *Chester Chronicle*, 3/7/1880.
5. ibid, 15/6/1878.
6. W. Bell Jones, History of Hawarden,Ms., vol 1 pp 308-9.
7. FRO D/GW/555/ FF. 157.
8. Cropper, op cit, p. 238.
9. Willett, op cit, p. 131.
10. *Chester Chronicle*, 1/5/1897.
11. C. Duckworth, 'Brass Bands in and around Buckley', *Buckley*, 8 and Rose Peters, Early Conductors of the Royal Buckley Town Band, *Buckley*, 30.
12. *Chester Courant*, 14/5/1851.
13. ibid, 8/12/1869.
14. From a newspaper report, probably the *Chester Chronicle*, 20/6/1917, found in FRO D/DM/434/166
15. ibid, 21/6/1917.
16. *Mold, Deeside and Buckley Leader*, 12/1/1923.
17. David Berry, *Wales and Cinema. The first hundred years*, (Univ. Wales Press, Cardiff, 1994), p. 73.
18. ibid, p. 119, and Neil Cropper, 'The Palace Picture House, Buckley', *Buckley*, 6.
19. ibid.
20. Neville Dunn, 'One family's connection with the Tivoli, Buckley', *Buckley*, 30.
21. *Mold, Deeside and Buckley Leader*, 29/5/1925
22. *Mold, Deeside and Buckley Leader*, 23/10/1925.
23. *Chester Chronicle*, 20/2/1965.
24. FRO D/DM/1048.
25. *Chester Chronicle*, 23/6/1945.
26. *Mold, Deeside and Buckley Leader*, 19/8/1927.
27. ibid, 2/3/1928.
28. ibid, 2/1/1931.
29. ibid, 19/8/1932, and 25/8/1933.
30. ibid, 26/1/1934.
31. A. G. Veysey, 'Buckley Amateur Pantomime Company', *Buckley*, 7, and Carol Shone, 'The most famous Amateur Pantomime in Great Britain,' *Buckley*, 24. I endeavour to present the history of the pantomime using the material to be found in Dennis Griffiths' manuscript deposited in Flintshire Record Office (FRO D/DG/). This use is made with the kind permission of his granddaughter Hannah O'Keefe.
32. *Mold, Deeside and Buckley Leader*, 22/1/1932.
33. Veysey, op cit, p. 6.
34. *Mold, Deeside and Buckley Leader*, 25/2/1933.
35. W. Alister Williams, *The Encyclopaedia of Wrexham* (Bridge Books, Wrexham, 2001), p. 265.
36. *Mold, Deeside and Buckley Leader*, 20/1/1933.
37. See annual newspaper reports, usually the beginning of March, and the large amount of material available in FRO Dennis Griffiths MS, D/DG/.
38. These are not reported by Veysey or Shone.
39. See Dennis Griffiths, *Out of this Clay*, op cit, p. 131f. The wording is slightly different.
40. FRO D/DG/19.
41. ibid, transcript of talk, January 1957, from BBC Bangor.
42. There is a complete set in FRO D/DG/7 a few contain illustrations.
43. *Chester Chronicle*, February 1938.
44. ibid, 18/2/1939.
45. *The Flint and Deeside Leader*, 6/3/1953.
46. ibid, 2/3/1956.
47. *County Herald*, 10/1/1890.
48. Sarbot, The origins of Buckley Football, *Buckley* (BYPCA) 1. (1944).

49. Information from *A Century in the Life of Buckley, 1897–1997*, p.47f.

50. ibid, p. 48.

51. Nemo (William Lindop), 'Memories of Buckley Cricket', *Buckley* (BYPCA) 1 (1944).

52. Dave Williamson, *Buckley Cricket Club, 'Digging In', 100 years at Lane End*.

53. ibid, p. 25

54. ibid, p. 37, for Webbert, (Mr James Griffiths) see *Buckley* 20, pp. 54–6.

55. The name of the old clay pit and brickworks.

Chapter 16
Postscript — the last sixty years, 1946–2006

The story of the making and shaping of Buckley has been told in the previous sections of the book. The purpose of this chapter is to bring together some of the main threads, make a summary and give a conclusion, if that is possible, to the rich heritage created over the centuries. It is obvious from what has happened in the last sixty years that society is continually changing and that those who have lived through the second half of the twentieth century have experienced more change than ever in western society. Here, very briefly, is an account of what happened in Buckley as seen through the eyes of the writer.

The Second World War, 1939–45, was a watershed in the history of Buckley for a number of reasons. Some of the older members of the community may think of the war as the end of the golden age of Buckley and the loss of traditional values; others will see it as the beginning of greater freedom and opportunity. At no time have there been such advances in democracy, educational opportunities, economic prosperity and technological development. But whatever our view, there is no doubt of great change and what is of more importance the ability of the community to adapt in a positive way to new circumstances.

The major post war development affecting Buckley is the beginning of industrial change. This in turn brought changes in employment patterns, house building, and movements of population. In Buckley these changes were dramatic. The lives of the workforce changed. Sons no longer followed their fathers into the same employment. They could no longer walk or cycle to work. Eventually they journeyed further distances to work often outside their community to the steel works, motor assembly plant, and aircraft factory. At first they travelled by public transport, the Works bus or train and later with their mates by car.

The coal industry, as we saw in section two, had ceased to operate in Buckley by the 1930s. At the end of the Second World War the last of the working potteries closed. This small-scale domestic industry was outdated and no longer able to survive the market forces of a modern industrial economy. Some stability in the community was achieved by the ability of the clay industry to adapt and survive in the climate of reconstruction after the Second World War. The demand for new houses set new targets for the production in Buckley of bricks, sanitary ware, and underground piping. The industry kept pace, to some extent, by means of take-overs, closures, and modernisation of plant. By the 1960s this process of survival was virtually completed, and, for a while, brought some security to a generation 'which had never had it so good'. The major players in Buckley industry in the closing rounds being John Summers (British Steel), Hancock's (Butterley, Hanson's) and Stein Refractories. The family connection of both Hancock's and Catherall's had ceased in the 1930s.

Quarrying the rock away from Lane End Brickworks, 1987. [Buckley Library]

The clay industry suffered in the economic climate of the late 1970s and 1980s. The effects of massive closures in the British Steel Works at Shotton seriously affected the Buckley community through the sale and eventual closure of the Castle Brickworks, a serious increase in numbers unemployed and future job prospects. Stein Refractories at Ewloe Barn, closed at the end of the 1970s, unable to weather difficulties in marketing their products because of increased fuel and transport costs. By the 1980s the Buckley clay manufacturers were reduced to Hancock, Butterley and Hanson. The closure of the last brickmaking site in 2003 meant the abandonment of traditional clay workings in Buckley. The industry, which had contributed more to the making of the Buckley district than any other, was now finished. The challenge to the question, what is the community going to do with its former industrial sites, will shape the future of Buckley. This response has already been made in various ways over the past fifty years.

Gradually the spoil tips of the collieries were carted away for road making. Over the last decades abandoned landscapes of flooded clay quarries with their derelict skeletal brickworks perched perilously above have become the haunt of artists, anglers, walkers and wildlife enthusiasts. The retention of this ugly industrial environment and its gradual transformation into beautiful nature reserves opened up an ongoing debate between conservationists, as preservers of the industrial heritage, and developers seeking land for housing. The landscape was 'up for grabs'.

The question of what is the community going to do with its industrial sites took the form of a competition in Buckley to re-use the ever increasing industrial sites available, for a number of purposes: industrial parks, landfill sites, heritage trails, conservation areas, and housing developments. This competition for land use has gradually brought about in the last fifty years the greatest change in Buckley since the last ice age, the transformation of the landscape. Such changes have occurred spasmodically, with no major planning programme, and subject to the pressure of a variety of interests.

The management of the environment, including the ancient commons, and changes in land use, has been the responsibility of many bodies. Local authorities: Buckley Town Council, Buckley Urban District Council (until 1974), Alyn and Deeside, (1974–95), Clwyd and Flintshire County Councils. Much land was taken up by building developers who made their contribution by filling up spaces and providing acres of private housing estates. Statutory supervision by environmental agencies and public pressure groups acted as watchdogs for conservationists and the provision of public amenities.

Foremost in the provision of public facilities was the building of a shopping precinct in the 1970s and a new library. Major development was halted to some extent in the 1970s by local government reorganisation and the economic climate. However further development was continued in the 1990s with the establishment of a link road to enable the pedestrianisation of the main shopping area and the creation of car parking space. Development has taken place across the Buckley area in all the satellite communities — Alltami, Bryn y Baal, Burntwood, Drury, Ewloe Place, Liverpool Road, Mynydd Isa, Nantmawr and Spon Green. In many areas, local authority sheltered accommodation, health clinics and sports centres have been provided with a general expansion in private housing development.

A major shift in the movement of population to the several satellite communities has meant that schools have followed people. Since the 1960s all the primary schools in the Buckley area built in the nineteenth century have gradually closed, been replaced, or relocated. The major educational development in the area was the opening of Buckley's first secondary school in 1954. The building of the Elfed School was in many ways a symbol of the coming of age of Buckley, and has more than fulfilled the dreams and aspirations of its patient advocates. In fifty years Buckley has acquired two outstanding secondary schools, Elfed in 1954 and Argoed in 1978. With a catchment area network of new feeder primary schools and other specialist educational institutions.

The continuing vitality of the several religious denominations in Buckley is marked every year by the annual jubilee procession and celebrations. Over the last fifty years attendances at places of worship have declined. This is reflected in Buckley. Religious buildings have either closed or been demolished in some cases because they were beyond repair, in others for development or as a matter of expediency to bring congregations together. The formation of the United Reformed Church, nationally in 1972, eventually brought together in Buckley the English Presbyterians from Zion and the Congregationalists from St John's. A result of this partnership was the opening of a new church and in this way both local denominations were

St. John's URC Church, 2002, interior and exterior.
[Buckley Society Archive]

renewed. At the same time, at the millennium, the Roman Catholic Church of our Lady of the Rosary, replaced its nineteenth century place of worship with a building designed to meet increased numbers of members and liturgical changes introduced by the Second Vatican Council. A few years earlier two Buckley Methodist congregations decided to share the same building. Square Methodist Church members migrated to the new Tabernacle whose former building was demolished in the 1970s. Members at Tabernacle were now resident across the road in the converted Sunday school. This is a substantial building designed in the Gothic style by the Mold architect Fred Roberts and erected by Hayes brothers in 1936 at a cost of £3,500. It is a first class building with a main hall to accommodate 450 people and two classrooms and a kitchen etc. This is now called Buckley Cross Methodist Church.

All the traditional churches mentioned in the early chapters are still thriving with improved community facilities. The former Roman Catholic Church building is now the centre for Bible christians and is an addition to the post war Buckley churches. For the past one hundred and fifty years the Buckley Jubilee has been the witness of christian unity in the area. Another symbol of unity, which has appeared in the post war period, is the creation of a body that is known as Cytun, which means, churches together. Gone are the days in Buckley of religious prejudice and sectarian strife and churches are finding new opportunities to work and witness together.

But in spite of the continuation of christian witness in Buckley and evidence for its reinvigoration there is no doubt of its loss of influence and the impact of secularisation on community life. This is shown in many ways. One of the first signs was the closure of faith schools in the primary sector and the disappearance of

The new Church of Our Lady of the Rosary, interior and exterior. [Buckley Society Archive]

Buckley Cross Methodist Church, interior and exterior. [Buckley Society Archive]

those linked to Emmanuel Bistre and St Matthew's Buckley.

The greater availability of public funding for expenditure on community needs has raised expectations and enhanced facilities. At first the major funding agency was the local authority whose funding has been supplemented in recent years by the national lottery. School sites have become the centre for these benefits.

There have been many changes. One of the most significant has been the loss of its dialect. Sixty years ago natives of Buckley could be identified by their speech. Intimacy was maintained through the use of language. It was the first language children spoke. Strangers were set apart by its use. Above all it was spoken by the close-knit work force, underground in the colliery, in the brick shed and quarry hole. Children used it in the school playground and old folk in their prayer meetings. Through it gossip was retailed, confidences shared and greetings exchanged, in the streets and corner shops. The dialect bred familiarity, endearment, and humour, which expressed itself in the identification of its local characters by well-chosen nicknames.

The revolution in transport, people tending to travel alone, and the reclusive television age has weakened the dependence upon work mates and neighbours. Although some of the friendly atmosphere still prevails in the informal meeting places of shopping precinct and public library.

Buckley people are becoming more aware of their industrial heritage through the pioneer work of local archaeologists like the late Jim Bentley and Martin Harrison, the publications and archive of the Buckley Society which has published regularly for over thirty years, and the Library Heritage Centre. Heritage has been allied to leisure through the establishment of the trail through Etna Park. Another outstanding feature of the history of the Buckley area is its 'Mountain' area and Common land. Although Knowle Hill gradually disappeared to provide the raw material for the clay industry the three major Commons are recognised and protected as amenity and conservation areas by Flintshire County Council. This provides another advantage and challenge to the people of Buckley to permanently protect its flourishing wild life, bird song, and flora. This is part of the future making of Buckley.

Here is a brief review of some of the major developments over the last sixty years.

New schools

Elfed High School – Ysgol Uwchradd Elfed
On the 19 May 1937 Mr Bevan Evans, Director of Education for Flintshire reported the approval of the Board of Education to the purchase of six-and-a-half acres for the site of the proposed Central School Buckley, and in March 1938 building plans were approved. Flintshire Education Authority was implementing the proposals made by Sir Henry Hadow, the leading influence in British Education between the wars. His report, the *Education of the Adolescent*, published in 1926, recommended the division of education into the

primary stage, 5–11 years, and secondary education for all after the age of 11 years. Secondary education was to be organised on a selective basis, with a division into grammar and secondary modern school entry. Central schools were to be the first pioneers of this proposal. The Deeside Central School was opened in 1929 and plans to build others at Mold and Buckley were advanced at the beginning of the war in 1939.

Buckley had to wait until 1952 before work began on building a new school. In the meantime the Education Act of 1944 made selection compulsory for 'grammar schools' and 'secondary modern schools'. Thus, in the first years after the war all Buckley children over the age of eleven had to travel outside the community to receive their education.

The new secondary school at Buckley was opened on 5 January 1954 with Mr L. W. Mothersole, BSc as headmaster. The major public event, however, was the laying of the foundation stone on 20 October 1952 by Alderman W. J. Hodson on behalf of the Flintshire Education Committee. It was reported in the *Flint and Deeside Leader* that:

> The school was started in January last year and it is expected that it will be completed in six months time at a cost of £200,000. The building in two storeys was designed by Mr W. Griffiths, county architect, and his staff. It represents the most modern development in school planning and will accommodate 630. Buckley now comes into its own in the educational sense. It's a modern secondary school and it means in the educational sense that eleven plus boys and girls will no longer have to travel to the school at Mold, once it has opened. This has always been a sore point with the Buckley people. They could never understand why Buckley should have to feed a school elsewhere with so many children of its own. Their boys and girls will have to continue to travel to Hawarden and Mold for their grammar school education.
>
> The new school honours Elfed (Dr H. Elfed Lewis) the former archdruid, and perpetuates his name as a Welsh scholar and Congregational divine who now lives at Penarth but still has intimate associations with the district. His daughter, Mrs Humphrey Llewellyn Jones, lives at Mold, whilst Elfed at the age of 19, became the minister at Buckley Congregational Church.
>
> Elfed Modern Secondary School has 30 classrooms, and was planned before the war. Economic austerity has, of course, put its imprint upon it, but nevertheless it is a beautiful building, and here are some of the facts which must be recorded: - All the bricks were made in Buckley; all the cement was made in Buckley; all the drain pipes were made in Buckley; all the electrical engineering was done by a Buckley sub contractor; the builders were Buckley people; all the steel windows were made in Flintshire; all the sanitary and door fittings were supplied by a local builders merchant.
>
> And what about the siting? Standing as it does within almost a stone's throw of Hawkesbury cultural centre, the garden of remembrance and the sports grounds, the school completes a perfect community centre without equal in the county. So that in every way Monday's ceremony was a memorable occasion in the history of Buckley. The ceremony took place in the lofty and spacious school hall.

Alderman W. Hodson placed the foundation stone in a wall in the hall. The builder was Mr Ken Shone of Buckley. Prayers were said by Canon A. W. Rees and the Reverend Wynn Parry. Alderman Hodson described the various parts of the school. The school hall was reported as being 90 x 45 ft, the stage 30 x 40

ft, with dressing rooms; 2 gymnasiums 70 x 40 ft, with changing rooms and showers; 17 acres of playing fields with football and cricket pitches; a dining and cooking unit, sufficient to accommodate every pupil attending.[1]

In 1967, Elfed School became a senior comprehensive and fully comprehensive in 1973 and now caters for pupils aged 11 to 18 years. The school site extends over 30 acres, 22 of which are used as sports areas. The school has been developed over the years to meet increased

Elfed School and Hawkesbury Bowling Green.
[FRO PH /11/424]

numbers and curricula requirements. The 30 classrooms have been complemented by wide ranging facilities which include — a purpose-built theatre used for both school and public performances, a media and music suite, science laboratories, technology, art and home economics rooms, information technology centre, satellite, language and weather recording facilities and a library.

There are excellent sporting facilities with a sports centre for use by school and community. To these have been added a floodlit all-weather sports area and a new swimming pool which replaces Buckley baths. It is not surprising that the school has an outstanding record for academic attainment and sporting success.

The school marked the 50th anniversary of the laying of the foundation stone by the unveiling of a commemorative sundial on 17 October 2002 by Mr Ken Shone, the main contractor who built the school in 1952/3. This was followed by a concert given by the Elfed High School Wind Orchestra under its musical director, Mr Barry Smallwood and the Royal Buckley Town Band under its musical director, Mr D. Roberts.

Mr Ken Shone unveils a commemorative sundial, 17 October 2002. [By courtesy of Mr Barry Smallwood, Elfed School]

The Reverend Elvet 'Elfed' Lewis, 1860–1953

It was an inspiration to name the new Buckley Secondary School after Elfed for it captured the affection and imagination of Buckley people, provided a link with the past, and gave them an outstanding role model for future generations. Elfed's reputation as an Independent minister, preacher and hymn writer was second to none in Wales. His long life of nearly a hundred years coincided with Buckley's golden age. His outstanding contribution to social justice and compassion towards the unemployed in the depression years were a great source of comfort and admiration to the nonconformists of Buckley.

Buckley people regarded Elfed, despite his short ministry in their midst, as their adopted son and lovingly felt that they had played a significant part in his nurture. To them he was 'the lad', remembering him when he came to them at the age of 19 years. They prayed with him, saw his growing fame as a preacher in Wales during the Revival, and treasured his hymns and poetry. He was their friend, a poor country lad, who by his brains and determination had made his mark in the world. He married Mary Taylor, of Cherry Tree Farm, Broughton in 1887 and returned often to preach in Buckley, the last time on 1 August 1953. It had already been decided to name the school after him and he must have seen the building, which was opened

a few weeks after his death. Elfed received two doctorates from the University of Wales, was a successful competitor in many eisteddfodau, and was given the distinction of being made a Companion of Honour by King George VI. One would like to think that he regarded as his greatest recognition Ysgol Uwchradd Elfed.[2]

Argoed High School

Argoed High School is the second secondary school built to accommodate children from Buckley and district primary schools. It takes children from Mynydd Isa, Southdown and other neighbouring schools. Argoed is an 11–16 mixed comprehensive school built in 1978, with a school population

Dr Howel Elfed Lewis, CH. From the cover of Howel Elfed Lewis *by E. Wynn Parry.*

Three head teachers present at the twenty-fifth anniversary of Argoed High School September 2003. L-R: Alison Brown (2000–), Janet Wright (1988-99) and Bryn Ellis (1978-88) . [By courtesy of Bryn Ellis]

over 550 with a teaching staff numbering 30 plus.

Primary Schools
New primary schools were built to replace the nineteenth century schools opened by the St Asaph Diocesan Board of Education in the parishes of St Matthew's (Buckley) and Emmanuel (Bistre) and schools built by the Buckley School Board.

Buckley Mountain Lane Primary School replaced St Matthew's and Lane End Schools in 1963.

Buckley Southdown Primary School replaced Emmanuel Bistre Church Schools in 1975.

Buckley Westwood Primary School replaced Buckley Council School, formerly Buckley Board School.

Drury Primary School. A new school opened in 1973 for pupils who previously attended St Matthew's and Buckley Mountain schools.

Mynydd Isa School Infants opened on 23 April 1906 with Miss Edwards as head teacher. Amongst the pupils enrolled the following year were two children of Thomas Cropper. The school premises were eventually situated at Bryn y Baal where a new school was built in 1914. This school remains as a junior school. The infants department was transferred to a new school, Wat's Dyke, opened in 1972, which now incorporates a unit for children with special educational needs.

Special School
Ysgol Belmont, a special local authority school on two sites. It caters for pupils aged 3–19 years of age, with buildings in Mill Lane and Nant Mawr road.

The Hawkesbury Community Centre

By 1944 there was in Britain a deep longing for a new and better society. This hope kept people going whether they were serving in the armed forces or making their contribution at home. If after the First World War there had been a determination to make a country fit for heroes to live in, the approach during the Second World War was more practical and realistic. This time nothing was to be left to chance. The planning for peace had already been begun by the publication of Sir William Beveridge's blue print for the Welfare State published in 1942–3 with its attack upon the giant evils of 'Want, Disease, Ignorance, Squalor, and Idleness'. All members of the new society were to be given equal rights to social security, health, education, housing and a policy of full employment. The nation's debate about its post-war future began during the War in the canteens and NAAFIs and on the radio with such programmes as the 'Brains Trust'. Discussions took place as lively as those of any democrats at a time of social change. It was a remarkable time to be alive. There was a sense of change felt by all generations. Food rationing had produced healthy young people who eagerly shared in the debate with their elders.

Evidence for this lively participation in the democratic process is what the foundation in 1944 of Buckley Young People's Cultural Association was all about. If young people had been disciplined and nurtured in their respective church vestries and Sunday schools they had their horizons broadened by war time radio, cinema, and a knowledge of the horror of war. They expressed the right to a better future, and a share in the peace prizes of freedom and opportunity. No one realised this better than Mr Dennis Griffiths and the dedicated company who had worked with him for over a decade to bring out the abilities of young people

Hawkesbury Community Centre, 1953.
[Buckley Society Archive]

in the pantomime. This revolution was guided by old-fashioned liberals and earnest churchmen. They did not wave the red flag. Their objectives were cultural rather than political.

Within six months of its establishment a home was found for BYPCA through the purchase of Hawkesbury Hall. The house, built by Jonathan Catherall in 1801, was to be the home of a new family who shared his independence of mind and pioneering spirit. An expression of this vision which Mr Dennis Griffiths shared with the four hundred young members of the Cultural Association was publicly announced in the *Buckley* magazine: 'Hawkesbury', he wrote, is 'to be used as a Community Centre, where we intend to promote many kinds of activities for both sexes. There we hope to arrange facilities for training in Music, Art, Drama, Dancing, Discussion and other subjects, and to provide physical cultural training and recreation in indoor and outdoor sports and games under suitable leadership. Both the residence and the grounds will be available for the widest possible use for the whole of Buckley and it will be our earnest endeavour to maintain warm social sympathy'.[4]

In June 1945 the BBC recorded a message from the young people of Hawkesbury to their contemporaries in Jacksonville, Florida. During the programme members of the drama section performed part of John Drinkwater's play *Abraham Lincoln*.[5]

By the time Hawkesbury was officially opened on 7 July 1945, the Germans had surrendered and before the end of July a Labour Government was in power with a large majority, a few weeks before Japan surrendered.

The opening was a grand occasion celebrated with a Garden Fête. The programme was designed to bring the whole of Buckley to Hawkesbury. Its serious objectives were presented in a carnival atmosphere to match the air of relief at the end of the war in Europe. Before the community centre was declared open there was a 'Victory Baby Show' that attracted fifty-one entries, judged by Miss Waring, Matron of Mancot Nursing Home, and Nurse Dyke. After the formal speeches there were two performances of 'The Pageant of the Nations', a display given by fifty children trained by the experienced Mrs Peter Wilcock and Miss Peggy Griffiths. Mr Dennis Griffiths was at the piano, assisted by several instrumentalists, and the attendance of the Royal Buckley Town Band. This was followed in the evening by open air dancing.

Over 1,500 people came to Hawkesbury to see the displays, wander round the stalls, sideshows and numerous attractions. A large marquee was erected in the grounds and what was described as 'a mammoth tea party' provided. The newly acquired Community centre with its eleven rooms was open to public inspection. One of the features was a display of Buckley ware and Roman pottery from Chester and a model of the hull of the sailing ship *William Shepherd*.[6]

The platform party gave significance to the purpose of the day. It was carefully chosen to represent the best in Welsh public life in terms of public career, ability and background. Lady Wynn

Mr Dennis Griffiths at the piano.
[By courtesy of Hannah O'Keeefe]

Dr Thomas Jones, CH.
[FRO D/DM/434/117]

Wheldon, the opener, was the wife of Sir Wynn Wheldon, a distinguished Permanent Secretary of the Welsh Department of Education, the Council of the University of Wales, who served the principality in many other capacities. He was a leading layman of the Calvinistic Methodists, and a distinguished soldier who was awarded the DSO in 1917. The main speaker was Dr Thomas Jones, CH. His presence in Buckley on this occasion was particularly poignant because his daughter Eirene was the unsuccessful Labour candidate for Flintshire in the 1945 General Election. Dr Jones, a former university professor, civil servant and administrator was one of the most famous and respected Welshmen of his day. He was deputy secretary of the Cabinet until 1930, the author of important diaries, a friend and adviser to both Lloyd George and Stanley Baldwin. He was influential in the National Library of Wales and National Museum of Wales, and as a founder of Coleg Harlech showed his interest in further education in Wales. At the time he was engaged on a biography of Lloyd George and his knowledgeable political background provided the advice he gave to the young people present. He criticised the cheap propaganda and partisan spirit in which the two great war leaders Lloyd George and Winston Churchill had conducted, when peace came, their election campaigns after their outstanding leadership in war time. He advocated democracy as the noblest ideal of government and warned that unless we learn to transmute the will to power, into the will to serve, we will experience failure. In replying to a vote of thanks, he said he knew of no place the size of Buckley which could compete with what they had done for young people.[7]

In 1945 the total membership of the various groups and organisations numbered over seven hundred of which four hundred were under twenty-one years of age. Group membership was enjoyed by a number of organisations. Amongst these were the Amateur Pantomime Company, Ambulance Association, Bistre Church Youth Guild, Buckley Boy Scouts, Congregational Young People's Circle, Drama Circle, Delta Players, First Buckley Girl Guides, Glee Party, Ladies' Hockey Club, Orchestral Society, the Hawkesbury Ladies Guild, Toc H, the St John's Ambulance Association, St Matthew's Church Young People's Guild, Swimming Club, United Methodist Young People's Guild and the VAD. To these organisations were added the Boys' Club, the Play Reading Circle and the Women's Guild.

Hawkesbury Hall had land, an orchard and three cottages for which the BYPCA paid £3,200. The eleven-roomed house gave space for their activities. Its first committee was under the chairmanship of Mr Dennis Griffiths, with Mrs Peter Wilcock, treasurer, and Mr J. E. Messham as secretary. In September 1947 the Hawkesbury Little Theatre was opened in a converted NAFFI hut by Mr Wilfred Shone, and the Buckley Drama Circle continued its productions there. Tennis courts were opened in 1950. The following year, in September, the Buckley Chamber of Trade held the first of their of their trade fairs in the Hall.

A great loss to Buckley was the demolition in August 1952 of the Hawkesbury bell tower. George Lewis recorded in his diary: 'The old bell tower at Hawkesbury, in front of the new school was demolished today. It was between 5 and 6 yards high and was built in the early years of the last century by Jonathan Catherall.

The Bell Tower at Hawkesbury before demolition in August 1952.
[Buckley Society Archive]

It used to be rung to summon people to a service held in the dining room of his house, Hawkesbury. When it was erected Nonconformists were not allowed to build a tower on their chapels. The bell was bought by Jonathan Catherall from Cork for £12. The Hawkesbury Community Centre Committee preferred not to demolish the tower, but the Flintshire Education Committee insisted because of the building of the new school. They are going to put a plaque on the wall where the tower stood.'

It reads 'This plaque marks the site of the Old Bell Tower built by Jonathan Catherall, a pillar of non-conformity early in the century.'

It was agreed to create a Garden of Remembrance and a cenotaph for the Buckley dead of two World Wars which was dedicated in September 1951 by the Bishop of St Asaph. In July 1953 Mr Dennis Grifffiths performed the official opening of the new Buckley Bowling Green at Hawkesbury.

Dennis Griffiths expressed his faith in the future of Hawkesbury and his belief in its high ideals by becoming its first warden. He held office from the beginning of the centre until 1965, when his protegé Derek Hollins succeeded him until he became County Drama Organiser. Vernon Hughes was the third and last warden.

Over the years the Hall has come very close to demolition and has survived several threats. In 1967 financial problems forced the Hawkesbury Trustees to sell the complex to Flintshire County Council and in 1980 Clwyd County Council agreed to build a new centre, the cost of which was shared in three ways, between the BYPCA, Clwyd County Council and Alyn and Deeside District Council. Mr J. E. Messham, the Secretary in 1945, opened the new community centre on 9 July 1982, with speeches by Mr Charles Duckworth and the Town Mayor Mrs Elizabeth Jones. It was well used by a number of organisations including the Camera Club, the Buckley Society, the Hawkesbury Playgroup, Toc H, the Hawkesbury Ladies Guild and a number of other groups.[8] For over twenty years Buckley Rovers and Buckley Wanderers Football Clubs had many successful seasons on the Hawkesbury ground and sharing the old tin bath after the game!

Among the organisations, which have used Hawkesbury over the years, are the following:

Mr J. E. Messham. [Buckley Library]

The Buckley Drama Circle

The Buckley Drama Circle was in existence for a quarter of a century and bridged the period from 1938 until the 1960s. It produced over fifty plays under the direction of Mr Dennis Griffiths, and when he was forced to retire in the 1960s Mr Derek Hollins succeeded him as producer. Under their leadership the Drama Circle successfully competed in the Denbighshire and Flintshire Drama Festivals where it won many cups. In the 1960s Derek Hollins produced around fifteen plays many of them classics, the work of Ibsen, Chekov, Moliere, Shaw, Obey, Dylan Thomas and other notable dramatists.

The Buckley Theatre Club

The Buckley Theatre Club grew out of the

The Buckley Drama Group rehearsing The Giaconda Smile, *1959. L–R: Margaret Bell, Rueben Dolby, Ken Lloyd, Muriel Barnes, Gerald Wright, Muriel Gould, Glenys Hughes, Robert Pownall. [Courtesy of Muriel Barnes]*

The Bistre Drama Group, 1960.
Winners of the Flintshire and
Wrexham Drama Festival with their
chairman and producer Mr Donald
Jones.
[By courtesy of Mr Donald Jones]

The Buckley Theatre Club at Elfed
School Theatre, 1977; a performance of
Babes in the Wood with Ken Davies as
the Baron and Ken Lloyd as the Dame.
[By courtesy of Mr Donald Jones]

Bistre Drama Group founded in the 1950s by young members of Bistre Church under the leadership of Mr Donald Jones. They used the Parish Room at Lane End for the performance of plays to which they added pantomime in 1960.

The Drama Group eventually became the Theatre Club and since 1960 have staged over forty pantomimes mainly under the direction of Mr Donald Jones (who wrote the scripts) and Mrs Joyce Hughes. In addition two plays were performed annually. In 1966 they moved from the Lane End to the Elfed Theatre. Since 2000 they have the refurbished Hawkesbury Little Theatre as their home. Amongst the pantomime stars over the year are Joan Jones, Margaret Shone, Ken Lloyd and Ken Davies.

The Buckley Society

Members of the Buckley Society have made a tremendous contribution to recording the history of the local community. The Society was established at Hawkesbury in 1946 with Mr J. E. Messham as secretary. He set a high standard for members and published a number of scholarly articles on medieval Ewloe and the Buckley pottery industry. The high esteem in which he is held was recognised by his appointment in 1998 as Life President of the Society.

Regular publications by the Society became established on its revival in 1969 and over thirty volumes have appeared since then. Mr J. E. Messham and Mr Charles Duckworth were responsible for the direction of the revived Society. It set out to promote historical interest in the local area, to collect and publish all available information and materials relating to Buckley and district in an annual magazine, and to arrange lectures and discussions that would interest and be beneficial to the public and the local community.

The late Mr Charles Duckworth, (1906–84), epitomised the enthusiasm of the local historian. He made valuable and systematic transcripts of the local newspapers from the end of the eighteenth until the end of the nineteenth century. He gave a series of lectures, under the auspices of the Workers Educational Association on the history of Buckley, which included a wide range of topics, and published some interesting articles in the *Buckley* magazine. One of his major interests was Nonconformity in Buckley.

Another local pioneer was the late James Bentley (1921–2004), a pharmacist who came to Buckley in the 1950s and had a shop on Daisy Hill from the 1950s. His enthusiasm and expertise as a local archaeologist made a significant contribution to the preservation of Buckley pottery and industrial sites. Mr Bentley was always ready to share his findings with others which he did through WEA classes and his writings on pottery for school children. He was also an artist who recorded Buckley's past through scenes painted in his own inimitable style. Some of these through the courtesy of Mrs Bentley are reproduced in this book.

One of the strengths of the Buckley Society is the variety of contributions made by members. Expert editorial work has been done over the years by Mr J. E. Messham, Mr Geoffrey Veysey (former County Archivist) and the present editor, Mr Ken Lloyd Gruffydd. A new dimension in the recording of history is being pioneered in Buckley through the setting up of a website and establishment of a multi-media archive under the direction of Mrs Carol Shone. Images are collected and sessions are held fortnightly on Wednesdays in the library. The society encourages people to research and publish their own topics of local history, the variety of which continues to

Mr Charles Duckworth.
[Buckley Society Magazine, 10]

enrich the heritage of Buckley. This follows in the footsteps of the first pioneer Thomas Cropper (1869–1923) whose book *Buckley and District*, provided a stimulating starting point for local historians.

The Buckley Society continues to hold regular meetings at Hawkesbury. In 1996 Clwyd County Council through their Libraries and Museums Service chose to use the Buckley Town Library as a Heritage Centre, which has a fine display of local pottery, and a centre for staging other short exhibitions. Another feature of the library is the opportunity it gives to local artists to display their work.

Mr James Bentley. [Buckley Library]

The Buckley Art Society

Buckley Art Society has produced, over the last sixty years, excellent work by local artists. A feature of some of their work is the way in which it has recorded the variety of landscape in Buckley. Included are the work place, street scenes, the railway, and the changing industrial sites and conservation areas seen through the splendour of the four seasons.

The Society has had its ups and downs, although this has not affected the enthusiasm and output of local artists. The first club, known as the Buckley Art Club, began at Hawkesbury in 1946. Amongst the first members were John Whormsley, Miss Terry Martin, Herbert Parker, Charles Kelsall and Clifford Jones.

Some of the Buckley Society Archive Group in the Library May 2006, with Bill Pritchard. L–R: back row — Emrys Williams, Bill Fisher, Mervyn Foulkes, Carol Shone, Paul Davies, Trevor Rowlands; front row — Wilf Owens, John Bright, Eric Hayes, Bill Pritchard. [Buckley Society Archive]

Mr Thomas Dempster Jones, late President of the Buckley Arts Society. [Buckley Library]

This first group met, until its decline by the 1960s, to be succeeded in 1970 by the newly named Buckley Art Society. Its chairman was Mr Joe Chesters, secretary D. J. Catherall and treasurer Miss S. Jones. This new Society was distinguished, as its predecessor had been, by an excellent 'school' of local artists who continued to provide pleasure for Buckley folk by the sensitive production of subjects with a local appeal. In 1971 the Paris Salon gold medallist Thomas Dempster Jones was elected the Society's President. The works of some of these artists, Joseph I. Chesters, John Whormsley, T. Dempster Jones and Jane Edwards, are featured in this book. In 1976 the Society moved to the Elfed School where it found a permanent home.[9] Annual exhibitions were held, mainly at Buckley Library. In 1986–7 it became the Buckley and Mold Art Society, later the Buckley and Mold Arts Society. The Society disbanded in October 2001.

The Coronation Garden, Lane End, 1953

The souvenir programme of the festivities, arranged to mark the Coronation of Queen Elizabeth II in 1953, announced that in commemoration of the event, 'we in Buckley are making a start in the beautification of our home town by planting a garden'. George Lewis chronicled the enterprise:

May 30 Sat. The Coronation Garden in Lane End, Buckley, was opened today by Mrs Rene Wilcock, who cut the red, white and blue ribbon. Mr W. E. Roberts designed the Garden, aided by Mr E. Watkin, Council Surveyor. Mr Charles Wilcock, former Chairman of the UDC, initiated the making of the Garden. It was completed by voluntary labour. The Garden measures a quarter of an acre and a thousand tons of topsoil was added free of charge. A few days before Coronation Day nearly two thousand red, white and blue roses were planted in the Garden. The head teachers of the Buckley Schools have promised that the children will donate four hundred and fifty rose trees to the Garden in the autumn. Mr Wilf Shone supervised the work and gave the stone.

The festivities on Coronation Day, 2 June, included arrangements for collective viewing of the service on television, children's sports, and a variety concert. Other events took place in the following week, a boxing contest, street dancing, the distribution of beakers to children, and a pensioners outing to Southport. Later in the month the Tivoli presented *A Queen is Crowned* — in glorious technicolour.

Industrial changes

In the introduction to this chapter we referred to the end of the old traditional industries in Buckley. Here we give a brief outline of what replaced the clay industry as works gradually closed in the last decades of the twentieth century.

Cement Manufacture at Padeswood.[10]

George Lewis noted in his diary: 'May 13 Mon. They started with mechanical excavators, to clear the ground to build a new Cement Works on Padeswood Hall for the Tunnel Cement Co.

Coronation Gardens, Lane End. [FRO PH /11/423]

The Cement Factory Padeswood.
Painting by James Bentley, 1988.
[By courtesy of Mrs M. Bentley]

In 1946 Tunnel Cement[11] purchased the Padeswood Hall estate from Flintshire County Council for £9,700 to build a new cement works. The first works consisted of two kilns, the first of which was fired in December 1949, and the second in May 1950. Padeswood is ideally situated with the essential materials for cement manufacture nearby: limestone from Cadole, sand from Hope and Bodfari, and water from bore holes at Kinnerton.

In 1966 a long dry process kiln was installed and modernisation has taken place since then. In 1982 Tunnel Cement became Castle Cement and in 1988 Castle was bought by Aker a.s. of Norway and the Swedish Company Eurco AB. In 1995 Eurco merged with Aker's cement and material division to form Scanlon AB. In 2005 a newly designed kiln came into production involving an investment of over £50 million in the plant.

Industrial sites

The list of industrial sites developed in the area over the past twenty-five years indicates the replacement of the clay industry by clusters of small business units. This development is a response to unemployment caused by the closure of Shotton steelworks. Over 5,000 jobs in a radius of five miles were lost when Shotton closed in 1980. Job creation became the priority of Clwyd County Council and Mr Barry Jones the local Member of Parliament. Funding was sought from many agencies including the European Economic Community and the Welsh Development Agency.

The first initiative in the Buckley area was the creation of the Pinfold Industrial Estate, where a wide range of small businesses were attracted to a group of 34 purpose built factory units of various sizes. The site was designed as a village in easy reach of the transport network. Financial assistance came from a £600,000 urban aid from the EEC and under the auspices of the government's Enterprise Allowance. These were officially opened in March 1982 by the Secretary of State for Wales. The scheme was intended to relieve unemployment and create diversification of industry in an area which had previously relied on steel and clay. Pinfold was the first of the area's many industrial estates.

Site	Size (in acres)	Place
Ewloe Barn Industrial Estate	22.44	Alltami
Pinfold Lane	25,75	
Catherall's Industrial Estate	11.64	Buckley
Drury Brickworks Industrial Estate	2.09	
Little Mountain Industrial Estate	25.63	
Pinfold Industrial Estate	5.65	
Spencer's Industrial Estate	9.71	
Lakeside Business Village	6.17	Ewloe
St. David's Business Park	27.18	

(information from *Flintshire Business Directory 2000*)

The development of Buckley in the late twentieth century

The late Councillor Arthur Jones saw the end of the Buckley Urban District Council in 1974 as a loss of decisive local government control which would have been the main influence in the redevelopment of Buckley. He stated:

> 1974 brought the reorganisation of the local government and again in 1996, both acts of parliament have proved to be disastrous … Buckley lost its status as an Urban District Council. Its power and authority over its local services had been transferred to another body. Only its identity by name was left. Local government as we knew it had gone. The Town clock, a gift to the Council was the only asset within its control. Since the reorganisation of the local government, large-scale plans for Buckley have been abandoned. Public services have declined.

However, the three-stage development plan of the 1970s, aimed at giving Buckley a civic centre, was only partially abandoned, and quite a number of building innovations were made eventually. A shopping precinct was erected and opened in November 1971. A new fire station was built. The Library, from 1974 under the direction of Clwyd County Council, moved in 1977, to a new building in the Precinct. However the proposed new council chamber, offices and a civic centre were not erected. There was a gap of over twenty years before the shopping centre received further development.

In the 1990s part of Brunswick Road between the Cross and Precinct was pedestrianised and excellent free car parking space was created in the vicinity. The Precinct was subject to improvements which cost half a million pounds, of which the Welsh Development Agency contributed £165,000. These included a glass roof, new floor, video surveillance and new security gates and the Library received its heritage centre and an improved art gallery. But what won the applause of Arthur Jones was the completion of the new link road proposed and planned by the former UDC and Flintshire County Council in 1971. This he said 'will go down in the annals of local government as the Jewel in the Crown'.[13] The Buckley Link Road and 'Town Enhancement' was officially opened on 2 December 1996. It was partly funded by the Welsh Office under the Strategic Development Scheme and by the Welsh Development Agency at a contract cost of £1.3 million. Messrs F. G. Whitley & Sons Co. Ltd, Buckley, carried out the work. Its purpose was to remove most of the existing Mold Road and Brunswick Road traffic through the centre of Buckley, relieving the congestion at the Cross, and providing a safer and cleaner environment for the main shopping area.

Improvements and new developments continued into the new millennium, the most conspicuous being the opening of a new swimming pool in 2005 within the grounds of the Elfed High School.

Conservation and Landscaping

Our concluding topic in the making of Buckley looks at the way in which new uses have been made of the old industrial sites. There is no doubt that there is a competition for land use, which has been an element in

The entrance to Buckley Shopping Precinct. [Buckley Society Archive]

the history of the making of Buckley from the time of the enclosures in 1800. Today the major competitors are housing developers, local authorities and other businesses interested in recycling household and industrial waste, and conservationists. Each of these interests has achieved some success in Buckley over the last thirty years.

Successive local authorities such as Alyn and Deeside Council, Clwyd County Council and Flintshire County Council, have managed landfill sites at Belmont, Brookhill, Etna, Standard and Mount Pleasant. Some of these sites have been reclaimed as conservation areas for the benefit of the local community. This has not always been easy and there has always been a mixture of controversy, compromise, and conservation.

Buckley Library ground floor area. On the first floor is a heritage centre, art gallery and reference section.
[Buckley Society Archive]

One group which has valued for over sixty years the importance of conservation is the Buckley Angling Association. Entries in George Lewis's diary have several post-war entries relating to stocking Buckley's clayholes: '1947 Sun. 21 Sept. The new Angling Association went to White Weir, Shropshire, and caught pike and put them into the clayhole at Ewloe Place. They made two other journeys within the year to Welshpool and Montgomery to collect pike for Ewloe Place.'

The Buckley Angling Association had 300 members in the year 2000 and built a new clubhouse at the Trap. In 1999 the Alltami Fishing Club, founded in 1978, with a membership of *c.*360 were threatened with the loss of the pool they leased free from Hanson Brick Co. The anglers are a strong lobby for preserving their tranquil preserves.

We conclude with two examples of conservation in the Buckley area, which have taken place in the last ten years.

Brookhill Quarry

In 1995 Brookhill Quarry in Pinfold Lane was designated as a tip site to be utilised when the Standard site was full. This led to a crisis in conservation circles when it was discovered that Brookhill was the habitat of large numbers of amphibians including great crested newts. Eventually the future of the wildlife was ensured when the Deeside Urban Wildlife Group reported in 1997 that 'a solution satisfactory to all the parties involved has been agreed. An area equal to that which is to be destroyed, has been bought or leased for the creation of a newt reserve (approximately 7.4 hectares)', and announced that, 'during the ten years that the landfill is in operation, the site will be progressively restored to create habitat specifically designed for enhancement of Great Crested Newts and other amphibians. Eventually on completion, the whole area will be designated a Local Nature Reserve amounting to approximately 12 hectares.'[14]

The Brookhill Nature Reserve grew into a network of 20 ponds. A bird hide, funded by AD Waste Ltd., was constructed from which were observed various water, woodland and hedgerow species including buzzard, sparrowhawk, kestrel, snipe, mallard, coot, reed bunting and sedge warbler. The Deeside Urban Wildlife Group (now called North East Wales Wildlife), manages the project.

The Buckley Heritage Trail[15]

A discussion of the Buckley Heritage Trail is a suitable subject to conclude this study of the making of Buckley. Although it does not relate to the whole of our book it provides an ideal point in that it sums up the area's industrial heritage.

What is the significance of the heritage trail? The purpose of the trail is 'to provide Buckley with a strong sense of identity'. 'To develop a Heritage Trail linking several old clay holes including Etna and Mount

Pools with the aim of explaining the changing land use in the area and the effects this has had on wildlife and people'. 'To create an Urban Park with opportunities for wildlife and people and promote the Park and Heritage Trail as a tourist attraction'. 'To develop the Park and the Trail in an innovative and artistic way using materials mined or made locally e.g. clay and brick.'

Where is the Urban Park and Heritage/Sculpture Trail? The sketch map shows its location on a site of 22 hectares on the northern side of Buckley, an area in which the Buckley coal and clay industry was concentrated. The trail encompasses an area which included the following brickworks and quarries — Globe, Standard, Drury, Mount Pleasant, Hancock's (Butterley, Hanson's), Knowle Lane and Etna. 'The pattern of changing landscape reflects the true story of Buckley', and 'the derelict land left by the coal mining and clay industries has re-colonised naturally or has been exploited for landfill and other industries. These sites in turn are now providing opportunities for wildlife and recreation. A recycling of the landscape has taken place.' This project brings together three separate initiatives Mount Pools, Etna Landfill and the Heritage Trail[16] and has been enhanced in an imaginative way by incorporating local brick and clay.

An 'artist in residence', Tina Gould, was employed by the Council. She worked with over 600 people from various community groups and schools to ensure the success of the venture. They undertook a variety of tasks, which included the carving of wet blocks of clay before they were fired at the brickworks. The Ranger Service, along with the bricklayers from Deeside College, then built the sculptures.[17]

The official opening of the scheme took place at Etna Country Park on 17 October 1999. The enterprise was led by Flintshire County Council who received funding and support from a larger number of groups, which in itself, was an expression of the belief in the principles of the project outlined above.[18]

The Heritage Trail embraces ten significant areas with a mixture of industrial sites and conservation areas.

Map of Heritage Trail. [Buckley Society Magazine]

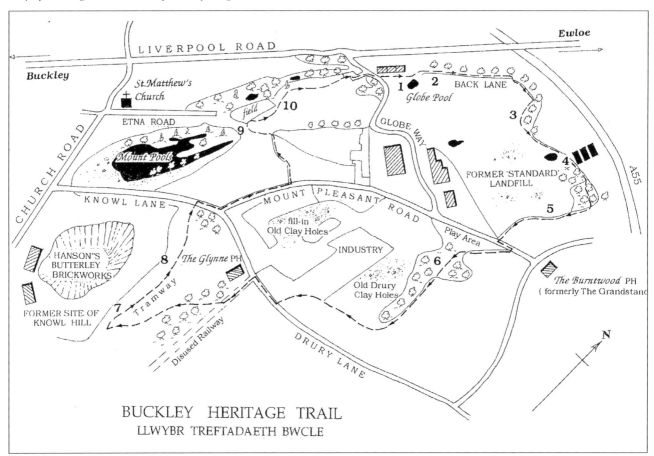

BUCKLEY HERITAGE TRAIL
LLWYBR TREFTADAETH BWCLE

Buckley Town Football Ground within Heritage Area. [Buckley Society Archive]

1. Globe Pool — clayhole and sculpture.
2. Back Lane — an ancient trackway — with a sculpture depicting pottery throughout the ages.
3. Cross Tree Opencast — a post-war coal extraction site.
4. Siltation Lagoons used for breeding the Great Crested Newt.
5. Standard Clay Hole — a former landfill site that has been landscaped — the sculpture includes ceramic pipe shapes.
6. Drury Clay Hole — depicts an area of former bell pit mining.
7. Lane End Brickworks — this stop demonstrates the extent of clay extraction in Buckley — as the former site of Knowl Hill, which once stood 563 feet above sea level, and is now reduced to a large clay hole. Here a sculpture with coloured ceramic bricks depicts the chimney demolished during the Second World War.
8. Knowl Hill — a sculpture commemorates the early tramways with reference to the Five Way Point junction — much beloved of the late James Bentley.
9. Mount Pools — former fire-clay pits now a wildlife habitat.
10. Etna Country Park — a former brickworks and restored landfill site which clearly demonstrates the way in which a changing landscape can herald a new beginning in the making of Buckley.[19]

Etna Sculpture No. 5, by Tina Gould, on Heritage Trail. [Buckley Society Archive]

Globe Pool, May 2006. [Buckley Society Archive]

Tree Planting on Etna, 1999. [Buckley Society Archive]

Notes

1. *The Flint and Deeside Leader*, 24/10/1952.
2. For Elfed see E.Wynn Parry, *Howel Elfed Lewis* (Independent Press Ltd., London: 1958). And the entry by Emlyn Glasnant Jenkins in the *Dictionary of Welsh Biography, 1941–1970* (Honourable Society of Cymmrodorion, London: 2001).
3. Grimly called 'Social Insurance and Allied Services'.
4. See the *Buckley* magazine (of BYPCA), vol. 1, 1944.
5. *Chester Chronicle*, 14/7/1945.
6. Named after the owner, a mid-nineteenth century brickmaker. The schooner traded from Connah's Quay.
7. *Chester Chronicle*, 14/7/1945.
8. See Brian D. Hodnett, 'Hawkesbury: 200 years of history', *Buckley*, 24. And the annual reports by the Warden of Hawkesbury, 1945–late 1960s in FRO D/DM/434.
9. See J. I. Chesters, The Buckley Art Society: 21 years, *Buckley*, 16.
10. See Mervyn C. Foulkes, 'The History of Cement Manufacture in Padeswood, North East Wales,' *Buckley*, 28.
11. Owned by F. L. Smidth.
12. Councillor Arthur Jones CBE, JP, *A Century in the life of Buckley, 1897–1997*.
13. ibid, p.11.
14. Deeside Urban Wildlife Group Publications, *Wild Life Matters*, No. 13, Spring, 1997.
15. This account is based on 'Proposals for Etna Park and Heritage Trail, a consultative document produced in October 1996, by Flintshire County, Culture, Leisure and Tourism, proposals drawn up by Paul Richards, Countryside Officer for Alyn and Deeside District Council', and Phil Hodges, Countryside Ranger for Flintshire County Council, A brief History of the Buckley Heritage Trail, *Buckley*, 25; and *Buckley Heritage Trail: Llwybr Treftadaeth Bwcle*, published by Dylunio Argraffu — Design Print.
16. The above references are from 'Proposals for Etna Park and Heritage Trail', see fn 15.
17. See Phil Hodges, op cit.
18. The following were named in the consultative document (see fn 15) as funding partners and supporting organisations with whom discussions took place: Buckley Town Council; Welsh Development Agency; Hanson Brick Ltd; AD Waste; Countryside for Wales; Wales Tourist Board; NEWI School of Art and Design, Wrexham; Cywaith Cymru; Forestry Authority; Community Group; Buckley Society; Deeside Urban Wildlife Group; Burntwood and Drury Residents Association; local primary and secondary schools; Millennium Commission.
19. See *Buckley Heritage Trail: Llwybr Treftadaeth Bwcle*.

Sources

1. Manuscript collections
Flintshire Record Office
Census returns
Nonconformist records
School Log Books
Glynne-Gladstone MSS
Buckley urban District Council Minutes
J. E. Messham Collection
James Bentley Collection
Charles Duckworth Collection
Dennis Griffiths Collection

2. Principal Journals
Annual Reports County Archivist
Archaeologia Cambrensis
Bistre Parish Magazine
Buckley Parish magazine
Buckley Society Magazine
Clwyd Historian
Denbighshire Historical Society Transactions
Flintshire Historical Society Publications and Journal

3. Official Publications
Report of the Commissioners of Inqiry into the State of Education in Wales, 1847
Royal Commission on the Church of England and Other Religious Bodies in Wales and Monmouthshire, 1906.
Royal Commission on Land in Wales and Monmouthshire.
Evidence of the Royal Commission on Land in Wales and Monmouthshire, 1894.

4. Books and Articles
These are given in the text notes at the end of each chapter.

5. Newspapers
Chester Chronicle
County Herlad
Mold, Deeside & Buckley Leader
Wrexham Advertizer

6. Photographic Collections
Buckley Society Media Archive
Buckley Library and the collections of Joe Chesters, Robert Lloyd and Stephen Wilkin
Flintshire Record Office
For individual sources see captions

Index

The index is arranged alphabetically in word-by-word order. Page numbers in italics indicate maps and illustrations.